HEALTH, ILLNESS, AND THE SOCIAL BODY

THIRD EDITION

HEALTH, ILLNESS, AND THE SOCIAL BODY

A CRITICAL SOCIOLOGY

Peter E. S. Freund
Montclair State University

Meredith B. McGuire
Trinity University

Prentice Hall   Upper Saddle River, New Jersey 07458

Library of Congress Cataloging-in-Publication Data

FREUND, PETER E. S.
    Health, illness, and the social body : a critical sociology /
Peter E. S. Freund, Meredith B. McGuire.–3rd ed.

    Includes bibliographical references and index.
    ISBN 0–13–897075-0 (alk. paper)
    1. Social medicine.   2. Sick–Psychology.   3. Medical care.
I. McGuire, Meredith B.   II. Title.
RA418.F753   1998
    306.4′61–dc21   97-39102
                                                                  CIP

Editorial director: Charlyce Jones Owen
Editor in chief: Nancy Roberts
Managing editor: Sharon Chambliss
Editorial/production supervision and
    interior design: Barbara Reilly
Copyeditor: Anne Lesser
Prepress and manufacturing buyer: Mary Ann Gloriande
Marketing manager: Christopher De John
Cover design: Bruce Kenselaar

This book was set in 10/12 Baskerville Book by DM Cradle
Associates and was printed and bound by Courier Companies, Inc.
The cover was printed by Phoenix Color Corp.

 © 1999 by Prentice-Hall, Inc.
Simon & Schuster/A Viacom Company
Upper Saddle River, New Jersey 07458

Printed in the United States of America
10   9   8   7   6   5   4   3   2   1

ISBN   0-13-897075-0

Prentice-Hall International (UK) Limited, *London*
Prentice-Hall of Australia Pty. Limited, *Sydney*
Prentice-Hall Canada Inc., *Toronto*
Prentice-Hall Hispanoamericana, S.A., *Mexico*
Prentice-Hall of India Private Limited, *New Delhi*
Prentice-Hall of Japan, Inc., *Tokyo*
Simon & Schuster Asia Pte. Ltd., *Singapore*
Editora Prentice-Hall do Brasil, Ltda., *Rio de Janeiro*

CONTENTS

PREFACE

Society has profound influence on human bodies, as well as on our ideas and perceptions about those bodies. For this text we have selected key themes in the sociology of health and illness that highlight the complex interrelationship of body, mind and society. Although we describe various interpretive approaches and review much conventional literature in several related disciplines, this is not a standard medical sociology text; instead, it presents a critical, holistic interpretation of health, illness and human bodies that emphasizes power as a key social-structural factor in health and in societal responses to illness.

Since the previous edition of this text, rapid and important changes in our society and its provisions for health and illness highlight the importance of power issues in health and healing. Some of the most interesting recent health-related research explores precisely those areas of social life where power differences are evident: gender, race and ethnicity, poverty and wealth, work and professions, abuse and violence, the physical and social environment, and health care financing and delivery, among others. The politics of the debate over U.S. health care "reform" also illustrates the importance of power and wealth—especially of corporate actors—in setting the very terms of discourse, not merely affecting the policy outcomes.

This text does not attempt to cover every relevant topic, but is organized as a set of core essays around which to build a course. Thus, for example, the topics of women's health issues, ethnic factors in health and illness, and AIDS are discussed in several different sections, rather than all under one heading. Students using the Index will find a wealth of information and references for further research on these and other important issues. Using this text as a core reading, instructors can assign related articles, monographs, or readings to complement their own emphases.

Chapter 1 is an introduction that outlines relevant problems and key concepts in the field, and especially shows how this text links materialist and social-constructionist theories of health and illness through the unifying theme of power. Chapter 2 introduces students to social epidemiology, and outlines broad patterns of morbidity and mortality. Chapters 3 through 5 describe the social production of unhealthy bodies and develop interpretations of the nature of connections among mind, body, and society. Chapters 6 through 9 discuss the social context of ideas and experiences of health and illness. Chapters 10 through 12 examine social and cultural factors in the medical system's treatment of sick persons and the political economy of health care in the United States.

While presented in an orderly arrangement, the book's chapters may be used in a different sequence. Each chapter introduces relevant key concepts and a limited number of sociological theorists or researchers. For reasons of practical flexibility, we have reiterated explanations of a few key terms in more than one chapter. Authors mentioned by name in the text generally have been selected for the importance of their theoretical contributions. Others are cited in the recommended readings and references, which have been included both to acknowledge our intellectual debts and to provide students with extensive useful references for further research.

Each chapter ends with an annotated list of some recent recommended readings; two appendices suggest further useful materials. Appendix A outlines major resources for a search of the literature in the field. Students preparing term papers or theses will find these resources essential. The book's extensive bibliography should also be invaluable for researchers. Appendix B is an annotated list of film and video resources. We have found good visual presentations to be excellent aids for concretizing and illustrating points that are often far from students' personal experiences, as well as for stimulating discussion.

In writing this third edition, we have received additional help from several persons, whose assistance we gratefully acknowledge: Miriam Fisher, Debra Kantor, George Martin, Jean Parks, Linda Podhurst. Also very welcome were the advice and encouragement of our editors, Nancy Roberts and Sharon Chambliss, and reviewers Jim Aho (Idaho State University), Erma Jean Lawson (The University of Texas), Georgeanna Tryban (Indiana State University), and Michael D. Quam (University of Illinois at Springfield). We appreciate the assistance of Linda Baird, Kathy Barrientos, Susan Goscinski, Kieran McGuire, and Janaki Spickard-Keeler in manuscript preparation. Finally, we want to thank our families, Miriam Fisher, Kieran McGuire, and Jim, Janaki, and Dmitri Spickard, for putting up with us during the writing of this book and for illustrating by their very lives why sociologists should care about health.

HEALTH, ILLNESS, AND THE SOCIAL BODY

A SOCIOLOGICAL PERSPECTIVE ON HEALTH, ILLNESS, AND THE BODY

CHAPTER OUTLINE

When we think of health and illness, we usually think of eating properly and other healthy habits, of institutions such as hospitals, and of health professionals such as doctors and nurses. Although we may be dimly aware that health has its social dimensions, we may not think of health as a topic for social scientists.

Sociological analysis emphasizes that the occurrence of illness is not random. Eckholm (1977: 18–19) notes:

> Individuals who enjoy good health rightly think of themselves as fortunate: But luck has little to do with the broad patterns of disease and mortality that prevail in each society. The striking variations in health conditions among countries and cultural groups reflect differences in social and physical environments. And increasingly, the forces that shape health patterns are set in motion by human activities and decisions. Indeed, *in creating its way of life, each society creates its way of death.* [emphasis added]

The sociology of health and illness studies such issues as how social and cultural factors influence health and people's perceptions of health and healing, and how healing is done in different societies. Social structures and cultural practices have concrete consequences for people's lives.

We like to think that a newborn infant is as yet untouched by these abstract forces and has possibilities for health limited only by the child's genetic makeup. Even at birth, however, these abstract forces have begun to inscribe themselves on the baby's body. The very life chances of this infant, including the probabilities that she will live, be well, acquire the skills for success in her culture, and achieve and maintain that success, are powerfully influenced by all of the social circumstances and forces she will encounter throughout her life. In short, the baby's life chances, including possibilities for health and long life or sickness and death, are shaped or constructed by society itself.

The baby's birth weight, for example, is influenced by her mother's diet, which in turn is partly a product of her society, her culture, and her social class. Other features of the mother's social context have direct consequences for the newborn's health, including the mother's smoking or drug habits, the housing and sanitary conditions in which the infant is born, and the like. Later, whether the baby is a victim of cholera, bubonic plague, schistosomiasis, or lead poisoning depends on public health measures taken in her environment. What other factors in the baby's home life and environment will shape her sense of self and self-esteem, and her ability to cope with stress and manage her environment? As she matures, how will her gender, race, ethnicity, and social class influence her life chances?

Later in life, her experiences as a worker will place her in various physical environments and social relationships that will affect her health. Her culture will shape what she likes to eat, how she experiences stress, whether she drinks alcohol, and how she feels about her body. How she experiences the process of giving birth will be shaped by her culture's meanings of childbirth as well as by the social context of birth, such as whether it takes place in a hospital under the supervision of an obstetrician trained in Western notions of pregnancy as a medical problem.

The infant is born into a social structure and culture that also powerfully influence what will be considered illness and how that illness will be treated. When this person gets sick, social forces play an important role in determining her chances of becoming well. How does she decide when she is sick and needs help? If she is sick, for example with a bad cold, how will others respond? If she develops multiple sclerosis, how will the attitudes and responses of others, and the quality of her social and physical environment affect her very life chances? What will happen if she develops a stigmatizing illness, such as leprosy or AIDS?

What resources are available to her in dealing with her needs when ill? If she approaches the medical system for help, how does she pay for it? How do her social class, age, race, and ability to pay influence the quality of her medical care? How does the institutional context of her medical care (for example, a public versus a for-profit private hospital, or a nursing home compared to a hospice or home care) help determine its quality? In addition to the quality of life, even the quality of death is linked with such social contexts.

Medical systems involve concrete organizations that reflect the economic interests of such groups as doctors and other professionals, insurance companies, pharmaceutical industries, manufacturers of medical equipment, hospitals, research organizations, government agencies, and medical schools. They all compete for resources, influence policy, and try to set health care and research agendas. Health care systems differ greatly from society to society in how they define and meet the needs of individual citizens. The baby's life chances are intimately intertwined, therefore, with these seemingly remote social organizations.

The fates of individual bodies are thus linked to the workings of the social body. A person's life chances are neither some deterministic fate nor a purely accidental, random result. Rather, a person's chances for illness and successful recovery are very much the result of specifiable social arrangements, which are in turn products of human volition and indeed deliberate policy choices made by identifiable groups and individuals. In large part, illness, death, health, and well-being are socially produced.

THE SOCIAL CONSTRUCTION OF THE BODY

To construct is to make or build something. Clearly, societies do not literally make or produce bodies, but they can influence, shape, and misshape them. Just as an artist can mold clay to construct an object (which is constrained by the physical properties of the clay), social groups and the cultures they share can shape members' bodies. Obvious examples of cultural shaping of the human body include the foot binding practiced in traditional Chinese society, the cradle boards used to shape infants' heads among the Kwakiutl Indians, the stays and corsets worn by nineteenth-century middle-class European and American women, and the high heels and pierced earrings favored today. Similarly, having to live in a polluted environment or to sit at a desk, to work on an assembly line, or to bend over all day in a mine shaft are examples of social conditions that can indirectly shape the body and in turn the body's health.

A biologist illustrates the physical consequences of social practices:

> If a society puts half its children in dresses and skirts but warns them not to move in ways that reveal their underpants, while putting the other half in jeans and overalls and encouraging them to climb trees and play ball and other active outdoor games; if later, during adolescence, the half that has worn trousers is exhorted to "eat like a growing boy" while the half in skirts is warned to watch its weight and not get fat; if the half in jeans trots around in sneakers or boots, while the half in skirts totters about on spike heels, then these two groups of people will be biologically as well as socially different. Their muscles will be different, as will their reflexes, posture, arms, legs and feet, hand-eye coordination, spatial perception, and so on. They will also be biologically different if, as adults, they spend eight hours a day sitting in front of a visual display terminal or work on a construction job or in a mine. (Hubbard, cited in Vines, 1993: 93–94).

Those things that happen to human bodies are closely related to the working and anatomy of the social body. Illness is not merely a physical experience but also a social experience. The sick body is not simply a closed container, encased in skin, that has been invaded by germs or traumatic blows; rather, it is open and connected to the world that surrounds it. Thus, the human body is open to the social body. Similarly, our material (or physical) environment, such as the urban landscape, the workplace, or our foods, are influenced by our culture, social structure, and relationships. And these, in turn, influence our bodies.

THE SOCIAL CONSTRUCTION OF IDEAS ABOUT THE BODY

Ideas, too, are constructions. Every society has many levels of shared ideas and practices regarding bodies: What is defined as healthy and beautiful in one society might be considered unhealthily fat and ugly in another; what is seen as thin and lean in one group might be defined as sickly in another. Aging may also be defined as a process to be either conquered, feared, accepted, or revered. Likewise, some societies picture the body as working like a machine, whereas others see it as a spiritual vessel.

Health Beliefs and Practices

Because they are social constructions, our ideas of the body and its health and illness are influenced by both our culture and our social position, such as class or gender. Both cultural and social structural factors are important in understanding people's behavior and health. People act as they do not only because of their beliefs about health (the cultural aspects) but also because of structural aspects, such as how power is distributed and relationships are organized. Thus, although we conceptually distinguish cultural and social structural aspects, in actuality they overlap.

Culture is the beliefs, values, practices, and material objects shared by a people. Culture includes such elements as language, beliefs about the universe and the nature of good and evil, ideals such as justice or freedom, and more mundane considerations such as what constitutes appropriate food, dress, and manners. It also encompasses objects that a people produce and share. Cooking utensils, automobiles, plays, cemeteries, blueprints, crucifixes, tools, musical scores, and flags are among the items that represent cultural values and notions.

How do our cultural conceptions of a person's physical abilities affect those abilities? In our society, we used to believe that women were unable to carry heavy objects. Although biology contributes somewhat to women's physical abilities, so do cultural ideas. In a patriarchal society, women's expectations that they will be weak, together with the experience of being treated as weak because of their social status, have a self-fulfilling result: Women do not become strong. Culture can affect health by shaping behaviors, such as diet, or by influencing how people change their environments, which in turn affects their health (Brown and Inhorn, 1990).

Social structure (or social organization) is the relatively stable, ongoing pattern of social interaction. In a particular society, recognizable patterns of interaction are appropriate to different social positions and relationships, such as parent-child, supervisor-employee, teacher-student, and friend-friend. Behavior in these relationships is regulated through a number of mechanisms, including social control and shared cultural values. Various persons in social relationships occupy different social statuses. These relationships are often part of larger social organizational contexts; for example, the supervisor and employee positions may be part of a business corporation.

Social status is an individual's position in any system of social ranking. People can be stratified or ranked according to such dimensions as class, ethnicity, age, and gender. Social class (often measured by income, occupation, or both) is one important indicator of social location; it influences how much power individuals have to manage their bodies and their external environment.

Class is not the only determinant of power. The particular position of power we occupy in our family (for example, child or parent) and our gender, race, and ethnicity are also all important factors. Even health status (being chronically ill, for instance) determines the stressors to which we are exposed and the coping resources available to us. Our position in institutional arrangements, such as being a hospital patient, can also affect our health (Volicer, 1977, 1978).

In understanding health and illness, cultural aspects to consider might include people's eating and hygienic practices and their ideas about health, illness, and healing. By contrast, structural elements might include a person's position and relationships in the workplace, family, and medical settings, as well as such social status indicators as gender, race, age, and class.

Both scientific and nonscientific ideas about health, illness, and the body are the result of social construction, as are the facts we assemble as evidence for our ideas about the world. All descriptions, including medical descriptions, are constructions in that they include some information and exclude other information. Similarly, definitions of health are social constructions. For example, the *International*

Dictionary of Medicine and Biology defines health as "a state of well-being of an organism or part of one, characterized by normal function and unattended by disease" (Becker, 1986: v. 2, 1276). This definition delineates well-being only in terms of bodily functioning and the absence of disease. But are we necessarily healthy if we simply lack disease? And are all diseases necessarily unhealthy? Is it healthy to function under all (however miserable) conditions? Why should functioning be such an important criterion? Is it because our society places so much cultural emphasis on certain forms of functioning?

The Medical Model

Our culture derives many of its ideas about the body from the Western biomedical model. A sociological perspective on health and illness, however, does not take this model as truth. Rather, medical ideas of the body and its diseases are also seen as socially constructed realities that are subject to social biases and limitations. Biomedical ideas are based on a number of historical assumptions about the body and ways of knowing about the body; the following are some of these historically created assumptions that have become embedded in the Western medical model. Chapter 9 develops these concepts in more detail.

One biomedical assumption is *mind-body dualism*. The medical model assumes a clear dichotomy between the mind and the body; physical diseases are presumed to be located solely within the body. As a result, biomedicine tries to understand and treat the body in isolation from other aspects of the person inhabiting it. The history of Western medical science suggests several of the sources of this image of the body as separate from mind or spirit.

Not only does the medical model dichotomize body and mind, but it also assumes that illness can be reduced to disordered bodily (biochemical or neurophysiological) functions. This *physical reductionism* excludes social, psychological, and behavioral dimensions of illness. One result is that medicine sees disease as localized in the individual body. Such conceptions prevent the medical model from conceiving of the social body or how aspects of the individual's social or emotional life might affect physical health. Thus, medicine generally ignores social conditions contributing to illness or promoting healing.

A related assumption of the biomedical model is what Dubos (1959) called the *doctrine of specific etiology*. This belief holds that each disease is caused by a specific, potentially identifiable agent. The history of Western medicine shows both the fruitfulness and the limitations of this assumption. Dubos noted that although the doctrine of specific etiology has led to important theoretical and practical achievements, it has rarely provided a complete account of the causation of disease. An adequate understanding of illness etiology must include broader factors, such as nutrition, stress, and metabolic states, which affect the individual's susceptibility to infection. As noted in Chapter 2, the search for specific illness-producing agents worked relatively well in dealing with infectious diseases but is too simplistic to explain the causes of complex chronic illnesses. Also, as Dubos observed, this approach often results in a quest for the "magic bullet" to "shoot and kill" the disease, producing an overreliance on pharmaceuticals in the "armamentarium" (stock of "weapons") of the modern physician.

The *machine metaphor* is another implicit assumption in the medical model. Accordingly, the body is a complex biochemical machine, and disease is the malfunctioning of some constituent mechanism (such as a "breakdown" of the heart). Other cultures use other metaphors; for example, ancient Egyptian societies used the image of a river, and Chinese tradition refers to the balance of elemental forces (yin and yang) of the earth (Osherson and AmaraSingham, 1981). In combination with the assumption of mind-body dualism, the machine metaphor further encouraged the notion that the physician could "repair" one part in isolation from the rest (Berliner, 1975).

Partly as a product of the machine metaphor and the quest for mastery, the Western medical model also conceptualizes the body as the proper *object of regimen and control* (Foucault, 1979), again emphasizing the responsibility of the individual to exercise this control in order to maintain or restore health. This assumption meshes with other values, resulting in the medical and social emphases on such standardized body disciplines as diets, exercise programs, routines of hygiene, and even sexual activity (Turner, 1984: 157–203).

THE CENTRALITY OF POWER IN THE SOCIOLOGY OF HEALTH AND ILLNESS

One of the unifying themes of this text is the social construction of both ideas about the body and the body itself. In this process, power and control play an important role. In the most general sense, **power** is the ability to get what we want and to get things done.

Power is a ubiquitous factor in our daily lives. It both enables us to accomplish tasks (such as to get enough food) and constrains the number and types of possibilities open to us. This text emphasizes the relationship between health and power, such as the power of workers over their work pace; the power of people to control the quality of their physical environments; the power of various groups or societies to shape health policy or to deliver what they consider healing; the power of people of different statuses to control, receive, and understand information vital to their well-being; and the power of the mass media to shape ideas about food and fitness. In addition to these objective manifestations of power, we also subjectively experience power. Our sense of personal empowerment—a feeling that we can handle stressful situations, for instance—is important to health and well-being and strongly related to our ability to manage our environment and feel safe and secure in it. The power of individuals is not simply personal but also usually has a social basis.

The concept of social power in particular implies that the will of one individual or group can prevail over that of others. Our statuses (such as age and social class) in society determine the resources available for the exercise of power. For example, if I own a business and control its resources, I can decide how they will be used; generally, I have power in my workplace and have more resources to enforce my will than do the workers in my business.

Often our experiences deal not with overt power or control but relative, implicit power. For example, if I feel in control of my family life, I thus feel able to resist others' attempts to wrest control, whether by direct confrontation or by subtle manipulation. For this reason, power is typically enhanced when its exercise is accepted as legitimate. Likewise, when people do not recognize that power is being exercised, they may submit to control unwillingly and unknowingly. Concepts like "social status" and "social control" thus are significant in understanding the relationship between power and the body. Control refers to the exercise of power in a particular situation. Like a sense of empowerment, control is related to our ability to manage our environment and to feel safe and secure in it.

Social control may be defined as those ways in which a society assures itself of its members' proper and respectable behavior, appearances, productivity, and contributions. Social control assures the relatively smooth functioning of the social order and the maintenance of hierarchical relationships such as class.

This control may rely on violence, force, persuasion, and/or manipulation. Internalized forms of control, such as individual conscience, are far more subtle and effective means of assuring uniformity. The standards by which people learn to measure themselves are another way in which society uses the social self as a means of control. Social organizations also use their control of information to maintain power. For example, the regulation that workers have to punch a time clock is a device for assuring work attendance. Social control measures also affect those who are in power, as when they become their own slave drivers.

THE PERSPECTIVE OF THIS TEXT

Although our focus is sociological, we have drawn from many other disciplines and subdisciplines, such as medical sociology, medical anthropology and economics, socio- and psychophysiology, sociology and anthropology of the body, sociology of health and illness, social psychology, history, philosophy of the body, and ethics. Each has its separate focus, and persons contributing to one discipline are often unaware of related work in other fields. We emphasize synthesizing work from several disciplines to achieve a more holistic appreciation of health and illness that views healing and prevention in the broadest sense: The body is not treated as a self-enclosed machine, and health and illness are understood in their social, cultural, and historical contexts.

A holistic perspective is necessary, but difficult because it requires us to go beyond the rigid separations of concepts about the body, mind, and society. As Scheper-Hughes and Lock (1986: 137) wrote:

> We are without a language with which to address mind-body-society interactions, and so are left hanging in mid-air, suspended in hyphens that testify to the radical disconnectedness of our thoughts. We resort to such fragmented concepts as the biosocial, the psychosomatic, the psychosocial, the somatosocial, as feeble ways of

expressing the complex and myriad ways that our minds speak to us through our bodies, and the ways in which society is inscribed on the expectant canvas of our flesh and bones, blood and guts.

We stress the interactions of mind, body, and society, and the importance of symbols and subjective experience in understanding health and illness. The narrow focus and unifactorial models of disease characterizing much of modern medicine and some of the sociology of health and illness deflect attention from the social issues implied by persisting inequalities in health status within most modern societies (Comaroff, 1982: 61), as well as the yet greater gaps of inequality between so-called developed and less developed nations.

SUMMARY

This text on the sociology of health and illness deals with the social construction of bodies, with an emphasis on how power shapes this construction. How cultural and social-structural factors and central power relationships influence us physically and how we perceive, care for, maintain, and "repair" our bodies constitute the major questions to be addressed. Our perspective is holistic, emphasizing the interpenetration of mind, body, and society.

The first part, Chapters 2 through 5, deals primarily with the ways in which society and culture affect physical functioning, and the material environments in which people exist. The second part, Chapters 6 through 9, emphasizes people's experience of their own and others' bodies, especially social aspects of the illness experience. The last part, Chapters 10 through 12, examines social and cultural factors in the medical systems' treatment of sick persons, and the political economy of health care in the United States.

WHO BECOMES SICK, INJURED, OR DIES?

Sickness does not just happen. Rather, discernible patterns are evident in the distribution and frequency of sickness, injury, and death in human populations. **Social epidemiology** is the study of these patterns and the *social* factors that shape them (Mausner and Bahn, 1985).

Noticing relationships between specific illnesses and people's social situation is hardly a new phenomenon: Early Greek and Egyptian writers made such connections (Sigerist, 1960). Popular lore also includes awareness of the linkage between, for example, an occupation and a sickness. *Alice in Wonderland's* Mad Hatter was a plausible madman because people had recognized a connection between the occupation of hatmaking and bizarre behavior long before the relationship was traced to the effects of the mercury with which hatmakers regularly worked (Stellman and Daum, 1971: 255). Similarly, long before medicine identified the problem, villagers living by the Niger River in Africa recognized that their proximity to the river was related to the prevalence of a horrible sickness characterized by intense itching and eventual blindness. Often they would move away, abandoning valuable farmlands, when the sickness had affected too large a proportion of the community (Eckholm, 1989).

During the late eighteenth and early nineteenth centuries, industrialization set the stage for the development of the disciplines of both sociology and epidemiology (Spruit and Kromhout, 1987). The changes that accompanied industrial capitalism created radically different conditions for health and illness:

> The rates of smallpox, typhus, typhoid fever, diphtheria and scarlet fever all increased: two cholera epidemics had swept through the warrens of the Great Towns, a third was on its way. . . . The reordering of the circumstances of everyday life . . . ensued. Industrial capitalism gave rise to novel physical arrangements for work and dwelling (the factory, the company town), created new patterns of economic exploitation (mass displacements from land, urban migration in unprecedented numbers, wage labor). . . . Hazardous and fatiguing work, damp cold and stifling living quarters, cheap gin and adulterated foods, demoralization–the legacy of disease bequeathed by early capitalism stems from such an environment. (Susser et al., 1985: 4)

Epidemiology, as a discipline, evolved from early studies of epidemics among people living in such environments. Like sleuths tracing the path of a suspected criminal, epidemiologists examined clues to the path of a suspected source of infection. For example, in 1854 a cholera epidemic broke out in London. Sir John Snow pinpointed known cases of the disease on city maps, thus narrowing the search to certain neighborhoods. He then interviewed survivors and neighbors of cholera victims about everyday behavior, such as what the victims had eaten, where they had played, and so on. Snow discovered that all of the victims had obtained their water from the same pump. He concluded that there was a relationship between this source of water and cholera infection, and he had the pump shut down, thereby ending the epidemic (Snow, 1855).

Although modern epidemiologists have far more sophisticated tools such as computers and complex bacteriology laboratories, their underlying method remains much the same as Snow's. They search for patterns linking the types and incidence of sickness of a people with their way of life. Thus, epidemiological studies often highlight the political and social contexts of health and illness (see Box 2.1). The famous nineteenth-century epidemiologist Rudolf Virchow declared, "Medicine is a social science, and politics is nothing but medicine on a grand scale" (quoted in Susser et al., 1985: 6). Political and social factors are readily evident in studies showing certain diseases to be characteristic mainly of the rich; others occur almost exclusively among the poor. Political implications also follow, for instance, from epidemiological studies demonstrating certain occupations to be the causes or major contributing factors in certain illnesses and death. Epidemiology is only one of many approaches to understanding the connections between social arrangements and sickness or death, but epidemiological data receive special attention from policymakers because they describe large-scale differences applicable to entire industries, communities, or nations.

COMPLEX WEBS OF CAUSAL FACTORS

Epidemiology examines the interaction of complex disease-producing factors: a "web of causation" (MacMahon and Pugh, 1970: Chapter 2). This web is composed of three main, intertwining aspects: agent, host, and environment. The agent is the source of a disease, such as a virus in an infection or asbestos fibers in asbestosis. The agent is a necessary but not sufficient cause of disease; disease does

BOX 2.1

Fur Fashions and Plague

The outbreak of Manchurian plague at the turn of this century constitutes a well-documented example of the role of living patterns in disease causation. The plague bacillus is widely distributed among the wild rodents of Asia. Manchurian marmots normally harbor this microbe, but they do not suffer from the infection under usual circumstances. Around 1910, a change in women's fashions in Europe suddenly created a large demand for the fur of the Manchurian marmot, and a number of inexperienced Chinese hunters began to hunt this wild rodent. Until then it had been hunted only by Manchurians who had a taboo forbidding them to hunt sick animals. In contrast, the inexperienced Chinese trapped every animal within reach, especially the sickest who were slower and easier to catch. As it turned out, the sick marmots were suffering from plague, and many Chinese hunters contracted the infection from them. When the hunters met in the crowded and ill-ventilated Manchurian inns, those who had caught the microbe spread it to their neighbors, thereby initiating a widespread epidemic of pneumonic plague. A change in women's fashions in Europe thus indirectly caused an epidemic of pneumonic plague in Manchuria.

Source: René Dubos, *Man, Medicine and Environment*. Baltimore: Penguin, 1968: 113.

not occur without an agent, but the agent alone is not sufficient to produce the disease (Mausner and Bahn, 1985).

The site within which an agent creates a disease is called the host. The host and agent interact within a biosocial environment, which includes the external conditions linking the agent to the host (such as unsanitary living conditions); the vector, or the means through which the agent is carried (such as diseased marmots or contaminated drinking water); and the condition of the internal environment of the host (such as relative immunity). To cause disease effectively, an agent must be able to survive in the environment and find a susceptible, fertile host (Johnson and Sargent, 1990). For example, a human body (host) may harbor tubercular bacilli (agent), but if the body's resistance is high, this disease agent cannot produce infection. Thus, disease is not the outcome of just one factor; rather, many factors contribute to the complex web of causation.

As the name implies, epidemiology arose from the study of widespread infectious diseases, or epidemics. The maturing field has more recently begun to include study of the distribution, spread, and cause of noninfectious diseases, such as heart disease or cancer. The epidemiology of these sicknesses is more difficult, however, because they develop more slowly, often over decades. The causal factors are thus obscured by time. A 60-year-old victim of a heart attack is not likely to be able to recall accurately relevant information about his life as much as 40 or 50 years earlier.

Noninfectious diseases also often involve multiple contributing factors rather than a single infectious agent. It is difficult to identify all possible factors and determine their relative weight. For example, the hormones in birth control pills have been implicated in the development, many years after their use, of breast cancer. But determining just how significant a factor they may be is complicated for several reasons. The disease does not develop in clinically observable forms immediately upon use of the pill. Other factors (such as the age of the onset of menstruation) are also involved and, in combination, greatly increase probability of developing the disease. Evaluating the relative importance of these various other factors (such as the woman's leanness, her age at the birth of her first baby, and whether she breastfed her babies) or even whether some possible factors are not being considered is difficult. It is hard to determine, many years after the fact, exactly how much or which type of hormones women received; formulations for early contraceptive pills contained much higher dosages of hormones and in different combinations than more recent formulations. If a woman is now 48, she may have taken several different formulations for many periods of varying length since the age of 18.

Although web of causation stresses *multiple* causes, this approach has a number of limitations. First, it still assumes disease to be a feature solely of *individual* bodies, divorced from their sociocultural contexts (Link and Phelan, 1995). Few epidemiological studies consider the "spiders" that "spin the web" (Krieger, 1994), that is, the fundamental social, cultural, and biological factors that interweave agent, host, and environment. Epidemiology needs an ecosocial approach incorporating historical, evolutionary, and sociopolitical determinants of health. In the chapters that follow, we suggest some of the spiders that weave the web of illness causation, for which we must look beyond epidemiological studies. Epidemiological studies, however, are a good starting place to describe general demographic factors linked to patterns of disease and death.

METHODOLOGICAL ISSUES

Epidemiology proceeds by observing statistical correlations between two or more variables pertaining to health, sickness, or death. The data for these statistical procedures are often drawn from records kept for other institutional purposes; researchers must therefore contend with discrepancies or errors created by the original records.

Statistical Associations

The existence of a statistical correlation between two variables is not sufficient evidence of a causal link between them. Many statistical relationships are spurious. For example, a nineteenth-century observer noted that the incidence of cholera was inversely correlated with the altitude of a community; low-lying places had higher rates of the disease than did those at higher altitudes. This correlation seemed to confirm a prevalent notion that stagnant air (miasma) caused cholera; accordingly, because their air was supposedly fresher, communities at higher altitudes had less miasma and thus less cholera. Later epidemiological discoveries showed that impure water was actually the vector (means of spreading the agent) for cholera. Because low-lying places were more likely to have both stagnant air and impure water, investigators had been led to a spurious correlation between the disease and miasma (Mausner and Bahn, 1985).

Historically, many epidemiological uses of statistical correlations have been seriously biased by racial or ethnic prejudice. Many late nineteenth- and early twentieth-century U.S. public health measures were justified by reference to epidemics allegedly caused by immigrants. An epidemic of smallpox in San Francisco between 1876 and 1877 was attributed to the immigrant Chinese, although deaths among Chinese San Franciscans accounted for only 77 of the 482 smallpox deaths in that epidemic. The city's public health officer attributed the epidemic to "unscrupulous, lying, and treacherous Chinamen who have disregarded our sanitary laws," merely on the basis of the statistical correlation between the influx of Chinese immigrants in the years prior to the outbreak and the increased morbidity compared to the previous epidemic (Kraut, 1994: 82).

Although epidemiology as a science has become more careful methodologically, similar misuse of epidemiological evidence arose in the early years of the AIDS epidemic, when oversimplified statistical correlations made AIDS appear to be linked to Haitian immigrants. In the early 1980s, the U.S. Centers for Disease Control announced that Haitian immigrants had been classified as a high-risk category for AIDS. A few years later, when it dropped this classification, the director of the Center for Infectious Disease acknowledged the spurious relationship, stating,

"The Haitians were the only risk group that were identified because of who they were rather than what they did" (cited in Kraut, 1994: 261).

It is often difficult to determine whether a statistical correlation is the product of an indirect relationship actually explained by intervening variables. For example, epidemiological data from the rural southern regions of the United States may show a statistical correlation between low birth weight and childhood deaths from diarrhea. Does that mean that low birth weight causes subsequent death from diarrheal dehydration? This is a plausible interpretation because birth weight may affect the child's susceptibility to illness, but birth weight may be only a by-product of some other causal factors. One clue to these other factors is to ask a somewhat oversimplified question: What kind of children are likely to experience both low birth weight and diarrhea? The profile of children with these conditions suggests several related features: They are likely to be from poor families in which the mother was young and received little or no prenatal care (Stevens, 1988). To establish a direct causal link between low birth weight and death due to diarrhea, it would be necessary to identify and hold constant all other factors. Any causal analysis must take into account multiple factors that may operate at several levels in the web of causality.

Bases of Data

Epidemiological studies may be based on seriously flawed records. Some statistics come from the records of schools, industries, insurance companies, hospitals, and public health departments. Because these data are kept for various other institutional reasons, they are often of limited accuracy for epidemiological purposes. For example, industrial accident statistics can be distorted by an industry's attempt to give the impression of a low accident rate.

Likewise, death certificates are very inaccurate and unreliable sources of information about the causes of death (Hill and Anderson, 1988, 1991). A Connecticut study found that 29 percent of death certificates inaccurately stated the cause of death, based on autopsy reports and patients' medical records (Kircher et al., 1985). In a further 26 percent of the cases, the autopsy and death certificate gave the same general disease category but attributed death to different specific diseases. More than half of the certificates thus provided seriously flawed data about the cause of death. Similar conclusions about the inaccuracy of death certificates were found in a Scottish study of postmortems (Cameron and McGoogan, 1981). Interviewing doctors in a Scottish city, Bloor (1991) found wide variations in how deaths were certified.

The usefulness of data from both medical records and death certificates may also be diminished by judgments made by the medical personnel who keep the records. Deliberate misrepresentations often occur when the cause of death is a stigmatizing sickness, such as alcoholism or AIDS. Such reporting problems make it difficult to assess the scope and actual impact of these important health problems. Not only the concern over stigma but also political, economic, and ideological considerations often figure into the deliberate underreporting of the incidence of AIDS. Data have been flawed, for example, by racist attitudes, fears of hurting tourism, and the assumption that AIDS affects only stigmatized minorities (Bolton, 1989: 93–94).

Death certificates also often state only a final cause of death, rather than the initial or contributing causes. For example, a person who dies of a gunshot wound may be listed as having died of internal bleeding. Although the bleeding is a fact in the case, the gunshot wound does not appear in the mortality statistics. Certain causes of death, such as adverse reactions to prescribed medications, are also systematically underreported (Altman, 1988).

The *International Statistical Classification of Diseases, Injuries and Causes of Death*, revised about every ten years by the National Center for Health Statistics of the United States, specifies standards to be used by attending doctors, coroners, and others in an attempt to produce internationally comparable data. Changes in these guidelines for classification, however, yield different rates of morbidity and mortality. One revision of the manual required coders to disregard medically induced (iatrogenic) causes of death, such as postsurgical bleeding or drug reaction, and instead to record the medical condition that first necessitated the treatment (Bloor et al., 1987). The proposed new form of death certificates in the United States asks for the immediate cause of death and a sequential listing of *all* underlying causes. These new data will likely result in the discovery of comparatively high rates of medically induced conditions leading to death.

Despite recent efforts to change the format of U.S. death certificates to allow for more complex and thorough reporting, the data entered on them remain problematic. Most death certificates are based on doctors' clinical judgments about the cause or causes of death; autopsies are expensive and performed for a decreasing proportion of cases. Whereas in the 1950s, autopsies were performed on about half of all patients who died in a hospital, current rates are only about 12 percent, performed disproportionately for forensic (that is, legal) evidence and, thus, hardly a representative sample (Hill and Anderson, 1991). Even when an autopsy subsequently contradicts the certificate or adds significant new information, physicians often do not amend it (Altman, 1988).

Even if autopsy findings are included on death certificates, these data may be slanted by the criteria used to select cases for autopsy. Women are less likely to be autopsied than men. In some states, nonwhite deaths are less likely to be investigated than those of whites (Bloor et al., 1987). Social status and/or the perceived social worth of the victim may also influence the thoroughness with which a death is investigated (cf. Sudnow, 1967). The cases autopsied are not a representative sample of all deaths.

So-called errors or variations in diagnosis are not random; they are often socially produced. For example, medical personnel's judgments may vary according to the perceived social class of the dead person. In earlier medical reporting, the cause of a professional person's death from heart disease was likely to be labeled "angina," whereas the cause of death of a working-class person with the same condition was usually classified as something else (Marmot et al., 1987).

Similarly, diagnoses (and thus morbidity statistics) are influenced by doctors' attitudes toward patients' social characteristics, such as gender, social class, or occupation, as discussed further in Chapters 9 and 10. For example, earlier data indicated that the rate of deaths due to alcoholism in Scotland was about twice those in England and Wales; these data are now in question, because studies show that doctors in England and Wales are much less likely than those in Scotland to attribute death to alcohol-related diseases such as cirrhosis (see Altman, 1988).

Cultural differences in medical practice, even among Western industrial nations and among doctors trained in modern biomedicine, account for some variations in diagnoses. For example, blood pressure readings considered hypertensive in the United States would be considered normal in England (Payer, 1988). Doctor characteristics may also affect the diagnosis or reported cause of death. Because of differences in their training, younger British doctors were less likely than older ones to report stomach cancer as a diagnosis (Bloor et al., 1987). Thus, a falling rate of mortality due to stomach cancer may be at least in part an artifact of differences in doctors' education.

These examples show that many health statistics may be *artifactual*, or produced by the social arrangements by which the statistics themselves are gathered and processed. Such artifactual evidence is misleading and often altogether incorrect. With these limitations in mind, let us examine some results of epidemiological investigation. The cautious use of epidemiological information can give us a broad picture of health.

CHANGES IN LIFE EXPECTANCY IN THE TWENTIETH CENTURY

American males born in 1900 could expect to live 46.3 years, and females, 48.3 years. By 1994, the life expectancy for both sexes had increased, but so had the gap between male and female rates. Males born in 1994 can expect to live 72.3 years; females born that same year could live on the average to the age of 79.0 years (USDHHS, 1996a). Figure 2.1 shows the dramatic increase in life span in the United States by decades from 1900 to 1990. A general decline of infant mortality and increasing difference in life expectancy between men and women began to emerge around 1920. In 1994, the infant mortality rate[1] for the United States was 8.4 deaths per 1,000 (USDHHS, 1996a). Figure 2.2 shows U.S. patterns of infant mortality between 1920 and 1990. There are also dramatic differences between blacks and whites in both general life expectancy and infant mortality.

Along with life expectancy changes have also come changes in the causes of death in Western industrial societies. Despite the recent development of some infectious diseases such as AIDS, there has been a long-term decline in death rates due to infectious diseases and an increase in death rates due to chronic degenerative diseases (McKinlay et al., 1989). Figure 2.3 illustrates this important change.

---

[1]The infant mortality rate is the number of children who die within the first year, calculated per 1,000 live births.

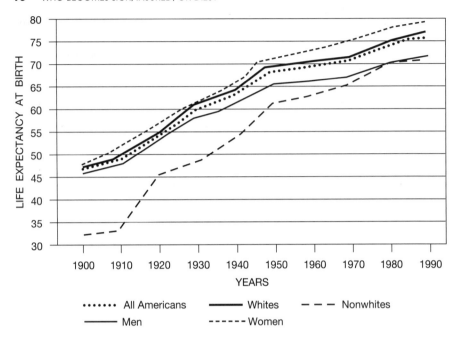

FIGURE 2.1   **Changes in U.S. Life Expectancy, 1900–1990**   *(Sources: U.S. Bureau of the Census, Statistical Abstract of the United States, 1992. Washington, DC, 1992; U.S. Bureau of the Census, Historical Statistics of the United States, Colonial Times to 1970. Bicentennial edition, part 2. Washington, DC, 1975.)*

Table 2.1, on page 21, shows the changing causes of death in order of their frequency. In 1900, acute infectious diseases (pneumonia, influenza, and tuberculosis) were the foremost causes of death in the United States. Chronic diseases (heart disease and cancer) were the major killers in 1994. Since the 1950s, the death rate from coronary heart disease in the United States has been decreasing, perhaps due to changes in diet, exercise patterns, and smoking habits (Sytkowski et al., 1990). Rates of death from cancer have increased during the same time (USDHHS, 1996a).

This shift from infectious to chronic degenerative diseases is part of *epidemiological transition*, characterizing changes in societies as they become more developed. Nevertheless, infectious disease can also be chronic (as is the case with AIDS) and infectious diseases are still a source of morbidity and mortality in developed societies (Radley, 1994). Some evidence indicates that since 1980, mortality from infectious diseases in the United States has been increasing, after years of steady decline. In 1980, infectious diseases ranked fifth as cause of death; by 1992, they ranked third (Pinner et al., 1996). Possible reasons for these increased rates include the spread of AIDS and diseases such as tuberculosis (of which some strains are resistant to antibiotics), especially in contexts of increased poverty (Pinner et al., 1996; Radley, 1994). Nonetheless, chronic degenerative diseases (including heart disease and cancer) still predominate as causes of death.

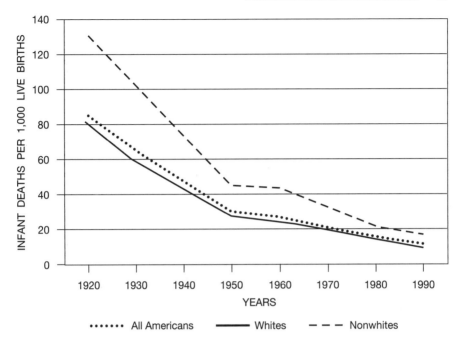

FIGURE 2.2   **Changes in U.S. Infant Mortality, 1920–1990** *(Sources: U.S. Bureau of the Census,* Statistical Abstract of the United States, 1992. *Washington, DC, 1992; U.S. Bureau of the Census,* Historical Statistics of the United States, Colonial Times to 1970. *Bicentennial edition, part 2. Washington, DC, 1975.)*

The increased incidence of chronic degenerative diseases cannot be attributed simply to the fact that people are living longer. It is true that the longer people live, the more likely they are to develop a chronic disease; however, increased longevity does not account for the fact that, beginning in the 1950s, even *younger* age groups have shown an increased incidence of these afflictions (Angier, 1991; Eyer and Sterling, 1977). This premature development of degenerative sickness may be the result of contemporary dietary, environmental, and social factors. Evidence that the social, biochemical, and physical environment of industrialized societies create new health problems, such as increased rates of cancer, comes from a comparison with preindustrial societies, which have lower incidence of these problems. Aspects of the way of life in industrialized societies are implicated because the rates of chronic degenerative diseases increase among groups that migrate from agricultural to industrial communities (Janes, 1986).

THE MYTH OF MEDICAL PROGRESS

Many people believe miracles of medical progress have been responsible for the improved health and longevity in Western industrial countries since the turn of the century. Media imagery often contributes to the notion, but much evidence

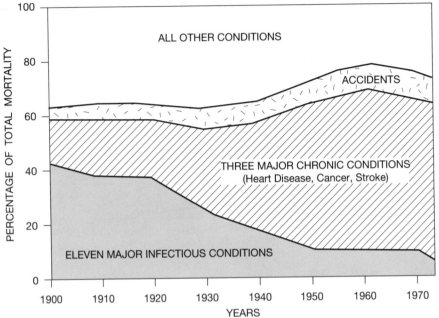

FIGURE 2.3 **Proportion of Chronic and Infectious Disease Contributing to U.S. Mortality 1900-1973** *(Source: John B. McKinlay and Sonja M. McKinlay, "The questionable effect of medical measures on the decline of mortality in the United States in the twentieth century,"* Milbank Memorial Fund Quarterly 55, *1977: 416. Reprinted by permission.)*

suggests the contribution of medical intervention to increased life expectancy has been rather limited. McKeown (1979) argues that improved nutrition and population control, the control of predators, and improvements in urban dwelling conditions and hygiene have played a much greater role in extending life expectancy than has medical technology. The impact of these various factors on health can be documented through epidemiological studies.

A study of mortality rates in the United States shows that medical intervention (such as inoculations) accounts for only a small percentage of the decline in mortality from infectious diseases during the early part of the twentieth century (Kates, 1996: 57; Wilkinson, 1996: 66–67). Figure 2.4 shows that, of nine common infectious diseases, only poliomyelitis began to decline significantly *after* the introduction of the vaccine. All the other major infectious diseases had declined dramatically *prior* to the introduction of a vaccine or antibiotic (McKinlay and McKinlay, 1977). The decline of tuberculosis likewise preceded the introduction of chemical therapies (Friedman, 1987). Nonmedical factors, such as improved nutrition, clean water, garbage and sewage disposal, and other public health measures, may account for the primary decline in mortality due to many infectious diseases.

The precise contribution of medicine to increased life expectancy, to the reduction of morbidity, and to the quality of life is difficult—if not impossible—to assess.

TABLE 2.1   **Causes of Death in the United States, 1900 and 1994**

	1900		1994
Causes of Death	Crude Death Rate (per 100,000)	Causes of Death	Crude Death Rate (per 100,000)
All causes	1,719.0	All causes	876.9
Pneumonia and influenza	202.2	Diseases of the heart	281.6
Tuberculosis	194.4	Malignancies	206.0
Diarrhea, enteritis, and ulceration	142.7	Cerebrovascular disease	59.2
Diseases of the heart	137.4	Chronic obstructive pulmonary disease	39.1
Senility, ill-defined or unknown	117.5	Influenza and pneumonia	31.3
		Suicide and homicide	21.5
Intracranial lesions of vascular origin	106.9	Diabetes mellitus	21.2
Nephritis	88.6	Cirrhosis, liver disease	9.9
All accidents	72.3	HIV infection	16.1
Cancer and other malignant tumors	64.0	Motor vehicle crashes	16.2

Sources: U.S. Department of Health and Human Services, National Center for Health Statistics, "Births, marriages, divorces, and deaths for 1985," *Monthly Vital Statistics Report* 34(12), 1986: 5; U.S. Department of Health and Human Services, *Health: United States, 1995.* Hyattsville, MD: National Center for Health Statistics, 1996: 161.

Some have argued that the iatrogenic (that is, medically induced) health risks of modern medicine and its institutions outweigh its benefits (Illich, 1975). This position probably overstates the harmful effects of modern medicine. Nevertheless, any evaluation of the contribution of medical intervention must take into account its iatrogenic consequences, such as unneeded surgery, over- and misprescription of drugs, the negative side effects of medication, and infections transmitted in medical settings.

Without a doubt medicine has made significant contributions to human health. It is effective in treating many acute diseases. Emergency medicine has saved many lives, and technological innovations in medicine since World War I have made it possible for many to survive previously mortal health crises. Medicine has also played a major role in the virtual eradication of some infectious diseases, such as smallpox and polio. The ability of medicine to treat or prevent chronic, degenerative diseases is more limited, however. Furthermore, the benefits from medical progress must be distinguished from social-environmental changes and public health measures that have played a major part in improving people's health. The contributions of public health measures are often devalued by modern medicine, resulting in social policies that allocate the vast majority of health care expenditures to medical research and treatments rather than to preventive programs such as maternal nutrition or workplace safety.

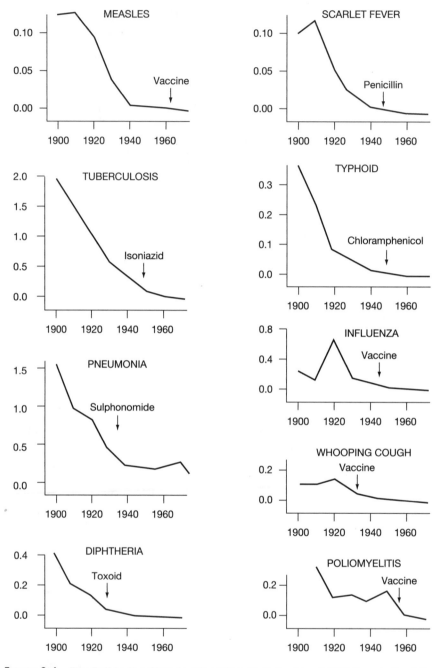

FIGURE 2.4 **The Fall in the Standardized Death Rate (per 1,000 Population) for Nine Common Infectious Diseases in Relation to Specific Medical Measures in the United States, 1900–1973** *(Sources: John B. McKinlay and Sonja M. McKinlay, "The questionable effect of medical measures on the decline of mortality in the United States in the twentieth century," Milbank Memorial Fund Quarterly 55, 1977: 422–423.)*

MORBIDITY AND MORTALITY IN THIRD WORLD COUNTRIES

The pattern of high rates of mortality due to infectious diseases seen in industrial-ized societies at the turn of the century still characterizes the health situation of many Third World societies. The average person born in Japan in 1992 can expect to live to about 79.5 years; in Sweden and Canada, about 77 years; and in the United States, 76 years. Contrast those estimates with the life expectancy of those born in 1992 in China, 68.5; in India, 60.4; in Haiti, 56.5; in Rwanda, 47.3; and in Guinea-Bissau, 43.5 (United Nations Development Programme, 1995). Average life expectancies are somewhat misleading, however, because they do not reflect the variations between subgroups (for example, class, gender, and rural-urban differ-ences) within each society. In Third World countries, as in nineteenth-century Europe and America, such factors as inadequate diet and unsanitary conditions contribute greatly to the high mortality rate and prevalence of infectious diseases. Twenty-five percent of people in the Third World lack access to safe drinking water (Kristof, 1997). Childhood diseases such as measles are much more likely to result in death where nutrition and sanitation are poor.

Many Westerners consider Third World countries to be inherently disease ridden, eagerly awaiting the benefits of modern civilization. In reality, the intrusion of so-called civilization from the West has introduced devastating infectious diseases to Third World peoples. Native peoples of the Americas and Polynesia were deci-mated by diseases introduced by European explorers, sailors, merchants, and colonists (Harkin, 1994; Kraut, 1994). Since Captain Cook's voyage there in 1778, more native Hawaiians have died of infectious diseases introduced by foreigners than of all other causes combined (Bushnell, 1993).

In the nineteenth century, Africa was viewed as a "white man's grave," a disease-filled "dark continent." Many diseases, however, such as smallpox, syphilis, measles, influenza, cholera, and tuberculosis, were introduced to Africa from Europe and Asia, devastating native populations, which had no immunity to diseases to which they had never been exposed. The colonization of Africa and the slave trade created massive sociocultural dislocations and altered patterns of land use. Migration to the cities and the attendant overcrowding, as well as the ecolog-ical disruption of the land, generated conditions that bred and spread certain infec-tious diseases. In epidemiological terms, alterations in the environment made for a changed relationship among host, agent, and environment. For instance, in western Africa the development of logging, commercial agriculture, roads, railways, and other changes in the landscape created sites (infection reservoirs) for breeding mosquitoes and thus for spreading malaria (Epstein and Packard, 1987).

In countries such as South Africa, radically different pictures of health exist side by side in the same society. As a whole, South Africa has a highly developed economy. Nevertheless, the policy of apartheid (1950–1993) produced the social and economic domination of a white minority over a nonwhite majority by radical segregation of housing, education, occupations, and legal status. This social arrangement resulted in very different living conditions for whites and nonwhites, and hence in different patterns of morbidity and mortality. The infant mortality for blacks in South Africa is approximately six times higher than that of whites. One-quarter of black children under 14 years of age are chronically malnourished or undernourished. By contrast, hardly any malnutrition or undernutrition exists among whites, and whites generally die of "diseases of affluence," which are linked with lifestyles characterized by high-calorie diets and sedentary occupations. Blacks are more likely to die of infectious diseases, such as typhoid, cholera, tuberculosis, and measles (a disease that is rarely fatal in affluent societies). Thus, in one nation, two very different ways of life produce different health profiles. These differences are a dramatic illustration of how social-structural arrangements (that is, apartheid) can produce different patterns of health, illness, and death (Frankel, 1986; Susser et al., 1985).

Not only are diseases themselves spatially and socially segregated, but various forms of segregation also reduce people's ability to know and understand others' way of life. Probably most members of the white minority in South Africa did not fully perceive the physical consequences of apartheid. The ability of the affluent to see the world of the hungry and poor is blocked by their spatial and social segregation from each other. Similarly, a reporter in Ethiopia noted that many members of the urban middle and upper classes did not have any knowledge of the famine in their own country until foreign correspondents wrote about it (May, 1985). A censored press can thus mute social conscience. In many cities in the United States, economically comfortable middle-class persons may likewise live only blocks from squalor and never be truly aware of it.

THE EPIDEMIOLOGY OF AIDS

By the year 2000, an estimated 210 million people worldwide will be infected with the HIV virus. As of 1995, approximately 1.5 million in the United States are infected with HIV, of whom 441,525 had been diagnosed with AIDS (Smith, 1996: 1). Worldwide, 985,119 AIDS cases were reported as of mid-1994: 523,777 in the Americas; 331,376 in Africa; 115,668 in Europe; 8,968 in Asia; and 5,330 in Oceania. In some countries, cases may be underreported because of the stigma attached to AIDS, the fear of losing tourism, and other cultural and political reasons (Bloor, 1995: 12, 13).

The transmission of the AIDS virus depends on the geosocial and cultural context in which it is spread. In North and South America, Western Europe, Australia, and New Zealand, AIDS affects mainly males. The mode of transmission often involves anal intercourse, whereas the rate from transmission by vaginal intercourse appears to be relatively low. In these countries, AIDS is concentrated primarily among homosexual men, contributing to the myth that it is essentially a gay plague. However, of all the adults estimated by the World Health Organization to be infected with HIV in 1991, three-quarters contracted the virus through heterosexual contact (Bloor, 1995: 72).

Many developed countries are now reporting an increase in AIDS cases due to heterosexual transmission (Bloor, 1995). Thus, the epidemiological profile of

AIDS in countries like the United States may be changing. As of 1989, women were increasingly likely to become infected (Corea, 1992). More people belonging to racial and ethnic minority groups—men, women, and increasingly, children—are becoming AIDS victims. In New York City, more than one-half of AIDS cases are among blacks and Hispanics (Shulman and Mantell, 1988). By the middle of 1994, AIDS replaced homicide as the leading killer of black Americans aged 25 to 44 (Muwakkil, 1996b). Among Hispanics, the rates are highest among Puerto Ricans, whereas the rates among Mexican Americans are similar to those of non-Hispanic whites (Selik et al., 1989; USDHHS, 1992).

The designation of groups as high risk is itself problematic. First, no one is at risk because of their membership in a group but because they engage in certain risky practices. Intravenous drug users are not at risk because they inject drugs but because they share equipment (Bloor, 1995: 29). Secondly, epidemiological use of broad categories (such as "Hispanic") obscures the wide variety of practices *within* groups (Becerra et al., 1991). So-called high-risk groups, such as prostitutes, show a great deal of variability in HIV prevalence with 0 percent in Las Vegas, Nevada, and 55 percent in Newark, New Jersey. Similar variations exist among European cities (Bloor, 1995). Thirdly, to single out certain groups as high risk may contribute to stigmatizing them. Finally, the practices of so-called high-risk groups may change over time. In the United Kingdom, for example, drug users may be reducing their risk behavior, much like the gay community.

The rates of new cases in the gay community are leveling off because of dramatic changes in sexual practices. Such changes preceded large-scale government health education campaigns and were partly due to social organizing, education, and condom distribution by the gay community (Bloor, 1995; Friedman, 1993).

In central Africa, the patterns of transmission to hosts and course of infection are quite different for those in Europe and the Americas. One-third to one-half of all those with AIDS are women, with a large concentration of cases among prostitutes. This suggests that in Africa heterosexual intercourse is a more common means of transmitting AIDS than homosexual contact and intravenous drug use. In parts of Africa, prostitution is encouraged by practices of migratory labor (a heritage from the colonial past) and poverty. Millions of couples are separated for months at a time while men go to cities or plantations for work (Lear, 1996). Men who resist the use of condoms and have multiple partners transmit the virus from place to place during their travels for work (Corea, 1992; Turshen, 1989). Female prostitutes, in contrast, often have few alternative means of survival. Prostitutes may also travel and thus spread the virus. Women's lack of power renders them more vulnerable to AIDS (see also Bloor, 1995; Doyal, 1995; Lear, 1996; McAuliffe, 1996).

The categories epidemiologists use are not neutral, and use of a particular system of classifying groups guides the way we interpret this information. In the early days of the epidemic, fixed ideas about AIDS as a gay plague kept American physicians from believing intravenous drug users with AIDS who denied any homosexual contact (Bloor, 1995: 56). Rather than simply looking at risk groups, it makes sense to focus on the variable sociocultural, political, and economic contexts in which HIV transmission occurs (Bloor, 1995; Friedman, 1993).

VARIATIONS IN MORTALITY AND MORBIDITY

The wide range of mortality (that is, death) and morbidity (injury and disease) within societies is distributed along basic sociological variables such as region, age, gender, ethnicity, and class. Variations in health and death are linked to people's different locations in social space and structure. The following discussion examines major variables in mortality and morbidity for the United States.

Age

As expected, death rates increase with age. Until the age of 40, U.S. death rates increase gradually. After 40, they virtually double for each decade of age (Mausner and Bahn, 1985: 120). Figure 2.5 shows population pyramids for the United States, which indicate, for a given year, the relative numbers of males and females in each age bracket. The data for 1910 take the shape of a conventional pyramid because the birthrates are balanced by death rates, for both sexes, in a somewhat even pattern. The 1995 pyramid, however, is less conventionally shaped because of decreased birthrates and lower death rates, a pattern that characterizes industrialized nations. This trend, in which fewer people are born and more live past the age of 50, has been called the graying of society because ever larger proportions of the population survive into old age. Demographic projections show that people aged 85 years or more are likely to be the fastest growing part of the population in the next few decades (Rice, 1990).

Although chronic degenerative diseases have been increasing in all age groups, their rates increase most dramatically for older people (Radley, 1994; Verbrugge, 1990). In 1965, one out of five Americans under 50 had chronic diseases; among those over 65, four out of five had such disorders, with heart disease most frequent (Susser et al., 1985). Only rates for death due to homicide, accidents, and suicide decline with age; rates of death due to chronic illnesses and disabling conditions increase. The increased number of people in our society with chronic illness and disabilities has raised a number of sociopolitical issues, discussed further in Chapter 7. Many chronic conditions are not a natural result of aging. For example, the rate of hypertension (high blood pressure) increases with age in American society but not in hunting and gathering societies. The nomadic !Kung bushmen of the Kalahari Desert in Africa consume large quantities of dietary salt, a factor that some have linked to hypertension, yet they do not show increased blood pressure with age (Schnall and Kern, 1981).

Although aging seems inevitably to involve increased morbidity, some researchers suggest the possibility of "compressing" morbidity. They argue that although the life span is biologically limited, it may become possible to limit the period when an aging person is infirm (Fries, 1990). Others point out that although the compression of morbidity is a desirable goal, it is not occurring now and little

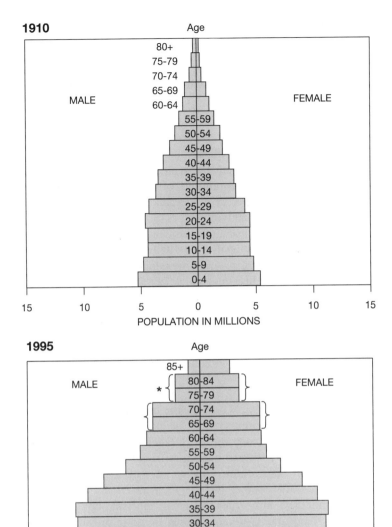

1910

Age

MALE   FEMALE

80+	
75-79	
70-74	
65-69	
60-64	
55-59	
50-54	
45-49	
40-44	
35-39	
30-34	
25-29	
20-24	
15-19	
10-14	
5-9	
0-4	

15   10   5   0   5   10   15

POPULATION IN MILLIONS

1995

Age

MALE   FEMALE

85+
80-84
75-79
70-74
65-69
60-64
55-59
50-54
45-49
40-44
35-39
30-34
25-29
20-24
15-19
10-14
5-9
0-4

15   10   5   0   5   10   15

POPULATION IN MILLIONS

*The bracketed data reflect the arbitrary disaggregation of 10-year age ranges into two equal 5-year sets, rather than estimation of the proportional distribution of the age groups.

FIGURE 2.5 **Age Composition of the U.S. Population, 1910 and 1995** *(Sources: Population Reference Bureau,* Population Bulletin *37 (2), 1982; U.S. Bureau of the Census,* Statistical Abstract of the United States, *1995. Wash., DC 1995.)*

evidence indicates it will in the near future (Guralnik and Schneider, 1990). Although compression of morbidity may be possible, it pertains mostly to higher socioeconomic groups, however. Widespread compressed morbidity would require greatly increased social equality (House et al., 1990).

Gender

In the nineteenth century, women typically died younger than men. One explanation of the difference is that frequent pregnancies and childbirth involved considerable health risks. Also, under conditions of general material scarcity, women often got what food was left after men and children ate their share. Poor nutrition then compounded women's health difficulties (Shorter, 1982). The female advantage in life expectancy became apparent in the United States and Europe by the late nineteenth century (Doyal, 1995). By the 1920s, the gender patterns in mortality rates had changed, and women generally were living longer than men. By 1994, the life expectancy at birth for U.S. males was 72.3 years; for females, 79.0 (USDHHS, 1996a). At all ages, males have higher rates of mortality than females (Verbrugge, 1992). Similar differences between men and women exist in most Western industrialized countries (Sagan, 1987; Waldron, 1994); however, in some Third World countries, male life expectancy is greater than, or the same as that of women (Doyal, 1995; Waldron, 1994).

Biological factors may partially account for the higher mortality rates of males, especially early in life (Doyal, 1995). Higher fetal mortality rates have been reported for males (Harrison et al., 1992). Because the male-female mortality rate difference occurs cross culturally, it cannot readily be explained by social factors. Female life expectancy is also higher among many other animal species (Sagan, 1987). This biological advantage for women may come from hormonal differences, although such differences may also produce higher rates of some sicknesses in women (Friedman, 1987).

Men die earlier and have more life-threatening illnesses, but in general women become ill more frequently. Chronic illnesses are more prevalent among women than men, but they are less severe and life threatening than those of men (Marks, 1996; Verbrugge, 1992). Women also report more episodes of illness and more contact with physicians (Susser et al., 1985: 71). Women's higher rates of sickness and doctor visits can be partly explained by gynecological or reproductive problems, which men do not have, but the incidence of these problems is not great enough to account for the difference in morbidity rates between men and women. Perhaps women are more willing than men to admit they are sick and/or to visit physicians. If this is true, then lower morbidity rates for men are deceptive, because they are a function of the underreporting of sickness rather than differences in rates of actual disease (see Waldron, 1976). Perhaps women learn more effective coping skills and ways of caring for themselves (such as seeking care and calling in sick), but no firm evidence exists for this hypothesis (Verbrugge, 1992). Gender differences in morbidity may be underestimated, however (MacIntyre, 1993). For such conditions as flu and the common cold, men are more likely than women to overstate the severity of their symptoms. Thus, rather than being stereotypical "chronic complainers," women may be underreporting their sickness.

Men are more likely than women to engage in high-risk behavior, such as smoking, violence, or unsafe driving (Stillion, 1995). Likewise, risks associated with work roles may be higher for men (Krieger and Fee, 1994; Waldron, 1991; Woods, 1995). The mortality gap between men and women may be narrowing in recent years. The gap may narrow further as women adopt such high-risk behaviors as smoking and enter workplaces with job stressors and other risks, and as men, by contrast, improve their health behaviors (Woods, 1995). There is some evidence that death rates due to smoking-related diseases are rising among U.S. women (USDHHS, 1996a). Although such biological factors as hormonal differences play some role, sociocultural factors linked with differences between men's and women's roles probably account for much sex-linked variation in mortality and morbidity rates.

Race and Ethnicity

Patterns of morbidity and mortality also vary among ethnic and racial groups in a society. Some differences may be explained by hereditary factors that are disproportionately characteristic of certain groups. Genetically transmitted sicknesses include sickle-cell anemia (among blacks and some other groups) and Tay-Sachs syndrome (among persons of eastern European Jewish descent).

Hereditary factors also combine with sociocultural factors to produce ethnic differences in morbidity and mortality. For example, Mexican Americans are more likely to have inherent lactose intolerance than Anglo Americans; lactose intolerance combined with social factors (such as higher rates of poverty) produces serious nutritional deficiencies (Schreiber and Homiak, 1981: 283). Similarly, genetic tendencies may be a component factor that, together with stressful living and working arrangements, leads to disproportionately high rates of diabetes among Mexican American migrant workers (Angel, 1989; Scheder, 1988).

Patterns of variation are linked indirectly to ethnicity through other factors: nutrition, housing and sanitary living conditions, employment and types of occupation, family patterns, and lifestyle. Epidemiological data reflect these variables, but cannot always separate them neatly to show just how much variance is explained by any one variable. Other connections are more obvious. For example, a study of the incidence of childhood lead poisoning showing a large number of the victims to be inner-city black preschoolers could determine rather easily whether the causal connection was in fact that disproportionate numbers of urban blacks live in substandard, older housing where the crumbling lead paint may be ingested by young children. The following discussion gives some of the highlights of U.S. data about racial and ethnic variation in morbidity and mortality.

Black Americans constitute by far the largest racial/ethnic minority in the United States. Epidemiological data referring to "nonwhites" are thus mainly describing blacks. The pattern of health of black Americans is very different from that of white Americans. In 1989, black life expectancy was 69.6 years compared to 75.9 years for whites (USDHHS, 1992). These rates represent a dramatic improvement since 1920, when life expectancy was 45.3 years for blacks and 54.9 years for whites.

One major factor in the lower life expectancy for blacks is their high rate of infant mortality. Figure 2.2 shows differences in infant mortality between white and nonwhite Americans between 1920 and 1990. Even though infant mortality has been steadily declining for both groups, the nonwhite rate has generally been about twice that of whites (La Veist, 1992). Infant mortality is especially high among newborns with low birth weight or very young mothers or both. The rate of live births of babies with low birth weight (less than 2,500 grams) was 12 percent for blacks compared with 6 percent for whites; 38 percent of black mothers did not receive prenatal care until after the first trimester of pregnancy, compared to 20 percent of white mothers (Anderson et al., 1987). These factors are clearly linked with socioeconomic factors (La Veist, 1992). Low birth weight is often the direct result of poor maternal nutrition and inadequate prenatal care. Drug abuse also contributes to poor infant health among African Americans. Thus, fetal alcohol syndrome is disproportionately higher among African Americans and Native Americans compared to other ethnic groups (Collins, 1996). Compared to other industrialized countries, the U.S. infant mortality rate is frighteningly high, largely due to this country's failure to address the problems of poverty, especially nutrition and health care. Indeed, since 1980 cutbacks in federal spending resulted in reduced or inadequate prenatal care for poor mothers (cf. Physicians' Task Force on Hunger in America, 1985).

Since the mid-1980s, there has been a slight decrease in black life expectancy (while whites experience a slight increase); changes in life expectancy of black males account for most of the decrease (Najman, 1993; USDHHS, 1992; Williams and Collins, 1995). This decrease may be partly due to the rise of infectious diseases such as AIDS and increased conditions of poverty[2] experienced disproportionately by blacks (Muwakkil, 1991). The proportionately higher rates of hypertension and hypertensive heart disease among blacks compared with whites illustrate the complexities of causal factors with which epidemiological studies must contend. Factors accounting for these differences include genetic factors in susceptibility, greater stress due to racism, lower socioeconomic status, less access to good medical care, and a higher rate of obesity among blacks (Friedman, 1987). The genetic susceptibility explanation seems doubtful because cross-cultural studies found no such patterns among genetically comparable peoples of Africa. Whereas American blacks show a rapid increase in blood pressure after the age of about 24, African blacks living in tribal communities do not have increased blood pressure as they age. Migration to industrialized, urban settings, however, does promote increased blood pressure (Janes, 1986). The lower socioeconomic status of many blacks probably accounts for much of the differences in hypertension and other problems (Navarro, 1991). Even after taking social class into consideration, however, some

---

[2]For example, the percentage of black children living in poverty increased from 41 to 44 percent between 1979 and 1988 (Williams and Collins, 1995).

small yet significant differences remain (Navarro, 1989). Such factors as stress produced by racism and residential segregation,[3] which influence even the more affluent blacks, may explain some of these remaining "racial" differences (La Veist, 1993; Mutchler and Burr, 1991; Reed, 1993).

Hispanics[4] (among them, Mexican Americans, Puerto Ricans, and Cuban Americans) are a fast growing minority in the United States. Some are at increased risk for diabetes, hypertension, tuberculosis, AIDS, alcoholism, cirrhosis, specific cancers, and violent deaths. Among subgroups of Hispanics, Puerto Ricans have the poorest health (Williams and Collins, 1995), due mainly to low socioeconomic status (Council on Scientific Affairs, 1991).

Some American ethnic groups comprise individuals whose families came to the United States in different waves of immigration. Comparative studies thus have the potential of identifying which factors in sickness and death are due to the particular living situation and lifestyle of a group in the United States compared with the country of origin. For example, although the rate of tuberculosis among Chinese Americans is higher than among the general population, it is nevertheless lower than in the old country. Similarly, both first- and second-generation Chinese Americans have more coronary heart disease than Asian Chinese; diet and stress are both implicated (Gould-Martin and Ngin, 1981). The experience of migration itself may contribute to poor health (Sundquist, 1995).

Patterns of morbidity and mortality among Native Americans reveal another set of factors. American Indians are among the most disadvantaged ethnic groups in the United States; their death rate is about 30 percent higher than that of the general U.S. population (Weeks, 1986). Like many peoples of developing nations, Native Americans are experiencing a demographic and epidemiological transition over a relatively short period of time.

Demographic transition refers to the changes populations undergo (usually in the course of so-called modernization) as they move from a situation of high mortality and fertility to a stage in which mortality has declined but fertility is still high. The third phase is characterized by low fertility and mortality (Omran, 1971). Native American groups have experienced more decline in mortality than in fertility, and the decline in mortality is largely due to the reduction of epidemic infectious diseases. The resulting rates of morbidity and mortality, at this stage of transition, reflect a shift in causes of death. For example, among Navajos, overall mortality has declined, especially mortality due to influenza, pneumonia, gastritis, and certain diseases of early infancy; at the same time, there is increased mortality due to accidents and alcohol-related diseases (Kunitz and Levy, 1981).

---

[3]Residential segregation may also mean less access to decent education, health services, housing, and recreational facilities. Toxic waste dumps, waste incinerators, and air pollution from traffic appear to be disproportionately found in black neighborhoods (Brown, 1995b; Williams and Collins, 1995).

[4]The term *hispanic* is a contested term for nonblack persons of Latin American descent. Because it arbitrarily lumps together, for national census categories and other record keeping, persons of highly diverse and often mixed ethnic backgrounds, it results in confusing generalizations. For instance, for hypertension, Mexican women are at lowest risk, Central American women at higher risk, and Cuban and Puerto Rican women are at highest risk (Krieger and Fee, 1994).

There thus appears to be considerable racial and ethnic diversity in the United States in rates of mortality and morbidity, but precise figures are not available because national epidemiological data do not differentiate among white ethnic groups or nonwhite ethnic groups (for critical summaries of various studies on urban black Americans, Chinese Americans, Haitian Americans, Italian Americans, Mexican Americans, Navajos, and mainland Puerto Ricans, see Harwood, 1981a; see also Polednak, 1989). Most differences, however, appear to be largely due to social-structural factors, especially class. Purely materialist explanations (that is, those that focus on the impact of different material conditions on health differences) may not always completely explain ethnic differences in such health indicators as infant mortality (Andrews and Jewson, 1993). Cultural factors also influence diet, reproduction, and such health-related behavior as smoking and drinking.

Social Class

Social class is probably one of the most useful shorthand indicators of a person's power. Class is usually measured by income, education, occupation, or a combination of these factors. Generally, a consistently significant relationship exists between class and health (Dutton, 1986). The lower the social class, the higher the rates of morbidity and mortality. This relationship is not surprising, considering the important part that social class plays in the quality of our everyday lives (Mausner and Bahn, 1985). Infant mortality and social class are also clearly linked. Although infant mortality has declined for the population as a whole in the past century, class differences are still quite large and have remained constant over the years (Wilkinson, 1986a).

Indeed, in the United States, class differences in health may have increased (Najman, 1993; Navarro, 1991; Williams and Collins, 1995). Differences in mortality between socioeconomic groups have generally increased in the United States since the 1960s (Kennedy et al., 1996). In recent decades, similar increases in mortality-rate disparity have been noted between socioeconomic groups in other countries (Pappas et al., 1993; Williams and Collins, 1995).

The relationship between social class and rates of mortality has been documented for England, Wales, Denmark, Finland, France, Japan, New Zealand, and the United States (Marmot et al., 1987). Table 2.2 shows some relationships between social class (measured by occupational classifications) and morbidity, mortality, and health behavior in England and Wales. Lower-class persons had consistently higher rates of perinatal (infant) mortality, maternal mortality (the mother's death from pregnancy- or birth-related problems), and mortality from all causes. Studies in the United States and Australia also show a relationship between social class and infant mortality (Najman, 1993). Class differences are also linked to rates of coronary heart disease and diseases of the respiratory system. Morbidity rates (measured by respondents' reports of long-standing illness and the number of restricted activity days per year) show a regular correlation with social class. Class differences are particularly pronounced between the highest class (professionals) and lowest class (unskilled manual workers) (Rice, 1991).

In Scandinavia, long-standing illness is reported more frequently among blue-collar than white-collar groups (Rahkonen et al., 1993). There is a relationship between people's self-assessment of health and their income levels. The higher the

TABLE 2.2   **Birth Weight and Mortality in England and Wales by Social Class.**[a] **Morbidity and Health Behavior in Great Britain by Socioeconomic Group.**[b]

		SOCIAL CLASS[a]				
		I	II	IIIN	IIIM	IV	V
Birth weight ≤ 2500 g, 1980 (%)		5.3	5.3	5.8	6.6	7.3	8.1
Mortality							
Perinatal mortality/1,000, 1978–1979		11.2	12.0	13.3	14.7	16.9	19.4
Mortality 1–14, 1970–1972	M	74	79	95	98	112	162
	F	89	84	93	93	120	156
Maternal mortality, 1970–1972 (standardized maternal mortality rate)		79	63	86	99	147	144
All cause mortality 15–64, 1970–1972 (SMR)	Men	77	81	99	106	114	137
	Married women	82	87	92	115	119	135
	Single women	(110)	79	92	108	114	138
Coronary heart disease, men 15–64, 1970–1972 (SMR)		88	91	114	107	108	111
Disease of respiratory system, men 65–74 (PMR)		60	74	82	105	108	123

		SOCIOECONOMIC GROUP[b]					
		1	2	3	4	5	6
Morbidity (age 45–64)							
% Reporting long-standing illness	M	35	31	41	42	47	52
	F	32	36	40	41	49	46
Averge number of restricted activity days per person per year	M	4	14	30	31	27	38
	F	22	23	28	27	33	39
Health behavior							
Prevalence of cigarette smoking, 1984	M	17	29	30	40	45	49
	F	15	29	28	37	37	36
Participation in active outdoor sports (%), 1977	M	42		34	23	17	15
	F	30		27	17	14	11

[a]Registrar-General's Social Class: I, Professional etc; II, Intermediate; IIIN, Skilled occupations (nonmanual); IIIM, Skilled occupations (manual); IV, Partly skilled; V, Unskilled.

[b]Socioeconomic group: 1, Professional; 2, Employers and managers; 3, Intermediate and junior nonmanual; 4, Skilled manual and own account nonprofessional; 5, Semiskilled manual and personal service; 6, Unskilled manual.

Source: M. G. Marmot, M. Kogevinas, and M. A. Elston, "Social/economic status and disease," *Annual Review of Public Health* 8, 1987: 113. Reproduced with permission from the *Annual Review of Public Health*, 8, © 1987 by Annual Reviews, Inc.

income level, the more likely self-assessed health is excellent; the lower a person's income, the more likely health will be self-rated as poor (Blaxter, 1990; Navarro, 1991; USDHHS, 1992).

These data illustrate that differences that at first appear to be individual are often actually social variations. Although smoking is an individual behavior, for example, those in the lowest socioeconomic positions are almost three times as likely to smoke as those in the highest positions (Marmot et al., 1987), which may partially explain the higher rates of respiratory diseases among the lower classes. Similarly, alcohol consumption is highest among the lower classes, as is the incidence of obesity (Dutton, 1986). Deaths due to accidents also increase as socioeconomic status decreases (Quick, 1991).

The Black report, a famous British study on the relationship between class and health, concluded that lack of personal control over one's life was an important factor linking low social status with poor health (Black, 1980; see also Gray, 1982). A 1987 update of the Black report not only documented persisting class differences in morbidity and mortality, but also showed a widening gap in health between the upper and lowest classes (Townsend, 1990).

Syme and Berkman (1976) have argued that this lack of control and other adverse features of lower-class life create a "generalized susceptibility" to disease (see also Blaxter, 1990). The issues of generalized susceptibility, control, and health are discussed further in the next three chapters.

The conditions of lower-class life include living and working in more polluted and crowded environments, exposure to higher noise levels and risks of accidents, and inadequate housing and transportation. Medical care for the poor is less accessible and of lower quality than that for higher social classes. Furthermore, health problems of the poor are typically more serious, complex, and difficult to treat (Dutton, 1986).

As the Black report shows, for England, improved access to medical care does not by itself significantly reduce social class differences in health. Scandinavian countries, which provide citizens with excellent access to high-quality health care, nonetheless exhibit some class differences in health. A study of the Scandinavian situation concluded that "health care without social welfare and economic policy will be ineffective in reducing social inequalities in health" (Rahkonon et al., 1993: 77). To seriously reduce the effects of social class on health requires far more basic economic and social reforms (Hurowitz, 1993).

Measuring social class variables is difficult. Occupation is one frequently used indicator of social class, but occupational categories are often broad and not neatly tied with a single social stratum. For example, the category "teacher" might include a nursery school teacher and a professor at a prestigious university. How would the classification scheme distinguish between a farmer who owns 50 acres and cultivates them for family subsistence, and a "farmer" who owns 4,000 acres and hires numerous workers to cultivate them (Susser et al., 1985)? Measures of class using occupation may use the husband's occupation as a measure of the wife's socioeconomic status, but such measures do not indicate whether a husband is, indeed, sharing his socioeconomic advantage with his wife and children. As more women enter the work force, such a measure is even less adequate (Krieger and Fee, 1994).

Despite such definitional problems, studies of many societies document a consistent relationship between social class and health. Rates of mortality and social class are clearly linked, but the relationship between class and specific causes of death is not so consistent, and may change over time. Rates of coronary heart disease in England and Wales, for example, first began to increase in the 1930s among men of the upper classes. By 1950 the disease was more common among the lower classes. A similar downward shift in the incidence of coronary heart disease took place in the United States (Susser et al., 1985). A possible explanation of the variation is that the upper classes were initially more susceptible to coronary heart disease as a "disease of affluence" (for example, they may have eaten much more meat and enjoyed more sedentary leisure time). As lifestyles changed, however, concern with dieting and exercise became values for many middle- and upper-class persons, and coronary heart disease declined. The lower classes did not adopt such lifestyle changes, and thus their rates of coronary heart disease remained high (Marmot, 1996; Susser et al., 1985).

The epidemiology of poliomyelitis also illustrates how the relationship between class and mortality from specific diseases may change over time. In lower-class areas, characterized by overcrowding and poor sanitation, children often developed antibodies and hence immunity to polio after being exposed to the virus early in life. Thus, the poor had lower risk of paralysis and death than the more "sheltered" middle and upper classes. When the polio vaccine was introduced in the mid-1950s, however, this relationship between class and vulnerability to the disease changed. Those upper- and middle-class children who were first vaccinated were the first to benefit. An education campaign eventually resulted in the wide-spread acceptance of immunization, but pockets of underimmunized persons still exist in the United States, particularly among lower-class minority groups (Susser et al., 1985: 229–231).

These examples show that the relationship between specific kinds of morbidity or causes of mortality may not follow the usual relationship with social class and may shift over time. At present, however, there are no major causes of mortality for which death rates are not higher among lower-class than upper-class persons. On the whole, the lower classes bear higher burdens of mortality and morbidity (Blaxter, 1990).

Even when data show a strong correlation between two variables, such as social class and health status, the direction of causality is sometimes difficult to determine. Does variable *A* produce variable *B*; does variable *B* produce *A*; or are they related in even more complex ways, mutually influencing each other or indirectly influencing each other through some third (intervening) variable? For example, do lower social status and the poor living conditions that accompany it produce poor health, or does poor health lead to downward mobility and lower income, or do both situations interact (Dutton, 1986)? The explanation that poor health results in downward mobility has been called the *drift hypothesis*, which suggests that those who acquire disabling diseases "drift" down the social ladder in the course of their lives (Lawrence, 1958).

Some evidence hints that serious illness in childhood is related to downward mobility in later life. Boys who were seriously ill are more likely than those who were healthy to gravitate to a social position below that of their fathers (Wilkinson, 1986b). Downward drift may be linked only to specific "diseases" such as schizophrenia (Marmot et al., 1987), so the drift hypothesis does not explain satisfactorily most of the relationship between class morbidity and mortality (Marmot, 1996; Wilkinson, 1996; Williams and Collins, 1995). The hypothesis does appear to hold more for chronic illness than for acute illness. The two explanatory models may, however, be complementary: Chronic illness may lead to lower socioeconomic status, the conditions of which may increase the likelihood the person will suffer acute diseases, thus producing a vicious downward circle for the disadvantaged (Wolinksy and Wolinsky, 1981).

Some of the relationship between social inequality and specific kinds of morbidity and mortality may be more artifactual–a product of the way the variables are measured–than real. An extensive critique of the Black report argues that the correlation between social class and mortality due to chronic degenerative diseases is essentially artifactual (Bloor et al., 1987). For example, the perceived social class of the deceased person influences whether the cause of death was classified as heart disease. The significance of such artifacts in the correlations between social class and health is not clear. Other reviews (compare Marmot et al., 1987) consider artifacts to be relatively unimportant in explaining the social class differences in health. They observe that a large number and variety of studies, done in several societies, indicate a strong relationship among class, health, and death.

SUMMARY

There are observable patterns to the frequency and incidence of human sickness and death. As opposed to the clinical-medical model, which focuses on individual bodies and a limited number of causal factors in disease, the epidemiological approach looks at social patterns of morbidity and mortality and the complex "web of causation." Epidemiological studies show that many patterns of morbidity and mortality are connected with social variables, such as the kind of society, race, ethnicity, age, social class, and gender. These epidemiological variables are also rough indicators of the social distribution of power and of the different power relationships people experience. With its broad generalizations, social epidemiology sets the stage for a more refined analysis of the ways a society produces, defines, experiences, and treats sickness and death.

RECOMMENDED READINGS

Articles

JOHN MCKINLAY and SONJA MCKINLAY, "The questionable contribution of medical measures to the decline of mortality in the United States in the twentieth century." *Milbank Memorial Fund Quarterly* 55, 1977: 405–428.

DAVID R. WILLIAMS and CHIQUITA COLLINS, "U.S. socioeconomic and racial differences in health: Patterns and explanations." *Annual Review of Sociology* 21, 1995: 349–386.

Books

MICHAEL BLOOR, *The Sociology of HIV Transmission.* Thousand Oaks, CA: Sage, 1995. Comprehensive review and analysis of the epidemiology of HIV transmission in developed and developing countries and a discussion of risk behavior.

GARY D. FRIEDMAN, *Primer of Epidemiology*, 3rd ed. New York: McGraw-Hill, 1987. A clearly written introduction to epidemiological concepts.

SOL LEVINE and ABRAHAM LILIENFELD, eds., *Epidemiology and Health Policy*. New York: Tavistock, 1987. An excellent collection of articles dealing with problems such as nutrition, coronary heart disease, cancer, injuries, and occupational health.

MEREDITH TURSHEN, *The Politics of Public Health.* New Brunswick, NJ: Rutgers University Press, 1989. Lively, critical analysis of public health and epidemiological issues in a global context.

THE MATERIAL FOUNDATIONS OF HEALTH AND ILLNESS

Certain social practices contribute to the production of a healthy body; others lead to its destruction. The very condition of our bodies—whether we are healthy or sick, whether we live or die—depends not on luck but on social circumstances.

In Chapter 2 we discussed some of the patterns of distribution of sickness and death according to social variables like socioeconomic status, ethnicity, race, and gender. In this chapter we examine certain social environments and practices that produce physical conditions contributing to these differences in health and illness. Basic health requirements—a satisfactory diet and a safe, clean physical environment—are very much influenced by many cultural and social-structural arrangements.

Much in our social activities endangers our health. How we organize production, and what and how we produce and consume are central to creating our way of life as well as to producing health or illness. This discussion begins by examining material (that is, physical) sources of health and illness, and how they are shaped by social factors, especially the power of different groups to control physical resources such as food and the quality of the physical environment.

FOOD

Hunger

Every few years the news media alert the public in economically developed nations to widespread starvation in parts of the world such as Ethiopia or Bangladesh. The public conscience is mobilized, and money and food are collected. The furor then dies down, and for a while the public forgets the routine starvation that plagues much of the world. In 1991 (when the world population was over 5 billion), more than half a billion adults experienced continuous hunger. About 1 billion people (20 percent of the world's population) lack the calories needed for an active work life (Cohen and Hoehn, 1991).

More common than outright malnutrition is undernutrition, or a diet that lacks enough basic nutrients such as protein or vitamins. Iron-deficiency anemia is common, especially among women between the ages of 18 and 45 and young children (Latham, 1987). Anemia, which results in symptoms of fatigue, exists in an estimated 51 percent of children between 0 and 4 and in 60 percent of pregnant women. An estimated 40 million preschool children in 37 countries have vitamin A deficiency (McIntosh, 1995). Iodine deficiency affects approximately 200 million people and about another 1 billion are at risk (McIntosh, 1995). Thus vitamin-deficiency diseases, such as scurvy, beriberi, rickets, keratomalacia (lack of vitamin A), pellagra, and mineral-deficiency diseases (for example, anemia) are still widespread in the Third World (Brown and Inhorn, 1990). Mortality rates from measles are much higher in Third World countries such as Mexico and Ecuador. Differences in vulnerability to an infectious disease such as measles (which kills few people in the United States), tuberculosis, and even diarrhea[1] are partly due to nutritional factors (Eckholm, 1977: 48). One-third of all children under the age of 5 in developing countries are undernourished to the point of permanent developmental impairment (Cohen and Hoehn, 1991). Although not starving, many people in the world suffer from stunted physical development, a greater vulnerability to disease, and a lowered quality of life brought on by under-nutrition.

An adequate diet is characterized partly by the quality of food consumed and by a certain amount of various vitamins, protein, fiber, and other components. An adequate diet also requires the consumption of a sufficient number of calories to support the body's activity. (A calorie is a measure of how much energy is generated by food eaten.) Table 3.1 shows variations in per capita calorie consumption in selected regions of the world. We can see from this table that the figure for some regions, such as Africa from 1988 to 1990, was a little more than half that of countries such as the United States. Per capita figures, however, do not show how these calories are distributed within the population. For example, in Africa some are well fed, whereas others consume far less than their minimum daily caloric requirement. Per capita indicators obscure age, sex, and social class differences within countries or regions, understating the existence of malnutrition (McIntosh, 1995: 42–43).

Although undernutrition and malnutrition are more common in Third World countries, ironically they are also features of well-to-do countries such as the United States, where an entire industry is devoted to producing foods that taste like the real thing but lack caloric substance, and where some use jogging and other exercises to cope with the tendency to overconsume and overeat. In the 1960s, however, studies such as *Hunger U.S.A.* (1968) showed the extent of undernutrition in America. The introduction of food stamps, increased health care and welfare benefits, school lunches, and other poverty programs since that time has helped decrease the incidence of hunger. Some evidence suggests that cutbacks in these programs since the Reagan administration in the 1980s have led to increased incidence of hunger. The 1985 report of the Physicians' Task Force on Hunger in America estimated that approximately 20 million Americans are hungry and about 500,000 children are undernourished. Approximately one child in eight under age 12 is vulnerable to hunger. The problem of hunger in the United States appears to be growing; indeed, in the 1990s, the U.S. food aid program helped a record number of eligible food stamp recipients (Cohen and Hoehn, 1991). Increased unemployment and under-employment created the "new poor" (former members of the middle and working

---

[1]Diarrhea is a major killer of children in the Third World; an estimated 4.5 million children die from it each year. In the United States, about 200,000 children under the age of 5 are hospitalized each year because of diarrhea, and several hundred a year die from it. Although vaccines against the virus that is the disease's primary agent are not yet available, the treatment of oral rehydration therapy is simple, safe, and inexpensive. The epidemiology of diarrhea shows that in America these preventable deaths occur disproportionately among poor black children in the rural South; social policies addressed to alleviating poverty, improving sanitation, and increasing access to health care and health care education could thus eliminate an entire category of infant mortality (Stevens, 1988).

TABLE 3.1   **Per Capita Calorie Consumption by Region (1969-1971, 1988-1990)**

	KCAL PER CAPITA/DAY	
Region	1969-71	1988-90
World	2,430	2,700
Developed regions	3,190	3,400
North America	3,230	3,600
Europe	3,240	3,450
Oceania	3,290	3,330
Former USSR	3,320	3,380
Developing regions	2,120	2,470
Africa	2,140	2,200
Far East	2,040	2,450
Latin America	2,500	2,690
Near East	2,420	2,920

Source: United Nations, Food and Agriculture Organization (FAO), *The State of Food and Agriculture, 1992.* Rome, 1992: 21.

class) and contributed to increased hunger in the 1980s. Neither wages nor public assistance benefits grew to keep pace with greatly increased costs of shelter, forcing many families to choose between hunger and homelessness (Poppendieck, 1995). Economic crises in the farming sector during the 1980s ironically increased hunger among the families of the nation's food producers (Schneider, 1987).

Overpopulation and Scarcity   One common theory explains world hunger as a matter of overpopulation combined with lack of natural resources, such as arable land and favorable climate. Accordingly, poor people exceed their ability to feed themselves by reproducing too fast. This is often called a Malthusian explanation, after Thomas Malthus, a nineteenth-century British economist whose theories of population growth still have influence (Hess, 1987). Malthus ([1798] 1965) argued that the growth of the world's food supply would not be able to keep pace with the growing population unless it were reduced by "natural" forces such as war or famine, or by poor people's abstinence from sex. Innovations in agricultural productivity, which were already apparent in Malthus's time, cast doubt on his theory. His interpretations nonetheless influenced many social scientists and policymakers, particularly the nineteenth-century social Darwinists, who argued that social life and survival could be explained using the principles of evolution and that evolution favored the "survival of the fittest." Malthus's predictions were correctly characterized as "dismal" and led some (including the social Darwinists) to believe that although food aid and improved sanitary measures might help the poor in the short run, they would simply encourage them to breed more, thus creating more long-term suffering (Hess, 1987).

The Malthusian notion of an absolute scarcity of food and thus the need for poorer nations to control population growth still prevails (McIntosh, 1995). Although there is some truth to this position, advocates often refuse to consider policy measures, such as land reform, that would more equitably redistribute the resources needed to grow food (Moore-Lappé and Collins, 1986).

Malthus, of course, could not fully grasp the potential of modern technology to stimulate the food supply. With existing levels of technology, some estimate that it is possible to feed a much greater number of people than the world's current population (Barraclough, 1991; George, 1982; Moore-Lappé and Collins, 1986). However, in many countries hunger seems to have increased just as the world food surplus has grown. In fact, many poor countries in which undernutrition and malnutrition prevail are *exporting* large quantities of food. During a 1984 drought, for example, Zimbabwe was exporting a record harvest of tobacco, soybeans, and cotton, and Kenya was exporting asparagus and strawberries (Bennett and George, 1987). During a famine in Mali, there were likewise increased exports of cotton and peanut cake, which is fed to European cattle (Moore-Lappé and Collins, 1986).

After the communist revolution, life expectancy in China increased dramatically, from the age of 24 in 1931 to 65 in 1982; infant mortality also sharply declined. Except for periods of famine in some areas caused by natural disasters, China has been able to feed its people not simply by increasing food production but also by distributing food more equitably (Barraclough, 1991; George, 1982; Lardy, 1983; Warnock, 1987). The improved standard of living brought population growth to China. Agricultural practices and land use for urban areas and industry have subsequently decreased the available arable land, which, relative to other countries, was already minimal (Warnock, 1987). To increase its living standards and diversify people's diet further, China may have to import food. If the nation continues to increase its use of energy-intensive agricultural methods to increase crop yields, it will become dependent on oil imports.

Nevertheless, China—an extreme example of the Malthusian problem of many people and few resources—has managed to bring about dramatic decreases in hunger through political changes (Barraclough, 1991). Population growth will be a significant factor in the long-term standard of living, but population is not the only factor, nor can the mechanisms that affect population growth be considered independently of sociopolitical and economic factors.

Emphasis on population control as the primary solution to hunger problems often places the burden of solutions on poor people whose attitudes toward birth control appear irrational to outsiders. High birthrates in developing countries may, however, be very rational to the people themselves, who believe they need more babies (in the face of high infant mortality) to care for them in old age and to provide a family labor force. Population growth is thus not simply the *cause* of poverty. Large families are a way of coping with impoverished conditions, and hence a *result* of poverty (George, 1982).

The scarcity argument also holds that many countries lack sufficient natural resources such as arable land. Only about 44 percent of the world's cultivatable land is being used to grow food. Much lies unused for investment purposes (that is, the owners are waiting for its value to increase). How land is used and who determines this use are thus important considerations. Colombia, for example, uses arable land for such export crops as carnations, which bring the large landowners more profit than subsistence crops. In Brazil, land that had once been used to grow food beans for local consumption is now cultivated in soybeans for export. Due to a diversion of land use for export crop production, bean prices tripled. At the same time Brazil's GNP (gross national product) increased, as did its supply of foreign currency. Brazil industrialized and its rich prospered while hunger grew among the poor (Brooke, 1993; George, 1982). Moore-Lappé and Collins (1986) have argued that every country has enough land to feed itself, and that hunger is often the result of patterns of land use and ownership which are shaped by the social distribution of power in these societies.

Although overpopulation and geography contribute to world hunger, more important reasons involve sociopolitical and economic factors as well as technology and knowledge.

Technology and Knowledge Modern technologies, such as farm machinery, allow people to work the land more effectively and often to increase food production. Indeed, some improvements in health in the Western world were the consequence of advances in agricultural production. Yet these technologies must be viewed in their sociopolitical and economic contexts.

Toxic substances are often a part of modern agricultural technologies, but developing countries do not have effective regulatory controls (Norris, 1982). Many of the world's countries have no effective legislation to control toxic chemicals. Many pesticides such as DDT and DBCP, which have been banned in the United States, continue to be sold and used in the Third World. Beyond their widespread and deadly effects on farmers who often do not know of their risks, these toxic chemicals often come back to our dining room as residues on vegetables and fruits, thus completing a "circle of poison" (Thrupp, 1991; Weir and Shapiro, 1981). Industrialized nations export substances that are banned in their own countries but subsequently are imported back into their own food supply.

The high yield these agricultural technologies produce has other negative consequences. They are typically energy intensive, requiring considerable quantities of oil to build and fuel machinery, and to make pesticides and fertilizers. Thus, a great deal of nonrenewable resources, like oil, is required to produce relatively little food energy. The need to import such resources for energy and for agricultural technology increases the foreign debts of many Third World countries, which means that more land must be devoted to producing export crops to pay those debts. Should the market price of a major export crop drop, the problem becomes more acute. When coffee prices dropped in 1981, for example, El Salvador had to spend 70 percent of its coffee earnings on oil imports (Everett, 1984).

Energy-intensive technology is a mixed blessing for many people. Small farmers cannot afford it, and its uncontrolled use may deplete the land and cause extensive pollution. Technological solutions alone are thus of little use to many developing nations. Many farmers would benefit from less energy-intensive ways of growing food, but such possible options are not likely to be developed by the companies that profit from existing technologies. In short, technologies do not develop in sociopolitical and economic vacuums.

Some critics attack many of the agricultural practices and consumption patterns of the Third World poor as irrational factors contributing to their hunger. On the surface, nothing appears more irrational than starving Hindus in India who will not eat their cattle. Harris (1985), however, has argued that many of these seemingly irrational practices make ecological sense, given local conditions. Cows can be used to plow land and produce milk, their blood (which can be drained without killing them) is a source of protein, and their manure provides fuel and fertilizers. In the context of Indian culture, large-scale meat production may actually be "ecologically impractical," because it takes about 20 pounds of grain to produce 1 pound of beef (George, 1982). In fact, much of the world's grain is used for animal feed. If the people of the world were to adopt a more vegetarian diet, the capacity to feed populations with existing arable land would increase greatly (Waggoner, 1996). The major barriers to subsistence are thus not the lack of technology, overpopulation, or a scarcity of land but rather economic, political, and social considerations that relate to land use, distribution, and control.

Land as a Resource: Use and Distribution In South America, 90 percent of the land is controlled by 17 percent of the landowners (George, 1982). In Honduras, one of the poorest countries in Central America, 4 percent of the people control 65 percent of the arable land (Wijkman and Timberlake, 1988). In El Salvador, another extremely poor Central American country, 81 percent of the arable land is used to grow coffee and is owned by 3 percent of the population (Kotzsch, 1985). In the 1980s, 3 percent of landowners controlled two-thirds of the land in Guatemala, and almost 90 percent of the peasants (mostly indigenous peoples) were landless (Barraclough, 1991). This pattern of land ownership and use is typical of many Third World countries.

Bangladesh is an example of how patterns of land control are significant in explaining world hunger. In that country, the per capita calorie consumption is considerably less than the necessary nutritional minimum, yet Bangladesh actually produces enough food to be able to feed its hungry. In fact, it exports large amounts of food. Between 1960 and 1984, the number of landless households (that is, those with less than 0.2 hectares of land) tripled (Barraclough, 1991). Those who own less than 0.2 hectares of land or who own *no* land consume an average of 1,924 calories per day. People owning 1.2 hectares or more consume 2,375 calories per day, and consume 28 percent more protein than those with less land (Brown et al., 1987: 31). In short, farmers' access to land and their ability to grow what their family needs are prerequisites to subsistence. Land reform that would make this subsistence possible is very difficult to institute, however, because the parliament is dominated by landowners (Crittenden, 1981).

In southwestern India, the state of Kerala managed to improve its life expectancy and infant mortality rates, despite the fact that it has one of India's lowest per capita income rates. (In 1986, life expectancy in Kerala was 68 years, compared with the national rate of 57 years; its infant mortality rate was 27 per 1,000 live births, compared to 86 per 1,000 for India as a whole.) The lower infant mortality rate and increased life expectancy were due to improved food intake. In

1969, a new state government instituted land reform, government control of food prices, large-scale public health actions, accessible medical care, and literacy training. Kerala was able to improve its health and nutritional status through political and social change rather than increased economic development and production (Franke and Chasin, 1992).

Hungry Bodies Are Socially Produced A basic requirement for health is a good diet. At first glance, it would seem that the problem of hunger in many parts of the world revolves around issues of scarce resources, a lack of technology, and overpopulation. These undoubtedly *are* factors, but technology depends on who controls it, whether it is available to all, and whether it is geographically and culturally appropriate. Most countries have the resources to feed even very large populations, but the key factors in determining whether they do so appear to be political considerations as well as corporate control of technologies and, often, of large amounts of land used to grow export crops.

Many have criticized food aid on the grounds that it is used as a political tool: Countries may withhold needed food aid from governments whose policies they disapprove of (Barraclough, 1991; Kinley et al., 1981). A more serious problem, however, is that much aid never reaches those who need it because of local power arrangements. A World Bank study of Bangladesh discovered that about one-third of the food aid went to police, military personnel, and civil servants; about one-third went to the urban middle class; and only one-third reached the rural poor, who constitute the vast majority of the hungry. A similar pattern prevails in other countries (Kinley et al., 1981; Parker, 1981).

Hunger in poor countries is affected by their relationship with rich nations. Many Third World countries must contend with the impact of colonialism on their society, physical environment, and system of food production. Furthermore, rich nations' models of industrial food production may be inappropriate for less developed countries, and their pressure to adopt "advanced" food production methods often hinders the development of culturally and ecologically viable alternatives. Many Third World countries also serve rich nations as a source of markets, raw materials, and export crops. Fluctuations in global food prices are furthermore affected by the capitalist world market in which rich nations are a dominant force (Warnock, 1987).

The basic requirement of health, a good diet, is linked therefore to the distribution of power. It is easier to blame nature, scarcity, a lack of technology, or individual reproductive practices than it is to indict social systems. Yet it is the social systems and the way power is distributed within them that shape the material world in which we live and hence the condition of our bodies.

The Sociocultural Dimensions of Eating Habits: "You Are What You Eat"

A society's practices of food consumption also play a role in nutritional problems. These eating habits are in turn influenced by sociocultural factors and issues of power. So-called affluent societies, with their diets high in animal fat, salt, and sugar, are often characterized by poor eating habits. At the end of the eighteenth century, sugar consumption in Europe (13 pounds per person per year) was already relatively high compared to previous times. With time, sugar found even more and more uses as a flavor enhancer and preservative. By the middle of the twentieth century, sugar consumption in the United States was over 120 pounds per person per year (Mintz, 1979). In some respects our diets have become healthier (increased consumption of protein, for instance); however, in other ways (significantly increased consumption of food additives, sugar, animal fat, and salt), they have become unhealthier. We tend to view eating habits as a matter of individual free choice. Although this is partly true, they also reflect sociocultural preferences, and the way we eat is shaped by sociopolitical and economic factors. In this section, we examine the interrelationships among society, power, and food from that perspective.

We do not eat merely to survive or because food provides us with sensuous pleasure. For humans, food takes on symbolic meanings, and activities related to the consumption of food have social functions and dimensions. Sharing food reflects social bonds. A family dinner is an occasion to communicate, affirm social ties, and remind members of their respective social statuses. Tastes in food are used by people to distinguish themselves socially. Middle-class people pride themselves in "good" taste in food choices, preparation, and consumption, as opposed to the "unhealthy," "unrefined" eating practices of the lower class. There are some gendered food preferences in our society: Men may prefer red meat and "man-sized" portions; women, salad and vegetables (Lupton, 1996).

Food taboos exist in virtually every society. For instance, Muslims and Jews prohibit the consumption of pork. A breach of a food taboo can affect one physiologically. A person who knowingly eats a proscribed food may get sick or even die. For example, when the Ponape, a people of the South Pacific, ate a forbidden fish, they would break out in hives (Farb and Armelagos, 1980). Cultures define what is edible or not, what is "good" food and "bad" food. For example, rural North American folk beliefs hold that too much pork, rich or red meat, and salt is "bad" food, causing high blood pressure (Lupton, 1996: 28).

Culturally rooted aversions to particular foods are not restricted to religious groups or preliterate societies. A priest in San Francisco once suggested that because Asian refugees in the area liked to eat dogs and cats, the humane society could supply them with stray animals (which unless adopted, would be killed anyway) to use as food; His proposal was met with a great deal of opposition. Many Americans would get physically ill if they discovered they had just eaten "puppy parmigiana," yet in some parts of the world dogs are a normal source of meat protein and even considered a delicacy. Americans enjoy cheese, but most Chinese people find it disgusting (Lupton, 1996). Cultural factors thus shape our food preferences, our reactions to food, and our very appetites.

The diets of specific cultures are often well suited to the physical environments and biological constitution of the people who inhabit them. A genetic intolerance of lactose, a prime component of milk, is not uncommon among *most* peoples of the world (Harris, 1985; Overfield, 1985). Such physical intolerance, common among the Chinese, may partially explain their aversion to cheese, for example. Biological variations are not the only reason some foods are defined as unpleasant or preferred. Cultures also adopt certain food habits for practical benefits, as exemplified by the Hindu prohibition against eating cows (Harris, 1985). Some foods may be too costly in their demand on land, human, and fuel resources. The Chinese custom, for example, of rapidly cooking food in a wok over a high flame developed because of fuel scarcity (Farb and Armelagos, 1980).

Sociocultural Change, Eating Habits, and Multinational Corporations
When external forces alter the eating habits or way of life of a culture, new nutritional problems can ensue. In many societies, dental cavities were rare until Western influences introduced large amounts of refined sugar into the diet (McElroy and Townsend, 1985). Several decades ago the Zuni Indians of the American Southwest had a very low incidence of diabetes. As farmers and hunters, their bodies had developed a capacity to store fat efficiently to survive periods of food shortage. Their cultural values defined being fat as healthy. As they "modernized," their lifestyle became more sedentary, and they replaced their traditional diet with the low-income food culture of fast food that was high in salt and sugar. Their biological capacity to store fat then became a liability, as they burned less energy and consumed more food. The incidence of diabetes subsequently increased (Peterson, 1986).

In recent years, multinational corporations have found new markets for their food products in the Third World. Often these products are promoted and introduced into sociocultural environments in which their widespread use may be inappropriate and unhealthy. Soft drinks and white bread, for example, have been aggressively promoted in countries like Malaysia and Mexico (Barnet and Mueller, 1974; Kaur, 1990). Advertising campaigns and the fact that these products are seen as coming from a "high-status" culture make them prestigious, and they may come to symbolize modernity and social status. Given the limited cash income of Mexican peasants, however, such products consume disproportionate amounts of the family budget and provide little nutritional return. In Malaysia, many farmers spend up to one-third of family incomes on cigarettes and alcoholic drinks (Kaur, 1990). In a marginally nourished population, this exchange is a poor trade.

In the 1960s and 1970s, several companies such as Nestlé promoted commercial baby formula in Third World countries. Their advertising presented bottle feeding as modern and healthy for babies. Bottle feeding, however, required much of the family cash income (from 15 to 85 percent, depending on the country), and many mothers diluted the milk to stretch supplies, thus unintentionally starving their babies. The lack of the clean water, fuel, and sanitary conditions needed for formula preparation and storage also prevented the product's safe use (Kaur, 1990). Even a marginally nourished mother can usually produce breast milk, which also transmits to the infant her natural antibodies that fight infection. As bottle-feeding practices were adopted in such places as Kenya, infant malnutrition increased. Doctors gave this form of commercially encouraged malnutrition a medical label: "bottle-baby syndrome." Because of an international boycott and other pressures, the transnational companies were persuaded to stop many of their practices promoting this inappropriate product in Third World countries (Norris, 1982).

The world's eating habits are increasingly influenced by global corporate interests, which not only control much food production but also influence the information disseminated through advertising. One author concluded, "Backed by such powerful advertising, the standardization of food values at a global level at the expense of the local specificities has divorced people's eating habits from their history and culture" (Mansour, 1987: 16). Large corporations have more and more control not only over the growing and processing of food, but also over advertising and information about their products. These factors increasingly shape the food habits of the world.

Nutritional and Commercial Practices in Industrialized Countries Commercial messages that promote foods are often directed at such vulnerable targets as children. A considerable portion of Saturday morning commercials on U.S. television, for example, promotes sugar-laden cereals and snack food. With the exception of a few token public service nutrition ads, most commercials imply that such food is consumed by the viewer's heroes, and that eating it will result in personal pleasure and status among one's peers (Barnouw, 1978: 91–92; Gussow, 1978: 229). One study indicated that children influenced by these commercials may exert significant control over their mothers' shopping habits (Barnouw, 1978: 92–93).

Not only do individual advertising messages affect eating habits, but their cumulative tone also suggests a cultural attitude toward food. The more implicit messages often have a greater effect. Bottled drinks, such as beer and soft drinks, are heavily advertised. The implicit message is less a matter of which product one drinks, but rather that one should want a commercial drink instead of water or a home-produced beverage to satisfy thirst. Advertising has thus sold a behavior, not just a product (Gussow, 1978: 222). Some ads suggest that when people are hungry and do not have time to eat, they should deaden hunger pangs by consuming a candy bar, which produces a sugar "high." Other ads urge the audience to eat or drink more, even after the hunger or thirst is satisfied; expanded appetites are thus created. To sell products, commercials often urge people to override their bodies' signals by either deadening them or overconsuming. Their messages are often contradictory: "Be thin," "control your eating," "eat, drink, and be merry," and "gorge, gorge, gorge."

Affluent societies often consume overly rich diets with too much sugar, fat, and salt, and too little fiber. Absence of fiber in a diet has been linked to the high incidence of colon cancer (Burkitt, 1973). Food processing enables modern societies to preserve, store, and transport a wide variety of foods, increasing their availability throughout the year in regions far from their origins. Processing also increases the convenience of preparing many foods. By its very nature, however, processing causes the loss of many nutrients (Farb and Armelagos, 1980: 211). It also frequently takes away some of the natural flavors; to compensate for lost flavor, manufacturers then add sugar, salt, or artificial flavoring (Silverstein, 1984).

The diet of our modern society is more varied, interesting, and in many ways more nutritious than that of our medieval ancestors, who, prior to the fifteenth or sixteenth centuries, subsisted on a plain fare mainly consisting of grains and vegetables with few spices (Braudel, 1973). Increased trade, the availability of new foods and seasonings, and advances in agricultural technology and food processing have made an improved diet possible. The growth of capitalism helped stimulate trade and technology to the benefit of many. Food processing, however, is also used to increase profit. Technologies have been developed to store foods longer, to increase yield of products (for instance, hormones make chickens grow faster and fatter), to enhance flavor in place of using expensive ingredients, and to disguise products with artificial colors, scents, and shapes (Center for Study of Responsive Law, 1982). Yet rather than reducing food prices, processing often increases costs (Silverstein, 1984). Corporate control over food production and distribution also affects the choices available. Relatively few people have access to and can afford to buy unprocessed foods, which are now sold as part of a growing health food industry. In many places, supermarket fare is the only option.

Dieting and Fitness From 1960 to 1980, approximately one-quarter of U.S. adults were overweight, but between 1980 and 1991, the figure grew to about one-third of the adult population (Burros, 1994). The motivation and opportunity to consume a healthy diet and to exercise are socially distributed (Goldstein, 1992; Townsend, 1990). Several studies show a relationship between social class and obesity (Chrisler, 1994). One study indicated that women from lower-class backgrounds are six times more likely to be obese than upper-class women. Eating disorders, such as anorexia, are more common in upper-class women (Yates, 1991). Some of this variation is explained by differences in availability of adequate nutrition (that is, starchy food satisfies hunger and is cheaper). Another factor is that people overeat to manage stress; also, different classes assign different social meanings to obesity. Obesity is not as heavily stigmatized in the lower class. Dieting and fitness rituals are primarily a middle- and upper-class phenomenon (Goldstein, 1992), not motivated simply by a concern for better health. In some cultures fat is a sign of prosperity; in middle-class American culture, however, fat symbolizes loss of self-control. In recent years, there has been an increasing concern with thinness. The pressures to be thin are greater for women than for men. In addition to socioeconomic factors, cultural-ethnic factors may also contribute to the tendency to be overweight, for example, among Mexican-American women (Burros, 1994).

What constitutes being overweight, and how much excess weight is unhealthy? Questions of overweight and overnutrition are difficult to calculate with precision. Although supposedly objective scientific facts bear on what is defined as normal weight, the facts change, and various groups challenge particular standards of evaluation. In 1959, standards for normal weights were established by the Metropolitan Life Insurance Company; these widely used standards ("Tables of Ideal Body Weights") were revised *upward* in 1983 and again in 1990 (Sobal, 1995). Groups like Weight Watchers, the American Cancer Society, and the American Heart Association do not accept these changed standards as valid. In short, no tidy, universal standard exists for how much we should weigh (Chrisler, 1994; Schwartz, 1986; Sobal, 1995).

Our cultural obsession with dieting and fitness reflects a concern not merely with health but also with self-control and physical appearances. In our society, looking good and feeling well tend to be confused (Lupton, 1996). In all societies, health is judged to some degree on the basis of appearances, but in our society, a person's image is especially important, due to the influence of mass media and other political-economic factors.

Concern about weight and fat is one expression of a generalized societal anxiety about physical appearances. Since the 1880s, societal tolerance for high weight may have narrowed, and the criteria for acceptable weight have become more demanding (Schwartz, 1986). Eating disorders are on the increase (Attie and Brooks-Gunn, 1987; Sagan, 1987: 55; Yates, 1991), and cultural standards for women's bodies have shifted from fat to thin. In recent decades, the number of articles and books about diets have increased (Hatfield and Sprecher, 1986). Weight loss organizations are a $30 billion a year industry (Sobal, 1995). Women's and increasingly men's anxiety about weight and fat constitutes a major source of profit. A 1985 survey found that in comparison to 1972 data, respondents (both male and female) showed more dissatisfaction with their body image. Although the proportion of women expressing such dissatisfaction was still higher than in 1985, the differences in the level of dissatisfaction between the sexes had narrowed. Weight was the one physical feature that evoked the most anxiety among these males (Cash et al., 1986). One study found that 63 percent of high school girls were dieting the day they were surveyed (compared to 16.2 percent of boys). Children become concerned about weight as early as 7 or 8 years old (Way, 1995).

Such fears are not totally without foundation. Obesity is strongly stigmatized in our culture, particularly among the middle and upper classes (Attie and Brooks-Gunn, 1987; Lupton, 1996; Sobal, 1995). Negative attitudes toward obese people tend to be learned at an early age (Yates, 1991). One study showed 10- and 11-year-olds pictures of a "normal" child, one with an amputated limb, one with facial disfigurement, one in a wheelchair, one with crutches and a wheelchair, and an obese child. When the children were asked to rank the pictures in terms of their preference for a friend, the majority made the obese child their *last* choice (Richardson et al., 1963). Discrimination against people who are obese has been found in education, rental housing, employment, and other areas of life. In the past 25 years, a number of groups have emerged to combat the stigma of overweight and to advocate "fat power" and "fat pride" (Sobal, 1995).

Obesity does contribute to physical problems such as high blood pressure. Although obesity functions to raise blood pressure because of the physical strain it puts on the body, other factors may also be involved. Perhaps the social meanings of obesity affect the body as well (Attie and Brooks-Gunn, 1987). Because obesity is perceived as a negative attribute, it may affect an individual's self-esteem. Anxieties about one's body may also contribute to increased blood pressure (Lynch, 1985).

Obesity has been linked to such health problems as high blood pressure and strain on the musculoskeletal system; however, the evidence linking overweight and sickness is not as strong as previously believed (Chrisler, 1994). Dieting and large fluctuations in weight may cause greater negative health effects than does obesity per se (Chrisler, 1994).

Society's stigmatization of those who are overweight is related to the social norm of control, but whether obesity is a metabolic disorder beyond some people's control is questionable (Brody, 1983). If this is the case, to focus on the individual's responsibility is cruel and futile. The regulation of appetites is not merely biological, however; social factors are important too. To regulate our appetites, we need to know whether we are hungry. It is possible that obese people are more vulnerable to social forces that short-circuit hunger signals from their bodies. One study found that "normals" were more oriented to internal cues as signals when to eat, whereas obese people relied on external cues such as the appearance, taste, and smell of food and the time of day. In one variation of the experiment, a wall clock had been moved forward a few hours, displaying the wrong time. Subjects of normal weight did not eat the available food, even though the clock falsely signaled meal time, whereas the obese subjects ate (Schachter, 1968).

Some have observed that our culture encourages people to rely on external signals for eating. Snack ads urge us to deaden hunger signals; meal schedules encourage us to look to the clock for signs of hunger. In a culture that encourages high levels of consumption, physiological hunger and nutritional considerations may be eclipsed by advertising messages designed to create demand (Silverstein, 1984). If there are natural limits to human appetites (and this is debatable), the economic system's impetus to sell must overcome them. This factor does not explain individual differences in responding to social pressures, but it does suggest that cultural pressures may affect the way people perceive their bodies, and hence how they control their eating.

All societies value some degree of self-control, but in modern societies such a concern is pervasive. Turner (1984: 112) observes:

> We jog, slim and sleep not for their intrinsic enjoyment, but to improve our chances at sex, work and longevity. The new asceticism of competitive social relations exists to create desire—desire which is subordinated to the rationalization of the body as the final triumph of capitalist development. Obesity has become irrational.

The contemporary emphasis on fitness, especially among the middle class, is not simply a matter of health but of conformity to the norms of an eternally youthful, lean body. Moreover, fitness activities may be a way of displaying control over one's body and hence over one's self in a culture in which control is valued and yet powerlessness seems to be a pervasive experience (Glassner, 1989; Lupton, 1996). The "ideal" body is not only slender, but also firm—tightly self-managed, self-constrained; this changed ideal may reflect society's increased emphasis on self-control and management, rather than externally imposed control and coercion (Bordo, 1990).

A study of workers in California's Silicon Valley suggests that their almost compulsive tendency to exercise and diet (along with compulsive shopping and extensive drug abuse) represents a way of coping with the powerlessness, alienation, stress, and loneliness of much of their lives (Hayes, 1989). As with dieting, a vast industry has arisen to meet fitness needs, producing endless streams of commodities and specialized technologies, from electronic rowing machines to digital pulse meters. Commercialized diet and fitness thus transform simple needs into marketable commodities (Glassner, 1989).

In modern society, appearances are very important in achieving success in work, play, and sexual relationships. A competitive society makes such successes important to the individual's sense of self. To achieve them, a rational mastery over the body and appearances becomes a central concern in life. By these norms, then, obesity reflects an irrational inability to control oneself, whereas dieting and fitness activities (beyond their contribution to health) promote a sense of self-mastery (Lupton, 1996).

Gender, Power, and Eating Disorders Much concern about weight is a concern about appearances. The standards for physical appearances or somatic (body) norms vary from time to time and place to place. The importance of conforming to such standards also varies. Our society tends to evaluate women by their appearances and men by their performance (such as occupational, athletic, and sexual). Despite some shift in attitudes, men are generally more anxious about functioning and women about appearances (Lakoff and Scherr, 1984; Melamed, 1983). Furthermore, the responsibility for whether one is successful in one's area of competence rests with the individual:

> Ours is a culture of personal responsibility; we are told to captain our own souls and "take responsibility" for our successes and failures. Traditionally, men have been able to demonstrate success through their achievements in work, but it has mainly been through what a woman does with her appearance that she has been able to exhibit her mastery and achievement to others and to herself. (Millman, 1980: 155)

Although this double standard is changing somewhat, it still prevails (Way, 1995).

Women are more likely than men to believe they are overweight when in fact they are not, if judged by so-called objective standards (which themselves are not so objective). A 1980 survey of college women found that 70 percent believed they were overweight, although only 30 percent actually fit the insurance chart definitions. Women's anxieties about weight are thus out of proportion to the facts. Fears about one's body and appearances are fueled by the mass media, which reminds audiences how inadequate their bodies are. One woman observes:

> The mass media tells us all day and all evening that we are inadequate, mindless, ugly, disgusting in ourselves. We must try to resemble perfect plastic objects, so

that no one will notice what we really are. In ourselves we smell bad, shed dandruff, our breath has an odor, our hair stands up or falls out, we sag or stick out where we shouldn't. We can only rook people into liking us by using magic products that make us products too. (quoted in Hatfield and Sprecher, 1986: 291)

Concerns about weight are a source of chronic stress for many women (Attie and Brooks-Gunn, 1987). Pressures on women to look thin may contribute to eating disorders like anorexia and bulimia (Fallon and Rozin, 1985), which are much more common among women than men. Anorexics lose the desire to eat and starve themselves. Bulimics binge, consuming vast amounts of food, and then purge themselves by vomiting or using laxatives. Although the initial motivation for disordered eating practices is cultural or social (Way, 1995), these practices over time may modify the body physiologically to make the person "addicted" to such practices (Brumberg, 1988). Self-starvation may become pleasurable and satisfying (Lupton, 1996).

Our culture gives members seriously conflicting messages about eating. On the one hand, people are urged to control their appetites and to diet in order to be sexy and desirable. At the same time, there is a conflicting message to enjoy life, to consume, to indulge ourselves and our appetites. The cultural contradiction of our times lies in the conflict between one set of messages, which emphasizes the importance of discipline as producers (that is, the work ethic), and another, which stresses our role as pleasure-seeking consumers (Brumberg, 1988; Lupton, 1996). Turner (1992: 224) argues that anorexia may, to some extent, be regarded "as an ascetic and moral response to contemporary consumerism." We are thus asked to be both ascetic (disciplined and in control of our flesh) *and* hedonistic (pleasure seeking and indulgent) at the same time. This dual expectation compounds problems for women, whose traditional role as nurturers and food providers places them in frequent contact with food (Charles and Kerr, 1987).

Anorexia can be interpreted as a woman's body discipline carried to an extreme. Families of anorexic adolescents often stress perfection and success (Yates, 1991). Eating disorders are extreme, self-destructive ways of responding to cultural conflicts that affect most women to some degree.

Advertising for a variety of products may promote the bulimic solution in a seemingly benign way. One "lite beer" commercial promises, "Oh, you can have it all!," trumpeting both a message of the good life and the promise of a beer that tastes like it has substance but in fact has little. A vast array of diet foods offers a "banquet without food," which promises all the pleasures of eating without its unwanted consequences (Schwartz, 1986).

Eating disorders are not really problems of appetite for food but rather self-destructive responses to cultural constraints and contradictions. Somatic norms of femininity limit female appetites (not only for food but also for public power, independence, and sexual gratification). Gender-role norms expect women to feed and nurture others, and not the self.

Similarly, overeating is sometimes a means of asserting control. Millman (1980) found that some of the obese women she interviewed experienced eating as the one area of a controlled life where they felt able to "let go," and others used eating as a way of protecting themselves against parental domination. One respondent reported that she ate and gorged herself as a defiant response to her mother, who was always harassing her about her appearance. Millman (1980: 73) observed:

> This woman (like several others I interviewed) has throughout her life used food and weight to assert and feel control in her relationships and her place in the world. And when these assertions run against the wishes of parents or husbands, eating and weight become associated with a refusal to bow to social control.

Others have argued that fat may represent a form of "armor" by which some women can protect themselves from unwanted sexual advances. Eating may also help alleviate the anxieties about identity and devalued sense of self that our society engenders in women (Chernin, 1981). The double standards of physical appearances, together with the strong link that our culture encourages between women's looks and their sense of self, have led some writers to declare that "fat is a feminist issue" (Ohrbach, 1981). This approach suggests that eating disorders are not simply a loss of control but may reflect an attempt to assert control (albeit in ultimately self-destructive ways). It is simplistic to view eating disorders as a sign of personal weakness or as a purely individual matter, independent of social factors (Lupton, 1996).

THE SOCIAL ORGANIZATION OF SPACE AND PRACTICES

Our fitness, health, and physical comfort depend in part on the quality of the physical space we inhabit and our options for activity within it. Those options depend greatly on the social organization of space, as well as the opportunities or constraints that social forces place on our movement. The social organization of space and activities (that is, practices) is affected by the distribution of power in any given society. Some people have more influence in shaping their physical surroundings than others; some have more freedom of movement.

Space, Practices, and Occupational Health

The design of physical environments reflects social status. One indicator of social status is the amount and quality of an individual's space. Large private offices with windows, for example, are reserved for executives (Lindheim, 1985). The vast majority of jobs in the expanding information service sector are low-level positions in which workers have little control over their environment, which is designed to maximize cost effectiveness and worker control. The following arrangement is characteristic of white-collar offices:

> Of the people surveyed in one large modern office building by our Columbia University research team, 34 percent could not decorate or personalize their work areas in any way. They couldn't even hang a picture or keep a plant. Ninety percent could not control the number of people passing by their desk area, and 69 percent had no say over whether others could come directly up to their desk at any

time without permission. Eighty-four percent of the office workers reported that they were always in the view of someone else and had no way to avoid this contact; 80 percent also reported that they had no control over whether their work or conversations were overheard. The overwhelming majority of office workers could not alter the ventilation (88 percent), open the windows (96 percent), adjust the lighting (83 percent), rearrange the furniture or equipment (75 percent), or change the temperature (75 percent). (Stellman and Henifin, 1983: 112)

How the workplace regulates our movements may literally shape or misshape our bodies. Friedrich Engels ([1845] 1973: 282–283), writing over 145 years ago, describes the crippling effects of their work on the bodies of women and children coal carriers:

> The first result of such over-exertion is the diversion of vitality to the one-sided development of the muscles, so that those especially of the arms, legs, and the back, of the shoulders and chest, which are commonly called into activity in pushing and pulling, attain an uncommonly vigorous development, while all the rest of the body suffers and is atrophied from want of nourishment. More than all else the stature suffers, being stunted and retarded.

These damaging effects result from how environments are organized, the design of tools and equipment, the pace of work, and the fact that certain repetitive work practices can cause disproportionate wear and tear on the body. Although musculoskeletal problems are more likely to be associated with certain work practices, their injurious impact of such practices can be significantly reduced by frequent breaks, job rotation, and the proper ergonomic design of work spaces and equipment. Musculoskeletal problems are often the result of a poor fit between the social organization of space, time, and practices and the person's body.

The occupational link with musculoskeletal injuries, such as "washerwoman's sprain," "bricklayer's shoulder" and "telegraphist's cramp" has long been recognized by medical science (Dembe, 1996; Goldoftas, 1991). In the early twentieth century, certain musculoskeletal injuries were attributed, not to workplace conditions, but to the special "sensitivity" of certain groups, especially women and Jews. This gender and ethnic bias among physicians who diagnosed such problems was related to societal fears about the movement of women and immigrants into the U.S. labor force (Dembe, 1996).

One musculoskeletal injury known as "cumulative trauma disorder" (or "repetitive strain injury") has captured public attention in recent years. Cumulative trauma disorders have increased in the United States more than tenfold between 1983 and 1993 and account for more than 60 percent of reported occupational health problems (Dembe, 1996; Lohr, 1996). In the United Kingdom and Australia, musculoskeletal disorders are also the most common work-related health problem (Reid et al., 1991; Wise, 1996).

People whose occupations require the use of their arms, wrists, or fingers in quick repetitive motions (such as cashiers, meat packers, computer operators, garment workers), may suffer from inflammation of their tendons (tendonitis) or from compression of their nerves (carpal tunnel syndrome) (Dembe, 1996). As the use of computers in colleges and universities becomes more common, cumulative trauma disorders may be becoming more prevalent—especially among those working under great pressure to be productive (Rimer, 1997). Among meat packers, carpal tunnel syndrome is estimated to be as high as 15 percent of the work force (compared to a prevalence of 5 to 10 percent in the industrial work force). The rise of carpal tunnel syndrome in the United States has been attributed to the intensification of work pace and the alteration of work practices so that the range of motion is decreased (Goldoftas, 1991).

Ergonomics is the study of the relationship among the workers, their movements, and the physical features of their work environment. For example, is the chair designed to minimize backaches after long hours of sitting? Is the control panel easily readable and within comfortable reach? Ergonomic studies have tended to emphasize designing machines and workplaces that will enhance productivity; however, less attention has been directed toward worker health or comfort (Goldsmith and Kerr, 1982). Furthermore, ergonomists design workplaces with the average person in mind, with little provision for those whose bodies are not average.

In many workplaces, even basic ergonomic considerations are often ignored to enhance productivity and profits. Workers may be forced to work in cramped, uncomfortable positions. For instance, one welder comments:

> I got moved to a new job spot-welding where I had to stand on my toes with my head all the way against my back and my arms stretched out all day long. I told my boss that we had to disassemble the piece in order for me to do the job without injuring myself, and he insisted that I could do it the way it was. Well, I did it until finally I hurt my back so bad that I was out for 5 months. (quoted in Back, 1981: 24–25)

Until a few decades ago, farm laborers were forced to use short-handled hoes, which raised productivity by increasing traction but also caused serious back pains. It was only after pressure from unions and workers that the farm owners finally allowed workers to use long-handled hoes. Healthy movements are thus related not just to the nature of the activity, but also to the design of the tools and environment.

Varying the position of the body frequently during the workday is important for orthopedic health and psychological well-being. Some workers come to experience themselves and their bodies as "split" when their work involves uncomfortable, uninterrupted, repetitive motions:

> I sit in one place all day facing a wall. My fingers are moving all the time, my eyes are staring into a machine that is placed so I have to hold my neck stiff to see the words clearly. Everyone is typing or using machines so there is a lot of noise. It's impossible to talk or even to turn around and look at someone else. My job is basically to copy numbers and letters all day, but most of the time I'm not even aware of them. *It's like my hands and my eyes are alive and my mind and my body are dead.* (quoted in Back, 1981: 41–42 [emphasis added])

People can adapt to unhealthy environments, but often at a cost. A significant portion of time in our everyday lives is spent on such unnoticed forms of body activities as walking up and down, pacing, stretching our limbs, tapping our feet, drumming our fingers, smoothing our hair, and hugging our body. These kinds of activities are integral to our self-image and contribute to stress reduction and to fitness (Csikszentmihalyi, 1990). They may also foster a sense of self-control and physical-emotional satisfaction. The social arrangements of many workplaces affect workers' ability to engage in these natural activities.

The workplace illustrates the relationship between the organization of space and the regulation of motion, and workers' psychophysical well-being. Disempowering spaces force people's bodies into standard forms or the motions of a machine. Workers need to vary their movements and to distribute more evenly the stressors that cause bodily wear and tear. The ability to control movements and to adapt work spaces to one's own well-being in turn depends on various political and economic factors.

Space, Practices, and Transportation

Transportation is another arena in which the organization of space and practices affects health. In many parts of the United States, someone with no automobile transportation has severely curtailed access to medical care, shopping, leisure activities, friends, and work. It has been estimated that more than 38 percent of U.S. households with incomes under the poverty level do not possess a car. About 24 percent of households of elderly persons lack a car (Freund and Martin, 1993). Similarly, most youths and many persons with disabilities are unable to transport themselves (M. Hillman et al., 1990; Rosenbloom, 1988). In American society access to transportation is thus unequally distributed, based on race, income, age, and class (Holtz Kay, 1997; Yago, 1985). The system of transportation dominated by the individual passenger car was created not merely by individual consumer choices but also by political and corporate interests. The major portion of public funds spent on transportation in the United States goes for highways as opposed to mass transit (Freund and Martin, 1993; Snell, 1982).

Reliance on automobile transportation is related to various problems of physical fitness. Difficulties in commuting can increase stress; for example, the heart rate of a train passenger is lower than that of a passenger in a private car (Lundberg, 1976). Driving causes increased levels of stress hormones, blood sugar, and cholesterol (Robinson, 1988), and can create problems like "motorist's spine" and "driver's thigh" (Homola, 1968). Persons who drive a car for 20 miles or more a day are at special risk for lumbar disk herniation (lower back injury). Truck drivers suffer a high rate of back injuries (National Institute on Disability, 1987).

The shape of modern transportation networks is the result not merely of society's love affair with the automobile but also of concrete economic and political decisions that affect the location of offices, shopping malls, industrial parks, and restaurants. These decisions thrust individuals into relying on private automobiles, whether they love or hate them. Advertising campaigns of automobile companies, furthermore, have imbued the car with symbolic meanings of masculinity, freedom, and social status; reliance on cars is thus not simply a matter of preference. Through their various interventions in the marketplace, manufacturers have shaped social space to the needs of automobile transportation. According to Snell (1982), from the 1930s to the 1950s the automobile industry (specifically General Motors) promoted the homogenization of the urban landscape by dismantling alternate transportation networks (such as trains and trolleys) and replacing them with inefficient, polluting trucks, buses, and automobiles. Once other modes of transportation had declined, the automobile became a virtual necessity rather than a luxury (Freund and Martin, 1993).

Accidents: An Individual or Social Problem?

Following heart disease, cancer, and stroke, accidents are among the foremost causes of death in American society. Automobile accidents constitute a large percentage of total accidents; work-related injuries are another important component (USDHHS, 1992). Accidents result from the interplay among an unsafe environment, unsafe equipment and tools, and the behavior of the individuals involved. Accidents are usually treated as the results of individual fault, but often social and environmental problems also play a significant causal role. Accidents are not random, unpredictable events but follow patterns (Smothers, 1991). The very definition of events as "accidents"—as opposed to socially produced, preventable incidents—has political and social policy implications (Freund and Martin, 1993).

Auto Accidents Despite long-term declines in the rates of fatalities and injuries from automobile accidents in the developed world, absolute levels of death and injury remain high and stubbornly resist reduction. In 1995, there were 43,900 U.S. deaths by motor vehicle, up from 40,982 in 1992 (American Automobile Manufacturers Association, 1996). Improvements in safety (both in vehicle-roadway technology and in driver behavior) have been offset by increases in auto use fostered by the expansion of auto-centered transport. In both the United States and the United Kingdom, reduction in the rate of traffic accidents has lagged behind declines in the rates of home and workplace accidents (Leichter, 1991: 181–182). Driving an auto remains a far riskier activity than other means of travel: Risk of death from an auto accident over a 50–year period is estimated to be 1 in 100, whereas risk of death from an airplane crash is 1 in 20,000 (*New York Times*, 1991; see also Royal Commission on Environmental Pollution, 1994). Auto accidents are a leading cause of death for young males 15 to 19. Just as auto accident fatalities are socially distributed along lines of gender and age, they also vary by social class. In Britain, lower-class persons have the greatest risk of auto accident fatality; because fewer lower-class persons drive, not surprisingly, their pedestrian death rate is also high (Quick, 1991).

Each year in the United States, approximately 4 to 5 million motor-vehicle related injuries occur. Of these, 500,000 people require hospitalization (averaging a stay of nine days). More deaths occur from automobile accidents than from any other injury-producing event. Motor vehicle accidents are the largest single trauma-induced cause of paraplegia and quadriplegia, and a major cause of epilepsy and head injuries in the United States (Holtz Kay, 1997).

Although traffic deaths and injuries remain an intractable problem—and an underappreciated public health issue—in the developed world, the worldwide picture is also not promising. About 1 million traffic deaths and about 40 million traffic injuries occurred in 1990 worldwide. Traffic accidents were the ninth leading cause of death, and the World Health Organization projects that deaths from traffic accidents will rise by 2020 to about 2.3 million, more than doubling the toll for 1990. Deaths will increase as developing nations adopt auto-centered transport systems, at the same time the proportion of young adults in their populations (those at most risk) grows (Murray and Lopez, 1996).

Why the automobile exacts such a high health risk is a complex question. Much public attention focuses on drunk driving. In 1990, 39.7 percent of U.S. road fatalities involved drivers with blood alcohol levels of 0.1 percent or more (a level defining intoxication). This figure represents a decline from 1982 when it was 46.3 percent (Smothers, 1991). These figures are somewhat misleading, however, because they include all traffic deaths in which any of the parties involved consumed alcohol, even if the person who was drinking was not at fault. Other estimates place the figure of alcohol-related deaths at 25 percent (Ross and Hughes, 1986). Many alcohol-related traffic fatalities, furthermore, involve cofactors such as fatigue, inexperience, poorly designed or inadequately lit roads, and unsafe cars (Gusfield, 1981).

Although individual drivers have a responsibility to drive safely, focusing merely on individual behavior neglects the social, cultural, and environmental dimensions of auto accidents. In many parts of the United States, the automobile is the only available means of transportation, pressuring drunken drivers and other impaired persons (for example, those with vision problems) into driving (Syme and Guralnik, 1987). Such factors in traffic fatalities are the result of social policies.

Policy responses to traffic accidents emphasize raising the *drinking* age, but few legislators would consider raising the *driving* age because in many parts of the country to be without a car is to be helpless, especially given an atrophied public transportation system. Social factors also explain why males are at particularly high risk. Many young males are socialized into taking lots of risks and into feeling or appearing invulnerable; media messages glorify speed and risk taking; many car-chase scenes convey a relatively carnage-free image of fast or reckless driving; advertisements glamorize cars as images of masculinity, speed, power, and excitement; and young men often view the use of seat belts as not "macho" (Horton, 1985b; Quick, 1991).

Economic pressures may also contribute to vehicular accidents by promoting reckless behavior on the road. Truck drivers have a high rate of drug consumption (especially stimulants). Economic considerations lead them to drive longer hours with unsafe equipment and larger payloads. Thus, social-structural forces contribute to trucking accidents (Rothe, 1991).

Public policy has not given much attention to the health costs of a transportation system centered on the auto. Accidents are only one of the costs, which also include health consequences from auto emissions (see Table 3.2 on page 63), noise pollution, and so on. Diet, smoking, exercise, and alcohol are in the limelight as health-lifestyle issues, but because we take cars for granted as the primary means of transport and because of the political power of auto interests, there has been inadequate analysis of the health implications of pervasive auto use (Hunt, 1989).

In addressing the problem of automobile accidents, most policy focuses on changing individual behavior through education or various sanctions (Gusfield, 1981). However, individuals are hard to reach, influence, and control; traffic penalties are not consistently and rapidly imposed on violators; and to monitor and educate all drivers is difficult and not very cost effective. By contrast, an ecological approach to the problem emphasizes changing the social and physical environment (for example, building safer highways), producing safer cars, and making many alternative ways of traveling available to drivers (Syme and Guralnik, 1987). These kinds of preventive measures have been consistently constrained by the market-place, however. The political and economic power of the automobile industry, in consideration of the cost of designing safer vehicles and highways, seriously limits the government's power or willingness to choose and implement solutions to prevent auto accidents (MacLennan, 1988).

Workplace Accidents: Unsafe Behavior, Unsafe Conditions? Workplace accidents (some prefer the term *injury* because an accident implies a random occurrence) differ from occupational diseases: In the former, the exposure to the source is sudden, and the damage as well as its cause is readily apparent (Baker et al., 1987: 177). By contrast, the cause of work-related diseases is not always apparent, and the effect may be gradual. Accidents are thus discrete, clearly identifiable events that happen suddenly but involve a multitude of causal factors (Dembe, 1996).

Between 1980 and 1989, occupational injury claimed the lives of 63,589 U.S. workers (*New York Times*, 1994a). Each year, workplace accidents cause 1.7 million disabling injuries (Moeller, 1992: 37). Mining was the most dangerous industry followed by construction (*New York Times*, 1994a). In 1993, the private sector reported 2,772,500 injuries with lost workdays (USDHHS, 1996a: 185). Like other health problems, their incidence and severity tend to be socially distributed. Lower-status jobs generally involve more accidents (Dutton, 1986). Because black males tend to work in high-risk occupations with little control over their work environment, they have 37 percent greater likelihood than whites of suffering occupational injuries or illnesses (Goldsmith and Kerr, 1982). The rate of injuries, particularly fatal ones, have generally declined somewhat in the past 50 years (Baker et al., 1987). The legislation of safety regulations, such as the 1969 Federal Mine Safety and Health Act, seems to have helped reduce injuries. Since 1994, however, the Occupational Safety and Health Administration's (OSHA) safety inspections have dropped by 43 percent (Cooper, 1997).

Data on workplace safety are highly problematic. Job injury rates are sometimes calculated in terms of the number of workdays lost per week, month, or year due to injury. However, employers often keep injured workers on the job or move them temporarily to easier jobs to keep injury rates down (Goldsmith and Kerr, 1982). Some companies simply do not report all injuries. In 1986, the Chrysler

Corporation was fined a substantial sum for failing to report 182 injuries at one work site alone (Noble, 1986). Because official government data are based on company self-reports, these figures also tend to underestimate injuries. In 1985, the U.S. Bureau of Statistics reported that 3,750 workers died on the job, whereas the National Safety Council (an independent agency) reported 11,600 worker deaths (Noble, 1986). Part of this discrepancy is due to the fact that the government does not count injuries in private businesses employing fewer than 11 people.

The concept of accident proneness, first coined in 1926, became the focus for whole generations of industrial psychologists who searched for specifiable characteristics causing some individuals to be especially likely to have accidents. In a chapter on industrial and occupational psychiatry, the 1966 *American Handbook of Psychiatry* described the "accident syndrome" as involving an "impulsive character" and "reaction of anxiety." The handbook does not suggest, however, that the psychiatrist should take into account the characteristics of the workplace in which the "accident-prone" behavior occurs (Berman, 1978: 23–24). Empirical research has been unable to isolate any personality traits, independent of specific situations, that could be categorized as "accident proneness" (Members of the Working Party, 1975).

Environmental factors also contribute to accidents. Workplace accidents involve "accident prone" tools and environments, as well as social pressures that encourage risky behavior. As for automobile accidents, the ecological model appears more useful than the individual behavior model for understanding workplace accidents. At one steel plant, for example, the higher the rate of production grew, the higher the monthly injury rate rose (Hills, 1987). Similarly, in the past decade or so as the meat-packing industry came under increased competitive pressure, wages decreased, but productivity pressures grew, simultaneously increasing the rate of on-the-job injuries (Dembe, 1996; Novek et al., 1990). Especially when linked with job alienation, situational pressures enhance the likelihood of accidents (Back, 1981).

Design of equipment itself is sometimes the source of accidents. Although machines can be built in an ergonomically sound fashion to reduce accidents, more often they are designed mainly to enhance productivity (Goldsmith and Kerr, 1982). The burden of accident prevention in these environments is thus on the individual worker. An assembly-line worker commented:

> When there are accidents they always blamed us for not using safety equipment. Six of us had to work with an acid solution and we were all given plastic goggles. But no one could wear them because they didn't fit and you couldn't see very well with them on. This was a piece work job and there was no way we were going to make our bonus if we wore our glasses. I always felt caught between being worried about my health and being worried about not making production. You know it could've been fairly easy to put a shield over the whole operation so we wouldn't have to worry about it. (quoted in Back, 1981: 15)

Engineering controls that alter the environment, such as putting a protective "shield over the whole operation," are typically more expensive than giving workers individual safety equipment, such as respirators to prevent breathing dust. So-called passive safety approaches, which rely on safe equipment and environment more than on behavior, are more effective but also more expensive (Baker et al., 1987). Although respirators are cheaper for corporations, they create problems for workers. Respirators are physically uncomfortable, especially if worn the whole day under conditions of high temperature and noise. They may also be ineffective or create such side effects as breathing difficulty or heart strain. Workplace physical stressors, such as high noise levels and toxins, may also affect workers' perception, alertness, and reflexes, thereby producing "accident proneness."

Some social scientists consider accidents to be related to the social structure of the workplace. In many work situations, there is a split between those who plan and organize work and those who execute it. This division may influence the perception and treatment of occupational health problems (Dembe, 1996; Navarro, 1981). Experts who study accidents and occupational health problems are often far removed from the day-to-day routine of the workplaces they analyze. Furthermore, management concerns with productivity and cost effectiveness are not always compatible with workers' needs for safe workplaces. Human error (for example, due to drug use) and carelessness *are* significant factors in workplace injuries. It is also important, however, to focus on how such variables as style of managerial control also contribute to workplace health problems (Members of the Working Party, 1975: 74–75). One basic issue in occupational injuries is the conflict between, on the one hand, managerial pressures to enhance productivity, control, and profit margins, and, on the other hand, the needs of workers to work in the safest technologically feasible working environment. Box 3.1 illustrates some structural ways of reducing workplace injuries.

BOX 3.1

Swedish Road to Better Conditions

The Swedish approach to health and safety has four main features.

First, Swedish workers have won real power at the local level to prevent hazards. Sweden's OSHA–the National Board of Occupational Safety and Health–sets standards and inspects work places, but unions view its role as secondary to their own efforts.

Second, Swedish workers have the information and training to enable them to use that power.

Third, unions have a major voice in safety and health research and research is often geared to finding practical solutions to hazards.

Fourth, Swedish unions are concerned about the total work environment, not just safety and health as narrowly defined in the U.S. They consider physical safety hazards, chemical and noise exposures, heat, and cold, speed-up, boredom, and stress as related problems. The Swedish unions are concerned not only about injuries and illnesses but also discomfort, an unpleasant work place and lack of job satisfaction.

They believe that workers are entitled to a humane work environment and control over their jobs.

Source: *In These Times*, January 18–21, 1986: 17. Reprinted by permission.

"Safety" experts tend to focus on the individual and to minimize the importance of *social* organization of space and practices (Williams et al., 1995). For example, one study concluded that safety experts overemphasized individualistic and psychological factors, such as "safety values," and needed to pay more attention to participants' local knowledge about the safety of environments (for example, poor housing, unsafe play spaces, transport and traffic conditions). Although having the right attitude about safety *is* important, to prevent accidents, it is also very important to consider such environmental arrangements as the organization of space, time, and practices (Roberts et al., 1995).

ENVIRONMENTAL POLLUTION

The concept of pollution usually carries the connotation of the fouling of the environment by humans, but volcanoes pollute the air and various nonhuman species pollute the environments with their excreta. In fact, most atmospheric pollution is not of human origin. Only 9 percent of the carbon monoxide in the air comes from human sources, such as automobile use. Of all particulates (that is, bits of metal and the like) emitted into the air, only 11 percent comes from human activity (for example, cars and industrial pollution). Various industrial processes account for 16 percent of the hydrocarbons in the atmosphere. About 45 percent of the sulfur dioxide in the atmosphere comes from human activity (Botkin and Keller, 1982: 172–173).

Approximately 130 million Americans are exposed daily to harmful levels of air pollution. An estimated 60,000 Americans die prematurely each year of heart attacks and respiratory illnesses linked to air pollution, and 250,000 children a year suffer from asthma attacks and respiratory disorders triggered by air pollution (St. Clair, 1997). Table 3.2 shows the quantities and sources of major pollutants emitted

TABLE 3.2 **Air Pollution in the United States in 1992 (Calculated Emissions Estimates)**

Type of Pollutant	All Sources	Transpor- tation	Stationary Fuel Combustion	Industrial Processes	Solid Waste	Other
Particulate matter[a]	7.1	1.6	1.8	2.4	0.3	1.0
Sulfur oxides[a]	20.6	1.0	17.7	1.9	0.0	0.0
Nitrogen oxides[a]	21.0	9.4	10.6	0.8	0.1	0.1
Volatile organic compounds[a]	20.6	7.5	0.6	7.3	2.1	3.1
Carbon monoxide[a]	79.1	63.5	5.6	4.6	1.5	3.9
Lead[b]	4.7	1.4	0.4	2.1	0.7	0.0

[a]Emissions in 10^6 metric tons per year.

[b]Emissions in 10^3 metric tons per year.

Source: U.S. Department of Health and Human Services, *Health, United States, 1994*, Hyattsville, MD: National Center for Health Statistics, 1995: 215.

in the United States. A significant decrease of lead emissions between 1975 and 1980 coincided with an approximately 50 percent decline in the use of leaded gasoline. Nevertheless, one-third of poor black American children between the ages of 1 to 5, who live in large cities, have hazardous levels of lead in their blood. Seventeen percent of Hispanic American children and only 6 percent of white children living under similar conditions have such high lead levels in their blood (Brody, 1995). Motor vehicles are a major source of carbon monoxide, a gas that interferes with the blood's ability to carry oxygen. Sulfur dioxides and nitrous oxides come from fuel combustion used to heat dwellings, generate electricity, and power motor vehicles (Renner, 1988). These emissions are important components of acid rain, which has a destructive impact on forests and the life in lakes and rivers, contributes to the erosion of building surfaces, and may contribute to human respiratory problems. Because acid rain often falls in regions distant from where the pollution originates, the economic activity in one region damages the environment in another, causing political strains between regions and nations, such as the United States and Canada.

Although humans are not the only sources of global pollution, their activities have increasingly produced ecological changes in climate, atmosphere, and the very shape of the earth's surface. Our social institutions may not be able to regulate the impact effectively (Shabecoff, 1987: A6). This impact of humans on the spaceship earth is not merely the result of technology or so-called progress but is also linked to the failure of political, economic, and social policy to regulate the use of technology or to create healthier technologies.

Poorer communities are more likely to be victims of corporate pollution. Several studies document the fact that toxic waste dumps are disproportionately likely to be located in poor neighborhoods, especially poor African American neighborhoods (Krieger and Fee, 1994). Roughly three out of five African Americans and Hispanic Americans live in communities with one or more hazardous waste sites. Childhood cancer rates are several times the national average in Latino farm communities where pesticides are used. Primarily because of poor air quality in inner cities, young black men die of asthma at three times the rate of young white men (Muwakkil, 1996a).

Along the U.S.-Mexico border, the waterways are becoming chemically and bacterially polluted. Unscrupulous U.S. developers have not provided safe water or sewage disposal in many new housing developments for poor workers, and many *maquiladora* workers on the Mexico side live in unregulated shantytowns. The border region has become an attractive area for legal and illegal dumpers of toxic chemicals and radioactive waste (Skolnick, 1995).

Sometimes it is community-based groups that call attention to the health consequences of polluting activities of corporations in their communities. In one Massachusetts community, ordinary citizens collected information to understand the sources and effects of pollution in their area. Their efforts led to lawsuits against two corporations that had been dumping toxic wastes (Brown and Mikkelsen, 1990). Increasingly, local lay activists fight against placing toxic waste dumps in their communities. These struggles for environmental justice have led to the emergence of what has been called "popular epidemiology" (Brown, 1995b), which involves the participation of community members who collect data and collaborate with experts using epidemiological methods. Popular epidemiology grows out of the concern of people living in communities that are polluted or in other ways perceived to be unhealthy (Brown, 1995b).

Discussions of pollution often pronounce that "we" (referring to humans in general) pollute. This expression, however, masks the sociopolitical dimension of environmental health by equating the individual litterbug with the corporate polluter whose impact on the environment is more far reaching and potentially dangerous than that of the individual (Bookchin, 1962). Not all of us citizens pollute equally, nor are we all equally affected by pollution. Not unlike passive smoking, polluted air affects even those who do not themselves pollute.

"Don't Let the Smoke Get in Your Lungs": The Individual as Polluter

Although tobacco smokers do not contribute significantly to atmospheric pollution, their habits do have a significant impact on health. They obviously pollute their own air and are at increased risk of coronary heart disease, emphysema, bronchitis, and lung, bladder, and esophagal cancer (USDHHS, 1987: 50). In 1990, 3 million adults in 1990 died from the effects of smoking tobacco, and the annual number of deaths is increasing. China is the largest developing country that consumes the most tobacco (*Journal of the American Medical Association*, 1996: 163). About 400,000 deaths per year occur in the United States (Nichter and Cartwright, 1991).

Some experts argue that smoking is as serious an addiction as heroin and, in the long run, perhaps even more damaging to the body (Weil and Rosen, 1993). Some research suggests a possible synergistic (that is, mutually enhancing) relationship between smoking and air pollution from other sources. For example, smokers in urban areas of high air pollution are at a greater risk of lung cancer than their rural counterparts who smoke (Epstein, 1978).

In the United States, smoking has declined at about 2 percent a year since 1974; however, some of this reduction has been offset by the number of teenagers (especially females) who have taken up smoking (Feder, 1996). In 1989, approximately 32 percent of males and 27 percent of females smoked (Nichter and Cartwright, 1991; see also Chesney, 1991). By 1991, daily cigarette consumption rates per man, woman, and child were 5.6 in the United States and 4.6 in Britain (Macalister, 1992). In the United States, smoking is considerably more common among blue-collar than white-collar workers. Blacks are more likely to smoke than other racial and ethnic groups. Cigarette industry advertising has increasingly targeted these vulnerable groups (Stebbins, 1991).

Individuals who smoke also affect the quality of air shared by others in the enclosed spaces of offices, homes, and restaurants. Passive smoking (the inhaling of someone else's cigarette smoke) has been linked to a variety of health risks. Parents' smoking has an impact on the respiratory health of their children, and a smoker's spouse may have an increased risk of lung cancer (Fielding and Phenow, 1988; Sandler et al., 1988). The effect of the smokers' habit on nonsmokers raises fundamental issues regarding individual rights as opposed to collective rights:

> Air pollution makes us take seriously the fact that we exist, not as isolated entities secure behind our fences, but as fellow creatures in a shared and threatened environment. While in some settings—when looking at second-hand smoke or workplace hazards—we can insist that individual consent remains fundamental, in others we may have to look beyond consent to autonomy and beyond the individual to a deeper sense of community. If anything is our birthright, it is the air that we breathe. (Center for Philosophy and Public Policy, 1985: 5)

The passive smoking issue has helped to define "personal" habits as a social problem (Chapman et al., 1990). Might other "habits" such as the "excessive" use of automobiles also be viewed as social problems because of their pollution of "community" air (Freund and Martin, 1993)?

Increased awareness of the hazards of passive smoking has contributed to wider smoking restrictions and affected smokers' cigarette consumption. The passive smoking issue thus poses another threat to the tobacco industry (Chapman et al., 1990). Movements to restrict smoking in public places are becoming widespread in the United States (Cummings, 1984). One company told workers that they would either quit smoking or lose their jobs (*New York Times*, January 25, 1986). The courts subsequently overturned the company's efforts to control its workers' private lives (that is, their smoking outside of work). Because the company manufactured accoustical tiles and insulation containing various fibers that may contribute to respiratory problems and lung cancer, union officials saw the company's emphasis on smoking as an attempt to evade the more costly issue of clearing the workplace air of these dangerous fibers.

Smoking is often a way of dealing with the stress induced by the workplace. To reduce employee smoking, employers might offer alternative ways for employees to cope with negative moods and work-related stress (Chesney, 1991). Are the employers who wish their workers to stop smoking willing to give them more breaks, alternative means of stress reduction, more relaxing work conditions, and a slower pace of work? The tendency to focus only on smoking may distract from issues of other sources of environmental pollution that are often heavily concentrated in workplaces (Fettner, 1987).

The tobacco producers form a major industry in the United States. On one hand, pronouncements and public service messages from the surgeon general and Department of Health and Human Services condemn smoking; on the other hand, the Department of Agriculture continues to subsidize tobacco growers heavily. Taxes on tobacco sales are also a source of revenue for the government, so there may be some conflict of interest on the issue. The tobacco industry has compensated for its loss of revenues in the United States by increasing its exports, particularly to the Third World (Nichter and Cartwright, 1991; Stebbins, 1991) and eastern Europe (Macalister, 1992). The U.S. government has exerted pressure on such countries as Thailand and South Korea to allow American cigarette sales and advertising or to face trade sanctions (Nichter and Cartwright, 1991; Stebbins, 1994).

Rather than deal with such massive economic and political issues, however, policymakers find it easier to focus on changing individuals' habits (Milio, 1985). Although smoking is an individual behavior and only the individual can decide to stop, the practice of smoking is firmly rooted in a sociocultural context (Townsend, 1990). Advertising has glamorized smoking, associating it with vigor, sexiness, and sophistication. Other social factors supporting the habit include peer pressure among teenagers and the use of smoking for sociability and for stress reduction (Lupton, 1994: 155). Smoke cessation programs, some argue, have little impact, because their focus is on changing individual behavior rather than addressing its sociocultural sources (Syme and Guralnik, 1987). As with accidents, an ecological method that considers individuals and their relationships to their social and cultural environment is a fruitful approach to supposedly personal addictions like smoking.

Pollution in the Workplace

Between 70,000 and 100,000 Americans die each year from occupational diseases—*not* including occupational injuries (Elling, 1986; National Safe Workplace Institute, 1990). About 390,000 new cases of disabling occupational diseases are diagnosed annually (Moeller, 1992). These estimates vary according to criteria for the category of "occupational diseases." Many respiratory problems experienced by coal miners, for example, were not immediately classified as black lung. They were so designated only after years of political conflict between mine owners, workers, unions, and various health professionals (Smith, 1981). The same symptoms were previously diagnosed as bronchitis, emphysema, or health problems resulting from workers' personal habits. In fact, occupational diseases are often hard to distinguish from "ordinary," nonwork-related problems (Elling, 1986: 18). To a physician untrained in diagnosing occupational diseases, lung cancer caused by asbestos looks like cancer due to smoking. Many cases of brown lung (a disease caused by inhaling cotton fibers) among textile workers go unrecorded because the symptoms may be misinterpreted as emphysema (Guarasci, 1987). Stress-related diseases (discussed in Chapter 4) are also not included in occupational disease statistics.

Obtaining sound statistics on occupational disease is a complicated process because they vary depending on who decides which health problems are job related. Company doctors, for example, are less likely to view symptoms as work related than union-affiliated doctors. One doctor working for the textile industry claimed that brown lung is "best described as a 'symptom complex' rather than a disease in the usual sense":

> We feel that this term may be preferable, first in order not to unduly alarm workers, as we attempt to protect their health and secondly, to help avoid unfair designations of cotton as an unduly hazardous material for use in the textile industry, raising the fear that the engineering control of it may be costly, and that it may be better, therefore, to switch to some less costly material. (quoted in Berman, 1978: 93)

Industry has focused on individuals, their lifestyle, and their "susceptibility" to occupational diseases (Epstein, 1990a). For years, instead of cleaning the air of cotton dust, the textile industry tried to identify hypersusceptible workers or "reactors" (Green, 1983). Employers' concern with workers' health is often inextricably tied to economic interests that influence what is or is not perceived and treated as occupational disease. As with accident prevention, management favors individual devices rather than passive engineering controls for the prevention of occupational disease. The issue of having the worker adapt to the workplace rather than adapting the workplace to the worker is thus not merely an economic one. Nelkin and Brown (1984: 70) observe the following:

> [T]he dispute over precautions extends beyond the question of immediate cost. Personal protective equipment places responsibility for protecting health on the workers themselves. Ill health can then be blamed on their failure to comply. Conversely, engineering controls place responsibility on management, shifting both the burden and the blame. To insist on personal precautions is to reinforce the belief that individuals are responsible for their own health and safety. To accept engineering controls is to accept the notion of corporate responsibility.

Because the people who study or make policy decisions about occupational health are often remote from the workplace (Dembe, 1996), workers' reports of symptoms are often ignored or invalidated, despite the fact that workers are often the first to recognize occupational health hazards. A Labor Department study found workers' self-reporting of health hazards to be highly reliable, except that workers tended to underestimate the effects of chronic diseases caused by occupational exposure (Nelkin and Brown, 1984: 31). Coal miners have known of "miner's asthma" and black lung for generations; their awareness is documented in song and popular writings. Such knowledge was dismissed as unscientific or as excuses for malingering, however. Although workers' reports are not based on scientific observation, ignoring their observations delays effective responses to occupational health hazards.

Workers do not always report work-related health problems, however; some may not complain out of fear of repercussions. Many others do not make the connection between low-level, long-term exposure to hazards and diseases that developed slowly or gradually. For example, the symptoms of asbestosis appear 20 to 40 years after asbestos exposure. Most private physicians have little training in occupational medicine and may not recognize patients' symptoms (Dembe, 1996). One study of worker deaths from asbestos exposure showed that only 48 percent were correctly diagnosed on the death certificates. Only about half of U.S. medical school programs require course work in occupational health; among those that require the topic, the median time spent on occupational health topics is four hours (National Safe Workplace Institute, 1990: 18). Many doctors do not record a patient's occupational and work history, and often they fail to connect symptoms to work conditions.

Tens of thousands of different chemicals are used in commercial production processes, and the list grows at the rate of about a thousand a year. Of the 2 million known chemicals, only a few thousand have been tested for their dangerous properties, and only a few hundred of these have been thoroughly tested. Production processes often use several chemicals in conjunction with each other, but very little is known about health hazards created when these chemicals (which individually may be harmless) interact with each other (Nelkin and Brown, 1984). Regulatory standards are typically set only after a problem has been identified among workers. In this sense, workers often function as human guinea pigs.

As Epstein (1990b: 455) notes:

> The regulatory system is potentially only as valid as the information generated is reliable. When the ingredients are not identified, when the proper studies are not conducted, when the results of studies are not published for review, and when the results of studies state conclusions contrary to the actual data, effective regulation becomes virtually impossible. . . . An overwhelming record confirms the premise that scientific information generated and interpreted by institutions and individuals with direct or indirect economic interests in its outcome must be regarded as suspect until proven otherwise by independent validation.

Institutional interests do not necessarily intentionally alter data. Sometimes, however, industries such as asbestos mining and manufacturing have collected occupational health data and then systematically suppressed it (Lilienfeld, 1991).

Regulatory agencies such as the Environmental Protection Agency (EPA) or OSHA must rely heavily on company data about various chemicals. However, the very companies with an economic interest in producing the chemicals are often the ones that test them. Cutbacks in funding to regulatory agencies, such as those in the 1980s, further limit effective research to determine regulatory standards. In many cases, OSHA has not set standards even for those chemicals known to be carcinogenic (that is, cancer causing).

Many dusts and particles inhaled by workers produce serious health problems. An estimated 10 percent of active miners have black lung disease (pneumoconiosis). The inhalation of various fibers (such as cotton dust) affects about 85,000 U.S. textile workers, 35,000 of whom are disabled by brown lung (byssinosis) and other respiratory problems (Hills, 1987). Tunnel workers' asthma (silicosis) comes from inhaling particles of sand. Table 3.3 shows the number of male deaths due to exposure to some of these substances. Exposure to chemicals used in many manu-

TABLE 3.3 **Death From Selected Occupational Diseases for U.S. Males, 1970–93**

Cause of Death	1970	1975	1980	1984	1989	1993
Malignant neoplasm of peritoneum and pleura	602	591	552	584	565	551
Pneumoconiosis	1,155	973	977	923	725	564
Asbestosis	25	43	96	131	261	308
Silicosis	351	243	202	160	130	123

Source: U.S. Department of Health and Human Services, *Health, United States 1995*, Hyattsville, MD: National Center for Health Statistics, 1996: 158.

facturing processes has also been linked to cancer and various other serious diseases.

Pollution in the workplace is not confined to blue-collar or industrial jobs. For example, the computer industry, which seems high tech and clean, exposes workers to solvents, chemicals, and gases that may be toxic. Adequate health and safety standards have not been established for this relatively new industry (Hayes, 1989; Howard, 1985). Supposedly clean office work sometimes involves inhaling ozone, a gas that can aggravate respiratory problems, from photocopiers or chemical copier fluids (Stellman and Henifin, 1983). Several studies document "office sickness" due to the high pollutant content of modern office buildings that are often airtight and rely on centralized air sources (Sterling et al., 1983). Persons who do housework may also be exposed to a variety of chemicals and air pollutants, such as fungal spores and bacteria (Chavkin, 1984).

The World Health Organization estimates that 30 percent of new and remodeled buildings, with efficient but "closed" ventilation systems, have indoor air quality problems (cited in National Safe Workplace Institute, 1990). Closed systems can spread infections such as the flu (Gilbert, 1997). Ironically, some workers in the EPA building itself wore respirators shortly after it was built because of indoor air pollution.

Workplace pollution spreads beyond the confines of the workplace, affecting workers' families. Factory pollution also tends to spread into the immediate vicinity. A high percentage of urban dwellers have some asbestos fibers in their lungs, even though they have not worked with asbestos. Atmospheric pollution from asbestos plants, construction sites, and even from auto brake linings spreads asbestos fibers into public spaces.

Just as the fruits of production are not equally distributed, so too are the costs of production, such as pollution, unequally shared. The average age at death of blue-collar workers is more than a decade earlier than that of white-collar workers (National Safe Workplace Institute, 1990: 11). People living in urban poverty areas are exposed to larger quantities of chemical and air pollution than their middle-class suburban counterparts (Dutton, 1986). Likewise, developing countries experience increasing pollution and industrial hazards, even while already industrialized countries are achieving greater environmental and workplace health and safety regulations. Many developing countries want to attract industry, but they lack technical information to evaluate processes, resources for testing products, effective power to set and enforce standards, and worker organizations to voice concerns (Navarro and Berman, 1981).

In the United States, the Occupational Safety and Health Act of 1970 was passed to "assure as far as possible every working man and woman in the United States, safe and healthy working conditions." This assurance has not been realized, however, in large part due to political abuses and to underfunding of the vast task of researching and enforcing standards (see Berman, 1978; Elling, 1986; Howard, 1985; Simon, 1983; Szasz, 1983). The United States spent $0.63 per worker on job health in 1986, whereas Finland spent $12.29 in 1986 and Sweden $12.33 in 1988 (National Safe Workplace Institute, 1990). Compared to Sweden, Finland,

Germany, and the United Kingdom, the United States ranked last, or tied for last place, on five out of six criteria for effective occupational safety and health: a strong national policy mandate for occupational health and safety; the provision and organization of services related to occupational health; workers' ability to control their work environment; the level of financing for occupational health activities; worker education; and the information about the workplace available to workers and experts. Sweden and (the former) East Germany ranked highest on all six criteria (Elling, 1986).

Comparative data on actual levels of occupational health and safety in each of these countries are scant and difficult to evaluate because countries use different methods of collecting and categorizing information. Elling (1986) argues that those countries with the most protection have the lowest rates of occupational disease and injury. Calculating admittedly crude work-related death rates, he finds that the United States has the highest rate, with 50 such deaths per 100,000 workers; the United Kingdom has 2.5 per 100,000, and Sweden has 3.6 per 100,000. Comparing rates of occupational disease and injury, Sweden and East Germany have the lowest; Finland and the United Kingdom fall in the middle; West Germany is next, and the United States has the worst (Elling, 1986: 22). The other countries appear to have stronger regulations and generally safer working conditions than the United States (Goldsmith and Kerr, 1982). For instance, Swedish workers have the right to veto plans for new machines, work processes, or construction on health and safety grounds. They are also trained in health and safety (including ergonomics) at the employers' expense. In one Saab automobile plant, the accident rate decreased 33 to 50 percent after some of these policies were implemented (Engler, 1986). Because a significant proportion of disease and disability in the United States is work related, issues of regulation and the politics of regulation have become important health considerations (National Safe Workplace Institute, 1990).

SUMMARY

Sociopolitical factors and culture construct our physical environments, our access to such resources as food, and hence our bodies. Cultural meanings, shaped by social status as well as corporate and other political interests, influence physical activities: working, eating, and fitness. Social and cultural factors shape people's opportunities for a healthy material environment and lifestyle. Thus, human activity produces important factors in bodily health and life, or illness and death.

RECOMMENDED READINGS

Articles

NICKE CHARLES and MARION KERR, "Food for feminist thought." *The Sociological Review* 34(3), 1987: 537–572.

CAROL A. MACLENNAN, "From accident to crash: The auto industry and the politics of injury." *Medical Anthropology Quarterly* 2(3), 1988: 233–250.

DAVID MICHAELS, "Waiting for the body count: Corporate decision-making and bladder cancer in the U.S. dye industry." *Medical Anthropology Quarterly* 2(3), 1988: 215–232.

MARK NICHTER, "Kyasanur forest disease: An ethnography of a disease of development." *Medical Anthropology Quarterly* 1(4), 1987: 406–423.

BARBARA ELLEN SMITH, "Black lung: The social production of disease." *International Journal of Health Services* 11(3), 1981: 343–359.

Books

ALLARD E. DEMBE, *Occupation and Disease.* New Haven, CT: Yale University Press, 1996. Discussion of social, cultural, and technological factors that affect the diagnosis and visibility of occupational health problems (such as back pain).

PETER FREUND and GEORGE MARTIN, *The Ecology of the Automobile.* Montreal: Black Rose Books, 1993. An analysis of the ecological, social, and health effects of automobile-dominated transportation systems.

DEBORAH LUPTON, *Food, the Body and the Self.* Thousand Oaks, CA: Sage, 1996. Good discussion of the sociological aspects of food and eating—including ideas about health and food.

MARCIA MILLMAN, *Such a Pretty Face: Being Fat in America.* New York: Norton, 1980. An excellent, highly readable empirical study of dieting, "fat camps," the social meanings of obesity, and the relationship of such issues to gender.

4

MIND, BODY, AND SOCIETY

CHAPTER OUTLINE

W e have briefly reviewed some of the ways in which social and political factors affect the quality and our use of our material environment. In previous chapters, we looked at physical determinants of health and at their social contexts. Here we examine other ways our bodies are affected less visibly, but perhaps more directly, by social relationships and structures. In this chapter and the next, we focus on the issue of sociopsychological stress and health. Stress and related concepts provide the basis for a holistic perspective in which individual minds and bodies are integrally interrelated with social environments.

"STICKS AND STONES MAY BREAK MY BONES, AND NAMES CAN ALSO HURT ME"

In everyday life, we are sometimes aware that sociopsychological factors affect our health. We might say, "I always get a cold after a tough exam."[1] Conversations contain various psychosomatic references such as, "You're a pain in the neck!" "She'll be the death of me yet!" "Grandma died of a broken heart!" These references show a commonsense awareness of the connections among the mind, body, and society. Particularly among middle-class persons, there appears to be a recent increase in self-consciousness about bodies and stress.

Despite this recent interest in mind-body relationships, psychological and social factors are not perceived to be truly important in determining health because they are not "real," that is, countable and tangible. Viruses, radiation, chemicals, and smoking are physical factors whose effects on the body can be measured and observed. Because medical science has viewed mind and body as separate entities to be studied and treated separately, doctors often do not assign these factors much reality or tangibility. Thus, although we may intuit the reality of psychosomatic connections, we also believe that "sticks and stones may break my bones, but words will never hurt me" (at least not physically!). Yet is this adage really true?

Some evidence suggests that a conversation with another person (even a nonthreatening one) will automatically raise our blood pressure; a conversation with our boss, even more so (Lynch, 1985; Lynch and Rosch, 1990). What are we to make of accounts of "voodoo death," when a chieftain utters a death curse at a woman who violates a tribal taboo, and the woman, who believes her death to be inevitable, soon dies of no clear physical causes (Cannon, 1942)?[2] Modern equiva-

---

[1]In fact, studies show that immunity to disease among medical students is lower than usual during finals (Kiecolt-Glaser and Glaser, 1991).

[2]Other mechanisms may be involved in voodoo death besides being scared to death. For example, other people, such as relatives, friends, and neighbors, withdraw their emotional support from the victim. Funeral rites may be carried out while the person is still alive, thus symbolically defining the individual as dead. (This has been called social death.) However, there may also be a withdrawal of material support. The literature on voodoo death differs on how the process works. Some argue that dehydration (loss of body fluids) is a vital factor. Relatives may withhold water, and the victim, believing he is doomed, loses the desire to drink or obtain water (Eastwell, 1982). Thus, according to some, voodoo death has mainly physical causes, with psychological causes being secondary. Others argue that although physical causes are important, psychologically giving up on life produces lethal physical consequences (such as cardiac arrhythmia). Some laboratory evidence indicates that animals who give up die because their physiological systems have been depressed to a point of death (McElroy and Townsend, 1985).

lents of voodoo death occur in such cases as sudden death after retirement or widowhood. Engel (1971) argued that such phenomena are due to intense emotional arousal, which interrupts the regular rhythm of the heart; in other words, it causes a cardiac arrhythmia that can be deadly. We do not wish to overstate the case that words can kill, but we do want to make the point, developed further later, that human physiology is responsive to its social environment and symbolic meanings can physically affect us.

Placebos: A Case of Mind or Body?

Research on placebos provides some suggestive linkages between mind and body. A placebo is a chemically inert or inactive substance (for example, a sugar pill) that looks like real medication. It is a sham treatment that is supposed to have no actual physical effects. The Latin word *placebo* means "I will please." Doctors sometimes give placebos to patients who want and expect treatment yet seem to have no physical, organic basis to their complaints. Placebos are also used in tests of drugs and treatments to determine how much of a drug's effectiveness is due to its specific physical properties and how much is due to subjective or psychological factors. The placebo is used as a standard (or a control) against which a drug being tested can be compared.

Although chemically inert, placebo "pain medication" can actually reduce pain in as many as 35 percent of patients (Beecher, 1959). In the late 1950s, there was even a controversial experiment with placebo surgery. (Recent tighter rules for experiments with human subjects prohibit such experiments.) It was found that an early version of coronary bypass surgery (called mammary artery ligating surgery) was no more effective than sham surgery, in which patients were put to sleep and had an incision made, although no actual surgery was performed on the heart arteries (Cobb et al., 1959). Some observers have suggested that current coronary bypass surgery may likewise derive part of its success from a placebo effect. Many bypass patients experience considerable relief, even though their surgery produced *no* working grafts (that is, surgery did not improve ventricular function). The operation's symbolic and metaphorical effects may thus account for much of the patients' relief from angina pain (Moerman, 1983). Because patients usually hope that treatment will work, almost all treatments involve an element of the placebo effect. Medical settings—with their impressive equipment, diplomas and certificates on doctors' office walls, white uniforms, clipboards, and stethoscopes—contribute to this faith or expectancy.

Some researchers view the placebo effect as being all in the mind, with no physical basis. Others suggest that placebos actually induce internal physical changes in the body (Bakal, 1979; Cousins, 1989; Eisenberg et al., 1993a; Horwitz et al., 1990; Weil, 1988). For instance, placebos may stimulate the body's production of natural opiates, called endorphins (Davis, 1984; Levine et al., 1978). If this is true, it may be an oversimplification to consider the pain-relieving properties of a placebo merely psychological. Doctors' bedside manner, or communication, may likewise have concrete physical effects, such as reducing pain or speeding recovery. As one physician notes,

But what if it is demonstrated in the future that reassurance provided by a health professional is capable of releasing endogenous morphine-like substances within a patient's brain? Without doubt, the phrase "laying on of hands" will acquire a new meaning. (Bakal, 1979: 251)

The Western assumption of a division between mind and body is not shared by all cultures. In many cultures being sick or being healed is neither all biological nor all psychological, but a psychophysiological process (Grossinger, 1990; Kleinman, 1978; Weil, 1988). We examine this issue in later chapters. For our present purpose, research on placebos illustrates that they may have a psychophysiological effect and that biomedicine's assumption of a mind-body split may not be supportable. A growing body of evidence suggests that the assumption of such a mind-body dualism limits medicine's ability to understand health and illness.[3] Furthermore, mind and body exist in a social environment with which they also interact. Thus, social meanings, pressures, and relationships have at least *some* impact on us. The following sections sketch some of the possible pathways through which social pressures (or stressors) can become the source of psychophysical troubles.

The value of placebos is sometimes misconstrued as a simplistic mind-over-matter argument, which leads to the trap of another form of mind-body dualism: the mind ruling the body. Mind and body must be seen as interacting and not as separate elements. Diseases clearly have biological components, but they also have a psychosocial dimension. Psychosocial factors, however, do not magically transform bodies. Psychosocial pressures generally take years to exact their toll; for instance, social stress does not generate coronary heart disease or hypertension overnight. Some health problems experienced in adulthood may have begun much earlier in the person's life, even early childhood, when the organism is not yet fixed in its patterns of physical responses. Physical damages brought on by long-term stress, for example, may not be easily reversible. The fact that a health problem is affected by social factors, however, does not make it any less real.

The Open Quality of Human Bodies: Dogs Don't Brood

All creatures interact intimately with their environments; they have an impact on their environmental conditions and in turn are affected by them. When studying organisms and their surroundings, we have a tendency to make a sharp distinction

---

[3]Much of the research is controversial but very suggestive. Evidence comes from a host of disciplines with a bewildering array of names, including psychological medicine (Bakal, 1979), psychosomatic medicine, psychophysiology (Suter, 1986), health psychology (Millon et al., 1982), sociophysiology (Barchas and Mendoza, 1984a, 1984b; Waid, 1984), and psychoneuroimmunology (Ader et al., 1991; Locke et al., 1985; Pelletier and Herzing, 1988). These names become less intimidating if we break them down into smaller units of meaning; thus, "psychoneuroimmunology" refers to the study of the interactions among the mind, the nervous system, and the immune system. A central theory underlying much research in this area is that the immune system may be the connecting point between psychosocial experiences and diseases (Solomon, 1985). Such factors as social stress may have an impact on immunity, which in turn lowers a person's resistance to disease.

between the environment and the creatures inhabiting it (Levins and Lewontin, 1985), but this distinction is misleading. We speak of animals adapting to their environments, but creatures also transform the world they live in, often modifying it to their needs and in turn being shaped by the world they have shaped. Humans, more than other creatures, can transform their social and physical environments, but they are also more liable to be affected mentally and physically by the world they create.

Creatures are shaped not only by physical surroundings but also by their social relationships and expectations. Social relationships affect physical responses. The social position of animals, for instance, affects their behavioral responses to amphetamines. Given amphetamines, both dominant and submissive monkeys increased dominant and submissive behaviors "appropriate" to their status. When a monkey changed its social position, so did its response to the drug. Thus, under amphetamines, a monkey with increased status changed its behavior from being submissive to being more threatening and making more dominant displays (Haber and Barchas, 1984).

In a similar experiment with humans, four subjects were told they would be given a sleeping pill, but one of the four was actually given a stimulant. All four subjects became drowsy and quiet (including the one who had unknowingly been given the stimulant). This study shows the importance of social expectations, the influence of the experimenter, and the behavior of one's peers (in this case the other three subjects) for one's physical response. Psychosocial factors were thus as important as the drug's biochemical properties in influencing people's behavior (Bakal, 1979: 180). Culture and social learning affect how the individual experiences the effects of drugs (Becker, 1967). The ability of the hallucinogen LSD, for example, to produce a psychotic episode does not depend merely on the chemistry of the drug but also on the sociocultural setting in which it is experienced.

Human physical functioning is more responsive than that of other animals to its environment (Berger and Luckmann, 1967: 47–50). This is true for a number of reasons:

1. Human beings leave the womb more unfinished than other creatures and exist in an extrauterine social womb of dependence on others. Social learning begins before we are biologically complete (for instance, our central nervous system is not fully developed) for an extended period after birth. Because human young are more open and malleable, early social learning has a deeper impact on them both physically and mentally. Although rats are far more "closed" than humans, studies show that activity and social stimulation can modify the brain of infant (and even adult) rats (Diamond, 1988). The role of early stimulation in constructing human physiology is much greater. Indeed, there may be critical periods in which the body is particularly "open" to social-environmental influences. Experiences early in life may influence how we respond physically to stressors later in life because they "become built into our nervous, immune and endocrine systems—our selves" (Evans, Hodge, and Pless, 1994: 184). Because human interconnectedness and dependence on others are thus partly a result of biology, human physiological functioning is more deeply affected by social surroundings (Birke, 1986: 85).

2. Humans communicate through the use of symbols, which allows them—unlike other creatures—to reflect on themselves and their bodies, and to attach meanings to events (Berger and Luckmann, 1967). Symbols allow humans to remember experiences in a way that other creatures cannot. Humans reflect on their past and anticipate their future, but dogs cannot brood about old grudges. This is not to say dogs do not remember past pain or wait in anticipation, but relative to humans, they tend to be more grounded in the here and now. Such a capacity to reflect on the meaning of events may generate a chronic, low level of stress because our brooding can contribute to a constant degree of psychophysical arousal. The capacity to symbolize widens the range of events to which humans respond as psychologically and physically stressful. A human can respond to the fear of being humiliated in the same way that an animal responds to physical threat. Unlike animals, however, humans do not generally respond to threats motorially (that is, by running or fighting) but by mulling them over in their minds. This response has an impact on our health, because the wider range of anxiety and guilt about our past, present, and future that may result can affect us physically.

3. Research shows ways in which seemingly involuntary physical processes, such as blood pressure, digestion, and the functioning of the immune system, can be changed in "lower" animals by conditioning (namely, reward and punishment) and in humans by learning (such as learning through biofeedback). People are capable of a great deal of voluntary self-regulation and, as yogic practitioners demonstrate, can initiate the regulation of even "involuntary" aspects of physical functioning (Pelletier, 1992). Whereas one can *condition* an animal to lower its blood pressure, humans can *place themselves* into states of mind that will alter their blood pressure. This means the regulation of blood pressure and other supposedly involuntary physical functions are not closed systems that simply operate automatically, but rather they are responsive to the psychosocial environments of which the person is a part. Human sexual responses are modulated by "higher" cognitive functions. Fantasies may amplify or diminish excitement (Cohen and Taylor, 1976). All organisms are capable of *self* organizing their physical functioning; in humans this capacity seems greater. This capacity may be affected by moods, emotions, and feelings about ourselves that are in turn connected to our social existence (Buytendijk, 1974).

In sum, one might loosely characterize human physiology, relative to that of other creatures, as more responsive to its environment and more capable of self-regulation. Humans have more open and more controllable bodies; hence, we are more "makeable." Our bodies have greater access to the outer physical and social world because humans are free from fixed instinctual patterns and have greater capacity for self-regulation. One human aspect of our bodily nature is this particular openness to the world. "Our body in its relative independence has an opening to a formed outer world" (Buytendijk, 1974: 19).

Through these mind-body thoroughfares, our movements are shaped by the physical constraints of our world, and our internal environment fluctuates to some extent with our experiences in the social and physical world. The way in which conversation can raise blood pressure serves as an example. Our way of life in a society and how we experience this way of life are linked to the functioning of our bodies through muscular, neurohormonal, cardiovascular, respiratory, and other systems. Due to our developed self-consciousness and capacity to reflect, the self can dampen or incite the physical systems and in turn be affected by them.

The ability to communicate symbolically (which is intrinsically tied with this open quality) makes us susceptible to a wider range of stressors than other forms of life experience. Humans respond physically to both physical and socially symbolic threats. Most psychosomatic illnesses are therefore peculiarly human. Humans also possess a greater ability to modify stressors' impact by the way we interpret them.

Body and society can intersect in many ways. We have reviewed some obvious connections, such as the impact of cultural and social factors on our diet and hence on our physical condition. Other interrelationships between body and society are more subtle, such as ways our biochemistry may be influenced by the temporal rhythms of social environments or relationships. Some body-society influences involve surface modifications of our muscular-skeletal structure, including our posture, movements, and the shape of our bodies. Others may penetrate our body by changing blood pressure or the responsiveness of our nervous system. Although showing relative internal stability, our bodily systems are "never completely withdrawn from a relationship to a way of existence" that is constantly changing and affecting these bodily systems (Buytendijk, 1974: 29).

Respiratory functioning, which is both voluntary and involuntary, exemplifies such body-society connections. We breathe automatically, yet can hold our breath. How we breathe may be affected by our mood. Anxious people breathe more shallowly. Anxiety in turn may be produced by social settings. What we have here is a kind of society-mind-body bridge (Lupton, 1994). Similarly, blood pressure, blood sugar, and immunity are affected by patterns of neuroendocrinological arousal (Gruchow, 1979), which are themselves linked to the way we live and respond to our life experiences. The early empirical and theoretical foundations for such linkages can be found in the pioneering works of W. B. Cannon (1929) and his student who became the father of contemporary stress research, Hans Selye (1956).

The Neurohormonal Connection: Stressor and Stress Response

The body's response to stressors appears to involve the immune, hormonal, and nervous systems. Previously considered self contained, these systems are now increasingly seen as interconnected (Evans, Hodge, and Pless, 1994).

A stressor, or a stress situation (Suter, 1986), refers to stimuli, or environmental conditions or events, that elicit stress. We include here those stimuli that come from our minds, such as recalling a frightening event. The threat of a dog's bite is a stressor, and our body's response to that stressor is called the stress response or fight-or-flight response. The stress response is the body's way of getting ready to deal with the stressor by mobilizing itself to either fight or to flee. This "fight-or-flight reflex," as Cannon (1929) called it, involves neurohormonal changes in the body (Suter,

1986: 73), which elicit a particular pattern of arousal or excitation in the nervous system and the release of certain hormones. One function of these hormones is to "stimulate and coordinate distant organs" (Selye, 1975: 148).

Hormones are released by the endocrine glands directly into the body, and they stimulate or depress various physical functions. These hormones act as the body's chemical messengers, telling it to step up or to slow down its activities. Adrenaline (also known as epinephrine) and noradrenaline (norepinephrine) are examples of a class of stress hormones known as catecholamines. The stress response involves changes in the central nervous system (CNS; the brain and nerves in the spinal cord) and the release of some of these hormonal substances.

Other examples of stress hormones are the corticosteroids. Research since Selye, however, has suggested that many other hormonal substances, including peptide hormones (for example, endorphins) play a role in the stress response. Thus, to speak of specific stress hormones may be misleading (Pelletier and Herzing, 1988; Weiner, 1992). We could think of hormones as "information substances" (Hill, 1989). One function of hormones is to stimulate and coordinate distant organs (Selye, 1975). Another may be to provide communication links between different physiological systems. Thus, peptide hormones, for example, influence communication between the brain and immune system (Pelletier and Herzing, 1988). Both the organism and its relationship with its environment can be conceptualized in informational terms, with neuroendocrinological functions acting as information networks within the organism (Weiner, 1992).

The fight-or-flight response, according to Selye, is a general physiological response that involves a number of systems throughout the body and can be evoked by any number of nonspecific stimuli (stressors) in the environment. Selye noted that his medical training encouraged a blind spot for the idea of nonspecific factors. In the course of his medical education, specific diseases and their causes "assumed an ever increasing importance and pushed the syndrome of just being sick, the question 'what is disease in general?' out of my consciousness into that hazy category of the purely abstract arguments that are not worth bothering about" (Selye, 1956: 17). In contrast to Selye, other researchers (Weiner, 1992) argue that stressors evoke physiological responses specifically attuned to those specific stressors. Furthermore, prior rhythms of the organism, genetic predispositions, social contexts, and other factors influence physiological responses to stressors. We examine some sources of variability in physiological responses to stressors later in this chapter.

The stress response, in the form of this neurohormonal activity, creates a number of nonspecific changes in the body[4] that adapt the organism for fight or flight (Sapolsky, 1990):

---

[4]The stress response can never be measured directly. In a sense, a stress researcher is like an investigator who tries to deduce what is happening inside a factory on the basis of noises he or she hears while standing on the outside (Suter, 1986). Some measures of stress include the calculation of the amount of electrical activity in the nervous system and the biochemical analysis of blood and urine, but all of these methods have problems. For instance, although the quantity of catecholamines in a person's urine reflects different levels of stress, it may also be a function of that person's unique way of metabolizing (processing) such substances because some people will excrete such hormones more rapidly than others.

1. Blood pressure is increased. Blood flows to the muscles and heart, and much is diverted from the peripheral (outer) parts of the body; this is why cold feet and hands are often a symptom of stress. Blood is also diverted away from functions, like digestion, not needed for fleeing or fighting.
2. Sugars and fats (including cholesterol) are released to give the body energy.
3. Immunity is temporarily depressed to allow the body to tolerate possible invasions, such as wounds.

These changes suggest how prolonged, uninterrupted stress might create physical problems. For example, does the continued release of fats and sugars into the blood help explain the connection between stress and coronary heart disease? Can prolonged stress affect the mechanisms that regulate blood pressure? These are some of the issues investigated by stress research.

Weiner (1992) suggests that research should focus on disturbances—what he calls "perturbations" of neuroendocrinological rhythms and ways in which stressful experiences relate to those disturbances. He advocates looking at both organic (disease) and functional (ill health) problems from this holistic model. Some researchers believe that stress-induced neuroendocrinological changes generally only contribute to causing disease (as a cofactor along with others, such as prior structural damage and genetic factors). Furthermore, they argue stress-induced changes contribute more to *ill health* than to the onset of disease. *Disease* (such as coronary heart disease) has a relatively clear biological basis. Bodies also manifest *ill health* in a wide range of symptoms such as sleeplessness, fatigue, hyperventilation, chronic pain, and so on. These symptoms, on the other hand, do not have a clear-cut organic basis (Weiner, 1992). Even though such forms of distress are common medical complaints, medicine has neglected them because they lack clear organic sources. Given the tendency for medicine to see mind and body as separate, often doctors do not take such problems seriously.

The events in modern life that elicit the stress response in humans are not usually physical but more typically social and symbolic in nature (for example, the threat of being humiliated). Furthermore, modern conditions do not always make the adaptive response of fleeing or fighting a practical one. We may be provoked by a boss to fight or run, but we have learned that neither response would be appropriate. Thus, the body may be continuously geared up for action but not allowed by the rules of civilized behavior to act.

Any demanding situation, such as climbing a dangerous trail for enjoyment or mining coal in a dangerous mine shaft for a living, can be stressful. Not all stressors are negative, however; some can energize and challenge. Stress itself is not inherently unhealthy. It is a part of life, and a totally stressless environment would be both impossible and boring.

Negative and positive stressors are not necessarily equal in their impact on us. Are there qualitative differences in how people respond to negative or positive stressors? Research (Dohrenwend and Pearlin, 1982; Glass, 1977) suggests that it is not just change or environmental demands that are stressful. The uncontrollability of the stressor event seems to increase its destructive consequences for the body.

Stressors are likely to have a negative effect when the individual feels helpless in the face of them.

The Relationship Between Physical and Sociopsychological Stressors

Just as physical factors affecting health (such as diet) cannot be separated from sociocultural ones (such as eating patterns), so too socio-psychological stressors may be difficult to separate from physical stressors. A physical stressor may have an impact on psychological states like mood (Bullinger, 1990). For example, noise levels may not only have physical consequences, such as damage to hearing, but may also influence mood and act as a psychological stressor. Furthermore, evidence indicates that physical and sociopsychological stressors interact with each other. By lowering immunity, stress can aggravate an individual's vulnerability to infectious microorganisms. Being physically rundown may also make it harder to cope with social stresses. Often different kinds of stressors interact with each other and may in fact increase one another's impact on the body. Such a mutually enhancing interaction is called a synergistic relationship. Each factor may "feed" into the other, amplifying effects that either one alone might have had.

The relationship between diet and stress exemplifies synergism. In our fragmented ways of looking at health and illness, we often focus on one factor (such as diet) as *the* determinant of health. Some think that eating properly will save them from heart disease and other woes, yet diet cannot be considered in isolation from other factors. A high cholesterol diet *combined* with high levels of social stress can increase the likelihood of atherosclerosis (hardening of the arteries), over and above the effect of diet by itself (Eyer, 1984; Kaplan et al., 1983). Smoking and stress combined may interact synergistically to raise blood pressure and heart rate (Karasek and Theorell, 1990; Ratliff-Crain and Baum, 1990).

Not only physical stressors (for example, workplace ergonomic conditions) but also mental ones can influence levels of muscular tension leading to musculoskeletal disorders (Lundberg et al., 1994). Mental stress can produce muscular tension in the absence of a physical workload; it can be aggravated by the fact that muscles are being "readied for use" but *not* being used. Mental and physical stressors can get together synergistically to increase muscular tension. For example, the combination of the inability to relax at home because of a "second shift" of household labor and physical work conditions (at a computer terminal, for instance) may lead to the high incidence of neck and shoulder problems among women (Lundberg et al., 1994).

A QUESTION OF SUSCEPTIBILITY

Why do two people react very differently to the same stressors? Some of us face stress with confidence; others with fear, despair, and a sense of hopelessness. Some people seem to weather life's crises without much damage; others break easily.

Clearly, it is not only the stressor itself that determines the reaction, but also how the individual experiences and deals with the stressor. Furthermore, research suggests that even physiological reactions to stress vary from person to person. Some people's bodies react very strongly to a stressor; others' less so. What factors account for such variations in individual susceptibility?

Although there are important individual variations in reactions to stress, we should avoid individualistic interpretations that ignore the social circumstances contributing to these variations. Such approaches tend to blame the victim of stress rather than to examine the social situations that might account for variations in individual susceptibility. Three interrelated kinds of individual variations in stressor reaction exemplify this problem; the mere presence of a stressor does not account for a person's physical reaction to it. First, there are differences in the way people's bodies respond to stressors (**physiological reactivity**). Second, there are variations in how people perceive stressors and assess what is happening to them (**cognitive-emotional appraisal**). Third, there are differences in the way people manage stressors (**coping**).

Physiological Reactivity

Although the basic pattern of the stress response remains essentially the same from person to person, researchers have found recurring *individual* patterns in the way people's bodies respond to stress. Some individualized physical responses are more fixed or rigid than others. Two people faced with the same stressor will show differences in the level to which their blood pressure rises. The pressure of persons who have hypertension tends to fluctuate more dramatically than that of those whose blood pressure at rest is "normal" (Buytendijk, 1974; Suter, 1986).

Individuals also differ in their patterns of neurological excitation. In some people the ergotrophic response, in which sympathetic arousal is high, is more easily elicited. Other people respond more quickly with a tropotrophic response, in which parasympathetic excitation predominates (Suter, 1986). Individuals may also differ in how readily their bodies shift between these two responses, physically changing from being in a state of fight or flight to being in a state of relaxation (Gellhorn, 1969).

Individuals have varying hormonal reactions (Bieliauskas, 1982: 5). In some laboratory studies, men produced more epinephrine in response to stressors than women did. A study of women in nontraditional "male" occupational roles, however, showed that women meet demands with almost no sharp increase in epinephrine like the men's (Frankenhaeuser, 1991). It is nonetheless possible that this difference has genetic and natural bases. Perhaps men overreact to stress, thus producing an inefficient excess of stress hormones (Frankenhaeuser, 1991; Overfield, 1985; Polefrone and Manuck, 1987). Some physiological variations may reflect differences in biological makeup. Perhaps men and women *do* differ biologically to some extent in hormonal reactions. Perhaps some individuals are genetically predisposed to hypertension or coronary heart disease. Such issues are by no means resolved, and the research results are mixed.

Variations in physiological reactivity, such as differences in catecholamine reactivity, may also be the result of social factors, at least to some extent. Men and women are socialized to deal with stress in different ways. It may well be that these learned patterns also affect their way of responding physically (Birke, 1986; Lowe and Hubbard, 1983). The fight-or-flight response tends to elevate blood pressure. A long-term exposure to stressors and a learned typical way of responding to them might eventually lead to a regular pattern of reacting physically, as some animal studies suggest (McCarty et al., 1988). One study suggests that chronic occupational stress in blue-collar workers may, over an extended period, modify the way the heart and blood pressure respond to stressors (Siegrist and Klein, 1990).

Moss (1973) has argued that given a certain cognitive-emotional orientation to stressors, over time the nervous system might become "tuned" into a particular pattern of arousal. Thus, the sympathetic nervous system's reaction to situations might become amplified and fixed in that amplified pattern. The parasympathetic nervous system would not, therefore, be as readily activated. The person could be easily excited and would find it hard to unwind. Individual physiological patterns in responding to stress might be partly the result of learning and other social experiences (Suter, 1986: 84). The distinction between physiological factors and social factors in health is thus not always clear cut.

Cognitive-Emotional Appraisal

Cognitive-emotional appraisal is the physiological impact of a person's interpretation and emotional reaction to a stressful event. In one study of this phenomenon, Lazarus (1966) and his associates showed male students different versions of a film that depicted ritual operations on the genitals: circumcision (cutting around the penis to remove the foreskin) and subincision (cutting the penis lengthwise). One version of the film had no sound and showed only the operations. Another version had a soundtrack that emphasized the harmlessness of the procedures and the fact that the participants in the rites saw them as an honor. A third version contained the narration of an anthropologist who, in an intellectual tone, constantly commented on events as the interesting and "exotic" customs of other societies. The researchers measured the level of physiological stress response of each member of the audiences. Those exposed to the second or the third version of this film showed lower physiological levels of stress. Lazarus concluded that one's physical reaction to a stressor is affected by how one interprets it. In this case, the soundtracks helped the audiences interpret the stressor as less threatening. Although watching a stressful event on a film is not the same as seeing it in person or having it done to oneself, such experiments illustrate that our interpretations of events have a significant effect on how we react to them.

Several theories emphasize the importance of an individual's cognitive-emotional appraisal of situations in linking stress to illness (see Moss, 1973; Totman, 1979). Antonovsky (1987: 13) proposes that people with a high "sense of coherence" are healthier:

[They have] a global orientation that expresses the extent to which one has a pervasive, enduring though dynamic feeling that (1) the stimuli deriving from one's internal and external environments in the course of living are structured, predictable and explicable; (2) the resources are available to one to meet the demands posed by these stimuli; and (3) these demands are challenges worthy of investment and employment.

Antonovsky (1990) conceptualizes this sense of coherence as "dispositional orientation" (rather than personal "trait") toward experiencing stressors as comprehensible, manageable, and meaningful.

Cultural factors and an individual's position in a social structure can affect this sense of coherence. Antonovsky does not, however, thoroughly examine the ways environments disempower people, nor does he systematically consider how conditions that attack a person's sense of coherence are built into the social organization of institutions such as the workplace and the family. He also does not explore in sufficient depth the impact of social and economic systems such as capitalism on individuals' sense of coherence.

These theories emphasize the importance to health of feeling a sense of empowerment or control.[5] What they clearly do not distinguish is how a person feels or perceives the world, as opposed to conditions that lead a person to emotionally and mentally appraise the world a certain way. The emphasis on cognitive appraisal in the stress literature often implies that how one perceives an event is the result of a psychological attribute or quality inherent in the person, independent of the event itself (Evans, Hodge, and Pless, 1994). This approach treats *how* we perceive things as almost unrelated to what we are perceiving. Such a focus may downplay common, objective environmental stressors such as poverty (Moos and Swindle, 1990). Furthermore, people may react physiologically to a stressor but not be consciously aware of it (Krohne, 1990).

Although individuals do vary in the way they appraise stressors at any given time, these differences are often the result of former social experiences with past stressors. Feeling helpless may come from some set of previous objective experiences. If, for instance, people were once overwhelmed and made to feel powerless by social class, economic, or familial events, later in life they may find it harder to

---

[5] Antonovsky (1979: 127–128) claimed that it is important to differentiate a sense of control from one of coherence, because a sense of control implies that "I am in control," which reflects a cultural bias equating sense of control with self-control. However, people do not have to be in control to have a sense of coherence. Rather, they need simply to be participants in shaping their fate, believing that who- or whatever is in control (their god or leader, for instance) is controlling events in the people's interest and is a legitimate authority. One can feel that the world is relatively safe and in control and yet not be in control.

But two issues must be raised: First, self-control is important in Western industrialized societies. Second, however much events can be "in the hands of the Lord," so to speak, individuals still must feel the world is manageable and not working against them. It is inconceivable that persons could tolerate feeling they were puppets or that their actions were not their own. To be unable to connect one's actions with more or less predictable outcomes would be most disturbing. Antonovsky admitted that, although control need not be totally in individuals' hands, they must feel themselves to be participants in their actions.

believe that a stressor now confronting them is a manageable one (even if it is!) (Evans, Hodge, and Pless, 1994).

Seligman (1992) observed that animals placed in laboratory conditions of helplessness for a long enough period were unable to cope with subsequent stress or possible activity. He has linked such "learned helplessness" to depression, poor health, and a generally heightened susceptibility to stressors. The experience of powerlessness in everyday situations at work or home may produce a similar learned helplessness in humans (Lennerlof, 1988). Other authors have introduced similar concepts, for example, the "giving-up complex" (Schmale, 1972) and the "paralysis of will" (Bakal, 1979). Likewise, the notion of "surplus powerlessness" (Lerner, 1992) suggests that if individuals were once made to feel powerless, the expectation that they will again be powerless builds up and keeps them from acting when confronted with stressors (even when they are able). People's present reactions to stressors are thus linked to their past experiences with empowering or disempowering situations. A lifetime of social exploitation or domination will certainly have an impact on whether a person feels empowered.

Coping

Coping refers to all of the ways of managing the tension a stressor produces (Mechanic, 1978: 51). As Syme and Berkman (1976: 6) observed:

> Generalized susceptibility to disease may be influenced not only by the impact of various forms of life change and life stress, but also by differences in the way people cope with such stress. Coping, in this sense, refers not to specific types of psychological responses but to the more generalized ways in which people deal with problems in their everyday life. It is evident that such coping styles are likely to be products of environmental situations and not independent of such factors.

One's cognitive-emotional appraisal of a situation is in itself a way of coping or managing stress. Some people overact emotionally; seeing the glass as half empty, they give up. Others see a glass that is half full and keep striving. Coping is not merely a matter of attitude, perception, or emotional response, however; it also involves action—that is, doing something about the stressor.

The focus of much stress literature on individual coping leads to two blind spots. First, these studies fail to consider how power affects people's ability to do something about stress. How does social class, ethnicity, gender, or work situation influence resources for effective coping? Second, much research tends to separate coping and stressor, thereby missing the fact that the conditions creating stress often also limit both the possibility of and options for coping. One's social position (such as one's status as a woman) often limits options for coping. In some areas of life, such as in friendships, certain personal styles of coping strategies are possible, but in much of everyday life people's options for managing stress are very limited. The world of work, for example, allows most people only limited coping strategies (Pearlin and Schooler, 1978). Coping ability tends to be viewed as primarily an individual phenomenon. This misconception comes from separating individuals from the social and cultural *contexts* in which they cope (Peterson, 1994; Valach, 1995).

The early literature on stress gives the impression that stress is a problem primarily for high-powered, white-collar workers. Yet research indicates that although these groups do face a great deal of stress, they also have access to resources that allow them to cope with it more effectively than those who lack resources. Even among animals the "top dog" generally has more resources to handle stressors than the "bottom dog." One study of baboons found that, in response to stress, high-ranking males showed faster increases in cortisol, a stress hormone, than subordinate baboons; however, their basal level (that is, the ordinary amount when not exposed to stress) of the hormone was lower than that of the subordinates. Furthermore, when the stressful event ended, the amounts of cortisol in high-ranking baboons returned more rapidly to the basal levels than did those of their subordinates. The more effective coping of these "top bananas" was attributed to such advantages as better choice of food, mates, and living conditions (Sapolsky, 1982, 1989, 1990; Wilkinson, 1996). Another researcher found that rats that can control the source of stress or predict when stress will occur also cope more effectively and show fewer pathological effects of stress than do rats that cannot control or predict stressors (Pelletier and Herzing, 1988: 32; Weiss, 1972). The blood pressure and cardiovascular reactivity of rats in response to stressors have been shown to be linked to their position in the social hierarchy (Bohus et al., 1991). A wide range of physiological patterns is associated with subordinate rank in animals; these patterns vary as the social status of the animal changes. They are thus a function of the animal's social status (Weiner, 1992: 176). Although animal studies cannot be used uncritically to generalize about human situations and behavior, executives and other "top bananas," whose job conditions allow for control and provide resources for coping (such as more control over the use of one's time), can probably cope with stress more effectively than those who do not experience such advantages.

One might argue that nonexecutive stress is a more serious health hazard than executive stress. A study of 5,100 Swedish and American men found the highest risk of coronary heart disease among workers with both heavy job demands and a "low ability to influence how their tasks are done" (Karasek and Theorell, 1990; Peterson, 1994). Thus, one's social position (such as on the job) may influence both the amount of stress one faces and the resources one has for coping. The most stressful occupations are those that combine high levels of stress with little control over those stressful conditions. Being a telephone operator or a waitress may therefore be more stressful than being a bank officer, sales manager, or physician. For example, a National Institute of Occupational Safety and Health study found that clerical women who had low control over their work with VDTs (video display terminals) showed higher levels of job stress than the highly pressured air traffic controllers, who also work with such terminals (Howard, 1985: 73). Similarly, a survey of U.S. Post Office mail handlers find them to be largely in the "high strain" job category—high job demands and low decision latitude (Cahill and Landsbergis, 1996). Thus, the social circumstances in which people find themselves influence not only the demands to which they are exposed but also their ability to handle those demands.

Corporate health programs have proliferated in the United States. Sponsored mainly by larger corporations, they emphasize exercise, meditation, diet control, and smoking cessation (Conrad, 1988; Pelletier, 1985). Although programs for blue-collar and lower-echelon white-collar workers exist, many are directed toward executives, who present potentially more expensive health-related losses for the corporation. These programs seem to have developed in an economic environment of escalating medical costs to corporations and governments (Alexander, 1988). However, there is no definitive evidence yet that, in the long run, they do prevent illness (Conrad, 1988). Indeed, they may be attempts to impose new forms of social control on the workers through a new corporate health ethic, by shaping values and attitudes of workers toward their lifestyles and also toward work. Such an ethic stresses the *individual* worker's fitness, strength, diet, and health habits while avoiding scrutiny of social contexts that affect health (Conrad and Walsh, 1992).

Although their overt function is to use prevention to reduce health care costs and loss of workdays, corporate health programs may also direct attention away from political and environmental issues in the workplace. They do not generally encourage workers to examine critically the social conditions under which they work, such as work pace, vacations, breaks, or participation in decisions affecting their work. The implicit message to employees is that their health (and the costs they incur by being sick) are their individual responsibility (Glassner, 1989). Such programs may even be used to justify cutting back on medical benefits. The corporate image also benefits by such programs, and other parts of the business sector profit by selling the equipment and services for these programs (Alexander, 1988).

Stress and Power

Young (1980: 133) observes that both scientific and lay discussions of stress tend to "subvert sociological reasoning" by removing people from their social contexts and from class and group conflicts. They tend to emphasize subjective factors and the way individuals *perceive* events, or in other words, psychological as opposed to sociological factors.[6] The way people see things gets confused with the way things are (Young, 1980: 145). Instead of beginning analyses of stress and health by looking at coping responses, cognitive-emotional appraisal, or individual forms of coping, why not begin by examining social conditions of inequality or structural arrangements, such as those that force a person to work under pressure or do not allow time to relax?

The incidence of diabetes among Mexican American migrant farm workers illustrates the relationship among psychosocial stress, limited options for managing

---

[6]We therefore do not agree with Mechanic (1978: 71), who after reviewing literature on helplessness and health, concluded that whether we in fact control our external environment is a "philosophical issue." What is significant, he said, is our subjective response to conditions, or our sense of helplessness.

stress, and social inequality. Much research on diabetes has focused on genetic factors, together with nutrition, obesity, and health behavior. Although these variables are important influences, exclusive emphasis on them obscures the role of such factors as social inequality. Diabetes is more common among low-status and low-income people. The exact role that psychosocial stress plays in the disease is not clear; however, some evidence suggests stress may influence its onset and course (Jacobson and Leibovich, 1984; Scheder, 1988).

Stress can also affect health behavior, such as excessive eating and drinking. The neuroendocrinological arousal generated by high levels of chronic stress may also affect blood sugar metabolism (Jacobson and Leibovich, 1984). One study found that rates of adult-onset diabetes (Type II diabetes mellitus) were much higher among those who had spent a long time as migrant farm workers and had frequent experiences of stressful life events. Obesity did not distinguish those who got diabetes from those who did not. Rather, the high levels of stress experienced by these migrant workers as a result of their low social position, disrupted social networks, social marginality (that is, being outsiders in American culture), discrimination, heavy workloads, job insecurity, poverty, and feelings of hopelessness and helplessness contributed to catecholamine-produced impairments in glucose levels (Scheder, 1988).

Folk diseases such as "nerves" (*nervios* or *nervos*) also reflect the links among stress, power, and sickness. "Nerves" are a form of ill health characterized by physical symptoms that appear to have no clear organic source, such as fatigue, trembling, headaches, fainting, and feeling of imbalance. "Nerves" are physical responses to situations of extreme powerlessness that characterize the lives of many poor people, especially women. That similar illness is widely experienced cross culturally suggests the importance of issues of power, personal sense of control, and psychosocial stress for people's health and well-being (Duffie, 1996; Low, 1994; Scheper-Hughes, 1992).

The social organization of time provides an excellent example of the complex interrelationship of physical, sociopsychological, and political (that is, relationships of power) sources of stress and illness. Our social material environments (such as the design of our work spaces and the pace of work demanded of us) are important influences on our bodies. Our everyday lives take place in social contexts in which time is organized in specified ways. These contexts constrain or empower us and can have an impact on our health.

SICKENING SCHEDULES

Control over time—our own or other people's—is a form of power. Powerful persons have the ability to regulate other people's time and labor. The ability to manage our own schedules is limited by our position in society. Wealthy persons have more resources for managing the stress of demanding schedules. A teacher can keep a student waiting, but students should not be late for their appointments with a teacher because a teacher's time is assumed to be more valuable. *Time is socially orga-*

nized, and the ability to schedule time and to manage it is socially distributed. Those with more power have more control over time.

From the moment we enter the world as babies, we are subject to a social calendar that is not of our own making, and we are taught to respect the constraints of time. The fragmentation and structuring of time and space in adult terms begins early. In some societies, however, adults and children do not experience such sharp time distinctions between work and play (Cherfas and Lewin, 1980).

In our society, the emphasis is on productivity. The social organization of our economic life is the basis of much of our social scheduling of time. This organization demands intense productivity. How members of a society collectively use time and the different degrees of control over their own or other people's time are central sociopsychological factors in health. They determine the frequency and intensity of stressors as well as the effectiveness of means of dealing with those stressors. For example, work time can be stressful for many people; factors such as social or occupational status influence how well they can cope with work time.

Time and Work

In the beginning of the twentieth century, the intense control by employers over work time, which had characterized the growing capitalist society of the nineteenth century, was further extended. Workers became more and more paced by the rhythms of the machine. With the emergence of the assembly line and "scientific management" of work activity, new, more systematic, "scientific" or rationalized forms of control predominated in the workplace. For instance, standards for workers were increasingly set by time-and-motion studies.

The work of Frederick Taylor epitomizes the attempt to impose rationalized, scientific controls over time and motion. In *The Principles of Scientific Management* ([1911] 1947), Taylor argued for a sharp division between those who plan work and those who do it. The planning was to be carried out exclusively by managers trained in scientific management. Jobs were to be divided and subdivided into the smallest, easiest-to-learn unit of activity. Time-and-motion studies would determine the most efficient way to move and the optimum unit of time each subdivided task should take. These studies would then set standards for precisely how and how fast all the workers would move. Taylor argued that such a system of management should take precedence over the idiosyncratic rhythms and needs of individual workers (Karasek and Theorell, 1990). Although his system is no longer widely applied in most workplaces, the attitudes and assumptions of Taylorism still prevail among many managers.

Work in industrial manufacturing in particular was highly regulated by machines and specific, limiting instructions. Tasks were broken down into short, simple, repetitive units of activity (Braverman, 1974). The result of this form of control, used in the pursuit of productivity, was to place workers increasingly into environments that moved too fast, were deadeningly boring, and controlled the motions of the body in an unnatural and uncomfortable way.

The quest for increased productivity has been most intense in industrial manufacturing. This drive has put greater pressure on industrial workers in the form of ever-increasing demands on pace and the effective use of working time, and decreasing options for variety, relaxation, and social interaction at work. Various studies show that poor mental health, psychosomatic disorders, and sick leaves are most common in low-status industrial manufacturing jobs (Frankenhaeuser and Gardell, 1976).

The pace and motion of factory work has been extended to white-collar office work. The movements of some typists, keypunch operators, and other office machine operators have taken on "automaton-like characteristics" (Stellman, 1977: 55). The growth of computer technologies since the 1950s has opened up new work possibilities, but it has also led to more highly repetitive, boring, machine-paced work in the office. Computer technology provides for increased control over individual workers. A terminal on a supervisor's desk can monitor the number of strokes made by each individual keypunch operator (Garson, 1988; National Safe Workplace Institute, 1990).

Bell Telephone computers print 15-minute summaries of how many operators were on duty, how many calls each operator handled, the average speed of an operator's answer, and how long they spent talking to each customer (Howard, 1985: 63). Citicorp Bank uses a computer information system that provides management with data about workplaces hundreds of miles away. Each clerk's printout shows the amount of time spent processing records, talking on the phone, and the like. The records are then evaluated according to standards set by Citicorp's time-and-motion specialist (Howard, 1985: 30–31). A National Association of Working Women's survey found that 35 percent of its members, in jobs as diverse as bank teller, data entry clerk, waitress, and truck driver, were monitored by computer (Howard, 1985: 62). Even middle-level managers and executives are subject to closely monitored time controls; some must submit accounts of work done every half hour (Garson, 1988). Thus, in bureaucratically controlled workplaces (including office and professional work) one trend, exacerbated by computerization, is toward greater standardization of work and control over time (Burris, 1993; Garson, 1988).

Load Balance   Some environments demand too much, too fast; others demand some degree of involvement but make too few demands and are boring. The different rhythms of working (and of living in general) may be conceived of in terms of load balance: Do they demand too much or too little? How much pressure (or how much of a load) is imposed on a person? A load imbalance may involve either overload or underload, or both, as temporal rhythms. A chronic load imbalance may adversely affect one's health. Although our examples of time rhythms are drawn from the workplace, the problem of load balancing may apply equally to the lives of the unemployed, the elderly, and persons with disabilities (Frankenhaeuser, 1981).

Underload and overload are products of the degree of control one has over the rhythm of one's work. Temporal demands are not as stressful when self-generated. However, they are stressful when they are imposed and combined with little control over how one's work is done (Karasek and Theorell, 1990). Such jobs are likely to be held by low-status workers. Overload may involve piecework, such as being paid by the number of letters typed each hour. Overload usually results from a work environment that moves too fast for comfort. Underload often involves machine-paced work, such as an assembly line. Workers' movements are standardized but also demand their attention. Underload tends to be boring and tiring work. Clearly some boring work need not be stressful. A night watchman can read, walk, and chat; this work may thus not be as stressful as boring work that requires sustained alertness and attention, such as watching a machine.

Work often involves both underload and overload (Frankenhaeuser and Gardell, 1976). A dramatic example is the labor process at a Canadian meat packing plant:

> Two lines run during the day, one on the night shift. The pace is maintained by the skinning machine operators who place the hams with skins removed on the conveyer. . . . Workers holding razor sharp knives are forced to match the pace of machine operators. If a worker cannot keep up, the others down the line must work faster just to maintain the pace. Arguments occur among workers, accusations of going too fast or too slow. Stress on the job is high due to the surrender of control to the machine-paced line combined with the need to maintain a constantly high level of attention. A momentary loss of attention can lead to error or injury. Indeed, the sense of stress is heightened by congestion as workers are sandwiched between the moving table and large vats for waste and trim located two feet away. From management's perspective, however, the changes are viewed positively, because workers put pressure on each other to keep up production speeds. (Novek et al., 1990: 49, 292–293)

One can imagine the multiplicity of health risks that characterize this job, such as the danger of injury from knives and sharp machines, as well as repetitive strain injury. There is also the psychosocial stress produced by the pressure of time and the boredom coupled with the demand for constant alertness. Many jobs involve such a combination of extremes of hectic and boring work, together with strict control over time and movements that is physically and psychologically uncomfortable. Postal and delivery service workers, particularly those like mail handlers whose work is machine paced, are under considerable stress aggravated by recent industry moves to increase productivity often at the expense of safety (Cahill and Landsbergis, 1996; Drew, 1995). The "tyranny of the schedule" is a risk factor in occupational health (Syme, 1996: 29).

Overload and underload have been linked to increased excretions of catecholamine, a stress hormone (Frankenhaeuser, 1981). A study of sawmill workers found that those whose jobs were characterized by a lack of control over their situation (as a consequence of overload and underload) were most likely to have increased catecholamine excretions in their urine. These workers also reported feeling tired, tense, anxious, and ill more frequently than other workers (Frankenhaeuser and Gardell, 1976). Low control coupled with fast pace increases cortisol and adrenaline excretions (Karasek and Theorell, 1990). Some research has linked chronic work overload among blue-collar workers to myocardial infarction (Weiner, 1992: 88). Higher hospitalization rates for myocardial infarction (heart attacks) were related in another study to hectic monotonous work, lengthy and irregular work hours, and low degree of influence over timing holidays (Haynes, 1991: 159).

Such research shows that the social organization of time can be both *physically* stressful (that is, contribute to bodily wear and tear) and *psychologically* stressful. It can contribute to ergonomic stress, affecting the body "directly" by forcing workers to a pace that puts an excessive strain on the musculoskeletal system and makes work unsafe. It can also be psychologically stressful, creating unhealthy neurohormonal changes in the body.

The machine-paced nature of much work means that, in a sense, the human body must function like a machine. Because machines can tolerate what humans cannot, the gearing of the body to the rhythm and movements of a machine may have destructive physical effects. A sociologist who worked in a Hungarian tractor factory described how the time pressure of machine-paced work affected the way workers paid attention to physical signs that they are tired or uncomfortable:

> The best way I can put it is like this: I cease to exist. When the huge side doors of the workshop are opened and the transporters rattle in loaded with material, I know—without having a thought as such, I simply know—that I am in a freezing draught, but I do not feel that I am cold. My back aches, there is a cramp in my fingers, the piece rate is ridiculous: I don't feel or think any of this. (Haraszti, 1978: 112)

Time pressures can thus put one out of touch with one's own body.

To argue that our contemporary work hours are long may seem absurd in comparison to the nineteenth-century workweek of around 70 hours (Friedmann, 1961: 105). That period, however, was not typical. Industrial capitalism was then becoming a dominant force in Western society, and productivity was being enhanced mainly by lengthening the workday. By contrast, in agricultural societies the workweek was shorter (around 30 hours a week) and more in gear with seasonal rhythms, and workers frequently labored only about 15 weeks a year (Eyer and Sterling, 1977; Johnson, 1978).

In the United States, the number of hours per year that people work has increased since the late 1960s. From 1969 to 1987, the increase for men was nearly 100 work hours per year and for women, about 300 more hours a year. In Europe in recent decades, work hours have decreased, perhaps because of stronger unions. Paid vacation time required by law in Europe ranges from four to five weeks a year (Schor, 1992); the United States has no requirements for paid vacations, and the standard paid vacation in the United States is less than half as long as in Europe.

Shift Work Working on shifts is another kind of temporal rhythm that is utterly unknown in many societies. As capitalism became the predominant form of economic and social organization in Western society, shift work became more common. By 1980, 11 percent of full-time U.S. workers were on late shifts (U.S. Department of Labor, 1981). Roughly 20 percent of U.S. workers are on some form of shift work (Blyton, 1985; Klinkenborg, 1997). In Europe the proportion of workers on shifts has increased overall since World War II, with the greatest increases among women and nonmanual (white-collar) workers (Blyton, 1985). Shift work became more common as the investment in machinery became greater and as it became profitable to sustain production around the clock. Some shift work is needed for technical reasons, such as a specific manufacturing process that cannot be interrupted. Certain service jobs (like those in hospitals) also require round-the-clock coverage. Most shift work, however, is instituted because it increases profits by maximizing the use of the equipment and space in which capital has been invested.

There are many different systems for arranging shifts. The most common is to have an early morning, late afternoon, and night shift (for example, 5 a.m. to 1 p.m., 1 p.m. to 9 p.m., and 9 p.m. to 5 a.m.). The number of days worked on the same shift is called the rotation period. The most common rotation period is one week (Baker, 1981: 109).

Shift work often goes against the rhythms governing many bodily functions. Heart rate, body temperature, the production of various hormones, and metabolic rates all vary with the time of day, and seem to follow a 25-hour cycle called a circadian rhythm (Åkerstedt, 1990). One researcher suggests that shift work often violates workers' physiological rhythms by not giving them enough time to adjust from one cycle to another (Levi, 1981, 1978). One study exposed 100 volunteers to rotation periods that shifted between three days and three nights of continuous work. It was found that the circadian rhythms, geared to being awake during the day, persisted. The author concluded that although the endocrine system will eventually adapt to the shift, long rotation periods are necessary to adapt (Levi, 1978). However, most shift arrangements do not allow for this.[7] Studies show higher rates of sleep and digestive disorders among shift workers (Åkerstedt, 1990). Although some argue that shift work has not demonstrated long-term serious effects on health (Poole et al., 1992), one study found a connection between cardiovascular disease and the amount of shift work done. Higher levels of serum cholesterol also were found among shift workers (Knutsson et al., 1986).

The time of the day a person must work affects sensory-motor performance (for example, quickness of reflexes). It also has an impact on the metabolism (the body processing) of various chemicals and toxins to which individuals are exposed in the course of their work. How quickly the body absorbs a medication depends on what time of day it is taken. Similarly, how chemicals and other physical stressors affect the body may depend on the time of day of exposure, an issue that has

---

[7]Some individuals adjust better than others; some prefer certain time cycles, and there are sometimes ways of arranging shifts so that workers have an opportunity to adjust. However, most workers do not have sufficient control over their work time to effect schedules compatible with their individual needs.

not received much attention in research on time, work, and health (Baker, 1981: 117). Social factors often interact with psychophysical stressors in complex ways.

Shift work, like overtime, may be formally voluntary in the terms of a union contract, but often financial pressures or fear of denying a superior's request may make what is formally voluntary in practice almost compulsory (Pfeffer, 1979: 87–88). Working overtime or on different shifts, furthermore, has social consequences for workers and their families. Shift work often intrudes into the worker's personal life, affecting leisure and social networks such as family and friendships. These changes in turn influence eating habits and sleep patterns, and may produce such adverse health consequences as digestive disorders (Klinkenborg, 1997). For these reasons, some countries, such as Sweden and Belgium, have laws that strongly limit the prevalence of shift work.

Some experiments allowing employees to have some control over their own time, by choosing to work longer days and shorter weeks or other alternatives to nine-to-five daytime hours, have been tried in the United States and Europe. In West Germany and Switzerland about 40 to 45 percent of the work force is on flextime; it is mainly a white-collar prerogative, but more blue-collar workers are on flextime in those countries than in the United States. About 8 percent of the U.S. work force has flextime, and those workers are concentrated in the service sector and among nonmanual workers in large-scale business enterprises (Blyton, 1985). Unfortunately, flextime experiments are often limited by overriding fears of declining productivity and managerial control. Unlike flextime, U.S. industrial use of "compressed" work weeks (more hours per day over fewer days per week) and mandatory overtime to achieve "just-in-time" production, is often not a matter of choice for employees. A 1996 survey found that 34 percent of large companies used compressed work weeks for some of their employees (Kilborn, 1996). Although this compression may be preferable for some workers, for others it is highly stressful.

Work Time, "Free" Time

A time urgency characterizes behavior not only in work time but also in free time. In fact, the character of leisure time is affected by work time. The two-week vacations common in the United States (compared to the average of four to six weeks in many other industrial countries) are directly affected by the other 50 weeks of work. Temporal rhythms of underload and overload affect life experiences other than work (Antonovsky, 1979: 187). A college professor who worked in a factory on his year of academic leave observed:

> Except for shopping at supermarkets that are open all kinds of hours, I could hardly run errands, go see a doctor, or do anything in the community. . . . I found myself torn between spending those few precious hours of waking leisure with my son, with my wife or by myself. I found myself, in short and with some important differences no doubt, trying to live with drastically curtailed and compressed free time as millions of American workers have learned to live, snatching moments of personal satisfaction largely from time not sold to others. (Pfeffer, 1979: 41)

People who work in dull and restricting jobs tend to be less likely than those with interesting jobs to engage in "leisure activities requiring planning, participation and effort" (Frankenhaeuser, 1981: 492). Workers do not typically compensate for dull jobs with exciting, challenging leisure-time activities.

Not only may the rhythms of work time seep into the lunch hour, weekends, and holidays, but the physiological responses to work stress may also continue long after the workday is done. The physiological effects of work overload may spread to leisure hours, thus delaying their full impact (Frankenhaeuser, 1991). Many of us have experienced a form of work time carrying over into our free time when we are unable to adjust our sleep patterns during vacations and continue to wake up to an inner alarm clock geared to the memories of work time. The inability to unwind is accompanied by the hormonal system's inability to slow down, even in the absence of environmental demands. Thus, workers who have been working overtime show elevations of catecholamines not only at work but through the next evening as well. The process of unwinding may be accompanied by an increase in psychosomatic problems (Levi, 1981: 53).

The inability to relax during free time is also the consequence of media and peer pressures to consume frenetically. Although some people may shop for enjoyment, often free time ends up as rigidly scheduled as work time. The activity of consuming requires that commodities be bought, kept, and maintained. More time must be scheduled and compartmentalized to allow for shopping, getting to sales on time, and having goods repaired, waxed, shampooed, trimmed, and polished. Because time spent consuming must to some extent be scheduled, leisure time is therefore regimented. Sports and amusements may also mirror the rhythm and movement of the work world. One observer commented:

> Even days ostensibly outside daily routine, holidays, are occupied with "organized" sports and amusements which, far from being liberating forms of leisure facilitating participation in subjective atemporality, are ritualistic reaffirmations of the daily grind, veritable sermons or morality plays on the value of efficient use of "on" time and the rewards of synchronized cooperation. Indeed, unprogrammed, "idle," or "non-productive," time, eagerly sought and jealously safeguarded in more subjective cultures, is experienced as malaise in machine culture. (Dye, 1981: 58–59)

A disciplined worker and a disciplined consumer go together hand in hand in our society.

So-called leisure time is often consumed by unpaid labor in the form of housework and the care of dependent children and elderly. In our society, this burden falls disproportionately on women. Parenting and housework are work, even though they are not socially recognized as paid, "productive" labor. These forms of work are characterized by recurring, boring, repetitive tasks; long hours; social isolation in the home; and many features, such as underload and overload, that characterize factory work (Chavkin, 1984; Doyal, 1995; Popay and Bartley, 1989). Working mothers thus carry a double burden from both paid work and housework (Hochschild, 1989; Schor, 1992).[8] Furthermore, those household tasks for which women are responsible tend to be those that must be done daily at a fixed time, whereas men's household tasks (such as fixing the car) allow for more flexibility in scheduling (Frankenhaeuser, 1991).

In one study, male managers "wound down" physiologically more rapidly after leaving work than did female managers, indicating the continued work pressures of a "second shift" that women face. Similar results have been found for women physicians (Theorell, 1991). Another study concluded that if men's and women's roles were more equal and they spent their time in the same way, "women would experience better health than men, more consistent with their greater longevity" (Bird and Fremont, 1991: 126).

The standardization of work time (such as the practice of working for eight hours from nine to five) also means that many people are excluded from paid work, including mothers who cannot afford child care, elderly people who must rest more often, and disabled people who may not function as effectively on a nine-to-five schedule. Since the industrial revolution, there has been a trend to separate spheres of activity. Paid work is increasingly done outside the home; in earlier days it was often done at home. This segregation of activities of work and home, together with the standardized workday, makes it difficult or impossible for mothers and others who cannot function on "normal" time to participate in the paid labor force.

It would be simplistic to assume that the unemployed poor merely have time on their hands, without examining the quality of this time. The poor, both unemployed and employed, are unable to enjoy the privileges of time use that go with higher social class levels. For example, they spend a great deal of time waiting for various services in places such as emergency rooms, clinics, welfare offices, and courts. Such waiting can cost precious wages, especially because many services are not available after working hours. Middle-class people can take time off, and upper-status people can have the service brought to them (Henley, 1977). One's social position also influences the degree of access to other people's time and control over one's own use of time (Henley, 1977; Schwartz, 1973).

Elderly or disabled persons sometimes find themselves in surroundings that overwhelm them because they are unable to function at the speed demanded. In the right context, however, they might still be able to function well. Older people's disorientation and inability to function are sometimes interpreted as signs of senility; others' inability to function at "full speed" may be seen as a sign of mental or social disturbance. Thus, instead of seeing these problems as responses to environments that move uncomfortably fast or slow, we tend to treat them as personal, internal states of mind. When the environment of college students was experimentally sped up so that they could not maintain the pace, they also began to show irritability and the inability to function (Kastenbaum, 1971). Retirement and institutionalization lead people to experience "standard" time as irrelevant, thus

---

[8]Despite the stress of this double burden, many women employed outside the home experience *positive* effects on health compared to women working only at home; the net health effects of the "second shift" thus are mixed (Hibbard and Pope, 1993; Lennon, 1994; Vågerö, 1992).

atrophying time-related coping skills and contributing to behavior that may be incorrectly interpreted as evidence of senility.

An important relationship exists between time and health. The standard ways of socially scheduling activity often conflict with one's personal pace or biorhythms. A sharp discrepancy between the two will have an impact on one's health. Scientists studying sleep and sleep disorders note the tension between the sociocultural organization of time and the rhythms of our bodies (Klinkenborg, 1997). Such a split between social time and our ability to keep up is prevalent in time-pressured, production-oriented societies. In a society as productive as ours, a shorter workweek with longer breaks, more flexible hours, and less time-pressured work should not be impossible. Despite two-day weekends and labor-saving devices, we seem to live in a world that is more time pressured than past societies and many present ones.

SUMMARY

Material environments and our interactions with them affect our bodies. Symbolic and social factors, however, may also influence bodies through neurohormonal and other physical changes, which in turn may even mediate the interaction between our bodies and the physical environments they inhabit.

Stress is not merely in the eyes of the beholder, nor are the ways in which people handle stressors merely a matter of our individual resourcefulness. The economic organization of a society, the various social pressures—such as time pressures—to which its members are subjected, and their membership in sociological categories such as class, race, ethnicity, gender, and age are very important considerations. In the next chapter, we continue to explore these ideas by looking at the emotional aspects of social relationships, power, and health.

RECOMMENDED READINGS

Articles

HOWARD BECKER, "History, culture and subjective experience: An exploration of the social bases of drug-induced experience." *Journal of Health and Social Behavior* 8, 1967: 163–176.

GEORGE L. ENGEL, "Sudden and rapid death during psychological stress: Folklore or folk wisdom?" *Annals of Internal Medicine* 74, 1971: 771–782.

GERARD J. HOUBEN, "Production control and chronic stress in work organizations." *International Journal of Health Services* 21(2), 1991: 309–327.

LENNART LENNERLOF, "Learned helplessness at work," *International Journal of Health Services* 18(2), 1988: 207–222.

Books

AARON ANTONOVSKY, *Unraveling the Mystery of Health: How People Manage Stress and Stay Well.* San Francisco: Jossey-Bass, 1987. An elaboration and application of Antonovsky's "sense of coherence" perspective.

ROBERT KARASEK and TÖRES THEORELL, *Healthy Work: Stress Productivity and the Reconstruction of Working Life*. New York: Basic Books, 1990. Excellent analysis of the conditions of work that are sickeningly stressful.

JULIET B. SCHOR, *The Overworked American.* New York: Basic Books, 1992. As the title suggests, an analysis of the causes and consequences of increased time pressure experienced by U.S. workers.

MARTIN SELIGMAN, *Helplessness: On Depression, Development and Death.* San Francisco: Freeman, 1992. An introduction to the concept of learned helplessness that presents evidence for its various applications.

STEVE SUTER, *Health Psychophysiology: Mind-Body Interactions in Wellness and Illness.* Hillsdale, NJ: Laurence Erlbaum, 1986. An introduction to the psychophysiology of stress, basic relevant anatomy, and applications of the psychophysiological perspective to several illnesses.

CHAPTER

5 | *SOCIAL ORGANIZATION, HEALTH, AND ILLNESS*

CHAPTER OUTLINE

As indicated in Chapter 4, social encounters—particularly those characterized by a great deal of social inequality—can be stressful. Because of powerful and complex links between our emotions and our physical responses, some social relationships can promote sickness and inhibit healing. At the same time, social relationships and a sense of being connected to others can positively influence our health. Social networks can protect us from stressors; they can influence our appraisal of, and our ability to cope with, stressors. Our daily social relationships are not random, however; they are organized in institutional contexts, such as the workplace, religious group, and family. Thus, society influences our health through its institutional arrangements and our social positions in those arrangements. This chapter examines some social-emotional aspects of interaction, their institutional contexts (especially work and family), and their link to social inequality in everyday life.

"I GET BY WITH A LITTLE HELP FROM MY FRIENDS": SOCIAL SUPPORT AND HEALTH

Humans' biological makeup, as Chapter 4 shows, makes them open to influences from the social environment, including relationships with other people. The importance of social relationships for health is demonstrated by studies that find loss of a spouse or intimate friend leads to risk of coronary problems (Pilisuk and Parks, 1986: 33), lowered immunity (Bartrop et al., 1977), or death (Engel, 1971). Mourning and separation from loved ones can affect levels of stress hormones (Pilisuk and Parks, 1986: 45). The absence of social support can affect immune competence. Strong relationships with others can increase resilience against illness (Fonagy, 1996: 128). Although the withdrawal of social support or a diminished quality of social relationships can have a sickening impact on us, social bonds also have the potential to heal us.

Social support is one source of the individual's sense of empowerment. It may seem strange and perhaps a bit clinical to think of our relationships with lovers, family, friends, and fellow workers or students in terms of *power*, yet social ties can serve as nets that hold us up or keep us from falling when we are threatened. They function as sources of information and financial or other kinds of aid and as mirrors that help reflect messages of self-affirmation back to us. Just as a fetus needs a womb to receive nourishment, shelter, warmth, and life support, human beings do not function effectively as isolated individuals.

Social support is a general term for the many different resources that aid persons in times of crisis and help them cope with life. Social relationships empower individuals by making them feel they are part of a larger social order. They are also a source of self-validation and a sense of personal security (Pilisuk and Parks, 1986). As symbols of those relationships, physical contact and intimacy can be empowering. Other people can remind us that we are alive and have someone to lean on and depend on when necessary. They can enhance our sense of security and self-confidence. Emotional support is one of the most important ways that social support empowers individuals (House, 1981).

This support may involve touch. Because many measures of social support use paper-and-pencil methods such as questionnaires, human touch has not been adequately investigated as a medium of emotional support. Giving social support may involve subtle cues like body language and tone of voice, which often go unnoticed by the researcher-observer (Pilisuk and Parks, 1986: 39). Although the effects of social contact may not be mentally perceived, nonetheless they may have an impact on our bodies. For example, a nurse's touch can affect the blood pressure of even a comatose patient (Lynch, 1979). Under the stress of electric shocks, dogs who were petted responded to these stressors with fewer pathological consequences than animals who were not touched. Similarly, rabbits on a high-fat diet that were not touched were more likely to develop heart disease than those that were cuddled and petted (Marmot and Mustard, 1994). Animal experiments should be used cautiously when generalizing to humans, but these studies do suggest that nonverbal aspects of social relationships may have health consequences.

Social support may have physical benefits by preventing the loss of self-esteem and aiding a sense of mastery (Pearlin, 1983). Social support empowers by giving individuals a sense that they are valued, esteemed, cared for, and belong to a network of mutual obligation. These are primarily *emotional* functions, but social support also serves *instrumental* purpose. A person's support networks often provide useful information and material resources (such as financial aid) as well as other help (Levin and Idler, 1981). Support can also encourage recovery from an illness, for example, by encouraging a family member to do therapeutic exercises. Other social networks also promote such health habits as regular exercise, good eating habits, and adequate sleep.

In the classic study *Suicide*, Durkheim ([1897]1951) found a relationship between rates of suicide and the degree to which individuals were integrated into their group, which he measured with indicators such as divorce rates. Thus, a group with high rates of divorce should show a high rate of suicide. Conversely, a more integrated group should have a lower rate.[1] Durkheim was the first social scientist to demonstrate that suicide was not simply an individual psychological issue but also to some extent a social and cultural phenomenon influenced by such factors as the strength of social bonds. Much of the literature on social support and health follows in this tradition by making similar associations between social isolation and poor health. We must also consider the possibility of a reverse causal relationship; that is, poor health may lead to social isolation (House et al., 1988).

Social isolation itself can be stressful. Some research indicates that low integration into social networks (or low social cohesion) contributes to poor health, even when significant stressors are absent (Gore, 1978: 158). In a comprehensive study of a large population in Alameda County, California, Berkman and Syme (1979) measured four types of social contact: (1) marriage partners, (2) close friends and relatives, (3) members of a church, and (4) informal or formal associations.

---

[1]Durkheim also recognized that groups fostering *too much* integration could encourage what he called "altruistic suicide," such as the deaths of Japanese kamikaze pilots who crashed their planes into Allied warships during World War II.

Persons who had contacts with any of these groups evidenced lower mortality rates than those who did not. The authors of this study recognized the problem of causal direction: Does illness cause a person to withdraw and others to withdraw from that person, or does social isolation generate sickness? Therefore, they analyzed groups with every kind of health status and found that, even among those who were sick, persons with higher levels of social contact had lower mortality rates. Persons with extensive social connections were likely to smoke and drink less, and to eat and sleep more regularly than those with few social connections. This finding suggests that social relationships also protect health by encouraging good health habits (Wallston et al., 1983).

Another study found that neither high stress nor lack of support, in and of themselves, increased pregnancy complications. When major stressors were combined with a low degree of social support, however, there were significantly higher numbers of complications. Women who had high stress and high levels of social support experienced fewer difficulties than those who had a lot of stressful events but not much support. When the levels of stress were low, the absence of social support did not have a notable impact on complications (Nuckolls et al., 1972). Most research finds social support to be either a primary *causal* factor in determining health or a *mediating* factor, which may protect the person from the full impact of the stressor.

The Quality of Social Support

Lynch (1979) argues that social isolation can both contribute to coronary heart disease and adversely affect a person's recovery from a heart attack. Lynch emphasized that social contact (or what he calls "dialogue") is of chief importance for health. Corroboration of his thesis comes from studies that find mortality rates are considerably lower among married persons than among those who are single or formerly married. Between 1970 and 1988 in Poland, changes in death rates among married men and women were low, but they were substantially higher among divorced men and women. A similar pattern was found in Hungary, where the highest increases in death rates were among widows (Wilkinson, 1996: 123–124). Likewise, death rates from such diseases as cirrhosis of the liver, tuberculosis, and pneumonia are higher for those who are not married (Levin and Idler, 1981; Lynch, 1979). Although such evidence is in line with our cultural assumptions about the importance of family life, it must be interpreted cautiously. Marital status tells us nothing about the *quality* of social contact. Many people are formally married but psychologically live alone and feel isolated from each other, whereas divorced and other single people may participate in rich social lives. Unhappy marital relationships can cause greater health risk than can the absence of a partner (Kiecolt-Glaser and Glaser, 1991: 860–861).

Social support is also important in the workplace, where it buffers work-related stress (Hibbard and Pope, 1993; House, 1981; LaRocco and House, 1980; Waxler-Morrison et al., 1991). A study of NASA workers found that good work relationships protected them from the effects of such stress (Caplan, 1972).

Unemployment can have negative health effects, but social support may buffer them by offering a sense of empowerment. A longitudinal study of men who were laid off from work found that those with higher degrees of social support reported fewer symptoms of illness and showed lower levels of cholesterol (Gore, 1978).

Further investigation is needed on how particular organizational forms encourage or discourage social support. For example, how do cultural factors, such as an emphasis on competitiveness and individualism, affect the possibility for supportive relationships in the workplace? Pilisuk and Parks (1986: 59) observed "social currents of careerism, autonomy, mobility, privacy and achievement that disrupt our traditional roots and ties also make difficult the continuity of new bonds." Not only do we need further research on how social support may be health promoting, but also we need to examine how control over work conditions (and other institutional settings) makes social support possible.

A Critical Appraisal of Social Support

Much of the social support literature makes several assumptions that are problematic. First, social support should not be treated as a stable, constant factor; levels of social support do not necessarily remain the same over time. Second, stressful events (stressors) and social support are not independent factors, but rather interact with each other (Atkinson et al., 1986). Just as social support may protect a person against a stressor (such as unemployment), so too may a stressor (such as unemployment) affect levels of social support. For example, a spouse's unemployment may put a strain on the entire family relationship and thereby reduce the support given by family members. High levels of kin involvement and family leadership have been associated with high blood pressure among low-income people. For those with more economic resources, such family involvement and status have been linked with low blood pressure (Corin, 1994: 107–108).

Perhaps the most significant blind spot in this area of research is the failure to consider the larger contexts of power relationships in which social support takes place. For example, people in economic need may have difficulties with their social networks. Their social and economic powerlessness may place a strain on their social networks, and may also limit their access to supportive social relationships. Working-class people on the whole have less developed social networks and group affiliations than middle-class people (Fischer, 1983). One study showed how poverty limits social involvement because of a lack of funds for transportation, recreation, or association dues (Pilisuk and Parks, 1986: 60). Income and education seem to have an impact on how much social support can reduce stress (Ratliff-Crain and Baum, 1990).

Existing research tends to focus only on the *beneficial* aspects of social support. Although it is popularly believed that it is always good to have family and friends around in times of trouble, social support is not necessarily helpful and at times can be counterproductive. For example, persons experiencing a health crisis can be overprotected, which slows recovery. Family members may also try to communicate supportive messages ("You can do it!") that may be interpreted by the ill person as a form of pressure to get well (Horton, 1985a). Social support may undermine sick people's sense of personal competence by making them feel that they cannot do anything on their own or they cannot possibly reciprocate the help they have been given (Pilisuk and Parks, 1986: 39). Indeed social contact (including intimate relationships) can be stressful and affect our ability to cope with and appraise stress. One study indicates that perceived support may be more important than received support in coping with stressful events.[2] It concluded that it is possible that "the perception of one's network being ready to act can be as important—if not more important—than actual supportive behavior" (Wethington and Kessler, 1986: 84).

Western researchers typically assume that social support essentially means support from close family or friends. Yet people from various cultural backgrounds differ in what they perceive as social support and where they turn for support. In some cases, it is one's spouse or one's children; in other cases, friends and neighbors. The feeling of "belonging" to a neighborhood may be more important than any specific source of interpersonal support (Corin, 1994: 124–125). Lack of social support, as well as lack of (socially affirmed) self-esteem and sense of mastery, may account for "differential vulnerability" in the face of illness and other life struggles (Thoits, 1983: 90). Thus, an important factor in determining individuals' ability to cope with stress is how *empowered* they feel themselves to be.

Nevertheless, there are problematic *ideological* biases implicit in emphasizing social support and deemphasizing other factors that produce illness. The social support approach puts the responsibility on the individual and private sphere institutions such as the family. One consequence of overemphasizing social support may be to force people to fall back on their own *private* resources (Fischer, 1983), for it is in the private sphere of family life and friendship in which people have some control (Pearlin, 1983). In such public settings as the workplace or school, social support may not be available—indeed, may be organizationally discouraged—and individual coping mechanisms may not be effective. Research and health policies need to address the health problems exacerbated by coping difficulties and limits to social support created by societal structures *outside* the private sphere (Wadsworth, 1996: 165).

Studies of social support make little mention of class and power. For example, how do controls in the workplace affect social support as well as self-esteem and self-mastery? How does the distribution of power in existing social networks such as families affect social support? How do institutional structures under capitalism generate competitiveness, individualism, and social mobility that make social support difficult? Social support can be a means of empowering the individual, but it exists in social and cultural environments that often reduce its quality and availability. The research emphasis on social support should not blind us to the many other ways these social environments can disempower individuals, making it more difficult for them to control their own bodies and well-being.

---

[2]A problem in this study is that measures of both perceived and received support were based on the recall of subjects; they are therefore highly subjective and may have been perceptually modified by the respondents.

Social Inequality, Support, and Health

Evidence indicates that physiological changes—some of which may contribute to illness—are associated with subordinate status. A survey of the biophysical evidence shows:

> [A] wide-ranging pattern of physiological changes is associated with subordinate rank. This characteristic pattern is conserved on the whole in different vertebrate species. It entails the adrenal-cortical and gonadal steroids, levels of adrenal cate-cholamine-synthesizing enzymes, indoleamines, raised LDL to HDL ratios, the progression of atherosclerosis and some measures of immune function. These physiological patterns change as the social status of the animal is altered. They are a function of rank. (Weiner, 1992:176)

Most of the studies on which this evidence is based are animal studies. Relationships between top-ranking baboons and bottom bananas (as studied, for instance, by Sapolsky, 1982, 1989, 1990) are obviously in many ways unlike those between office worker and boss. The "underlying threat among humans is not of being bitten so much as that of economic sanctions like losing your job or missing promotion" (Wilkinson, 1996: 196).

Human relationships are more complex and involve symbolic aspects. We are creatures capable of reflecting on our situation (as described in Chapter 4). Thus, unlike other creatures, we can dramatize insults and injustices in our minds—either playing them down or dramatically enhancing them. The very process of talking to ourselves and others about events can function to minimize or dramatize their significance. Animal studies can suggest some ways by which social status affects human bodies (Evans, Hodge, and Pless, 1994). A number of similarities exist in the way risk factors for coronary heart disease are affected by social status both among baboons and humans (Brunner, 1996; Wilkinson, 1996: 195). The activities involved in establishing and maintaining hierarchies—such as activities of social control—may have physical consequences for humans and other animals (Weiner, 1992: 195).

It has been argued that there is a relationship between the distribution of power in a society (such as levels of economic equality or inequality), levels and quality of social support, and health. Some evidence links U.S. income distribution, social cohesion, and mortality (Wilkinson, 1996: 136). Economic stressors and the amount of support available tend to be socially distributed by class: "It's as simple as that. If you are poor, you have more stress and less supportive resources" (Pilisuk and Parks, 1986: 58). Indeed, some observers argue that the more egalitarian a society is, the more socially integrated, and thus healthier, it is (Wilkinson, 1996).

Social inequality thus not only affects the distribution of material resources available to individuals, but one's position in a social structure also influences the psychosocial resources available (Evans, Hodge, and Pless, 1994). Inequality has an impact on the social fabric of a society, affecting the quality of social relationships not only in the family but the public sphere as well. In societies characterized by narrow income distribution (one measure of social equality), one finds that "Instead of a moral and social vacuum mediated only by market relationships, life beyond the family has a well developed social structure. . . . [P]ublic life is explicitly part of social life" (Wilkinson, 1996: 133–134).

LIFE AS THEATER: SOCIAL INTERACTION IN DRAMATURGICAL PERSPECTIVE

Social interactions are often not only not beneficial, but downright harmful. What makes everyday social encounters, such as talking to one's boss, particularly stressful? Viewing social interaction from a *dramaturgical perspective* can help us understand some of the sources of stress in social relationships. In his early work, *The Presentation of Self in Everyday Life* (1959), Goffman views social life as theater, describing dramaturgical strategies as means of information control through which individual actors, small groups, institutions, and even whole societies manage how information is presented and expressed, in order to accomplish a desired impression. Using such resources as costumes, props, and settings, actors seek to control their *presentation of self* (that is, how they show themselves) and to monitor information presented to them by other actors. If everyday life is to some extent theater, then being a competent actor requires correctly interpreting "cues" provided by others and managing the information one presents to them. Actors seek to maximize the visibility of some information, to minimize the visibility of other information, and to gain access to information about others. How we feel about ourselves (our self-image) is related to how effectively we present ourselves and whether various encounters validate or invalidate our self-conception. Because much social life involves performing, it is easy to identify with the "stage fright" of an actor about to go on stage or that of a social actor about to present herself as a competent candidate at a job interview. Performances in everyday life can be stressful–indeed, under some circumstances, very stressful.

Emotion Work as Stressful

The stress connected with one's presentation of self and with dramaturgical strategies for monitoring other people's displays, we call *dramaturgical stress* (Freund, 1982, 1990, 1998). Dramaturgical stress is generated by role playing, the effort of managing the impressions one makes on others, and particularly by struggling to keep up social appearances that are inconsistent with deeply held feelings and conceptions about oneself.

A significant part of performing in social life involves managing our own and other people's emotions. Everyday situations call for appropriate emotions and feelings as well as appropriate displays of emotions. Many skills of self-presentation thus require what Hochschild (1983) calls **emotion work**–the activities through which we manage our own and other people's emotions. Emotion work involves repressing displays of undesirable or inappropriate emotions and evoking appropriate ones. For example, it is considered improper to laugh during a funeral. What does one do to keep from displaying such inappropriate emotions? One might try to think of something sad, engaging in emotion work to both appear to have the proper demeanor and to "feel" the appropriate emotions.

Because performing is part of all social life, some dramaturgical stress is inevitable. Societies such as ours, however, exacerbate dramaturgical stress because the manipulation of appearances and emotions is an important skill and a highly complex and self-conscious act. Not only are emotions and bodily expressions very much controlled, but also the very activity of manipulating appearances is itself more stressful (Elias, 1994 [1978]). It takes energy to constrain feelings and actions and to manage emotional communication while monitoring that of others. Self-presentation and role playing, together with the emotion work required by these roles, can be dramaturgically stressful (Williams and Bendelow, 1996: 41). Under certain social conditions such stress becomes particularly intense and chronic, promoting illness.

Dramaturgical Stress and Social Inequality

Dramaturgical stress is heightened when a person's performance in a given situation is inconsistent with his or her concept of self (Cockerham, 1978: 49). Stress may be generated by "the task of managing an estrangement between self and feeling and between self and display" (Hochschild, 1983: 13). Considerable pressure may come from the effort to protect and to control emotional information. Actors in subordinate social statuses (that is, those with less power) may be more likely to encounter such stressful situations and lack the dramaturgical resources to cope with them.

As noted in Chapter 4, some actors are in social positions that make them particularly vulnerable to stress: those who occupy subordinate positions in various institutional contexts (such as school, family, or work), members of minority groups, and those whose identities are potentially stigmatized (disabled or gay people, for instance). Actors in subordinate positions may lack *status shields* (Hochschild, 1983) to protect their sense of self (Freund, 1998). Lower-status individuals often lack such dramaturgical resources, leaving their very selves vulnerable to attacks by those in power (Williams and Bendelow, 1996). For example, institutional rules protect teachers from having their authority, character, or competence challenged in class, whereas students lack such status shields.[3]

Inability to protect the boundaries of self and to counter the intrusion of others may lead to depression and anxiety. Individuals' social positions determine their resources for protecting their self-concepts and for controlling how they experience themselves. Subordinate status, combined with social controls that prevail in a situation (such as a service job that demands emotion work), require intense feelings to be suppressed, denied, or relegated to another sphere (such as family).

---

[3]A poignant example of how such vulnerability translates into ill health is the response of a woman living in an extremely poor community in Brazil to a question about "anger nerves," a culturally recognized illness. She replied, "That's like when your 'patron' says something that really ticks you off but because she's your boss you can't say anything but inside you are so angry that you could kill her. The next day you are likely to wake up trembling with anger nerves" (Scheper-Hughes, 1992: 175).

Persons in subordinate status are thus especially vulnerable to dramaturgical stress, and the stress is intensified by their powerlessness in the face of controls and demands of others.

The social organization of time and social/physical space influences our emotion work and dramaturgical competence, the availability of "backstage"[4] respites, and our levels of security about our psychological space, and hence levels of dramaturgical stress. Having to interact in the same physical space with coworkers, bosses, or family members, we are less likely to express disruptive emotions there. "Physical containment may support emotional containment" (Newton, 1995: 84).

Social status is a key factor determining how much each individual can control this organization. For example, higher-status persons enjoy more private space and means of segregating audiences (such as a secretary who controls who is allowed into one's private office). Their dramaturgical stress is likely to be reduced because these spatial arrangements enable them to sustain a consistent presentation of self and effective performance. The organization of space and time also influences the degree of surveillance to which an actor's performance is subject and hence levels of stress.[5] Actors in subordinate statuses are more likely to find themselves subject to greater surveillance than persons in dominant statuses. For example, a reservations clerk is more likely to have her phone conversations electronically monitored by her supervisor than is the hotel sales manager. Subordinate status also reduces power over one's body and personal space. For instance, a boss can touch employees, but the employees cannot freely reciprocate.

Humans in subordinate social positions are particularly vulnerable to dramaturgical stress, not only because they often face heightened and conflicting emotional demands, but also they lack resources and options for coping or resisting. Williams and Bendelow (1996: 41) observe, "Less powerful people, therefore, face a structurally in-built handicap in managing social and emotional information and this handicap may, in turn, contribute to existential fear, anxiety and neuro-physiological perturbation."

Stressful Social Interactions

Because dramaturgical stress is linked with structural factors, especially social status, it is likely to be a feature of regular social interaction in which social stratification and power are embedded in social relationships.

Work In corporate and bureaucratic jobs, a great deal of control over the presentation of self is an important part of their work skills. Manners and politeness become tools for the efficient and effective accomplishment of work

---

[4]Backstages are "places" (for example, restaurant kitchen), where a waiter, for instance, can relax in his role, share talk about troublesome customers, and rehearse his role.

[5]Goffman (1961) argued that the social and physical arrangements in "total institutions" (such as monasteries, prisons, mental hospitals, and nursing homes) may work to short-circuit inmates' abilities to *control* their self-presentation.

(Mumford, 1963: 139). In postindustrial economies, the proportion of jobs providing service has increased. Occupations involving selling (salesclerk, stockbroker, for instance) or providing emotional services such as friendliness or reassurance (nurse, flight attendant) have increased dramatically (Hochschild, 1983). These service jobs demand elaborate skills in self-presentation and in managing one's emotions (both of which entail emotion work). Fromm (1965: 268) observed:

> If you do not smile you are judged lacking in a "pleasing personality" and you need to have a pleasing personality if you want to sell your services whether as a waitress, a salesman or a physician. Only those at the bottom of the social pyramid, who sell nothing but their physical labor, and those at the very top do not need to be particularly pleasant.

In his description of bureaucratic white-collar workers, Mills (1956: xvii) noted that the management of one's personality had increasingly become an essential work skill "of commercial relevance and required for the more efficient and profitable distribution of goods and services." Demand for pleasing personalities, particularly in the face of job conditions that are anything but pleasing, can be highly stressful and often require workers to deny their emotional responses. A study of bank employees found that when the emotional and physical appearances demanded of workers conflicted with their own sense of self, they began to experience self-artificiality. Bureaucratized structures, particularly those with commercial goals, are most likely to produce this tension between the public face and private self (Jackall, 1977; Karasek and Theorell, 1990: 33). The rude customer who "is always right," the demand for geniality in the face of social isolation within the office, the interpersonal competitiveness, and the hierarchical pressures all produce dramaturgical stress in the workplace (Freund, 1982, 1998). Box 5.1 illustrates how dramaturgical stress, combined with time pressures, affects health.

Emotion work entails more than merely assuming a smiling mask, because that might appear insincere. Rather one must convince oneself, to some extent, that one's angry reaction is not valid. Hochschild (1983) describes how flight attendants are taught to see the nasty customer as a victim and one's own angry response as unnecessary. They were expected to convince themselves that they felt something other than what they were feeling. Such invalidation of one's emotions may have long-term health consequences, especially as the split between what one feels and what one shows may become automatic, no longer a temporary mask that one assumes voluntarily.

Race and Ethnicity Over 30 years ago, Franz Fanon, the Algerian psychiatrist, wrote about the connections between racial and colonial domination and psychological and physical well-being. In the following passage, he linked muscular tension and illness in Algerians to their powerlessness in the face of French colonial authority:

This particular form of pathology (generalized muscular contraction) had already called forth attention before the revolution began. But the doctors described it by portraying it as a congenital stigma of the native, an original part of his nervous system where it was stated, it was possible to find the proof of a predominance of the extra-pyramidal system in the native. The contracture is in fact simply the postural accompaniment to the native's reticence and the expression in muscular form of his rigidity and his refusal with regard to colonial authority. (Fanon, 1963: 293)

Because it was not possible for the colonized Algerians to express anger openly toward colonial authority, it was held in, but manifested itself in the form of muscular tension. Note also that the effects of a social problem (colonial rule) were viewed by the colonial doctors as an inherited, individual problem. The individual could not leave the social space of a racist encounter and thus expressed somatically the resistance that could not be shown openly. The particular form and distribution of muscular tensions throughout the body represented how the body was used to create an impermeable boundary between self and other. This muscular armoring keeps the other and their claims on one out of one's psychological space.

Racism may be linked to other illnesses, such as hypertension, which is prevalent among African Americans. Their elevated rates of hypertension cannot be explained simply by diet or genetics (Johnson and Gant, 1996). One study of African American women concluded that face-to-face encounters with racist provocation can affect cardiovascular reactivity (e.g., heart rate, blood pressure). Cardiovascular reactivity increased more among those individuals who were able to

BOX 5.1

Dramaturgical Stress and Blood Pressure: The Case of a Hospital Administrative Aide

Researchers placed blood pressure and pulse monitors on participants in one study and correlated the changes in these stress indicators with activities and social pressures throughout the day. The case of one hospital aide exemplifies workplace stress.

Her peak reading at the office—a diastolic pressure of 77—came in the morning when she was mediating a dispute between two secretaries. She hit this level again just before lunch when she was in that perennial secretarial bind: politely taking orders from someone who annoys you.

In this case, it was a patient, a tense, well-dressed suburban matron convinced that something was wrong with her despite repeated tests showing she was healthy. At that moment, there were two real emergencies going on—doctors were rushing in and out of the office to consult about a woman near death on an operating table, and a cardiac patient from another hospital needed to be transferred by helicopter to the medical center. In the midst of all this, Collins spent 15 minutes negotiating appointments for the matron; her voice remaining pleasant, but her diastolic pressure peaking and her pulse hitting 90.

Source: John Tierney, "Wired for Stress," *New York Times Magazine*, May 15, 1988: 81.

speak during a racist provocation compared to those who were simply listening, but support from another person in responding to the provocation helped reduce reactivity (McNeilly et al., 1995). Another study showed that black women who responded actively to unfair treatment were less likely to have high blood pressure than women who held their responses "inside" themselves (Krieger and Fee, 1994).

Similarly, African American males may be exposed to more anger-provoking encounters with arbitrary authority (in regard to housing, employment, and the law, for instance) than other groups, but they cannot express their anger. The suppression of their emotional responses might well contribute to their greater incidence of hypertension (Johnson and Gant, 1996). Socialization to suppress hostility may be especially high among upwardly mobile, upper-lower-class persons, who emphasize the importance of politeness and respect higher-status people (Harburg et al., 1973). One study, comparing hypertensive African Americans with those with normal blood pressure, described those with hypertension as humble, docile, sober, serious, and controlled (Johnson and Gant, 1996: 98). The demand that one always be polite and civil—no matter how rude someone else may be—represents a form of social control. Strict control over anger is a norm in our society (Elias, 1994; Stearns and Stearns, 1986).

Sexual Orientation Those who must cope with a social stigma by concealing their identity under a cloak of normal appearances face special stresses. For example, in our society widespread homophobia (fear of homosexuality) pressures homosexuals to hide their true selves in order to perform according to social expectations; however, trying to pass as heterosexuals may cause considerable dramaturgical stress. In addition to the self-hatred that comes from internalizing society's antihomosexual values and the repressed anger from discrimination, they may suffer from the constant fear of disclosure:

> Visible lesbians are treated as outcasts or queers. They are ignored, fantasized about, and played with. Lesbians are subject to verbal and physical harassment. Closeted lesbians live in fear of being found out. A lesbian's family may be a source of stress for her as coming out to one's family can often mean risking anger, pain or exile. Drifting apart from one's family may be the result of not coming out. (O'Donnel, 1978:14)

"Closets" are the refuge of the powerless, but the use of this refuge has its price. "Closets are a health hazard" was a slogan first used by the physicians marching in the 1981 Gay Freedom Day Parade in San Francisco.

Family Not all situations that demand a split between self-presentation and feelings are equally stressful. One may more easily distance oneself from work relationships than from intimate, primary group relationships (such as family or loved ones). Pearlin (1983: 6) observed:

> [T]he family does have a dimension to its place in the stress process that sets it apart from occupations, however. It is, of course, a major reservoir of problems

and tribulations. Multiple facets of marital relations, parent-child encounters, and the transitional points along the family life cycle have been viewed as fertile ground out of which stress can grow. It is likely, too, to be an arena in which problems generated elsewhere are transplanted. But the family domain, unlike occupation, is also the place where the wounds that people incur outside are most likely to be healed. The family is truly many things to its members: it is commonly an active and rich source of pain, and it is just as commonly where people turn to find relief from pain. In the stress process, it stands in a uniquely pivotal position.

Several studies suggest that persons whose families make them feel powerless, force them to surrender their autonomy, or inhibit their displays of anger in response to arbitrary authority will experience subsequent health problems (Doherty and Campbell, 1988; Laing and Esterson, 1965; Pratt, 1976; Sagan, 1987; Schneider, 1975; Seligman, 1992).

Noting the high incidence of somatic symptoms among people who live in totalitarian societies, Griffith and Griffith (1994: 55) observe:

> In non-totalitarian, Western societies, we find remarkably similar examples of somatic symptoms that have been fostered within micropolitical systems of abusive families, where a child sexually abused at home hides the abuse at school and church, even defending her father as if he were a wonderful parent; or where a wife is physically beaten at home by her husband but hides the abuse even from friends or coworkers, believing that she cannot or should not escape and will only suffer more if she were to disclose.

Thus, micropolitical circumstances (such as marriage, family), like oppressive macropolitical contexts (such as totalitarian state), may require a distressful containment of feeling that can be expressed only somatically.

Situations in which sexual abuse or gendered violence occur are intensely stressful interactions. Griffith and Griffith (1994: 55–56) present a case of a woman who was sexually abused but had to contain her distress while routinely encountering her abuser in the micropolitical context of the home:

> In meeting with Jana alone, however, the story widened. With specific questioning about possible abuse, she told how during the summer, while out of school, she stayed at home with her stepfather on days that her mother worked. When they were alone, the stepfather had sexually fondled her and warned her not to tell anyone. She had not spoken out of fear that she would not be believed, that she would be punished by him, or that the revelation would threaten her mother's new marriage. She was terrified that he would touch her again but spoke to no one. Instead her body began jerking violently out of control.

Such situations create what the authors describe as "unspeakable dilemmas," because these women must live with their abuser and dramaturgically conceal their distress. Women with young children, few job skills, and no alternative place to live often feel trapped in abusive situations. Children who are victims of sexual abuse, when seen in emergency rooms, often show symptoms of seizures that are nonepileptic in origin (Griffith and Griffith, 1994: 55). Gendered violence (sexual abuse, rape, domestic violence, or the threat of abuse) attacks the victim's psychophysical boundaries, sense of self, and security in their world. The threatened person's feelings often cannot be acknowledged or expressed; they must be dramaturgically hidden.

Dramaturgical Stress and Health

As discussed in Chapter 4, certain kinds of prolonged or acute stress can lead to physiological responses and, ultimately, sickness. Dramaturgical stress, affecting body and emotions, may promote illness in a number of ways. Contradictory psychosomatic states are responses to dramaturgical demands and the result of dramaturgical stress. Interviews of patients with "somatoform symptoms" showed the following:

> [T]he bodily experience of such a dilemma is that of mobilizing the body for action (e.g., an aggressive emotional posture), while expressing a contradictory emotional posture (e.g., a warm welcoming with smiles and attentive listening, belying privately held seething). In essence, the body receives two conflicting directions for organizing its physiological readiness to act. (Griffith and Griffith, 1994: 61)

These physical symptoms are one way of responding to social situations in which a profound disjuncture exists between how one desires to present oneself and a contrary self-presentation, demanded by a social situation in which the actor cannot leave the field. Thus, the body may cope with such a "push me-pull you" situation by expressing somatic symptoms.

Several studies have examined the relationship between the expression of such emotions as anger and physiological responses. In one early experiment some subjects responded to provocative situations by expressing overt hostility ("anger out"). Persons displaying "anger in" responses were more likely to blame themselves and not express overt hostility. "Anger in" respondents exhibited more extended physical stress reactions than the "anger out" group (Funkenstein et al., 1957). In another experimental situation, anger was induced experimentally by having a colleague arbitrarily harass and insult subjects while they were trying to solve a problem. The subjects' anger resulted in increases in their blood pressure, but those who could express their hostility by giving the harasser what they believed was a mild electric shock returned to normal blood pressure levels more rapidly. Those who were not allowed to express anger in this fashion continued to show signs of elevated blood pressure long after the harassment had stopped (Hokanson and Burgess, 1962). Such experiments point to how emotion work might influence us physically.

Some evidence links the denial of feelings to coronary heart disease (Karasek and Theorell, 1990: 114). Yet this evidence is by no means unproblematic: Some studies find the *inhibition* of anger expression to be linked to coronary heart disease; others find the *expression* of anger to be the link (Engebretson and Stoney, 1995). A study of airline pilots concluded that both those who inhibit their anger a lot *and* those who often express their anger are prone to have higher levels of cholesterol in their blood than their more moderate colleagues (Engebretson and Stoney, 1995); this finding may account for the apparently conflicting prior evidence. Such studies are suggestive of how one's presentation of self, emotion work, social inter-action, and the body might be linked.

Individuals develop coping strategies in distressful situations, particularly those situations of heightened dramaturgical stress in which a sincere performance that belies distress is demanded. This coping is accomplished by compartmental-izing, by dissociating feelings (separating "gut" feelings from conscious feelings), thereby convincing oneself that "all's well." Such dissociation may separate bodily activities of expression and internal functions such as blood pressure–akin to what has been called "schizokinesis." A person whose demeanor appears "cool" on the exterior, but whose internal response to stress involves such dramatic bodily changes as sharp increase in blood pressure, exemplifies this dissociation (Lynch, 1985). How do social and cultural factors encourage such compartmentalization? A consequence of such splits is *emotional false consciousness* (Freund, 1990), which occurs when emotion work disrupts the body's equilibrium and our ability to interpret embodied feelings. Such false consciousness involves a split between bodily expres-sions and an awareness of internal psychosomatic sensations, on the one hand, and continued heightened physiological reactivity to distressful situations, on the other (Freund, 1990, 1998; Williams and Bendelow, 1996). It is as if the levels of consciousness come to be more or less permanently split between bodily appraisals and cognitive appraisals of situations.

An effective social performance (that is, one that appears sincere) may be accomplished through subjectively redefining relationships and emotional responses to them (Hochschild, 1983, 1989). For example, a flight attendant dealing with a rude customer who refused to abide by smoking rules tried subjectively to convince herself, "I shouldn't be angry, because it's not his fault; he may have had a miserable business trip." Problems arise, however, if feelings are reworked on only one level as consciousness and not also on the level of somatic or body conscious-ness; this emotion management thus short-circuits the signal function of emotion (Hochschild, 1983). Emotions "lie at the juncture between mind, body, culture and biology and are often considered crucial to our survival by their signal function in relation to danger" (Bendelow and Williams, 1995: 151). Emotion work strategies may seem effective for the short term, but on another level of consciousness continue to produce feelings of insecurity. These feelings are apprehended as free floating because one has redefined the source of the threat out of one's wide awake consciousness.

In social interaction, people may *collectively reproduce* emotionally oppressive and distressing situations (Newton, 1995). Indeed, oppressive situations produce individuals who collude in their own social control to reproduce distressing arrange-ments. The splitting of emotional consciousness facilitates the smooth functioning of hierarchical relationships, even while they produce distress. Furthermore, chron-ically disavowing one's feelings may also blur the boundaries between self and other. By affecting one's ability to experience social situations clearly, this process makes it harder for the victim of oppressive situations to identify accurately those situations as oppressive.

SUMMARY

In this chapter we continued our discussion of mind, body, and society relationships, emphasizing the role of emotions in social interaction. Some research on social support was critically reviewed. The distribution of power is an important factor in influencing the availability and quality of supportive social relationships. We then looked at some of the stressful aspects of interaction that come from role playing. Those in subordinate social statuses may be more vulnerable to dramaturgical stress and more likely to lack resources to cope with such stress. The chapter concluded with a discussion of dramaturgical stress and health.

RECOMMENDED READINGS

Articles

PETER E. S. FREUND, "The expressive body: A common ground for the sociology of emotions and health and illness." *Sociology of Health and Illness* 12(4), 1990: 452–477.

JAMES S. HOUSE, KARL R. LANDIS, and DEBRA UMBERSON, "Social relationships and health." *Science* 214, July 1988: 540–545.

Books

ARLIE HOCHSCHILD, *The Managed Heart: Commercialization of Human Feeling*. Berkeley: University of California Press, 1983. Introducing the concepts of emotion work and emotional labor, this study of flight attendants discusses the increase of emotion work in the service sector.

VERONICA JAMES and JONATHAN GABE, *Health and the Sociology of Emotions*. Oxford: Blackwell, 1996. This collection of essays applies a sociological perspective on emotions to various health and illness issues.

ROBERT WILKINSON, *Unhealthy Societies*. London: Routledge, 1996. Discussion of the relationship among social inequality, social cohesion, and health.

What does it mean to be sick? In some ways a tree's disease is similar to a human's disease: Trees can recover or they can die of disease; branches become lifeless, leaves wither, and roots and trunks function poorly. Unlike trees, however, humans must also grapple with the experiential aspects of sickness. Humans are capable of reflecting on themselves, their bodily conditions, and their self-perceptions. This capacity to reflect means that humans typically suffer not merely from disease but also from their experience of illness and the meanings that they and others attach to it.

Sickness is upsetting to the social group too. Because it is a breach of the ideals or norms of the society, it can be disruptive. Illness represents a threat to the order and meanings by which people make sense of their lives and organize the routines of their everyday existence. Sickness also raises moral questions, such as, "Who (or what) is responsible for this misfortune?"

ILLNESS AS DEVIANCE

The very notion of health is a social ideal that varies widely from culture to culture or from one historical period to another. For example, in the nineteenth century the ideal upper-class woman was pale, frail, and delicate. A woman with robust health was considered to lack refinement (Ehrenreich and English, 1978). In other periods, cultures, or subcultures, however, the ideal of health might be identified with traits such as strength, fertility, spirituality, righteousness, the absence of pain, the presence of certain pain, fatness, thinness, or youthfulness. The ideal of health thus embodies a particular culture's notions of well-being and desired human qualities. Standards of health in any culture reflect that culture's core values. Through ritual action and symbols (especially language), the social group continually reproduces these central, shared meanings (Durkheim, [1915] 1965).

Durkheim ([1895] 1938: 68–69) observed that deviance serves to remind the entire social group of the importance of certain collective values. Like crime, sickness is a form of **deviance**, or departure from group-established norms. Society typically imputes different kinds of responsibility for crime than for sickness. Durkheim asserted that the very existence of social norms—however defined—means there will be deviance in all societies. The way a society reacts to sickness and crime reaffirms its core values. Furthermore, the practices for sanctioning deviance (such as punishing the criminal or treating the sick person) reaffirm and revitalize the collective sentiments and maintain social solidarity. Durkheim ([1893] 1964: 108) argued that societal reaction against deviance "is above all designed to act upon upright [non-deviant] people." This function suggests that the treatment of the sick in all healing systems serves to reaffirm cultural norms and ideals for the sick and the well alike.

Thus, deviance is more a description of the social group that defines it than a quality of the individual considered deviant. Labeling of an attribute or behavior as deviant is, in fact, a social product (Becker, 1963; Waxler, 1980). Cultures vary widely as to whether they consider deviant such bodily conditions as facial scars, obesity, shortness, and paleness. One cultural standard, for example, considers a certain amount of hair on a man's chest to be desirable, representing fortitude, robustness, and manliness. Much less hair on the chest is treated as too effeminate; much more is considered coarse and animal-like. Other cultures (and subcultures), however, have different definitions of desirable body hair and different connotations of deviance from those norms.

As Chapter 9 illustrates, defining deviance is a social process involving factors such as power and stratification. Power in a society includes having significant influence in setting social norms and labeling deviance. It also involves having control over the social mechanisms by which these norms are taught and enforced. Indeed, one function of social control is to perpetuate the dominance of those in power in the establishment of norms. Socially established norms are *imposed* on people, regardless of their own beliefs. Power is a factor in both the creation of a deviance label and its application to some individual persons.

The Sick Role

Like all social roles, the sick role is primarily a description of social expectations (including those of the sick person). Although these expectations strongly influence behavior, the sick role does not describe how sick persons actually behave (cf. Twaddle, 1981: 56–58).

According to Parsons (1951: 428–447), the sick role entails certain responsibilities as well as certain privileges:

1. The individual's incapacity is a form of deviance from social norms, but because it is not deliberate, the individual is not held responsible;
2. The sickness is legitimate grounds for being exempted from normal obligations, such as work or school attendance;
3. The legitimacy of this exemption is, however, predicated on the sick person's intent to get well;
4. The attempt to get well implies also seeking and cooperating with competent help to treat the illness.

The sick role of someone with pneumonia exemplifies Parsons's use of this concept. A person with serious pneumonia would not be expected to report to work, to do housework, or to keep an appointment. Failure to perform such basic social obligations is a form of deviance that is typically sanctioned, for example, by firing an employee. Having pneumonia, however, is usually considered an acceptable, but temporary, excuse for not meeting these obligations. The employer does not hold the sick person immediately responsible. How society responds to an instance of perceived deviance depends largely on its determination of the individual's responsibility for the deviant behavior. This part of the sick role concept is thus connected with Parsons's larger concern with how societies maintain their equilibrium in the face of deviance and disruptions such as sickness.

Although having pneumonia is a legitimate excuse for not reporting to work, the sick person is expected to act sick and try to get well. The employer would be less than happy to see the supposedly sick employee at a baseball game later that day, for example. According to Parsons, part of trying to get well involves seeking competent health care from a trained physician. The social expectations for a person with pneumonia thus include going to a doctor, obtaining and taking the doctor's prescription, and otherwise conforming to whatever regimen the doctor ordered. Thus, he tied the sick role inevitably with the role of medical professionals. (Parsons was especially interested in the development of professionalism as a feature of modern society.) In his usage, the sick role directly implies the patient role; by contrast, we explore the patient role as a separate role, which sick persons may or may not enter, depending on whether their sickness is brought to the attention of medical professionals (see Chapter 10).

Parsons's concept of the sick role is valuable in that it highlights the social control functions of how society treats sickness. It also emphasizes the extent to which social definitions of sickness reflect larger cultural values of modern Western societies (Parsons, 1972: 124). The cultural narrowness of this concept is partly due to Parsons's explicit focus on mid-twentieth-century American values (for example, individual achievement and responsibility). The sick role, however, is not as clear cut as Parsons's model suggests. Four problems with his approach are discussed next.

The Sick Role Is Not Necessarily Temporary Parsons's conception of the sick role is based on only one, relatively narrow class of health problems. The obligations and exemptions described in his model appear to fit serious, acute illnesses reasonably well. **Acute illnesses** characteristically occur suddenly, peak rapidly, and run their course (that is, result in death or recovery) in a relatively short time. Examples include influenza, measles, and scarlet fever.

Chronic illnesses, by contrast, are of long duration–typically as long as the sufferer lives. They often result in the steady deterioration of bodily functioning. Examples include emphysema, diabetes, multiple sclerosis, epilepsy, and heart disease. Furthermore, some acute illnesses are considered chronic when they become a continuing pattern in an individual's life; examples include chronic bronchitis, asthma, and ulcers. Additionally, a number of chronic, disabling conditions (such as paraplegia from a car accident) do not involve any ongoing disease, but may result in an ambiguous, lifelong sick role.

Although many acute conditions can be cured (or are self-limiting), most chronic conditions are permanent. Treatment of chronic illness is aimed at best at controlling the deterioration caused by the disease and at *managing* the illness. Many of the most dangerous acute (usually infectious) diseases of earlier generations have been brought under control in developed countries through improved sanitation, nutrition, housing, and the like. Inoculations, antibiotics, and other medical treatments have also had some effect in curing infectious diseases (although, as Chapter 2 shows, their role has been somewhat overstated). The proportion of persons suffering chronic illnesses has greatly increased, however; modern medical intervention does not appear so potent in the face of such conditions.

The nature of chronic illness does not fit Parsons's sick role pattern (Radley, 1994). Obviously, his assumption of the necessity of an "intent to get well" is irrelevant if the illness is, by definition, permanent. His sick role conception presumed that the benefits were conditional, but chronic illnesses make most of the conditions meaningless (Alexander, 1982). Unlike acute infectious disease, chronic ailments are more likely to be considered partly the fault or the responsibility of the sufferer. Whereas few people consider a case of chicken pox, for example, to be the sick person's fault, lay and medical conceptions of many chronic conditions, such as lung cancer, high blood pressure, and cirrhosis of the liver, are believed to be brought on—at least partially—by the sufferer's own lifestyle.

Feelings about whether a chronic illness is sufficient grounds for exemption from normal responsibilities are also ambiguous. Because the condition is not temporary, the exemptions are all the more problematic for both the sufferer and those who would grant the exemptions. Just how disabling is the condition? Is a partial exemption feasible? Often persons suffering chronic illnesses do not want total exemption from normal responsibilities, but the illness prevents them from fulfilling some usual duties. As Chapter 7 shows, due to societal values enforced by the sick role, persons with chronic illness have considerable difficulty negotiating such concessions. As a means for maintaining stability and social control, the sick role allows temporary exemptions from normal role requirements *without changing those requirements.*

Similarly, many other "deviant" health conditions do not fit the sick role model of acute diseases and thereby lead to ambiguities about expectations. Should a person born with a physical handicap be treated as sick? What about accident victims or the mentally ill? Should such normal conditions as pregnancy or menopause be treated as sickness? Considerable ambiguity surrounds the role expectations of those whose health conditions are treated as somehow "deviant" yet do not fit the (acute) sick role.

The Sick Role Is Not Always Voluntary Parsons's model holds that the sick person, in exchange for the advantages of the sick role, is motivated to assume that role and voluntarily cooperate with the agents of social control in the appropriate therapy for the deviant condition. In the preceding example of the worker with pneumonia, for example, the person's discomfort and fear of complications would presumably motivate the individual to see a doctor, have blood tests and X-rays, get bed rest at home or in a hospital, and take medications. Parsons thus assumed that, in contrast to criminal deviance, the sick person voluntarily enters the socially prescribed role.

Not all persons, however, want to enter the sick role, even when they feel ill. Many people resist the expected childlike dependency the role often entails; many others have strong aversion to medical treatments, especially in the hospital. A Scottish study of lower-class women found considerable negative moral evaluation of persons who give in, or "lie down," to illness (Blaxter and Paterson, 1982). Some people, furthermore, simply cannot afford to withdraw from normal obligations; the sick role is a threat to their subsistence (Kasl and Cobb, 1966).

Some sicknesses carry a negative connotation or stigma. Although the sick person would obtain some benefits (such as exemption from work or other duties) from the sick role, these negative attitudes toward that illness could be worse than the condition itself. For example, a person suffering epilepsy may actively avoid being socially identified as having the disease because of the repulsion and often outright discrimination associated with the illness (Schneider and Conrad, 1980).

Many persons are placed into the sick role by others, regardless of their own wishes. Children and the dependent aged are generally not considered competent to decide for themselves whether to assume the role; instead, their caretakers make the decision for them. Likewise, some conditions (for example, loss of consciousness) force an involuntary entrance into the sick role. Other ambiguous situations arise when someone's family (or unrelated caretakers, such as doctors, social workers, or police) decide that an individual is too sick to have good judgment and then place the person into the sick role. Because many people thus do not enter the sick role voluntarily, their cooperation with the medical regimen cannot be assumed. In many such cases, the social control functions of the sick role are more coercive and less benign than portrayed by the model.

By contrast, some persons seek to enter the sick role and are denied access. A process of subtle social negotiation occurs when an individual claims the sick role. This claim must then be accepted as legitimate by others, especially authoritative others. Often medical personnel such as the school nurse and the company doctor are the critical *gatekeepers* who have the power to determine who will be admitted to the sick role in their institutional setting. Informal negotiation also typically takes place as the person claiming the sick role attempts to convince family and others of the legitimacy of the claim, and the others judge—and sometimes test—that legitimacy. Entry into the sick role is thus essentially a social and political process. This link between social control and medical personnel's gatekeeping roles is developed further in Chapter 9.

Variability in Sick Role Legitimacy

Variability in Sick Role Legitimacy   Parsons's conception of the sick role also presumes that a single, stable value system is operative for all persons in a society. Historically, however, the legitimate exemption of sick persons from various obligations has been highly variable. The criteria for such an exemption may also differ according to gender, social class, and subcultural expectations.

Legitimate exemptions from work obligations, for example, vary enormously, typically according to social class. Unskilled workers, for example, often have no paid sick days, whereas many white-collar workers are given an annual allowance of such days of absence proportionate to their rank or seniority. Indeed, the idea that absence due to sickness should not be a basis for dismissal is relatively recent; even today sickness is not a legitimate exemption for many workers, and they have no legal protection of their jobs.

The meaning of the sick role itself varies considerably according to social class. The same sickness has different connotations according to the class or gender of the sufferer. For example, in the nineteenth century, consumption (tuberculosis) was a romanticized illness among the middle and upper classes. This sick role implied a "consuming" passion as expressed in artistic sensitivity and creativity.

Some of the physical effects of tuberculosis were considered beautiful: slenderness, fever-bright eyes, pallor, and a transparent complexion accompanied by pink cheeks. One young woman with consumption wrote in her diary:

> Since yesterday I am white and fresh and amazingly pretty. My eyes are spirited and shining, and even the contours of my face seem prettier and more delicate. It's too bad that this is happening at a time when I am not seeing anyone. It's foolish to tell, but I spent a half-hour looking at myself in the mirror with plea-sure; this had not happened to me for some time. (Marie Bashkirtseff's Journal of 1883, quoted in Herzlich and Pierret, 1987: 81)

The well-to-do sufferer was " 'apart,' threatened but all the more precious for it" (Herzlich and Pierret, 1987: 25). Although the disease was more prevalent and devastating among the lower classes, no such privileged or positive sick role was available to them.

The sick role was considered especially appropriate for women of that era because it was thought to reflect ladies' refinement and delicacy. It was expected and even stylish for well-to-do women to faint frequently and to retire to bed for "nerves," "sick headaches," "female troubles," and "neurasthenia." Lower-class women, by contrast, were considered to be more robust, as evidence of their coarse-ness and less civilized nature (Ehrenreich and English, 1978).

Upper-class Victorians could obtain exemption from normal obligations by claiming the sick roles of neurasthenia or hysteria, illnesses of the "nerves" believed to afflict particularly intellectual or sensitive persons. The label of neurasthenia appears to have been especially useful for men, whose normal role expectations of fortitude and active participation in the world outside of the home made it difficult for them to exhibit dependency or weakness. The vague symptoms identified as neurasthenia, however, were a legitimate basis for men to assume the sick role (Sicherman, 1978; see also Drinka, 1984).

Cultural expectations of the sick role also vary, perhaps widely. Some evidence indicates that cultures differ in the degree of legitimacy they accord various illnesses and their resulting claims to exemption from responsibilities. For example, neurasthenia is a legitimate basis of the sick role among contemporary Taiwanese, whereas in the United States it is a far less common diagnosis or cultur-ally recognized reason for assuming the sick role (cf. Kleinman, 1980). Similarly, persons of Hispanic background would be more likely than those of Anglo-Saxon heritage to consider a certain "fright" (*susto*), such as being startled by an animal or a possible assailant, to be a legitimate basis for the sick role (Rubel et al., 1984). Because cultures vary in how they understand various illnesses, they also have different expectations for the behavior of persons occupying the sick role, such as the amount of pain and disability they may experience (cf. Angel and Thoits, 1987). These examples illustrate that the expectations identified as a sick role change; problems that were identified in the past as a legitimate basis for claiming the role are no longer appropriate, whereas other problems—formerly unrecognized or discounted—are now accepted as legitimate.

Responsibility for Sickness Parsons's model of the sick role held that, unlike crime, sickness was not the responsibility of the deviant person. Furthermore, he considered the professional diagnosis and treatment of medical deviance to be purely technical, neutral, and unbiased. As Chapter 9 illustrates, however, the very definition of illness is socially constructed, and social groups often impute responsibility for illness to the sick person.

Freidson (1970) observed that certain conditions are typically viewed as the responsibility of the sick individual and thus are treated relatively punitively, like crimes. Examples include various sexually transmitted diseases as well as substance abuse and conditions derived from such abuse. Freidson noted that the attitudes of both the society and the medical profession, although greatly expanding the range of conditions considered to be properly "medical" problems, do not necessarily abolish the negative moral connotations attached to these conditions. He also described another category of sicknesses that, although not technically considered the fault of the sick person, are nonetheless stigmatized (Freidson, 1970: 234–237). **Stigma** is a powerful discrediting and tainting social label that radically changes the way an individual is viewed as a person (Goffman, 1963: 2–5). For example, being an illegitimate child was (in the past more than now) an enormous barrier to presenting oneself as a "normal," upright citizen.

Many sicknesses carry a stigma. Leprosy, epilepsy, and AIDS, for example, all carry connotations of disreputability and even evil. The sick role for someone with a stigmatized illness is clearly different than that for a person with a neutral sickness. Stigmas can result in various forms of discrimination: Persons with epilepsy, for instance, have experienced job discrimination, difficulty in obtaining insurance, and prohibitions against marrying (Schneider and Conrad, 1980). Even after someone has been treated and pronounced cured of such a condition, the stigma often remains on that person. Furthermore, the stigma frequently spreads to the family and close friends of the sick person in what Goffman (1963: 30–31) calls a "courtesy stigma." For example, families and friends of persons with epilepsy, cancer, or AIDS sometimes find themselves shunned or harassed (Conrad, 1986).

The source of stigma is not the disease itself but rather the social imputation of a negative connotation. Leprosy is highly stigmatized in India, but far less so in neighboring Sri Lanka. Lepers in India are treated as outcasts, whereas many lepers in Nigeria remain in the village and carry on normal social lives (Waxler, 1981). Because cultures vary in the stigma imputed to different sicknesses, the sick role for those illnesses varies accordingly.

The degree of stigma and responsibility attached to a sickness may also change over time, often as notions about an illness change. In the nineteenth century, when tuberculosis was considered to be a somewhat romantic sickness resulting from an inherent disposition of passion and creativity, the illness had relatively little stigma. Later, however, when tuberculosis was considered infectious, those with the disease were seen as carriers to be avoided, isolated, and feared (Herzlich and Pierret, 1987).

Specific social and historical conditions lead to the stigmatizing of a sickness. Before the middle of the nineteenth century, leprosy in Hawaii was of minor importance and not stigmatized. As international trade and colonialism began to change the islands' social and economic situation, however, many outsiders came to the islands. Large numbers of Chinese immigrants arrived to work on the plantations, and the Hawaiians believed they had brought leprosy. Although the Chinese immigrants were hard working and frugal, they were viewed as an inferior ethnic-racial group that threatened the jobs of other working-class persons. In 1880, Hawaii enacted laws to exclude the Chinese, partly based on the belief that they carried disease. Health data suggest that the Chinese were not, however, an important source of leprosy, which more likely came to the islands through the ethnically mixed crews of ships from countries where the disease was prevalent. The Chinese were stigmatized in part because they were thought to be the source of leprosy, which at the same time became stigmatized because it was identified with the Chinese. A relatively unknown and unimportant disease was thus transformed into a morally threatening sickness (Waxler, 1981).

The stigma attached to AIDS in recent years is a parallel situation. AIDS can and does affect all kinds of people, including many newborns. However, because most people identify the disease with homosexuals and drug users, it carries a considerable stigma. The widespread imputation of responsibility and stigma to sick persons suggests that Parsons's sick role model understates the moral judgment and social control aspects of sickness.

The Medicalization of Deviance

Religious, legal, and medical institutions have all contributed to the definition of deviance in society. For example, "Thou shalt not steal" is a religious norm: Stealing is a sin. Legal systems define similar norms of behavior, and violation of the norms is a crime. In a process called the **medicalization of deviance**, medical systems increasingly also define what is normal or desirable behavior: Badness becomes sickness (Conrad, 1996).

The relative influence of religious, legal, and medical institutions in defining deviance has shifted in Western societies. As the Middle Ages waned and these three institutions became increasingly differentiated from each other, the religious organizations still had the greatest weight in defining deviance. This preeminence continued into the eighteenth century, but in America and France (and later in other European countries), the legal mode of defining deviance gained ascendancy (see Freidson, 1970: 247–252). In America, the increasing preeminence of the legal definitions was promoted by religious pluralism and by the increasingly rational organization of the nation-state (cf. Hammond, 1974).

The significance of legal definitions of deviance has diminished somewhat in the twentieth century, and medical definitions have gained in importance. This shifting balance is clearly reflected in the 1954 precedent-setting case *Durham* v. *United States* (214 F.2d 863), in which the court ruled that "an accused is not criminally responsible if his unlawful act was the product of a mental disease or mental defect." The shift in balance favoring medical definitions of deviance corresponds chronologically with a period of the rapid professionalization of medicine, when medical discoveries and technology proceeded quickly, and public faith in science and medicine was increasing.

Part of the reason for the declining importance of religious definitions is that they appear too nonrational and, in a religiously pluralistic country, lack society-wide acceptance. Legal definitions, although more rational, seem to hinge too greatly on human decisions, such as the judgment of 12 ordinary citizens on a jury. Medical definitions, by contrast, *appear* to be more rational and scientific, and based on technical expertise rather than human judgment.

The concept of sickness, however, far from being a neutral scientific concept, is ultimately a moral one, establishing an evaluation of normality or desirability (Freidson, 1970: 208). The medical profession (especially its psychiatric branch) has defined a wide range of disapproved behavior as "sick": alcoholism, homosexuality, promiscuity, drug addiction, arson, suicide, child abuse, and civil disobedience (Conrad and Schneider, 1992; Peele, 1989). Social stigma adheres to many sicknesses, such as leprosy, AIDS, pelvic inflammatory disease, and cirrhosis of the liver.[1] Moral judgment is also applied in the evaluation of good patient behavior, defined as acknowledging the necessity of medical care and following doctors' orders for various conditions, which may include receiving prenatal care, accepting blood transfusions, obtaining inoculations for one's children, and following prescribed drug and dietary regimens. Issues of moral judgment and responsibility are at stake.

Zola (1983: 261) argued that "if anything can be shown in some way to affect the workings of the body and to a lesser extent the mind, then it can be labelled an 'illness' itself or jurisdictionally 'a medical problem.' " Thus, even normal and healthy physical conditions or processes, such as menstruation, pregnancy and childbirth, body and facial shape and size, and aging, have been brought under medicine's jurisdiction (Dull and West, 1991).

The Medicalization of Moral Authority

The same historical processes that brought about the preeminence of medical definitions of deviance also led to a much stronger role for medical authority in moral issues, such as what is right or wrong?, what is good or bad?, and whose good should prevail? Sometimes court events involve a clash of several sources of authority.[2]

In one representative court case, claims were made from legal, medical, parental, and religious bases of authority. A young person had been comatose for months, and was as good as dead in the commonsense view. Her body was being kept alive by technological intervention, and eventually her parents sought legal permission to terminate these extraordinary measures. Because no single authority held uncontested legitimacy, the case was complicated. Medical experts gave their

---

[1]Cultures vary, however, as to which sicknesses are stigmatized. For example, in China, diseases attributed to socially unapproved emotions such as anger are more stigmatized than those attributed to purely physical causes (Ots, 1990).

[2]This section is adapted with permission of the publisher from *Religion: The Social Context* (4th ed.) by Meredith B. McGuire ©1997, by Wadsworth/ITP.

opinions on the medical definitions of death. Legal experts raised issues of the legal rights and guardianship of comatose patients. Theological experts offered briefs on the borderlines of life and death, and the girl's father made a thoughtful personal statement about his request. The relevant issue is not merely the uncertainty of the outcome, but also that it was the court in which medical, legal, religious, and parental figures vied to have their statements taken seriously (Fenn, 1982; Willen, 1983).

The growing legitimacy of medical authority, relative to other sources of judgment, is further illustrated by contemporary court decisions upholding medical judgments to perform Caesarian sections. Caesarian sections are increasingly common, now accounting for about one in four births in the United States. They involve major abdominal surgery, with its concomitant risks and complications. An investigation of court cases between 1979 and 1986 showed that courts often accept physicians' decisions to operate over the objections of patients, their families, or religious persuasion, even though subsequent medical developments suggest that many of these operations were not necessary (Irwin and Jordan, 1987). Nevertheless, nontechnical judgments are often involved in decisions to impose medical treatment, even a serious breach of the bodily integrity of the unwilling patient. Court-ordered surgical delivery was disproportionately used on women of color, poor, and non-English-speaking women. These factors appear to be linked with doctors' moral evaluation of some women as incompetent, ignorant, or "bad" mothers, who cannot take the interests of their child into account (Daniels, 1993: 31–55). Similarly, medical authority has legitimated the legal prosecution of women charged with "prenatal endangerment," for example by engaging in childbirth without medical assistance or failing to follow doctors' orders to stop smoking or drinking (Tsing, 1990).

Medical dominance has effectively reduced the legitimacy of actions of other "encroaching" institutional areas such as religion and the family. Several courts have overruled religious or moral objections to various medical procedures. Jehovah's Witnesses, for example, believe that blood transfusions are forbidden by scripture, but the courts have generally upheld the medical authorization of such treatments, even for unwilling recipients (*United States* v. *George*, 239 F. Supp. 752, 1964). Medical authority was also ruled to supersede parental authority in decisions presumed to determine life or death (precedent cases in 1952, 1962, and 1964 are cited in Burkholder, 1974: 41). Even in instances in which the medical ability to prevent death is more doubtful, greater legitimacy is given to medical rather than parental authority. In 1994, for example, a California court ordered that a Hmong Laotian child suffering from leukemia be removed from her parents' custody because they refused medically prescribed chemotherapy for her; more than 200 Hmong demonstrated against the decision, which overruled the parents' ethnic and religious objections to Western medical treatment (*New York Times*, 1994c).

Social Control and Power

The labeling of deviance is an issue of legitimacy on another level as well, for the power to define sickness and to label someone as sick is also the power to discredit that person (Zola, 1983: 276–278). If a person's mental health is called into question, the rest of society does not have to take that person seriously. The individual then becomes the locus of the so-called problem. During the Vietnam War, a physician refused to train medical personnel for the army, claiming that his religious conscience compelled him to refuse this service. The army insisted that his compulsions were psychological rather than religious (Fenn, 1978: 57). By thus raising doubt about his psychological health, the army was able to evade his religious dissent as well as his legal claim to protection under the First Amendment of the Constitution.

Medical control in defining deviance also produces medical power in certifying deviance, which is another aspect of social control. The societal acceptance of medical definitions of deviance gives the medical profession unique power to certify individuals as sick or well. If a back disorder is a legitimate basis for taking the sick role (and thus to be excused from work or to claim insurance), a physician is considered the appropriate agency for certifying a valid claim. Sick persons typically use "feeling" terms to describe internal states that they experience as illness; they say, for example, "I don't feel good" or "I feel too dizzy to stand." When the bodily source of feeling sick is not obvious to their audiences, they need doctors' substantiation to legitimate their claims (Telles and Pollack, 1981). Putting a medical label (known as a "diagnosis") on an illness can be beneficial when it validates and demonstrates serious concern about patients' symptoms and gives some meaning or coherence to their distressing experience, thereby supporting their efforts to manage the illness (Broom and Woodward, 1996). Doctors, however, often resist diagnosing ambiguous illnesses (especially contested categories such as chronic fatigue syndrome) because they do not want to encourage patients to take the sick role. They are thus caught between conflicting roles for themselves: physician as patient advocate and patient-claimant versus physician as agent of social control.

One of the social control functions of physicians is the role of gatekeeper (Stone, 1979a, 1979b), making them responsible for separating the "deserving" from the "undeserving" claims for sympathy and social support, sick leave, disability pay, health insurance, hospitalization, and so on. Physicians became the chief arbiters of claims for workers' compensation for repetitive strain injuries; not surprisingly, company doctors selected by manufacturers or insurers typically were less likely to certify the injury or provide sympathetic care than were personal physicians (Reid et al., 1991). Similarly, from 1952 to 1979, when homosexuality was considered a legitimate basis for denying a person U.S. citizenship, psychiatrists were given the power to certify that a homosexual should be thus denied (see Szasz, 1970).

When a person is certified as deviant, the agency of social control must then deal with this offender. Religious responses to deviance include counseling, moral indignation, confession, repentance, penance, and forgiveness. Legal responses include parallel actions, such as legal allegations, confession, punishments, rehabilitation, and release with or without the stigma of a record. In the medical model, the responses entail other parallels: diagnosis, therapy, counseling.

The process of reintegrating the deviant individual into the social group is therapy, which for even relatively minor deviance involves a form of social control (such as getting a young mother "back on her feet" so she can resume her family responsibilities). The social control functions of therapy are most clearly evident in such situations as the kidnapping and forcible "deprogramming" of persons with deviant religious or political views (Robbins and Anthony, 1982) and the mental hospitalization of political dissidents (Freidson, 1970: 246; see also Turner, 1977; Medvedev and Medvedev, 1971).

The use of psychoactive drugs for social control is one area of particular concern. Several U.S. and Canadian studies have documented the very large proportion of the elderly receiving drugs that affect the central nervous system, such as tranquilizers, analgesics, antidepressants, sedatives, hypnotics, and anti-convulsants. One function, deliberate or not, of the use of these drugs is the management of elderly persons. For example, older persons need shorter but more frequent periods of sleep than younger adults, but sedatives are often prescribed in many institutions to try to keep the elderly in an eight-hour sleeping pattern, so the staff can better supervise them at night (Harding, 1981; see also Harding, 1986).

Similarly, difficult-to-manage schoolchildren are often prescribed Ritalin to calm their excess activity and get them to pay attention to their learning tasks. In the mid-1990s, between 1.5 and 2.5 million (approximately 3 to 5 percent) of U.S. school-age children were being medicated daily with Ritalin, according to a U.N. report (*New York Times*, 1996a).

Social control is also involved in the use of drugs to make it possible for persons to accommodate themselves to an unsatisfactory social role. When workers experience severe stress in the workplace, treating their stress-related health conditions with drugs keeps them performing their roles without challenging the work conditions or the appropriateness of those roles.

One pharmaceutical company was investigated in 1987 by the U.S. Food and Drug Administration for sending doctors an advertising brochure depicting on the cover a very tense air traffic controller at the computer monitor in a hectic control tower. The caption read, "He needs anxiolytic [tranquilizer] therapy . . . but alertness is part of his job." Inside the folder, the worker is portrayed as cheery and smiling, and the text reads, in part, "BuSpar. . . . For a different kind of calm." Although the ad was criticized as misleading in its downplaying of negative side effects of the drug, the more serious sociological issue is that a tranquilizer is being promoted as a solution to workplace stress brought on by specific policy decisions. According to a U.S. Government Accounting Office study, air controllers suffer very low morale, extreme overwork, and other pressures due to chronic and serious understaffing—a major problem since President Reagan had fired 11,000 striking air traffic controllers in 1981 (*Health Letter*, 1987; Hinds, 1987).

Research in the United States, Canada, and Europe shows that women have been the overwhelming majority of recipients of prescriptions for tranquilizers and sedatives (Ashton, 1991; Harding, 1986). Pharmaceutical company advertising to doctors specifically recommended such psychoactive drugs to deal with women's dissatisfaction with their social roles. An advertisement for Valium (diazepam) showed a troubled young woman sitting at a table in a school gymnasium; the photo was labeled as follows:

> Symbols in a life of psychic tension: M.A. (Fine Arts), PTA (President-elect), GYN repeated examinations, normal (persistent complaints). . . . Rx: Valium . . . M.A. (Fine Arts) . . . PTA (President-elect) . . . representations of a life currently centered around home and children, with too little time to pursue a vocation for which she has spent many years in training . . . a situation that may bespeak continuous frustration and stress: a perfect framework for her to translate the functional symptoms of psychic tension into major problems. For this kind of patient—with no demonstrable pathology yet with repeated complaints—consider the distinctive properties of Valium (diazepam). Valium possesses a pronounced calming action that usually relieves psychic tension promptly, helping to attenuate the related somatic signs and symptoms.

Like the air traffic controller, this young woman is identified as suffering from the stress and frustration of her social role. The solution of prescribing tranquilizers serves the social control function of keeping people in their roles without questioning the role demands themselves (for a review of the literature on prescription of psychotropic drugs for women, see Ettorre and Riska, 1995).

In the 1990s a newer form of medicalized social control became evident in the United States, Canada, and several European countries. In the name of improving health, the medical establishment (in the form of national health services, public health programs, corporate wellness programs, and managed care organizations) promoted *moral* judgments attached to "lifestyle" decisions. These lifestyle expectations were highly individualized: It became solely the individual's responsibility to maintain a "healthy" lifestyle, for example by getting lots of exercise, eating "right," ceasing smoking and drinking alcohol, reducing stress, maintaining the "right" weight, and so on. Although the promotion of behaviors that might help prevent diseases is an appropriate part of public health measures, by individualizing the concept of "lifestyle" these programs had the effect of distracting from the *social* and *public* causes of disease, such as environmental pollution, illness-producing work and workplaces, and socioeconomic constraints that prevent individuals from achieving a healthy "lifestyle" (Bunton et al., 1995). Notice the moral connotations of such notions as eating "right," with little or no recognition of the difficulties of obtaining a good diet on a poverty-level income. These moral judgments are readily medicalized because of biomedicine's paradigm that treats disease as a feature of the individual (see Chapter 9).

Social control may seem more pleasant or humane when the deviance is treated as sickness rather than as crime or sin, but the potency of the control agencies is just as great. Certain medically defined deviance can permanently spoil the individual's identity (cf. Goffman, 1963). Even when the condition is considered medically cured or under control, stigma still adheres to such illnesses as alcoholism, drug abuse, mental disorders, syphilis, and cancer. This problem of stigma is especially evident in the case of epilepsy and other conditions involving deviance from one very important cultural norm: self-control.

Chapter 7 further examines the problems of stigma and control in chronic illness and disabilities.

Sickness and Social Dissent

The social control functions of the sick role and of some medical interventions demonstrate that society's constraints on individual behavior are real, even when individuals do not agree with the norms for behavior. Although social control measures may be objectively powerful in a society, their effect is never total. Society's members are never fully socialized and compliant. Thus, deviance such as sickness can also be a form of social dissent—usually unorganized, but sometimes organized—against existing social arrangements.

Sickness is, as the sick role concept shows, an act of refusal that is potentially threatening to the established order. In effect, the sick person is saying, "I will not . . . any longer." By claiming the sick role, the individual may refuse to go to school or work, to be responsible for dependents, to serve in the armed forces, and to participate in everyday social obligations. Indeed, in its extreme form, sickness is a refusal to cope, to struggle, and to endure. As such, claiming the sick role resembles the political activist strategy of passive resistance (Lock and Scheper-Hughes, 1990; Scheper-Hughes and Lock, 1991; see also Herzlich and Pierret, 1987: 183–184; Kleinman, 1992). Taking the sick role is thus often a way of expressing dissent from other social roles. Many social historians consider the epidemic of hysteria among Victorian women to be an expression of their dissent against the constraints of their social roles (Ehrenreich and English, 1978; Sicherman, 1978). Similarly, workers' job dissatisfaction is often expressed by high rates of absenteeism for sickness.

Sickness is not necessarily an effective form of dissent, however. Waitzkin (1971) suggested the sick role has latent (that is, not recognized or intended) functions that maintain the status quo in society and reduce conflict and change. For example, if disgruntled workers take sick leave to relieve the tensions of their job satisfaction, the sick role reduces the likelihood that those tensions will be addressed politically, such as in a confrontation with management. The sick role instead provides only a *temporary* safety valve to reduce pressure in various institutional settings, such as the family, prisons, and the military.

Although the sickness may not be able to change social arrangements, such as social class or gender hierarchies, it may be effective in obtaining actual advantages or relief for the sick person. Some secondary gains of sickness, such as receiving extra attention in the family, may be such a result. For example, many African societies have special healing cults for women, such as the *zar* cult of the predominantly Muslim peoples in Ethiopia, Egypt, Sudan, and Somalia. Some anthropologists have interpreted the *zar* affliction, in which the sick person is believed to be possessed by spirits, as women's assertion of dissatisfaction with their lack of social and economic power (Lewis, 1971). Taking the sick role can be a relatively successful (albeit manipulative) assertion of power of the subordinate members of the society. It poignantly expresses women's dissent, but does not fundamentally alter the social arrangements.

Similarly, sickness is sometimes the attempt to cope (although not always constructively) with an intolerable social situation, as discussed in Chapter 4. Sickness expresses frustration, dissatisfaction, and anger turned against oneself. Alcoholism and other substance abuse, depression, and suicide exemplify this potentially self-defeating attempt. To interpret, for example, the alcoholism of a middle-aged, unemployed, impoverished Native American on a reservation as a purely individual sickness is thus to miss the likelihood that it is the expression of his frustration and hostility in the face of his utterly marginalized social condition (Scheper-Hughes and Lock, 1991). Likewise, to interpret an immigrant woman's severe case of "nerves" as a quaint relic of old-country folk beliefs misses the meaning of nerves (or "*nervios*," "*nevra*," and so on) as a physical expression of real distress (Finkler, 1989; see also Guarnaccia et al., 1989). Her distress, expressed in the physical symptoms of "nerves," may be produced by the perceived disorder of daily life in a society where she experiences exploitation as a worker and discrimination as a member of an ethnic minority. Her "nerves" may be a reaction to a lack of meaning and perceived assault on self-esteem from living in a culture that lacks the values by which she would have been honored in her native culture (Lock, 1990).

Scheper-Hughes and Lock (1991) argued that modern medicine has so thoroughly individualized its image of sickness that it has lost sight of the extent to which sickness may be the expression of social dissent about frustrated and unmet human needs. They stated:

> In summary, we wish to stress that while illness symptoms are biological entities they are also coded metaphors that speak to the contradictory aspects of social life, expressing sentiments, feelings, and ideas that must otherwise be kept hidden. As patients—all of us—we can be open and responsive to the hidden language of pain and protest, rage and resistance, or we can silence it, cut it off by relegating our complaints to the ever expanding domains of medicine ("It" is in the body) or psychiatry ("It" is in the mind). Once safely medicalized, however, the social issues are short-circuited and the message in the bottle—the desperate plea for help and the scream of protest—is forever lost. (Scheper-Hughes and Lock, 1991: 422–423)

Some of these metaphorical aspects of the body and sicknesses are described in more detail next.

PROBLEMS OF MEANING AND ORDER

Illness is upsetting because it is experienced as a threat to the order and meanings by which people make sense of their lives. Suffering and death create problems of meaning not simply because they are unpleasant, but also because they threaten the fundamental assumptions of order underlying society itself (cf. Berger, 1967: 24). For the individual, illness and affliction can likewise be experienced as assaults on the identity, and on the ability to predict and control central aspects of one's own and one's loved ones' lives. Healing, in all cultures, represents an attempt to restore order and to reassert meaning.

Illness disrupts the order of everyday life. It threatens our ability to plan for the immediate or distant future, to control, and to organize. Even a relatively minor malady, such as a head cold, can disturb the order of daily life; how much more so can serious, potentially fatal, or debilitating illnesses, such as cancer or polio, throw our lives into disorder! A study of the impact of childhood leukemia found two characteristic experiences of sufferers and their families: uncertainty and the search for meaning (Comaroff and Maguire, 1981).

Medical systems in all cultures restore order in the face of illness in a number of ways. Diagnostic action, whether accomplished by divination or CT (computer tomography) scan, divine revelation or physical examination, is a means of naming the problem and giving it a culturally recognizable form. Naming the illness imposes order on a previously chaotic set of experiences, thereby giving the sick person a set of expectations and some basis for acting. Etiologies likewise contribute to restoring a sense of order, because they reflect important values of the social group, especially by identifying a causal relationship between sickness and socially prescribed normal or ideal social relationships. In applying particular etiologies to a given illness episode, the medical process ritually reaffirms these values (Young, 1976).

In many cultures, the healing process addresses not only individual disruption but also disordered *social* relations. The healing role of the African Ndembu diviner is to identify (in symbolic guise) the agents of affliction. Sickness is understood as an eruption of social conflict and divisiveness in one symbolic place. For example, the Ndembu attribute menstrual disorders to *chisaku* (misfortune due to displeasure of ancestral shades or breach of taboo). The healing ritual propitiates the ancestors and exorcizes the evil influences of both living and dead. Significantly, it involves the woman's matrilineal kin, with whom there may be a problem for the woman and her husband. The larger aims of the healing ritual include restoration of problematic kinship ties, reconstruction of the woman's relationship with her husband, and enhanced procreation, thereby benefiting both the marriage and the lineage. Because the disordered body is the expression of disordered social relations, healing consists of reunifying and reordering the entire group, of which the sick person is only an individual expression (Turner, 1968, 1969).

Similarly, faith healing in many Christian groups restores order through healing the metaphorical body (McGuire, 1982). For example, some Christian groups believe that healing a troubled marriage should involve bringing the "body" (wife and children) into proper relationship (namely, submission) with the "head" (husband and father). The importance of the body as a natural symbol suggests that, even in Western cultures, illness and healing may be ways of symbolizing order and meaning on several levels.

The Body as a Symbol

The human body is a natural symbol. The meanings of the symbol are not intrinsic in it, but are socially constructed and attached to it. As Douglas (1970: 93) stated,

> The social body constrains the way the physical body is perceived. The physical experience of the body, always modified by the social categories through which it is known, sustains a particular view of society. There is a continual exchange of meanings between the two kinds of bodily experience so that each reinforces the categories of the other. As a result of this interaction the body itself is a highly restricted medium of expression.

Thus, she argued that bodily control is social control, and attitudes toward the body reflect the social concerns of the group (Douglas, 1970: 11–18; see also Douglas, 1966).

Body symbolism works on several levels; often the body and its parts are used as metaphors. For example, when we say a person is upright, we are referring to both a moral evaluation and a physical posture. Similar body metaphors are applied when we evaluate people as spineless, underhanded, open-eyed, heartless, cold-blooded, brown-nosed, blue-blooded, sinister, thick-skinned, or gutless. Social relations are likewise reflected in body metaphors, such as, "He is a pain in the ass," or "They are thicker than blood."

Consider all the symbolic meanings we give to various body parts and body products, including hands, heart, womb, hair, eyes, milk, blood, spit, feces, and sweat. These meanings are not inherent in the physical properties but are applied by a social group. In socialization, we learn our society's meanings. A baby is not born with an aversion to the sight of blood. A young child must learn to be disgusted by the feel of feces (usually only after having played with them and receiving several reprimands).

Through the meanings attached to the body, social structure shapes individual bodily expression. At the same time, bodily expression reflects the social structure. Numerous studies of various cultures, including Western industrialized societies, have shown how core values are revealed in body-related beliefs and practices, such as eating (Banks, 1992; Lupton, 1996; Turner, 1982); beauty and adornment (Kunzle, 1981); birth and death (Comaroff, 1984; Davis-Floyd, 1992); sex (Foucault, 1978; Turner, 1984); pollution and cleanliness (Classen, 1994; Douglas, 1966; Elias, 1994 [1978]); fitness and healthy "lifestyle" (Bordo, 1993; Lowenberg and Davis, 1994; Lupton, 1995; O'Brien, 1995); and health and healing (Comaroff, 1985; Crawford, 1984; McGuire, 1988; Westley, 1983).

The Meaning of Affliction

Illness is also upsetting because it raises the questions of meaning: Why is this happening to me? Why now? Who's responsible? How could God allow this to happen? Why do the good suffer and the evil prosper? In many cultures, the medical system and the religious system are inextricably interwoven. Religious meaning is thereby connected with illness explanations.

In his analysis of religious systems, Weber noted the importance of **theodicies**, or religious explanations of meaning-threatening experiences, for sickness, suffering, and death ([1922] 1963: 138–150). Theodicies tell the individual or group that the experience is not meaningless but is rather part of a larger system of order, a religious cosmology (see also Berger, 1967: 24). Some successful theodicies are in fact nothing but assertions of order. A woman discussing her personal meaning crisis after her husband's premature death said, "I finally came to understand that it didn't matter whether *I* understood why he died when he did, but that God had a reason for it, and that was all that mattered." For this believer, knowing that an order exists behind events was more important than knowing what that order was (McGuire, 1982). Theodicies do not necessarily make the believer happy or even promise future happiness; they simply answer the question, Why do I suffer?

At the same time that Western societies are experiencing the increasing medicalization of authority, Western medicine is having difficulty dealing with sufferers' problems of meaning. Anthropologists remind us that however well Western medicine deals with the symptoms the sick person suffers, it fails to address the problem of "who sent the louse" (Comaroff, 1978). Illness etiologies in Western medicine typically deal with such proximate causes as germs, viruses, and genetic defects, but these notions are not adequate explanations for many people, because questions of meaning frequently beg for ultimate causes.

A foremost characteristic of the institution of medicine in modern Western societies is its differentiation from other institutions that provide meaning and belonging. **Institutional differentiation** is the process by which the various institutional spheres in society become separated from each other (see Parsons, 1966). For example, religious functions are focused in special religious institutions, which are separate from other institutions, such as the educational, political, and economic. The medical institution has limited itself to the cure of disease, as a biophysical entity, and to the physical tending of the diseased individual. Provision of meaning and belonging is treated as relatively unimportant for healing and relegated to the private-sphere institutions of family and religion. These private-sphere institutions are allowed, even encouraged, to handle the meaning problems of the sick, but only so long as their beliefs and actions do not interfere with the medical management of the disease (McGuire, 1985).

Just as the physical body is a potent symbol of one's selfhood, so too are experiences of suffering linked with one's identity (see also Chapter 7). Practically, being unwell implies being disabled, in the sense of being made unable to do what one wants or needs to do; it implies reduced agency. It means losing some control (an especially important quality in this society), and it involves losing one's routines— the very patterns by which daily existence is ordered (Cassell, 1982; see also Comaroff, 1982).

Suffering is not connected with disease or pain in any precise causal or proportionate way. The pain of childbirth, for example, may be more severe than the pain of angina, but it generally causes less suffering because it is perceived as temporary and associated with a desired outcome. A disease may be incurable yet cause little suffering if it does little damage to the person's sense of self and ability to engage in everyday life. For example, a chronic fungal infection of the big toe may cause less suffering than a temporary but disfiguring episode of Bell's palsy. Many people may seek help and healing less for disease itself than for suffering and affliction.

Cassell (1982: 639) has suggested that suffering poses difficulty for the biomedical system because it is "experienced by persons, not merely by bodies, and has its sources in challenges that threaten the intactness of the person as a complex social and psychological entity." He observed that medical personnel can unknowingly cause suffering when they do not validate the patient's affliction, and when they fail to acknowledge or deal with the personal meanings the patient attaches to the illness. Cassell (1982: 642) noted that "people suffer from what they have lost of themselves in relation to the world of objects, events and relationships." One woman still suffered greatly from a hysterectomy she had undergone six years earlier. As she explained, "It meant losing a huge part of my future." Unmarried, childless, and only 29 years old, she lost hopes and dreams for the future. She expressed enormous anger at the insensitivity of physicians and hospital staff who had treated her "like an ungrateful child, crying over spilt milk" (quoted in McGuire, 1988). The medical personnel, even if thoroughly well intentioned, probably felt their sole duty was the correct treatment of her specific uterine problem; the woman's suffering was not their problem, nor relevant to their tasks.

Whether brought on by a physical problem or not, affliction often results from a threat to the *coherence* of a person's world. As noted in Chapter 4, a sense of coherence itself is related to health and healing. People suffer from a loss of connectedness—links with loved ones, valued social roles, and groups that are important to them. As Chapter 7 shows, the illness experience often involves such losses. In the face of affliction, people seek meaning and order to address this essential coherence (Cassell, 1982; see also Antonovsky, 1984).

SUMMARY

Sickness is not merely the condition of an individual, but is also related to the larger social order. It is connected with moral issues and the imputation of responsibility for deviance from social norms. Society deals with such deviance through social control mechanisms, including the sick role. Sick role expectations, however, vary historically and cross culturally. The discrepancies between the ideal image of the sick role (based on certain forms of acute illness) and chronic and other nonacute conditions result in ambiguous expectations for those whom society defines as sick. The medicalization of deviance and the social stigma of illness highlight the social control functions of medicine, which are yet another connection between power and health. The medical profession has successfully asserted primacy in the defining deviance and the corollary function of certifying deviance, thereby becoming a primary moral authority in modern societies.

A related issue is the problem of meaning created by illness, suffering, and death. Because of the importance of the human body as a natural symbol, bodily control and healing practices reflect social relationships and concerns. The problems of meaning brought on by illness are particularly difficult in modern Western medical settings, due to the differentiation of medical institutions from meaning-providing institutions such as religion and family. The biomedical model, with its nearly exclusive focus on physical conditions, does not deal adequately with suffering and the subjective experience of affliction.

RECOMMENDED READINGS

Articles

JEAN COMAROFF, "Medicine: Symbol and ideology," pp. 49–68 in P. Wright and A. Treacher, eds., *The Problem of Medical Knowledge: Examining the Social Construction of Medicine.* Edinburgh: Edinburgh University Press, 1982.

ROBERT CRAWFORD, "A cultural account of 'health': Control, release, and the social body," pp. 60–103 in J. B. McKinlay, ed., *Issues in the Political Economy of Health Care.* New York: Tavistock, 1984.

MARGARET LOCK and NANCY SCHEPER-HUGHES, "A critical-interpretive approach in medical anthropology: Rituals and routines of discipline and dissent," pp. 47–72 in T. M. Johnson and C. F. Sargent, eds., *Medical Anthropology: A Handbook of Theory and Method.* New York: Greenwood Press, 1990.

NANCY E. WAXLER, "Learning to be a leper: A case study in the social construction of illness," pp. 169–194 in Elliot G. Mishler, Lorna R. AmaraSingham, Stuart T. Hauser, Ramsay Liem, Samuel D. Osherson, and Nancy E. Waxler, *Social Contexts of Health, Illness, and Patient Care.* Cambridge: Cambridge University Press, 1981.

Books

SUSAN BORDO, *Unbearable Weight: Feminism, Western Culture, and the Body.* Berkeley: University of California Press, 1993. Amply illustrated with commercial advertisements, this readable theoretical book critiques the ideological uses of commodified women's bodies, including somatic norms for weight, control and self-management, plasticity and malleability.

PETER CONRAD and JOSEPH W. SCHNEIDER, *Deviance and Medicalization: From Badness to Sickness.* Philadelphia: Temple University Press, 1992. This highly readable volume explains the medicalization process, illustrating it with detailed examinations of the medicalization of mental illness, alcoholism, opiate addiction, hyperkinesis, child abuse, homosexuality, and criminality.

CHAPTER OUTLINE

Illness is a profoundly human experience that calls into question normal expectations about our bodies and capacities. When illness is not part of our life, we take the relationship between our bodies and our selves for granted. Indeed, we are not likely to think about our bodies or be particularly conscious of many bodily sensations. In health, we expect our bodies to be able to function and to sustain a presentation of our selves as normal, reliable participants in social interaction (Dingwall, 1976: 98). What we call illness is a disturbance in body processes or experience that has become problematic for the individual.

ILLNESS AND SELF

The experience of illness, even if only temporary, reminds us of our limitations, of our dependencies—present and potential—and of our ultimate mortality. When ill, our bodies inform us that they cannot always be counted on to be able for what we want them to do. Because our very sense of who we are and our important social relationships are intimately connected with our bodies and their routine functioning, being ill is disruptive and disordering. We identify our selves with our bodies, as evidenced by one physician's introspective account of his own accident and gradual recovery. He exclaimed, "What seemed, at first, to be no more than a local peripheral breakage and breakdown now showed itself in a different, and quite terrible, light—as a breakdown of memory, of thinking, of will—*not just a lesion in my muscle, but a lesion in me*" (Sacks, 1984: 67).

Thus, the illness experience is much more than a biophysical event; it has far-reaching social, emotional, moral, and spiritual implications. Kleinman's (1978, 1988) distinction between disease and illness is useful. According to his definitions, **disease** refers to the biophysical condition—the problem as seen from the biomedical practitioner's perspective. The physician transforms the patient's and the family's expressions of illness into terms that fit the theoretical models of disease. By contrast, **illness** refers to "how the sick person and the members of the family or wider social network perceive, live with, and respond to symptoms and disability" (Kleinman, 1988: 3–6). Because doctors of Western medicine have been trained to focus almost exclusively on disease, they have difficulty dealing with the illness experience (Kleinman, 1978).

This chapter focuses on the experiences of illness and pain, especially as shaped by social structure and culture. Although even the most minor illness can be problematic for the sufferer, we emphasize those illnesses most likely to have a damaging effect on the person's identity and sense of self (see Oleson et al., 1990). Most everyday illnesses are not profoundly disruptive, although they too remind the sufferer of personal limits and dependencies. If I have a bout of the flu, I may be very miserable, fall far behind in my work, and be temporarily dependent on family and friends, unable to reciprocate their care; however, such illness does not significantly challenge my relationships and my identity. Likewise, many accidents wounding the body and many acute illnesses, although temporarily very discomforting or even seriously threatening, do not damage the ill person's sense of self. If I suffer acute pneumonia, the condition may be life threatening and require dramatic medical intervention—hospitalization, antibiotics, and intense nursing care—but I emerge to retain my essential relationships and identity. Other illnesses, however, are deeply disruptive, threatening the ill person's important relationships and very sense of self (Bury, 1991; Kelly and Field, 1996; Radley, 1994; Toombs, 1995).

Loss is one factor that can make an illness experience profoundly disruptive. People actively grieve because the loss of body parts (for example, amputation of an arm) or functions (such as partial blindness) represent loss of integrity—the wholeness of the person (Cassell, 1982). People suffer not only from the loss of present capacities and roles, but also from being robbed of their future: the teenager who is a paraplegic after a car accident, the childless young woman who has a hysterectomy, the middle-aged lawyer who loses her eyesight, the elderly musician whose arthritis makes playing a beloved instrument impossible. One woman with breast cancer said, "The loss of being able to dream for the future is the most significant effect of cancer. This makes me feel like I'm left out and on a separate track from others" (quoted in Fife, 1994: 313).

Chronic illness and pain in particular force the sufferer to come to new terms with the experience of time. Sometimes a life-threatening acute illness or a serious accident has such impact, but an acute condition is—by definition—temporary. Chronic illness, by contrast, often leads to a radical reassessment, in light of changed and yet-changing capacities, of one's self in relationship to one's past and future. The experience of chronic illness thus involves both a sense of loss and a heightened self-consciousness (Charmaz, 1987, 1991). Chronic illness often demands complex strategies for managing symptoms. Adhering to drug regimens must be balanced against the side effects of drugs; symptoms may be concealed from other people; life must be scheduled around symptom flare-ups or to avoid flare-ups (Bury, 1991; Pinder, 1988). These strategies break up taken-for-granted rhythms and activities of daily life and heighten self-consciousness.

Illness is especially damaging to the self when it is experienced as overwhelming, unpredictable, and uncontrollable because it paralyzes the person's ability to manage life, to plan, and to act. Enormous attention must be given not merely to actual crisis periods in the illness but also to minute, mundane worries such as these: Can I visit my friend's apartment without having an asthma attack? Can I make it to the bathroom quickly enough? If I attempt sexual intercourse, will my back pain flare up? Do I risk a heart attack if I take on this interesting project at work? Can I negotiate the path from my car to the store? (cf. Kleinman, 1988: 44). Unpredictability and uncontrollability result in a disjunction between the person and the body; the functioning that was once taken for granted is gone, and the person in effect feels, "I cannot count on my body. *It* fails *me*." The body becomes an "other"—at best an unpredictable ally.

Illness that results in ongoing social marginality is also particularly damaging to the self. Much of our web of social relationships is predicated on the assumptions that members will be able to reciprocate, that one member will not be utterly dependent on others, and that all give and receive. Some illnesses undermine the assumption of reciprocity and thus make social relationships precarious. Losing independence is threatening to one's sense of self not just because of pride in self- sufficiency (a related value in our culture), but more because it impairs one's ability to participate as an equal in important social relationships. Valued friendships and social roles become strained or lost altogether. Often the individual lives in a deliberately collapsed world because the larger world becomes unmanageable or threatening. One woman commented,

> What is really so awful is that illness, I believe, really makes you very lonely. . . . One is really out of the world. *When there is illness one is, and one stays, alone.* It's very hard to get help. . . . It destroys what one would like to do, it isolates you. . . . If I got into very poor health, I could no longer take care of them as I do. . . . I would be cut off from my family, life would have to be organized without me, I would not play the role that I play now. I believe that one who is sick is outside of normal life. (quoted in Herzlich and Pierret, 1987: 178)

Pain and treatment often become a focus for the chronically ill, forcing them to withdraw into themselves. Lack of access to everyday activities also fosters isolation. Others, unable to deal with chronic problems, socially withdraw, and thus a spiral of increasing isolation is set into motion: The less one can or wants to do, the less one socializes; but the less one socializes, the more others withdraw, and in turn the more the person with a chronic illness withdraws (Radley, 1994). One man with severe rheumatoid arthritis said,

> Now the only place I go now is down to the local club. Everybody knows me sort of thing. They might say it's a shame for him, but nobody bothers me, they accept me as I am. But if I go anywhere else . . . people are embarrassed. People say "bloody hell, is that . . .? Dear me, what's the matter with him?" And they try not to catch your eye, if you will. People tend to stay away from you. I don't know, they just don't want to be involved. You tend to do the same then. (quoted in Bury, 1982: 176)

All the more marginalizing are illness experiences involving stigma, which by definition has the potential to discredit the self that the individual is trying to present to others. For example, one young woman had undergone a colostomy in which a large part of her colon was surgically removed, necessitating the perpetual wearing and cleaning of a device that collected and held the contents of her bowels. She exclaimed,

> I feel so embarrassed by this—this thing. It seems so unnatural, so dirty. I can't get used to the smell to it. I'm scared of soiling myself. Then I'd be so ashamed I couldn't look at anyone else. . . . Who would want a wife like this? How can I go out and not feel unable to look people in the eyes and tell them the truth? Once I do, who would want to develop a friendship, I mean a close one? How can I even consider showing my body to someone else, having sex? (quoted in Kleinman, 1988: 163)

Because control is so strongly valued in our culture, loss of control is especially problematic. People experience an assault on their sense of self when their illnesses involve losses of control, such as incontinence, loss of bowel control, flatulence, seizures, stumbling and falling, tics and tremors, and drooling. We rely on relative control of our bodies to present ourselves in socially valued ways (Goffman, 1963), but chronic illness and disability disrupt that control (Radley, 1994; Schneider and Conrad, 1983). Furthermore, in a culture in which productivity, vigor, beauty, and youth are very important values, disability and aging are especially threatening. Disability and chronic illness may remind people of their vulnerability (Livneh, 1991; Murphy, 1987). Thus, certain chronic illnesses and disabilities are especially likely to threaten the individual's sense of self and connectedness with others.

There may be gender differences in response to chronic illness. Men whose identities are invested in being autonomous, independent, dominant, problem solvers, and having personal power may experience narrow options for preserving their sense of self and social relationships in the face of chronic illness. Women can be more flexible and resourceful (Charmaz, 1995).

Even with nonfatal chronic illnesses, such as arthritis, the illness experience requires individuals, families, and personal networks continually to confront problems of uncertainty, dependency, and understanding. It also necessitates the negotiation of new role relationships with others. Sometimes a chronic illness may result in outright conflict or rejection (Bury, 1988; see also Schott and Badura, 1988). A retired lawyer described the effects on himself and his family of his wife's ten years of decline with Alzheimer's disease:

> Our children come and they cry. And I cry. We reminisce about old times. We try to recall what Anna was like before this happened. But I can see it wears them out just being here for a day or two. They've got their own troubles. I can't ask them to help out any more than they do already. Me? It's made a different person out of me. I expect you wouldn't have recognized me if you had met me ten years ago. I feel at least ten years older than I am. I'm afraid what will happen if I go first. I haven't had a half hour free of worry and hurt for ten years. This illness didn't just destroy Anna's mind, it has killed something in me, in the family, too. If anyone asks about Alzheimer's, tell them it is a disease of the whole family. (quoted in Kleinman, 1988: 183)

Illness is not experienced merely by the individual in whose body the symptoms are located; often the family and other close members of the sufferer's social network also feel the disruptiveness of illness. For example, the husband of a woman with cancer said,

> I keep saying we felt, like I guess I feel like this is my disease, too. That's because it's so drastic. It's a fight that she has to undertake, so it's partly mine, too. It's a psychological thing, the helplessness for the husband. This is not just her disease, it is my disease, too. (quoted in Wilson, 1991)

The human response to illness is to give it meaning, to interpret it, to reorder the disordering experience. To make sense of what is happening to us, we draw on socially available categories from a large cultural repertoire and from personal and family stories and meanings absorbed from our particular ethnic and religious backgrounds (see Fife, 1994). In the case of minor illnesses, the interpretations might include our underlying definitions of health and illness, and our notions about why we got sick and how to get well. Seriously disruptive illnesses are likely to evoke further interpretations about the meaning of life, moral responsibility, suffering, relationships, and death.

LAY CONCEPTIONS OF HEALTH

How do you know you are sick? How do you know if your condition is potentially serious enough to warrant doing something about the illness? Long before any outside help (medical or otherwise) is sought, individuals interpret their own condition. Underlying all such evaluations is a set of ideas about health and illness. The concepts and logic of these ideas are not those of science or medicine, although they may be borrowed, accurately or inaccurately, from those formal systems of knowledge. Rather, they are the concepts and logic of ordinary people whose experiences, socialization, cultural background, and immediate social network shape and continually develop their notions of health and illness.

Many people think of health as simply the absence of illness. For example, a Scottish study of older persons found that key dimensions of health mentioned were an absence of illness, a reserve of strength, and a feeling of being generally fit or capable of accomplishing daily tasks (Williams, 1990). Corroborating evidence came from a study of middle-aged French subjects, who described health in terms of an absence of illness, an equilibrium in daily life, and a capacity to work (Herzlich, 1973; Herzlich and Pierret, 1987).

Other research found that although both working-class and middle-class persons shared the notion that health meant the absence of illness, working-class people tended to emphasize health as a tool in their everyday lives: It enabled them to carry out their tasks, especially job and family duties (Blaxter and Paterson, 1982; see also Pierret, 1993; Williams, 1990). Middle-class persons were more likely to mention broader, positive conceptions of health that included such factors as energy, positive attitudes, and the ability to cope well and be in control of one's life (Calnan, 1987; Herzlich, 1973; Saltonstall, 1993). These views are illustrated by the following comments of a middle-class woman:

> I think that [truly healthy persons] . . . are very spontaneous and flexible, and I think they have more options that they experience. . . . They are feeling connected to a larger purpose and connected with other people. . . . I would also say that being in power, feeling powerful in your life, feeling responsible for your life is a very important part of it. (quoted in McGuire, 1988)

The sense of being in control may be particularly important to the middle class, for it meshes with their experiences of making decisions and having a degree of control in their work and daily life. By contrast, because working-class persons have control over far fewer areas of their lives, this value may be remote or inconceivable to them. Crawford (1984: 78) argued that middle-class values have expanded the notion of health to something that must be actively achieved and proven, because "to be healthy [in this culture] means to demonstrate to self and others appropriate concern for the virtues of self-control, self-discipline, self-denial, and will power." A Canadian study of lay conceptions found important differences between how respondents defined "health" (an abstract state) and how they understood "being healthy" (an ongoing negotiated status). Embedded in "being healthy" is a moral code by which one is judged (Litva and Eyles, 1994).

Important differences are apparent in lay conceptions of health and illness within various subcultures as well. Persons raised in different ethnic subcultures—Chicano, Irish, Appalachian, or Polish, for example—typically learn their group's ideas about health and illness, including: What is health? What can cause illness? What does a given illness mean? How can I protect myself and loved ones from illness? How can I counteract illness when it occurs? What can I expect to experience with different illnesses? What resources can I turn to for help in the face of illness?

Religious subcultures likewise influence not only their members' responses to illness but also their very definitions of health and illness. One member of a Christian healing group stated, "Health, wholeness—all these words to me are Scripture and salvation. It all goes together. A healthy person to me would be one that was whole in spirit, soul, mind, and body" (quoted in McGuire, 1988: 39). A study of middle-class spiritual healing groups found that, as persons became more actively involved, they expanded their notions of what needed healing in their lives. Because health was an ideal encompassing all their religious ideals, healing was a continual part of the process of striving for those goals (McGuire and Kantor, 1987; McGuire, 1988).

Although few studies have been done about other kinds of subcultural groups, it is probable that they too influence members' conceptions of health, illness, and healing. For example, to what extent is an adolescent subculture (and not just chronological age) a factor in the health notions of teenagers? Are there health belief systems communicated by other subcultures, such as homosexuals or the military? We have only begun to explore the diversity of lay conceptions of health and illness. The sketches we have thus far, however, illustrate the importance of lay conceptions for understanding people's behavior in the face of illness.

LAY UNDERSTANDINGS OF ILLNESS

Just as laypersons' notions of health are shaped by their social and cultural background, so too are the ways people understand their illnesses. People seek to comprehend what is wrong with them: What is the nature of this illness? Where did it come from? Why me? Why now? What can be done about this illness? What can be done to protect myself from other illness? Individual belief systems about illness are typically drawn from, but not necessarily rigidly determined by, larger cultural belief systems, which give shape to the illness experience, help the individual interpret what is happening, and offer a number of choices about how to respond.

Lay images of various diseases reveal why certain responses make sense. A study of middle-class New Yorkers found that people regularly refer to disease and diseased body parts as "its"—as objects separate from the person. This image allows ill persons to distance themselves from their problems. The concept of disease as an "it" also meshed with notions that the problem had its source in some external agent that invaded the body (Cassell, 1976). Because lay images of illness reflect people's diverse experiences, they vary by such factors as social class, gender, ethnicity, and religion. For example, some religious subcultures promote fatalist interpretations of disease causation and others tend to be activist (Mullen, 1994).

A study of Scottish women showed the predominance of the image of disease as a thing that one "has," "gets," or "catches." Accordingly, "it" attacks, strikes, or sets in. One respondent said, "My family wis never bothered wi' their chest . . . it wis always their throats. It always went for their throat, not their chest" (quoted in Blaxter, 1983: 61). The regional idiom of "taking" a disease distinguishes temporary (typically infectious) illnesses from chronic illnesses or a clear physical abnormality. One might "take" pneumonia, measles, bronchitis, or scarlet fever, but not a tumor, cyst, arthritis, or cancer (Blaxter, 1983).

People employ their lay conceptions to explain the nature and causes of specific maladies. In one English community, respondents tended to think of their illnesses in terms of hot or cold and wet or dry; for example, a chest cold fit the wet-cold image, whereas a fever was depicted as hot-dry. By extension, then, certain maladies were linked especially with damp, cold weather or house environment. People held explicit images of the germs and viruses to which they attributed some illnesses. They often depicted these agents as clouds of tiny particles or as minute, invisible insects. Medical professionals sometimes participated in the use of these images, for example by explaining a problem as "a tummy bug" (Helman, 1978).

The causal categories used by laypersons may not be correct in bioscientific terms but are generally rational and based on the kinds of empirical evidence available to laypersons. One Scottish study showed the most commonly invoked lay causal categories were, in rank order: (1) infection; (2) heredity or familial tendencies; (3) agents in the environment, such as "poisons," working conditions, and climate; (4) secondary products of other diseases; and (5) stress, strain, and worry (Blaxter, 1993, 1983; similar categories were found by Locker, 1981: 67).

The interpretation of illness is an ongoing process. People reinterpret their situation at various stages of their illness. They look back at earlier experiences and actions and reinterpret them to make sense of subsequent events and new beliefs. Interaction with physicians is only one source, among many, of people's reinterpretations (Hunt et al., 1989). Interaction with important others is another source of new interpretations. One purpose for this ongoing reconstruction is to make sense of a whole sequence of events, rather than viewing each part as an episode that just "happened." Thus, for example, cardiac patients retrospectively noticed the symptoms that had built up to their heart attack. Their reconstruction of the meaning of the sequence of events made the heart attack seem less threatening and more understandable (Cowie, 1976).

Cross-cultural research suggests that several explanatory logics are used by laypersons, including those in modern Western cultural settings. One category of logic is that of invasion, in which an outside agent is believed to come into the body to cause the illness. Examples include notions of possession, germ theory, or object intrusions. Another logic involves degeneration, in which the illness is explained as due to the breakdown of the body or its parts from such causes as exhaustion or the accumulation of toxic substances. Mechanical models provide another logic, explaining illness as the result of misalignment of body structures, or blockages of digestive or nervous channels, for example. A fourth logic commonly used is the notion of equilibrium, which attributes illness to the failure to maintain harmony (individual or social), balance, and order (Chrisman, 1977). Although these categories can be used to analyze the logics of other cultures, they are all used extensively by laypersons in modern Western societies.

Lay understandings of illness typically address the broader issues of meaning, such as those discussed in Chapter 6: Why must I suffer? Why me and not someone else? Why now? Have I done something bad to bring this on myself? Indeed, in much lay thinking, cause and meaning are not separate interpretive categories. Serious illnesses in particular evoke broader causal interpretations that are often used in combination with medical interpretations. For example, one young woman accepted the medical etiology of her vision problems, but simultaneously employed a broader causal meaning to her illness: " 'With my eye problem, there was something that I didn't want to see. I couldn't get well until I opened my eyes to that something' " (quoted in McGuire, 1988).

NOTICING ILLNESS

How do people know they are ill? In addition to these underlying ideas about health and illness, a number of other social factors influence whether an individual will perceive a particular disturbance and come to define it as distressing enough to warrant further attention. People react to the meaning of a symptom, not merely the symptom itself. The significance of symptoms is not self-evident; the person must actively give attention and interpretation to them. Sometimes a bodily disturbance is sufficiently acute and obvious to merit certain treatment. A person with a gaping and painful wound that is bleeding profusely is not likely to ignore the bodily disturbance. Other disturbances, however, are more open to varying interpretations, including those that make the person less likely even to notice them. Mechanic (1976) suggested that the ordinary response to such disturbances involves testing hypotheses by observing the situation over time. Part of this process involves assuming a wait-and-see stance to test such hypotheses as these: This is something minor, the body will heal itself, and further symptoms may develop to give a better idea of what this could be.

Typically, people try to normalize their symptoms. They interpret disturbances as within the range of "okay," or at least understandable. A man who was hospitalized for a heart attack stated,

> I just felt rotten and I had a pain in my chest and I thought it was indigestion. I'd been rushing in the lunch hour and lifted a heavy box and all this sort of thing, and it was, oh three quarters of an hour after the actual rush that I felt the pain. (quoted in Cowie, 1976)

Normalizing a disturbance, however, does not necessarily make it unimportant or less real. For example, a person might normalize an excruciating abdominal pain by interpreting it as a bout of recurring gallbladder problems. For this reason, the response to acute illnesses is typically different from the response to chronic illnesses. One U.S. study found that for acute problems, people focus on the symptoms. The amount of effort the individual puts into some form of treatment often depends on the severity of the symptoms themselves. For chronic problems, by contrast, people develop strategies of management over the long term. When problems flare up, the response is routinized and not necessarily directly related to the severity of symptoms of that single episode (Verbrugge and Ascione, 1987).

PAIN AND ITS PSYCHOSOCIAL DIMENSIONS

The sociocultural and psychological dimensions of pain demonstrate how profoundly greater the illness experience is compared to its mere biophysical aspect. Because the medical model does not adequately encompass these dimensions, it often fails to meet the needs of pain sufferers. Pain is a form of biofeedback essential to our survival. Occasionally someone is born without the capacity to feel pain. In one such case, the person was deformed by the age of 25 because he had severely burned his hand and suffered other injuries without feeling them. Further, the ulceration and wearing down of bodily extremities characteristic of leprosy were once thought to be symptoms of the disease, until it was discovered that they were produced by its deadening of the victim's ability to feel pain (Neal, 1978: 47–50). Although pain is an essential warning system for the body, it can also be a scourge and a terrible existential reality, a source of fear and anxiety that in some cases becomes all-consuming and overwhelming.

Pain is the symptom that people report most frequently when they see a doctor. Musculoskeletal problems (lower back pain, joint pain, or arthritis, for example) are the leading causes of disability among people in their working years; back pain is second only to respiratory problems as a reason for missing work (Osterweis et al., 1987). Approximately 7 million Americans have serious back problems (Bogin, 1982). A nationwide sample of 1,254 adults revealed that about 75 percent of Americans suffer from occasional headaches and more than 50 percent from back and muscular pain. People who reported high levels of stress also reported high levels of all kinds of pain (Schmeck, 1985). Pain seems to be a very individual and personal matter. As a physical sensation, it does not seem to be subject to sociocultural influences, yet there are many ways in which the private world of pain interacts with the sociocultural world.

The clinical reality of pain is complex, however, and involves three components: a person's actual sensation of pain; a person's tolerance *threshold* for pain; and a person's expression of pain. Pain is unique as a medical phenomenon because its measurement relies on individuals' accounts of what they are feeling as well as the doctors' observations of pain-related behavior. The doctor can observe a person's gait or flex limbs to see if pain is inhibiting movement, but all indicators are based on what the patient says or does. In other words, pain measurement depends on patients' intended or unintended expressions of the pain they are feeling. Although of limited reliability, several laboratory techniques (such as thermography and positron emission tomography, or PET, scans) attempt to measure organic signs of pain without relying on patients' reports, but these are only indirect measures of the manifestations of pain, such as the degree of sympathetic nervous system activity (Osterweis et al., 1987: 141–142). Thus, clinicians must rely heavily on the individual sufferers to describe or show what they feel.

Pain as a Biosocial Phenomenon

Pain is obviously a sensation; a cut finger produces a "simple" physical sensation. Pain generally involves more than simply a physical sensation, however, because it is imbued with meaning. For some ballet students or athletes, the pain that comes with a workout is "good pain," or a normal, acceptable consequence of well-done exercise, whereas a sharp, sudden new pain of unknown origin would signal that something fundamental has gone wrong. One doctor observed that the wounded soldiers he was treating during World War II complained of less pain and requested less pain medication than civilians who had suffered equally serious wounds. The soldiers, for whom the wounds meant leaving the battlefield and further danger of death, apparently experienced and tolerated pain differently (Beecher, 1956).

Although pain obviously involves physical sensations, it is often more than just sensations. As something that accompanies disease or a serious injury, pain takes on meaning as a form of suffering. "People in pain report suffering from pain when they feel out of control—when the pain is overwhelming, when the source of pain is unknown, when the meaning of the pain is dire or when the pain is chronic" (Cassell, 1982: 641). In short, when pain threatens one's integrity as a person and one's physical existence, it becomes suffering (Cassell, 1982). These negative meanings of pain may in turn amplify the physical sensations the person experiences (Kleinman, 1988).

In Chapter 4, we argued that the mind and the body should be seen as an interrelated whole. Placebos, for example, do not merely relieve pain "in the mind" but can also generate physical changes by stimulating the release of pain-relieving endorphins. The spinal-gate control theory of pain suggests another mind-body-society thoroughfare by proposing that activity in the nervous system affects the opening and closing of gates in the spinal cord that modulates the flow of pain messages. Most theories of pain hold that a specific pain stimulus produces an input in the form of a pain message that travels upward along the spinal cord to a pain center in the brain, where an alarm is set off. In contrast, the spinal-gate control theory argues that pain messages from the frontal cortex (a higher brain center), from the limbic system (a midbrain area that controls emotions), and from other parts of the body can affect the opening and closing of these spinal gates, and thus modify incoming pain messages (Melzack and Wall, 1983). The experience of pain is more than an incoming sensation, however, because it is affected by emotional states and higher-order cognitive mental functions (Bendelow, 1993; Osterweis et al., 1987). Indeed, pain does have important biopsychosocial and cultural dimensions (Bates, 1987; Freund, 1982).

There may be ethnic variations in the experience of pain as well (Bates, 1987). Some studies suggest that men and women may differ in pain tolerance, with the male threshold allegedly being higher. Racial differences have also been indicated; whites appear to have the highest tolerance for pain, and blacks and orientals, less (Woodrow et al., 1972). Of course, major individual variations within groups exist, and all of these measures of tolerance are based on pain expressions and the way they are interpreted. The research is by no means conclusive, but it strongly suggests that such variations exist. But are they biological, cultural, or biocultural (Bates, 1987; Overfield, 1985)?

Sociocultural Variations in Pain Expression

Pain expression refers to how a person shows and behaviorally responds to pain. Pain expression is clearly influenced by sociocultural factors. Cultures in which emotional control is valued encourage stoicism about pain. "Big boys don't cry!" reveals a cultural expectation that adult males should repress the expression of pain. The ability to control the social presentation of pain even under conditions that inflict a great deal of pain may be a sign of one's moral status (that is, one's "manhood," moral uprightness, or reliability). An elder of the Kuranko society of Sierra Leone in Africa, for example, describes the circumcision of an adolescent going through a puberty rite:

> Even when they are cutting the foreskin you must not flinch. You have to stand stone still. You must not make a sound from the mouth. Better to die than to wince or blink or cry out. (quoted in Jackson, 1983)

In the Kuranko society, control over pain expression symbolizes the ability to assume an adult male role. Painful procedures such as tatooing and scarification are endured by adolescents partly because the expression of pain is negatively sanctioned, and perhaps because the meaning and honor of the procedure affects the experience of pain itself. Many athletes endure pain that most other people would not. On the whole, however, our culture teaches that pain can and should be avoided, and we tend to medicate it extensively (Bogin, 1982; Kleinman, 1988).

Under some situations, persons suffer excruciating pain, yet must quickly learn to manage their expression in order not to threaten a group's morale or its ability to function. Medical settings are an excellent example of this. Were one to scream hysterically in a dentist's chair, what influence would this have on waiting patients, especially small children? In hospitals the treatment for severe burns, which includes scrubbing the wounds, scraping away dead tissue, and applying new dressings and medication, inflicts a lot of pain in addition to the extreme pain of the burns themselves. However, burn victims are socialized into enduring the pain by the "coaching" of staff as well as of other patients who have been through similar experiences (Fagerhaugh and Strauss, 1977).

People from varying cultural backgrounds present their symptoms, including pain, in different ways (Good and Good, 1981). Zborowski's (1952, 1969) study of hospitalized male patients suffering from back pain and spinal lesions found that Jewish and Italian men were particularly vocal and disturbed about their pain. Whereas Italians were concerned with immediate pain relief, the Jews worried about the pain's implications for their future. Anglo-American patients wanted the pain taken care of but were not as vocal in their pain expression. Irish patients were the most stoic and likely to deny pain. Zborowski's work has been criticized for its limited sample, broad and overly stereotypic generalizations about ethnic groups, and the fact that subjects were studied only in a medical setting. Yet Zborowski's study pointed the way to understanding cultural variations in the expression and possibly also the experience of pain. Zola (1983) found ethnic differences in how people showed and talked about their symptoms. Italians, for instance, described their symptoms more expansively and emotionally. Another study found ethnic differences in responses to pain from Asians, Afro-West Indians, and Anglo-Saxons (Thomas and Rose, 1991).

Generalizations about different groups' responses to pain must be used cautiously and not become the basis of stereotyping. Although we may have typical ways of expressing ourselves, social situational factors can affect how we will express ourselves. Expressing pain must not be confused with *feeling* pain; for instance, acting stoic does not mean that one feels no pain. Even if people from various social categories (social classes, gender, or cultures) do present their pain differently, social and cultural factors also influence how observers interpret their pain expressions.

Responses to other people's pain expressions are influenced by cultural assumptions about what those expressions mean. An African woman's response to stomach pain due to infection may seem exaggerated to a Western-trained male doctor, but the woman's response is reasonable given her fears about infertility, a source of shame in her culture. The same woman, however, may handle the pain of childbirth without complaints (Susser et al., 1985: 136). One study of burn patients found Samoans (in contrast to, for instance, American burn patients) were calmer, more "stoic," accepting of the situation, and less complaining (Ablon, 1986). Zborowski (1952, 1969) and Zola (1966, 1983) found that because Italians expressed their pain so dramatically, non-Italian doctors tended to question the credibility of their Italian patients, interpreting their problems as "psychiatric." Such differences in the social and cultural backgrounds of doctor and patient can thus lead to very different interpretations of pain. One study reported the following:

> [T]he pain of women was treated later and less directly than the pain of men. Women suffered longer before being referred to the Pain Unit. They were less often treated with procedures specifically intended to cure the pain. The men in a shorter period since pain onset were operated upon twice as often as the women. Paradoxically, women reported twice as many surgical procedures unrelated to pain. (Lack, 1982: 62)

Women were also given more minor tranquilizers, antidepressants, and analgesics, and fewer narcotics than men. This difference implies that the doctors took women's pain less seriously, interpreting it as of psychological origin; however, they accepted men's pain as "real" and prescribed painkillers. Was this difference due to variation in how men and women showed pain, or because of how male doctors interpreted women's presentations of pain? Other studies (such as Bendelow, 1993) suggest that health workers were more likely to believe that women's pain was psychogenic.

The visibility of the source of pain is another significant factor in determining how seriously people take another's pain symptoms. It is often hard to see the cause of pain. Patients with chronic back pain may, for example, learn to conceal signs of pain, such as masking a limp caused by sciatic nerve pain. Because they look healthy, their pain may not always be taken seriously (Fagerhaugh and Strauss, 1977). By contrast, a bloody gash—even on a part of the body with relatively little nerve sensitivity—is taken seriously as a source of pain.

Chronic Pain

Approximately 17 percent of U.S. adults have suffered chronic pain lasting at least six months (Kolata, 1994). By definition, chronic pain is recurring or ongoing. It is not simply continuous but is experienced qualitatively differently from acute pain episodes. Because it is ongoing, chronic pain often has profound implications for a sufferer's life and very identity. People with chronic pain face continuing problems in symptom management (Strauss, 1975). How does one deal with pain and live life as normally as possible? People in chronic pain may not be able to tolerate regular employment, to follow schedules, or even to meet the demands of home life. Chronic pain is not always constant, but is often intermittent and unpredictable, flaring up unexpectedly (Bogin, 1982). Each day sufferers must manage a host of problems associated with activities that are taken for granted by others: They must pace their activities in order to tolerate or not aggravate the pain, and they must balance the undesired side effects of medication against the benefits of pain reduction.

Chronic pain also poses basic problems for the sufferer's sense of self. One person explained,

Our personalities have been shaken to the core, and what we most counted on—our close relationships, our marriages, our jobs—may well have fallen by the wayside. Our whole sense of life has radically changed since pain became a part of it, yet no one seems to understand our listlessness, our loss of hope, our lack of optimism. Other people can't see our pain, so how can they imagine what it's done to us? Only someone who has lived with chronic pain knows how insidious the process is. (Bogin, 1982: 4)

Acute pain goes away and does not become an ongoing, major focus of everyday existence. Chronic pain, by contrast, is a "somatic reminder that things are not right and may never be right. This reminder, phenomenally situated in one's own body, is inescapable" (Hilbert, 1984: 370; see also Good, 1994). The body as subjectively experienced is transformed into an object with pain. One "moment one is one's body, the next one has a body" (Bergsma, 1982: 111). Chronic pain demands constant attention and can become all-consuming. Indeed, it can alter one's consciousness of the world, changing one's sense of time and state of alertness. Chronic pain alters one's relationship with one's own body and bodily experience; "it" cannot be trusted and is experienced as acting unpredictably (Good, 1994). The phenomenon of pain highlights how inextricably mind and body are meshed; it is simultaneously sensation and emotion (Jackson, 1994; see also Bendelow and Williams, 1995).

People in chronic pain often face invalidating responses from others, particularly if their pain is not believable or if an organic basis of pain is not apparent. One sufferer stated that she had considered unneeded surgery so she would have a scar to show (Hilbert, 1984: 373). Another believed his several surgical treatments had worsened the pain but at least gave him scars that symbolized, to himself and others, the physical reality of the pain (Kleinman, 1988: 68). Core values in American culture may contribute to the invalidation experienced by chronic pain sufferers. Some anthropologists (Good et al., 1992: 205), writing on chronic pain, observed,

A number of our subjects complained of something akin to a North American *tyranny of health*. The dominant images in the popular culture extol physical vitality and deny anything short of robust health. Blemishes, illnesses that cannot be rapidly cured, and especially grave infirmities that suggest disability or death are banished from everyday life. A strong will, we are told, can influence the body, so infirmity is often associated with a lack of individual strength. The chronically ill feel great discomfit in this ethos. They are discredited as burdensome, anomalous, and, in some unspoken but definite way, responsible for their condition. Suffering is accorded no positive value. To bear distress and pain is not the same thing in the post-Reagan era as it was in Colonial, Jacksonian or Victorian America. It now carries no moral virtue. Quite the contrary, in the society of instant crises and quick remedies, of risk management for the unexpected, the very idea of *chronicity*, of predictable, serious long-term trouble, is unacceptable. Thus, the chronically ill—especially those with conditions that are at the borderline of respectability—feel that they are culturally illegitimate, unaccepted in the wider society.

Invalidating responses often come from doctors (Hilbert, 1984: 368), particularly when they are frustrated by their inability to treat effectively or find an organic cause for the pain (Bogin, 1982; Kleinman, 1988). Chronic pain challenges doctors' sense of competence and control. More significantly, chronic pain raises issues about mind-body relationships that threaten sharp distinctions between "real" versus "imagined," "psychological" versus "physical" pain (Good, 1994; Williams and Bendelow, 1996). "Physical" experiences of pain may be influenced by "perturbed" neuroendocrinological rhythms (Weiner, 1992). Physicians are unlikely to look for those factors and, given their assumptions about the nature of pain, would not "notice" them.

Invalidation of the reality of the experience of pain is particularly disconcerting because sufferers are being told that what their bodies are telling them is not real. Because our bodies and physical sensations are primary sources of our sense of reality, this invalidation is especially devastating (Kleinman, 1992; Ware, 1992; see also Ewan et al., 1991; Hilbert, 1984; Kotarba, 1977). Chronic pain sufferers find themselves in a bind. On the one hand, concealing signs of their pain reduces the likelihood that their claims to being in pain will be taken seriously. On the other hand, persons who regularly display and dramatize their pain risk wearing down other people's sympathy, placing a strain on their social support networks.

Somatization

In all cultures, the body serves as a means of expressing and communicating cultural, as well as personal, messages. No tidy distinction exists, however, between physical and emotional pain (see Jackson, 1994); a person in pain or distress may be simultaneously expressing and experiencing *both* physical and emotional pain inseparably. Like language, pain and illness are *idioms* in which people sometimes "encode" their distress (Good, 1977; see also Blair, 1993). For example, a young adult's parents may be stifling her autonomy, but to leave home means to alienate them and to face an uncertain, perhaps hostile, existence away from home. Pain may be both a way of delaying the difficult decision and a means of communicating something about the conflicts she is experiencing (Kleinman, 1988).

Somatization is "the communication of personal and interpersonal problems in a physical idiom of distress and a pattern of behavior that emphasizes seeking of medical help" (Kleinman, 1988: 57). To understand pain as "somatization" does not mean it is inauthentic. Pain may be physical in origin but sustained and amplified by sociopsychological factors. Social distress may create the physiological changes that amplify existing pain or create an experience of pain (Kleinman, 1988). In her study of Mexican women's sickness and pain, Finkler (1994) refers to the damaging effects of women's distresses, social situation (especially gender roles), and cultural beliefs as "life's lesions." Kleinman (1995) reminds us that somatized pain, as well as psychological suffering such as depression, may be the traumatic products of political violence such as war or repression and oppressive cultural forms, for example, abusive family structures.

Each person's particular idiom of distress is drawn from a cultural repertoire. For example, in Iran "heart distress" is a meaningful expression linking an entire set of social concerns: infertility, attractiveness, sexual intercourse, pollution, and old age. Thus, when an Iranian complains of a "pressed heart," that complaint must be understood in terms of its cultural meanings (Good, 1977; cf. Guarnaccia and Farias, 1988). Similarly, just as there are class and gender differences in how people encode their meanings in language, so too does somatized distress differ according to social class and gender (Blair, 1993).

Even when it has sociopsychological sources, however, pain is not simply "in the mind" but also is a bodily phenomenon.[1] Labeling an illness "psychosomatic" or "psychogenic" delegitimates people's real suffering. Because their pain is expressed in body idioms, it is too easily medicalized and, thereby, distorted or trivialized. For example, to label the suffering of a Salvadoran refugee as posttraumatic stress disorder is to isolate and euphemize the consequences of pervasive political violence (Kleinman, 1992, 1995; Kleinman and Kleinman, 1991).

CHRONIC ILLNESS AND DISABILITY: THE POLITICS OF IMPAIRMENT

Because chronic illness and disability more seriously disturb the person's essential relationships and very sense of self, they result in a very different illness experience than acute illness. An **impairment** is the loss of some physiological or anatomical function, whereas a **disability** is the consequence of such an impairment, such as the inability to walk, climb stairs, or travel (Barton, 1996; Oliver, 1996). Many people with disabilities object to the term *handicap* because of its negative connotations, especially when it implies that the whole person is handicapped. We therefore speak of persons with disabilities (Zola, 1993).

Although some people with chronic illnesses are impaired and disabled, chronic illness does not inevitably lead to disability. For example, diabetes may interfere only minimally with some people's functioning. Some people with an impairment and a disability (for example, from an automobile accident) are not sick and may object to being defined as such. The sick role (described in Chapter 6) temporarily exempts people from normal activities; however, people with disabilities who are treated as though they were sick may find themselves prevented from participating in normal social activities and placed in a state of perpetual depen-

---

[1] Although pain always involves sociopsychological aspects, this should not detract from the reality of the physical aspects. A doctor who cannot discern organic sources of pain should not assume there are none; biomechanical causes, for example, that were not detectible by earlier technologies (for example, X-rays or myelograms) may appear through newer imaging technologies. Is it possible that painful social experiences at one point in one's life (for example, sexual abuse in childhood) may alter a person's physiological reactivity to pain later in life? Can socially distressing life circumstances increase pain sensitivity or amplify the painful effects of physical trauma? Perspectives such as Kleinman's (1988) that stress the biopsychosocial aspects of pain recognize the relationship between social life and pain, including the subjective reality of somatized pain.

dence. Nonetheless, many people with chronic illness have impairment and share problems with those who have experienced a loss of functioning at birth or due to a trauma such as an accident.

Impairment is relatively verifiable in "objective" medical terms.[2] Disability, however, is not as easily defined separate from the social and cultural context of impairment. Disability is not a bodily or mental attribute but results from the interaction between person and environment: "Disability is something imposed on top of our impairments by the way we are unnecessarily isolated and excluded from full participation in society" (Oliver, 1996:22). In a small Egyptian village, for example, trachoma (an infection that affects the eyelids) is widespread, but the "Western" standards of blindness do not apply to those who are afflicted. Instead, the social and cultural arrangements make it possible for many villagers with severely impaired vision to function without disability:

> Most visually impaired adults are illiterate, so they do not need signs to read. There are no street signs or house numbers to read in the hamlet. The structure of the village changes very slowly. If a new house is built every five years the visually impaired can learn to find their way around it. . . . Plowing, sowing seed and harvesting ripe produce do not require much vision. If there is some small task they are unable to do, their extended family does it for them. Thus, they do not perceive themselves as disabled. (quoted in Cockburn, 1988: 13)

Until the 1940s, a significant proportion of the inhabitants of Martha's Vineyard in Massachusetts was deaf. The whole community knew sign language, and hearing people used it even among themselves. Sign language became a natural and ordinary form of communication. People with impaired hearing worked, married, and were not thought of as separate, significantly different, or as "special" (Whyte and Ingstad, 1995).

Thus, whether an "objective" impairment becomes a disability depends on the environment, the expected daily activities, and the attitudes of others. A disability is not just the result of the limitations of a person's sensory, motor, cognitive, or other capabilities, but a "function of the interaction between the individual's condition and the environment, both physical and attitudinal—in which they live" (Gartner and Joe, 1987: 1). Impairment is universal, found among people in all societies; however, social and cultural responses and the "design" of social environments vary (Oliver, 1996). The sociological focus, therefore, is not on disabled people but on disabling attitudes and environments.

One definition used in the United States considers disability to be "an inability to engage in gainful employment"; more broadly, it refers to a reduction of activity, a "restricted activity day" (Mausner and Bahn, 1985: 113). Estimates of the number of Americans with disabilities range from about 35 to 43 million people (National Institute on Disability and Rehabilitation Research, 1993; Shapiro, 1993: 6–7). Fifteen percent (37.7 million people) of the noninstitutional-

---

[2]Even in this respect, there is still the question of what is a "normal" body.

ized U.S. population have a limitation of activity caused by chronic illness or impairment. The most prevalent sources of activity limitation are musculoskeletal impairments that affect walking, climbing, and lifting (La Plante, 1996). Nonwhite disabled people outnumber white disabled people by a ratio of about two to one (National Institute on Disability and Rehabilitation Research, 1986). These figures suggest that disabilities are not as uncommon as many believe. Our perceptions are based partly on the fact that Western society, especially the United States, tends to deny and to segregate disability, old age, and death. Furthermore, the likelihood of having a disability is socially distributed, as are individual resources for coping with disability.

Categorizing people as disabled has implications for social policy, as Zola (1982: 242) pointed out:

> By trying to find strict measures of disability or focusing on "severe," "visible" handicaps we draw dividing lines and make distinctions where matters are very blurry and constantly changing. By agreeing that there are 20 million disabled or 36 million, or even that half the population are in some way affected by disability, we delude ourselves into thinking there is some finite, no matter how large, number of people. . . . Any person reading the words on this page is at best momentarily able-bodied. But nearly everyone reading them will, at some point, suffer from one or more chronic diseases and be disabled, temporarily or permanently, for a significant part of their lives.

Being disabled is a "normal" condition of humanity, and categorizing people by disability status can create misleading distinctions. Such definitions are social and political constructions, as illustrated by the fact that the boundaries are historically shifting and cross-culturally variable (Brzuzy, 1997; Osterweis et al., 1987).

Chronic illness is, by definition, ongoing, recurrent, and often degenerative. Conrad (1987) suggested different types of chronic illnesses, each with its own social implications: "lived-with" illness, such as asthma and diabetes; "mortal" illness, such as some cancers; and "at risk" illnesses, which include inherited, "environmental," or "personal" behavior risks. Chronic illnesses and pain pose special problems that stable, predictable conditions such as trauma-induced paraplegia do not (Pinder, 1995). Living with chronic illness requires coping with the very uncertainty of the course of the illness itself (Royer, 1995). People with disabilities or chronic illnesses in our society face a number of common problems regarding the social organization of their environments, the attitudes of others, and their sense of self.

Disability, Chronic Illness, and the Social Organization of Space and Time

The organization of the spaces in which people move and the time arrangements of their practices are related to the quality of life and health. Building codes, government ordinances, financial considerations, and many other factors structure the qualities of the buildings in which we work, live, and play (Hahn, 1988). Social and political considerations influence the quality and accessibility of transportation. Zola (1982: 208) described the inhospitable nature of many environments for a person wearing a leg brace:

> Chairs without arms to push myself up from; unpadded seats which all too quickly produce sores; showers and toilets without handrails to maintain my balance; surfaces too slippery to walk on; staircases without bannisters to help me hoist myself; buildings without ramps, making ascent exhausting if not dangerous; every curbstone a precipice; car, plane, and theatre seats too cramped for my braced leg; and trousers too narrow for my leg brace to pass through. With such trivia is my life plagued. Even though I am relatively well off, mobility is a daily challenge.

Imagine trying to walk about in a physical space designed only for those in wheelchairs. The doors would be too low, the floors would be too slippery for walking, and no chairs would be provided for sitting. People with physical impairments simply have more specialized or individual physical needs than those without impairments. The failure of social environments to account for individual rhythms and patterns for comfortable movement contributes to problems in health and the quality of life for all people, but to a greater degree for people with impairments.

Although technological advances have made it possible for many people with disabilities to survive and potentially to function, such advances have not generally been applied to the design of public, work, and living environments. We live increasingly in human-made, artificial spaces that are not currently adapted to a wide spectrum of bodies but could be so modified. In recent years, however, there has been a slight shift toward creating more environments of "universal" or "transgenerational" design, geared to the needs of persons with some physical impairment (Shapiro, 1993). Although no environment can accommodate everyone's needs, "universally" designed spaces are intended for use by the widest possible range of bodies. One example is a park built for access both by able-bodied and disabled people; its tennis, pool, and special swings are designed for use by people in wheelchairs (Brown, 1988).

Much research on chronic illness and impairment focuses on malingering and whether government financial benefits motivate people not to work; instead, however, research should examine how work and economic conditions themselves discourage the chronically ill from maintaining their jobs. During World War II, people with disabilities who had been defined as unemployable were placed into full-time employment. The need for labor, *not* the impairment, defined employability (Oliver, 1996). For all workers during that time, there were lower rates of absenteeism, work-related accidents, and turnover, and higher rates of production. After the war, workers with disabilities were replaced by returning "able-bodied" veterans (Struck, 1981: 26). The nature of the job, such as the pace of work and the physical design of the workplace, is an important determinant of work disability (Osterweis et al., 1987; Yelin, 1986). Shorter, more flexible work schedules, opportunities for breaks, and general social-temporal arrangements that accommodate slower or differently paced rhythms would allow individuals with impairments to function more effectively.

People with chronic impairments do not usually challenge disabling time limitations and pressures. They do not generally question the arrangements of work and living spaces in which they must function; rather, they typically assume such arrangements to be natural and given (Charmaz, 1983). People come to believe that their inability to squeeze their bodies and rhythms of movement into inadequate social-spatial arrangements are signs of their *personal* inadequacy. Disabling environments and attitudes thus contribute to a loss of sense of self and to suffering among those who have chronic physical impairments (Charmaz, 1991).

Disabling Attitudes and Sense of Self

Our society often places people who violate somatic norms into institutions or segregates them behind the scenes of everyday life (Baird, 1992). One woman with multiple sclerosis commented,

> I once asked a local advertiser why he didn't include disabled people in his spots. His response seemed direct enough. "We don't want to give people the idea that our product is just for the handicapped," he said. . . . If you saw my blind niece ordering a Coke, would you switch to Pepsi lest you be struck sightless? No, I think the advertiser's excuse masked a deeper and more anxious rationale: to depict disabled people in the ordinary activities of daily life is to admit that there is something ordinary about disability itself, that it might enter anybody's life. If it is effaced completely or at least isolated as a separate "problem," so that it remains at a safe distance from other human issues, then the viewer won't feel threatened by her or his own physical vulnerability. (Mairs, 1987: C2)

The suffering created by such discrediting attitudes is not just a matter of the personal attitudes themselves but also the social conditions that engender them (Charmaz, 1983).

The stigmatizing opinions of others have a strong impact on one's sense of self. A stigma is a deeply discrediting attribute that, when visible, can brand a person as less than human, as pitiable, horrible, and publicly discreditable. The degree to which an attribute is stigmatizing depends on its sociohistorical context and the status of the person who possesses such an attribute:

> Conjure in your mind a military man with an eye patch. Is there not something romantic and heroic about the injury? Doesn't it suggest a dark and complex past, a will of uncommon strength, perhaps a capability for just enough brutality to add a trace of virile unpredictability to the man? Now replace the image of the mysterious man who wears an eye patch with the image of a 7-year-old girl who wears one. For most people, something strange happens. The romance and mystery disappear; what we see is a handicapped child. There is something sad and even pitiful about her; we fear for her future and worry about her present. We think: this poor kid is going to have a hard time growing up and making it in this world. (Gliedman and Roth, 1980: 29)

In all societies, certain deviations from somatic norms are considered stigmatizing, but there are no inherently stigmatizing attributes. Rather, stigma is a social construction that depends on person and context (Susman, 1993).

In our society, those with "severe" impairments are sometimes viewed as "visually repulsive; helpless; pathetic; dependent; too independent; plucky, brave and courageous; bitter with chips on our shoulders; evil (the 'twisted mind in a twisted body'); mentally retarded; endowed with mystical powers and much else" (Sutherland, 1981: 58). People with disabilities may be targets of hate crimes. One woman recalled a man who grabbed her cane, threw it down an escalator, spat on her, and told her "move, blind lady . . . you people belong in concentration camps" (cited in Wolfe, 1995). Given the cultural obsession with health and bodily control, people with disabilities may be experienced as threatening (Norden, 1995; Susman, 1993). Some of these attitudes are changing. The mass media, however, still perpetuate stereotypes that associate disability with evil and criminality (recall Frankenstein's hunchbacked assistant), a loss of self-control, an attempt to compensate for their impairment, and a tendency to either be asexual or deviantly sexual (Longmore, 1987; Shakespeare, 1996).

Media images project some heroic role models: the blind skier, the one-legged pitcher who made it to the major leagues, and Helen Keller and her many achievements.[3] These examples show people's ability to transcend the most limiting of conditions, and in that respect they are inspiring. They may, however, imply another message: "that if a Franklin Delano Roosevelt and a Wilma Rudolph could *overcome* their handicap, so could and should all the disabled. And if we fail, it is our problem, our personality, our weakness" (Zola, 1982: 204–205). Many media success stories similarly communicate a message in tune with the American ethos of rugged individualism and responsibility for oneself. This imagery, however, deflects from an understanding of the mundane problems faced by those with impairments and the many barriers that most humans simply cannot overcome.

Sexual expression is an important source of pleasure, tension release, and sense of self. Until recently, however, the prevalent attitude, even among many professionals working with people with disabilities, was to deny or avoid recognition of their sexuality (Lonsdale, 1990). The deviation of persons with disabilities from somatic norms often arouses an aesthetic anxiety in others, particularly in Western societies, which put a high premium on "supernormal standards of bodily perfection" (Baird, 1992; Hahn, 1994). Our sexual fantasies are saturated with images from advertising and the entertainment world. Media-driven standards of sexual attractiveness, particularly for women, result in even greater disadvantages for people whose bodies deviate from the ideal (Sutherland, 1987: 27). Zola (1982) described a Swedish experiment in which counselors acted as sex surrogates with their clients who had disabilities; the experiment was stopped, however, because the counselors began to enjoy their contacts. The fear that "deviant" bodies may

---

[3]Very few people know that Helen Keller was displayed for a while as an exhibit, like the Elephant Man, in a vaudeville show.

be "deviant" only in the eyes of the beholder made this experiment a threat. Some societies have begun to accept sexual pleasure as a *right* for the disabled. In 1992, a government agency in the Netherlands ruled that a municipality must pay a person with a disability a monthly stipend to cover the services of a sex surrogate (Stalk, 1992).

People with disabilities also face special problems in the management of such emotions as anger. The impairment itself may inhibit anger expression. Being physically weak or on crutches may make the direct, motoric, dramatic expression of emotions difficult. Furthermore, disabling attitudes and environments force people into a state of dependency beyond the biological consequences of their impairments.

People with disabilities are also socialized out of their anger. They are expected to be grateful for what help they receive and cannot "afford" the luxury of overt anger expression for fear of risking the alienation of the people on whom they depend (Zola, 1982). Like fat people, people with disabilities are expected to tolerate their situation quietly and to be cheerful and jolly (Charmaz, 1991: 201). When people regularly and vocally respond to frustrating or disempowering conditions, they further risk having their anger treated as a by-product of their impairment rather than as an appropriate response to their social environment or living conditions. The docudrama "Captives of Care" depicted a resident of an institution who was angry with the staff for the arbitrary limits imposed by institutional life. In one encounter, he lashed out at a nurse for invading his privacy. The nurse did not understand his reaction, and a colleague explained to her that "that's the way he is because he is twisted." Because his physical impairment was thus seen as explaining his behavior, his protest over institutional conditions was invalidated.

The constant emotional work involved in managing anger often results in repressing the anger, and turning it inward and against oneself. Zola (1982: 222) argued that depression among those with disabilities is partly due to constraints against getting angry. This depression is often viewed as the individual's problem rather than a normal response to social pressures. Turning socially provoked anger inward is thus socially functional, but individually repressive. Another destructive emotional response to lack of privacy and autonomy, to stigma, and to the "threatened integrity of the body" is dissociating and "switching off" oneself from one's body (Shakespeare, 1996: 207).

One strategy for avoiding the potential stigma of some disabilities is *passing*, or concealing a discrediting social status or stigmatizing attributes. In some cases, disclosure or "selective telling" can act as a means of forestalling a negative reaction from another person. For example, people with epilepsy weigh the stigma potential of their condition against positive consequences (for example, having someone to help in case of seizure) of revealing the fact (Schneider and Conrad, 1983). Concealing one's condition is sometimes a way of avoiding stigmatizing attitudes. *Because* people with impaired vision may consider a cane to be a stigma symbol or an overt sign of disability, they may prefer a less obtrusive folding cane, even though it may not be as effective an instrument. Charmaz (1991: 151) observes, "An appliance that simplifies logistical problems and arduous tasks can confound self-image and social identity. Hence some ill people prefer to stay at home or risk heart failure, a fall or exhaustion rather than use a walker, wheelchair or a handicapped parking space." The refusal to use highly visible prosthetic devices, however, is not necessarily irrational, but may be based on well-founded fears of being viewed as a "cripple."

In Chapter 4, we suggested that assaults on one's sense of self may have physical consequences, including an impact on the immune system. Certain chronic illnesses, such as herpes, epilepsy, and AIDS, carry a load of powerful negative meanings that define afflicted persons and our perception of them. In addition to the fear of death, disfiguring treatments, and the usual threats to one's self-concept that accompany any debilitating disease, sufferers of AIDS are also faced with highly stigmatizing responses from others. It has evoked irrational fears of contagion, not unlike leprosy did in the past. Because of its association with homosexuality, it has also evoked intense homophobic reactions. People with AIDS have been dismissed from their jobs, evicted from their homes, rejected, and isolated by friends and relatives. Even the family, friends, or colleagues of victims may become stigmatized by association, a pattern that Goffman calls "courtesy stigma" (Goffman, 1963). AIDS victims may also be ostracized by medical personnel whose fears override their knowledge about contagion. Studies indicate that the risk of spreading infection from AIDS patients to health care workers is minute (Heyward and Curran, 1988), yet one patient with AIDS commented,

> The nurses are scared of me; the doctors wear masks and sometimes gloves. Even the priest doesn't seem too anxious to shake my hand. What the hell is this? I'm not a leper. Do they want to lock me up and shoot me? I've got no family, no friends. Where do I go? What do I do? God, this is horrible! Is He punishing me? The only thing I got going for me is that I'm not dying—at least, not yet. (quoted in Kleinman, 1988: 163)

Such attitudes contribute to distress and unneeded suffering; they may also have biophysical consequences. Further research is needed on the impact of the social stress produced by the stigma of AIDS in further assaulting a person's immune system (Kaplan et al., 1987).

Disability as a Minority Status

People with disabilities constitute a minority group because of their relative powerlessness and their identifiability, both of which promote discrimination and stigmatization. Unlike other minority groups, however, the disabled do not usually share a subculture, a geographical location, or history. Their cultural status is ambiguous: They are "betwixt and between," neither healthy nor sick. Murphy (1987) argues that because such ambiguity is threatening to normals, the isolation and discrimination faced by those with disabilities may come from their anomalous and ambiguous status in our system of cultural classification. Nevertheless, like other minority groups, such as women, blacks, Hispanics, and gays, they do experience similar problems of being powerless objects of stereotypes and discrimination.

A Harris poll in 1984 showed that 74 percent of persons with disabilities do identify with one another, and that 45 percent consider themselves a minority in the same sense as blacks or Hispanics (Fine and Asch, 1988). Some people who are deaf, for instance, are resistant to "technical fixes," such as cochlear implants (in which the inner ear is wired to a receiver), precisely because the technology denies people who are deaf their identity in a deaf culture, such as participating in the use of sign language (Barringer, 1993). Some studies suggest that physically "normal" people view those with impairments, such as blindness, as inferior to members of ethnic minority groups (Susser et al., 1985). One study found a hierarchy of attitudes toward persons with disabilities, with those who were blind ranked below those with cerebral palsy, total paralysis, or epilepsy. Other studies show that blacks as a group were ranked close to the blind in terms of social preference. Such biases develop as early as the age of 6 (Gliedman, 1979).

Perhaps the most important feature that people with disabilities share with racial and ethnic minorities is the tendency for others to attribute their perceived inferiority and "differentness" to biological factors alone, rather than to social conditions. Disabling attitudes and environments create a self-fulfilling prophecy that legitimates individualistic and biologistic assumptions about the disabled. Because such environments and attitudes exclude people with disabilities from the community and from workplaces, the nondisabled conclude that this exclusion is evidence that the disabled cannot function in such settings. "Like racists, able-bodied people often confuse the results of social oppression with the effects of biology" (Gliedman and Roth, 1980: 28).

Disability Civil Rights Movements: Recapturing Self and Access

Stimulated by the 1960s civil rights movement, people with disabilities became politically active, working from the assumption that they constituted a minority group deprived of their civil rights. Shifting their focus from individual problems to attacking unfair social structures, they began demanding equal access to housing, jobs, transportation, and health care. The activism of the 1960s had widened the definition of political issues to include the personal, everyday problems faced by various groups. Disability rights activists realized that definitions of disability were sociopolitical (Scotch, 1988).

Groups like the Center for Independent Living in California and Disabled in Action on the East Coast, staffed largely by people with disabilities, sought to define issues such as access not as charity or welfare, but as basic civil rights. Many workers in human services, however, still view people with disabilities as clients with problems to be treated. By contrast, the disability rights movement emphasizes the involvement of citizens with disabilities in shaping their own fate (Shapiro, 1993).

Such activist movements remind us that socially created environments are designed for a narrow range of bodies. Humanly authored landscapes, cities, workplaces, and transport systems favor healthy young bodies. Furthermore, the disability rights movement has highlighted the pervasiveness of disabling attitudes in our society, calling attention to the social, political, and economic contexts of such attitudes and environments (Oliver, 1996).

In the United States, the disability rights movement contributed to the passage of the 1990 Americans with Disabilities Act, the first comprehensive civil rights legislation for people with disabilities (Shapiro, 1993). This law prohibits employers from discriminating against people with disabilities; it requires businesses to provide reasonable accommodations to workers and customers with disabilities, and it orders accessible public transportation and other reasonable public accommodations for persons with disabilities. The United Kingdom passed similar legislation, the Disability Discrimination Act (Brindle, 1996).[4] It is difficult to judge the efficacy of such legislation (Oliver, 1996). At very least, they provide legal foundation for civil rights of people with disabilities.

SUMMARY

Illness is the complex set of ways in which the sick person (and family and friends) perceive, manage, and respond to symptoms and disability. The experience of illness reminds us of our limitations, dependencies, and ultimate mortality. Although ordinary, even minor illnesses disrupt one's life, certain illness experiences are likely to have a damaging effect on the sick person's identity and sense of self. Certain disabling conditions and chronic pain and illnesses are especially problematic, because they involve a sense of loss; they are overwhelming, unpredictable, and uncontrollable; and they produce social marginality for the sufferer. The chronic illness experience is not limited to the sick person but often involves family and friends as well. People interpret their illness, giving it meaning, form, and order. These meanings in turn shape their perception of their symptoms and pain.

Disability and pain are important features of the illness experience, especially chronic illness. Social and political factors are involved in both the definition and management of disability. Disabling social and physical environments and attitudes are responsible for many of the problems suffered by persons with chronic illness or impairments. Similarly, both the experience and expression of pain are linked with sociocultural factors. Suffering is often increased, however, when others invalidate the reality of the pain. Because the majority of serious illnesses today are chronic, in contrast to the acute illnesses predominant in the recent past, we need to appreciate their powerful impact on the sufferer's daily life, social relationships, and very self.

---

[4] Two perspectives on disability—the "minority group" model in the United States (Hahn, 1994) and the "social model" in the United Kingdom (Barton, 1996; Oliver, 1996)—emphasize addressing disabling attitudes and barriers that come from the social organization of space, time, and practices, in contrast to the biomedical and clinical perspectives which emphasize treating the individual.

RECOMMENDED READINGS

Articles

LINDA ALEXANDER, "Illness maintenance and the new American sick role," pp. 351–367 in N. J. Chrisman and T. W. Maretzki, eds., *Clinically Applied Anthropology*. Dordrecht, Netherlands: D. Reidel, 1982.

KATHY CHARMAZ, "Loss of self: A fundamental form of suffering of the chronically ill." *Sociology of Health and Illness* 4, 1983: 167–182.

SHARON R. KAUFMAN, "Toward a phenomenology of boundaries in medicine: Chronic illness experience in the case of stroke." *Medical Anthropology Quarterly* 2(4), 1988: 338–354.

Books

SHIZUKO FAGERHAUGH and ANSELM STRAUSS, *Politics of Pain Management: Staff-Patient Interaction*. Reading, MA: Addison-Wesley, 1977. A study of the social organizational contexts—especially power relations—for the perception of pain and pain management.

ARTHUR KLEINMAN, *The Illness Narratives: Suffering, Healing, and the Human Condition*. New York: Basic, 1988. A sensitive witness to narratives of illness experiences, especially those that are chronic and disabling or disfiguring.

ROBERT F. MURPHY, *The Body Silent*. New York: Henry Holt, 1987. An anthropologist's account of his increasing paralysis due to a spinal tumor and his personal perspective on the sociocultural aspects of disability.

JOSEPH W. SCHNEIDER and PETER CONRAD, *Having Epilepsy: The Experience and Control of Illness*. Philadelphia: Temple University Press, 1983. A sociological look at epilepsy, and the management of its symptoms and stigma.

JOSEPH P. SHAPIRO, *No Pity: People with Disabilities Forging a New Civil Rights Movement*. New York: Random House, 1993. A very readable account of the disability rights movement in the United States.

IRVING K. ZOLA, *Missing Pieces: A Chronicle of Living with a Disability*. Philadelphia: Temple University Press, 1982. An excellent combination of sociological insights and Zola's personal experiences with disability, as well as his participant-observations as a guest in a Dutch village adapted to the needs of people with disabilities.

SEEKING HEALTH AND HELP

CHAPTER OUTLINE

How do people conclude that they are ill, and what actions do they choose to take in response? There are a number of implicit and often utterly incorrect assumptions about how people seek health and respond to health problems. Probably each one of us can think of instances in our own experiences when these assumptions did not hold:

> People know for sure when they are ill.
>
> As soon as they realize they are ill, they seek competent help, specifically a medical doctor (or dentist, psychiatrist, or other appropriate professional).
>
> When they consult the professional, they give an explanation of the problem that is as medically correct as possible.
>
> The doctor understands what they are saying about their problem.
>
> The doctor's explanation of the problem makes sense to them.
>
> When the doctor prescribes therapeutic action, they follow that advice carefully until it takes effect or until the doctor changes the instructions.
>
> People know for sure when they are well, and they are satisfied when this state of health is restored.

The fact that these assumptions are rarely accurate is a source of considerable tension and outright dissatisfaction on the part of both medical professionals and patients. One key reason for this tension is the enormous, and generally unrecognized, chasm between the medical models of illness and the conceptions used by laypersons in understanding and making decisions about their own health and illnesses. This gap is built into the structure of professionalized medicine, where—by definition—the layperson does not share the specialized body of knowledge used by the professional (Freidson, 1970: 278–279).

Most modern societies tend to treat professional interpretations as vastly superior to lay understandings. Medical professionals tend to demean lay conceptions, often labeling them as superstition, ignorance, foolishness, or instances of persons being unwilling to take proper care of themselves. From this perspective, the doctor is viewed as the expert whose rational pronouncements are the result of legitimate authority, whereas the patient should be passive and obedient, deferring all judgment to the expert.

By contrast, West (1979: 162) argues that attention should be directed to "the person as a conscious, reflective actor engaged in the process of making sense of various kinds of body changes within the framework of his own 'lay' knowledge." Studies of decision making in health matters show that most laypersons *do* make conscious choices that are rational, within the framework of their understanding of the illness (Locker, 1981). We examine the vast range of interpretations and decisions the ordinary person makes in seeking health.

Contrary to the common misconception, health seeking is largely *not* a process of getting professional medical care. Most health-enhancing or preventive measures are nonmedical, and only a very small portion of ailments are ever brought to a physician's attention. As Zola (1983: 111) commented,

> Virtually every day of our lives we are subject to a vast array of bodily discomforts. Only an infinitesimal amount of these get to a physician. Neither the mere

presence nor the obviousness of symptoms seems to differentiate those episodes which do and do not get professional treatment.

This observation is corroborated by studies documenting the "iceberg of morbidity"—the vast majority of physical problems that are never brought to medical (or formal health statistics) attention (Verbrugge, 1986). The Health in Detroit Study found, on the basis of health diaries, that persons over 18 experienced an average of 23 health problems in 16 days within a 6–week period (Verbrugge and Ascione, 1987). This means that people experienced discomfort sufficient to be considered a health problem more than one-third of the days of the study (which itself was scheduled to avoid the height of hay fever and winter colds seasons, so this figure is probably conservative). The *least* commonly mentioned action in response to these problems was medical care; on only 5 percent of days on which they experienced problematic symptoms did respondents have medical contact of any kind (office visit, appointment scheduling, medical advice by telephone, or hospital visit). The study found that people typically responded promptly to symptoms, but that "for most symptoms of daily life, people opt to do something on their own without medical help" (Verbrugge and Ascione, 1987: 549).

This society generally and medical professionals in particular hold an ambiguous norm: Responsible persons *should* get professional medical care for all serious, medically treatable ailments and, at the same time, *should not* bother doctors or use medical facilities for unimportant or nontreatable ailments. This norm furthermore assumes that people share the professional definition of which ailments are serious or treatable and are able to assess their own situations adequately to determine into which category they fit. Although physicians strongly urge professional attention for health problems, they simultaneously dislike being bothered with trivial problems or problems they do not know how to treat effectively (Klein et al., 1982). One emergency room doctor who objected to dealing with worried mothers of young children who were not "real" emergency cases, commented to a researcher, "Anxious mothers, I sometimes think that they haven't got the sense that they were born with" (quoted in Roberts, 1992: 119).

A British study found that 25 percent of general practitioners surveyed complained that patients consulted doctors for unimportant reasons. At the same time, 56 percent complained that patients did not have enough humility in accepting the medical expert's judgments (Cartwright, 1967). The contradictory or ambiguous norm is that laypersons should be actively expert in judging correctly which ailments to refer to the professional, and then assume a humbly passive role when under the care of the professional.

SELF-TREATMENT AND THE DECISION TO GET HELP

The vast majority of actions people take to prevent illness or to treat everyday health problems are done without expert help, either medical or nonmedical. A British study found that women respondents most frequently listed the following ways of keeping healthy: good diet, exercise and fitness, no smoking, sufficient sleep and rest, and fresh air. Very few respondents (less than 10 percent) mentioned medical checkups or screening (Calnan, 1987: 101–130).

Likewise, the individual or family typically responds directly, without lay or professional help, to ordinary health problems (see Dill et al., 1995). The Health in Detroit Study found that self-dosing with prescription or nonprescription drugs was the most common response, used during 58 percent of the days on which people experienced symptoms. Self-imposed restriction of activities (such as cutting down on errands and chores) was also common, used on nearly 24 percent of the days on which symptoms were noticed (Verbrugge and Ascione, 1987).

British researchers found that although 91 percent of adults studied reported symptoms during the two weeks prior to interview, only 16 percent had consulted a physician. Indeed, only 28 percent had consulted their doctor at all during the previous 12-month period, even though, under the British National Health Service, the cost of consulting a doctor is not a deterrent, as it is for many in the United States. A far more frequent action in response to symptoms was taking medicine. In the 24 hours before the interview, 55 percent of adults had used some medicine; in the two weeks before the interview, they had taken an average of 2.2 different items of medication. Some were taken for preventive purposes, but most were taken in response to specific symptoms: a temperature, headaches, indigestion, and sore throats. Self-medication also includes the decision to take medicines prescribed and often kept for long periods, to be taken "as needed." Prescription drugs for the central nervous system (such as tranquilizers and sedatives) were frequently self-dosed. In a sample of households in England, Wales, and Scotland, 99 percent of homes kept one or more medicines; the average number was 7.3 nonprescribed and 3.0 prescribed. A fifth of the households kept sedatives, tranquilizers, or sleeping pills, and two-fifths kept some medication that the respondent could not identify (Dunnell and Cartwright, 1972).

Some responses to illness are not merely physical. If the person's belief system attributes illness to nonphysical causes, such as emotions or spiritual factors, then it is logical for a sick person to choose nonphysical approaches to treating the illness. If, for example, a person believes that she is especially vulnerable to infections when she is lonely or "blue," she might choose to treat an ailment by doing things that cheer her up or by visiting a close friend. Similarly, if someone believes that God will intervene to heal his illness, then prayer for healing constitutes a therapeutic action.

Such nonphysical responses are rarely done to the complete exclusion of physical treatments, and often they are meshed in interesting combinations. For example, when a person chooses to treat a bad case of the flu by consuming a bowl of steaming chicken soup or a concoction of milk toast, is the treatment merely the ingestion of a therapeutic substance or the soothing emotional connotations of the food, or both? Likewise, when a sick person says a blessing prayer over a bottle of prescription pills, is the treatment purely a physical response to illness?

The Health in Detroit Study found that about half the time people responded to their health problems by talking with family or friends (Verbrugge and Ascione, 1987). This response is both therapeutic in itself and also a way of consulting with other laypersons about what to do. Laypeople rely on their own networks of contact for advice, including suggestions about where to seek further help. Family, friends, neighbors, and colleagues at work, school, a religious group, or a social club all constitute potential sources of advice. The sick individual, however, must decide whose advice is sought and whose advice is heeded. For example, your grandmother might be a valued source of home remedies, and her burn ointment may be more effective than any commercial salve you have tried, but you might not want her advice on what might be a sexually transmitted disease because the advice is likely to come with a lecture on sin. Individuals are typically selective in their choices of lay advice.

Some evidence indicates that these lay advice networks rely especially on women as knowledgeable sources of referrals and as the seekers of health advice both for themselves and for members of their families (Graham, 1985). The division of labor in many households allocates to women more than to men such duties as caring for sick family members or selecting and arranging for appointments with medical and/or nonmedical practitioners.

Not all lay advice comes from existing networks, however. Sometimes people seek out new sources of advice or create a new network of lay advisers. A person with Parkinson's disease, for example, may look for a group of fellow sufferers, whose advice on some matters may be more valued than that of longtime friends or even doctors who have not experienced the disease themselves.

One specific form of advice is the lay referral to a source of help (Freidson, 1970: 290). Through lay referrals, the individual learns of many treatment options (which are usually linked with their lay advisers' evaluation of what might be the problem), including a favorite (or least favorite) doctor; the type of specialist to try; less orthodox practitioners, such as an herbalist or acupuncturist; self-help health groups; and alternative healing groups, such as a psychic healing circle, prayer group, or meditation center.

A study of Puerto Ricans in a small northeastern city, for example, found that sick persons with effective networks of kin and fictive kin (*compadrazgo*) received much concrete assistance in selecting and negotiating entry to both institutional health resources (for example, prenatal care programs) and noninstitutional help (such as *espiritistas*–spiritual healers). The study concluded that such kin networks should be viewed as health educators because of their role in teaching members where to seek help, how to select among available help resources, and how to deal with bureaucratic and other roadblocks to getting help (Schensul and Schensul, 1982).

Social interaction with family, friends, and acquaintances often plays an important part in the decision to seek help. One study of the decision to take a health problem to a clinic found that the individual rarely sought help at the physically sickest point. Rather, the nature of symptoms themselves appeared to be less significant than social interaction in prompting the decision to see a doctor:

> For our patients the symptoms were "really" there, but their perception differed considerably. There is a sense in which they sought help because they could not

stand it any longer. But what they could not stand was more likely to be a situation or a perceived implication of a symptom rather than any worsening of the symptom *per se.* (Zola, 1983: 118)

For example, a person might be motivated to seek help after a friend's description of some serious disease that could possibly be related to her symptoms; symptoms that were formerly not worrisome then become significant, even though she had experienced no change in the symptoms themselves. Similar factors are probably involved in the decision to seek nonmedical forms of help. Thus, the motivation to do something about a health problem often results from social interaction that heightens the significance imputed to the symptoms.

People do not always seek help mainly to *cure* a health problem. For example, a person might go to a *shiatsu* (Japanese acupressure) therapist for pain relief but not accept the diagnostic interpretations the therapist gives. Some people consult medical doctors for diagnoses more to rule out feared serious outcomes than actually to treat the symptoms. Similarly, some people want the medical diagnosis but distrust the medical treatment (especially certain drugs or surgery). One middle-class American woman said, "I still think they give you too much medication, which I accept gratefully and then don't take" (quoted in McGuire, 1988). We have too little data on what patients actually hope to accomplish by consulting medical and nonmedical health experts, but probably much of what professionals call noncompliance (discussed further in this chapter) is due to the fact that the doctors' orders are not necessarily what laypeople want when they seek professional help.

THE HIDDEN HEALTH CARE SYSTEM

Far too often, when people speak of the health care system, they refer only to the professionalized, institution-oriented *illness care* system of doctors and other professional health workers, hospitals, clinics, insurance companies, pharmaceutical companies, and government agencies. This form of care is important, because it is complex and powerful. It also has extensive economic significance, as discussed in Chapters 11 and 12. There is, however, another highly important system of health care.

Home and Family Care

The **hidden health care system** refers to all the laypersons who are often the real *primary* health care providers (Levin and Idler, 1981).[1] The vast majority of efforts to maintain health takes place in the home and other private spheres of action, including diet, rest, recreational exercise and relaxation, hygiene, adequate

---

[1]This usage differs from the common one in the literature, where "primary providers" refers to general practitioners, pediatricians, and other medical doctors or nurse practitioners who, in contrast to specialists, are supposed to be the first to evaluate patients' needs.

shelter, avoidance of dangerous substances, and prevention of accidents and injuries (Pratt, 1976).[2]

Likewise, most health care takes place in the home and is either self-administered or given by members of the family. Virtually all care of minor illnesses occurs outside the formal health care system. Imagine how many people in any given day may be taking care of themselves or someone else who is miserable with such illnesses as chicken pox, a bad head cold, or stomach flu! Even for health problems that have been treated in the formal system, most of the actual care is done at home: giving medications, tending a person restricted to bed, changing dressings, and monitoring symptoms.

Furthermore, throughout the society enormous amounts of energy and time are also required to care for persons with chronic illnesses, disabilities, and mental retardation, and those who are dying. In 1994, more than 5 million persons in the United States received some form of paid health care help in their homes, rather than in institutions such as nursing homes or hospitals (Dey, 1996). The majority of these were living with their families, also receiving family help with everyday activities such as walking, bathing, dressing, preparing meals, and eating. Note that these figures do not include persons receiving only unpaid care. Older adults accounted for the vast majority of persons (about 70 percent) needing home care, and the rates of persons needing assistance increased dramatically for those over age 85. The graying of modern societies, described in Chapter 2, results in a larger proportion of members surviving to an age at which they need long-term care for chronic health problems.

Even in nations with large government expenditures for health care, the *formal health care system is predicated on the expectation that most care will be given at home*. Indeed, the transfer of even part of these services (for example, complete care of all victims of Alzheimer's disease or AIDS) to the public sphere would probably swamp the system. Informal health care, which provides care at little or no cost to the government or insurers, has thus remained a part of the domestic economy.

There are several health-related benefits to self-treatment and home treatment, especially compared with treatment of the same problems in a formal, usually institutional, setting. Those who participate in the care of their own illness are more likely to experience a sense of independence, mastery, self-confidence, and control than those who are the passive recipients of care. A number of studies show the benefits of self-care, especially in treatment of chronic illnesses such as diabetes, hemophilia, and kidney disease (see Levin and Idler, 1981: 79–80).

---

[2]As Chapter 2 shows, much of the great reduction in mortality between the 1870s and 1950s was due to improved living standards (especially better nutrition and hygiene) rather than medical measures. Although one important factor in this improvement was rising real wages, another major factor was increased domestic labor created by the consolidated role of "full-time housewife and mother." The domestic labor required to cook meals, boil water, wash clothing, and so on (with few "modern" conveniences such as running water, much less washing machines) was a *key social practice* producing health for the family, even though the women *doing* the domestic labor themselves often experienced chronic ill health due to childbearing and overwork (Thomas, 1995).

Home care of illness and injury is typically more personal than formal or institutional care, although personal ties can be problematic because care givers can have negative as well as positive feelings for the sick person. Home care is also likely to involve more nurturance than perfunctory tending, although the actual care too varies from home to home. Another advantage of home care is greater continuity; the patient will not have to face an unfamiliar shift of nurses or a new specialist. Finally, home care is usually not as isolating as institutional care.

Just as persons with disabilities need special enabling environments, so too is the optimum setting for recuperation or the management of chronic illness one that is enabling. For example, a person with a debilitating chronic illness may require assistance with treatments (such as injections), the management of routine activities (like bathing), and ambulation (for instance, climbing stairs). Much home care, like many institutional settings, is disabling. Like institutional care, home care given by families, volunteers, or paid workers sometimes subordinates the sick person's needs to other household goals, such as keeping to a certain schedule. Home care sometimes increases sick people's dependency rather than enabling them to manage on their own as much as possible.

For most of us, the idea of home care raises cozy images of our comfortable room, surrounded by our favorite home entertainments, with Mom bringing us whatever we want for comfort: home-cooked special foods, a hot-water bottle, or a soothing drink. This image is, however, not the reality for many sick persons. For instance, what is the reality of home care for the widowed elderly person living alone in a bare furnished room, or the single mother who is seriously ill?

Nor are all families loving sources of nurturing care. Many families offer their members—especially children and elderly dependents—daily lives of negligence or outright abuse (Steinmetz, 1988; Straus et al., 1980). Indeed, the very health-related problems for which they need care may exacerbate these victims' abuse by other family members. Constant demand for help negotiating stairs or bathrooms, for example, might drive a tired care giver over the edge to abuse or neglect. Some long-term or demanding tasks can strain the emotional and physical resources of even the most caring family.

The expectation that most health-related care will be given at home also fails to take into account that poverty prevents many people from maintaining a healthful home; a growing proportion of U.S. families are utterly homeless, and many more live in seriously substandard housing. Unlike previous patterns, the period of the 1980s and 1990s saw a dramatic number of women and children and entire families become homeless (Link et al., 1994). Children now constitute about 15 percent of the officially recognized homeless population, and that proportion is growing rapidly (Burt, 1992; see also Leath, 1995), especially in the wake of 1996 changes in welfare legislation that makes many families ineligible for federal aid.

Homeless children tend to have particularly great health problems: low birth-weights, poor nutrition, generally poor health and poor access to regular health care and preventive medicine, high rates of preventable infectious diseases and lead poisoning, more developmental, cognitive, and emotional problems (NIAA and NIMH, 1992). Without decent shelter and basic means to make a home, family care givers find it impossible to maintain their family's health or to care for the sick. For example, a homeless mother living without utilities or sanitation in an abandoned tenement would lack control over her family's living conditions necessary to maintain a therapeutic regimen of serving a sick child prescribed foods or giving perishable medications at specified hours daily. Given such absolute lack of control in their lives, many poor patients give up trying to adhere to therapeutic recommendations (Hilfiker, 1994).

U.S. health care policies have barely begun to explore (much less fund) a vast range of physical and social arrangements that would support such enabling environments as noninstitutional collective living situations, copatienting, adequate services to sick persons living independently, barrier-free physical settings for chronically ill persons, and well-trained and well-paid institutional and home health workers. Adequate funding must address the full range of help needed to meet the home-care needs of persons who are chronically ill or have disabilities, or are recuperating from accidents, surgery, or acute illnesses (Soldo, 1985). Few families can afford many of the time- or labor-saving arrangements that might relieve care givers' burdens; domestic help and hydraulic lifts, for example, are expensive. Where they exist, some community nursing and social service agencies and volunteer groups do help families with certain of these needed resources. Some communities also have subsidized adult day care centers, hot meal delivery services, and visiting physical therapists. Especially in the United States, however, very few of the costs of home health care are provided under the terms of health insurance or government medical programs, and many Americans lack adequate insurance coverage to pay even for available services (see Moroney, 1980).

Women's Roles

When people speak of home care, they mean care by a *woman* (typically a wife, mother, or daughter), an assumption that becomes particularly problematic in light of women's changing roles within the larger society. It is estimated that three-quarters of care given in the home is provided by unpaid relatives, of whom 70 percent are women (Shapiro, 1993: 252). Approximately one in four U.S. workers—mostly women—are providing unpaid health services to at least one disabled elderly family member (Brody, 1994). The assumption that it is the wife-mother who should care for the family's sick results in real restrictions on women's opportunities in the public sphere, especially the world of work. Mothers, far more often than fathers, nurse sick children. Employed mothers reported three times as many hours of work lost due to family (primarily children's) illnesses compared to employed fathers (Carpenter, 1980). Missing work to care for a child who has a throat infection is not a mere inconvenience; it may also seriously reduce a woman's job opportunities. The world of work assumes key participants will not be taking off time to care for dependents; anyone (female or male) who takes home responsibilities more seriously than work risks losing promotion opportunities or even the job itself.

Furthermore, the care-giving role requires many women to forgo paid jobs to care for a chronically disabled relative. Although there may also be some rewards for such duties, caring for some homebound sick persons can be a 24-hour-a-day responsibility, leaving little time for personal needs. One study found that, in order to care for their elderly disabled parents, 11.6 percent of caregiving daughters had to leave their jobs, 23 percent had to reduce their hours of paid work, and 35 percent had to rearrange their work schedules (cited in Brody, 1994). A report issued by the Older Women's League noted that women spend an average of 17 years caring for children and 18 years assisting aged parents (cited in *New York Times*, May 13, 1989; see also Abel, 1991; Braithwaite, 1991; Brody, 1994; Hooyman and Gonyea, 1995).

The view that the health and illness care role belongs to the wife-mother is so pervasive that media and health education programs assume women will rearrange their lives to provide for the health of their families. One British health education project published a pamphlet urging measures women should take to prevent their husbands from having heart attacks. It recommended, for example, the following:

> The sensible wife will first decide whether her husband should lose weight, and then plan his menu accordingly. Pressure and pace at work, family responsibilities and general worries can be controlled to some extent by the man himself. . . . But perhaps more important is the tolerance and understanding of his wife. Let your husband talk about his worries, and whenever possible take the work from him—draft letters, pay bills, arrange for the plumber to come yourself. (quoted in Graham, 1985)

In efforts to reduce medical costs, insurers (including Medicare) and hospitals have emphasized outpatient surgery and other treatments while reducing the length of hospital stays (discussed further in Chapters 11 and 12). The result of these policies is that recuperating patients return home needing more extensive lay nursing care for longer periods. New technologies make possible the home administration of some fairly sophisticated therapies, such as kidney dialysis and intravenous feeding and medicating. The cost savings of performing these procedures at home is considerable. For example, in 1988 feeding by tube cost about $23,800 a month in a hospital, but only $6,000 a month at home (Findlay, 1988). These procedures usually cannot be done by the sick person without help, however. In addition to requiring visits from skilled nurses who teach the procedures, supervise home treatment, and monitor the sick person's condition, much home care involves the extensive commitment of family members. Their unpaid labor increasingly includes providing complex nursing medical care previously done only by physicians, registered nurses, or therapeutic specialists (Glazer, 1990).

In recent years, policy changes by government, private insurers, and hospitals have resulted in considerable **work transfer** for women providing health care, paid and unpaid. Economists and public policy analysts typically conceptualize domestic production (that is, work done in the home) as separate from the larger (public) economy, but the ability of these public-sphere institutions to extract cost savings or profits by transferring labor "costs" to unpaid women workers in the home shows how inaccurate such an idea is. Indeed, it suggests that public-sphere institutions use the notion of duty to one's family as an ideological legitimation for extracting unpaid labor (Glazer, 1993; see also Braithwaite, 1991; Hooyman and Gonyea, 1995).

This cost-cutting policy shift toward home care is developing precisely at a time when women are beginning to achieve somewhat greater equity in educational and occupational opportunities. Not only are women workers less eager to take on such additional care burdens, but the larger proportion of women in the work force also results in fewer (women) volunteers available for neighborhood assistance to those who need help at home. The policy shift also comes as nurses and other health care workers are struggling to achieve greater recognition (and pay) for the work they do (Brown, 1983).

Although moving more care of the sick to the home superficially appears to be demedicalization, note that it is not mainly the *doctors'* tasks or fees that are being reduced by earlier release from the hospital, but rather the more so-called menial tasks of care, which are being transferred to the family or family-paid workers. Whereas previously these tasks would have been done in the hospital or nursing home by low-paid nurses' aides and licensed practical nurses (LPNs), they are now transferred to unpaid relatives, who are sometimes assisted by very low-paid home health workers; nearly all are women (see Fine, 1988). It is nurses—not doctors—who usually make the home visits and monitor acute episodes of the homebound sick. Cost-cutting measures during the 1980s, however, severely restricted the amount of actual nursing care given by visiting nurses and greatly augmented their caseloads at the same time that patients were increasingly released from hospitals while seriously ill (Glazer, 1990).

The nature of professional home nursing does appear to be a move away from a highly medicalized model because ideally the nurse treats the patient as a whole person in the emotional and social context of home and family relationships. Home nursing also emphasizes teaching the sick person and family to care for themselves.[3] One community health nurse noted that her work was unlike that of doctors or hospital nurses because she works with the patient in the physical and social context of the family and home life, emphasizing the personal caring aspect of nursing. She added, "In a holistic sense, community health nurses are healers."

The trend to community-based health care has *not* usually reduced medical control, however. The home birth movement, for example, has been vigorously suppressed. In the United States, although some physicians have supported the practice of out-of-hospital births, professional organizations such as the American College of Obstetricians and Gynecologists have vigorously opposed it. Certification for trained midwives is available only to registered nurses who have

---

[3]The work of community health nurses (including many nurse-practitioners and nurse-midwives) is comparable to that of their predecessors, public health nurses, who since the 1920s enjoyed greater professional autonomy and respect in their work than did hospital- or office-based nurses (see Melosh, 1982: 113–157). Physicians, however, have perceived them as professional competitors and have often fought to prevent laws that would permit these nurses to work independently. Because nurse-practitioners can provide primary care, comparable to physicians, for about 80 percent of the patients in ambulatory clinics, there are many possibilities for status and role conflicts between the two gender-stratified occupations (Little, 1982; see also Lurie, 1981).

taken extra training, but even these certified nurse-midwives have been severely restricted in their attempts to practice independent of physician control and have had great difficulty obtaining malpractice insurance. The virtual monopoly of obstetricians and hospitals has thus been protected (Levin and Idler, 1981: 83–103; Romalis, 1985).

Mutual Aid

Self-help and mutual aid groups are another form of hidden health care. These voluntary associations offer *reciprocal* help, usually among persons with similar health needs. The mutual quality of this aid is the key feature distinguishing these groups from professional health care. Members exchange roles as provider and receiver of health and illness care (see Katz, 1979; Katz and Levin, 1980; Katz et al., 1992; Levin and Idler, 1981). Examples include support groups such as those for persons with certain diseases (such as epilepsy and Parkinson's disease) or disabling conditions (chronic pain, for example), or who have undergone certain operations (like mastectomies or colostomies) or other traumatic experiences (for instance, the suicide of a loved one, or a rape).

Self-help groups typically offer their members much mutual social support, concrete suggestions about how to manage the many day-to-day problems, information about their condition and various therapeutic possibilities, and advice about dealing with family, friends, and medical professionals (cf. Droge et al., 1986; Morgan et al., 1984). One aim is to break the isolation of those whose regular networks may not include anyone in a similar situation. As one member explained, "In the beginning one is truly cut off, one feels completely different from everyone else. . . . The healthy cannot understand the sick, one really belongs to a world apart" (quoted in Herzlich and Pierret, 1987: 220).

Mutual help groups appear to be a feature of lay health care especially in the United States, where they mesh with cultural values and historical experience of mutual and self-reliance (see Risse et al., 1977). The mutual help movement is also widespread in much of Europe (World Health Organization, 1981). Interestingly, in recent years, long-distance telephone connections and the Internet have provided lay mutual help networks a way of communicating beyond their immediate communities to exchange experiences with their disease and ideas about how to deal with it.

Considerable diversity characterizes the social organization of these groups, with many of the long-term groups imitating professional, bureaucratic health care organizations, yet many others remaining adamantly loosely organized lay groups. Some are formed at lay initiative; others have been created by helping professions for their clients. Thus, there is a difference in the degree of independence of power experienced, for example, by a group of chronically ill persons who organize to do something for themselves and each other, as compared with a therapy group organized by the outreach staff of a hospital.

Mutual help groups also vary greatly in the degree to which they have assumed any political agenda or recognized any of the political issues implicit in self-care or mutual aid. The Independent Living Movement for persons with disabilities and chronic illnesses and the Women's Health Movement have taken a politically activist stance (see Crewe and Zola, 1983; Doyal, 1983; Ruzek, 1979; Tudiver, 1986). Out of one such women's support group emerged the now famous "handbook" for women's health: *Our Bodies, Our Selves* (Boston Women's Health Collective, new edition, 1992).

Assuming self-care and mutual responsibility in the face of illness, however, also has *implicit* political consequences because the sick persons take an active and often knowledgeable role in the treatment of their own sickness. They often consider their proficiency in treating their particular illness to be superior to that of the professionals (cf. Herzlich and Pierret, 1987: 217–218). For example, diabetics who must give themselves frequent injections and persons with renal (kidney) failure who may perform their dialysis at home often distrust having those services performed in the hospital. People who have had long experience managing their chronic illness or disability often gain considerable expertise about their condition and are more likely to expect doctors and other medical personnel to share power with them.

Our recognition of this hidden health care system helps us to understand better the full range of activities people engage in to keep well or to treat illnesses. Not all outside help is professional medical care. Beyond the lay help of home, neighborhood, and mutual aid groups are a number of nonmedical healing alternatives that people may seek.

ALTERNATIVE HEALING SYSTEMS

People's belief systems inform their decisions as to when they need help and which kinds of help are appropriate. Even in modern Western societies, where biomedicine is the dominant medical paradigm, people may use several healing systems simultaneously with biomedicine. A study (McGuire, 1988) of middle-class Americans who used various alternative, spiritual healing approaches (such as Christian faith healing, psychic healing, and Eastern or occult healing) found that virtually all adherents used both biomedical *and* alternative systems. Furthermore, their beliefs shaped how they combined these various approaches. For example, one man had his broken arm X-rayed and set in a cast by medical professionals at the hospital, but followed this treatment with frequent prayers at home and in his religious group. He believed that the prayers resulted in faster and more effective healing. Adherents of the various alternative healing approaches felt that medical doctors were not necessarily the best source of help for such problems as chronic pain and illness, because they "treat the symptoms, not the cause." These adherents believed that the "real" causes of such illnesses were spiritual (or the socioemotional by-products of spiritual problems). Thus, by definition, modern medicine alone was not a sufficient source of help (McGuire, 1988).

Even people who are not consciously using alternative belief systems seek different sources of healing help, depending on how they understand or express their problems. Someone with back pain, for example, might consult a pharmacist, massage therapist, orthopedist, physiatrist, or chiropractor, depending on how the person interpreted the pain, its seriousness, and its possible causes. For many people, seeking help for health or illness includes several options in addition to orthodox medical care.

Nonallopathic Practitioners

One longstanding alternative source of health-related help is a professional practitioner from a formal healing system other than allopathy. Although allopathy is only one approach to doctoring, as described in Chapter 10, it has attained a virtual monopoly of medical education, licensing, and practice in the United States and Canada. It is also the dominant form of medicine practiced in most of Europe, although several nonallopathic approaches have greater legitimacy and freedom there than in North America. Medical systems that dissent from the dominant one have often been called sects, perceived as analogous to religious sects that dissent from the established church (see Jones, 1985). These medical systems are based on completely different, competing paradigms of illness causation and cure.

Probably the best known alternatives in the United States are two nineteenth-century challenges to allopathy: chiropractic and osteopathy, therapeutic systems based on the idea that malalignments of the musculoskeletal system also produce problems in the neuroendocrine system. Osteopathy has become largely subordinated within regular (allopathic) medical practice and licensing. Until the 1980s, chiropractic was actively suppressed by the AMA and licensing legislation, and it had to fight several court battles to force the AMA to change its prohibition against MDs referring patients to chiropractors. Chiropractic treatment has since gained greater legitimacy and is now covered for limited services by much health insurance (Wardwell, 1994; see also Albrecht and Levy, 1982; Coburn and Biggs, 1986; Singer and Baer, 1995; Wardwell, 1993).

There are few studies on how patients combine the use of both chiropractic and medical doctors. In Canada (where chiropractic has been officially recognized and is reimbursable by the national health insurance), one study found that, although all the low-back pain sufferers in the study had gone initially to medical doctors, those who subsequently sought help from chiropractors were part of lay referral networks (family, friends) that informed them of a wider range of alternative healing approaches (Wellman, 1995). Although chiropractors appear to be widely used alternative practitioners in the United States as well, patients seem to seek their services only for narrowly focused problems, especially back-related complaints, rather than general health or preventive care (Coulter et al., 1996). Early chiropractic was far broader in scope, but chiropractors today appear to have sacrificed that role to acquire legitimacy (Moore, 1993).

Homeopathy, a holistic form of pharmacological therapeutics developed in the early nineteenth century (Kaufman, 1971), is now more common in Europe and Latin America than in the United States. In England, for example, homeopathic physicians are licensed to practice and are reimbursed under the National

Health Service. The homeopathic movement also encourages laypersons to self-treat certain illnesses and to learn to use some of the homeopathic medicines (Coulter, 1984).

Like homeopathy, naturopathy utilizes presumably milder medicines, primarily herbs. One form of naturopathy, Thompsonism, was influential in the United States in the eighteenth and nineteenth centuries because it was linked with the rising tide of political populism and the needs for lay modes of healing in frontier and other rural communities (Cassedy, 1977; Numbers, 1977). The various natural health movements were generally suppressed in the United States, but in some European countries, such as Germany, these practices have long been more acceptable as a complement to biomedicine (Maretzki and Seidler, 1985; Roth, 1976). Contemporary versions of naturopathy as well as homeopathy appear to be used increasingly in the United States and Britain, perhaps as a result of dissatisfaction with the dominant, allopathic medical system (Baer, 1992; Sharma, 1992; Taylor, 1984; Thomas et al., 1991).

Another extant nineteenth-century alternative to allopathy is hydrotherapy, which utilizes water (in the form of baths, mineral water, and mud) for treatments. So-called new age alternative healing practices include some indigenous and religious healing approaches (described further in this chapter), but also include such alternative techniques as reflexology, iridology, aroma therapy, colonic irrigation, and radionics.

Some traditional Oriental medical practices have recently been introduced into Western societies.[4] The paradigms of illness and healing of such therapies as acupressure, acupuncture, *qigong*, and Oriental herbal medicine are very different from those of Western biomedicine. Acupressure, or shiatsu, is generally administered like a massage, so it is not in direct competition with licensed medicine, but neither is it typically covered by medical insurance. Acupuncture, which involves the insertion of needles, is under tighter legal control. In most of the United States nonphysician acupuncturists are required to work under the supervision of licensed doctors, although some states have made allowances for licensing nonphysician acupuncturists (who, ironically, are often better trained as acupuncturists than physicians who took relatively brief training in the method). Patients who utilize acupuncture alongside regular medical treatment often do not tell their own physicians for fear of alienating them (Kotarba, 1975; see also Wolpe, 1985).

There are few sociological studies of the extent of use of these nonallopathic therapeutic systems, but evidence suggests that they are used in conjunction with biomedicine, although without the knowledge of the patients' medical doctors (Eisenberg et al., 1993b; McGuire, 1988). One German study found that an estimated 30 to 40 percent of patients of medical doctors also consulted such nonallopathic practitioners as homeopaths, naturopaths, and hydrotherapists (Haehn, 1980). Surveys indicate that in Europe roughly one of every five persons has used

[4]Professionalized practice is also a feature of other Asian medical traditions, such as Ayurvedic and Yunami medicine, but these have not been extensively "borrowed" by Westerners (see Leslie, 1976).

alternative healing approaches (Fulder, 1993; Johannessen et al., 1994; Menges, 1994). Using a much broader definition of "alternative," a large U.S. survey indicated as many as one in three persons may have used some kind of alternative therapeutic approach (Eisenberg et al., 1993b).

Because these nonallopathic professional healers are in direct competition with allopathic medicine, political and legal maneuvers regarding their practice have concrete economic effects. Like allopathic medicine, these alternatives are organized as professional practices, with their own body of knowledge, training and certification standards, code of ethics, and organizations (see the review of literature in Cassidy et al., 1985; see also Budd and Sharma, 1994; Cant and Calnan, 1991; Saks, 1992; Sharma, 1992). They also rely largely on learned diagnostic and therapeutic techniques, which do not require the patient to understand or agree with the underlying paradigm in order to be treated effectively. Like biomedicine, many nonallopathic therapeutic approaches tend—despite their more holistic ideals—to locate illness in the *individual* (separate from social context) and to treat patient's bodies as reified objects (Sharma, 1995).

Indigenous Healers and Religious Healing Groups

The acceptance of an underlying belief system is more likely to be a feature of **indigenous healing**, or native, folk, or popular practices for health and healing. Anthropologists have documented a vast array of such systems around the globe. The early literature, however, generally assumed that as societies became modernized and Westernized, they would shed these "primitive" beliefs and practices and substitute the biomedical system, but this expectation has not been borne out (Kleinman, 1984). Furthermore, indigenous healing has remained widespread in modern industrialized societies. Social scientists once interpreted these beliefs and practices as remnants of peasant, old-country traditions or as characteristic of uneducated, lower-class persons who could not afford modern medical treatment. By contrast, some anthropologists now argue that—rather than a negative reflection on lower-class persons who use indigenous healing approaches—this persistence may be a form of resistance to the "racist and class features of the American dominative medical system" (Singer and Baer, 1995: 196; see also Snow, 1993).

Although there appear to be different healing systems operating in the various subcultures of modern societies, indigenous and other nonprofessional alternative healing beliefs and practices are in fact relatively widespread also among educated, fully acculturated, and economically secure persons (McGuire, 1988). A 1990 survey estimated that 34 percent of Americans had used some kind of alternative therapy that year; 72 percent of those using nonmedical therapies did not tell their doctors they were using other approaches in their treatment (Eisenberg et al., 1993b).

The sheer diversity of indigenous health and healing beliefs and practices makes it very difficult to generalize about these alternative options. Some indigenous practices are conducted by healers—lay specialists who have particular knowledge and/or spiritual or natural "gifts" for healing. Other indigenous healing is done by the sick person or nonspecialists in the group. In the United States, for example, indigenous healing approaches include those of spiritual healers, mediums, shamans, herbalists, lay midwives, fire doctors (for burn pain), bone setters, leg lengtheners, astrologists and spiritual advisers, and occult healers. Indigenous healing also includes a wide variety of meditation approaches, prayer, spiritual exercises, massage and other body work, exercise disciplines, and martial arts. These nonprofessionalized forms of healing alternatives are more likely than professionalized forms (such as chiropractics and homeopathy) to be integrative— not only linking the patient's body to a wider social context, but also addressing both body and emotions in therapeutic practices (see Csordas, 1994; Csordas and Kleinman, 1996; McGuire, 1996).

Although most indigenous healing occurs outside orthodox medical practice and is generally denigrated by the medical establishment, a number of medical doctors are open to some of these alternative practices. One study of these physicians found that their personal web of experiences, including religion and spirituality or their own illness or pain experiences, led them to integrate alternative approaches with mainstream medical practices. It concluded that many mainstream physicians hold views about health and healing and behave in ways that deviate from norms promulgated by their professional organizations (Goldstein et al., 1987).

One small fringe of both indigenous *and* orthodox medical practice includes what has been called "quackery," or fraudulent healing, usually for financial gain. Much labeling of quackery has been the effort of the medical profession to suppress any competition to its professional dominance. For example, the AMA funds a Bureau of Investigation to trace "quacks" and aid in their legal control and prosecution (Young, 1992). This effort also polices the AMA's ranks because many "quacks" are medical doctors who deviate from acceptable professional standards (Roebuck and Hunter, 1975; Young, 1992).

Because indigenous and other nonprofessional alternative healing, by contrast, is loosely organized, there are no clear-cut boundaries for acceptable practice. To the extent that indigenous healers are members of an established community in which they work, however, ordinary social control is operative. Someone who is believed to be pretending to heal and exploiting neighbors' needs in time of trouble would almost certainly be punished. When indigenous healing occurs more anonymously (for example, by a traveling healer or advertised nostrums), there is greater potential for deliberately fake healing. Most indigenous healing, however, is sincere; it is practiced by people—healers and patients alike—who, to some degree, share a belief system in which that approach to healing is plausible and indeed advisable (see Box 8.1).

Some of these alternative approaches are systematized by recognized movements; others are developed by independent healers, often drawing eclectically from a wide range of Western and non-Western traditions. The various spiritual healing approaches are generally based on a larger religious belief system. For example, healing done in pentecostal prayer groups is not an isolated activity of the group but an expression of the groups' larger belief that God acts directly in believers' everyday lives in response to their prayer and faith.

BOX 8.1

One American Healer[5]

Marge is a 48-year-old pediatric nurse employed full-time in a large hospital in a suburban community. She is successful in her career, with the appropriate advanced degrees and experience for high level positions, although she has not chosen to leave active nursing for administration. Her husband is a senior partner in a law firm in a nearby city. The couple has four grown children. . . .

Marge is involved . . . in several groups using alternative healing. She personally utilizes some Eastern methods . . . but she does not teach these methods nor is she affiliated with a group in which Eastern spirituality is a focus. As a nurse, she has used Therapeutic Touch for about three years. She uses her psychic healing methods to "get in touch with" the pain and suffering of the children in her ward; patients do not need to know that she is "sending" them healing energies. Privately, she has been practicing psychic healing for about six years; her methods are eclectic and she tries new "modalities" as she learns about them, discarding some approaches, keeping others. Her main support group is a psychic healing circle that meets each week in members' homes. . . . When she seeks healing for herself, she usually turns to the members of this group. In addition, she attends the monthly or weekly meetings of three regional holistic health and metaphysical societies. These meetings are important sources of new ideas and techniques. She has also taken numerous workshops and short courses on various alternative methods: foot reflexology, rebirthing, and crystal and color healing.

Marge does healing almost any time, any place and with anyone—including many people who do not know she is "sending" them healing energy. Marge described working on healing herself and others even while doing the dishes or in the elevator at work. Sometimes she engaged in it deliberately; other times, she felt, it was simply a part of her being. She stated: "I believe that in every moment of my life I release energy to those around me. I think everybody needs it every moment. . . . I feel that whoever makes connection with me or I make connection with them, I'm using my energy to heal."

She is also a good example of the general lack of clear financial motivation on the part of many "expert" alternative healers. She charges private clients only a nominal fee (from $15 to $30, depending upon ability to pay) for a thirty-to-ninety-minute session, and she earns about $100 to $150 (depending upon the number of registrants) for teaching a day-long workshop. These services are, however, occasional and minor sources of income for Marge. Her professional salary, combined with that of her husband, supports a high standard of living; Marge views her paid work as healer as a sideline, done mainly as a service.

[5]This is a composite portrait to protect the identity of the actual healers studied.

Source: From *Ritual Healing in Suburban America* by Meredith B. McGuire with the assistance of Debra Kantor. Copyright 1988, by Rutgers, The State University. Reprinted with permission of Rutgers University Press.

Spiritual healing is rather widespread, even in modern Western societies. Obvious examples include Christian faith healing, Christian Science and other New Thought healing, psychic healing, and healing approaches imported from various Eastern spiritual traditions such as Zen and Tibetan Buddhism and Jainism (Csordas, 1974; English-Lueck, 1990; Johnson et al., 1986; McGuire, 1988, 1982; Poloma, 1985; Skultans, 1974; Tipton, 1982; Wagner, 1983; Westley, 1983).

Ethnic and other subcultural belief systems inform the indigenous healing practices of most ethnic groups in the United States (and elsewhere). The healing actions of such persons as the Mexican American *curanderos*, Navaho singers, Puerto Rican *espiritistas*, Hawaiian *kahunas*, Eskimo shamans, or Haitian vodou healers are based on complex systems of ideas about illness and power (Brown, 1991; Fontenot, 1994; Garrison, 1977; Gill, 1981; Harwood, 1977; Kiev, 1968; Payne-Jackson and Lee, 1993; Roeder, 1988; Snow, 1993; Trotter and Chavira, 1981; Vogel, 1970).

The Effectiveness of Indigenous Healing

The foremost reason why people use indigenous healing is that *it makes sense* to them. Indigenous healing beliefs are plausible, especially to people who grew up in a culture or subculture in which they were common. Indigenous healing "works" partly by fitting into people's understandings of their world and how it operates. Young (1976: 8) pointed out that therapies are considered efficacious not merely when they are a means of curing sickness, but "equally important, [when] they are a means by which specific, named kinds of sickness are defined and given culturally recognizable forms."

Indigenous healing forms and transforms the illness experience. It utilizes symbols and ritual action, meaningful to believers or members of that culture, that can produce change on several levels: social, bodily, and emotional.[6] A number of studies of symbolic healing suggest that just as mind, body, and society are linked in illness causation, so too are they (potentially at least) part of the healing process (Csordas, 1994; Csordas and Kleinman, 1996; Dow, 1986; Laderman and Roseman, 1995; Lyon, 1990; McGuire, 1983, 1996; Moerman, 1979).

The therapeutic practices themselves also make sense to members of the subcultural group. To an outsider, the Vermont folk remedy of a honey-vinegar mixture may seem nonsensical and repulsive. To persons raised in that rural New England subculture, however, it may be a plausible and appealing way of conceptualizing problems of health and illness; the remedy invokes images of benign nature, living "near to the soil," and being in harmony with the laws of nature by which health is maintained and produced (Atkinson, 1978).

---

[6]Biomedicine also uses symbols of power to enhance its effectiveness. For example, a pill may symbolize medical power to cure inside the body (Pellegrino, 1976). Surgery, lab tests, and diet regimens may likewise be used as ritual practices (cf. Posner, 1977). Medical costumes and settings (for example, stethoscopes and white uniforms) symbolize professional expertise. Such symbols increase trust and expectancy and, indirectly, may increase healing effectiveness (Frank, 1973). Much of what is called the "placebo effect" may in fact be related to symbolic healing (Moerman, 1983).

In summarizing several outcome studies, which generally evaluate the results of healing efforts in terms of Western medical as well as indigenous standards, Kleinman (1984: 150) observed, "These studies document three things: that folk healers are frequently effective, that there are limits to their efficacy, and that, while toxicities of folk healing are infrequent, they do occur."[7]

This summary, along with Kleinman's caution that each form of healing has to be viewed in its own social context, probably also applies not only to folk healers but to the full range of healing practices in modern Western societies—including biomedicine, which some anthropologists refer to as our culture's "ethnomedicine."

ADHERENCE TO THERAPEUTIC RECOMMENDATIONS

Part of the health-seeking process is whether and how the sick person follows the recommended therapeutic procedures. For example, is a recommended diet followed? Are prescriptions filled and medicines taken? A medical doctor's recommendations may not be the only course of action to which a sick person would adhere; the advice of a lay consultant, an herbalist, a massage therapist, or spiritual healer might also be considered. Some sick persons deliberately seek several opinions—medical or otherwise—and therefore obtain several therapeutic recommendations. Adherence thus implies actively choosing which advice to follow.

Some formulations of the sick role have included following the doctor's orders as a role expectation (see Chapter 6). Many doctors, likewise, consider it a patient's duty to comply with their therapeutic regimen. The very notion of patient compliance implies a power relationship: The doctor is treated as authoritative and powerful, the patient as powerless and appropriately obedient (Chrisman, 1977; Stimson, 1974). The idea that the patient should comply thus may have ideological functions for the physician (Trostle, 1988).

A number of studies show that health care professionals greatly underestimate the amount of patients' nonadherence to medical regimens (see the review of literature in DiMatteo and Friedman, 1982: 35–57; Kasl, 1975; Stimson, 1974). One estimate suggests that some 20 percent of prescriptions are never filled; 30 to 50 percent of medications prescribed are taken incorrectly (National Council on

---

[7]We need to keep in mind that the *exact* same generalizations could be made about healing by medical doctors: They are frequently effective, their efficacy is limited, and some treatments are dangerous. This evaluation does not mean, however, that one should not consult a doctor, but it does imply we should be cautious about naive assumptions that medical treatment is necessarily beneficial or safe just because it is more scientific than other healing approaches. Likewise, we should avoid romantic notions that indigenous healing is necessarily beneficial or safe. The effort to evaluate or compare the effectiveness of indigenous or religious healing with medical healing is greatly complicated by the fact that, because they operate with totally different paradigms, their notions of what constitutes a "successful" healing are very different. Although there is much overlap in what problems they consider to need healing, indigenous or religious healing usually have very different goals from those of medicine.

Patient Information and Education, as cited in Brody, 1992). When doctors' orders involve major lifestyle changes (such as changing eating or exercise patterns), compliance is even less common. Doctors often experience patient nonadherence to their recommendations as an affront to their authority; they blame patients as irresponsible.

Often, however, there are many other reasons why patients do not adhere to recommended therapies. Because patients do not want to alienate their doctors, they often hide their nonadherence to the doctors' recommendations and the extent of their search for other opinions. Many patients, especially those dealing with chronic illnesses, develop their own strategies for managing their illness. Such strategies include the selective use of biomedical approaches, but often also involve other therapeutic approaches, advice from more than one doctor, and/or their tailoring of the doctor's advice. From the patients' point of view, such noncompliant health-seeking behavior is rational, and it preserves for them some element of control (Herzlich and Pierret, 1987; see also Alexander, 1982).

Rather than conceptualizing the sick person's role in terms of degree of compliance with doctors' orders, it is useful to understand the meaning of medications and other therapies from the perspective of the sick person. One study found that many people with epilepsy modify and self-regulate their use of prescribed medications in an attempt to assert a degree of control over their condition (Conrad, 1985; see also Donovan and Blake, 1992; Trostle et al., 1983). In a similar assertion of control, hemodialysis patients from a wide range of educational and ethnic backgrounds utilized nonprescribed treatments (for example, special diets and exercises, religious and folk healing, herbal treatments, massage, and acupuncture) without the knowledge of their medical doctors (Snyder, 1983).

Noting the extent of nonadherence to doctor's recommendations, Zola (1983: 217) argued that "to 'take one's medicine' is in no sense the 'natural thing' for patients to do. If anything, a safer working assumption is that most patients regard much of their medical treatment as unwanted, intrusive, disruptive, and the manner in which it is given presumptuous." The patient is engaged in an ongoing process of evaluation of recommended therapies; whether the recommendation is medically correct is only one, sometimes minor criterion in this evaluation. Other criteria include such matters as these: Does the doctor appear to understand my illness correctly? Do the doctor's methods of diagnosis, interpersonal style, and treatment meet my expectations of competent? Is there a safer, more pleasant, or less drastic alternative (especially to surgery and powerful medications)? Does it feel like this therapy is working? When dissatisfied, patients may try to modify the treatment either by negotiating with their doctor or by modifying the plan by themselves (known as noncompliance). Both approaches represent patients' attempt to assert some control (Donovan and Blake, 1992).

Much patient nonadherence can be traced to difficulties of understanding and communication in the doctor-patient interaction (Svarstad, 1976), as described further in Chapter 10. Part of the problem, however, is due to important differences in the perspectives and goals of doctors and their patients. The doctor's focus is typically on curing or managing the specific disease presented by the patient.

Laypersons, by contrast, are more likely to have a broader notion of health and illness and to be concerned with all aspects of their life, not merely one health problem, no matter how serious. For example, a patient may feel that the depression experienced as a side effect of blood pressure medicine is so debilitating that continuing the medication is not worth the struggle (cf. Twaddle, 1981).

Often the decision not to follow the doctor's recommended course of action (or not to seek professional help in the first place) is due to a discrepancy between the layperson's and the professional's understandings of the sickness. For example, a Louisiana study of black women with hypertension (high blood pressure) found that their cultural beliefs and folk-illness models affected their adherence to the medical regimen prescribed. Many of these women conceptualized their sickness as "high blood," a subcultural term implying the blood is too rich, thick, and hot, and total blood volume is too great; this conceptualization is not what doctors mean by high blood pressure. When health professionals failed to understand that medical diagnostic terms invoked a whole different set of cultural meanings for these patients, they inadvertently contributed to patient noncompliance (Heurtin-Roberts and Reisin, 1990).

A Massachusetts study of sufferers of specific chronic illnesses found that primary care physicians and nurse practitioners showed very limited knowledge of their patients' conceptions of these illnesses. Although professionals were more likely to know the beliefs of college-educated patients than those of less educated patients, overall they understood the lay explanatory models used by less than half of the patients in the study (Helman, 1985). This lack of shared understanding of the nature of the illness is likely to lead to considerable nonadherence to doctors' orders and to dissatisfaction on the part of both medical professionals and their patients.

Adherence to any therapeutic regimen is likely to require some effort. The sheer logistics of putting all recommendations into effect are enormous, especially for chronic illness, for which the therapeutic regimen must last a lifetime and is likely to become more demanding as the condition deteriorates. Health seeking is an active process throughout, but the active participation of the sick person is especially evident when it comes to choosing and putting some or all therapeutic advice into effect.

SUMMARY

The process by which people seek health is an active one. Both preventive care and the treatment of problems involve numerous decisions about the body and its needs. Self-treatment is far more common than treatment by professionals, medical or nonmedical. In addition to professional medical care, a vast hidden health care system provides advice, preventive and therapeutic care, emotional and practical support, and guidance in the search for professional care.

Orthodox Western biomedicine is only one of several healing systems available in most societies. Other options include nonallopathic practitioners and various indigenous healers and healing groups. The individual, then, has a range of health-seeking options. Even after consulting outside help, the individual also chooses which advice or therapeutic regimens to accept and put into practice.

RECOMMENDED READINGS

Articles

HILARY GRAHAM, "Providers, negotiators, and mediators: Women as the hidden carers," pp. 25–52 in E. Lewin and V. Olesen, eds., *Women, Health, and Healing: Toward a New Perspective.* New York: Tavistock, 1985.

Books

ALAN HARWOOD, *Rx: Spiritist as Needed: A Study of a Puerto Rican Community Mental Health Resource.* New York: Wiley, 1977. This highly readable ethnography describes the beliefs and practices underlying the use of Puerto Rican spiritual healers in a U.S. urban environment.

LILY M. HOFFMAN, *The Politics of Knowledge: Activist Movements in Medicine and Planning.* Ithaca: State University of New York Press, 1989. The author presents case studies of activist movements that challenged the occupational self-interest of professions, especially the medical profession.

LOWELL S. LEVIN and ELLEN L. IDLER, *The Hidden Health Care System: Mediating Structures and Medicine.* Cambridge, MA: Ballinger, 1981. A highly readable synthesis of the literature on the role of families, self-care, religious groups, community groups, and mutual aid in the larger system of health care.

MEREDITH B. MCGUIRE, with the assistance of Debra Kantor, *Ritual Healing in Suburban America.* New Brunswick, NJ: Rutgers University Press, 1988. This study describes the beliefs and practices of middle-class, educated suburbanites who use various nonmedical healing alternatives (such as faith healing, meditation, psychic healing, acupressure, and massage) in addition to medical treatment.

Our culture and social structure shape the way we understand and interpret our bodies, illness, and disease as well as whether or how we perceive illness. This chapter examines how what we know about illnesses is socially constructed, used, and changed.

A sociological approach to knowledge about illness differs from the biomedical approach in that it does not assume the objective existence of what medicine categorizes as disease.[1] The sociologist does not take for granted that disease entities exist in nature and await discovery. This perspective does not mean that people's health conditions have no objective foundation. People do experience real pain, sickness, and death. But this approach does mean that both laypersons' and professionals' ideas about illness are **social constructions**, or the result of human activity. Therefore, no matter how empirically precise these ideas are, they are always open to the influence of social factors in their production, transmission, and development. Medical ideas are bound by assumptions implicit in the language and cultural rules for producing knowledge (that is, epistemology). Thus, they are always delimited in their representation of the real world (see Young, 1978).

MEDICAL IDEAS AND SOCIAL FORCES

These ideas about body, health, and disease are nonetheless very powerful in shaping a society's medical reality. The knowledge held by any given culture or group is the product of its social history. Western medicine's knowledge of its disease categories is a social-cultural product, as is the knowledge of diseases in other medical systems, such as Ayurvedic medicine in Asia and *curanderismo* in Latin America.

In Chapter 8 we described lay conceptions of health, illness, and the body. By contrast, formal medical knowledge in Western societies is typically highly specialized and based on bioscientific theories and categories of thought. The contemporary medical paradigm represents a major historical change in how the body is viewed. Scientific **paradigms** are frameworks of formal knowledge that members of a given scientific community share, mainly due to having undergone similar educations and professional initiations; to sharing a common professional language, rules of evidence, and conceptual schemes; and to relying on the same professional literature and communication of the same scientific community (Kuhn, 1970: 176). Paradigms are rather like lenses; the world viewed through one paradigm looks very different from the world viewed through another. We examine briefly the recent history of current medical paradigms and how they have come to have such a powerful impact on the practice of medicine and the development of the medical profession.

Although Western medical practice is based on scientific knowledge, the practitioners themselves are not typically scientists. The scientist's objective is to gather

---

[1]Any social constructionist approach to knowledge must recognize how sociological ideas are likewise influenced by social processes and historical developments.

empirical data, and to analyze, interpret, and generalize from these findings. Scientists are not necessarily concerned with the practical application of scientific knowledge. By contrast, the practitioner's goal is more pragmatic: to deal with the specific conditions of individual patients or clients. What the practitioner needs to know is likewise more practical. The only portion of medical knowledge relevant to doctors is that which relates to conditions they are most likely to encounter in clinical practice. Much medical knowledge is thus often "recipe knowledge," or "knowledge limited to pragmatic competence in routine performances" (Berger and Luckmann, 1967: 42). For example, pediatricians' use of immunizations does not require their detailed understanding of the latest scientific theories about the operations of the body's immune system (although their medical education typically introduced this subject). Rather, they rely on recipe knowledge of which immunizations are recommended for children, at which ages, and with what common side effects and contraindications. They also rely on knowledge of where to turn when a situation is no longer routine.

A person's access to or possession of a valued form of knowledge can be an important factor in determining his or her power and prestige in any society. For example, if the knowledge of how to make a valued ritual potion is held only by the women of a particular family, then their knowledge is the basis of some power or honor. Knowledge is unevenly distributed in a society, often along lines of gender, social class, age, ethnicity, and the division of labor (Berger and Luckmann, 1967: 76–81). Access to and possession of specialized, formal knowledge, such as medical knowledge, is particularly uneven. Because very few people in modern societies possess advanced medical knowledge or technical skills, being able to control such knowledge is the basis of rewards (such as high fees), power, and privilege. People who control specialized knowledge are thus in a position to limit the access of others to that knowledge (for instance, by controlling professional school admissions and discouraging laypersons from gaining knowledge). The social distribution of knowledge both reflects and shapes social distinctions of power and prestige.

"Discovering" Disease: A Historical Example

Many diseases that were diagnosed frequently in the past either are not commonly found today or are no longer recognized as diseases. Similarly, some conditions diagnosed as disease nowadays may very well cease to fit any disease category in the future. The forces shaping the so-called discovery of disease categories are not purely objective, scientific factors; rather, value judgments, economic considerations, and other social concerns frequently enter the process. For instance, a famous physician during the American Revolution identified a disease he called "revolutiona," which was characterized by presumably irrational opposition to the "natural rule" of the English monarch (Conrad and Schneider, 1992: 49). In the 1850s, the classification of "diseases of the Negro race" included "drapetomania," which caused slaves to run away from their masters, and "dysaethesia aethiopis," which accounted for laggard work habits among slaves (see Cartwright, 1851).

Disease categories thus have political uses, and those on whom they are imposed may suffer serious consequences.

A prime example of changing medical definitions is a disease prevalent in the latter half of the nineteenth century and the first part of the twentieth century that had the following characteristics:

> It retards the growth, impairs the mental faculties and reduces the victim to a lamentable state. The person afflicted seeks solitude, and does not wish to enjoy the society of his friends; he is troubled with headache, wakefulness and restlessness at night, pain in various parts of the body, indolence, melancholy, loss of memory, weakness in the back and generative organs, variable appetite, cowardice, inability to look a person in the face, lack of confidence in his own abilities.
>
> When the evil has been pursued for several years, there will be an irritable condition of the system; sudden flushes of heat over the face; the countenance becomes pale and clammy; the eyes have a dull, sheepish look; the hair becomes dry and split at the ends; sometimes there is a pain over the region of the heart; shortness of breath; palpitation of the heart . . . ; the sleep is disturbed; there is constipation; cough; irritation of the throat; finally, the whole man becomes a wreck, physically, morally and mentally.
>
> Some of the consequences of [this disease] are epilepsy, apoplexy, paralysis, premature old age, involuntary discharge of seminal fluid, which generally occurs during sleep, or after urinating, or when evacuating the bowels. Among females, besides these other consequences, we have hysteria, menstrual derangement, catalepsy and strange nervous symptoms. (Stout, 1885: 333–334)

This serious disease was onanism, better known as masturbation. The fact that the doctor writing this description of symptoms slips easily into referring to it as an "evil" alerts us to the strong moral connotations that this disease label carried. This supposedly scientific medical category thus clearly reflected the moral and social judgments of the doctors who applied it (cf. Engelhardt, 1978).

What functions did the identification of masturbation as a disease serve? For the distraught parents of a moody teenager, the label explained a wide range of behaviors. It is less likely that the young person experienced much relief at having this diagnosis applied to symptoms such as poor appetite, headaches, or split ends. Another important function was to establish this "disease" within the proper jurisdiction of the medical profession. The author of the preceding description concluded emphatically that "the treatment of this disease should be undertaken only by a skillful physician" (Stout, 1885: 334).

Applying the category of disease to masturbation implied etiological explanations. The **etiology** of an illness is a set of ideas about its causality in general or about the origins of a particular illness episode. Like all ideas, they are human constructions that change over time. Early etiological theories of masturbation implicated the loss of seminal fluid, whereas later theories emphasized the overstimulation of the nerves, which led to general debility. Several authorities held that all sexual activity was potentially debilitating, but that masturbation was especially injurious because it was "unnatural" and thus more likely to disturb the nerve tone (Engelhardt, 1978: 15–17). The diagnosis of masturbation as a disease syndrome is no longer common; indeed, in many medical and lay conceptions it is now considered to be quite normal and healthy.

Identifying a person's problems as the disease of masturbation subsequently implied a particular course of therapy in accordance with etiological ideas about the disease. Therapies were supposed to first, eliminate the practice, and second, calm the nerves and rebuild the person's sapped strength. Some of the more tolerant therapies included hard work, a simple diet, tonics, cold baths, sedatives and narcotics such as opium, and alternative sexual outlets such as prostitutes or mistresses (Engelhardt, 1978: 19). If these therapies were not successful, more drastic measures were often recommended, such as restraining devices, acid burns and rings inserted in the foreskin to make masturbation painful, circumcision (of males and females), clitoridectomy (surgical removal of the clitoris), vasectomy, acupuncture of the prostate or testicles, and even castration (Barker-Benfield, 1975; Engelhardt, 1978; Groneman, 1995). Such a seriously debilitating disease required serious measures, including drastic surgery.

Those symptoms once clustered and classified as signs of the insidious disease of masturbation may still exist (for example, some teenagers still have variable appetites, split ends, and dull, sheepish looks), but the characteristics are no longer classified as a disease. Conversely, new classifications, such as premenstrual syndrome (PMS), have been defined into existence as a disease. The diagnostic category of PMS is a social construction which, like the diagnosis of onanism, embodies a set of cultural ideas and values. The considerable controversy within the American Psychiatric Association over whether to include the diagnosis (called "Late Luteal Phase Dysphoric Disorder") in the revised *Diagnostic and Statistical Manual* (DSM-III-R, 1987) illustrates the political and social value considerations implicit in the definition and diagnosis of PMS, or LLPDD (Figert, 1995; John Richardson, 1995). The attempts by medical doctors to define PMS are similarly problematic; some definitions are so broad that they classify as PMS the normal variance during as much as 17 days of the 28-day cycle in virtually all women with menstrual cycles. Accordingly, they define almost all adult women as having a medical problem (and presumably needing medical treatment). Despite lack of strong empirical evidence, doctors, lawyers, psychologists, journalists, and laypersons have used the notion of PMS and other hormonal cycle variance to purportedly explain women's violent crimes, automobile driving patterns, accident proneness, suicidal impulses, and quarrelsomeness. Thus, like the nineteenth-century diagnosis of hysteria, a "modern" medical diagnosis—seemingly factual and empirically based—comes to embody old cultural assumptions that women's reproductive systems cause irrationality and "sick" behavior (Rodin, 1992).

Such new categories both justify medical control and legitimate the expense of medical care for that disease. For example, in the United States socially constructed disease categories are the only basis for most insurance reimbursement. These categories, accepted as legitimate by the medical establishment, become the basis for funding research, treating patients, and institutionally establishing treatment programs. By putting these ideas into practice, medicine gives the disease categories a reality of their own. The process by which symptoms are selectively clustered and defined as disease is a social process and reflects cultural assumptions and power relationships (see Johnson, 1987).

Science as a Social Product

With its emphasis on a scientific model, biomedicine has developed increasingly complex **nosologies** (typologies of diseases). The medical model held that each particular disease could be characterized by a specific pathological configuration and attributed to a definite, unique cause. Thus, medicine has emphasized the classification and description of all diseases. The movement toward ever more precise differentiations of medical nosologies and etiologies is based on the assumption of **disease specificity**—the medical belief that each disease or syndrome has characteristic qualities and causes specific to that category of disease. This assumption has led to a focus on the individual rather than the social and contextual locus of sickness (Cassell, 1986; see also Dingwall, 1976: 50).

Medical ideas are the product of social processes and are continually changing. All scientific work involves the social construction of facts and interpretive schemes (Berger and Luckmann, 1967: 60–72; Latour and Woolgar, 1979: 243). Modern medical science strives to be as empirically neutral as possible, for example, by conducting blind experiments in which neither administrator nor subject knows whether a substance being given is the experimental substance or an inert control substance. Nevertheless, much medical research cannot be readily conducted neutrally, because—among other reasons—live human bodies are not readily detached from the persons who inhabit them. Thus, neither the scientific observers nor the objects of scientific observation can have their influential social characteristics and attitudes eradicated.

Social, economic, and political factors greatly influence the scientific discovery of new diagnostic categories. Funding for research largely depends on what is socially defined as a serious problem at the moment. For example, a disease syndrome known as GRID (Gay-Related Immune Deficiency) received relatively little medical attention or research funding, but when the same syndrome was later considered to be a national threat to the heterosexual population and redefined as AIDS (acquired immune deficiency syndrome), enormous increases in research funding enabled scientists to identify several variants of the syndrome and to describe some of the complex ways it can damage the body (see Shilts, 1987). Funding for research on what is now recognized as a serious international health problem was thus significantly delayed due to the politics surrounding a stigmatized illness.

Similarly, research on women's problems has been funded at a much lower rate than men's. In 1988, only 13.5 percent of the National Institute of Health's budget was used to research women's health problems, such as heart disease, cancers, and osteoporosis (Rosser, 1994). New funding initiatives (created in 1991, in response to public outcry) are only beginning to improve the situation. Furthermore, most clinical studies (for example, tests of the effectiveness of pharmaceutical and surgical therapies) have been done almost exclusively on males. Although this testing bias may protect some women (and offspring) from harmful effects of drug testing, it also results in potentially harmful misdiagnosis and treatment when symptoms, course of the disease, and response to drugs and surgery are different in women's bodies than in men's (Mastroianni et al., 1994).

Coronary heart disease (CHD) is the foremost cause of death among women, accounting for approximately half of their deaths, yet physicians learn to diagnose CHD using symptoms and methods of testing derived from studies of *men's* heart disease. Thus, doctors are more likely to misdiagnose and undertreat women's heart disease, not recognizing that the disease has different manifestations: For example, in men the most common initial manifestation is myocardial infarction—an acute symptom, whereas for women it is angina pectoris—serious pain but often continuing for years before a more acute symptom occurs (Mastroianni et al., 1994). One study showed 192 randomly sampled male internists videotapes in which "patients" (actors) with different characteristics (age, gender, race, socioeconomic status) presented the exact identical clinical information, and physicians were asked what they would do for their own patients in similar circumstances. Despite the fact that all tests and symptoms were identical, for the heart "cases" doctors were much less likely to diagnose cardiac disease in younger women compared to men, to consider medical treatment for (younger and older) women to be necessary, or even to recommend therapeutic lifestyle changes involving diet and exercise for women (McKinlay, 1996). The lack of solid research about heart disease in women may produce a vicious circle: Doctors fail to diagnose women's CHD because they do not expect to find it, but they do not expect to find it because the morbidity statistics showing low rates of CHD in younger women may be faulty due to failure to recognize the disease in women.

Thus, bias in scientific research is not merely a matter of levels of funding. Both scientific knowledge and medical practice are shaped by *social, cultural,* and *political* factors. These determine which research tasks are considered worth pursuing, how research questions are framed, and how the research is connected to a larger body of knowledge. Biomedical science is clearly a social product.

Often the development of new disease categories is connected with the emergence of a new occupational specialization. Considerable professional prestige is attached to "discovering" and describing a "new" disease or syndrome. In psychiatry, for example, the 1987 *Diagnostic and Statistical Manual* (DSM-III-R; APA, 1987) recognized 292 disorders. It included a novel appendix subtitled "Proposed Diagnostic Categories Needing Further Study"; subsequently, nearly 100 new diagnoses were proposed for the next edition (Pincus et al., 1992). The process of proposing and gaining acceptance of new categories of diagnosis is partly political and often based on cultural assumptions rather than "pure" empirical evidence (Gaines, 1992). Corporate interests also promote "discovering" legitimation for new disease categories, especially when they purport to have a marketable "treatment" for the newly labeled condition (Conrad and Schneider, 1992; Peele, 1989: 115–143). Finding new diseases is thus an active process; medicine is consciously oriented to creating disease categories where previously there were none (Freidson, 1970: 252). The case of menopause as a medical syndrome illustrates this process.

Creation of Medical "Problems": The Case of Menopause

Social and economic considerations promote the search for new diseases. For example, menopause, the period of women's lives in which menstruation naturally ceases, is now indexed in the *International Classification of Diseases* (USDHHS, 1989: 524–525). Although menopause is a normal biological process, in the last 50 years, it has come to be seen as a medical problem in the United States and many other Western societies. The Western biomedical literature generally treats menopause as an estrogen deficiency disease or ovarian dysfunction that produces various physical and emotional problems (see Bell, 1990; McCrea, 1983). Considerable cross-cultural variation is noted in its biophysical, social, and emotional concomitants, however.

In our culture, symptoms such as hot flashes, headaches, dizziness, fatigue, anxiety, insomnia, irritability, depression, and general emotional problems are typically associated with menopause. Cross-cultural data suggest, however, that women's responses to the cessation of menstruation may be connected to the structure of society and its cultural expectations for women (see Bowles, 1990; Lock, 1991, 1993). For example, in Islamic and many African societies, menopause brings relative freedom from many of the restrictions of women's lives: They are no longer required to be secluded, veiled, and restricted in the male company. These women experience few of the physiological and psychological symptoms attributed to menopause in Western societies (Townsend and Carbone, 1980). Menopause is thus a good example of how social meanings influence individuals' physical experiences and perceptions of their own bodies.

The Western medical construction of menopause, however, ignores these social meanings, reducing the experience to a set of biochemical processes presumed to characterize all female bodies, regardless of cultural or socioeconomic factors. Medical knowledge often becomes detached and independent of the research on which it is based. Thus, limitations in the original research are not taken into account in the accumulated stock of knowledge. For example, the medical construction of menopause is based in part on clinical studies with small numbers of subjects, typically drawn from patient populations—women whose menopause was surgically induced (as through oophorectomy) or whose problems with menopause had already been medically defined as severe enough to warrant treatment. There are severe methodological limitations to such studies, and cautious researchers know not to generalize too extensively from them to the general populace. Unfortunately, once in the medical literature, these ideas are treated as facts that are presumably generalizable to all women (Kaufert, 1988).

Recent studies of a wider population of middle-aged women have found relatively little evidence of pathology or medical problems. One U.S. study followed the self-reported experiences of 8,050 women over several years before and after menopause; the majority of women did not seek help for menopause-related problems, and those who did experience significant "symptoms" were disproportionately those who reported prior poor health, independent of menopause. The researchers concluded with concern that physicians may be too quickly assuming that these women's problems were due to menopause and, thus, failing to diagnose or treat other, more probable causes such as chronic illnesses, stressful social situations, or preexisting psychological problems like depression (McKinlay et al., 1991). Part of the reason for doctors' acceptance of the methodologically flawed studies is that the medical construction of menopause meshes with physicians' assumptions about bodies and diseases. Thus, to define and treat a normal process as a disease fits the medical model, and the idea that menopause is a disease implies a concrete medical course of action.

In the United States, the definition of menopause as a deficiency disease resulted from the professional efforts of a small elite segment of the American medical profession during the 1930s and 1940s. A study of the medical literature during this transition shows that this process involved both the "discovery" of a theory of etiology of this "disease" and the development of pharmacologic methods of treatment. Using the paradigms of sex endocrinology, doctors attributed menopause to the deficiency of hormones (in particular, estrogen) regularly produced by the woman's body before cessation of menstruation. The development of an inexpensive synthetic estrogen replacement, DES (diethylstilbestrol), subsequently made the medical management of this "disease" possible (Bell, 1990).

Although these specialists acknowledged that most menopausal women (a common estimate was 85 percent) experienced few or no problems, the efficacy of DES created the possibility of treating *all* menopausal women. Indeed, despite growing criticism and concern over the safety of estrogen replacement therapy (some studies had linked it to cancer and some other serious conditions), by 1975 estrogens had become the fifth most frequently prescribed drug in the United States. A survey done the same year found that an estimated 51 percent of women had taken estrogen for at least three months, with a median use of ten years (see Kaufert and McKinlay, 1985; McCrea, 1983). In 1975, one gynecologist stated,

> I think of the menopause as a deficiency disease like diabetes. Most women develop some symptoms *whether they are aware of them or not*, so I prescribe estrogens for virtually all menopausal women for an indefinite period. (quoted in Brody, 1975: 55 [emphasis added])

In the mid-1970s the scientific literature firmly began to implicate estrogen therapy in iatrogenic diseases (that is, those caused by medical treatment). Debates over the curbing of estrogen replacement therapy involved conflicts between the pharmaceutical companies and the Food and Drug Administration, which ruled in 1976 that the industry must prepare a warning on the risks of estrogen for insertion in packages. In subsequent years, the pharmaceutical industry fanned women's fears of menopause and postmenopausal health problems such as osteoporosis. The heavy involvement of the drug industry in the writing and publication of medical literature itself (see Foster, 1995: 83) makes it difficult for physicians, as well as laypersons, to judge competing claims.

The conflict generated a debate within the medical profession itself, highlighting the differences in perspective between biomedical researchers and physicians in clinical practice (Kaufert and McKinlay, 1985). The definition of menopause as a deficiency disease resulted from the efforts of a small elite of specialists, together with the development of a disease etiology that lent itself to medical management and the promotion of a pharmacological agent that could be used in the treatment of the newly created disease.

Denial of Medical "Problems": Tardive Dyskinesia

Despite the general disposition to find new diseases and syndromes, the medical profession sometimes *resists* accepting new disease categories. Social and political factors also account for some constraints against medical "discovery." Tardive dyskinesia is a seriously debilitating, often irreversible disorder of the central nervous system, characterized by a variety of involuntary movements, most notably of the lips, jaw, and tongue. It is a seemingly new disorder partly because it is a pervasive, iatrogenic side effect of antipsychotic (neuroleptic) drugs, such as chlorpromazine, which came onto the market in the 1950s. In the 1960s and 1970s, the prevalence of tardive dyskinesia increased because neuroleptic drugs were being prescribed more frequently and in higher doses. Even after the syndrome had been identified and named in 1960, many clinicians did not accept or use the diagnostic category (Brown and Funk, 1986: 116–124).

One significant factor in this resistance was that acknowledging the existence and pervasiveness of tardive dyskinesia hurt the economic and political interests of many clinicians. The institutional and professional mandate to control the deviant behaviors of patients often superseded concerns for the drugs' physical risks for patients. The researchers and others who called attention to tardive dyskinesia were generally identified with the National Institute of Mental Health, medical schools, and research institutes, whereas the clinicians who dealt with patients with the syndrome were working in mental hospitals and private psychiatric practice.

Many clinicians simply did not *observe* the disease, even in patients with obvious symptoms. The professional self-interest of these psychiatrists was involved; they relied heavily on pharmacological methods in their claims for efficacy in the treatment of psychoses, and their claims for recognition and remuneration as medical professionals were linked with their emphasis on biopsychiatry and psychopharmacology. Because the patients were generally already defined as mentally ill, their complaints could be readily discounted and their overt symptoms attributed to other problems, such as brain disorders (Brown and Funk, 1986). The economic and political interests of these physicians prevented them from recognizing the disease they were creating.

IDEAS AND IDEOLOGIES

Despite the supposed value-neutrality and objectivity of so-called scientific medicine, the knowledge produced, held, and used by its practitioners is, with considerable regularity, connected to their personal social location and the larger social situation of medical institutions in that society. In particular, social stratification (by criteria such as social class, age, political power, gender, and race) appears to be closely correlated with ideas about the body, health, illness, and healing. Thus, medical ideas often reflect or serve as ideology.

Ideology is a system of ideas that explains and legitimates the actions and interests of a specific sector (class) of society. For example, when the coal mining industry was in conflict with coal miners' representatives over black lung disease, the medical ideology of the industry promoted a very narrow definition of the disease, thereby diminishing the industry's legal responsibility toward the victims and its social responsibility for prevention of the syndrome (see Smith, 1981, 1987).

Ideas about health and illness frequently serve as legitimations for the interests of one group over another. A **legitimation** is any form of socially established explanation that is given to justify a course of action (see Berger and Luckmann, 1967: 92–128). In Chapter 6, we examined how ideas of health and illness legitimate the larger social order. Here we focus on legitimations for the interests of certain social groups in the stratification system.

In Western industrialized societies, the medical profession has organized itself, as we describe further later, specifically to promote its interests. Different professional interests pertain to other health-related occupations, such as nurses, pharmacists, X-ray technicians, midwives, and physical therapists. Incorporated into their ideas about health and healing are legitimations for their occupational statuses and income.

The 1975 so-called discovery of Lyme disease, a tick-borne spirochetal infection, illustrates how American rheumatologists successfully claimed the "discovery" and right to define treatment for the disease, superseding the "turf" claims of European dermatologists, who had "discovered" the same (or closely related) condition decades earlier and identified it as ECM (erythema chronicum migrans). By presenting Lyme disease as new and threatening, the mass media enhanced public attention to the disease, and commercial interests fanned public fears to promote a growing range of antitick products for people, pets, and property. Rather than being a discrete, objective entity that was simply medically "discovered," Lyme disease exemplifies the complex process by which a legitimized diagnosis is socially negotiated and developed (Aronowitz, 1991).

Other interests served by medical legitimation include those of the health-related industries: pharmaceutical industries, biotechnological industries, hospitals, nursing homes, and the medical, life, and disability insurance companies. Medical legitimations are especially important for various agencies of social control, such as the courts, mental hospitals, prisons, hospitals, and schools; this role is discussed further later. Ideas about health and illness are also used to legitimate the interests of such parties as employers, workers, producers, consumers, polluters, environmentalists, and the military.

Ideology influences actions subtly, most often without the actors' awareness. It is incorporated in the language and rituals of everyday interaction, and thus comes to be taken for granted and unnoticed or unexamined (cf. Emerson, 1970; Fisher, 1986). For example, the language used in referring to a patient as "the broken hip in room 305" depersonalizes the ill person, transforming her into a case that can be managed more readily by a professional team. Even matters of professional dress (such as a uniform, clipboard, and stethoscope) subtly symbolize status differences.

Ideological aspects of thought and practice often go unnoticed because they are often self-confirming. Because ideology shapes people's expectations and what they consider to be evidence, it often produces evidence that confirms those expectations. If, for example, I expect old people to be befuddled, my observations of them are likely to confirm my expectation. Indeed, if an individual protests that he is not befuddled, I may interpret his protestations as further evidence that he is so confused he cannot see the validity of my judgment. Also, when I treat him as befuddled, he may come to act that way and further confirm my prejudgment. The supposed evidence that confirms my expectation is a self-fulfilling prophecy.

Although interest groups tend to be attracted to ideas and practices that mesh with their particular interests, the concept of ideology does not adequately predict any given individual's behavior. We should avoid using this term in any simplistic or deterministic sense. Material interests are not the only motivating force for individuals; for example, spiritual or altruistic motives might lead people to work for conditions that are not in their personal interest. Nevertheless, in general, people tend to hold ideas and engage in practices that serve or at least do not conflict with their own interests.

Some examples of medical practice in Western industrialized societies show the influence of ideological elements, but there are also ideological aspects to healing practices in other cultures as well. The following examples illustrate some ways that interests influence ideas of health and illness, medical research, and individual diagnosis and treatments in Western bioscientific medicine.

Medicalization, Demedicalization, and Professional Interests

Medicalization is the process of legitimating medical control over an area of life, typically by asserting and establishing the primacy of a medical interpretation of that area (see Conrad and Schneider, 1992; Illich, 1975; Zola, 1983). The process of medicalization is illustrated by the medical treatment of pregnancy and childbirth, as doctors took over a substantial business previously done primarily by midwives.

With the medicalization of childbirth, aspects of women's reproductive lives that are not pathological were brought under the canopy definition of illness (Davis-Floyd, 1992, 1994; Foster, 1995). Medical education for the new specialization of obstetrics and gynecology fostered the notion that the events of childbearing—pregnancy, labor and delivery, and puerperium (the period immediately following childbirth)—could best be understood in purely physical and pathological terms (Hahn, 1995: 209–233). More recently, sexuality, potency, fertility, and the process of conception have also become increasingly medicalized (Becker and Nachtigall, 1992; Sandelowski, 1991; Tiefer, 1992, 1994).

The medical profession persuaded the public and the regulators of health care that women needed doctors to manage their pregnancies and childbirth; however, that initial medicalization was linked more with doctors' professional interests than with patients' well-being. Indeed, when medical control over childbirth was first being consolidated, doctors and hospitals had abysmal records, especially for spreading infection to both mothers and babies (Oakley, 1984; Wertz and Wertz, 1979).

Artificial insemination has similarly been medicalized for reasons unrelated to health per se; the actual process of artificial insemination can be safely and effectively done without advanced technology or medical procedures. Rather, medicalization serves social control functions, for example, by screening applicants (and denying insemination to many). Physicians medicalize the process by representing it as a response to a husband's fertility problems, rather than as a response to a woman's wish to become pregnant. By medicalizing the artificial insemination, physicians retain a monopoly over the market and their control is protected by law in several states (Wikler and Wikler, 1991).

Just as medicalization is a largely political process, so too are efforts to undo previously medicalized conditions. For example, after considerable politicking in the American Psychiatric Association, homosexuality was removed from its earlier classification as a disease. Patients' interests are rarely the foremost political force for demedicalization; often more powerful interests such as competing professionals, insurers, pharmaceutical companies, and government agencies engage in the effort to medicalize or demedicalize a category. For example, if normal childbirth were redefined as a nonmedical event, insurers would be less likely to pay for physicians and hospitals for delivery. Similarly, for cost savings many hospitals now discharge patients early while they still need extensive nursing care; this hardly represents a trend toward demedicalization. In general, medical institutions and medical professionals still retain vast and culturally respected authority over anything they have defined as "disease."

As Chapter 6 shows, some medicalization results from redefining "badness" as "sickness" and bringing the treatment of deviance under medical control. In this process, too, the medicalized ideas about the problem serve professional interests. When sicknesses thus labeled are defined as "bad," the doctors who join or organize efforts to eradicate or control them function as "moral entrepreneurs" (Becker, 1963: 147–163), or those who make an enterprise out of moral concerns.

The "discovery" of an illness category called hyperkinesis (more recently subsumed under the label "attention deficit disorder") involved such entrepreneurial action. Virtually all of the persons labeled with this syndrome have been children; most are boys. Behaviors identified as characteristic of hyperkinesis include excess of motor activity, short attention span, restlessness, impulsivity, and inability to sit still in school and comply with rules. These behaviors, however, have been frequently observed among schoolchildren, probably since the invention of the institution of the school. Although no organic basis was identified, the medical category of hyperkinesis resulted in part from social factors, such as the development and vigorous promotion of psychoactive drugs (specifically, Ritalin [methylphenidate]) for controlling hyperkinetic behavior and the crusading efforts of moral entrepreneurs, including doctors, educators, and parents. Although hyperkinesis has been a medical category for only a brief time, it rapidly became an attractive diagnosis, and the drug Ritalin accounted for significant proportions of the pharmaceutical industry's profits (Conrad and Schneider, 1992: 156–158).

The promotion of ideas about a disease category is thus a political effort, by which professionals are promoting their own interests; ideas function as ideologies. The attempt to define participation in religious cults as a medical problem illustrates how the illness label is a product of specific political efforts (Robbins and Anthony, 1982). The 1980 and 1987 editions of the American Psychiatric Association's *Diagnostic and Statistical Manual of Mental Disorders* (DSM-III and DSM-III-R) contained several changes from previous editions in order to characterize participation in new religious movements or in non-Western religions in the United States as characteristic of mental disorder (Post, 1992). For example, in the definition of paranoid personality disorder, the revised manual stated that "individuals with this disorder are over-represented among leaders of mystical or esoteric religions and/or pseudoscientific and quasipolitical groups" (American Psychiatric Association, 1987: 308). Thus, an evaluation of someone's mental health includes a judgment as to whether the individual's religious, scientific, or political persuasion is deviant (Lukoff et al., 1992). Interestingly, the efforts to define participation in new religious movements as sick were primarily those of a relatively small number of therapists who made their living "deprogramming" former members or testifying as expert witnesses in court cases involving such religious or other social movements. These moral entrepreneurs were establishing a specialized professional territory for themselves by creating illness labels (Richardson, 1993).[2]

Although the boundaries of what is called mental illness are generally more malleable than those of physical illnesses, similar political processes are often involved in classifying physical ailments. Ideas about the etiology of an illness (and, by extension, responsibility for it) are often debated politically. For example, a syndrome called miners' nystagmus has been the subject of continual political negotiation as a medical category. In the nineteenth century, this syndrome was a recognized diagnostic category (characterized by such symptoms as oscillation of the eyes and spasms of eyelids, dizziness, headaches, and sensitivity to light). Later, however, it had become an expensive item of compensation, so the British mining industry engaged in continual medical-legal debates as to whether it was

---

[2] The 1994 edition (DSM-IV) reduced some bias, dropping reference to "terrorists and cultists" in its definition of dissociative disorder; however, it added a new code (V62.89) to legitimate psychiatric treatment for persons with spiritual distress (James Richardson, 1995).

a legitimate illness. The incidence of nystagmus complaints was often related directly to changes in conditions of work (such as production schedules) in the mines. As the result of complex social interactions involving doctors, management, labor, and government agencies, this illness was eventually psychologized, and thereby both recognized as a problem yet invalidated as a compensable illness (Figlio, 1982).

By trying to define the issues as mere medical problems with purely technical responses, some researchers and their commercial sponsors are evading profound social and moral issues. For example, in justifying experiments involving injections of healthy children with the genetically engineered human growth hormone, researchers framed short stature as a deficiency disease with a purely technical solution. It is a debatable ethical issue whether an inherited characteristic previously considered to be within the range of normal should be redefined as a "medical problem" needing medical treatment (Hotz, 1993).

Corporate Interests

A good example of how ideology figures into the definition of, diagnosis of, and response to illness can be seen in ideas about occupational health hazards. In recent years, manufacturers, unions, workers' rights groups, medical authorities, and several government agencies have been involved in a growing confrontation over issues of the genetic protection of workers and their offspring. One episode occurred in 1979, when the Department of Labor cited and fined American Cyanamid for requiring women to be sterilized to keep their jobs at the company's lead pigments manufacturing operations in West Virginia. Numerous chemicals central to the manufacture of paints, pesticides, herbicides, plastics, and heavy metals have been strongly implicated in reproductive damage. Sterility, miscarriages, and birth defects have been identified with workers' exposure to these chemicals.

In 1984, the UAW (United Automobile Workers union) sued Johnson Controls, the nation's largest producer of batteries, over its exclusionary policies for workers' exposure to lead, the basic raw material of batteries. One worker had undergone sterilization to keep her job; another worker was transferred to a nonexposed job at loss of pay, despite very low probability of becoming pregnant; but a male employee's request to transfer to a nonexposed job to avoid reproductive risk was denied. This case eventually resulted in a 1991 landmark decision by the U.S. Supreme Court that personnel practices limiting the employment of fertile women in jobs posing reproductive health hazards constituted sex discrimination and thus were illegal under the 1964 Civil Rights Act. This court decision will undoubtedly have long-term policy implications related to several health issues: Are women more at risk than men (who also contribute genetic material to their offspring)? Is the risk to the fetus the most important concern, or should there be concern for male and female workers as well? Are these reproductive problems only one manifestation of health threats (such as cancer) that might affect all workers? (see Daniels, 1993; Robinson and Giacomini, 1992).

Captive Professionals

The company doctor is a good example of what Daniels (1969) called "**captive professionals**," or those whose presumed professional autonomy is compromised by organizational pressures from the bureaucracies that employ them. Daniels's study noted that psychiatrists practicing in the armed services accommodated their professional judgments to the military's manpower needs and values. Whereas psychiatrists working for mental hospitals tended to diagnose patients as mentally ill (in accordance with the expectations of the employer institutions), psychiatrists working for the military (where sickness reduced active manpower) tended to deny soldiers' claims of illness (Daniels, 1969, 1972; cf. Rosenhan, 1973). The diagnoses made by both of these "captive professionals" served to legitimate administrative decisions of the bureaucracies that employed them (cf. Ingleby, 1982: 136–137).

Similarly, many medical personnel employed by industry are "captive professionals." One Canadian study found that company doctors exhibited a "lack of sympathy with or intolerance of workers' attitudes towards health and safety in the workplace," and often perceived workers' health concerns as "fashions" or unreasonable fears. Rather than press the company to engineer changes in the production process or to initiate expensive monitoring programs, these doctors often emphasized workers' use of protective equipment and the screening and exclusion of supposedly "hyper-susceptible" workers (Walters, 1982). Although the corporate physician is potentially in a position to influence improved occupational health for employees, the professional's employer—not the individual worker—is still the "client," so ethical ambiguity and conflicting pressures are inherent in the structure of the job (Walsh, 1987).

Although some professionals' organizational situation makes them clearly vulnerable or "captive" to their employers' interests, all professionals are likely to be influenced by their identification with certain class or status interests. Source of income indirectly affects medical decisions and doctor-patient relationships. For example, doctors employed by industry tend not to diagnose occupational diseases, whereas doctors employed by unions or workers' health clinics frequently do (Lewin, 1987). Doctors at for-profit hospitals are likewise more likely to urge patients to undergo Caesarian sections, whereas those working at public hospitals are much less likely to decide to perform such operations (Stafford, 1991). And doctors who have mastered a new surgical procedure are less likely to recommend it for patients than doctors who are eager to practice that procedure (Scully, 1980: 195–196).

Whose Interests Are Served?

Although ideologies legitimate certain interests over others, they are often accepted by people whose interests are not necessarily served by those ideas. Ideological elements are often subtly diffused in a society through popular culture, educational institutions, mass media, and commercial advertising. For example, whose interests were served by the turn-of-the-century glorification of women's domesticity? Throughout the first half of this century, this ideal was meshed with popular ideas and fears of bacterial contagion to create much more work for house-wives, who were taught in school and in women's magazines that they should be occupied with "scientific cleaning" and buying numerous products to protect their families from these dangerous invisible agents (Ehrenreich and English, 1978: 127–164). Interest groups exert power to shape ideology and to have it accepted and disseminated through channels such as the mass media and public education (Berger and Luckmann, 1967: 119–124).

Ideologies are not peculiar to medicine under capitalism and absent under other social and economic arrangements. *All* medical systems embody ideologies, but the nature of these ideologies varies according to the structure of that society. In capitalist societies, the treatment of health and healing as **commodities** to be bought and sold under market conditions produces certain economic benefits for various individual and corporate interests. Medical systems in noncapitalist soci-eties, however, also utilize ideologies to legitimate and promote the interests of certain groups, such as state bureaucracies, dominant ethnic or tribal groups, or patriarchal powers (Donahue and McGuire, 1995).

Reification: Diseases and Bodies as Objects

Ideas that serve as ideologies often come into use subtly, frequently without explicit intention or awareness that the ideas have ideological uses. One such set of ideas are contemporary medical conceptions of the nature of disease and of the body. The product of this development is the notion that diseases are discrete, iden-tifiable (or potentially identifiable) entities—in short, objects. The body is likewise treated as an object, separate from the person who inhabits it.

This conception illustrates the process of reification and its ideological func-tions. **Reification** is the "apprehension of human phenomena as if they were things," or something other than human products (Berger and Luckmann, 1967: 89). Reified reality confronts people as something outside themselves, as a nonhuman object. Institutions, social roles, norms, and other social processes are often reified; they come to assume a greater-than-human authority and inevitability. Reification thus entails a certain amount of mystification, as the human roots of phenomena are veiled (see Taussig, 1980).

Reification of disease means conveniently forgetting the social processes by which the concept of disease is produced. It means denying the social meanings embodied in symptoms, diagnoses, and therapy, and in the very experience of illness itself. Reification of the body results in an even greater dehumanization because of the close connection between the body and the identity of the individual. For example, an anesthetized body lying on a gurney before surgery on its testicles is medically no more than an object with a pathological entity (disease) in its tissues (things) that must therefore be surgically removed. To the person himself, however, that body and those testicles are an important part of who he is—his very self.

Reification creeps pervasively into the practice of bioscientific medicine because the guise of the scientific process masks the human factors involved in the creation of medical knowledge, as illustrated earlier in this chapter. It also occurs when any individual practitioner fails to acknowledge that a diagnosis or medical disposition is a human creation. The diagnostician constructs a disease identification from an assortment of ambiguous signs and symptoms elicited by human processes, and interpreted in the context of a human evaluation of the patient's social and psychological—as well as physical—condition.

Diagnoses are the product of social interaction, yet rarely does a physician accept authorship of a disease identification. Rather, the disease comes to be seen as a feature or property of the patient (Taussig, 1980). For example, the complex process by which a physician applies the diagnostic label "diabetes" to a patient's condition is forgotten, and the diabetes is treated as an objective thing that the patient "has." The reified disease identification often assumes primacy; if it conflicts with the patient's subjective illness experience, the objectified disease-thing is often treated as more real than the sick person's feelings. To the extent that patients internalize this image of their bodies and diseases, the reified reality shapes even their self-perception and experience.

One of the ideological functions of the reification of disease and the body is an emphasis on individualistic rather than social or political responses to disease. In the example of workers' health risks in a chemical factory, the location of disease as a property of individual bodies led to an emphasis on finding which individuals were more likely to be susceptible to workplace toxins. It promoted the idea that those who were identified at risk should be counseled to change jobs, rather than reducing the exposure of all workers or eliminating the industrial processes that required the use of toxic substances. Reification transforms occupational disease into a thing that befalls some individuals instead of the result of specific human decisions affecting workers' health.

The emphasis on disease as an object that occurs within an individual also produces a tendency to locate responsibility for illness in the individual. It is thus one form of **blaming the victim** (Ryan, 1971), a type of legitimation which argues that the victim rather than the agent of a misfortune (such as rape, homelessness, or family abuse) was actually responsible for the occurrence. In the case of illness, the sick person is assumed to be responsible for having taken health risks, such as accepting a hazardous job, failing to use seat belts, or moving to an area with polluted water. As described in Chapter 4, the individual is often held accountable for unhealthy lifestyle choices, such as smoking, drinking, poor eating habits, and lack of exercise. The individual's emotional style and characteristic response to stress are also blamed (Crawford, 1977; see also Nettleton and Bunton, 1995).

Such attention to the individual as the locus of disease often results in inattention to the sick person's whole situation. Even extremely caring physicians can lose sight of the sociostructural roots of patients' suffering by focusing on an utterly individualized image of disease. For example, one study of doctor-patient communication noted the extent to which the patient's larger social predicament (for example, an extremely stressful workplace) was generally ignored or reduced to individualistic treatments, such as recommendation of tranquilizers or a vacation (Waitzkin, 1984). Medical *ideas* about disease thus serve subtle *ideological* functions, legitimating an individualistic–rather than social–approach to prevention and healing.

THE DEVELOPMENT OF MODERN BIOMEDICINE

We sometimes view the present nature of medical practice as a cultural given. When we think of medical care, our ready mental images include doctors, hospitals, nurses, medical laboratories, operating rooms, X-rays, hypodermic needles, and pills. But the institutions, occupations, and technologies we identify with medical care are the peculiar result of specific political, economic, and social interactions. The history of modern medicine shows that many alternative courses were possible, and the particular form that medical knowledge and practice have taken in this society made certain medical advances possible but also limited the field by cutting off other potentially fruitful approaches to health and healing.

The paradigm of modern scientific medicine incorporates a number of assumptions about the nature of the body and disease. Ideas do not just happen; rather they are produced, accepted, and transmitted in a political and social context. The elevation of this particular paradigm to become the medical mode for understanding disease and the body occurred in connection with the political process by which the medical profession gained dominance relative to other social authorities and healers.

Professional Dominance

In the nineteenth century, most medical doctors were barely considered professionals. Their credentials were relatively easy to achieve (or fake), their body of medical knowledge was skimpy, their tools for diagnosis and therapy were primitive and often dangerous, and their abilities to heal were not particularly impressive. Several kinds of physicians, each having very different ideas about the causes and treatments of sickness, competed for patients and social legitimacy. Furthermore, physicians were only a small percentage of the total number of persons practicing various healing arts, who included, among others, midwives, bone setters, nurses, pharmacists, barbers (who performed minor surgery), herbalists, and folk and religious healers.

Within just a few decades, however, in the early part of the twentieth century, medical doctors had achieved virtually total professional dominance. In the process described next, they had successfully eliminated, coopted, or subordinated all competing health professionals and acquired a state-legitimated monopoly over the health care market in the United States. Although medicine enjoys similar professional preeminence in other nations, it lacks the degree of state-legitimated dominance over the entire health care system that characterizes the American situation (cf. Berlant, 1975; Coburn et al., 1983; Freidson, 1970; Herzlich and Pierret, 1987; Schepers, 1985; Willis, 1983).

A profession is a service occupation characterized by legitimate control over the market for its services and over a body of specialized knowledge or expertise.

The **professionalization** of medicine as an occupation is thus a sociopolitical move-ment organized to achieve a "monopoly of opportunities in a market of services or labor and, inseparably, monopoly of status and work privileges" (Larson, 1979: 609). For medicine to achieve professional status, three main developments were necessary: (1) achieving standardization and cohesion within the profession; (2) convincing the state at various levels to grant a monopoly, for example, by requiring medical licenses to engage in healing practices; and (3) gaining public respect and persuading the public to accept the profession's definitions of what problems properly should be brought to it for service.

One definitive characteristic of a developed profession is its autonomy, which is an organizational product of its ability to dominate its area of expertise in the divi-sion of labor. In the case of the medical profession, autonomy is evidenced by doctors' legal protection from encroachment by other occupations. A second factor in medical autonomy is the profession's control over the production and application of medical knowledge and skill, especially the training and licensing of physicians. A third indication of medicine's status as a developed profession is its presumed self-regulation with a code of ethics (Freidson, 1970).

In 1847, the American Medical Association (AMA) was established as a professional organization for physicians from the medical belief system dubbed **allopathy**, which was characterized by "heroic" and invasive treatments such as bloodletting, purging, blistering, vomiting, and medicating with powerful drugs (such as opium) and poisons (like mercury and arsenic). Allopathic physicians called themselves "regular" or orthodox physicians, but the public was, under-standably, attracted to some of the less dangerous forms of medicine practiced by competing approaches such as homeopathy, naturopathy, and hydropathy.

The initial program of the AMA was relatively straightforward: to create internal professional cohesion and standardization by controlling the requirements for medical degrees and by enacting a code of ethics that would exclude "irregular" practitioners from the ranks. These efforts were aimed primarily at reducing the influence of the chief competitors, homeopathic physicians, who had organized the American Institute for Homeopathy in 1844. Between 1850 and 1880, the two camps became increasingly polarized, as the AMA censured members who continued to have dealings with the "enemy." For example, in 1878 the local medical society expelled a Connecticut doctor for having consulted with a homeopathic physician—his wife. "Regular" physicians lost considerable ground in the latter half of the nineteenth century while homeopathy gained as much public respect and legal considerations as allopathy. So-called regular practitioners accounted for nearly 90 percent of all doctors, but the proportion of irregular physicians increased in the mid-1800s. For the latter half of the century, irregulars commanded approx-imately one-fifth of the market (Starr, 1982: 88–99).

The AMA and the irregular physicians cooperated, however, in their political efforts to have states enact licensing laws, because they shared a common interest in eliminating competition from persons who had not attended any form of medical school, such as midwives, ministers, pharmacists, and folk healers. From its outset, the AMA has been especially interested in exposing and prosecuting what it calls "quackery," which is practically defined as all forms of medicating or healing outside the profession's control. A related campaign successfully eliminated much competition from patent medicine manufacturers and eventually subordinated the practice of pharmacy to medical control. Licensing legislation began to specify the quality of the medical education required, and some states set up boards of medical examiners, initially making allowances for various irregular forms of professional training alongside the regular. The courts and legislatures had begun to grant professional prerogatives to thus-approved doctors. Gradually, regular medicine coopted and absorbed most irregular physicians, but rejected and actively opposed later organized alternatives such as chiropractic (Starr, 1982: 99–112; see also Baer, 1984; Wolpe, 1990).

Scientization of Medicine and Medical Training

The most dramatic change in the medical profession's dominance occurred after the turn of the century. The adoption of scientific medicine and the insistence on standards of rigorous medical education were central strategies in the professionalization process. Science and education did not, however, characterize the actual practice of regular medicine at that time. In fact, scientific training was available to only a small elite of physicians, mainly researchers and educators, who had the money to study in Europe (Berliner, 1976).

Control of medical education was critical to a monopoly in the market. In the early 1900s, practicing physicians made relatively poor incomes; one comparison suggests that they earned less than an ordinary mechanic of the day (Berliner, 1976: 584). There appeared to be a growing oversupply of physicians relative to the market of paying clients. Licensing laws had not resulted in fewer physicians but merely more medical schools. The national population grew between 1870 and 1910 by 138 percent; the number of physicians increased by 153 percent. Many professional leaders objected not only to the numbers of new physicians these medical schools were graduating but also to the fact that they had recruited "undesirable" students: women, blacks, immigrants, and working-class persons. Advocates of reforming medical education believed that medicine could not become a respected profession if its ranks included such lowly elements. Shortly after the turn of the century, the AMA underwent a major internal organization and subsequently made such "reform" its primary focus (Starr, 1982: 112–117).

After a preliminary review of medical colleges, the AMA invited an outside group, the Carnegie Foundation, to conduct a through investigation of the appoximately 160 medical colleges in the United States and Canada. The resulting report in 1910 was devastating to many medical education programs (Flexner, 1910). The report's foremost objection was to the lack of medical science in the curriculum and training experiences. It recommended that the great majority of medical schools should be closed; the first-rate schools should be strengthened on the model of Johns Hopkins, which had a singularly science-oriented program; and a few medium-quality schools should be greatly improved to meet the upper standard. With the support of state legislatures and many universities themselves, the governing body of AMA subsequently became the de facto national accrediting agency for medical schools. The report's recommendations were dramatically supported by funding from numerous philanthropic foundations. By 1934, the nine largest U.S. foundations had given over $154 million to implement reforms (Berliner, 1975).[3]

These reforms of medical education had exactly the kind of effects the AMA wanted: increased internal cohesion of the profession and increased control of the market. Not only had the supply of licensed physicians been dramatically cut, but the homogeneity of the profession had also been assured by greatly limiting access to medical education for women, blacks, Jews, and all who could not afford the newly required four years of college and four full-time years of medical school. The declining numbers of new physicians adversely affected poor and rural areas. Flexner had expected that the new highly trained graduates would disperse throughout the country, but in practice they gravitated to the wealthiest regions. The increased cost of their medical education reduced the likelihood that they would accept the modest incomes of practices in small towns and rural areas (Starr, 1982: 123–127). There were likewise fewer doctors for blacks. Due to widespread discrimination and segregation, blacks received treatment mainly from black physicians, but the reforms dramatically reduced their numbers (Starr, 1982: 124). Only two of the seven medical schools for blacks survived the reforms. Because the medical colleges run by irregular physicians had been somewhat more open to interracial admissions, their disproportionate demise also reduced opportunities for blacks to become doctors.

In the latter part of the nineteenth century, considerable numbers of women had entered medical practice. In the decade from 1880 to 1890, women doubled their proportional representation of all doctors in the United States (from 2.8 to 5.6 percent); 17 medical colleges for women were founded in that period. After considerable struggle, women began to be admitted to elite medical schools after 1890, and by 1893–1894, women constituted 10 percent or more of the student body at 19 of the coeducational schools (Starr, 1982: 117).

Women's acceptance into coeducational settings was far from smooth, however; they experienced considerable harassment from male professors and students (Morantz-Sanchez, 1985). Many physicians believed that women's menstrual cycles made them incapable of professional work. For example, one doctor declared, "periodical infirmity of their sex . . . in every case . . . unfits them for any responsible effort of mind . . . [and that during their menstrual] condition, neither life nor limb submitted to them would be as safe as at other times"

---

[3]The conspicuous role of the capitalist philanthropies, notably the Rockefeller Foundation (which gave some $66 million to just nine medical schools in the aftermath of Flexner's report), has led some to suggest a direct affinity between capitalist classes and the type of medicine they chose to support (see Brown, 1979; and the critique in Starr, 1982: 228). Even if there were no deliberate collusion, it is true that the outcome was a version of medicine that necessitated extensive expenditures on pharmaceuticals, medical technology, and capital-intensive hospitals, as described further in Chapters 11 and 12.

(quoted in Wertz and Wertz, 1979: 57). After the turn of the century, women were increasingly excluded from the profession of medicine. All but 3 of the 17 women's medical colleges closed, and coeducational medical colleges maintained quotas that, until the 1960s, limited women to about 5 percent of admissions (Starr, 1982: 124).

Because they were excluded from mainstream medicine, some women turned to the less prestigious area of public health, such as campaigns for better hygiene, nutrition, and mother-and-child health care. The medical profession often opposed these efforts, which it perceived as threats to its dominance and as competition for health expenditures. For example, female public health advocates campaigned for the Sheppard-Towner Act of 1921, which provided health care for mothers and infants until 1929, when the AMA pressured Congress not to renew funding (Morantz-Sanchez, 1985).

Professional Autonomy and Control

By the 1930s, the medical profession had achieved significant autonomy. It controlled the recruitment and training of new physicians, including the length and content of medical education, as well as the examination and licensing by which new doctors could be admitted to practice. The profession defined (and regularly expanded) the scope of its work, specified its own standards of practice, and maintained the right to enforce them (Freidson, 1970).

The prerogative to define the scope of medical work is connected with the process of *medicalization* by which increasing numbers of areas of life were brought under medicine's purview and control. Childbirth, alcoholism, obesity, infant feeding formulas, and menopause are just a few of the areas that previously were not defined as properly "medical" matters but, through the medical profession's influence, were redefined as issues needing doctors' attention, regardless of whether the medical approach was more effective than nonmedical. Other efforts to expand their markets included the campaign to persuade well persons to get an annual checkup.

In defining the scope of its work, the medical profession also eliminated much of its competition. Some professional competitors, such as homeopaths and osteopaths, were coopted; others, such as pharmacists, nurses, anesthetists, and X-ray technicians, were subordinated; whereas still others, such as midwives, clergy, and barber-surgeons, were driven from legitimate practice outright (Gritzer, 1981). The AMA also worked to limit public health authorities severely; medical professional interests campaigned (usually successfully) against public dispensaries, the compulsory reporting of tuberculosis, municipal laboratories and vaccination programs, the provision of health services in the public schools, and national public health programs, which were all viewed as competitors in the provision of services and as threats to the profession's autonomous authority over its domain. By controlling licensing, the access to facilities (such as hospitals and labs), access to other physicians as backups, and the legitimacy of third-party reimbursement, the medical profession greatly reduced its competition (Dolan, 1980).

The medical profession rapidly consolidated its control over the conditions of its work as the organization of hospitals specifically reflects. In recent years, however, the profession may have lost some of its control in many institutional settings, such as the new for-profit hospital corporations described in Chapters 11 and 12. Because of its market monopoly, the medical profession also asserted its control over the terms of its remuneration. American medicine is organized on a fee-for-service basis in which, rather than receiving a set salary, most doctors charge each patient a fee for each service performed. The profession's model of the ideal economic relationship was one of direct payment by the patient-receiver to the health care provider. The rise in importance of third-party payment from the government, insurance companies, labor unions, or fraternal organizations, who paid part or all of some patients' medical fees, represented an intrusion and danger to medical dominance. As Starr (1982: 235) observed, "to be the intermediary in the costs of sickness is a strategic role that confers social and political as well as strictly economic gains." Over the years the medical profession has vehemently asserted its interests in campaigns against national health insurance, Social Security health benefits, Blue Cross and Blue Shield, prepaid health plans, Medicare, and Medicaid. As shown in Chapters 11 and 12, the role of third parties has nevertheless increased, resulting in some regulation and limitation of medical practice and payments.

Modernization and Medical Practice

The features of modern medicine are in many ways the products of the broader process of modernization, which has similarly shaped other institutional spheres, such as industry, education, and communications. The specific historical development of the medical profession also contributed to certain structural features of modern medicine.

Several aspects of modernization apply to the development of medicine. One is the trend toward **institutional differentiation**, in which various institutional spheres in society become separated from each other, as each comes to perform specialized functions. Differentiation resulted in the separation of healing functions from the institutions of religion and the family. A second aspect of modernization is **rationalization**, the application of criteria of functional rationality to many aspects of social and economic life. When applied to the division of labor, rationalization promoted bureaucratic forms of organization and an emphasis on efficiency, standardization, and instrumental criteria for decision making. The structure of the modern hospital reflects this rational principle of organization.

Rational ways of knowing emphasized the use of empirical evidence to explain natural phenomena without reference to nonnatural categories of thought. Weber ([1904] 1958: 139) observed that this led to the "disenchantment" of the world, meaning that phenomena once held in awe or reverence were stripped of their special qualities and became ordinary. The human body itself has been thus disenchanted. For example, the modern view of the body contrasts strongly with the medieval notion that the body should not be dissected lest it be unfit for reuniting with the soul in resurrection. Bodies that are considered spiritual temples must be respected; bodies that are disenchanted entities require no special reverence. The key feature of the rationalization process is not so much the particular explanations of phenomena but the belief that all phenomena can be rationally explained. A by-product of this belief is an increased emphasis on technology and technique by which rational knowledge can presumably be translated into control. Modern societies particularly value rational mastery. For example, we believe that if we can explain what causes a disease, then it is only a matter of time before we can develop a technology or technique for healing or even preventing the disease.

Although the process of rationalization occurred in all modernizing medical systems, an additional feature in capitalist societies was **commodification**, or the process by which such qualities as health, beauty, and fitness are transformed into objects that can be bought and sold in the marketplace. Not only material objects such as pharmaceuticals and prosthetic devices but also the entire range of health services become commodities to be bought and sold. Commodification encourages both the sick and the well to become avid consumers of the nebulous product known as health (Featherstone, 1991).

Although these aspects of contemporary Western medical systems are linked with the larger process of modernization, many of the specific characteristics of modern medicine are the products of the historical-political struggle for professional dominance and the assumptions implicit in the biomedical belief system described next. Indeed, it is entirely likely that if different factions and competitors had won those early battles for legitimacy and a share of the medical market, we would today have an entirely different model of medical knowledge, of what constitutes health and health care, and of what it means to be a doctor.

Assumptions of the Biomedical Model

The present system of medical knowledge is based on a number of assumptions about the body, disease, and ways of knowing. Although many of these assumptions have a long history, they do not necessarily produce better medical care. They also deflect attention from nonmedical measures for promoting health, such as nutrition and public health, and as the last part of this chapter illustrates, contribute to serious problems in doctor-patient communication.

Mind-Body Dualism The medical model assumes a clear dichotomy between the mind and the body; physical diseases are presumed to be located within the body (Engel, 1977; see also Benoist and Cathebras, 1993; Gordon, 1988; Kirmayer, 1988; Leder, 1984). The medical model also holds that the body can be understood and treated in isolation from other aspects of the person inhabiting it (Hahn and Kleinman, 1983).

The philosophical foundations for this split may go back to Descartes's division of the person into mind and body. The practical foundations, however, probably lie in medicine's shift to an emphasis on clinical observation toward the end of the eighteenth century and pathological anatomy beginning in the nineteenth century. Foucault (1973) demonstrated that medicine shifted its ways of viewing the body and developed a "clinical gaze." Previously, physicians saw the body indirectly, mainly through patients' descriptions of their experience of a malady. By contrast, the clinical gaze emphasized direct clinical observation and physical examinations; technological developments, such as the invention of the stethoscope in 1819, gave physicians access to direct (and presumably more objective) clinical knowledge than previously could be gained only indirectly. Foucault noted that the way the body is viewed has profound political implications. The ascending medical perspective saw the body as docile—something physicians could observe, manipulate, transform, and improve (see also Armstrong, 1983). Increasingly sophisticated pathological anatomy meant that diseases were conceptualized in terms of alterations in tissues that were visible upon opening the body, such as during autopsy. This mode of conceptualizing disease had a profound effect in splitting body from mind in the practice of clinical medicine (Sullivan, 1986: 344–345).

Physical Reductionism The medical model not only dichotomizes body and mind, but also assumes that illness can be reduced to disordered bodily (biochemical or neurophysiological) functions. This physical reductionism, however, excludes social, psychological, and behavioral dimensions of illness (Engel, 1977). The result of this reductionism, together with medicine's mind-body dualism, is that disease is localized in the *individual* body. Such conceptions prevent the medical model from conceiving of the *social* body, or how aspects of the individual's social or emotional life might impinge on physical health. Another result is medicine's general inattention to social conditions (as described in Chapters 3–5) that contribute to illness or could aid in healing (Bologh, 1981).

Specific Etiology A related assumption of the biomedical model is what Dubos (1959: 130–135) called the "doctrine of specific etiology," or the belief that each disease is caused by a specific, potentially identifiable agent. It developed from the nineteenth-century work of Pasteur and Koch, who demonstrated that the introduction of specific virulent microorganisms (germs) into the body produced specific diseases. One primary focus of scientific medicine became the identification of these specific agents and their causal link to specific diseases. The doctrine of specific etiology was later extended beyond infectious diseases and applied to other diseases, such as deficiency diseases in which the specific etiology was not an intrusive microorganism but the lack of a necessary element, such as a vitamin or hormone.

Although the doctrine of specific etiology has led to important theoretical and practical achievements, Dubos noted that it has rarely provided a complete account of the causation of disease. He asked why, although infectious agents are nearly ubiquitous, only some people get sick some of the time. Accordingly, an adequate understanding of an illness etiology must include broader factors, such as nutrition, stress, and metabolic states, that affect the individual's susceptibility to infection. As noted in Chapter 2, the search for specific illness-producing agents worked relatively well in dealing with infectious diseases but is too simplistic to explain the causes of complex, chronic illnesses. Also, as Dubos (1959) observed, this approach often results in a quest for a medicinal "magic bullet" to "shoot and kill" the disease, producing an overreliance on pharmaceuticals in the "armamentarium" (stock of weapons) of the modern physician.

The Machine Metaphor One of the oldest Western images for understanding the body is a comparison with the functioning of a machine. Accordingly, disease is the malfunctioning of some constituent mechanism (such as a "breakdown" of the heart). Other cultures use other metaphors; for example, ancient Egyptian societies used the image of a river, and Chinese tradition refers to the balance of elemental forces (yin and yang) of the earth (Osherson and AmaraSingham, 1981). Modern medicine has not only retained the metaphor of the machine but also extended it by developing specializations along the lines of machine parts, emphasizing individual systems or organs to the exclusion of an image of the totality of the body. The machine metaphor further encouraged an instrumentalist approach to the body; the physician could "repair" one part in isolation from the rest (Berliner, 1975). Such mechanical metaphors further justify, as a medical procedure, the replacement of nonworking parts by organ transplants, pacemakers, and artificial joints, for example.

Regimen and Control Partly as a product of the machine metaphor and the quest for mastery, the Western medical model also conceptualizes the body as the proper object of regimen and control, again emphasizing the responsibility of the individual to exercise this control in order to maintain or restore health. Modernizing trends toward rationalization have further encouraged the notion of the standardization of body disciplines, such as diets, exercise programs, etiquette, routines of hygiene, and even sexual activity (Foucault, 1979; Turner, 1984: 157–203).

This brief history shows that the knowledge and practice we know as medicine have their roots in sociopolitical processes. The ideas and assumptions of biomedicine forcefully influence economic and power relationships both within the relationship between practitioner and patient and in institutions (for example, law) of the larger society. We must remember that these medical realities are socially produced.

SUMMARY

What we know about health, illness, and the body is socially constructed. Both lay and professional medical knowledge are influenced by social, economic, and political factors. The categories and even the very language for describing and understanding diseases are likewise subject to powerful social influences. Diseases and disease syndromes are discovered and professionally accepted through concrete social processes; other disease categories are similarly denied, dropped, or disavowed by social processes. Such social influences shape not only ideas but indeed also the experiences of our own and others' bodies and bodily conditions.

The nature of modern medicine is partly determined by the larger process of modernization, especially the extension of rationalization to the body and ways of knowing about and treating the body. In capitalist societies, the additional societal process of the commodification of health and health care has altered the economic meaning of medical services, as health has become an ambiguous product to be bought and consumed.

Medical knowledge sometimes serves ideological purposes, legitimating the interests of certain persons or groups. Ideological aspects of thought and practice are typically very subtle, and often go unnoticed by people who believe and use them. The medicalization of various areas of life and the uses of medicine in service of various institutional goals illustrate some of the ways ideology influences medical ideas and practice. The tendency of bioscientific medicine to treat diseases and bodies as objects masks the social history of ideas of disease and the social processes of finding disease. Reification also leads to a view of disease as a property of the sick person, thus reducing the significance of the social and environmental causes of the disease and the social context of the person's illness.

Many characteristics of the contemporary medical establishment can be traced to political developments in the recent history of the profession. Certain features of modern medicine are the results of the assumptions of the biomedical approach itself, which is characterized by its dichotomization of mind and body, physical reductionism, the doctrine of specific etiology, the machine metaphor for the body, and an emphasis on bodily regimen and control. These assumptions have concrete implications for the delivery of health care.

RECOMMENDED READINGS

Articles

PHIL BROWN, "Naming and framing: The social construction of diagnosis and illness." *Health and Social Behavior*, 1995 (extra issue): 34–52.

H. TRISTAM ENGLEHARDT, "The disease of masturbation: Values and the concept of disease," pp. 15–24 in J. W. Leavitt and R. L. Numbers, eds., *Sickness and Health in America*. Madison: University of Wisconsin Press, 1978.

FRANCES MCCREA, "The politics of menopause: The discovery of a deficiency disease." *Social Problems* 13(1), 1983: 111–123.

BRYAN S. TURNER, "The government of the body: Medical regimens and the rationalization of diet." *British Journal of Sociology* 33(2), 1982: 254–269.

VIVIENNE WALTERS, "Company doctors' perceptions of and responses to conflicting pressures from labor and management." *Social Problems* 30(1), 1982: 1–12.

Books

SAMUEL BUTLER, *Erewhon*. New York: New American Library, [1901] 1960. A fictional utopia based on dramatically different definitions of health and illness.

PEGGY FOSTER, *Women and the Health Care Industry: An Unhealthy Relationship?* Buckingham: Open University Press, 1995. A balanced but critical examination of the medicalization of women's health issues.

ELIOT FREIDSON, *Profession of Medicine: A Study of the Sociology of Applied Knowledge.* New York: Dodd, Mead, 1970. This classic study of the structure of medical knowledge and professional autonomy serves as a useful basis for understanding current debates about the status and proper roles of medicine and various other health-related occupations.

PAUL STARR, *The Social Transformation of American Medicine.* New York: Basic, 1982. A sweeping history of the medical profession's rise to professional dominance.

MODERN BIOMEDICINE: KNOWLEDGE AND PRACTICE

Social constructions enter the practice of Western medicine not only through the ideas and professional organization of biomedicine, but also through routine social practices, such as interactions between medical personnel and their patients. Detailed analyses of doctor-patient interactions show how professional dominance affects the interpersonal level of health care. Many problems of doctor-patient relationships are due to social-structural aspects of medical training and practice. Other very important factors are embedded assumptions of the medical model of disease and treatment. Some of these medical assumptions also make it difficult for physicians and society as a whole to deal effectively with emerging dilemmas in modern health care: the proper ends of medical treatment and the limits of medicine.

When people turn to medical professionals for help, they typically enter the patient role. Unlike the sick role, which is defined by broader social expectations (see Chapter 6), the patient role involves primarily the *reciprocal* expectations and norms held by the doctor and patient.[1] These expectations are emotionally charged; doctors and patients alike are often deeply dissatisfied with the actual situation.

Although each patient negotiates a different relationship with each particular doctor, a number of general social-structural factors shape the doctor-patient relationship. Two factors in particular are at the root of many of the problems in Western medical practice: (1) professional dominance, and (2) rationalization of the body in the medical model. Professional dominance creates and exacerbates social chasms between doctor and patient, and the medical model's rationalization of the body creates enormous discontinuities between medicine's paradigm of disease and curing, on the one hand, and patients' experience and understanding of their illness and their needs, on the other.

Although individual doctors could do much to overcome these problems in their own work with patients, these two characteristics are thoroughly embedded in the *structure* of the profession, medical education, hospital and other medical institutional structures, and the organization of medical practice. Without structural change, they will continue to limit the potential for individual change in the doctor-patient relationship. Although the issue of patient (or consumer) dissatisfaction is a genuine concern, a more serious problem is that inadequacies in the doctor-patient relationship may gravely impede the very process of healing. The following discussion suggests some of the ways these social-structural factors may diminish the healing effectiveness of medical practitioners.

PROFESSIONAL DOMINANCE

The professionalization of medicine produced social distance between the practitioner and the sick person. The doctor is assumed to be the knowledgeable expert; the patient, the relatively ignorant recipient of the doctor's professional services.

---

[1]The role of patient is qualitatively different relative to other professional and nonprofessional workers (such as nurses, technicians, or hospital aides), and varies dramatically according to institutional context (such as doctor's office, hospital, patient's home, clinic).

Indeed, typically the patient is limited in ability to judge whether the doctor is using adequate medical knowledge, making competent treatment recommendations, and providing good service.

The greater the social distance between two people, the less sensitivity either is likely to have toward the other's problems. **Social distance** refers to a sense of separation, difference, and inability to identify with each other produced by a myriad of social characteristics and experiences (for example, social class or gender differences). Doctors who themselves have had extensive experience in the patient role may be more empathetic toward their own patients (cf. Hahn, 1995: 234–261). Considerable social distance is inherent in the expert-layperson dichotomy.

Social distance produced by divergence in *ascribed* statuses (such as race or gender) appears to be more important than other status differences in causing doctor-patient miscommunication (Richey et al., 1995). One study found that (female) nurse-practitioners interacted with women patients with far less social distance than did male medical doctors. Although promoting better communication with their patients, however, the nurse-practitioners did not succeed in overcoming social distance based on barriers of social class and expertise (Fisher, 1995).

The sick person who wants medical help is in an intrinsically weak position. As medicine and other professional domains become increasingly specialized, mediated by high technology, and based on a growing, complex body of knowledge, the gap between laypersons and various experts grows wider. The gap is further exaggerated when a position of professional power is used to legitimate physicians' economic rewards and professional autonomy. When patients are in awe of doctors' knowledge and skill, they are more likely to defer to physicians' judgment and to consider high fees reasonable. Although this awe and deference to doctors' expertise may promote healing by raising patients' confidence, hope, and cooperation in the therapeutic process, they may also be a source of unrealistic expectations and anger, such as that leading to malpractice lawsuits (cf. Fielding, 1995).

Professional power protects physicians from potentially damaging problems such as therapeutic failure. If a diagnosis is incorrect or a treatment does not work, the distance in knowledge between doctor and patient reduces the likelihood that the patient would be able to evaluate whether the failure was due to the doctor's lack of knowledge or skill. Professional dominance also legitimates the power and prestige of some health care professionals over others. For example, there is an ongoing "turf war" (with profound implications for the well-being of birthing mothers) among obstetricians, family practitioners, nurse-midwives, and lay-midwives (Good, 1995).

Information Control

One of the foremost ways doctors protect their professional power is by controlling the flow of information to the patient. On the one hand, the doctor cannot possibly, even in a long-term relationship, communicate to the patient everything the expert knows relevant to the limited actual circumstances of the patient's condition. On the other hand, patients need information about their condition: What is wrong with me? How serious is it? What is the expected outcome? What are my treatment options?

The more information patients have, the better able they are to understand their situation, evaluate options, and participate in treatment decisions. But such evaluation and decision making is often threatening to the physician's control of the case. As a result, some physicians consider the "good" patient to be one who trustingly accepts the doctor's judgment and complies with doctor's orders, full of unquestioning appreciation of the doctor's ministrations. Especially in hospital settings, professionals use control of information as a protective device in managing medical mistakes (Millman, 1976). Withholding information after treatment may, however, have the opposite effect of increasing patient anger and litigiousness (Fielding, 1995). Sometimes keeping patients ignorant of their condition enables the doctor to manage them more effectively by preventing emotional responses that the physician might find disruptive or unpleasant. Although individual doctors do not necessarily engage consciously in these protective legitimations, the very structure of the profession promotes them.

Although the doctor-patient relationship is based on reciprocal role expectations, many doctors cast patients in stereotypical roles that serve to justify information control and doctors' dominant position relative to patients. One such expectation is the notion that patients are generally medically ignorant and childlike, unable to comprehend explanations of the causes, alternative treatments, and expected outcome of their conditions (Segall and Roberts, 1980). Several studies have found that the majority of physicians consistently and markedly underestimated their patients' level of comprehension (McKinlay, 1975).

Information control involves both information gathering and information giving. The doctor controls the medical interaction, deciding how much and which information to seek, and how much and which information to impart to the patient. The rationale and method for this model of a medical encounter are discussed further later. The medical interview and clinical examination consist of many such information-gathering and -giving decisions. Doctors control the information-gathering aspect by framing questions, cutting off patients' statements, ignoring certain patient input as irrelevant, and actively eliciting other input. The doctor decides whether and how extensively to conduct a physical examination, which tests to have done, and what follow-up study is needed; these aspects of a consultation are highly variable, a matter of the doctor's discretion (Fisher, 1983).

The medical interview is a constrained, prestructured form of talk. West (1983) found that patient-initiated questions are "dispreferred." Her detailed analysis of 21 medical exchanges showed that only 9 percent of the 773 questions were initiated by patients. Patient assertiveness often resulted in less response from doctors, whose pervasive dislike of patient-initiated questions was linked with the physicians' reluctance to answer "too many" such questions (West, 1984: 156). Patients sensed that their questioning was not the preferred pattern for the interaction; when they did pose questions, nearly half (46 percent) exhibited some anxiety, such as stutters or nervous giggles.

How patients express themselves and certain of their personal characteristics are also important factors influencing the amount and quality of information that physicians give them. One study of a hospital family practice clinic found that doctors gave more information to their patients who appeared to be better educated, younger, or more anxious about their health problems. Patients with communicative styles that were more active and affectively expressive tended to receive more information; patients who were more passive, asked few questions, and exhibited few worries or emotions about their conditions received less information about their conditions and treatments. Because well-educated patients were also disproportionately represented among those with active communicative styles, these findings suggest that some patients are doubly disadvantaged in doctor-patient communication (Street, 1991; see also Street, 1992).

Information-giving and question-asking exchanges between doctor and patient vary significantly according to social class. A British study of general practitioners' consultations found that patients' social class differences accounted for a significant proportion of the variance in both the information doctors gave in answer to questions and in the explanations volunteered by the doctors. Doctors may misinterpret working-class patients' reticence to ask questions as due to their lack of interest, but this study suggested that such patients' diffidence may be due more to the social distance between them and the doctor, and perhaps also to learned patterns of deference to higher social classes (Pendleton and Bochner, 1980).

Social distance between doctor and patient affects not only the quality of the medical interview and information giving, but also the likelihood that the patient will cooperate with the doctor's therapeutic recommendations. Men physicians typically couched their treatment recommendations as explicit commands, resulting in compliant responses among patients less than half the time. By contrast, women physicians' communicative style was more collaborative, reducing some social distance from the patient. By giving directives in a characteristically "feminine" mitigated form (for instance, "Now that we've got your blood pressure stable, let's make our plan about the next steps in treatment"), women physicians achieved a more symmetrical doctor-patient relationship, which produced a far higher rate (67 percent) of patient "compliance" (West, 1993; see also Ong et al., 1995, for a review of the literature on doctor-patient communication).

Uncertainty and Control

Uncertainty and fallibility are built-in features of medical practice, and the boundaries between an "acceptable" versus an "unacceptable" error (and "avoidable" versus "unavoidable" mistake) are themselves uncertain (Paget, 1988; Rosenthal, 1995). One physician, describing his experience with medical mistakes, commented,

Many situations do not lend themselves to a simple determination of whether a mistake has been made. Seriously ill, hospitalized patients, for instance, require of doctors almost continuous decision-making. Although in most cases no single mistake is obvious, there always seem to be things that could have been done differently or better: administering more of this medication, starting that treatment a little sooner. . . . The fact is that when a patient dies, the physician is left wondering whether the care he provided was inadequate. . . . Medicine is not an exact science; errors are always possible, even in the midst of the humdrum routine of daily care. Was that baby I just sent home with a diagnosis of mild viral fever actually in the early stages of serious meningitis? Will that nine-year-old with stomach cramps whose mother I just lectured about psychosomatic illness end up in the hospital tomorrow with a ruptured appendix? . . . A doctor has to confront the possibility of a mistake with every patient visit. (Hilfiker, 1984)

Medical uncertainty is an inherent difficulty for both doctor and patient. Although precision, certainty, and control are goals of bioscientific medicine, clinical practice rarely comes close to meeting such goals. Real patients' problems are often complex, and even highly trained physicians cannot know everything about every possible problem. Diagnoses have, at best, only a certain probability of accuracy; straightforward diagnoses of well-known diseases have only a higher probability of accuracy than those of complex, poorly understood diseases. Pressures for certainty in diagnosis may lead to excessive medical testing (Kassirer, 1989). Control in treatment is likewise often elusive; much therapy is a matter of trial and error. Rather than resolve ambiguity, technological medicine often produces greater expectations at the same time as more arenas for uncertainty. For example, technological capabilities for keeping alive premature infants who would otherwise have died shortly after birth but now may survive with serious debilities increase the range of medical uncertainty for doctors who must decide whether to use these technologies for a particular infant (Beresford, 1991).

Medical training provides some preparation for dealing with clinical uncertainty (Fox, 1957), but routine medical practice often involves judgments whose accuracy and effects are uncertain and, in some cases, unknowable. Although practicing physicians do acknowledge a number of areas of uncertainty (Gerrity et al., 1992), they are uncomfortable with uncertainty as an indicator of personal inadequacy, failure, error, or lack of knowledge.

The patient's situation in the face of uncertainty is even more anxiety producing because the patient lacks medical expertise. Doctors sometimes prolong patients' uncertainty, even after their own uncertainty about the disease or therapy has been reduced or resolved. Physicians may use their control over patient uncertainty to preserve their power and keep their options open (Waitzkin and Stoeckle, 1972). For example, the head of one pediatric ward had a policy of aggressively treating children with leukemia up to the moment of death; no child was ever labeled terminal, no matter how unsuccessful the treatment. The mother of a child who was obviously succumbing asked this doctor, "Is my child critical?," to which the doctor replied, "No." Another member of the staff asked him privately, "Why did you tell her the child is not critical, when we know he has only a few weeks to live?" The doctor's answer: "He is not technically critical until he is on some life-support system." To control information about the child's status further, he ordered that the records not be shown or otherwise divulged to the distraught mother. He believed that if the mother knew how near to death her child was, she might refuse the course of chemotherapy he had ordered for the boy.

By contrast, many physicians consider informing patients a necessary part of involving patients in their treatment. One surgical oncologist said,

> If it's malignant, I want them to have enough information so that they have the truth, but also so that they have some hope. They know that there are things that can be done that will help them. I think the hardest thing is uncertainty, and also I think it's extremely hard if you begin to think that your doctors are not telling you things. Then you don't know if you can ever believe them. . . . When patients start out being involved from the beginning and being in control from the beginning, it's much better. (quoted in Good, 1995: 177)

Doctor-patient negotiations over information vary according to the type of illness. In the course of the long-term treatment of chronic illness, the balance of power is often altered, requiring a renegotiation of the doctor-patient relationship. Patients are likely to become increasingly expert about their specific condition and thus more assertive in challenging their doctors (cf. Calnan, 1984; Herzlich and Pierret, 1987: 212).

Doctor-patient communication is especially problematic in the face of the uncertainty related to diseases such as multiple sclerosis (MS), a gradually debilitating, incurable disease of the nervous system. Because many MS victims are in young adulthood, when serious chronic illness is least expected, doctors at first may not consider the diagnosis. MS creates uncertainty for both the doctor and patient partly because its early symptoms are unclear or elusive. Another reason is that the diagnosis is fearsome to both the sufferer and the doctor because MS is incurable and potentially severely debilitating. Physicians thus frequently fail to diagnose MS correctly or postpone telling their patients of the diagnosis until it is inevitable.

One study suggested that this protective strategy for the doctor can create significant problems for the patient, perhaps leading to iatrogenic emotional difficulties (Stewart and Sullivan, 1982). Lacking physician confirmation that their symptoms were indeed related to a "real" illness, many MS patients were viewed by family, friends, and doctors as hypochondriacs or as "imagining things." As a result many sufferers experienced symptoms of stress that were actually more troublesome than the MS-related symptoms themselves. They lost faith in their doctors, shopped around for others, challenged physicians' diagnoses, and self-diagnosed (actions that typically elicited very negative reactions from physicians). Similarly, a study of interactions in a clinic for chronic illness sufferers showed that a major concern of the patients was to convince others—especially doctors—of the reality of their diseases. This was done by elaborating their illness behavior, but the sicker they behaved, the less likely doctors were to believe them. Their "doctor shopping" to confirm the fact of their illnesses also increased the likelihood that doctors would label them as "crocks" (Alexander, 1982).

Especially when medical knowledge about repetitive strain injuries was in the early stages of development, sufferers engaged in a similar search for doctor-patient communication in which their expression of pain would be taken seriously, as a legitimate problem. The medical consultation thus became a situation in which patients needed to convince the doctor of the reality of their symptoms, especially pain and disability. They feared being labeled as "neurotic," "crocks," or "malingerers." When physicians must serve as both curers and gatekeepers (in determining whether workers' compensation or disability leaves are legitimate), doctor-patient communication can be even more strained or adversarial (Reid et al., 1991).

One researcher analyzed in detail the transcripts of three problematic doctor-patient encounters that were marked by tension, ambiguity, and no apparent resolution (Paget, 1983). Without much background about the patient, the reader sees in the transcript an apparently neurotic woman, overly preoccupied with little details of her body's functioning. After these three meetings, her doctor's assessment was that the patient's health was good and that her problem was "nerves." The transcript takes on an entirely different meaning, however, when we realize that the woman had recently had an operation for cancer. Her primary agenda in each of these encounters was clearly to address her fears that her cancer would metastasize or was not fully excised, but those fears never once became a topic of discourse. The doctor did not acknowledge that her fears existed or might be legitimate; he only heard her seemingly minor complaints about her teeth and her scalp. Indeed, an analysis of the doctor's responses to her input shows that he was not really listening to any of her expressions, perhaps because he had already defined them as the product of her "nerves," and therefore medically unreal or unimportant. She too contributed to the ongoing misunderstanding between them by referring only indirectly to the operation in the first encounter and not at all thereafter. She was afraid to express her fears and yet afraid to ignore them. The doctor's response—disconfirming the reality of her problem—produced further ambiguity, which only exacerbated the woman's fears.

Often such patients come to view physicians as evasive, nonsupportive, insensitive, uncaring, or dishonest. One MS patient said,

> I went to seven or eight doctors in less than two years. I'd tell them about my pins-and-needles feelings, or my numbness, or my weak arms and they'd all do the same thing—nothing. I really got upset with those doctors. They'd usually just say that my problems were normal for a woman my age (25) and things like that. And I'd get really uptight because they would just give me a Valium and not try to find out what was really wrong. Some of them thought I was going off my rocker. They thought I was imagining the problems. . . . One of them just threw up his arms and said he didn't know what was wrong with me. Now isn't that some way for a doctor to act! I got so I didn't believe any of them. I knew something was wrong and felt they could find out if they would just try. (quoted in Stewart and Sullivan, 1982: 1401)

In such situations the doctors' inability or unwillingness to communicate a diagnosis resulted in the patient's suffering and loss of trust in the doctor-patient relationship.

At the same time, however, total disclosure of all information is neither possible nor helpful for the patient. For instance, too great a barrage of information about a diagnosis and multiple treatment options can overwhelm the patient and, in effect, make patient participation in decision making impossible. Similarly, if a doctor discloses all of the remotely possible diagnoses, it would unnecessarily raise the patient's anxiety.

Information control includes basic communication about diagnosis and treatment. Sometimes, even long after a doctor has a working diagnosis, the patient is not told what the problem may be. Before the enactment of a series of laws in the United States in the 1970s, it was possible for doctors to perform surgery, put patients on medication, and order other treatments without the patients' informed consent.

The issue of informed consent is particularly problematic in medical experimentation and clinical trials of treatments not yet proven safe or effective. One notorious instance of medical science misconduct was the Tuskegee syphilis study, begun in 1932 and continued until 1972, when a Public Health Service worker blew the whistle to the press. The U.S. Public Health Service had recruited in Alabama some 400 black men who had syphilis at the time they were enrolled in the project; it also monitored 200 uninfected control subjects. The research was supposed to document the course of untreated syphilis, including autopsy after the subject died. Research subjects were recruited with misleading promises of "special free treatment" (actually spinal taps done without anesthesia–lab tests, not treatments), and they were denied antibiotic therapy in the 1940s when it became the effective treatment for syphilis (Edgar, 1992; Jones, 1981; King, 1992). Outrage over the Tuskegee study led directly to the 1974 National Research Act, which established procedures to guard the rights of human subjects of research.

The central principle of protection for research subjects also applies to medical treatments: informed consent. This principle means that researchers and physicians should give enough information about the procedures, their risks, and benefits so that the subject or patient can decide whether to consent to the treatment. Just what kind and how much information is necessary or desirable, however, is still debated. Unfortunately, the requirement of informed consent has been routinized (especially in institutional settings) into one more procedure that is performed on the patient. For example, a senior surgeon may ask an assistant, "Did you consent the patient yet?"–implying the patient is a passive recipient of a purely bureaucratic procedure.

In the treatment of potentially fatal or particularly fearsome diseases, such as cancer, many doctors prefer to tell their patients as little as possible. As recently as the 1960s, most physicians routinely withheld from patients diagnosis of feared diseases and prognosis of impending death. One study found that 95 percent of physicians did not disclose a diagnosis of cancer to patients (Oken, 1961; see also Glaser and Strauss, 1968). The same questionnaire, distributed nearly two decades later, found a complete reversal: 90 percent of the physicians claimed they disclosed all information (Novack et al., 1979). But although physicians believe they are giving their patients all relevant information, many patients are dissatisfied with both the amount and the quality of information they receive (McIntosh, 1974). One explanation for this dissatisfaction is that although doctors now usually disclose even unpleasant diagnoses such as cancer or AIDS, their information giving is still selective. For example, a physician may give considerable information about treatment options while downplaying or withholding information about prognosis (that is, prospects for recovery or probable course of the disease). Thus, the physician retains considerable control, especially over the patient's willingness to accept the recommended treatment (Miyaji, 1993).

Even for nonfatal illnesses, many doctors do not communicate their full diagnosis or prognosis. Doctors may want to protect patients from unpleasant information. This paternalistic approach may simultaneously protect the doctor from dealing with the unpleasant reactions such knowledge might evoke. Giving bad news is very uncomfortable for physicians, as one surgeon explained:

> I really hate this part of the work. I feel terrible . . . always . . . it never seems to get easier. . . . I know it's not my fault . . . I didn't give the patient the disease . . . but I always somehow feel that it is . . . and besides . . . I never really know what to say. They sure never had a course on this part of medicine when I went to school, but let me tell you, I could sure use it now . . . and I usually don't ever get to know these patients who think their lives are in my hands. How am I supposed to deal with it? I hate doing it . . . but I can't avoid it! (quoted in Taylor, 1988)

In response to this stress, physicians adopt complex strategies to routinize the painful task: telling the truth, professing uncertainty, evading the issue, and dissimulation. One study found that the majority viewed their role as selecting and interpreting information for patients (Taylor, 1988). In deciding where and how much to tell, they considered such factors as the certainty of the diagnosis, whether medical science understands the disease's natural course, whether there are potentially effective therapeutic options, and whether the patient is competent to understand information and make decisions on the basis of that information (Drickamer and Lachs, 1992).

Brody (1992) argues for a new ethic for doctor-patient relationships in which most power is shared with patients, without eschewing the beneficial aspects of the doctor's power as expert. He suggests the following:

> [P]hysicians most effectively empower patients neither by reflexively disclosing nor by reflexively withholding any particular sort of information. They empower patients by creating an atmosphere that encourages participation and dialogue. (Brody, 1992: 136)

The Micropolitics of Professional Dominance

When a patient interacts with a doctor, the relationship is not symmetrical. In addition to the physician's presumed medical expertise, a number of microstructural factors increase the relative power of the doctor in the medical encounter. The professional dominance of doctors is enhanced by their control over minute parts of their interaction with patients.

Language Use   Doctors control even seemingly medically irrelevant aspects of the doctor-patient interaction, such as humorous exchanges and other sociability (West, 1984: 152; see also Todd, 1983). Several patterns of language use reflect the subtle ways in which dominance is asserted. For example, interrupting is an assertion of whose input to the interaction is more important. Doctors frequently interrupted their patients, whereas they were seldom interrupted by their patients.

Doctors' unilateral use of false-familiar terms increases the gap between doctor and patient. For example, many doctors expect to be addressed deferentially by their title ("Dr. Jones"), but regularly address patients—regardless of age or other status—by their first names. Likewise, the use of diminutives is a subtle assertion of doctors' dominance and condescension. One study of doctor-patient interactions in a gynecological clinic and in private practice found that doctors frequently used diminutives in talking to patients. For example, a doctor teaching women to perform breast self-examinations said, "Just march your little fingers . . ." (Todd, 1983).

The Dossier   The doctor typically has far more information about the patient than the patient has about the doctor. Such one-sided familiarity serves to remind the patient that the doctor is dominant (Stimson and Webb, 1975). The medical record functions as a third agent, introducing the patient (and personal details about the patient, such as marital status and age) even before the face-to-face interaction. One researcher observed that doctors often appear to be more oriented to the patient's objectified record or chart than to the patient (West, 1984: 132–133). Records can indeed take on a reality greater than that expressed by patients themselves. Patients' narratives of their illness experiences often bear little resemblance to the case record (see Berg, 1996; Kleinman, 1988).

Patients typically lack access to or control over these records. They are prevented from seeing their charts, reading their records, or challenging items of information in their files. Particularly in institutional settings such as hospitals, control over medical records is a form of social control over inmates (Goffman, 1961). In ordinary office practice too, patient records often contain discrediting information. For example, a doctor in a group practice may read a colleague's comment that a patient is a constant complainer and accordingly decide not to give that person's current problem serious attention.

Social Organization of Space   The physical setting of most medical encounters is likewise supportive of the physician's dominance. Medical staff have the uniforms and props of authority—white coats, stethoscopes, framed certificates, and complicated equipment. Office and hospital consultations are on doctors' home field, which is organized to their specifications. For example, rarely is the doctor's office arranged so that doctor and patient are seated in equally important positions; much of the interaction may in fact occur in the examining room with the patient undressed and in an awkward posture. Studies of the uses of space, posture, and gesture demonstrate that such differences are related to power and stratification (Henley, 1977).

Social Control of Time   Significantly, doctors exert considerable control over the time spent with patients. One useful indicator of relative power in a dyad (that is, a two-person interrelationship, such as teacher-student) is which party is in a position to make the other wait for access to his or her presumably more precious time. Typically, the patient waits to see the doctor rather than the reverse. In private practice, physicians often overbook patients to assure that every block of office consultation time is filled, but they are more sensitive to the need for customer satisfaction than doctors in clinic or institutional settings, where patients are not free to take their business elsewhere.

The allocation of time spent with patients depends partly on the expectations and rewards for doctors in a particular institutional setting. One study found that prenatal clinic patients experienced different waiting times and received very different amounts of doctor time depending on whether they were being seen in the obstetrics or the family practice clinic. Reflecting different organizational—as well as health care—objectives, residents in obstetrics spent an average of five to ten minutes with a prenatal patient, and expected clinic nurses to do the job of communicating information about pregnancy and delivery. By contrast, family practice residents spent up to 45 minutes with patients. Family practice residents were encouraged and rewarded for the time spent with patients, whereas obstetric residents were discouraged from devoting time to "normal" pregnancies and were informally sanctioned if they failed to process their share of the patient workload fast enough (Lazarus, 1988).

Another study found that 73 percent of patients' visits to doctors lasted 15 minutes or less (Lawrence and McLemore, 1983). Because doctors' goals include the efficient, task-oriented use of this brief time, the interview and examination are directed to gathering information that they believe is directly relevant to fairly routinized diagnostic decision rules. A British study corroborated the impact of a sense of time constraints on doctor-patient communication. Even when time is actually available for more medical work, doctors narrow the objectives of their routine (and typically uninteresting) practice by thinking not "What can I do for this patient?" but "What can I do for this patient in the next six minutes?" (Horobin and McIntosh, 1983: 328). One physician commented on his tight control of patient interactions:

> The doctor's primary task is to manage his time. If he allows patients to rabbit on about their conditions then the doctor will lose control of time and will spend all his time sitting in a surgery [office consultation] listening to irrelevant rubbish. Effective doctoring is characterized by a "quick, clean job." (quoted in Byrne and Long, 1976: 93)

Patients are unlikely to know the criteria by which doctors are judging their input, and often doctors interrupt or discard information about problems that patients want to communicate. One study found that, on average, doctors cut off patients' descriptions of their complaints within the first 18 seconds (Beckman and Frankl, 1984). This practice is particularly problematic because patients only rarely readily reveal the important reasons that triggered their visit (Good and Good, 1982). For example, a patient may start out by presenting a "simple" problem such as a persistent rash, but may have really come to the doctor mainly to obtain reassurance that he does not have heart disease like his brother who recently had a heart attack. If given the time to present all their concerns, patients frequently identify three or four problems, of which the first mentioned is often not the most serious.

Doctors' information-giving time is likewise greatly constricted by the brevity of the ordinary medical encounter. One study found that only about 9 percent of a session was devoted to communicating information about the illness to the patient. If an average session is ten to fifteen minutes, the information-giving part is barely one minute. An analysis of 336 encounters in several outpatient settings showed that doctors spent little time informing their patients, overestimated the time they did spend, and underestimated their patients' interest in obtaining information (Waitzkin, 1985).

THE DOCTOR-PATIENT RELATIONSHIP

Broader structural factors also shape the pattern of miscommunication between doctors and their patients. As described in Chapter 8, patients come to the medical encounter with fundamentally separate (and often irreconcilable) expectations and goals from those of their doctor: What am I doing and why? What are the central facts about my situation? How should we proceed to make sense of this? What is my expected outcome?

Rationalization and the Medical Model

Modern biomedicine has developed a conception of disease as separate from the person experiencing it. Rationalized medicine views the body as an object; the body is incidentally inhabited by a person who can potentially help or hinder the task of treating diseases of the body. But people cannot simply leave their bodies at the repair shop. Although individual doctors may choose to relate to their patients as persons and not just bodies, such an approach is not an essential part of curing in the biomedical model. In many ways, the training and socialization of medical personnel actively discourages them from understanding their patients as whole persons with social, emotional, aesthetic, spiritual, and other health-related facets to their lives.

Medical training emphasizes technical skills in diagnosing and treating pathologies (physiological deviations that constitute or characterize disease). Thus, doctors are trained to approach a medical encounter with a patient with the goal of efficient diagnosis of a pathology and active treatment intervention. By contrast, the patient comes to the doctor with a broader, and more often vague, set of goals. The patient's needs may be related to a range of problems, some of which are unrelated or only indirectly related to an identifiable pathology or bodily condition. The patient may be experiencing illness but lack a clinically detectible pathology. The illness may also be a chronic condition in the face of which the doctor's active intervention is not very effective, although the patient may suffer from certain socioemotional aspects of the illness and its management. With a narrow disease-oriented training, doctors are likely to misunderstand completely what these patients need.

Most persons seeking medical help do not need the kind of medical intervention that physicians have been trained to appreciate. In medical school, internships, and residencies, the emphasis is on the interesting cases, which are typically acute and dramatic, and thus challenging—but not impossibly so—for the doctors' diagnostic skills. Cases often are defined as interesting if they offer the chance to practice new surgical techniques; once the doctor has mastered these procedures, such cases become less interesting (Scully, 1980: 166–171). In ordinary office practice, however, such interesting cases are proportionately very rare, and doctors are likely to be bored and impatient with the majority of patients' health problems.

One hospital's head midwife, who was involved in training obstetric residents, noted:

> It is a rare medical student who wants to sit with a woman in labor. Residents will even pass on watching normal deliveries. They see people as pathology, as a uterus. I rarely see the art of medicine, the understanding of seeing a patient as a total entity—where she is going, where she has been. I heard a resident say that "If I never do another normal vaginal delivery, it won't be too soon." They train for pathology but go into private practice with normal patients. There is more money in it, and it is the least amount of time for the most amount of money. (quoted in Lazarus, 1988: 39)

In general practice, which includes most of the work done by general practitioners, pediatricians, family practitioners, internists, and obstetrician-gynecologists, only about 15 percent of consultations are for the kind of acute, major, or life-threatening conditions that are likely to be interesting. By far the largest proportion of office visits are for seemingly minor, self-limiting conditions or for well-person preventive care; chronic illnesses are the second largest category. Physicians whose medical training was oriented toward interesting cases find such routine work far less rewarding. One doctor exclaimed,

> Our skills are absolutely wasted . . . frustration and boredom set in. There are days when you go home and think, "Have I got to do this for another twenty years?" You've done a lot of work but you really haven't done anything for anybody. . . . There's no stimulation at all. (quoted in Horobin and McIntosh, 1983: 321)

Labeling Patients

Doctors' socialization leads to negative stereotypes of patients. The use of such stereotypes does vary according to the institutional setting; doctors in private practice are less likely than doctors on hospital staff to use pejoratives openly to refer to patients, although they may hold some of the same negative attitudes (cf. Hahn, 1995: 173–208). Nevertheless, the values reflected in these attitudes toward patients are encouraged in both the self-selection of doctors and their medical education. Doctors learn that real medicine is about pathologies, not patients.

In a U.S. study, 439 family physicians anonymously answered a questionnaire about those patient characteristics to which they responded negatively (Klein et al., 1982). The doctors reacted negatively not only to various social and personal traits of their patients but also to certain medical conditions, especially those for which medical treatment offered little or no likelihood of cure or clear alleviation. The authors suggested that physicians particularly dislike certain situations, such as emphysema, senility, diabetes, arthritis, psychiatric conditions, and obesity, that challenge their faith in the potency of bioscientific medicine. Although they may find a challenging case with a high probability of a dramatic cure "interesting," they dislike conditions such as back pain, chronic vague pains, headaches, and chronic fatigue that offer little probability of cure while bringing their competence or diagnostic skills into question. Furthermore, they dislike conditions for which they believe the patient or others are responsible, such as sexual behavior, auto accidents, suicide attempts, and other self-inflicted injuries (Klein et al., 1982; see also Hahn, 1995; Jeffery, 1979; Roth, 1972; and Smith and Zimmy, 1988).

One study found the leading common characteristics of patients that doctors label as "gomers" ("*get outta my emergency room*") were illnesses and/or personal characteristics that created management difficulties for the hospital staff (Leiderman and Grisso, 1985). Many patients were identified as gomers because their conditions defied solution by modern medical intervention. Their deterioration under treatment was thus a source of frustration and ideological doubts for doctors, especially the beginning doctors who typically staff hospital emergency rooms and clinics.

Many of the other derogatory terms used for patients reflect similar values. A widespread distinction in doctors' stereotyping of patients is between "sick people" and "trolls." The latter term is applied to patients whom doctors believe lack a "real" disease and to those held culpable for the cause of and/or the failure to control their condition. Other derogatory terms for undesirable patients include "albatross," "turkey," and "crock." Medical education encourages compassion for "sick people" but contempt for "trolls." Such negative stereotypes often supersede even the medical model itself in informing the doctor's understanding of a case, thus leading to failed empathy (Stein, 1986).

Medical students, interns, and residents learn and use extensive slang terms for their patients, patients' conditions and bodies, hospital situations, and working conditions. Although use of slang serves other psychosocial functions, such as a safety valve for stressful working conditions and emotionally charged work, it also serves to distance doctors from their patients and confirm negative stereotypes (see Coombs et al., 1993; Yoels and Clair, 1995). Even though patients generally do not understand the meanings of insider talk among the medical staff, the terms reflect and produce problems of doctors' empathy. Consider, for example, the effect on interns' attitudes of routinely referring to patients under their care by such terms as: "BW" (*b*eached *w*hale, meaning obese), "slug" (not motivated to move around out of bed), "dud" (not an interesting case), "supratentorial" (patient's problem is considered to be psychological, not physical), or "HOWDY" (*h*ypertensive, *o*bese, *w*hite, *d*iabetic, *y*ahoo). Medical professors' routine use of vulgar or derogatory humor about patients and their conditions to make lectures more entertaining may encourage such stereotyping and failed empathy among medical students (Konner, 1987).

Contempt for "trolls" is particularly encouraged in the United States by the use of student doctors to staff emergency rooms and clinics that serve a disproportionate number of these "undesirable" patients compared to private practice. The characteristic contempt is illustrated in this quote from a junior resident in an emergency room:

> At least 40–50 percent are gomers. Some weeks there is nothing but alcohol-induced diseases. The other night on call I met only three people with genuine diseases—having nothing to do with anything they ever did to themselves. I spend hours [with them] and check them everyday, but some guy who comes in with alcoholic pancreatitis—I'll tune him up and fire him out the door, and not give two shakes about him. (quoted in Mizrahi, 1986: 102)

Hospital staff generally admitted that they often treated undesirable patients less thoroughly. Sometimes the stereotypes led to misdiagnoses and other medical mistakes (Mizrahi, 1986). For example, a homeless person brought unconscious to the emergency room may be treated as a gomer under the assumption that the condition was alcohol induced, whereas a thorough treatment might discover that the symptoms resulted from a serious neurological problem.

Doctors' negative stereotypes of patients are also based on social and personal characteristics. Doctors tended to consider "undesirable" those patients whose behavior violated the physicians' personal norms, even norms with little or no relevance to health. The largest category of social characteristics (33 percent) eliciting negative responses from doctors included such violations as being dirty, smelly, vulgar, chronically unemployed, promiscuous, homosexual, malingering, or on welfare, Medicaid, or workers' compensation. Doctors' expectations of patients are based largely on white, middle-class values that are accentuated by the self-selection and professional training processes. Social class differences also appear to figure into some negative stereotypes (Klein et al., 1982).

Doctors' often unrecognized value judgments of patients can result in failed empathy and less adequate care (Stein, 1986), as illustrated by one resident who admitted that he had detested patients who demanded Vistaril (an antianxiety drug often used in pain control). He had viewed them as not legitimately sick but rather as weak, irresponsible, and dependent. Coming from a religious, rural, self-sufficient background, he valued patients who were self-sufficient in their health care and who rarely complained. Until he himself experienced considerable pain from minor surgery (and quickly wrote himself a prescription for Vistaril), he had a strong negative stereotype of patients whose requests for pain medication did not mesh with his personal values.

A study of the medical education process showed how both the structure of medical training and professional ideology work against the development of humanistic doctor-patient relationships.[2] New physicians are taught to avoid inter-action with patients, to restrict the time spent with them, and to limit the patient input they listen to in medical interviews (Mizrahi, 1986: 118–119). This study concluded that the very structure of internship and residency teaches doctors to get rid of noninteresting patients. Reflecting both the attitudes of his supervisors and his personal experience with enormous time pressures, one junior resident said, "There are different kinds of ideal patients. When you're an intern, the ideal patient is someone you can get out and get out quickly" (quoted in Mizrahi, 1986: 74–75). Interns and residents, for example, were informally rewarded for quickly and effi-ciently taking patient histories, and they learned not to bother with inquiring about social aspects of the cases because nobody noticed or appreciated if that were done.

Medical students learned, formally and informally, that what their professors and supervisors really wanted them to do was to narrow their clinical findings effi-ciently to biophysical data relevant to possible pathology. One senior resident explained,

> I guess I could use the excuse that I don't have the time to do that [deal with patient's social problems]. . . . It would be nice to bullshit with your patients for an hour or so and get a feel for their social situation. . . . It may affect the complaints they present with. . . . If I was Marcus Welby [a former TV physician] and saw one patient per week, maybe I would be more concerned. I doubt it though, because it's really not appealing to me. If I really wanted to do it, I would have majored in social work or psychiatry. What appeals to me is treatment of sick people by diagnosing their diseases and giving medications. *I like good hard facts and physical findings*–things I can deal with on a tangible basis–not some intan-gible nebulous feeling of what their social situation is. (quoted in Mizrahi, 1986: 95 [emphasis added])

This attitude reflects the medical model's separation of the disease from the socio-emotional aspects of the patient's illness; doctors are socialized to view the nonbio-physical aspects as "fuzzy," "soft" facts that are ultimately irrelevant to their essential task.

TRANSFORMING THE SICK PERSON INTO A CASE

Just as the medical paradigm views the body as separate from the person, so too does the interaction between doctor and patient often involve isolating salient infor-mation about the sick body from the sick person. One effect of most medical encounters is to transform the sick person into a medical case. Drawing from their medical training and the biomedical paradigm for interpreting disease and pathology, physicians use the medical encounter for relatively narrow goals: the effi-

---

[2]For more detailed and textured description of the medical education process and its impact on treatment of patients, see Becker et al., 1961; Cassell, 1991; Coombs, 1978; Davis-Floyd, 1987; Good, 1995; Groopman, 1987; Konner, 1987; Light, 1980; Merton et al., 1957; Mizrahi, 1986; Scully, 1980.

cient eliciting and honing of facts relevant to a medical diagnosis, the precise application of a set of decision rules for proceeding, and active therapeutic intervention.
Although their understanding of the medical encounter is informed by rational
biomedicine, it is also the product of situational factors, cultural biases, and subjective influences that are often subtly embedded in the doctors' practice of medicine
itself (Stein, 1986; see also Good, 1995; Mishler, 1984).

Social Influences on Medical Judgments

The process of locating and interpreting medical evidence is always socially
mediated. Such medical judgments as the factors the diagnostician considers relevant, the clues that are thought worth seeking and thus are elicited in conversation
and testing, and those that should be overlooked or discarded often entail *social*
attributes. For example, doctors treating elderly persons sometimes do not carry out
routine tests in physical examinations, because they assume patient problems are
due to senility or old age (Glassman, 1980).

Both the patient and the doctor often treat the diagnosis as a conclusion
rather than a working hypothesis. Even before the diagnosis is reached, the physician's expectations and hunches may limit the clues examined. A study of medical
thinking showed that doctors tended to develop hypotheses very early in an intake
interview, often basing their hunches on only the patient's general appearance and
one or two presenting complaints (Kassirer and Gorry, 1978). The physician's
expectations are often subsequently self-confirming; contradictory clues are neither
noticed nor sought (Jones, 1982: 156–161).

Medical evidence is typically ambiguous and multifaceted. In both scientific
and other medical systems, the process of reaching a diagnosis is one of pattern
forming. Despite extensive diagnostic technologies, the art of diagnosis in modern
medicine is highly imprecise. A study of diagnostic failures in myocardial infarction
(heart attacks) showed that physicians who relied on technological assessment, in
place of their own observation and clinical skills, were likely to make a mistaken
diagnosis (Zarling et al., 1983). U.S. data on autopsies show that in biomedical
terms, at least one out of five diagnoses were mistaken, and that in half these cases
the correct diagnosis could have saved or prolonged the patient's life (Landefeld
and Goldman, 1989; Landefeld et al., 1988; see also Rosenthal, 1995). To form a
pattern, one must actively select pieces of evidence to cluster into an understanding.
This process necessarily entails deciding which pieces of information to include and
which to exclude (see Locker, 1981).

Similarly, in the interpretation of evidence and treatment decisions,
nonphysical elements, such as the emotional or social situation of the ill person,
become part of the pattern.[3] Often the person creating the pattern is not aware of
these elements; instead, moral judgments and ideological assumptions enter the

---

[3]This is not a criticism; effective treatment probably takes the sick person's entire situation into
consideration. The issue here is the extent to which uncritical assumptions and ideological biases often
enter the process and are treated as part of so-called objective reality, without the participants' awareness.

process under the guise of objective physical observations. For example, in examining X-rays of workers' lungs for symptoms of asbestosis, company physicians saw very different patterns than did doctors not connected with the industry (Brodeur, 1974: 174).

No necessary connection exists between the many diagnoses and possible treatments. Numerous, sometimes contradictory treatment options exist in any single medical system, and social factors influence which one the doctor recommends. Individual practitioners differ in the *decision rules* they follow in choosing certain treatments for the same condition. (Decision rules are a form of knowledge that provides a set of minimally acceptable criteria for selecting a mode of treatment, such as surgery or medication.) A British study of ear, nose, and throat specialists revealed that widely varying decision rules determine whether an adenotonsillectomy should be performed. Some relied heavily on a physical examination (and practitioners disagreed about what to look for in the examination); others attached no significance to examination findings and relied instead on the case history. Some recommended surgery only when several signs were present on examination; others considered the existence of only one sign sufficient (Bloor, 1976).

Social judgments also enter into physicians' decision rules. Often the therapy proposed by a doctor varies greatly from patient to patient, even when the same biophysical conditions are present. When recommending hysterectomies (surgical removal of the uterus, resulting in sterility), physicians often included in their decision rules such factors as the woman's age, ethnicity, poverty, marital status, and whether she was on welfare, had had multiple abortions, and had already had children (Fisher, 1986). A more serious biophysical condition in a 25-year-old white woman with no children thus might be less likely to be treated with a hysterectomy than a less serious condition in a 35-year-old black woman with four children.

Similarly, studies show that the social attitudes, beliefs, and personal characteristics of physicians influence the treatment options they offer their patients with breast cancer. For instance, although breast-conserving surgery is medically recommended for the majority of women whose cancer is in an early stage, older women (the vast majority of cancer patients) are significantly less likely to be offered this treatment option than younger women (Ganz, 1992).[4]

Judgments of social worth also enter into medical decisions. Studies of treatment decisions and other actions in hospital emergency services show that the young are treated as more valuable than the old, and welfare cases are treated as less worthy than those not on welfare. Especially disvalued persons, such as those labeled "drunks" and "PIDs" (women with pelvic inflammatory disease, often assumed to be due to promiscuity), are given even less prompt and considerate treatment (Roth, 1972; see also Sudnow, 1967).

---

[4]Another interpretation of these differences is that the physician's financial gain influences medical decisions (see Chapter 11). Several studies have shown surgery rates to be much higher where physicians are paid on a fee-for-service basis, and surgeons (and hospitals) earn far more for a radical mastectomy than for breast-conserving surgery (Montini and Ruzek, 1989).

An appreciation of the social construction of ideas of illness helps explain how cases are constructed. Medical decision making is powerfully influenced by social assumptions that are often implicit and unacknowledged. The creation of a medical case shows that not only medical knowledge but also medical practice is a social construction.

Depersonalization of the Patient

Patients also bring an understanding—sometimes fragmented and contradictory—of the nature of their illness. They enter the medical encounter with an array of important social, emotional, and situational concerns. Drawing from cultural models, the patients have some interpretation of their own illness. Furthermore, they are likely to be struggling with problems of meaning, at least in the instance of feared, serious illness, including these concerns: Why me? Who is responsible? Why this disease? What will this do to my identity and my future?

Serious miscommunication and depersonalization occur when the doctor disconfirms or ignores patient concerns and understandings. Box 10.1 illustrates a gravely flawed exchange between doctor and patient. The doctor, intent only on his biophysical assessment, has failed to hear the person, ignoring or interrupting her attempts to explain her illness. In conducting the interview and writing his report, the doctor is using the technically correct forms he learned in his training. However, in the medical record he produces, the patient is dehumanized and transformed into a reified, thing-like case, very unlike the person who, as revealed in the transcript, speaks eloquently of her commitments, fears, stresses, economic and social problems.

In transforming Mrs. Flowers into a medical case, the doctor reduces the person to her hypertension, her noncompliance with the medical regimen, her early signs of heart failure, and her medications. The doctor, following the technically correct approach to interviewing and treating, has completely missed the person with her complex social, psychological, and economic problems. His control of the interview consistently constrains Mrs. Flowers's presentation of her concerns; she is frequently ignored or interrupted when talking about the very matters that brought her to see the doctor. The doctor permits her to speak about her physical complaints, but disallows her psychological or social problems. The interview elicits only facts about her biophysical diseases and medical treatment. Even though Mrs. Flowers's human suffering is very much a part of her chronic illness, it is relegated to a perfunctory referral to a social worker (Kleinman, 1988: 134–136).

The disease orientation of the medical model and the doctor's professional distance from the patient combine to turn the complex person into a rationalized case with its biophysical parts neatly separated from its social, emotional, spiritual, and economic elements. In this situation, the doctor is also so culturally distant from the patient, he is ignorant of the ideas and social practices that inform her own understanding of her situation. For example, she refers to her "high blood"—a folk illness in lower-class black American subculture. Because "high blood" is believed to result

BOX 10.1

The Creation of a Medical Case

Background: Mrs. Flowers is returning to the clinic, where she had previously been treated for her hypertension. She is 39 years old, black, the mother of five children. She lives with four of her children, her mother, and two grandchildren in an inner-city ghetto. She works at present as a waitress in a restaurant, but periodically she has been unemployed and on welfare. She has been married twice, but both of her husbands have deserted her. As a result, she is a single head of household. Mrs. Flowers is an active member of the local Baptist church, which has been an important source of support to her and her family for many years. She is also a member of a community action group.

In the household of eight, she is the only wage earner. Her mother, Mildred, is 59 and partially paralyzed owing to a stroke that was the result of long-standing and poorly controlled hypertension. Her oldest daughter, Matty, the unmarried 19-year-old mother of two small children, is at present unemployed and pregnant; in the past, she has had a drug problem. Mrs. Flowers's 15-year-old daughter, Marcia, is also pregnant. Their 18-year-old brother, J.D., is in prison. Teddy, a 12-year-old, has had problems with truancy and minor delinquency. Amelia, 11, the baby of the family, is said by her mother to be an angel.

A year ago, Mrs. Flowers's long-time male companion, Eddie Johnson, was killed in a barroom brawl. Recently, Mrs. Flowers has been increasingly upset by memories of Eddie Johnson, by concern for how prison will affect J.D., and by fears that Teddy will get involved with drugs like his older brother and sister before him. She is also concerned about her mother's worsening disability, which includes what she fears may be early signs of dementia.

DR. RICHARDS: Hello, Mrs. Flowers.
MRS. FLOWERS: I ain't feelin' too well today, Doc Richards.
DR. RICHARDS: What seems to be wrong?
MRS. FLOWERS: Um, I don't know. Maybe it's that pressure of mine. I been gettin' headaches and havin' trouble sleeping.
DR. RICHARDS: Your hypertension is a bit worse, but not all that bad, considering what it's been in the past. You been taking your medicines as you ought to?
MRS. FLOWERS: Sometimes I do. But sometimes when I don't have no pressure, I don't take it.
DR. RICHARDS: Gee whiz, Mrs. Flowers, I told you if you don't take it regularly you could get real sick like your Mom. You got to take the pills every day. And what about salt? You been eating salt again?
MRS. FLOWERS: It's hard to cook for the family without salt. I don't have time to cook just for me. At lunch, I'm in the restaurant and Charlie, he's the chef, he puts lotsa salt in everythin'.
DR. RICHARDS: Well, now this is a real problem. Salt restriction, I mean a low-salt diet, is essential for your problem.
MRS. FLOWERS: I know, I know. I mean to do all these things, but I just plain forget sometimes. I got so much else goin' on and it all seems to affect the pressure. I got two pregnant daughters at home and

BOX 10.1 (*continued*)

	my mother is doin' much worse. I think she may be senile. And then I worries about J.D., and here comes Teddy with the same problems startin' up. I–
DR. RICHARDS:	Have you any shortness of breath?
MRS. FLOWERS:	No.
DR. RICHARDS:	Any chest pain?
MRS. FLOWERS:	No.
DR. RICHARDS:	Swelling in your feet?
MRS. FLOWERS:	The feet do get a little swollen, but then I'm on them all day long at the restaurant–
DR. RICHARDS:	You said you had headaches?
MRS. FLOWERS:	Sometimes I think my life is one big headache. These here ain't too bad. I've had 'em for a long time, years. But in recent weeks they been badder than before. You see, a year ago last Sunday, Eddie Johnson, my friend, you know. Uh huh, well, he died. And–
DR. RICHARDS:	Are the headaches in the same place as before?
MRS. FLOWERS:	Yeah, same place, same feelin', on'y more often. But, you see, Eddie Johnson had always told me not to bother about–
DR. RICHARDS:	Have you had any difficulty with your vision?
MRS. FLOWERS:	No.
DR. RICHARDS:	Any nausea?
MRS. FLOWERS:	No. Well when I drank the pickle juice, there was some.
DR. RICHARDS:	Pickle juice? You've been drinking pickle juice? That's got a great deal of salt. It's a real danger for you, for your hypertension.
MRS. FLOWERS:	But I have felt pressure this week and my mother told me maybe I need it because I got high blood and–
DR. RICHARDS:	Oh, no. Not pickle juice. Mrs. Flowers, you can't drink that for any reason. It just isn't good. Don't you understand? It's got lots of salt, and salt is bad for your hypertension.
MRS. FLOWERS:	Uh huh. Ok.
DR. RICHARDS:	Any other problems?
MRS. FLOWERS:	My sleep ain't been too good, doc. I think it's because–
DR. RICHARDS:	Is it trouble getting to sleep?
MRS. FLOWERS:	Yeah, and gettin' up real early in the mornin'. I been dreamin' about Eddie Johnson. Doin' a lot of rememberin' and cryin'. I been feelin' real lonely. I don't know–
DR. RICHARDS:	Any other problems? I mean bodily problems?
MRS. FLOWERS:	No, 'cept for tired feelin', but that's been there for years. Dr. Richards, you think worryin' and missin' somebody can give you headaches?
DR. RICHARDS:	I don't know. If they are tension headaches, it might. But you haven't had other problems like dizziness, weakness, fatigue?
MRS. FLOWERS:	That's what I'm sayin'! The tired feelin', it's been there some time. And the pressure makes it worse. But I wanted to ask you about worries. I got me a mess o' worries. And I been feelin' all down, as if I just couldn't handle it anymore. The money is a real problem now.

DR. RICHARDS: Well, I will have to ask Mrs. Ma, the social worker to talk to you about the financial aspect. She might be able to help. Right now why don't we do a physical exam and see how you're doing?

MRS. FLOWERS: I ain't doin' well. Even I can tell you that. There's too much pressure and it's makin' *my pressure* bad. And I been feelin' real sad for myself.

DR. RICHARDS: Well, we'll soon see how things are going.

After completing the physical examination, Dr. Richards wrote the following note in the medical record:

April 14, 1980

39-year-old Black female with hypertension on hydrochlorothiazide 100 mgs. daily and aldomet 2 grams daily. Blood pressure now 160/105, has been 170/80–110/120 for several months alternating with 150–/95 when taking meds regularly. Has evidence of mild congestive heart failure. No other problems.

Impression: (1) Hypertension, poorly controlled
          (2) Noncompliance contributing to (1)
          (3) Congestive heart failure—mild
          (1) Change aldomet to apresoline
          (2) Send to dietician to enforce lower salt diet
          (3) Social work consult because of financial questions
          (4) See in 3 days, regularly until blood pressure has come down and stabilized

Signed: Dr. Staunton Richards

Dr. Richards also sent a terse note for a consultation to the dietician, which read: "39 year old Black woman with poorly controlled hypertension who does not comply with low salt diet. Please help plan 2 gram sodium diet, and explain to her again relationship of salt intake to her disease and that she must stop eating high salt foods and cooking with salt."

Source: *The Illness Narratives: Suffering, Healing, and the Human Condition*, by Arthur Kleinman, M.D. Copyright 1988 by Basic Books, Inc. Reprinted by permission of Basic Books, Inc., Publishers.

from blood rising to the head, her consumption of pickle juice makes sense as a folk remedy because it is believed to thin or "cut" the blood. Cultural and social factors, such as the limitations posed by her job, make it unlikely that the sick woman would actually follow the difficult instructions for managing her serious illnesses. Rather than understanding these factors, the doctor views what he labels her "noncompliance" as a moral failing. She is not a "good" patient because she does not do what he tells her to do to control her biophysical condition (Kleinman, 1988: 135–136).

An interesting contrast is the inner-city clinic experience of a young black internist from a middle-class background; her understanding of a patient like Mrs. Flowers is remarkably different:

The more I see, the more appalled I am at how ignorant I have been, insensitive to the social, economic, and political causes of disease. . . . Today I saw an obese hypertensive mother of six. No husband. No family support. No job. Nothing. A world of brutalizing violence and poverty and drugs and teenage pregnancies and—and just plain mind-numbing crises, one after another after another. What can I do? What good is it to recommend a low salt diet, to admonish her about control of her pressure? She is under such real outer pressure, what does the inner pressure matter? What is killing her is her world, not her body. In fact, her body is the product of her world. She is a hugely overweight, misshapen hulk who is a survivor of circumstances and lack of resources and cruel messages to consume and get ahead impossible for her to hear and not feel rage at the limits of her world. Hey, what she needs is not medicine but a social revolution. (quoted in Kleinman, 1988: 216–217)

In learning the medical model and the specific techniques of clinical practice, doctors are trained to transform the patient into a case. A study of case presentations—a standard training method in which interns, residents, and fellows in a teaching hospital present formal case studies to their superiors—found that the standard discourse depersonalized patients, referring to them as objects: their disease, their treatment procedure, or a shorthand term for their health status (Anspach, 1988). For example, a pregnant woman is transformed into a "Gravida III, Para I, AbI, black female at 32 weeks gestation" (Anspach, 1988: 363). Furthermore, by using the passive voice and referring to technological procedures, doctors' case presentations also failed to acknowledge the *human agency* in observing or treating. For example, they state, "He was put on phenobarb," rather than "I decided to put him on phenobarb," or "The arteriogram showed that this AVM was fed . . .," instead of "I requested an arteriogram and interpreted its findings to mean . . ." (Anspach, 1988: 366–368).

Learning to present cases according to these norms affects doctors' interactions with patients; student doctors describe editing out patients' own stories and structuring their conversations with patients around the categories considered relevant for a case presentation. One study of medical education noted, "Case presentations are a genre of stories, through which persons are formulated as patients and as medical problems" (Good, 1994: 79).

The very language and interviewing techniques of the standard doctor-patient interaction result in losing sight of the patient as person and the patient's concerns. For example, physicians recode the patients' expressions into medical terminology, which becomes a shorthand for their medical condition and glosses over possibly relevant nonphysical aspects of the patients' description of their problems (Mishler, 1984; Waitzkin, 1991). In the preceding example, Mrs. Flowers's expressions are transformed into "hypertension, poorly controlled," "noncompliance," and "mild congestive heart failure." In recoding the language for conceptualizing the problem, the patient's perspective is obscured (Cicourel, 1983: 238).

Likewise, the structure of the medical interview leads to inadequate doctor-patient communication and truncated, distorted understandings of the patient's problem. Doctors are trained to use a set of formulas for conducting interviews with patients. One such formula is a "decision tree," a sequence of small decisions that culminates in a diagnosis and treatment plan. Accordingly, doctors elicit information from patients that enables them to narrow the range of possible medical problems down to smaller and smaller "branches." While they are talking with patients, doctors are simultaneously mentally testing hypotheses. Thus, doctors experience patient input not immediately relevant to the part of the decision tree they are considering as disruptive to their line of thought. Similarly, doctors are trained to proceed in the interview by reviewing each of the bodily systems (respiratory system, circulatory system, and so on), often in a verbal checklist format. This routine device guarantees a certain thoroughness, but doctors often become irritated by the "disruption" of a patient who introduces a question or a point relevant to some area of concern other than the immediate item on the checklist (West, 1984; see also Waitzkin, 1989).

Furthermore, the process by which the medical record (that is, the institutional, written medical file for each patient) is constructed reflects the construction of the patient as an *object* of medical practice. This medical record also transforms subsequent doctor-patient interaction, affecting the content of further medical decision making. The medical record does not contain *all* potentially relevant information for all the patient's problems; rather, it is a highly selective, abstract representation focused on a problem that is manageable in the doctor's (and/or hospital's) routines (Berg, 1996). Although this selective representation is efficient for the expert's decision making and routine practice, it both depersonalizes and distances the patient nonexpert from the physician expert.

Thus, the typical patterns of doctor-patient communication produce a case, a reified representation of a sickness in which the sick *person* is remote or absent. Often subsequent interaction between the patient and doctor as well as other medical staff is based on this representation, rather than on any fresh input from the sick person. Such depersonalization results when the focal object of doctors' work is the medical case.

THE ENDS OF MODERN MEDICINE: MORAL DILEMMAS AND SOCIAL POLICIES

Implicit in the medical model of disease and curing are a number of assumptions about life and death and the proper ends of medical intervention. These assumptions are so deeply embedded that rarely are they acknowledged, much less examined. They have contributed to major contemporary problems for medical personnel and for society as a whole about how to deal with death and dying, life and potential life, and "normal" and "abnormal" life. In short, should the foremost goal of medicine be preserving and extending life for all patients?

The Medical Model and the Conquest of Death

Comaroff (1984) suggested that the biomedical model's interventionist stance against disease, which is defined as the disruption of the body's organic functioning, led to the acceptance of the conquest of death as a major goal of medicine.

Although acknowledging that ultimately all persons will die, the medical model makes it difficult and sometimes impossible to *decide* that any given person shall be allowed to die (cf. Muller and Koenig, 1988). The focus on the conquest of death also reduces medicine's attention to other needs, such as ameliorating suffering or making mundane improvements in the sick (or dying) person's quality of life.

Contemporary medical dilemmas are in part the result of biomedicine's very successes. Modern technologies enable doctors to prolong lives, even though often they cannot actually cure the disease. For example, the technology of dialysis allows persons with otherwise fatal kidney failure to live three or more years longer. Technological developments enable neonatal intensive care units to reduce the rate of respiratory distress syndrome among undersized infants who would have surely died soon after birth in earlier decades. Other technologies simulate virtually every organic function, artificially supplying the body with breath, food, water, immune responses, heartbeat, excretion, and blood cleansing. Similarly, the extremely expensive technology of organ transplantation extends some lives, often for many years.

Whereas in the recent past, people expected that death was inevitable and would occur at its appointed time, now they expect medicine to intervene to prevent death and to prolong life. In modern societies, medicine—especially the promise of its technical efficacy—offers a nonreligious version of "salvation" from human sickness, death, and finitude (Good, 1994). Indeed, in promulgating the successes of scientific medicine, the profession itself may have raised people's expectations unrealistically high.

The idea that medicine can and should intervene to prolong life is consonant with both the medical model and physicians' professional ideologies. Doctors want to assert their control over sickness and the loss of life; many physicians view the death of a patient as a failure. The expectation that the goal of medicine is to prevent death has many negative consequences, however.

Our culture is profoundly uncomfortable with death and dying. It does little to prepare people for their own and others' deaths. Ariès (1974) documented the historical development of modern taboos about death. Accordingly, as society failed to provide a consensus about how to die a "good death," it segregated sickness and death from normal social interaction. Medical institutions perform the latent function of segregating the unpleasantness of sickness and dying while aspiring to the manifest function of curing (Kearl, 1993; see also Elias, 1985). As recently as 40 years ago, more than half of American deaths occurred in people's homes; by the mid-1990s, 80 percent took place in health care institutions under medical care (Stryker, 1996).

Death and dying have become medicalized partly because of expectations that medicine will be able to intervene in the process, and partly because many people are relieved to have their family members' dying supervised by medical personnel in a hospital setting. Death is perhaps less threatening if it is thus removed, sterilized, and routinized. At the same time, however, the dying process is partly cut off from the very institutions of society most likely to be able to provide meaning in the face of death: religion and the family. Some alternative arrangements for dying, such as the hospice movement, encourage demedicalizing and rehumanizing the process.

Nevertheless, to choose an alternative arrangement for dying requires that alternatives be available, affordable, and legally allowed; that doctors and family members be aware and consciously accept the patient is dying; and that mechanisms are in place to help dying persons consider their options and express their intentions regarding death. Many social structures and attitudes in our society make it difficult for people to die with dignity (see Rosenthal, 1997b). The specter of an unavoidable, overmedicalized end is not unrealistic: Medical technology makes possible keeping the body "alive" with respirators, feeding tubes, intravenous hydration and antibiotics, heart resuscitators, and the like, long after the person in the body has lost the ability to consider or express a desire to live or die.

The Technological Imperative

Another cultural value that makes it difficult to decide to let nature take its course and allow death to happen is the **technological imperative**, a prevalent idea in most Western societies (especially the United States) urging us that if we have the technological capability to do something, we should do it. The technological imperative implies that action in the form of the use of an available technology is always preferable to inaction. Indeed, once a technology becomes available, its use becomes almost inexorably routinized and considered standard. The failure to apply this standard care—no matter how inappropriate for the individual patient—would be reprehensible (Koenig, 1988).

The technological imperative is deeply embedded in many institutional responses to health crises. Institutional decisions to invest in technology are often driven by financial incentives, such as government subsidies (cf. Anspach, 1993). For example, most hospitals have created (and thus need to use in order to pay for) several high-technology wards, such as coronary and neonatal intensive care units, equipped and staffed to provide maximum multiple technological responses to patients' conditions. Similarly, many health insurance plans cover hospital care and high-tech medicine (such as treatment in a coronary care unit) but not low-tech or nontechnological responses (such as therapeutic massage or nursing home care). One study of therapeutic escalation (that is, the physician's decision to order more extensive and expensive treatments after prior therapy failed) found that the source of payment (such as private insurance) and the organizational setting (hospitals' internal incentives, for example) significantly affected doctors' decisions about whether to increase, maintain, or withdraw treatments (Ross and Albrecht, 1995).

In arguing that the proper goal of medicine should not be the unquestioned prolongation of life, the ethicist Callahan (1987: 173) wrote, "The existence of medical technologies capable of extending the lives of the elderly who have lived out a natural life span creates no presumption whatever that the technologies must be used for that purpose." Similar but perhaps more difficult questions need to be posed about the uses of technology for prolonging the lives of persons who have not lived out a natural life span (see Hilfiker, 1983). What medical intervention should be used, for example, for an accident victim left in a persistent vegetative state, for a medically unsalvageable patient (for instance, a person with cancer of the esophagus who subsequently has a heart attack), or for an irreparably damaged newborn (with anencephaly–congenital lack of a brain)?

There are also serious ethical questions about the use of medical responses that themselves cause pain or other suffering. For example, under what conditions should a patient or a patient's family be allowed to refuse a prescribed treatment, such as chemotherapy or surgery? The technological imperative has considerable legal support in many states; patients and their families must go to court to assert (and sometimes lose) the right to decide to refuse treatment or life supports. Other legal and ethical rights are also uncertain. Does a person have the right to obtain a particular treatment, even if it will not cure or even provide certain benefits for that individual? For example, does every person with kidney failure have the right to a transplant?

Because they underlie legal and social policies, such ethical issues are matters for the entire society as well as individual practitioners, patients, and families to consider. These issues are difficult for the courts, in part because the courts have increasingly deferred to the medical profession itself as the proper authority on matters of defining life and death. As noted in Chapter 6, the medicalization of moral authority has undermined the authority of other institutions, such as religion and the family.

On issues such as these, however, there is no technical, purely medical answer. The boundaries of life and death are blurred, and biomedicine is incapable of clearly delineating them for the courts in purely technical terms, as illustrated by the ambiguities of court cases involving the abortion of second trimester fetuses and the passive euthanasia of patients in a persistent vegetative state. As Callahan (1987: 179) observed, "The 'sanctity of life' has to be the sanctity of personhood, not merely the possession of a body." Moral and legal rights adhere to *persons*, but there are no neat biomedical criteria to distinguish when or whether a body is a person. The choice of such criteria must come from outside scientific medicine, although they may include medically measurable determinants, such as brain death.

Policy Implications

Our society must come to terms with these issues in order to develop sensible social policies: How shall we pay for the care needed by the sick and dying? Toward what ends shall we train doctors and other medical personnel? How shall we allocate our society's research funding? What kinds of institutional support are required to fulfill our health care goals; for example, should society's focus be on high-tech hospital care, or is more societal support needed for other institutional settings, such as public health programs, real homes for the aged, or home health aides? Such policy decisions regularly require difficult choices because no society can possibly meet every need of all citizens and thus must set its priorities.

These policy decisions have been thrust on us by the burgeoning costs of high-tech medicine; by the medicalization of birthing, dying, and other areas of life;

and by the increasing numbers and proportions of the population who are old and very old. Medicare expenditures to physicians and hospitals are rising dramatically and threaten to deplete those funds. About 27 percent of annual Medicare expenditures pay for the medical costs of only approximately 5 percent of the enrollees—those in their last year of life. And about half of all Medicare costs in the last year of life were incurred in the last 60 days of life (Scitovsky, 1994).

Furthermore, as recently as 15 years ago, babies born very prematurely died shortly after birth. Now many of these babies live, although a substantial proportion suffer serious physical and mental disabilities and chronic illnesses. The main factors in their survival are the new technologies in neonatal wards and intensive nursing. In many hospitals, the technological resuscitation of very premature babies is done automatically, without consulting the parents about their wishes; this process then necessitates considerable later agonizing over whether to sustain the infants on life supports and whether to perform invasive, sometimes painful procedures to keep them alive (see Anspach, 1993).

Neonatal intensive care requires extremely expensive services; the necessary three or four months of hospitalization may cost $90,000 or more. In many parts of the United States, the rates of premature birth are rising (French, 1989). Furthermore, the rates of severely disabled survivors is also increasing, ironically at a time that the U.S. government is decreasing its support for disabled persons (Anspach, 1993). Because of the burgeoning cost of such care, even though it is medically effective for some babies, society must examine whether this expenditure is the best use for its moneys (see Guillemin and Holmstrom, 1986; Rhodes, 1992; Young and Stevenson, 1990). Might it not be better to spend health care dollars on public health programs that could prevent premature births, such as prenatal care and nutrition programs for women of childbearing age?

Similar allocation questions also apply to decisions about who shall receive high-priced organ transplants and other expensive surgery. What proportion of the nation's health care resources should go to care for the elderly and the dying? What priorities should be given to heroic interventions (such as bypass surgery) compared to palliative efforts (such as pain relief) or to simple care and nursing? The United States operates with a de facto system of rationing health care: The wealthy buy whatever they want; the middle classes buy what their insurance allows and have the option to deplete their other resources to buy more; and the poor get whatever the state and Medicaid systems, public hospitals, and Medicare (if they are elderly) offer. This form of rationing results in enormous inequities (Fein, 1986; Gill and Ingman, 1986). The nation needs to confront the ethical issues that have been only implicit in its health care system and must examine its priorities.

SUMMARY

Modern biomedical forms of knowledge and practice are the particular result of social, political, and economic processes. The accomplishment of professional dominance by medical doctors in this century gives them both preeminence in the medical division of labor and control over the definitions of health, illness, and healing practices.

Medical professional dominance also creates problems for the treatment of the sick. The layperson-expert gap and other sources of social distance often result in poor communication and failed empathy. Doctor-patient relationships may reflect other social distance, such as that produced by gender and class stratification. Much interaction between doctor and patient serves to protect the power of the physician, which often directly disempowers the patient. Both the socialization of physicians and the social structure of medical practice promote patterns of doctor-patient interaction that disrupt real communication and lead to unsatisfactory treatment.

Assumptions implicit in the medical model have made it difficult for doctors and laypersons to admit to the limits of modern medicine and to consider setting different goals for its practice. By focusing on the conquest of death, medicine overemphasizes an interventionist approach to treatment and has difficulty coming to terms with death and dying. Not only do doctors and their patients need to reconsider the proper ends of medicine, but society as a whole is also confronted with massive ethical, legal, and policy issues about health care and medical treatment.

RECOMMENDED READINGS

Articles

ERIC J. CASSELL, "The nature of suffering and the goals of medicine." *New England Journal of Medicine* 306, 1982: 639–645.

JEAN COMAROFF, "Medicine, time, and the perception of death." *Listening* 19(2), 1984: 155–169.

BYRON J. GOOD and MARY-JO DEL VECCHIO GOOD, " 'Learning medicine': The constructing of medical knowledge at Harvard Medical School," pp. 81–107 in S. Lindenbaum and M. Lock, eds., *Knowledge, Power, and Practice: The Anthropology of Medicine and Everyday Life.* Berkeley: University of California Press, 1993.

ROBERT ZUSSMAN, "The patient in the intensive care unit," pp. 535–547 in P. Brown, ed., *Perspectives in Medical Sociology* (2nd ed.). Prospect Heights, IL: Waveland Press, 1996.

Books

DANIEL CALLAHAN, *Setting Limits: Medical Goals in an Aging Society.* New York: Simon & Schuster, 1987. Callahan outlines the ethical problems posed by the medicalization of aging and dying, together with the burgeoning proportion of society in the old and very old age brackets. In the context of alternative ideas about the proper role of the elderly, he proposes carefully considered guidelines for setting limits for health care expenditures on persons who have lived a full life span.

MELVIN KONNER, *Becoming a Doctor: A Journey of Initiation in Medical School.* New York: Penguin, 1987. A reflective ethnographic account of experiences of an anthropologist who entered medical school at the age of 33; although not very critical of the medical model of health and illness, the book gives excellent insight into the problems of medical education, hospital structure, and doctor-patient relationships.

MARY-JO DELVECCHIO GOOD, *American Medicine: The Quest for Competence.* Berkeley: University of California Press, 1995. Using several ethnographic inquiries as a spring-board, this book addresses how medical competence and risk are constructed, how competence is contested, and how it is defined, produced, and demonstrated in medical education.

EMILY MARTIN, *The Woman in the Body: A Cultural Analysis of Reproduction.* Boston: Beacon Press, 1987. This book analyzes how medical conceptualizations of women's bodies, particularly menstruation, menopause, pregnancy, and childbirth, embody cultural assumptions about women and their life purpose.

TERRY MIZRAHI, *Getting Rid of Patients: Contradictions in the Socialization of Physicians.* New Brunswick, NJ: Rutgers University Press, 1986. Mizrahi has studied various stages in the training of physicians with a particular emphasis on what they learned (formally and informally) about how to deal with patients; the serious contradictions in values imparted have important implications for the care of patients.

STRATIFICATION AND POWER IN HEALTH CARE SYSTEMS

Enormous variety characterizes how societies respond to the health needs of their members. Economic and social-structural arrangements determine how a society cares for members' sick bodies, frail elderly bodies, disabled bodies, infant bodies—the well-being of all its members. This chapter explains the importance of social power in shaping these economic and social-structural arrangements. Each society's political economy creates its health care system's goals and the policies for achieving those goals.

A health care system is the "aggregate of commitments or resources which any national society 'invests' in the health concern" (Field, 1973: 763). As a system, all parts mutually influence each other, for better or for worse. Changes in one part of the system result in changes in another part. For example, cutbacks in government reimbursements for hospital patients under Medicare may drive up costs of health insurance premiums paid by workers and their employers, as hospitals compensate for lost revenues.

U.S. PROBLEMS IN COMPARATIVE PERSPECTIVE

In this society health care has been equated with medical care, and most data in Chapters 11 and 12 refer only to medical care, its organization, and its costs. U.S. social policies have not conceptualized—much less accommodated—a *total* health care system. The development and possible effectiveness of social policy are ultimately a political process in which powerful interest groups vie to define the agenda. The present emphasis on medical care of disease (rather than, for example, preventive medicine or public health) is itself the political product of the relative muscle of various interest groups (see Evans et al., 1994). Any attempt to set a broader agenda for the health of the nation would almost certainly be contested by powerful interest groups benefiting from the present pattern of spending for medical care.

It is useful to compare the health care systems of nations because they show alternative ways of arranging the parts of the system.[1] For example, the Swedish

---

[1]The following sources are useful for comparisons among various health care systems with particular reference to industrialized societies: Abel-Smith, 1992; Banta and Luce, 1993; Culyer and Jonsson, 1986; Dahlgren and Diderichsen, 1986; Deppe, 1992; Field, 1989; Gabe, 1997; Kaufman, 1987; Light, 1997; Light and Schuller, 1986; Marmor and Mashaw, 1997; Mechanic, 1995; Morone and Goggins, 1995; Norbeck and Lock, 1987; Organisation for Economic Co-operation and Development, 1990, 1994; Rodwin, 1989, 1995; Roemer, 1991, 1993; Rosenthal and Frenkel, 1992; Saltman, 1991; Twaddle and Hessler, 1986; Vågerö and Illsley, 1992; Wilsford, 1991.
    Although many commentators treat developing nations' health care issues as utterly different from those of industrialized countries, we would argue that many of the problems are the same: attention to broad social causes of illness and disease, appropriate technology, the most desirable training and deployment of health care workers, effective public health and preventive measures, and maximum utilization of all health-related resources toward a genuinely humane treatment of people in need. Some sources that deal specifically with health care systems of developing countries include Banta, 1986; Donahue, 1986, 1989; Donahue and McGuire, 1995; Elling, 1986; Good, 1987; Green, 1989; Heggenhougen et al., 1987; Lassey et al., 1997; Low, 1985; Morgan, 1989; Rosenthal, 1987, 1988; Rowland, 1991; Sidel, 1993; Simonelli, 1987; Spickard and Jameson, 1995; Stebbins, 1986.

system regulates and controls doctors and hospitals more extensively than the U.S. system. It is more holistic in its concern for health-related issues like nutrition, child care, environmental pollution, and occupational health and safety. The Swedish system has also achieved a healthier nation by all international standards.

The United States could learn from developing nations as well as industrialized ones because our health care system is having to face real limits in the nation's human and financial resources for dealing with health needs. We need to find ways to maximize the health-producing results of how we use our resources. For example, China has achieved remarkable health gains at relatively little cost per capita (Sidel, 1993). The Chinese system incorporates indigenous health practices and utilizes nonprofessional providers (like the "barefoot doctors," paraprofessionals deployed to rural districts); China also emphasizes public health measures and nutrition. From such comparisons we might derive policy directions for our own health care system.

Among industrialized societies are four broad types of health care systems. The U.S. system, exemplifying the first type, is in principle a *laissez-faire, commodified* arrangement. Health care is sold in an economic marketplace. Lack of central planning or significant government controls results in a diverse and relatively uncoordinated mixture of many different institutional programs that provide health services. Profit is a significant motivating factor for many of the system's providers, institutions, insurers, and producers of products and technologies. The medical profession enjoys relatively large amounts of autonomy in regulating its affairs, conditions of work, and income.

The second type, a *national health insurance* system, is similar, except that all citizens are insured by third parties (such as government agencies or labor unions) that have a significant degree of regulatory control over practitioners and health-related institutions. The Canadian system exemplifies this model. The British National Health Service (NHS) is a prime example of the third type, a *health service* system, in which most facilities are owned by the nation and most physicians (whether in private practice or on hospital staff) are paid from state moneys. Physicians have relatively large amounts of professional autonomy, although the state has greater control over salaries and institutional arrangements than in laissez-faire or insurance systems. *Socialized* health systems, such as Russia's, give the state even greater centralized control. In this fourth type, the state owns and manages health facilities and employs almost all health personnel (see Field, 1973).

In the United States, the power of competing interest groups, together with the ideology of free-market competition, has resulted in an amazingly complex, unwieldy, and expensive health care system that is now in crisis. The ideology of a laissez-faire market has obscured the fact that relatively few parts of the health care system are amenable to real market conditions; thus, the notion that competition governs this type of health care system is a fiction. Nor has the United States maintained pure private enterprise, implied in its rejection of national health plans like Canada's. Indeed, nearly half of all U.S. health care expenditures are directly from public moneys, collected by city, state, or federal taxes, and much more is indirectly subsidized by government agencies (such as by tax writeoffs to employers who pay employee health insurance). The U.S. system fits the ideal type of a laissez-faire health care system only in that health care has become *highly commodified*, and the *drive for profits* is, indeed, a central dynamic, making it even more difficult to control or plan to meet the entire society's needs.

The contradictions implicit in the U.S. health care system have driven it to the brink of crisis. U.S. health care expenditures have grown dramatically—much faster than other expenses in the consumer price index. Figure 11.1 shows how greatly the proportion of the total U.S. gross national product (GNP) consumed by health care costs increased between 1940 and 1990. These figures include only expenditures for *formal* health care (including doctors, hospitals, pharmaceuticals, and medical supplies); they do not include most costs of informal care (for example, assistance with daily living for persons with chronic illnesses) or most health maintenance and sickness prevention expenses (such as nutrition, pollution control, and accident prevention).

Runaway health care costs have eroded the nation's ability to address other public needs, such as education and scientific research. Total health expenditures in the United States as a percentage of the gross domestic product[2] (GDP) grew from 7.4 percent in 1970 to 13.6 percent in 1994; by contrast, Canada's expenditures

FIGURE 11.1 **U.S. Health Care Expenditures as a Percentage of Gross National Product** *(Source: U.S. Department of Health and Human Services, Health, United States. Hyattsvillle, MD: National Center for Health Statistics. Note: These data differ from those given in previous editions of this publication, due to Department of Commerce revisions of the gross national product (GNP).)*

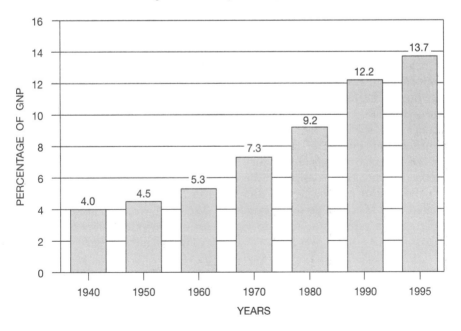

grew from 7.1 percent to only 10.3 percent of its GDP, Germany's from 5.9 to 8.7 percent, and the United Kingdom's from 4.5 to 7.1 percent in the same 19 years (Lassey et al., 1997: 14–15; Schieber et al., 1991). The U.S. cost increases are particularly troubling, because unlike Canada or European countries, the U.S. health care system is not accessible to many of its citizens who are uninsured or underinsured. Although the United States has been less successful in controlling costs, it shares with other developed nations the growing problem of meeting citizens' needs for basic social well-being–health, education, affordable housing, nutrition, old age security, basic support for children–while participating in a globalized economic system in which paying for citizen well-being reduces corporate profit and international competitiveness. Thus, all nations are struggling to find a way to provide for their citizens' well-being, but the U.S. system is in a worse crisis, because it has *never* had an adequate safety net to protect its citizens in times of economic troubles.

The vast majority of Americans are highly dissatisfied with their health care system. Public opinion polls show that between 82 and 90 percent of Americans consider the U.S. system to be so inadequate that it needs fundamental change or complete rebuilding. By contrast, in 1988, only 43 percent of Canadians and 69 percent of the British polled were so dissatisfied. By 1994, huge cutbacks in funding had reduced levels of Canadian satisfaction, but most citizens liked the system itself and wanted funding levels restored. In 1994, only 12 percent of Canadians (and 11 percent of Germans), compared to 28 percent of U.S. respondents, believed their health care system was utterly unsatisfactory and needed complete rebuilding. Both surveys found that under the American system, a much larger proportion of citizens are faced with financial barriers to receiving health care than in Canada (or Britain or Germany), and that substantial numbers are either not covered by health insurance or severely underinsured (Blendon et al., 1990, 1995; Donelan et al., 1996).

Another study found that approximately half of Americans polled worry about premium and health care costs, as well as whether they will be denied needed care due to inadequate insurance or lack of money for out-of-pocket health expenses (Smith, 1992). International comparisons suggest that their fears are well founded. U.S. spending, for every category of health expenditure, is the highest of all nations, but the rate of utilization (calculated by number of doctor visits per person or average number of and length of hospital stays) is well below the average of other industrialized nations (Schieber et al., 1991).

Because of inadequate cost controls, even those Americans who are fully covered (that is, older persons covered by Medicare) receive considerably less needed health care service than do Canadians, whose system pays far less per person for their care (Welch et al., 1996).[3] These figures suggest that many

---

[3]Canadian elderly received 44 percent *more* evaluation (doctor visits) and management services (such as physical therapists) but 25 percent *fewer* surgical procedures. Canadian surgery rates for procedures known to be medically beneficial (hip replacement, for example) were the same as the United States, but much lower for procedures (such as knee replacement) about which there was low consensus as to medical benefit (Welch et al., 1996).

Americans who experience the kinds of health problems that would be treated by the medical care system in other countries are not getting treatment in the United States. Extremely high costs in the United States may be one important reason why many Americans cannot obtain needed services.

By contrast with the United States, in the three decades since the inception of Canadian national health insurance, substantial gains have been made in making medical services accessible to all Canadians, regardless of ability to pay, and greatly reducing mortality disparities between wealthier and poorer, urban and rural regions (Badgley, 1991). Although some economic barriers still exist, the poor are far less at risk of being denied needed health care, and the middle classes are not in fear of being made poor by health care expenses.

The United States and the Republic of South Africa are the only industrialized nations without some form of comprehensive health care system for all citizens (Roemer, 1985). In 1993, a U.S. presidential commission urged a system guaranteeing coverage for all citizens. One alternative set of bills proposed a national health insurance program, comparable to Canada's. At the time, surveys showed that the majority of Americans preferred the Canadian arrangement of national health insurance financed by tax money to the present form of public and private health insurance (*New York Times*, 1992). The various interest groups, especially the insurance industry whose profits in this sector would be eliminated were the country to adopt a system similar to Canada's, spent enormous amounts of money on media campaigns, lobbying Congress and other influential politicians and jockeying for a favorable position relative to other interest groups in the resulting program.[4] No significant program developed, and the problems in the U.S. system have grown worse.

At the same time, however, there is little support in the United States for a national health service like Great Britain's. Indeed, the British are increasingly dissatisfied with their system. The British NHS has been seriously underfunded, resulting in shortages, understaffing, and growing waiting lists for nonemergency hospital services (Lyall, 1997). Indeed, in the 1980s and 1990s, conservative administrations encouraged competition from for-profit, private health care providers, with the effect of creating a two-tier system: NHS for the poor, middle, and working classes, and private providers for the as yet small proportion of the upper classes and upper-level employees with private insurance (Lattimer and Garfield, 1996; Whitney, 1991).

Although Americans spend much more than citizens of other industrialized nations on health care, they do *not* enjoy generally better health. In 1994, Americans paid an average of $3,086 per person for health expenses—far more than countries with the next highest expenditures: Canada, $1,950, and Germany,

---

[4]During the 1993–1994 debate over national health care policy, campaign contributions from the health and insurance industries reached $37.9 million, an increase of 51 percent over the same time period in the previous election cycle (Podhorzer, 1995). Total special interest spending (including paid lobbyists, mass media advertising, and so on) may have totaled over $100 million, making health care reform the most heavily lobbied legislative initiative in recent U.S. history (Center for Public Integrity, 1995).

$1,775, per capita (Lassey et al., 1997: 15). Despite being the industrialized nation with the highest total private and public spending on health care, on several important measures of the health of its people (such as life expectancy and infant mortality), the United States ranks far lower than other countries, such as Canada, Japan, and Sweden, which spend considerably less on health care (Lassey et al., 1997: 21–22). The enormous cost disparity is not purchasing Americans generally better health.

Japan, with a highly developed economy, spends much less per capita than the United States or Canada but has a worse medical care system. Japan's system does provide for all citizens through a weakly controlled national health insurance program. Its system of providers, however, is laissez-faire, with little government planning or control. Most hospitals are small, badly run, physician-owned, for-profit operations, with families of the sick providing most nursing care; public hospitals are better but congested and chaotic. Many Japanese doctors and hospitals overmedicate because a large part of their incomes is profit from medicines they sell directly to their patients—a useful reminder that *spending* on medical care does not necessarily produce better health. At the same time, however, due to good nutrition, prenatal care, public health measures and education, and a relatively high standard of living for working-class citizens, Japan has achieved the best rates of longevity and the lowest of infant mortality in the world (Marmor, 1994).

High expenditures do not guarantee better health because they are at best only indirectly linked with health-promoting or curing practices. For example, two nations may pay the same amount of money for a program of inoculations, but one nation may obtain far fewer inoculations per capita if the profit margins for the materials or provider services are higher in that health care system. Furthermore, health care expenditures are typically only *medical* care costs; these figures do not account for important differences in other health-promoting expenditures, such as nutrition.

As we examine the allocation of resources for health care, we should not assume that all expenditures necessarily benefit health care recipients; in fact, some health care procedures and practices are detrimental to people's health. The poor are not necessarily worse off for not being able to afford Caesarian sections and lots of tranquilizers. The expensive high-tech practices that characterize much of modern medicine produce varying results: Some are indeed medical wonders, some are merely satisfactory, and still others are negligible relative to the cost, effort, and sometimes pain they involve. Other medical practices are downright iatrogenic, creating illness rather than healing it. In being denied the benefits of medical treatment, the poor have thus been also spared some of the risks.

The U.S. health care system is the product of a long history of considerable political maneuvering, haggling, and contesting. This system places a particularly heavy emphasis on medical treatment rather than on health care. As a corollary, its focus is on institutional and professional forms of care. Furthermore, the U.S. system—even more so than other capitalist systems—emphasizes the **commodification** of health and health care; making money is one important driving force in the system (cf. Riska, 1985). The interplay of numerous conflicting interests created the existing system, and the same interests are exerted vigorously whenever change to the system is proposed. To understand this complex system, we must first appreciate the relative power among these interest groups and how they use their resources to further their interests.

The following is a greatly simplified sketch of the various economic interests represented in the U.S. health care system. In this chapter we consider the social organization and interests of some of the people involved in receiving or providing health care, especially those whose income is derived from providing such care. With the development of high-technology and specialized medicine, work within the medical care system has become heavily reliant on large bureaucratic organizations. The structure and functions of these medical organizations reflect the structure of the larger society. Workers in the medical care system are stratified largely according to the class, gender, ethnic, and other divisions in the whole society.

In Chapter 12 we describe the economic interests of large-scale organizations involved in the system, especially hospitals, medical industries, insurance companies, and government agencies. These interest groups vary dramatically in their relative power at various historical moments. The development of economically powerful interest groups as major institutional actors in the U.S. health care policy debates was a nearly inevitable result of the combination of the laissez-faire ideology of the system and the relatively recent expansion of health care profits and markets.

In order to think critically about a better future, we need to understand the structural sources of the present crises and the systemic problems that make the existing health care system so ineffective in providing good, affordable health care to all citizens. There appears to be a general consensus that the U.S. health care system requires significant changes, but there is less consensus on what parts to change and what the long-range objectives should be.

If we could build the system anew, what might it include? It is useful to imagine alternatives that might better address some of the health needs poorly met by the existing system. We need to consider many criteria—not merely cost—for a better system. Our nation could try to provide better access to care for rural and inner-city communities and more preventive measures for all age groups. We could reshape medical education to discourage overspecialization and encourage better doctor-patient relationships. Our country could restructure payments to providers to promote better decision making about use of surgery, medications, and medical technology, as well as to create hospitals that emphasize caring and skilled service, rather than cost-effective tending of patients.

At root are also some fundamentally moral issues, which we rarely acknowledge or discuss in a public forum. For instance, *what kind of nation do we want to be*? Do we want to consider health as a commodity that the wealthy can buy in abundance, that the middle classes can afford occasionally in limited measure, and that the poor cannot have at all? Or do we, as a nation, want to consider health, like education, as something we should try to provide for all in order to promote the good of all?

RECIPIENTS

Decades ago, the prospect of catastrophic medical costs was remote, even for poor persons, because the level of medical knowledge and technology did not command high prices. Hospitals were relatively low-tech, generally not-for-profit organizations that subsidized costs of care for those who could not afford to pay. Doctors, who lived in the very communities they served, charged for their services according to what people there could afford to pay. The implicit contract that protected the recipients of medical services also protected the doctor: affordable service for patients, even at inconvenient times, in exchange for community respect, deference to professional judgment, and a good standard of living for the physician. That kind of social contract, based on long-term communitywide commitments and loyalties, no longer pertains in most modern life (see Rubin, 1996). In its place have come impersonal, short-term commitments.

Recipients of health care now fear catastropic medical costs, because they sense that their interests are not being protected in a laissez-faire system of powerful corporate interests. Health care costs have taken much larger portions of the family budget (in premiums, taxes, and out-of-pocket expenses), but the families themselves have little or no say over these expenditures.

The U.S. system has been portrayed in political rhetoric as an open market of competing providers that (in theory) would lower prices if only patients would be more savvy consumers. In reality, however, the patient is in an inherently weak position as a consumer, primarily because medicine has become so sophisticated that the patient typically lacks the expertise to evaluate services (from doctor or hospital) and products (pharmaceuticals or technological devices, for example). Unlike standardized products, medical services are highly variable. Although an individual can do much to become an informed consumer of medical services, the enormous disparity in expertise between professional and patient places the consumer in a relatively weak position.

The market model also assumes the consumer is the one making the choices in the marketplace, but in medical care the recipient rarely makes such decisions. Ideologically the U.S. system emphasizes the patient's freedom to choose doctors, but actual choice may be severely constrained by the limited availability of doctors in a region, by insurance that is limited to certain providers, or by the assignment of a patient without private insurance to a clinic, military, or other institutional doctor. Before the 1980s, most employees' health insurance allowed the open choice of a provider, but in less than a decade nearly all employees lost this choice (Califano, 1989). Furthermore, most insured individuals do not even choose their own health insurance program; insurance plans are typically marketed to *employers*, rather than to the health care consumers themselves. Insurers compete only to insure the most profitable pools of employees—those who need the least health care—so market principles do not help reduce prices overall (Altman and Rodwin, 1988; Bodenheimer, 1990; Bodenheimer and Grumbach, 1997).

The recipient's doctor or insurance plan determines in which hospital to place the patient. Unlike most other industrialized countries, U.S. doctors do not relinquish care of (or income from) their hospitalized patients. Doctors maintain "admitting privileges" with certain local hospitals, and they bill their hospitalized patients separately from the hospital bill (Gabel and Redisch, 1979). This arrangement makes the hospital and private practitioner mutually dependent. Patients insured through various forms of managed care plans are further limited to hospitals that have negotiated favorable rates with the managed care organization. The patient thus rarely actually chooses a hospital, and hospitals do not compete for customers in an open market. Like insurance companies, hospitals try to attract doctors who will bring in only the most desirable pools of customers—those with ample insurance and whose care is most likely to result in net income for the hospital.

The doctor is probably the foremost guide of the patient's decisions about health services (Gertman, 1981). The doctor selects pharmaceuticals and treatment procedures; the doctor refers the patient to specific other doctors for specialized care and to specific outpatient labs and clinics for diagnostic or therapeutic services. Lacking significant decision-making power, the patient is hardly a consumer in an open, competitive marketplace.

Another feature of health care decisions that makes them difficult to weigh rationally as in a market situation is the high value our culture places on health and life. When we say our health is priceless, we imply that we cannot imagine what limit we would pay to preserve that health. The consumer's medical treatment decisions are even more complicated because they often must be made quickly and under stress. Unlike buying a house, the consumer may have to decide to commit several hundred thousand dollars with no opportunity to shop around or even consider other options.

Recipients of medical care are among the least powerful interest groups in the U.S. system. Collectively, some groups of potential patients have wrested benefits from the system, but their successes are related to their political clout (as is the case with senior citizens protecting funding of Medicare benefits) and/or their powerful socioeconomic position (for instance, upper-middle-class workers achieving substantial health care benefits from their employers). Less powerful groups of recipients, such as the working poor, have little or no influence against the interests of other parties in the system.

PHYSICIAN-PROVIDERS

As a profession, physicians collectively constitute one of several "countervailing powers" contending for economic advantages and control of the organization of health care delivery (Light, 1993). Historically, medical doctors' achievement of professional dominance (described in Chapter 10) accomplished both their preeminence over other medical occupations and their extraordinarily high level of income. Other occupational groups also have asserted their interests: to define their domains of expertise, to achieve recognition and pay as professionals, to have more control over the structure of their jobs. The resulting hierarchy of specialized health care occupations is fluid and changing, but all occupational interest groups utilize whatever resources of power they have to protect their interests. The prestige, power, financial success, and professional autonomy of medical doctors is, however, something of a standard against which other occupational groups measure themselves.

Just as the long-term social contract binding a community with its physician(s) is a relic of the past, so too is doctors' high degree of autonomy and control of their own incomes, treatment of their patients, and the terms and structure of their work. The prior system of medical work was vulnerable to the pressure of countervailing powers, in large part because of excesses or inconsistencies within that system itself, but the emerging arrangements are creating new problems for health care workers and for recipients of their services. In the last two decades of the twentieth century, U.S. medicine has come to be practiced largely in the context of large-scale corporations, most of which operate for *profit*–hospital corporations, insurance corporations, health maintenance organizations, and so on (Salmon, 1995; Starr, 1982: 420–449). Technocratic control of the labor process has transformed work in many professional fields including medicine (Burris, 1993: 120 ff.), for example by allowing computerized surveillance of each worker's performance. Although still prestigious and high-paying work, all medical fields are increasingly constrained, either by external regulations or by direct control of a corporate employer.

Corporatization of Medical Production

Whereas at mid-century, most U.S. doctors were in private, entrepreneurial practice, by 1989 about one-half of licensed physicians were salaried employees (Altman and Rosenthal, 1990). In the 1990s this trend has accelerated as large hospital corporations have bought out numerous doctors' practices and clinics nationwide (Goldsmith, 1993; Rodwin, 1993; Segal, 1996). Even when not directly employed by corporations, few doctors practicing in urban or suburban settings are independent of the corporate reach of insurers, hospital corporations, and managed care organizations. The projected oversupply of physicians, new patterns of hospital ownership and management, and changes in third-party insurance and government regulation make it likely that yet greater proportions of physicians will be employed in salaried or other corporate-linked arrangements. These developments are discussed further later in this chapter and in Chapter 12.

As a result of these new structural arrangements, health care providers are losing some of the autonomy they gained in their ascent to professional dominance (Hafferty and Light, 1995; McKinlay and Stoeckle, 1988). The same development of technologically advanced, hospital-based medical practices that enhanced the prestige and authority of the medical profession in the first half of the century has, in the second half, also produced conditions of the profession's corporate dependence. Modern medicine is capital intensive; few solo practitioners can afford to finance even modest practices. So they turn to corporate sponsors–medical groups, hospitals, and managed care corporations–to provide the necessary equipment and support services (Derber, 1984; Rodwin, 1993).

Physicians' relations with their economic sponsors are hardly as disempowering as those faced by nonprofessional workers because the medical profession retains near-monopoly control over much needed, complex skill and knowledge (Hafferty and Light, 1995; Navarro, 1988). Interestingly, corporatization has created a new elite within medicine—physician administrators, whose loyalties to the corporation supercede those to the profession (Montgomery, 1992). In the context of institutional cost cutting, however, even such highly expert employees as physicians may experience their jobs and entire incomes as vulnerable. For example, when two hospitals merge, much of the professional staff could be redundant; doctors, therapists, and nurses—especially the experienced ones with larger paychecks—may be dismissed (Rosenthal, 1997a).

Government agencies and private insurance companies (that is, "third-party payers" of medical bills) also increasingly monitor and regulate doctors' work. In an effort to curb rising costs and overuse of hospitals, diagnostic tests, surgery, and so on, these organizations have added new layers of bureaucratic management of health care, increasing standardization, surveillance, and sometimes countermanding physicians' professional judgment (see White et al., 1994). Loss of autonomy and increase of hassle connected with regulations and monitoring are major sources of dissatisfaction among doctors. One study found that British cardiologists were dissatisfied mainly with their heavy workloads and the health system's lack of resources; by contrast, American cardiologists were dissatisfied at being forced into a bureaucratic system of rules and regulations, hierarchical authority, and rationalized procedures, which reduces their autonomy (Gross, 1994). Another comparative survey found serious dissatisfaction with the nation's health care system among 77 percent of U.S. physicians, compared to only 33 percent of Canadian and 48 percent of German doctors (Blendon et al., 1993).

The corporate interests of hospitals and insurers have thrust considerations of cost effectiveness and profit maximization into the fore. Who speaks for the interests of the patient-recipient? In the former model, the doctor was supposed to be a "palladin" agent, whose implicit contract with the patient included advocacy on behalf of the patient's interests (White et al., 1994). If a doctor said, "This patient needs to be hospitalized," that decision was once accepted as authoritative by third-party insurers and hospitals. Physicians' sponsors today, however, are more likely to discourage, question, and even override their professional opinions. Although not all physicians are trustworthy guardians of their patients' best interests, for-profit corporations may be even less trustworthy because they are remote, impersonal, and their profitability depends on minimizing the costs of patient care (Gray, 1997; White et al., 1994).

Doctors' loss of total autonomy and control of patients' care was, however, largely the result of several countervailing powers—especially insurers and government—that developed policies and procedures to counteract abuses and excesses in the former system of provider reimbursement and incentives. One problem was the system of *fee-for-service billing*, which made it difficult to control escalating health care costs. A related problem was the extent of *perverse incentives* for a doctor to order unnecessary tests or perform extra procedures. *Conflicts of interest* due to sources of secondary income were another systemic problem. Unresolved problems with the system's response to *medical malpractice* created further cost escalation.

Fee-for-Service Payment and Capitation

As noted in Chapter 10, physicians achieved a legally recognized monopoly over the provision of most paid medical care, as well as the training and admission of new personnel. Historically, the economic basis of physicians' service has been a fee-for-service system in which the doctor typically charges the patient for each service provided at each visit. In principle, this system establishes an economic link between physician-provider and patient-recipient, but few contemporary doctor-patient relationships are so simple because only about 18 percent of physician service expenditures are paid "out-of-pocket" by patients (Baker and Newhouse, 1995). Various third parties, such as the government or insurance companies, direct the vast majority of payments. The idea that the mode of payment forges a direct link between provider and consumer is thus more a myth, harking back to an era of more personal doctor-patient relationships. This ideology supports the interests of physicians because the fee-for-service arrangement has allowed them great freedom to set their own terms of remuneration.

Many doctors themselves have been dissatisfied with how the fee-for-service arrangement has affected their everyday practice of medicine. One thoughtful physician described his realization of how detrimental these economic considerations had become:

> An aged patient had come in to the office and was talking about her aching feet. She not only had several very real physical problems but she was also very lonely and quite hypochondriacal. . . . As she continued to tell me how tired she was, I realized I wasn't listening. I was angry. What she needed was someone to sympathize with her, gently encourage her, and to make some simple suggestions that might alleviate her suffering. I knew from past experience that that kind of listening and empathetic presence would require at least half an hour, but I would only be able to charge $20 for an intermediate call, Medicare would discount the charge significantly, and my half after overhead, would be, maybe, $8. I also knew that if I just stood up, cut the woman off by giving her a prescription for a pain medicine and scheduled her for next month, I could charge the same $20 and move into the next room where another patient was waiting with a small laceration from which I would earn about $30 in perhaps 10 minutes.
>
> As soon as I recognized what I was angry about, I was ashamed. But the truth of my feelings was nonetheless real. . . . I was looking at my interactions with patients more and more as business transactions. (Hilfiker, 1986)

These problems show how unsatisfactory for both patient and provider is a system of highly commodified health service, in which each aspect of care is delivered as a discrete entity.

In the face of escalating medical costs, critics have questioned how doctors set their fees. The practice of medicine in the United States has been essentially entrepreneurial (that is, incomes are made in the business of selling of goods and especially services). What, then, are these services worth? Considerable evidence indicates that the level of fees is governed primarily by physicians' desired standard of living (Reinhardt, 1987). Overall, the profession is exceptionally well paid–in the top 3 percent of all earners in the United States (Altman and Rosenthal, 1990). If market principles drove the prices of physicians' services, U.S. medical services would cost less than comparable Canadian services because in the United States there are more doctors per capita (that is, "supply") and because a far larger proportion of U.S. citizens cannot afford needed health care, thus reducing the demand for physician services. But physician fees have been relatively impervious to market principles, and U.S. doctors charge more than twice what Canadian doctors charge for the same services (Fuchs and Hahn, 1990).

Specialists, particularly surgeons, earn far more than general practitioners and other doctors engaged in the more labor-intensive primary care. Furthermore, during the 1980s, when national spending for physician services nearly doubled, surgeons' and other specialists' incomes grew very rapidly, whereas primary care doctors' incomes gained by only 5 percent (Pope and Schneider, 1992). By 1992, cardiac surgeons averaged $575,000 annual net income (that is, earnings after paying costs of offices, insurance, and so on) and neurosurgeons averaged $449,000–several times more than the $119,000 average income of family practitioners or $124,000 of pediatricians (Eckholm, 1993).

Because the U.S. health care system has no centralized planning or effective controls over the numbers of doctors in the various branches of medicine, there are dramatic and growing imbalances in the supply of specialists (cf. Fryer, 1991). In 1992, the Council on Graduate Medical Education projected a serious and growing oversupply of doctors by the year 2000 relative to the nation's needs and ability to pay. Most of the surplus consists of surgical specialists; the supply of family practitioners and pediatricians is about the same as the amount needed, but there are nearly twice as many neurosurgeons and cardiologists as needed (Bencomo et al., 1995). These imbalances are expected to grow dramatically because only about 20 percent of medical graduates want to practice in primary care (such as family practice) rather than medical specialties (Gamliel et al., 1995; Rivo and Kindig, 1996).

Interestingly, the oversupply of specialists has not led to competitive pricing. Indeed, rather than competition driving physicians' fees down, the existence of an oversupply of physicians in an area generally increases health care costs because the doctors compensate for the fact that each has fewer patients by raising their fees for each procedure and by recommending more procedures for each patient they treat. For example, the dramatic increase in the number of prostatectomies (for nonmalignant enlargement of the prostate gland) performed in the United States is not due to any disproportionate increase in prostate disease (compared to other countries). Only a small fraction of the increase is explained by the existence of Medicare coverage for men over 65. Rather, the oversupply of competing specialists has made this surgery a financial mainstay of urologists' practices, motivating them to convince patients that prostate enlargement is a health problem and the surgery is necessary, effective, and acceptable (McDade, 1996).

Fees charged for the same procedure vary enormously from community to community. For example, in 1993 an appendectomy cost as little as $909 in Denver or as much as $1,377 in Los Angeles; a person in New York City spent $5,123 for a hysterectomy, and the same operation in Dallas cost $1,996 (Health Insurance Association of America, cited in Morganthau and Murr, 1993). Although variations in physicians' costs of practice (including office expenses and malpractice insurance) account for a portion of these dramatic differences in fees, they do not adequately explain them (Reinhardt, 1987).

The medical profession never has been effective in policing itself for illegal and unethical fiduciary practices, such as fee splitting, kickbacks, and self-referral (Rodwin, 1993). There is a fine and imprecise line between uniform pricing among doctors in a community and illegal price fixing. Nevertheless, doctors who set fees according to what the market will bear rarely undercut the going rate; rates are thus seldom competitive within a single community. No matter how honest the fee schedule, the patient typically is not able to evaluate its appropriateness.[5]

Between 1980 and 1989, when physician costs were soaring, the components of doctors' income that accounted for those increases were the volume of procedures performed (calculated by the number of surgical procedures and diagnostic tests per physician) and increased price per service. On average, doctors had not increased the amount of time spent with patients and other medical work. Rather, insurance and Medicare reimbursement policies made these fees for service *less* sensitive to market forces (Pope and Schneider, 1992). These excesses of the 1980s may have seriously undermined physicians' autonomy in the long run, because they brought into question whether the surgery, testing, and other increased utilization of medical services were really necessary for the patient's health.

Fee setting is in a state of flux because of the considerable struggles among the countervailing powers (for example, doctors, hospitals, the federal government, insurance companies, and managed care corporations). A 1988 government study found that the existing system of payments overcompensated doctors for invasive procedures such as surgery and for diagnostic tests, characteristic of much specialist care, but did not encourage them to spend time with patients in office visits and other time-consuming medical work, more characteristic of primary care (see Smith, 1992, for a thorough analysis of the Physician Payment Review Commission and policy debates). In 1992, Medicare began to phase in a new fee schedule, called Resource-Based Relative-Value Scale, based on the commission's recommendations (Lassey et al., 1997). In the same period, managed care corporations tried to hold down expenditures for physician services by such restraints as utilization reviews and negotiated discounts in fees. Average physician income did decrease slightly in 1994, after years of dramatic increases; the decrease was most pronounced among

---

[5]This analysis focuses on economic pressures experienced by all physicians, honest and dishonest alike; illegal behavior is one response to the opportunities for gain. Initially, it was only individual unscrupulous physicians who profited from illegal kickbacks and fraudulent billing (Rodwin, 1993).

those at the upper end of the spectrum whose incomes had soared in the preceding ten years (Simon and Born, 1996).

In an effort to cut costs, many managed care organizations have negotiated contracts with physicians to pay for their services by a different method. **Capitation** means the doctor is paid a fixed rate per month per patient (the amount varies according to age and sex of the patient), regardless of how much physician service is actually needed. A 1995 survey found 70 percent of health maintenance organizations[6] paid their primary care physicians by capitation (Friedman, 1996). Capitation is advantageous to the doctor because it simplifies billing and ascertains a regular flow of income. At the same time, however, because these doctors are not on a salary, they must fill their patient load with enough patients–often a mixture of capitated and fee-for-service clients–to bring in enough income. The third-party insurers have thus transferred some of the risk of their business to the doctors. It is the doctor–not the insurer–who must compensate when patients have serious, medical service-consuming illnesses.

This risk shifting has several deleterious effects on their patients. Embedded in capitation is the *perverse incentive* to deny care to capitated patients, because the physician is rewarded for taking on more patients and doing less for them (Gray, 1997; Poplin, 1996; Rodwin, 1993; Rosenthal, 1996). A related problem is that it creates incentives to avoid serving the needs of high-use patients. One doctor whose services were paid by capitation said, "I hate to talk about patients this way, but if I get a 50-year-old diabetic who I have to see every month, it's a major economic disaster" (quoted in Rosenthal, 1996). Precisely those patients who most need to utilize doctors' care are those most likely to be avoided by doctors paid by capitation.

Clinical Decisions and Economic Considerations

The fee-for-service arrangement is riddled with **perverse incentives**–built-in financial encouragements to treat the patient inappropriately by increasing services, overprescribing medications and diagnostic tests, or to choose treatment sites according to physician rather than patient interests (Rodwin, 1993; see also Frazier and Mosteller, 1995). When doctors can increase their own income by having their patients get medical services from which they personally profit, there is a significant conflict of interest often resulting in questionable medical treatment (Rodwin, 1993). Furthermore, many unneeded tests are ordered as part of "defensive" medicine to protect against malpractice suits, whereas others are requested by patients to allay fears of certain illnesses. Some estimates suggest that between 20 and 60 percent of these tests are unnecessary, adding nothing to the patient's diagnosis or treatment (Califano, 1989; Luft, 1983).

Likewise, the fee-for-service system gives incentives to doctors to use surgery rather than less invasive treatments. The decision to operate is based on a number of discretionary choices, perceptions, evaluations, and decision rules that vary

---

[6]Chapter 12 explains the various types of managed care.

considerably among physicians and medical situations. *All* surgery involves assessing the probability that the operation will improve function, reduce pain, or increase the quality of life as balanced against the risks of complications from the surgery itself. The fee-for-service system complicates the medical decision-making process with the added criterion of financial gain for doctor and hospital. For example, if a woman in labor does not give birth quickly, the physician experiences considerable incentive to perform a Caesarian section, a serious abdominal operation for which fee-for-service reimbursement is high and time required is relatively short, rather than work with the mother for a normal vaginal delivery for which the reimbursement is far lower proportionate to the time required. One study of rates of Caesarian sections for women whose previous deliveries had been Caesarians found that financial considerations were a significant predictor of the decision to operate (Stafford, 1991).

Especially for new and unproven procedures, there is considerable potential for physicians to conduct surgery for inappropriate reasons relative to the patient's health and needs. For example, a 1987 study found that only 35 percent of carotid endarterectomies (an operation to clear blockages in the major artery leading to the brain) were performed for "clearly appropriate indications" (Chassin et al., 1987). Similarly, critics assert that the U.S. rates of coronary bypasses, hysterectomies, and Caesarean sections are at least double the appropriate level (cf. Angier, 1997; Califano, 1989; McDade, 1996; Notzon, 1990; Rasell, 1993). Compared to other industrialized countries, the United States has exceptionally high rates of surgery without concomitant lower rates of mortality. For example, U.S. surgeons perform coronary bypass operations at six times the rate in England where, under the NHS, surgeons' income is not directly related to the number or type of operations performed, and mastectomies three times more frequently (Payer, 1988). We cannot infer that the difference is due only to unnecessary surgery (see Schwartz, 1984), but the socioeconomic incentive of fee for service is certainly one factor promoting high rates of surgery.

In principle, the physician is an advocate for the patient, representing the patient's interests to insurers, hospitals, and other specialists on the case. An inherent conflict of interest exists, however, even for physicians who take their role as advocate seriously, when they are in a position to order for their patients certain procedures that also happen to be an important source of their own income (Gray, 1991; Luft, 1983; Rodwin, 1993). Physicians' judgment may be also influenced by their hospital affiliates' pressures to fill beds. The number of operations performed per capita varies widely from community to community; two significant predictors of these differences are the rate of empty hospital beds and the local supply of surgeons (Evans, 1974; Lewis, 1969; see also Barron, 1989; Dartmouth Medical School Center for the Evaluative Clinical Sciences, 1996; Roth, 1984).

Some for-profit hospital corporations have made such financial incentives even more explicit by asking doctors who practice at their facilities to buy shares in the hospital itself. A 1997 study found that physicians who had invested in a Columbia/HCA-owned hospital in Miami increased their referrals to that hospital by 13.4 percent, and their referrals to other hospitals dropped by 22.4 percent in the first two years after the chain took control of the hospital (Gottlieb and Eichenwald, 1997).[7]

Financial incentives have even more impact on the kinds of physician services performed in response to patient demand rather than because of clear-cut medical need. Medical services for fertility or potency problems, sterilizations or abortions, obesity, or chronic pain exemplify these financial interests. A cosmetic surgeon is not likely to counsel a prospective patient that her nose is lovely without surgery.[8] So long as the U.S. health care system continues to provide economic incentives for inappropriate surgery and other medical procedures, both doctors and hospitals will continue to be subject to the influence of economic considerations in deciding on patient treatment.

Even greater potential for conflict of interest is involved when the physician can receive **secondary income** from the treatment. When physicians own a joint venture, such as a free-standing radiation therapy facility, diagnostic imaging facility, nursing home, or psychiatric hospital, they benefit financially by referring their patients, while evading antikickback laws (Mitchell and Scott, 1992). A California study of patients covered by workers' compensation found that physicians who referred patients to physical therapy, psychiatric, or magnetic resonance imaging (MRI) facilities of which they were owners tended to order significantly more services, including a higher proportion of medically inappropriate services, than did a control group of doctors with no financial interest in those facilities (Swedlow et al., 1992).

In 1993, federal regulatory agencies investigated some health care producers who had questionable financial relationships with physicians. For instance, one corporation recruited local doctors who made an initial investment in both a local home health business and the parent corporation. By referring all their patients to this business, the local doctors reaped investment income of thousands of dollars annually depending on how much business they sent themselves—in addition to profits on their shares in the parent company and over and above their incomes for their professional practice (Meier, 1993b).

By 1991, more than 10 percent of U.S. doctors had invested in businesses to which they refer their patients; in some states, such as Florida, more than 40 percent of all doctors have such investments (Pear, 1991; Pear and Eckholm, 1991). Contrary to claims of proponents of joint ventures, such facilities do not increase access to needed medical services for underserved populations. One study of joint ventures in radiation therapy in Florida found that none of the facilities were located in inner-city neighborhoods or rural areas, compared to 11 percent of

---

[7]This kind of hospital investment scheme is aimed at areas in which a large proportion of patients have Medicare or other kinds of insurance that does not limit doctors' selection of hospital. A reverse of this perverse incentive is characteristic of HMOs and other managed care programs, which reward physicians for *not* recommending hospitalization or other services (see Chapter 12).

[8]Because cosmetic surgery, fertility treatments, and many of these other elective physician services are done outside hospital contexts and are not reimbursable by insurance, they are particularly poorly regulated for cost, safety, effectiveness, malpractice, or fraud (Sullivan, 1993; see also Gingold, 1996; Glassner, 1995).

nonjoint-venture facilities. Joint ventures received 39 percent of their revenues from patients with good insurance coverage, in contrast to 31 percent for nonjoint-venture facilities. Furthermore, the principal personnel at joint-venture facilities spent 18 percent less time with each patient than those at nonjoint-venture facilities. Both the frequency and costs of radiation therapy at free-standing investor-owned facilities were 40 to 60 percent higher in Florida than the rest of the United States, despite the absence of other factors that might explain the difference in use and costs (Mitchell and Sunshine, 1992).

The program for end-stage renal disease (ESRD), a chronic, debilitating, and often fatal disease of the kidneys, illustrates the murky causal link between physician-investors' conflicts of interest, medical judgments, and escalating U.S. health care costs. One treatment for ESRD is hemodialysis. When it was first developed, hemodialysis was such an expensive technology that it was systematically rationed. In response to a concerted political campaign by well-organized groups of patients and providers, however, in 1972 the U.S. government passed an amendment to Medicare legislation that provided federal reimbursement for ESRD treatments, even though most ESRD patients were not old enough to qualify for Medicare.[9]

Even in the first year of the program, the actual costs were many times the projected costs, and subsequently national expenditures for ESRD treatments escalated dramatically. By 1991, the ESRD program annual per-patient cost ($29,000) was nine times higher than the average Medicare per-patient cost (Iglehart, 1993). The enormous cost escalation occurred because the legislation created incentives to put all sufferers of ESRD on dialysis, even though it is not an appropriate or even beneficial treatment for many (Simmons and Marine, 1984). Ironically, the United States, a nation with no program for equitable distribution of health care, became the most liberal subsidizer of dialysis for all. In 1989, the U.S. rate of treatment for renal failure was 2.2 times that of Canada and 3.8 times that of all European countries (Iglehart, 1993).[10]

A second reason for the dramatic escalation of ESRD therapy costs was that in the United States, unlike other countries, the dominant mode of treatment was in-center dialysis, rather than the less expensive home dialysis or kidney transplants (Kutner, 1982). After the passage of the ESRD program in 1973, in-center dialysis became a booming business; the number of for-profit dialysis facilities more than tripled in the 1980s alone. To curb runaway costs, in 1983 Medicare greatly reduced the reimbursement rate, but for-profit dialysis facilities continued to proliferate and earn profits, compensating for lower reimbursement rates by

---

[9]The existence of a single organ-specific program of government provision medical services illustrates the inefficiency of the U.S. health care system. If, instead, the system guaranteed that all Americans received care for hypertension and diabetes, before kidney complications developed, far fewer people would need ESRD treatment (Adams, 1995).

[10]The overutilization of dialysis (that is, using it for patients who have a low probability of benefiting from it) may be a significant factor in why the rate of death of persons on dialysis in the United States is extremely high (23.6 percent in 1992) compared to other developed nations such as France (11 percent) and Japan (9.7 percent). Another significant factor may be the cost-cutting measures used in the U.S. dialysis centers to turn a profit (Eichenwald, 1995a).

increasing billable services (for instance, by giving more injections), giving dialysis to more and more patients, including a much larger proportion of patients for whom the treatment was of questionable benefit. The dialysis centers also maintained profits by reducing their operating costs; they substituted less skilled staff for registered nurses, used dangerously obsolete dialysis equipment, and reused dialyzer fluids on multiple patients. Such changes raise questions about the quality of their care (Eichenwald, 1995a, 1995b, 1995c, 1996; Iglehart, 1993; see also Miller, 1983; Riska, 1985). Although many sick people have been helped by the ESRD program, the drive for profits by many participating physicians and dialysis centers have propelled the costs (more than $6 billion in 1996) and influenced professional judgments.

The potential for physician profits on such secondary gains has dramatically increased in recent years with the expansion of high-tech medicine. Government attempts to curb abuses have been limited, because both Medicare and Medicaid use mainly fee-for-service reimbursement, which is hard to monitor. Although outright fraud is illegal, the system has too few controls to prevent it (Sparrow, 1996). Many other secondary income schemes are not illegal, merely unethical. In 1991, the AMA adopted a policy discouraging physician referral to businesses in which they have an interest, but the policy is only advisory and voluntary, so it carries little weight and no sanctions. The organized American medical profession has been historically very ambivalent about ethical problems tied to financial interests; it did not seriously address financial conflicts of interest as a professional ethical issue until the 1980s. Even though fee splitting, kickbacks, and other questionable commercial practices have been a problem in professional practice since the turn of the century, in the second half of this century, the AMA steadily weakened its stance against abuses to placate its members and reflect their economic interests (Rodwin, 1992, 1993).

Regardless of whether physicians are conscious of their economic interests in clinical decisions, the profit connection in the United States results in a very different pattern of patient care than in countries where doctors cannot profit from the treatments they recommend. The ESRD program provides at least one important lesson for U.S. policymakers as they consider how to expand health care access to all citizens: the necessity of restructuring physician payment programs such that conflicts of interest cannot affect physicians' decisions about whether or how to treat their patients.

Malpractice: Economic Burdens and Regulation

The issue of malpractice is related to the socioeconomic basis of provider-recipient relationships. Around the turn of the century, medical societies provided for the mutual defense of members against malpractice suits. Courts deferred to local doctors' judgment as expert witnesses, which made it virtually impossible for aggrieved patients to get one doctor to testify against another. Furthermore, medical societies were so successful in protecting members from suit that they were able to obtain very favorable insurance rates, whereas nonmembers were often unable to obtain insurance at all (Starr, 1982: 111).

In the latter half of the twentieth century, however, the legal and cultural climate changed. Patients became more willing to take doctors to court, partly because of the growing impersonality of all economic relationships. Rising expectations of the wonders of medical science may also have both enhanced doctors' prestige and remuneration while creating unrealistic public beliefs about what doctors could accomplish. Simultaneously, courts allowed the wider use of outside experts and cosmopolitan rather than local standards of care, and legislation—especially since the 1970s—clarified patients' rights, such as the right to informed consent for procedures. The result has been a dramatic increase in malpractice litigation, increasingly large awards to patient-plaintiffs, and increased malpractice insurance premiums, the cost of which is generally passed on to the consumer (Hay, 1992; Horwitz and Brennan, 1995). Although the costs of malpractice insurance and litigation (probably only 1 percent of total health care spending) have been exaggerated by state legislators calling for reform, the system of handling malpractice in the United States is particularly ineffective and inefficient in protecting the recipient of medical services (Horwitz and Brennan, 1995).

The expansion of malpractice litigation has created a number of additional powerful interest groups in the health care arena. Malpractice insurance is typically offered as part of a for-profit insurance industry. Lawyers, courts, and layers of legal paper-processing organizations have likewise become major recipients of the health care dollar. An estimated 60 percent of the billions paid annually for malpractice insurance goes not to aggrieved patients but to the insurance and litigation industries (Califano, 1989). At the same time, however, the expense of litigation prevents the vast majority of injured patients from going to court to obtain any compensation (cf. Rosenthal, 1988).

Most cases that reach the courts are reasonable claims. One study of over 30,000 patients who had been hospitalized found that 3.7 percent had suffered some injury as a result of medical care; of those, 28 percent were injured due to doctor negligence or substandard care. Although 14 percent of the injuries were fatal and nearly 3 percent were permanently disabling, only 1 out of every 9.6 cases of injury due to negligence resulted in a lawsuit (Brennan et al., 1991). Another study found that most malpractice cases won by patients were, in fact, well-founded cases of substandard care and the amount of payment awarded closely correlated with the severity of the injury (Taragin et al., 1992).

Furthermore, the fear of malpractice suits encourages doctors to practice defensive medicine in which clinical decisions are made with an eye to protecting themselves from lawsuits. By practicing defensive medicine, hospital staff often construct a patient's chart as a case record designed more to stand up in court than to describe the patient's actual situation. Communication about the patient then takes place informally, off the record, such as by one specialist writing notes to another (Millman, 1976: 145). Defensive medicine also results in unnecessary tests and procedures (Califano, 1989; Freudenheim, 1987a; Reinhardt, 1987). For example, fearing lawsuits if they deliver imperfect babies, obstetricians are more likely to order fetal monitoring during labor and are more likely to perform possibly unnecessary Caesarian sections if the monitor indicates any signs of fetal distress. Furthermore, doctors may avoid treating high-risk patients or may shift their practice to a lower-risk specialization.

The problems of malpractice are due to two unmet needs in the U.S. health care system. First, the system has had no adequate method of identifying, controlling, or punishing physicians who were incompetent, negligent, or otherwise detrimental to the health of their patients. One of the prerogatives achieved by medical dominance was the right to peer review: Only doctors could identify and punish malpractice. Historically, however, once a physician passed the credentialing process and obtained a license to practice, fellow doctors were highly unlikely to constrain that practice, much less to take it away. The United States has only a loose system of state medical boards with authority to discipline malpractice, and no coordinated national monitoring is in place to prevent negligent or incompetent physicians from simply obtaining a license to practice in another state. Fewer than a third of the doctors disciplined for serious incompetence or misconduct lose their license to practice medicine (Hilts, 1996). Furthermore, the U.S. practice of dealing with medical negligence through lawsuits fails to deter doctors from negligent behavior (Horwitz and Brennan, 1995).

A second reason for the rise in importance of malpractice suits is that the nation provides few other avenues for a family to obtain recompense for the actual costs created by medical mistakes. Iatrogenic medical practices often create years of additional medical expenses as well as the loss of income due to disability, yet the U.S. health care system offers little assistance with such costs. Most patients have no safety net of economic help for serious medical problems. Thus, malpractice suits become the last-chance effort to obtain economic relief. Litigation is a highly unsatisfactory way to provide recompense for medical mistakes, however, because few people with legitimate claims can afford the long and expensive courtroom route. In the United States, the vast majority of persons injured by medical mistakes ultimately receive no financial help whatsoever.

By contrast, in Sweden, where equitable access to health care is a citizen's right, these functions are addressed by the nation's health system. Their Patient Compensation Fund is publicly financed no-fault insurance that compensates both economic and noneconomic aspects of injury, and settles claims rapidly according to a predetermined schedule. The mere fact of injury is sufficient for compensation; claimants do not have to prove that anyone was at fault. Relatively very few claims are arbitrated beyond this point, and patients are generally satisfied that compensation is equitable and objective. A completely separate mechanism, the Medical Responsibility Board—a free-standing national governmental body—deals with malpractice complaints against physicians. It investigates reported incidents and can employ a range of sanctions, from a reprimand to a recommendation that the National Board of Health and Welfare revoke a physician's license to practice. In 1982, the Responsibility Board's rate of disciplinary actions was 3.3 per 1,000 physicians, compared to an average rate of 2.4 per 1,000 by U.S. disciplinary boards (Rosenthal, 1988).

NURSE-PROVIDERS AND OTHER HELPING PROFESSIONALS

As noted in Chapter 10, the rise of the medical profession was achieved by a legal monopoly over the labor market for its services. By the 1990s, however, the countervailing powers of managed care and government insurers had encouraged labor market competition for medical work by allowing other professions (for example, nurse-practitioners, chiropractors, and nurse-midwives) to do previously monopolized work. At the same time, they also opened some professional employment to paraprofessional and nonprofessional workers, resulting in their substitution for workers with higher credentials (Hughes, 1996).

The historic professionalization of medicine also entailed the subordination, cooptation, or elimination of virtually all competing health care professions. For example, as early as 1906, the AMA's campaign against patent medicines (that is, proprietary drugs) produced laws granting doctors monopoly over the prescription of powerful medicines. Commercial medicine companies had to market their products to doctors rather than to customers (Starr, 1982: 127–134). The nascent profession of pharmacy was subordinated to the medical profession by requiring patients to consult doctors to obtain prescriptions for medicine.

Nonphysician practitioners in the predominantly male professions of dentistry, podiatry, optometry, pharmacy, and chiropractic were able to retain relatively independent practices, even while the medical profession exerted its organizational control. Traditionally female health care professions, such as nursing, did not fare so well; they were kept subordinate in pay, working conditions, educational programs, and bureaucratic organization. The vicissitudes of nursing as an occupation are almost prototypical of the larger historical process of rationalization of health services delivery, which promoted the ever-increasing specialization of tasks interwoven in complex–usually bureaucratic–organizations. The development of nursing and various allied health professions, such as laboratory technology, physical therapy, and radiological technology, is a result of *nearly total gender stratification of medical work.*[11]

The Development of Nursing

Early nursing was typically private care by an unpaid member of the family or a paid family helper. It was part of the domestic economy and inextricably linked with women's roles. One of the founders of professional nursing, Florence Nightingale, wrote, "Every woman is a nurse" (1860: 3). She also argued that women should not aspire to be doctors because nursing meshed with their "natural" abilities. Nightingale's hospital reforms envisioned genteel nurses competently running hospitals as domestic managers, completely supportive of and

---

[11]Even when women are allowed to practice medicine, they have been generally segregated in the lower paid primary care specialties such as pediatrics. Studies find that male physicians earn significantly more than female physicians, even after differences in the number of hours worked, speciality, type of practice, and other work characteristics are taken into account (Baker, 1996; Bird, 1996; Kopriva, 1995).

dependent on doctors, who were analogous to the male heads of household (cf. Ehrenreich and English, 1973; Melosh, 1982).

Even today, nursing is a predominantly female occupation; in 1990, 94.8 percent of all registered nurses (RNs) were women, but only 20.1 percent of physicians were women. Table 11.1 shows the distribution of women among several health occupations. The gender segregation of these two jobs means that gender-role expectations figure prominently in the working relationships between doctor and nurse (Brown, 1983). Traditionally, the nurse has been expected to be deferential, nurturing, and submissive, even while taking an active role in the patient's care. In the 1960s, researchers observed a series of strategies by which nurses communicated their recommendations without appearing to make a recommending statement; physicians asked for nurses' recommendations without appearing to be asking for help (Hughes, 1988; Stein, 1967). Although recent studies show nurses to be less deferential and more assertive than in the 1960s, changes in the doctor-nurse interaction occurred more in the behavior of nurses than in the reciprocal roles or expectations of doctors (Porter, 1992; Stein et al., 1990). Societies with less hierarchical medical work roles have developed different patterns of interaction (Svensson, 1996). Nevertheless, the historical emphasis on "womanly" qualities in nursing has been simultaneously an ideological hindrance to professional recognition and a basis for nurses to seek a distinctive, caring way of relating to patients in contrast to the impersonality of the bioscientific medical model (Reverby, 1987a).

In the early twentieth century, two major developments in medical care shaped the direction of nursing: the shift to hospital-based care and the growing emphasis on scientific medicine. The latter, together with many technological developments, created the need for highly trained assistance for doctors; the knowledge and skills required of nurses expanded rapidly. RNs are the single largest group of health care professionals, accounting for about one-fifth of all health workers (Melosh, 1982).

TABLE 11.1   **Selected Health Occupations by Total Employment (1990)**

Occupation	Total Employed (in thousands)	Black (%)	Hispanic (%)	Female (%)
Physicians	575	3.2	4.4	20.1
Dentists	150	1.5	2.7	10.1
Registered nurses	1712	7.1	2.4	94.8
Laboratory technicians and technologists	317	13.4	6.8	75.7
Dental hygienists	84	1.1	3.3	99.8
Licensed practical nurses	445	16.5	4.4	95.0
Nursing aides and orderlies	1506	31.2	6.9	89.2

Source: U.S. Bureau of the Census, *Statistical Abstract of the United States, 1992.* Washington, DC, 1992: 392–394.

Previously hospitals had been little more than sick wards of the poorhouse, staffed by minimally qualified nurses drawn from the lowest social classes. Male attendants worked in men's wards and female attendants in women's wards. Only those who had no family or means of private care were nursed in hospital settings. As middle- and upper-class persons began to use hospitals for sickness, surgery, and childbirth, and as medical and nursing education became hospital centered, hospitals became more prestigious and profitable rather than totally charitable institutions. Their new fee-paying clientele accordingly expected a much higher standard of care (Melosh, 1982: 15–35; Rosenberg, 1987: 212–236).

Hospitals were expanding rapidly and needed the very kind of disciplined, trained workers they found in nurses; however, the profession was further subordinated as it lost control over nursing education. Hospital administrators established nursing schools so that the student nurses would serve the hospital. Student nurses put in 60- and 70-hour workweeks for two or three years of ward service in exchange for their subsistence and a small sum (typically $10 a year) for uniforms and books (Rosenberg, 1987: 220–221). The economic disincentives and the structural subordination of nurses made the occupation increasingly unattractive to men. For women, however, nursing was one of the few occupations deemed respectable and was considered an appropriate preparation for marriage as well as a source of income.

In the early decades of the twentieth century, many voices within nursing urged greater professionalization and standardization of training. By mid-century, there was considerable division between those nurses advocating hospital training and those urging higher education (Melosh, 1982: 67–76). At stake was the relatively greater professional independence of nursing as well as ideas about the proper role of the nurse.

Technological developments in medicine, especially in the second half of the century, further increased specialization in hospital nursing. After World War II, when hospital-based medical care expanded rapidly, nursing was organized according to stratified functions, with routine bedside tasks and lower-skill nursing tasks relegated to LPNs (licensed practical nurses), aides, and orderlies, under the direction of RNs (registered nurses). Although this practice resulted in cost savings in hospital payrolls and some organizational prestige for RNs, it also resulted in RNs serving as managers more than as nurses. Greater prestige and pay were incentives for some upper-echelon nurses to specialize for work in the intensive care unit, cardiac unit, or operating room.

During the 1970s and 1980s, many hospitals reorganized the nursing labor process in a system called primary nursing, in which a single professional nurse (RN) was responsible for completion of all physicians' orders for a set of patients. Although primary nursing emphasized the professional role of nurses, few hospitals were willing to pay for sufficient nursing staff to enable workers to do both the professional work and the work of nonprofessionals who were displaced. Combined with the fact that hospital patients were increasingly seriously ill, the restructuring greatly intensified nurses' workload, increased time pressures, stress, and the likelihood of dangerous errors (Noble, 1993). This reorganization also significantly tightened the hospital management's control by unambiguously identifying a single employee responsible for all nursing tasks for each patient (Brannon, 1994). It was symptomatic of a larger shift in the social contract in which employers generally were pressing for wage and benefits concessions from workers (Brannon, 1994, 1996; Rubin, 1996).

In the 1990s, however, the "restructuring" of nursing work was more a matter of "downsizing" entire hospital work forces–laying off expensive employees and replacing them with cheaper, lower-skilled workers, or not replacing them at all (Rosenthal, 1997a). Between 1981 and 1993, nursing personnel as a percentage of the hospital work force decreased from 45 percent to 37 percent (Aiken et al., 1996). Some hospital corporations justified these job cuts by arguing that they are responsible for medical treatment, but not for care during patients' convalescence, recovery, and learning to cope–labor intensive medical work central to nursing (Gordon, 1995). Recent restructuring of nursing work appears to be designed, not only to cut costs (and raise corporate profits), but also to increase managerial control:

> [I]n addition to an emphasis on cost containment rather than quality improvement, work redesign is being applied in a manner that, rather than empower workers, is designed to reduce the level of professional staffing and destroy work jurisdictions that interfere with the further rationalization of the labor process. (Brannon, 1996: 649)

Ironically, although nurses are the health care provider most respected and supported by the public (Hart, 1990: 10), they are also the health care profession structurally most vulnerable to the power of other countervailing powers.

Stratification and Predominantly Female Health Professions

The structural subordination of nursing relative to both physicians and hospital bureaucracies has worked severely against the economic interests of nurses. Nurses' wages have historically been low, and between 1971 and 1987 pay raises failed to keep apace of increases in the cost of living. In 1989, the average salary paid by hospitals for nurses at the top of the pay scale was only $32,160 (Tolchin, 1989), or less than one-third of the average nonspecialist physician's net income.

Patients and their insurance companies are not generally billed separately for nursing services, as they are for the services of MDs, such as surgeons, radiologists, and anesthesiologists. Thus, employers of nurses try to keep wages low and to maximize the labor they can extract for those wages. Relative to other professions with comparable years of training, hospital nurses experience several other important occupational disadvantages: unfavorable hours and shift work (sometimes with forced overtime), high stress, and little opportunity for advancement in status or pay. The hospital nurse shortage of the 1980s was, in part, a by-product of changes in the labor process, although it was also due to the unattractively low salaries identified with nursing and the expanded opportunities for women as health professionals outside hospital nursing (in roles such as doctor or nurse-practitioner). As hospitals and managed care corporations reorganized nursing work, they pitted RNs against less well paid LPNs and nursing aides (Hughes, 1996).

In the health care industry, most occupations are gender segregated (that is, one gender accounts for 70 percent or more of those employed). Table 11.1 shows that the health-related occupations of greatest power, prestige, and income are concentrated mainly among white men. Women make up at least 75 percent of all health industry workers, although constituting only about 42 percent of the national work force. Not only are predominantly female occupations generally low paid, but women also earn less than men in the same job categories (Aries and Kennedy, 1986).

Predominantly female health care occupations are also characterized by relatively low amounts of professional autonomy. Nurses, medical technologists, dental hygienists, and other auxiliary workers frequently assume many of the less interesting and more time-consuming tasks of hospitals and doctors' offices. These "physician extenders" are able to do as much as 80 percent of the routine tasks of office medical practice; similarly, dental assistants can assume tasks such as cleaning, patient education, and X-ray work that would otherwise account for most of the dentist's time. The amount the doctor or dentist can charge for these services is roughly the same, regardless of whether they are done by the doctor or dentist or delegated to a relatively low-paid assistant. Masculine behavioral norms are deeply embedded in the organizational life of hospitals and clinics and, indeed, the very definition of a profession (Davies, 1995).

The medical profession has used its regulatory and educational controls to prevent serious competition from these auxiliary professions (Brown, 1978, 1983). Their control also enables them to suppress the wages paid to other health care professionals. For example, by using the states' Medical Practice Acts to abolish private X-ray laboratories, radiologists (MDs) were able to control the terms of employment of X-ray technicians and technologists, and to prevent them from competing with radiologists' own labs and those of hospitals.

Similarly, the independent practice of medicine by physicians' assistants was made illegal in all states where the licensing boards are controlled by doctors. Since 1971, however, a majority of states have amended their Medical Practice Acts to allow nurses to diagnose some conditions, prescribe some drugs, and perform other medical duties under certain conditions; similarly, since 1978, federal guidelines have allowed direct reimbursement to nurse-practitioners for Medicare patients. Home health care is one area in which nurse-practitioners have been particularly active; they have also served extensively in locations (such as the inner city and remote rural areas) considered undesirable by many physicians. The growing surplus of physicians (particularly of specialists such as obstetricians) puts nurse-practitioners in direct conflict with physicians for health care employment.

The tension between physicians and other health care professionals is best illustrated by the competition posed by a recent professional classification, the nurse-midwife. Obstetricians vehemently opposed allowing them to deliver babies and lobbied for legislation limiting the conditions under which nurse-midwives could practice (see Good, 1995). Nurse-midwives' inability to obtain independent insurance also prevented their practice in many states. There is a marked over-supply of obstetricians (Bencomo et al., 1995). As a surgical specialty, obstetrics initially responded to its market condition by greatly increasing the number of Caesarian sections and other procedures; the rate of Caesarian sections soared from 10.4 percent in 1975 to 22.7 percent in 1985 (Rosenblatt et al., 1997). Another strategy was to turn investment in hospital corporations into privileged control of deliveries in those hospitals, thus edging out nonspecialist MDs and midwives. By contrast, nurse-midwives are trained to help the mother to have her baby naturally; they emphasize a more holistic approach to the mother and child, including both prenatal and early infancy care and education. Their market strategy has been to offer comprehensive services at a much lower cost while appealing to consumers looking for a more satisfying birth experience (Little, 1982; see also Good, 1995). A study of healthy low-risk patients found that nurse-midwives' patients had fewer Caesarian sections, received less anesthesia, and had lower rates of episiotomies and induced labor than physicians' patients (Rosenblatt et al., 1997).

For patients, there is no obvious immediate benefit of these conflicts among health care professionals. For example, giving nurses greater professional recognition, autonomy, and pay may create a more satisfied work force, which may or may not result in better patient care. It may also increase the professional distance between the nurse and patient. Greater emphasis on nonphysician providers should be more cost effective, but the patient will not necessarily realize any financial benefits if the savings go to a hospital corporation, insurance company, or group medical practice. Although many of the predominantly female health care professions hold ideals of providing greater caring and patient service compared to the medical profession (Fisher, 1994), trends toward their specialization and professionalization may promote the further disempowerment of the patient.

NONPROFESSIONAL HEALTH CARE WORKERS

The health industry employs a vast number of nonprofessional workers, such as orderlies, clerks, receptionists, kitchen help, and housekeeping staff. Employment in the health industry reflects patterns of stratification in the larger society, especially occupational segregation by gender, class, and race. White men from well-to-do families disproportionately occupy the jobs at the top of the health industry; health care work at the bottom of the stratification heap is typically done by black women. Black workers are overrepresented in the menial and low-status occupations, such as practical nurse or home health aide (Aries and Kennedy, 1986). Black women are particularly concentrated in the nursing home and home care labor markets, and are far more likely than white women working in such nonhospital services to have earnings below the poverty level (Feldman et al., 1990).

Furthermore, women and blacks are concentrated in occupations with the least opportunity for advancement. Especially in hospital settings, there is almost total lack of job mobility, even though various workers can and do perform tasks appropriate to higher echelon workers. The resulting structural inequality promotes conflict, with the technical and managerial elite (doctors and administrators) separated from and opposing the interests of the lower-status workers. Although some of this conflict is muted by the professional ideals of nurses and others, there is a growing pressure for unionization and other collective expressions of worker dissatisfaction (Ehrenreich and Ehrenreich, 1978; Sacks, 1988).

The interests of nonprofessional health workers, like those of nurses and doctors, do not necessarily coincide with the interests of patients. At the same time, however, the health care system's failure to compensate, regulate, and educate its lower-level care givers adequately has been seriously detrimental to patients. One study of patient abuse in a nursing home noted that the personnel recruited were socially marginal, poorly educated or trained, and generally uncommitted to their work. Their low-paid, low-prestige custodial care of a powerless population of elderly patients promoted neglect and abuse (Stannard, 1973).

Similarly, the U.S. health care system's recent emphasis on home care has resulted in a new cadre of underpaid, undervalued aides who help the infirm with cooking, cleaning, bathing, dressing, and moving about their homes. Although some home health aides work for nonprofit agencies, many are employed by commercial agencies contracted by Medicare, state or city agencies, or insurance companies.

By the end of 1987, there were some 50,000 such workers in New York City alone. Most earned less than $7,000 per year (an income at or below the poverty level), and had no job security, no overtime pay, and few or no medical benefits (Iverem, 1988). A 1985 study by the Hunter College School of Social Work (Donovan, 1987) found that 99 percent of these workers were women with a median age of 47; 70 percent were black, 26 percent were Hispanic, and nearly half were immigrants. The typical home health aide was the primary breadwinner for her household, with three to four children to support. Because of their poor remuneration, these women and their families had had no health insurance for 92 percent of their own health problems in the previous year (cf. Feldman et al., 1990).

Thus, while federal, state, and private insurers enjoy the cost savings of home care compared with hospitalization, their savings are subsidized by a large number of poor working women. Home health aides are even more disadvantaged than similarly unskilled workers in hospitals because they have none of the social interaction, reassurance, job stability, economic rewards, or prestige associated with working in a medical setting. Further incentives to exploit home health aides exist when the agency employing them operates as a for-profit health industry (Fine, 1988).

SUMMARY

The social organization of health care services in any health system reflects the stratification and power of various interest groups in that society. Because of the commodified, laissez-faire system in the United States, these interests are particularly obvious as they compete for available resources and control. Social stratification and power are important considerations for understanding the quality of health services. Stratification is related to the social distance between patient and providers and between various levels of health service workers; it is also related to imbalances in the socioeconomic power of recipients and providers.

The stratification and power of these interest groups are also linked to structural incentives and disincentives that affect the quality of health services. Some of the rapid changes in the nature of medical work, such as the corporatization of doctors' and nurses' work roles, are the result of changes in these structural incentives. Many of the problems of the U.S. health care system can be best understood in light of these powerful socioeconomic structural features, which any attempt to solve the problems of quality, access, and cost must address. In Chapter 12 we continue examining the socioeconomic interests in U.S. health care with a discussion of the large-scale organizations that are increasingly powerful in this system.

RECOMMENDED READINGS

Articles

DORIS R. FINE, "Women caregivers and home health workers: Prejudice and inequity in home health care." *Research in the Sociology of Health Care* 7, 1988: 105–117.

SUE FISHER, "Is care a remedy?: The case of nurse practitioners," pp. 302–329 in A. J. Dan, ed., *Reframing Women's Health*. Thousand Oaks, CA: Sage, 1994.

FREDERIC W. HAFFERTY and DONALD W. LIGHT, "Professional dynamics and the changing nature of medical work." *Journal of Health and Social Behavior* 1995 (extra issue): 132–153.

JOHN B. MCKINLAY, "A case for refocusing upstream: The political economy of illness," pp. 519–533 in P. Conrad, ed., *The Sociology of Health and Illness*. New York: St. Martin's Press, 1997.

Books

CELIA DAVIES, *Gender and the Professional Predicament in Nursing*. Buckingham: Open University Press, 1995. Using the example of health care occupations, especially nursing in the context of Britain's National Health System, this book examines how cultural codes of masculinity and feminity are embedded in the day-to-day conduct of work organizations.

SUSAN REVERBY, *Ordered to Care: The Dilemma of American Nursing, 1850–1945*. Cambridge: Cambridge University Press, 1987. A thoughtful reexamination of the role of nursing in its economic and organizational setting.

CHAPTER 19

ECONOMIC INTERESTS AND POWER IN HEALTH CARE

The health care system in the United States has changed dramatically and rapidly; it has undergone major shifts even in the last five years. As noted in Chapter 11, considerable evidence indicates that the American health care system is in crisis. Many Americans are hard pressed to afford the health care available; a large number are simply not served by the system at all, and many of those who are served receive insufficient and inferior care. Despite many cost-cutting efforts, the amount spent on health care consumes an enormous proportion of the nation's gross national product, and the costs of most medical treatment continue to spiral upward.

Yet, as a nation, we are not getting as satisfactory health care as other nations spending far less. The cost-cutting efforts of the 1990s, however, often failed to make health care more affordable to the ordinary family because employers, hospitals, and other agencies shifted more of their costs to the recipients themselves. As the weakest of the interest groups, the recipients of health care have little control over and little understanding of their predicament.

The medical care system is a major part of the larger system of economic production and consumption; it is structured to allow various interest groups to make significant profits and to control considerable resources in medical production. Although we tend to think of medical care as a small-scale service offered by individual providers, such as a family doctor or a nurse, in the U.S. system most medical care is *big business*. The powerful economic interests involved in medical businesses—insurance companies, hospital corporations, pharmaceutical companies, medical technology corporations, and so on—often supersede the interests of both sick people and health care workers. These same powerful interests have also been successful in getting their products and services defined as *primary* expenditures in the health care system, to the detriment of needed expenditures on public health, preventive care, and palliative care (for example, long-term care for infirm elderly persons).

The dramatically increased scale of profits and power commanded by medical businesses has been itself a factor in the crisis of the U.S. health care system. Cost-accelerating profits that in the 1950s seemed like merely deplorable inconsistencies in the system escalated by the 1990s to an unsustainable burden, depriving many people of their sense of security in matters of health and illness, and threatening to tear apart a minimally integrated health care system. Well-financed interest groups have poured resources into influencing government attempts to rethink health care policies; each is vying to protect and enhance its power and profits. In this chapter we offer an overview of some of these large-scale medical care organizations.

In addition to examining the structural power of health care businesses, we hold the U.S. system up to three criteria for evaluation: quality, cost, and access. We describe some of the social-structural factors that influence these three aspects.

ECONOMIC INTERESTS AND THIRD-PARTY PAYMENT

The complexity and inadequacies of the *system of payment* for health care in the United States are probably the foremost causes of the crisis. This unwieldy system, as it has developed, fails to provide access to health care for tens of millions of

Americans, makes the guarantee of quality difficult to monitor or regulate, and drives up costs. The very complexity of the system itself makes it more costly than other nations' systems.

Ultimately, the *American people pay all health care costs*, but health care dollars are directed from the people to the providers via three main patterns: by direct payment by the consumer; from government taxation at various levels; and through private insurance. The U.S. method of financing health care is highly *regressive*; low-income families pay twice the share of income paid by high-income families. Out-of-pocket expenditures and payments for private insurance premiums are the most regressive because they are not priced according to the families' ability to pay. Expenditures financed by local, state, and federal taxes are generally progressive. A more equitable health care system would eliminate or greatly decrease reliance on expenditures made out of pocket and on premiums (Rasell et al., 1994).

Both the private insurance pattern and the government taxation pattern of collecting and disbursing health care dollars have resulted in large and powerful organizations to administer the transfer of funds to providers. Their reimbursement policies and regulations become, in effect, nationally significant health policies. In addition, because the choice of most private insurance is made *not* by the health care recipients, but their employers, the interests of business and other employers figure into this complex system.

Despite our national rhetoric regarding private enterprise, *public* funding is the single largest source of payments for health care, and reliance on public funding has steadily increased. In 1965, public funds (from federal, state, and local governments) covered only 25 percent of all health care expenditures, but by 1994, public funds accounted for 44.3 percent of all health care expenditures (USDHHS, 1996a). Indeed, if payments made by all level governments for health insurance premiums and Medicare for their own employees are included in the total, the public sector paid more than 50 percent of all U.S. health care (Rasell et al., 1994).

The existence of insurance for *some* citizens encouraged the inflation of costs for *all*, thus increasing the disparity in the affordability of health care for those with ample coverage and those with insufficient or no coverage. In the health care marketplace, *demand is not a function of need.* Many people need health care but cannot demand it because they lack the means to pay. Insurance functions to create the demand for goods and services among persons not wealthy enough to afford them easily otherwise. For example, when Medicare and some private insurance began to cover home health care products and services, the new demand created a profitable market, so prices for home health care rose far faster than other consumer prices.

The sense of crisis is largely due to the perception—especially on the part of ordinary citizens and payers of private health insurance—that the present arrangement of health care insurance does not *secure* their health care. Americans have become afraid they will be denied good medical care when they and their loved ones need it, afraid they will lose their health insurance coverage, afraid their insurance will not cover important medical needs, afraid they could be thrown into poverty by uninsured costs of catastrophic illness or long-term nursing care. The following discussion documents the extent to which many Americans' fears are well founded. Until the health care system in the United States provides the security that all citizens will obtain good quality health care when they need it, the crisis will not have been resolved.

C. Wright Mills (1959) reminds us that we are often trapped in our private "troubles" and fail to realize they are the result of public issues. The private struggles for health care and health insurance experienced by families across the United States are, indeed, the product of government and corporate policies which need to be reevaluated and changed. Boxes 12.1, 12.2, and 12.3 use a composite portrait of one family's private troubles to illustrate the larger systemic source of the U.S. crisis in health security.

Private Insurance

The very idea of and need for health insurance is a relatively recent development. Early in the twentieth century, medical services consumed a small proportion of a family's budget. Doctors and other healers charged comparatively modest fees, which often were adjusted according to a person's ability to pay. Pharmaceuticals were simple and inexpensive. The family itself provided most of the nursing care.

With the rapid expansion of technologically sophisticated, hospital-centered medicine, costs quickly began to climb, increasing the risk that treatment expenses would exceed the family's ability to pay. The Great Depression of the 1930s created another major impetus for insurance as voluntary hospitals experienced massive income reductions due to patients' inability to pay. Hospitals financially underwrote health insurance as a way to stabilize their incomes (Feigenbaum, 1987; Fein, 1986; Starr, 1982). The idea of using health insurance to spread the financial risks over time and across a population of insured thus came to fruition.

In industrialized countries of Europe such as Sweden, Denmark, and Switzerland, national programs of compulsory health insurance were developed as early as 1883. These state-subsidized programs were not instituted mainly for medical costs (which were as yet small proportions of people's expenses) but rather for income maintenance—"sick pay." Nevertheless, their existence later enabled European nations to expand national coverage to include medical costs not just for workers but for all citizens (Starr, 1982: 237–240).

Blue Cross, created in the 1930s, was the foremost early form of health insurance in the United States. Actively encouraged by the American Hospital Association, Blue Cross was a not-for-profit hospital insurance plan based on noncompeting territorial divisions in which participants paid premiums according to communitywide ratings. Although labor unions favored a national health insurance program instead, they accepted the Blue Cross alternative indirectly by including such insurance in bargaining agendas for labor contracts. The hospitals benefited by insurance because their incomes were stabilized; however, the system sowed the seeds of its later crisis, because *having health insurance became linked with having a specific job.* It also resulted in the hospitals (and later, physicians and other

BOX 12.1

An Insurance Nightmare*

Barbara was 40 when her husband divorced her, changed jobs, and moved out of state, leaving her and her two daughters without health insurance. Although she had been trained as a cosmetologist, workers in that field are often not able to obtain affordable health insurance. With little previous clerical experience, she considered herself lucky to find a job as a clerk-typist at a small university. The job had low pay—only $820 per month when she began in 1989, but at least it had a good benefits package—or so Barbara thought.

As the university struggled with soaring premium costs for employee health care, it made employees pay a greater and greater share. Shortly after Barbara began her job, the university announced that it would pay only a fixed amount per employee annually for all insurance premiums; the employees who wanted to be covered under the plan would have to pay the balance. In the first year of this so-called flexible benefits plan, the university paid a total of $110 per month toward Barbara's insurance coverage (life, disability, medical, and dental), but the premiums for family medical insurance alone cost $220 each month. The next year, the university's health insurer significantly increased the premiums (to $320 per month) because two employees had incurred significant medical expenses the preceding year. Although health costs had increased nationally by over 10 percent, the university increased its benefits "contribution" by 4 percent. The cost to Barbara amounted to nearly 30 percent of her after-tax income!

For a look at the larger picture, statistics show the following:

- At least 5 million women between 40 and 65 have no insurance as a result of divorce, death, or retirement of their spouse (Bodenheimer, 1990).
- Health insurance companies "redline" (that is, do not offer coverage to) workers in entire industries, such as barber and beauty shops, convenience stores, hotels, restaurants, and construction (Light, 1992).
- Many insurers also engage in "policy churning," a practice that deliberately creates a regular turnover each year. By offering employers attractively low first-year prices, they sign on new group accounts but pay out very little because they build in a 12–month waiting period for most expensive health needs. The next year, they increase the premiums dramatically for all but the lowest risk groups, knowing that those companies can and will change to cheaper insurance elsewhere. Small companies are particularly vulnerable because risk cannot be spread over a large number of employees. (Light, 1992)

*This story is a hypothetical composite of two persons' actual problems; features have been changed to protect their anonymity.

"covered" services) being paid "off the top"; thus, in times of economic downturns, employers and workers were committed to pay regular premiums even when their incomes were reduced. Because initially medical care costs were low, employers and workers did not realize this structural disadvantage.

Later, Blue Cross developed its companion plan, Blue Shield, for nonhospital services, such as doctors' services and lab tests. At first, the AMA (American Medical Association) opposed Blue Cross and other forms of third-party payment on the ideological grounds that they came between the doctor and patients, and restricted doctors' decisions about treatment. The AMA also committed considerable energies and funds to prevent Congress from creating national compulsory health insurance. Eventually, the AMA agreed to accept Blue Shield, because the profession was given some control over the program. By preventing a national comprehensive program, the medical profession gained a large measure of control and greatly increased its income (Starr, 1982: 290–334; see also Law, 1974).

Blue Cross had been conceived as a plan for an entire community, and premium rates were based on local experience with participants' hospital utilization and costs. Risks were thus widely spread. The initial institutional goal was to stabilize hospital use and income; income from insurance itself was not important. Blue Cross began to lose its competitive edge in the 1950s. Commercial insurers, explicitly seeking to maximize profits, began to approach employers of low-risk groups and offer them much lower premiums than possible by the community-rating method of Blue Cross. Commercial insurers, rather than spread risk widely in a large pool of insured, made their profits by insuring only the low-risk groups. Eventually, Blue Cross had to abandon its communitywide risk rating (Feigenbaum, 1987; Starr, 1982: 327–331). Indeed, in the 1990s many formerly nonprofit Blue Cross/Blue Shield programs were completely taken over by for-profit corporations (Bond and Weissman, 1997).

The enduring effect of this method of setting premium rates has been that only certain employers (such as very large corporations and those with mainly young, healthy workers) can obtain reasonably priced insurance coverage for employees. Other workers are likely to receive little or no employment-related health insurance because commercial insurers price premiums too high for employers to absorb. Furthermore, because the federal government subsidizes employer-arranged private insurance with a tax write-off (Barer, 1995), large and profitable companies have further advantages.

One of the most serious problems with the U.S. insurance system, as it has thus developed, is that most private insurance is employment related. Americans have relied since the 1920s on a largely private welfare system—available particularly to corporate employees—to provide health care benefits, old age pensions, job security, and vacations. The public welfare system, which encompasses Social Security, Medicare, and Medicaid, was loosely constructed to fill gaps in the private, employment-based system and to regulate benefits (for instance, by controls on corporate pension plans). Beginning in the 1970s and accelerating in the 1980s and 1990s, dramatic changes in the social contract have resulted in job insecurity (through "downsizing," "outsourcing," involuntary retirements, and increased use of part-time and temporary employees), producing haphazard and uncertain social welfare (Morone, 1995; see also Rubin, 1996).

A growing problem is the lack of regulation of the insurance industry. Like the savings and loan industry in the 1980s, some insurance companies in the

BOX 12.2

The Insurance Nightmare Continues

Barbara began to look for a better job, but she was trapped by her insurance needs. Because her younger daughter had a history of asthma, no insurer would offer affordable individual coverage for the family. Barbara needed a job with group insurance, but many employers offered no health insurance whatsoever; others had group policies that excluded coverage for preexisting conditions, like Mary Ellen's asthma. So Barbara kept her job at the university and began to work a second job (with no benefits) at night.

Meanwhile, the insurer again steeply increased the premiums, so the university changed insurers. Barbara was relieved that her new premiums were only $235 per month. Her relief was short lived, however, because eight months later the insurance company declared bankruptcy, leaving employees struggling with mountains of paperwork for claims and negotiations with unpaid providers. Although eventually the state covered the employees' insured health expenses for the remainder of their contract, the university again searched for an affordable group insurance plan.

The larger picture shows the following:

- An estimated 6 percent of Americans have been denied coverage because of conditions such as diabetes, high blood pressure, birth defects or other problems indicating the potential for needing expensive care (Himmelstein et al., 1992).
- With very little federal regulation and uneven regulation by the states, insurers can become precipitously undercapitalized; when health insurance companies and prepaid health care programs declare bankruptcy, the persons they were supposed to cover lose not only the health care for which they have prepaid but also their protection for coverage of preexisting conditions and other excludable health problems.

1990s have been severely undercapitalized. When they become insolvent, persons who thought they were insured are left unprotected. State and federal regulatory legislation and oversight of the industry has not adequately protected consumers (Akula, 1997).

The financial collapse of several HMOs, including the giant Maxicare, which once covered over 2 million persons, paid substantial dividends to investors, and was touted as the best managed HMO in the industry, left many enrollees uninsured and providers unpaid, highlighting the inadequate regulation of the industry (Freudenheim, 1989; Holden, 1989). The number of HMO failures per year increased from 1 in 1984 to 53 in 1988, and HMO mergers increased dramatically in the same period, leading to regulatory legislation in most states. The long-term effectiveness of highly political state-level insurance regulations for protecting consumers remains to be seen (Christianson et al., 1991).

For-profit health insurance companies make money primarily in two ways: by paying out less in benefits than they receive in premiums, and by investing premium funds before disbursing them as benefits. For example, United Healthcare, one of the nation's largest for-profit managed care companies, obtained 35 percent of its pretax profits from investments in 1995. Thus, for-profit insurance programs involve strong incentives[1] for insurers to *deny* coverage of claims and to *delay* paying claims. For example, by the end of 1996, three of the largest health care corporations (Oxford, United Healthcare, Humana) had seriously delayed paying doctors' and other providers' bills (Fein and Rosenthal, 1996; Freudenheim, 1997b).

Furthermore, insurance companies' portfolios frequently include investments in other for-profit health care ventures, such as hospitals, nursing homes, home health care agencies, and medical supply companies. Control over such large sums for investment is a significant source of economic and political power for major insurance corporations (Salmon, 1995). The scale of their financial interests and power is indicated by the fact that insurance lobbyists to state legislatures outnumber lobbyists representing other interests (Bodenheimer, 1990). The insurance industry's contributions to congressional candidates in 1990 was $10.9 million (Makinson, 1992). As health care reform became an issue in the 1992 national elections, the industry spent $18.6 million in congressional campaign contributions (Podhorzer, 1995; Pear, 1991; see also Brightbill, 1991; Center for Public Integrity, 1995; Kemper and Novak, 1993). Clearly, for-profit health insurance has become a big business, exceeding in power (and often buying out) the hospitals that originated the idea of health insurance.

Forms of Private Insurance   In the early years of private insurance, in order to gain a desirable profit margin most commercial insurers offered indemnity plans, rather than Blue Shield's original service coverage. *Indemnity plans* specify limits to the costs borne by the insurer by imposing deductibles, limits on per-service payments, and annual and/or lifetime ceilings on payments for various types of service (Feigenbaum, 1987). Indemnity plans involve no incentive for the insurer to keep costs down because the excess is borne by the insured. Because individual health care recipients often have little choice or leverage over hospitals and other providers, many persons covered by limited indemnity plans find themselves underinsured.

Indemnity plans have accounted for a decreasing proportion of the group insurance market since the mid-1980s, as employers and insurers shifted to some form of managed care for cost savings. Whereas in 1988, 71 percent of employer-arranged insurance was indemnity insurance, by 1996, only 26 percent was that type (Jensen et al., 1997; Toner, 1996).

Managed care forms of private insurance control what they spend on health care by intensely screening prospective utilization of insured medical care. They also manage expenditures by limiting coverage to care provided by doctors and health care facilities (including hospitals, clinics, laboratories, and therapeutic centers) that have accepted their discounted payment rates or are directly operated

---

[1]As HMO and for-profit insurers' stock values and profit margins soared, the company executives received cash and stock awards greater than those in *any* industry; in 1994, the CEOs of the seven largest for-profit HMOs were paid over $7 million on average (Freudenheim, 1995b).

or employed by the managed care corporation. Thus, managed care severely limits, either directly or indirectly, the choice of physician and hospital. By 1990, various forms of managed care accounted for 25.3 percent of group health insurance premiums, compared to less than 1 percent in 1984 (Hoy et al., 1991). By 1996, 75 percent of workers were in managed care plans (Toner, 1996).

Managed care plans proliferated in the 1990s, each arranged differently to represent the interests of their sponsors: insurance companies, hospital corporations, physician networks, and employers themselves. One type, Preferred Provider Organizations (PPOs) involves an employer's or insurance company's contract with a limited number of doctors, hospitals, and other providers to offer services for the insured at a discounted rate. Insured patients who choose other providers must bear the difference in cost and often a higher copayment as well.

Health maintenance organizations (HMOs) are prepaid health plans utilizing preferred providers who are either independently contracted or employed by an HMO group practice. Some HMOs, such as Kaiser in California, are not-for-profit organizations; most, however, are profit seeking. Many HMOs try to control costs by using staff physicians as gatekeepers to prevent overutilization of expensive specialists and hospitalization. Some HMOs further cut costs by paying contracted physicians on the basis of capitation rather than fee for service. As explained in Chapter 11, **capitation** means physicians are paid a preset amount per patient per month, regardless of how much medical service those patients actually need. This method of payment forces health care *providers* to assume much of the risk that insurance is supposed to assume. If the patient pool is large and not disproportionately sick, physicians could earn as much as under fee-for-service plans and would (presumably) save on some costs of billing.

Two serious problems with capitation are now evident. It creates perverse incentives for doctors to provide *too little* service because they earn the same regardless of whether they do little or much for each patient. Similarly, it encourages doctors to refuse to accept patients, such as those with diabetes, whose need for medical services is predictably high (Gray, 1997; Poplin, 1996; Rodwin, 1993; Rosenthal, 1996).

Cost and Access   Since the 1970s the federal government has encouraged managed care, hoping it would contain health care costs better than other forms of insurance, but the anticipated efficiency gains and cost containment have not resulted. Indeed, several studies have shown that most HMOs in the 1980s were not more cost efficient than conventional insurance plans, yet cost more in employee contributions, contributed to overall inflation of premium costs for all types of private insurance, and were sometimes engaged in outright fraudulent practices (Morone, 1990; PROPAC, 1988; see also Altman and Rodwin, 1988).

By 1990 most HMOs were owned by commercial insurers (Bodenheimer, 1990) for which the HMO structure realized profits by controlling in one single agency: patient utilization, provider reimbursement, and hospital costs. Increasing evidence suggests that patient dissatisfaction with HMOs is due largely to the limitations most HMOs impose to increase profitability, such as waits to schedule appointments, long hours in the waiting room, too little time with the doctor, severely limited selection of doctors, barriers to seeing specialists, and impersonal treatment (Rubin et al., 1993; see also Freudenheim, 1997c). For example, some HMOs imposed "gag" rules on physicians, forbidding them from telling patients about treatment alternatives that might be more expensive for the HMO (*New York Times*, 1996b).

Many HMOs and other prepaid plans create a conflict of interest for doctors whom they employ or contract because they base their remuneration on expectations of low rates of referral to specialists and hospital utilization. With these incentives, doctors can maximize their earnings by *decreasing* medical services for their patients. This conflict of interest, which is the reverse of the conflict of interest under fee-for-service payments, can have adverse effects on the quality of care (Rodwin, 1993).

One of the biggest problems for persons counting on private health insurance is that, as health costs have escalated rapidly, insurance companies and employers have passed on a significant part of that burden to the insured.[2] Some companies have dramatically raised the deductibles, copayments, and out-of-pocket expenses to be paid by the employee. Whereas in 1987, 43 percent of workers with single coverage and 36 percent of those with family coverage had employers who paid their full premiums, by 1994, these proportions had dropped to 34 and 26 percent, respectively (Holahan et al., 1995). Overall, between 1980 and 1989, the share of employees' health premiums paid by employers declined from 80 to 69 percent, leaving the employee paying the rest (Levit et al., 1989). Between 1980 and 1991, the premium cost for an employee and family increased by 241 percent; employee out-of-pocket expenses increased by over 500 percent (Rasell, 1993). These cost-shifting measures hurt the working poor disproportionately, causing many workers to forgo insurance because they simply could not afford the employee share of the premiums (Holahan et al., 1995; Seccombe, 1996; Seccombe and Amey, 1995). Box 12.3 illustrates how these wider developments affected one family.

Exact figures are not available on the number of persons who are underinsured due to seriously limited health plans; often employees do not discover how poorly they are insured until they are denied benefits during an actual health crisis. Although hospital care costs may be largely covered by insurance, consumers typically must pay most or all of outpatient medical services, prescription drugs, dental care, and long-term nursing care, as well as a large proportion of physicians' services (Knickman and Thorpe, 1995). Some policy analysts argue that patients should have to pay, in the form of copayments, a substantial share of the costs of each use of health care services in order to make them more selective and cost conscious. The Rand Health Experiment (1974–1982) found, however, that

---

[2]A growing problem has been that cost-cutting practices by insurers (especially private companies) and providers have made sick people themselves responsible for most of the paperwork for insurance claims. As a result, debilitating illness often results in an inability to collect insurance benefits while bills mount. An entire new business has arisen to process a claimant's paperwork in exchange for a percentage of the resulting benefits, thus further reducing the insured person's actual health care coverage.

BOX 12.3

An Unending Nightmare?

Subsequently, Barbara's employer decided to self-insure; that is, the university collected employees' premiums, added its own contributions, chose a Preferred Provider Organization (PPO) to negotiate discounts, and contracted an outside agency to screen claims. Thus, the employer saved some of the expense of commercial insurance, especially marketing costs and profit margin, and simultaneously controlled the assets, while briefly collecting earnings on the insurance pool. Under the new plan, Barbara's premiums were $255 per month. The university paid $130 toward her premium, with nothing left over for her life or disability insurance premiums.

The self-insured plan retained the terms (including deductibles and copayments) of the prior commercial plan, but added "managed care" PPO regulations. If Barbara's family used doctors and hospitals not on the preferred provider list, she had to pay considerably larger deductibles and copayments each visit. So Barbara had to find completely new doctors, selected from the ones covered by the PPO. After she established relationships with the new doctors, she had to change twice more because the approved list was continually changing.

Although the self-insured plan is more stable, Barbara's worries are not over. Next year her older daughter starts college. She has a good scholarship offer to an excellent college in a distant state, but Barbara worries whether her daughter ought to go to a nearby state college in order to be near the preferred provider hospitals and doctors. Barbara also worries whether her employer will decide to retroactively exclude her younger daughter's asthma from coverage. Just this year, the university excluded coverage for AIDS, hospitalization for mental illness and substance abuse, and dependent teenagers' pregnancies. Will they, in the near future, exclude or limit coverage for her family's needs, too?

The larger picture shows the following:

- Employer self-insurance is an important recent trend; in 1975, only 5 percent of employees were covered by self-insured plans. By 1985, more than 50 percent were in self-insured plans, which now control a market share greater than that of commercial insurers or Blue Cross/Blue Shield plans (Bodenheimer, 1990; Sullivan and Rice, 1991).

- Self-insured employers are not restricted by the same regulations as the insurance industry. In the 1990s, a U.S. Supreme Court decision affirmed the employer's power to set limits on coverage, including retroactive changes in the nature and level of coverage, so employees can find themselves seriously underinsured and without recourse.

---

although cost sharing did reduce the demands for health services, it did not result in good decisions about those demands. In fact, financial barriers reduced the use of health services even when those services were needed and appropriate (Lohr et al., 1986). Greater cost sharing likewise does not lead to more competitive pricing and consumer "shopping" (Marquis, 1984). In the United States, lack of adequate insurance essentially means severely limited access to health care.

The U.S. system of private insurance is structurally inefficient and expensive to administer because it is based on the exclusion and discrimination of *denying coverage* to precisely those who need the most health care. In order to maximize profits, insurance companies compete to *avoid* insuring higher-risk persons–those likely to actually need health care (Light, 1992). They issue complex policies with elaborate exclusions (for instance refusing to pay for care for any conditions that patients had before becoming covered by that insurance policy) and different terms of coverage for different groups of employees. To screen all claims by insured patients to enforce these exclusions and other restrictive terms, commercial insurance companies spend 33.5 cents for each dollar of benefits provided. These administrative costs are 14 times those of Medicare (2.3 cents per dollar) because all persons covered by Medicare have the same coverage and terms (Brandon et al., 1991).

This estimate of insurers' administrative inefficiency does not include the cost of paperwork on the part of the providers and claimants, which further add to the costliness of the U.S. health care system. The administrative, overhead, and marketing costs of commercial insurance companies have increased faster than the costs of providing health care. Administrative/bureaucratic costs consume about one-fourth of U.S. total health care spending. Some analysts have suggested that a public program of universal coverage would save enough on these costs that efficiency savings alone would pay for insurance for tens of millions of Americans who are presently without adequate coverage (Hellander et al., 1994).

Public Programs

The number, type, and quality of health care programs financed from tax revenues by various levels of government demonstrate the complexity and inadequacy of the U.S. health care system. The federal government, for example, directly provides care for large numbers of persons in the military and their dependents, veterans' hospitals, and federal prisons. The largest federal health insurance programs subsidize some care for the poor (Medicaid) and elderly (Medicare). The federal government also finances much health-related research, and has at times supported medical education and other training programs. State, county, and municipal governments also fund health care, by maintaining, for example, public hospitals, nursing homes, community health services, and public health programs. State governments are also cosponsors of Medicaid and other health services for the indigent; they pay directly for health care in state institutions, such as prisons and mental hospitals. The quality of and access to medical care provided by these many programs vary widely across the nation, but no national organization or central planning coordinates or regulates even the public efforts, much less connects public and private programs.

Medicare Medicare was enacted in 1965 to finance acute medical care mainly for elderly Americans. It quickly accomplished one of its objectives–to protect elderly persons unable to obtain private insurance from impoverishment due to health costs; the proportion of persons over 65 living in poverty dropped dramatically in the first few years of Medicare (Tynes, 1996). Medicare coverage was expanded in 1972 to include people of all ages with chronic kidney disease or long-term disabilities. By 1995, Medicare covered 37 million Americans. The program has two parts: Part A is hospital insurance, funded by a portion of the Social Security payroll tax. Part B is supplementary medical insurance (SMI) for physicians' services, outpatient care, laboratory fees, and home health care; because it is funded through general federal revenues, its growth as a budget item pits health care financing against other expenses, such as defense. Partly in response to the influence of hospitals, doctors, and other interest groups, from the outset Medicare was aimed at the acute medical care of the elderly. Chronic illness and long-term care were not part of the plan, even though they affect the health status and economic well-being of the elderly as much or even more than acute illness. Thus, as Box 12.4 illustrates, Medicare does not cover many needed health services and products.

Before Medicare, only about one-third of the elderly had health insurance; private insurance rates were outside the means of most older Americans. The enactment of Medicare immediately increased the average health care utilization rate among the elderly by more than 30 percent (Sorkin, 1986). Whereas in 1964, 21 percent of elderly had not seen a doctor in the last two or more years, by 1993 that rate was down to 7.4 percent (Davis and Burner, 1995). Although it dramatically increased access to health care, Medicare failed to protect beneficiaries from destitution in the face of health care costs, because its cost-sharing provisions did not limit liabilities in the event of catastrophic illness and did not cover most long-term (for example, nursing home) care or prescriptions (which increased in cost at a rate many times the rate of inflation most years since 1970).

The financing of Medicare has been problematic from the outset. Medicare legislation created less of a public health care program and more of an infusion of public money into *private* channels (Fein, 1986: 69–92). Initially, there were few cost-control regulations in the program. Partly because of the increased utilization of health care services but largely because of rapidly increasing charges by various providers, the expenditures were far more than anticipated. A limited cost-control measure was introduced in 1972, but it was largely ineffective. Between 1979 and 1982, expenditures under Medicare grew much faster than general inflation: hospital care by a rate of 17.2 percent per year, physician services by a 19.2 percent rate (Gibson et al., 1982; Sorkin, 1986). Part of the costliness was due to the fact that high-tech medicine and labor-intensive medical care are not as responsive to efficiency and other cost-savings measures as other industries; and part was due simply to overexpansion, greed, and in some cases outright fraud on the part of providers, hospitals, and insurance administrators (Sparrow, 1996).

At first, the AMA fought against the creation of Medicare, but the medical profession has been among its prime beneficiaries and now generally supports the program and its expansion. To secure the cooperation of physicians, the initial Medicare legislation allowed reimbursement of doctors' "usual and customary fees," so long as those fees were "reasonable." Such vague language, especially in the context of a seldom competitive fee-setting process, led to rapid inflation. Fees

BOX 12.4

Regressive Impact of Health Care Expenditures on Family Budgets: The Elderly

Dorothy and Frank are in their mid-70s and rely on their Social Security income of $1,400 per month for all their living expenses. They have Medicare coverage, but noncovered health care expenditures consume about 50 percent of their entire family budget, leaving them scrimping to pay for food, utilities, and other basic needs. Their monthly costs include modest Medigap insurance policy, $200; Medicare premiums, $85; prescriptions and other medicine, $250; deductibles and other charges not covered by Medicare or Medigap, $50; long-term care insurance (for Dorothy; Frank is not eligible because of preexisting health conditions), $200.

Clarissa is an 85-year-old widow, living alone on Social Security payments of $650 per month. Her health care needs not covered by Medicare consume 40 percent of her fixed income. They include Medicare premium, $42; prescription and other medicine, $120 (but she spends only $80, because she can't afford prescription painkillers for her arthritis); Medigap insurance, $80 (for a minimal policy); other charges not covered, $20.

She cannot afford long-term care insurance, but fears she will be sent to a third-rate nursing home when Medicare stops providing the home health aide who enables her to stay in her own apartment.

The figures show the following:

- An increasing proportion (in 1992, nearly one-third) of aged persons rely on Social Security for 80 percent or more of their income (Davis and Burner, 1995).
- Elderly families in all income brackets pay a *higher* proportion than nonelderly families of their total income on health care premiums (8.3 percent, compared to 4.9 percent) and on out-of-pocket expenditures (8.3 percent, compared to 3.2 percent)(Rasell et al., 1994).
- The 1993 median annual income of older men living alone is $14,983; older women, living alone $8,499; 58 percent of women 85 and over are poor or nearly poor (Butler, 1996).
- Elderly women are more likely than elderly men to have long-term, chronic disabling diseases. Assistance with tasks of daily living is required by 30.2 percent of women aged 75 and older, compared to 17.2 percent of men that age. Women constitute three-quarters of all nursing home residents; half the costs of U.S. long-term care are paid by Medicaid (see Barringer, 1992; Butler, 1996).

increased disproportionate to other rates of inflation; the number of elderly treated increased, and the number of medical services ordered by doctors for their Medicare patients rose markedly. After Medicare began, doctors who had previously reduced their fees for the needy elderly could receive their "customary" full payments. Physicians who had previously been frustrated by their inability to treat their pensioner-patients with the best available methods could, under Medicare, prescribe therapies without prejudice of ability to pay. Medicare funding provided stability for both physician and hospital income, much as private health insurance had done three decades earlier (Fein, 1986: 80–92).

Administration of Medicare regulations and reimbursement paperwork, however, add to the cost of the program. The waste of resources on administrative costs in the United States is particularly highlighted by contrasts with Canada and Great Britain, where insurance company intermediaries are eliminated and providers deal directly with the government rather than struggle with billing and collections (Himmelstein and Woolhandler, 1986; see also Fein, 1986: 157).

A major ongoing problem has been that some providers do not accept Medicare rates of reimbursement, so patients must bear the cost of the difference either out of pocket or by buying a relatively expensive ("Medigap") insurance policy (Davis and Burner, 1995). Because most Medicare reimbursement is still based on fee-for-service rates, there is no incentive for physicians to reduce the number of services or recommend less costly services. New Medicare regulations are regularly being proposed to try to contain costs, to ascertain greater physician cooperation, and to get better care for the moneys spent. The process is a political one, however, in which providers and insurers have disproportionately powerful voices (cf. Marmor et al., 1983b). The general failure of 1980s state and federal efforts to contain costs by prospective hospital rate setting (described further in this chapter) demonstrates how powerful interests can manipulate regulatory and reimbursements systems to their own advantage (McDonough, 1997).

In the 1990s the government encouraged (again, in concert with corporate interest groups) special Medicare HMOs, with the hopes that managed care corporations could contain costs. However, studies show that elderly (Medicare) and low-income (Medicaid) patients have generally done worse in health status in HMOs than in fee-for-service programs (Ware et al., 1996). Medicare HMOs often engage in "cream-skimming"—recruiting only younger, healthier senior citizens, whose care under traditional Medicare payment would have cost the government only 89.3 percent of the average. The proposal of "medical savings accounts" is another "cream-skimming" measure. These would allow participants to pocket a portion of the unused Medicare-paid premiums if their medical expenditures are very low, but they must accept the risk of much higher deductibles and copayments when they do need medical care, thus encouraging postponing needed care. Only very healthy and financially comfortable elderly persons could afford to take this risk, so others would remain in traditional Medicare. And as they aged and developed serious illnesses, those with "medical savings accounts" would drop such a risk-laden program. Because the government still has to cover the needs of the older, sicker elderly not in HMOs and other cream-skimming plans, its share of costs for the elderly is actually *increased* (Himmelstein and Woolhandler, 1996; Lynch and Minkler, 1997).

Although Medicare has been an important contribution to the health of covered citizens, it is less and less sufficient for their needs, and less able than ever to cover the increasing proportion of the eligible population. Without major restructuring and massive new sources of funding, Medicare is not a program on which citizens may rely for the future.

Medicaid   Medicaid was created at the same time as Medicare, but was organized very differently. Because Medicaid is funded through general revenues rather than a trust fund and is perceived as charity rather than deserved aid, the program is particularly vulnerable to cutbacks at every funding level. Each state operates its own program, with federal contributions varying according to the scope of the state's program, relative level of income, and certain features of providers and recipients. The federal program includes health care for persons covered by federal Supplemental Security Income (SSI), which assists blind, disabled, and elderly persons; members of families eligible for Aid to Families with Dependent Children (AFDC); and pregnant women in certain income brackets. Many states have defined the criteria for Medicaid so stringently that they exclude more than half the people who could be covered under federal guidelines (Fein, 1986: 108–112). Less than 35 percent of Americans living in poverty have health care coverage through public assistance, mainly Medicaid (Ries, 1991).

Due to deficiencies in Medicare coverage, Medicaid has become a significant source of funding for health care for the elderly. Some states use Medicaid to pay Medicare premiums, deductibles, and copayments that poor elderly persons cannot afford. Medicaid also covers services, such as long-term care, not provided by Medicare. More than 65 percent of U.S. nursing home residents are supported by Medicaid (Levit et al., 1996). The House Select Committee on Aging reported that 90 percent of single elderly patients "spend down" to the poverty level after paying one year of nursing home charges; half of the couples with one spouse in a nursing home reach poverty level within six months, and unless Medicaid helps pay for the nursing home, the well spouse is left destitute, often with many years of life ahead. Thus, Medicaid has become the de facto long-term care supplement to Medicare.

Children constitute 49 percent of Medicaid recipients, but consume only about 16 percent of Medicaid funds; the elderly used 31 percent of Medicaid dollars, representing only 11.5 percent of those eligible (USDHHS, 1996a: 165). Thus, Medicaid has *not* functioned primarily as a source of health care for lower-class persons, especially children, among whom poverty rates are at a 30-year high. Rather, its main recipients appear to be those who were made poor by the costs of health care in disability and old age (Fein, 1986: 112).

The administrative costs of Medicaid are higher than for Medicare. Many states parcel out portions of the program to various local agencies or institutional providers; the several layers multiply administrative costs. Furthermore, unlike Medicare, Medicaid eligibility must be determined by complex formulas and continually reviewed because agencies have a state-directed imperative to trim rolls and discourage coverage. A substantial portion of the funds that Americans believe are used for health care is actually going to the mere administration of public insurance programs (Fein, 1986).

Ironically, the greatest documented abuses of Medicaid funding have been on the part of unscrupulous providers, often abetted by the politically motivated purchasing policies of state and local agencies. For example, in 1971 the California legislature passed the Medical Reform Act, facilitating the assignment of Medicaid recipients to HMOs contracting with the state. The legislature had reasoned that these large health care contractors would be more efficient, reduce unnecessary utilization of health services, and thus be more cost effective than previous arrangements with independent providers. In fact, however, the welfare HMOs charged more. Compared to other HMOs, which spent about 10 percent of the premium dollar on administration and profits, welfare HMOs used 52 percent of state payments for administration and profits (Lewis, 1976). Subsequent investigations also showed that the utilization of services had been cut by using foreign physicians who spoke limited English, by contracting with proprietary hospitals 30 to 50 miles from the client population, by offering only brief office hours, and by denying emergency services and referrals to specialists (Gabel and Redisch, 1979). Later research found that persons enrolled in Medicaid-paid HMOs suffered considerably worse health outcomes than those whose Medicaid paid for conventional fee-for-service visits (Ware et al., 1996; see also Davis, 1991).

The structure of Medicaid has thus encouraged a two-tiered system of medical care, with the service to those covered by Medicaid being distinctly inferior. Medicaid has, however, increased the access of the poor to some medical assistance; after the implementation of the program, poor families used significantly more physician services and hospitalization. Likewise, in the 1980s when government cutbacks reduced Medicaid rolls, the poor with no insurance had significantly less access and utilization than those with Medicaid (Davis, 1991). In the 1990s, as the proportion of children covered by employer-based private insurance dropped dramatically, Medicaid coverage was again expanded. It now covers more than one-fifth of all U.S. children, unfortunately without reducing the proportion of children who are still uninsured (Newacheck et al., 1995).

It has not given the poor access to mainstream medical care, however; for example, poor children are particularly likely to be treated in hospital outpatient services rather than by private physicians, and they are highly likely to be seen by different doctors, if at all, rather than have a regular source of care (Kogan et al., 1995). Nor has the program enabled the poor to obtain sufficient medical attention relative to their generally greater health needs (Callahan and David, 1995; Lyons et al., 1996).

The Uninsured and Underinsured

In 1995, an estimated 43.4 million Americans had *no private or public coverage* for their medical expenses. Furthermore, an estimated 61 million—more than one-quarter of the entire U.S. population—were without health coverage for part of the year (Bradsher, 1995; Summer, 1994; Swartz, 1994). Despite large, steady increases in government health spending for Medicaid and Medicare, the number of persons uninsured increased significantly throughout the 1980s and 1990s (Rowland et al., 1994; Summer, 1994). Whereas in 1977, only 13.8 percent of the under-65 population was uninsured, by 1994, at least 18.7 percent were uninsured (Bradsher, 1995; Rice, 1991). Table 12.1 shows the comparison of 1984 and 1994 rates of private insurance coverage, Medicaid coverage, and lack of insurance for persons under 65. Welfare cutbacks in 1997, resulting in loss of Medicaid for many persons previously

TABLE 12.1 **Health Care Coverage in 1984 and 1994: Percentages of Persons under 65 Years of Age**

Characteristics	PRIVATE INSURANCE		MEDICAID		NOT COVERED*	
	1984	1994	1984	1994	1984	1994
TOTAL	77.2	70.5	5.6	9.4	15.6	18.3
Under 15	71.9	63.0	10.8	19.8	16.1	16.1
15–44	77.0	69.9	4.4	6.7	17.6	22.0
45–64	83.6	80.5	2.7	3.6	10.2	12.2
Family Income†:						
under $14,000	34.1	24.7	26.5	38.0	37.8	35.0
$14,000–24,999	71.3	54.0	4.2	12.3	22.1	30.4
$25,000–34,999	88.3	78.4	1.2	3.5	8.7	15.6
$35,000–49,999	93.1	88.5	0.4	1.3	4.8	8.7
$50,000 and more	95.2	92.7	0.4	0.7	3.1	5.6

*Includes persons not covered by private insurance, Medicaid, Medicare, or military plans.
†Income categories for 1984 (when the dollar bought less) were under $10,000; 10,000–18,999; 19,000–29,999; 30,000–39,000; and 40,000 and more.
Source: U.S. Dept. of Health and Human Services, *Health, United States, 1995*, Hyattsville, MD: National Center for Health Statistics, 1996, p. 260.

covered under the Aid to Dependent Children program, will dramatically increase this proportion, especially among unemployed or working poor mothers and their children (Hellander et al., 1995).

The working poor have been particularly hurt, because their jobs are less likely than middle- and upper-class jobs to provide health insurance benefits, but they earn somewhat too much to be eligible for Medicaid and yet far too little to afford private, nongroup insurance. Employed persons and their dependents account for approximately 75 percent of the uninsured population (Cantor et al., 1995). Furthermore, because these estimates are based on those uninsured at the time of the survey, the number of those uninsured at some time in the year is probably far higher because many workers become reemployed after layoffs. Another 50 million Americans are **underinsured**; they have some health insurance but it is inadequate to protect them from financial disaster in case of serious or prolonged illness (Himmelstein et al., 1992).

Changes in the U.S. labor market in the 1980s and 1990s have worsened the health care crisis, because in this country health care is closely linked to employment status. Layoffs and forced retirements caused by "downsizing," "deindustrialization," and other dramatic economic shifts left many Americans without health insurance. Many workers accepted early retirement with the promise of continued insurance benefits until they became eligible for Medicare, only to have their former employers slash or eliminate retiree coverage. In an effort to divest themselves of obligations (such as insurance benefits) to a steady work force, many employers made increased use of temporary workers and converted even professional jobs into "outsource" work (see Newacheck et al., 1995; Rubin, 1996). Due to the decline in employment-related coverage, the proportion of *non*-poor people without health insurance has increased dramatically, as shown in Table 12.1 (Summer, 1994). Cost shifting by employers makes it difficult even for middle-income families to afford coverage.

Blacks and Hispanics are particularly likely to be uninsured because they are disproportionately represented among the working poor, in jobs paying no insurance benefits, and in regions of the United States where labor is less commonly unionized and Medicaid insurance is least available (see Ginzberg, 1991). For example, the percentage of Mexican Americans under the age of 65 who are uninsured is approximately three times that of white, non-Hispanics. Among the uninsured Mexican Americans, more than half were gainfully employed but were living at or below the poverty level (Treviño et al., 1991).

Women are also disadvantaged in access to health insurance. About 75 percent of the nation's uninsured women are employed but receive no work-related insurance. One study found that women's chances of being covered by employer-arranged insurance were lower than men's, even when factors such as hours worked, years tenure on the job, and company size were taken into account (Institute for Women's Policy Research, 1994). Only 9 percent of all poor women under 65 are insured by employer-provided insurance (Lyons et al., 1996). Furthermore, because employers have reduced their contribution to family insurance, many nonworking wives have become uninsured. Divorce and widowhood also leave many women without a source of private health insurance (Meyer and Pavalko, 1996).

Particularly troubling is the high proportion of children who are without any form of health insurance. In 1994, more than 10 million (or 16.1 percent) of children in the United States had no health insurance at all. Only about three-fifths of the nation's children have any health coverage from employer-based insurance, and this proportion has been steadily dropping for two decades (USDHHS, 1996a).

Public assistance becomes the only possible source of health coverage for many children because, without employer-based group insurance, families cannot afford private insurance. States vary widely in the income threshold for Medicaid coverage, such that in some states more than half of all children whose families earn less than the poverty level are not covered by Medicaid. For example, whereas Wisconsin, Rhode Island, and Maine had only about 10 to 11 percent uninsured children among those below the poverty level, New Mexico excluded 44 percent, and Texas excluded 51.4 percent of poor children from Medicaid coverage (Cartland and Yudkowsky, 1993).

Having no health insurance severely limits people's access to health care, often forcing them to postpone care that could prevent a problem from becoming a serious or even life-threatening illness. For example, uncontrolled diabetes and hypertension can lead to serious (and expensive) complications. In the 1960s and early 1970s, the gap in access to medical care between the nonpoor and the poor or near-poor had been steadily closing, but in the 1980s and 1990s the gap widened dramatically (Davis, 1991; Rice, 1991).

Lack of health insurance led to fewer women getting prenatal care, and their newborns were disproportionately likely to have serious health problems

(Braverman et al., 1989). Large numbers of children were not getting minimally necessary inoculations during their preschool years, and more families were using hospital emergency rooms as their only accessible entry to any health care. When children's parents were laid off work, they temporarily lost coverage; about one-quarter of U.S. children were without insurance for at least one month in their first year of life, resulting in serious discontinuities of care (Kogan et al., 1995). Several studies have documented the significantly higher morbidity and mortality rates of the poor or near-poor and uninsured, who are limited in or denied access to physicians and hospitals (Callahan and David, 1995; Lyons et al., 1996).

Furthermore, public insurance programs rarely cover all needed expenses. Elderly families pay, on average, nearly 17 percent of their incomes for noncovered health expenses. Medicaid coverage is less adequate than that of Medicare, so many poor persons are simply denied access to care and go without needed medicine. Even after the contribution of public assistance, poor families pay, on average, an estimated 14 to 15 percent of their meager incomes, compared to roughly 8 percent for middle-income families and less than 3 percent for wealthy families (Rasell et al., 1994). Even seemingly small medical expenditures become financially catastrophic for families with low incomes and inadequate health insurance (Berki, 1986). Box 12.5 illustrates the impact of inadequate public insurance for the working poor.

Because of rising proportions of uninsured and underinsured Americans, together with the inadequacies of existing programs of public insurance, the health care crisis now affects all but the wealthiest citizens. In place of the fragmented for-profit health insurance industry, some policy experts have called for a nationwide program guaranteeing universal access to health care.

National Health Insurance: The Canadian Model

National health insurance is a perennial issue in the United States. As early as 1914 and with increasing fervor in the 1930s and 1940s, some American health reformers were urging social insurance legislation comparable to that in Europe. Insurance companies and the AMA vigorously fought these proposals (Starr, 1982: 240–289). The idea of a national health insurance has been raised in Congress many times since, but America has not yet enacted any comprehensive health care program for its citizens.

In light of the large numbers of uninsured and underinsured Americans and the rapidly escalating burden of health care expenditures, policymakers need to look again at the merits of the Canadian national health insurance as a model for the United States. Since 1972, a national program has covered all Canadian citizens for hospitalization, physician care, and many ancillary services. Each province maintains its own insurance plan, but federal approval and funding require the following minimal criteria: (1) universal coverage (all citizens must be covered); (2) comprehensive coverage (it must pay for all conventional hospital and medical care); (3) access (for instance, no extra charges that make the insurance regressive); (4) portability (each citizen's insurance must be accepted throughout the country);

BOX 12.5

Regressive Impact of Health Care Expenditures on Family Budgets: The Working Poor

Esperanza and Roberto both work, but their combined incomes cannot raise them out of poverty. Esperanza's job offers no group health insurance and Roberto's offers only minimal coverage for which the employees must pay substantial premiums. They rely on public clinics and emergency rooms for most care for themselves and their two children, but earn too much to be eligible for Medicaid in Texas, a state with a very high rate of uninsured working poor. Even by doing without needed doctor visits and medications, their health care expenses consume 15 percent of their combined take-home pay of about $1,500 per month). They pay Roberto's insurance premium, $85; doctor and clinic fees, $35; hospital bills being paid back a little each month, $65; prescriptions and other medicine, $40.

Connie is the divorced mother of two school-aged children. She works full time as a home health aide, with take-home pay of less than $1,000 per month. She has no employer-provided insurance for herself or the children, one of whom has been diagnosed with sickle-cell anemia (a hereditary chronic disease affecting mainly African Americans). The child is not yet sufficiently harmed by the disease to qualify for public insurance for the disabled, but does have frequent infections and needs far more medical attention than non-anemic children. Connie's family health expenditures consume nearly 30 percent of her income. They include doctor and clinic fees, $80; hospital bills being paid back, $100; prescriptions and other medicine, $50; taxi to doctors, hospitals, and clinics not located near public transportation, $35.

Not only do these families lack adequate access to health care, but also they must forgo spending on food, clothing, and shelter, in order to pay such a high percentage of their income on health care. They are not alone. The figures show the following:

- Low-income families pay a much higher proportion of their incomes for health care than do high-income families. Families in the first and second deciles (highest income 20 percent) spend 0.9 percent and 1.2 percent for out-of-pocket expenses, compared to middle-income families' 2.4 percent, and low-income families' (ninth and tenth deciles) 5.9 and 9.8 percent. Likewise, families in the first and second deciles spend only 1.9 and 2.8 percent of their incomes on health premiums, compared to middle-income families' 5 to 5.5 percent, and ninth and tenth decile families' 6.1 and 6.7 percent (Rasell et al., 1994).
- Minority families are particularly unlikely to be able to obtain affordable private health insurance (see Ginzberg, 1991; Reed, 1993; Treviño, 1991). Only 45.8 percent of Mexican Americans have any private insurance coverage, compared to 52.4 percent of African Americans and 77.4 percent of white, non-Hispanic origin Americans. Due mainly to the exclusion of working poor families from Medicaid insurance, the rates of persons with *no* private or public insurance coverage are 37.2 percent of Mexican Americans, 21.1 percent of African Americans, and 14.6 percent of white, non-Hispanic origin Americans (USDHHS, 1995:260).

- Only 9 percent of all poor women under 65 are insured by employer-provided insurance (Lyons et al., 1996).
- Chronic illnesses (such as hypertension, diabetes, sickle-cell anemia) that disproportionately afflict certain minority groups are particularly likely to be inadequately treated among the working poor, because the diseases are often not sufficiently disabling to qualify for Medicare disability insurance, but the patients are not poor enough to qualify for Medicaid—yet they are too poor to afford the increased levels of care their conditions need (Hill, 1995).

and (5) nonprofit, public administration. Private insurers are legally excluded from the health care arena. Doctors and other health care providers are mostly in the private sector, but the government controls expenses by an annually negotiated, binding fee schedule. Incentives for excessive surgery and other costly procedures have been eliminated (Marmor, 1993).

Canadian doctors have many incentives to work in primary care and to locate their practices in the kinds of communities, such as rural or inner-city areas, that are seriously underserved in the United States. The Canadian government maintains a smaller proportion of specialists (about one for every four primary care physicians, compared to one to one in the United States). Canadian doctors are paid far less than U.S. doctors, but they remain the best paid professionals in Canada. Doctors are paid on a fee-for-service basis, according to a fixed, annually negotiated schedule, but there are some caps on the total amounts doctors can earn. No evidence indicates that Canadian doctors are sufficiently dissatisfied with their system to leave to practice elsewhere, and Canada has a higher proportion of applicants for medical school than in the United States (Adams, 1993; *Consumer Reports*, 1990; Rosenthal, 1991; Wolfe, 1990).

Patients are free to choose their own doctor, although they must be referred by a primary care physician to use services of many specialists. When Canadians consult the doctor or go to the hospital, they simply show their medical card; they are not billed at all. Health care providers may not add on any charges, such as copayments, over those covered by the national insurance program. Canada's program covers most medical services, including many (such as long-term home care and nursing home care) not covered by medical insurance in the United States. The provinces are allowed but not required to cover additional services, such as physiotherapy, eyeglasses, and adult dental care (Kane, 1993; Rosenthal, 1991; Wolfe, 1990).

Control over the hospital sector also keeps costs down. Diagnostic tests are centralized, which provides no profits to physicians or labs. Hospitals are run by each province on an annual budget basis, with no incentives to overbuild or invest in duplicates of expensive technological devices. Authorization for purchase of new technology is more conservative in Canada than in the United States. The policy in Canada is to wait until there is strong evidence of the medical effectiveness, safety, and usefulness of expensive technology, and then to purchase gradually while gauging the actual rate of use of facilities. These controls have enabled the

Canadian system to keep its health care expenditures to a much smaller portion of the country's GNP while providing very high rates of access to health care for all citizens (Marmor, 1993; Wolfe, 1990). Because all citizens are covered by the same level and kind of insurance, administrative costs in Canada are far lower than in the United States; for instance, U.S. hospital administrative costs average 24.8 percent of overall spending—about 2.5 times the rate of Canadian hospitals (Woolhandler et al., 1993).

The Canadian system does have several drawbacks, however, compared to health care services afforded by upper-class Americans. Substantial waits may be involved, especially for nonemergency hospital procedures. Provincial facilities for some high-tech procedures and testing may not be located conveniently. The system also has an operative form of rationing, especially of very expensive services such as organ transplants. For example, a person with unfavorable prospects for long-term health benefits from a kidney transplant would be less likely than in the United States to be able to obtain one. Despite these drawbacks, even in years of underfunding, Canadians are highly satisfied with their system (Blendon et al., 1990). In a survey of ten industrialized nations, Canada had the highest proportion (56 percent) of citizens who stated the health care system needed only minor changes (the Netherlands, France, and Germany were the next most satisfied). The United States was at the bottom, with only 10 percent agreeing that only minor changes are needed (L. Harris Associates, cited in *New York Times*, 1991).

Had the United States enacted a national health program such as Canada's several decades ago, it might have realized similar cost controls and universal health care access. Now, however, vested interests profiting from the laissez-faire American system have become so entrenched, economically centralized, and powerful that it would be extremely difficult to establish any economical national health plan, even one as limited as national health insurance. A few decades ago, U.S. hospitals could have been organized as public facilities, but now many are organized as for-profit businesses with major investments to protect. Expensive high-tech medical equipment has already been purchased; excessive hospital rooms have already been built. Likewise, health insurance is big business; without eliminating the profit and paperwork of third-party payments, a national health plan could not realize the kinds of savings achieved in the Canadian system. Stringent government controls could prevent national health insurance from creating yet another inflationary spiral of health costs, but is there sufficient political will to take such a strong stand (Marmor et al., 1983a)?

A national insurance program would probably resolve one major aspect of the current crisis in the U.S. health care system: the access of poor and middle-class people to adequate physician and hospital care. National health insurance also has the potential, if implemented with certain regulatory safeguards, of improving the quality of care received by nonwealthy citizens. Absent major structural changes to eliminate or greatly restrict profit taking, however, a national health insurance program would probably not be able to reduce or even control costs.

The American people could decide that affordable health care for all is a sufficiently important value to warrant such structural changes. The enormous political and economic power of the vested interests of hospital corporations, insurance companies, medical industries, and health care providers would almost certainly be utilized to fight those changes.

HEALTH CARE INSTITUTIONS

The provision of health care in large-scale institutions, such as hospitals, is a relatively recent phenomenon. In the nineteenth century, most sick people were treated and nursed in their homes. Almshouse wards were the main form of hospital, nursing home, and insane asylum, offering a modicum of care and custody to indigent persons lacking family members to provide care. They were run as charitable institutions, with utterly paternalistic organization as well as little real curative function (Rosenberg, 1987).

The Development of the Modern Hospital

By the time of the early twentieth-century reformation of the medical profession (described in Chapter 9), hospitals too had changed dramatically. Both hospitals and medicine were becoming more rationalized: science oriented, specialized, and bureaucratized. Many towns established community hospitals, which lacked the stigma of the poorhouse wards. The rapid development of new medical "tools," such as antiseptic conditions for surgery, X-rays, and clinical laboratories, provided an important rationale for centering care in hospitals, which could capitalize these facilities and provide the necessary support staff. Hospitals' prestige and growth hinged on the practice of surgery (Rosenberg, 1987: 337–352).

One reason for the increase of middle- and upper-class hospital patients was the growing faith in the efficacy of medicine; another was the concerted advertising by hospitals, depicting well-appointed private rooms and immaculate conditions. Income from private patients made community hospitals economically viable. Hospital-admitting privileges became crucial to physicians' careers; hospitals in turn became dependent on doctors to bring in private patients (Rosenberg, 1987: 237–261).

Nursing too was changed from an untrained domestic task to a hospital-oriented and -trained occupation, bringing discipline and efficiency to the care of paying patients. By the 1920s American hospitals were, therefore, being transformed from charitable enterprises to bureaucratic organizations selling medical commodities in an impersonal marketplace. The very technology and specialization of tasks that made hospitals plausible sites for the centralized practice of medicine were subsequently major sources of the spiraling costs leading to the present U.S. health care crisis.

Hospital Ownership and Control

One of the biggest changes in the last 40 years has been in how hospitals are owned and controlled. Before the 1970s most hospitals were operated primarily as not-for-profit enterprises. Some not-for-profit hospitals are public institutions, funded mainly from tax revenues of a city, county, state, or national government; this includes most teaching hospitals, where the training of new doctors is combined with the care of indigent patients. Private not-for-profit institutions include community hospitals run by local boards as well as hospitals run by various religious and charitable organizations. Since the early years of private patient hospitalization, there have been private, for-profit hospitals, typically proprietary hospitals set up by several doctors in a community, but small groups of investors could not readily keep pace with the costs of capitalizing modern high-tech hospitals. Since about 1980, increasingly, for-profit hospitals are owned by large business corporations with investor-stockholders.

The numbers of public and not-for-profit hospitals are dwindling, and they are increasingly operating with huge financial losses because they have been left caring for a disproportionate number of the sickest and poorest patients, who are turned away from for-profit hospitals (Freudenheim, 1995c, 1997d; Goldstein, 1995; Gray, 1991; Preston, 1996; Rosenthal, 1996, 1994). The failure of the U.S. health care system to provide adequate insurance coverage for all citizens has wreaked havoc on the budgets of hospitals. A growing proportion of Americans—more than one-fourth of the nation—lack adequate health insurance, and government cost cutting has reduced the levels of funding of care for many poor, disabled, and elderly previously provided by Medicaid and Medicare. Only hospitals whose patients have good private insurance coverage can "break even" in operating costs; indeed, they can make sizable profits. As the private for-profit hospitals increasingly control this desirable market, other not-for-profit hospitals suffer financial losses and bankruptcies.

A rapidly growing trend in the United States is toward the proprietarization and corporatization of health care facilities, such as hospitals, nursing homes, psychiatric hospitals, and free-standing clinics and outpatient surgery centers. **Proprietarization** is the process by which a greater proportion of health care institutions are operated explicitly for profit. **Corporatization** is the process by which a relatively small number of investor-owned corporations control a greater concentration of proprietary interests.

For example, Columbia Healthcare Corporation bought a number of small failing hospitals to get a market toehold in cities such as Houston and Miami; then it acquired Galen Health Care, a 73-hospital chain. In 1993, Columbia merged with the HCA (Hospital Corporation of America), making it the world's largest investor-owned hospital group (Jones, 1993; see also Bond and Weissman, 1997). Although it was unsuccessful in its attempt to take over Blue Cross-Blue Shield of Ohio, by 1997 Columbia/HCA owned 343 hospitals, 136 outpatient surgery centers, and 550 home-care agencies, and numerous other medical services (Freudenheim, 1997a). As of 1991, about a quarter of all nonfederal acute-care hospitals were owned by investor-owned corporations (Lindorff, 1992). The proportion of investor-owned specialty hospitals, such as short-term psychiatric hospitals and nursing homes, was even greater.

For-profit hospitals have been highly profitable for investors. Interestingly, studies have found that for-profit acute-care hospitals are not more cost efficient than their not-for-profit counterparts, but rather are more expensive to operate. At the same time, however, the study found no evidence that patients admitted to for-profit acute-care hospitals were treated less well than those in not-for-profit hospitals (Institute of Medicine, 1986; Sloan, 1988). For-profit hospitals spend much less of their income on patient care than the national average for all kinds of hospitals, and they spend much more on administrative costs and profits (Woolhandler and Himmelstein, 1997).

Rather than cost efficiency, their profitability appears to depend on controlling patient-mix (that is, limiting the served population to the well insured), as well as dominating or monopolizing specific markets. For-profit takeovers of nonprofit health organizations has resulted in several instances of plunder of publicly created assets. For example, several Blue Cross insurance funds, as well as numerous community or religiously supported hospitals, have been acquired by for-profit chains with little or no return of the real value of the assets of the institution that community had created or supported with its donations of time and money (Bond and Weissman, 1997; Lewin and Gottlieb, 1997).

Although initially, after a corporate buyout of a hospital, for-profit hospitals may realize some economies of scale (for example, better prices on supplies bought through the united purchasing power of the chain), these studies suggest that for-profit hospitals cannot in the long run further reduce costs and maintain the same quality without seriously diminishing their profits. Indeed, if they eventually buy out or drive their nonprofit competitors to bankruptcy, they may be in a position to increase their profits by driving up prices (Jones, 1993). Because profits are their foremost reason for existence, investor-owned hospitals have no incentive to return cost savings to the payers of medical costs. The unprecedented power and potential for market monopoly of for-profit hospitals is a significant and growing problem that any viable U.S. health care policy must address.

Another change in the structure and power of medical businesses is that they are frequently connected within large integrated nationwide or international corporations. The corporatization of health care has involved both horizontal and vertical integration. Horizontal integration is the process by which a corporation acquires large numbers of productive facilities, such as hospitals or nursing homes, across widespread markets (Salmon, 1995). Vertical integration describes the conglomerate control over several levels of production, such as hospitals, nursing homes, hospital supply companies, pharmaceutical companies, prosthetic supply companies, medical office complexes, and home health care agencies. Vertically integrated industries have increased capacity to control diverse aspects of the market and to shift resources when one part of the business becomes less profitable. Many "managed care" organizations are vertically integrated, thus concentrating considerable control of the market.

Hospital Costs and Financing

Any effort to address the U.S. health system crisis must confront the costs of hospital care. Payments to hospitals account for the largest single category of national health expenditures. Not only have costs of hospital care risen far faster than the cost of living in the United States, they have also consumed an ever greater proportion of total national health expenditures. Whereas in 1929, the costs of hospital care amounted to 18 percent of all U.S. health spending, they were 30 percent by 1950, 37 percent by 1970, and 44 percent in the early 1990s (Gibson, 1980, 1982; Letsch, 1993). Hospital costs have been notoriously difficult to control.

One source of spiraling hospital costs has been the proliferation of sophisticated and expensive technologies. Many of these expensive investments are, however, not really needed in the community; many services are duplicated (see Glaser, 1991). For example, all five hospitals in one city may have purchased and staffed an expensive magnetic resonance imaging (MRI) unit, but none of them may have real use for more than one-fourth of the MRI's capacity, so the costs for each use must be high. Then in order to recoup more of the expense of the unit, the hospitals encourage their physicians to order more MRI scans for their insured patients. State regulatory agencies tried to contain these cost-escalating practices by requiring a certificate of need before purchases of certain equipment, but most such regulations failed to reduce costs substantially (Roth, 1984) and sometimes resulted in bribes and fraud (Lindorff, 1992). One important reason that states cannot adequately limit technology purchases, however, is that the medical profession quickly accepts many technologies, even if not yet of proven benefit, as the "standard" for care.

The proliferation of technologies from the minor (such as blood tests) to the massive (neonatal intensive care units, for example) have driven up hospital costs not only because they are expensive to acquire and house but also because they require costly specialized support workers. Whereas modernizing capital expenditures in industrial production usually decrease labor costs, technological investments in hospital production generally increase labor expenditures.

U.S. hospitals are far more labor intensive than their European counterparts. In 1985, they employed 2.75 hospital personnel per occupied bed, compared to 2.13 in Canada, 1.85 in Sweden, and 1.21 in Germany (Glaser, 1991). U.S. hospitals have higher rates of staffing of skilled medical personnel—an expensive part of hospital budgets. Another difference may be low hospital occupancy rates because many U.S. communities have an oversupply of hospital beds relative to the population, especially the insured population.

A further explanation is that U.S. hospitals employ far more personnel to administer their fiscal and bureaucratic operations. Lacking universal or standardized health insurance, in the United States every patient must be screened for type and amount of insurance coverage or other method of payment, and the hospital must communicate with payers for review and approval of specific services, as well as conduct elaborate billings and payment collections. Taken together, these labor costs contribute to enormous disparity between U.S. and European hospital costs. In 1987, the United States spent $969 per capita on hospitals, compared with $754 in Canada, $422 in Germany, and $296 in Belgium (Glaser, 1991).

Hospital Reimbursements In 1983, in an effort to contain spiraling hospital costs, the federal government adopted DRGs (Diagnosis Related Groups) as a basis for Medicare reimbursement (Ruggie, 1992; Smith, 1992).[3] In this system, each procedure or service that can be provided to a hospital patient is placed in a diagnosis-related category, each with a price fixed by computing what similar hospitals had been charging for like cases. The hospital is not paid more if the actual services cost more; if the actual services cost less, the hospital keeps the difference. Before DRGs, hospitals had strong financial incentives to use many procedures and services for each patient, because they could charge for each and every item in the patient's treatment. There were unforeseen negative effects of DRGs, however, including pressures on doctors not to request services that may be beneficial, and the early discharge of patients—"quicker and sicker."

Rather than contain costs, the DRG system actually increased them (Reinhardt, 1996). Hospitals shifted the costs of patient care, for example by sending postoperative patients home to be cared for by the family, sometimes aided by visiting nurses or home health aides. The costs of subacute care (such as in a convalescent facility) and home health care (which Medicare and other insurers paid separately, even when delivered by a subsidiary of the very hospital corporation that discharged the patient) rapidly escalated, more than equaling what had previously been paid for in-hospital care. The system was also vulnerable to outright fraud in hospital billing. For example, in 1997, a federal probe indicted the nation's largest hospital chain, Columbia/HCA Healthcare Corp., for systematically "upcoding" patient diagnoses in order to increase the bill to Medicare. By claiming a more serious condition (bleeding ulcer with complications rather than bleeding ulcer, for instance), the corporation more than doubled its charges (Lagnado, 1997).

The DRG system of Medicare payment, together with cost controls instituted by private managed care corporations (such as HMOs), may have also financially weakened many hospitals leading to acquisitions by for-profit chains or to closure. Shorter hospital stays left many hospitals underutilized. Between 1980 and 1993 there was a 36 percent cut in hospital inpatient days per thousand population, but the per capita spending on health services rose by 65 percent. In the name of cost controls, many hospitals were gutted, but their actual care of patients was diminished and, ironically, cost more overall (Reinhardt, 1996).

Hospitals can remain financially stable—and in some cases even highly profitable—if they can control the mixture of payers of their patients' bills. Those in a position to accept very few patients with payers (such as Medicaid) that severely restrict how much the hospital is paid, and to reject patients without adequate insurance or other means of paying, can be economically comfortable. Indeed, evidence shows that for-profit hospitals realize profits not by managing their health care delivery more efficiently but by effectively manipulating the reimbursement system (Pattison and Katz, 1983). Hospital competition for high-paying patients has led to serious problems of access to needed care.

---

[3]Several states also had statewide DRG controls, but by the mid-1990s their programs were abandoned in failure.

Problems of Access Most inner-city and rural hospitals, however, do not have the luxury of controlling the mixture of payers because they are often the only hospital available to a population. Many of them end up in dire financial straits, and their patients experience serious problems of access to needed health care. Many rural hospitals serve a relatively small, widely dispersed population; rural poor or uninsured persons including many farm families who cannot afford private insurance must rely on these hospitals to partially subsidize their care.

Rural hospitals accounted for a disproportionately large number of the more than 500 hospitals that closed between 1980 and 1987 (DeFriese et al., 1992). Some failed hospitals were outmoded and/or substandard, but many were the only ones available to the populace (Reinhold, 1987). Many rural areas have difficulty attracting physicians to practice in their areas, and losing a local hospital to which physicians can admit patients may further disadvantage the community. Closure of rural hospitals also decreases access to emergency medical care. Although the vast majority of the U.S. population lives in urban areas, some 70 percent of trauma fatalities occur in rural areas. There are workable substitutes for small rural community hospitals (outpatient satellite clinics and paraprofessional emergency teams, for example), but these require national or statewide policymaking and funding for restoring access to health facilities in rural areas (Rutledge et al., 1992; Straub, 1990).

Another problem of access is the use of the hospital emergency room (see Albrecht et al., 1996). All communities need access to some trauma center, open 24 hours a day, staffed and equipped to handle a vast range of possible medical emergencies. But emergency rooms are rarely profitable; indeed, they are unlikely to generate enough income to cover costs, because emergency rooms are used disproportionately by uninsured and underinsured patients who lack any other source of medical care. In predominantly poor areas, emergency rooms create massive losses to hospitals. Unable to afford primary care, poor persons appear at emergency rooms when they are extremely sick, requiring extensive medical attention. Furthermore, because many poor people lack the resources and safe conditions to be adequately nursed at home, hospitals must keep them longer. Many nonpublic hospitals have responded by eliminating their emergency room services. In Los Angeles, where 27 percent of all nonelderly adults and 30 percent of all children have no health insurance, 15 hospitals closed or downgraded their emergency rooms between 1986 and 1988; the remaining hospitals were posting multimillion-dollar annual losses on their emergency services (Reinhold, 1988).

In the inner cities, public hospitals, operated by city or other government bodies, are where most of the urban poor, the underinsured, and the uninsured go for treatment. These hospitals are gravely underfunded because of their inability to control their patient mix. They receive only about 12 percent of their revenues from private insurance, and nearly one-third of their patients, on average, have no insurance—public or private—and cannot afford to pay for their care (Kassirer, 1995). In the early 1990s, nationally, hospitals averaged profit margins in the range of 4 to 6 percent (while investor-owned hospitals earned considerably more). By contrast, inner-city hospitals operated at huge losses. For example, not-for-profit Presbyterian

Hospital (New York City) suffered a 3.1 percent loss in 1993, and New York City's 13 municipal hospitals sustained an 8.5 percent loss (Freudenheim, 1995c). Underfunded, many public hospitals have been forced to close. In the early 1980s there were more than 1,800 public hospitals, but by 1993 only 1,390 remained open, leaving the poor and uninsured even more vulnerable (Kassirer, 1995).

For-profit hospitals frequently refuse to serve patients who cannot pay or transfer them—often in medically unstable conditions—to public hospitals or those nonprofit hospitals willing to accept indigent patients. This extensive "dumping" of undesirable patients puts an added burden on inner-city hospitals, especially the publicly financed hospitals that become the poor's last resort. In Chicago in 1983, after the governor had placed a ceiling on state payments for hospital services to the poor, transfers of patients from private hospitals to the county public hospital increased from an average of 100 per month to 450 per month. A subsequent study found that of 467 patients transferred to Cook County Hospital from private hospitals, 89 percent were black or Hispanic, 81 percent were unemployed, and nearly a fourth were medically endangered by the transfer (Schiff et al., 1986). In outrage over this and similar instances, Congress outlawed the "dumping" of patients in April 1987. Seven years later, however, a study found that federal agencies were not enforcing the act and had punished only 9 percent of the 268 hospitals cited for the illegal practice (Public Citizen Health Research Group, 1993; see also Himmelstein et al., 1984).

The trend toward proprietarization and corporatization of health care in the United States is closely linked with this underfunding of accessible care for the poor and underinsured (Whiteis and Salmon, 1987), especially when for-profit hospitals displace previously not-for-profit hospitals (see Gray, 1991). For example, in the 1980s, when Medicaid hospital payments did not rise proportionate to payments by commercial insurers or Medicare, for-profit hospitals reduced their share of Medicaid patients (Davis, 1991).

For-profit hospitals (and sometimes, too, not-for-profit hospitals that emulate big businesses) engage in marketing and demarketing strategies to maximize their revenues. Demarketing is a euphemism for the practice of actively discouraging "undesirable" patients who seek their services.

For example, economically depressed Brownsville, Texas, is served by two hospitals, both owned by for-profit chains. Despite their very low occupancy rates (40 and 50 percent), they regularly turn away all but the most critical emergency cases if patients cannot pay. In addition to these hospitals' concern for profitability, the plight of poor patients is made more desperate by the fact that Texas has one of the least adequate of all state programs of health services for the poor; only those whose income is below 60 percent of the poverty level are covered by Medicaid insurance. The administrator of one Brownsville hospital said, "We ask all the patients for money. . . . We work with the poor patients and tell them we'd be happy to set up a payment program" (quoted in Tolchin, 1988b). Critics charge that the hospitals aggressively intimidate patients into leaving without health care service (Tolchin, 1988a). One survey of physicians found that those practicing at for-profit hospitals were two to three times as likely to report their hospital discouraged admissions of uninsured, Medicaid, and Medicare patients (Schlesinger et al., 1987). Nonpaying or low-paying patients also may be subjected to long waits and inferior facilities compared to full-paying patients.

A more subtle marketing strategy of profit-oriented hospitals is cream skimming, or the targeting of a market of highly desirable patients, typically middle- and upper-class persons with good insurance who need treatments that cost the hospital relatively little. Frills, such as cozy birth centers that provide champagne for the new parents, are advertised to attract well-insured patients. To the extent that some hospitals are successful in attracting the cream of patients, others are worse off, because their patient mix no longer includes those who are least expensive to treat.

A related form of cream skimming is the investment in specialty hospitals. By 1987 more than one-third of the 1,375 for-profit hospitals in the United States were devoted exclusively to specialty care, such as psychiatric care, treatment for substance abuse, and physical rehabilitation. This emphasis was prompted partly by the fact that specialized care is not subject to much federal cost-containment pressure; nearly all patients are privately insured, are younger than Medicare recipients, and tend to stay about three times as long as patients in acute care hospitals. Another feature that yields higher profits is that little expensive technology is required. Although the long-term profitability of specialty hospitals may be greatly reduced by government or insurer cost-containment measures, the immediate impact has been to siphon desirable patients away from general hospitals (Freudenheim, 1987b).

The nursing home industry—75 percent of which is controlled by for-profit companies—is somewhat less profitable than other specialty hospitals because it relies very heavily (over 60 percent) on government subsidies through Medicare and Medicaid. When government reimbursements were liberal, nursing home chains made huge profits and expanded rapidly. In California the average nursing home made a profit of 41 percent on net equity in 1978–1979. In those boom years, for-profit chains grew as much as 900 percent in just four years (see Harrington, 1984). Government funding became more restrictive in the 1990s; however, profit margins still outranked those in other industry groups. For example, in 1994 Manor Care had an 18 percent return on equity and a profit margin of 6.9 percent (Harrington, 1996).

The profit motive in specialty hospitals, especially those such as nursing homes and psychiatric hospitals where patients are relatively isolated and powerless, raises serious questions about the quality of care. The nursing home industry has had a long and continual history of patient neglect and abuse, physical danger, filthy conditions, and inadequate nursing care (see Harrington, 1996, for a review of the literature on quality of nursing home care). Such institutions have a very high proportion of unskilled workers, barely earning the minimum wage, with an annual turnover rate of 70 to 100 percent, leading to frequent understaffing. Understaffed nursing homes relied heavily on psychotropic drugs and physical restraints to control patients. Changed federal regulations in 1987 and 1991 significantly reduced the rate of restraint, but many nursing homes still use improper restraints. The government sanctioned 18 percent of surveyed facilities in 1993 for this violation (Harrington, 1996). Despite federal efforts to enforce standards, for-profit nursing homes provide far fewer nursing care workers—especially professional nurses—per patient than do the nonprofit and government nursing homes (Strahan, 1997).

The profit motive has also made specialty hospitals particularly prone to fraud, unethical marketing, and overcharging. For example, in 1991, Psychiatric Institutes of America, the nation's largest and most profitable chain of private psychiatric hospitals with 73 psychiatric hospitals nationwide, were implicated in systematic fraudulent practices. Investigators identified such abuses as inflating bills for medications and services, billing for services never rendered, altering diagnoses and treatments to match insurance coverage, admitting insured patients who did not need hospitalization, keeping patients against their will, and releasing patients—regardless of their condition—as soon as their insurance was exhausted (Kerr, 1991a, 1991b).

Overcharging and outright fraud contribute to the rapidly rising costs of medical care both directly, as when fraudulent Medicare claims are paid, and indirectly, as insurance companies pass on inflated costs by increases in premiums (Sparrow, 1996). Although many hospitals do not engage in such unscrupulous business practices, the added costs created by those that do are enormous. Federal, state, and local government regulatory agencies must then spend additional moneys trying to detect and control abuses of the system, adding yet more to the actual costs of the health care system. The trends toward proprietarization and corporatization are not inevitable; the government could, for example, decide to redirect funds into public health care programs or public or not-for-profit hospitals for all. These growing hospital corporations, however, wield massive political and economic force that they use to influence government policymaking to keep the hospital industry and their position in it as profitable as possible.

MEDICAL INDUSTRIES

Vast and profitable industries have developed to supply products and processes for medical care. They manufacture, distribute, and market known products while continuously researching and developing new ones. The most obvious example is the pharmaceutical industry, which markets large numbers of both prescription and over-the-counter drugs. Other industries supply everything from the simplest devices to the most complex, including monitors for various organ functions, radiological equipment, laboratory equipment, prosthetic devices, surgical equipment, medical office and hospital supplies and equipment, and intravenous solutions.

Costs

Changing medical technologies involve not only innovations in material objects (such as drugs, equipment, and devices), but also the development of new procedures and scientific and technical knowledge bases. Rapidly changing medical technology has been a major source of the increases in hospital and physician-related costs to pay for new technological equipment, to build and adapt spaces to use it, and to hire and supervise the specialized workers to operate it. Between one-third and three-quarters of increased expenditures for medical care is due to the costs of medical technology (Lassey et al., 1997).

Expenditures for prescription drugs also contributed a disproportionate amount to the rapid increase in U.S. health care expenditures. In the 1980s, the prices for prescription drugs increased more than 150 percent, or three times the rate of inflation (Novak, 1993). A considerable portion of these price increases went to corporate profits. Between 1988 and 1992, the pharmaceutical industry's pretax profits were five times the profit levels of other U.S. industries. A study done for Congress by the Office of Technology Assessment asserted in 1993 that the pharmaceutical industry had made "excess profits" of more than $2 billion per year (Freudenheim, 1993). In Britain, where government agencies limit drug prices, prescription medications cost a fraction of what the same drugs cost in the United States (Guell and Fischbaum, 1995). For example, in 1994, Premarin (a synthetic estrogen taken over a number of years by postmenopausal women) cost 9 cents per dose in Britain but 28 cents in the United States[4] (Pear, 1994). Although drug manufacturers held back price increases for two years in the mid-1990s, while Congress was debating health care reform, as soon as federal policy efforts failed, they raised their prices (and profit margins) dramatically (Freudenheim, 1995d, 1996).

New drugs are often extremely costly because they involve expensive research and development processes, including the costs of clinical trials required for federal approval, marketing, product liability insurance, as well as corporate profits. Drug manufacturers estimate that 16.7 percent of their revenues are used for research. The majority of that research is *not* devoted to finding remarkable cures, however. Much research is in order to find patentable alternatives to drugs made by rival companies or to drugs whose patent is soon to run out. FDA officials estimate that only about 40 percent of new drugs approved in 1993 represented any significant medical advancement (Rosenthal, 1993).

A more important component of the cost of pharmaceuticals in the United States is marketing expenses, which account for an estimated 20 percent of pharmaceutical corporations' entire budgets (Rosenthal, 1993). Marketing is a particularly important factor in profits on prescription drugs. Advertising aimed at the physician-prescriber attempts to achieve brand loyalty, especially when there is little real difference among the competing products. Drug companies spend, on average, more than $5,000 per doctor promoting their products (Wilkes and Shuchman, 1989). Doctors—not consumers—decide which drug to order, so drug companies have little incentive to compete by lowering prices. Some managed care programs have tried to negotiate deep discounts for pharmaceuticals in exchange for restricting covered drugs to one manufacturer's product. Unfortunately, this practice indirectly hurts persons on Medicare and others whose insurance does not cover pharmaceuticals, who must pay full drugstore prices and have no leverage

---

[4]Subsequently, after federal approval to advertise Premarin as a treatment for osteoporosis, the price was raised significantly (Freudenheim, 1995c).

to demand affordable prescriptions. Simultaneously, powerful pharmaceutical companies have bought out managed care drug benefit programs, acquiring enormous market control (Freudenheim, 1994, 1995a), further reducing incentive to compete by pricing.

One reason that many medical technologies and drugs are so expensive over the course of a patient's lifetime is that they are *"halfway" technologies*, that is, not resolutions of a problem but merely partial responses to it. For example, the iron lung was a response to some needs of polio victims but did not resolve the problem of the disease itself; a resolution came with the development of the polio vaccine. Although they may prolong some people's lives, improve some people's functioning, or hold some people's dangerous symptoms in abeyance, even impressive technological developments often do not fully resolve the medical problem for which they were invented. For example, as described in Chapter 11, end-stage renal disease (ESRD) is fatal, but dialysis technology can keep many patients alive, although it is very expensive—some $30,000 per year (Iglehart, 1993). Dialysis cannot cure the diseases that cause kidney failure, nor can it restore patients to full health. Such medical costs are, thus, not onetime expenses for a single illness episode, but rather continue to mount so long as recipients live.

Modern medicine is struggling to respond to many chronic illnesses that are not so amenable to a "technological fix" as were the acute infectious diseases prominent a few decades ago. For example, in 1993, the five top-selling prescription drugs, together generating annual U.S. sales of about $5.5 billion, included two drugs for high blood pressure, one for ulcers, one for high cholesterol, and one for depression (Freudenheim, 1993). The most frequently dispensed drugs are predominantly for chronic illnesses or conditions that the drugs are not actually able to cure: ulcers, hypertension, anxiety, heart disease, arthritis, angina, and menopause. Patients must typically take such medications for many years, often for the rest of their lives.

Some new drugs and technologies do save money, however. For example, new vaccines can prevent outbreaks of serious diseases. New screening devices can detect illnesses earlier when they are more readily cured. New inventions can make surgery safer or simpler. New drugs for conditions such as ulcers can make costly surgery unnecessary; however, whether this substitution saves money depends on whether the course of drugs is less expensive than the operation.

Another major reason for the increased costs of drugs and medical technologies has been the medicalization of problems not previously treated as medical issues (as described in Chapter 9). The medicalization of menopause, childbirth, old age, hyperactivity, alcoholism and other substance abuse, emotional troubles, and the like, has resulted in the prescription of a number of technological medical responses—drugs, devices, and procedures—that have all contributed to the greatly increased cost of treating these "conditions."

Regulation

Many interest groups are involved in the creation and utilization of new medical technologies. Three obvious parties are the manufacturers who profit from their sales, the physicians and hospitals who may choose to employ them, and the regulatory agencies that have varying degrees of power and responsibility over them. Other groups, including research scientists, political figures, media representatives, consumer groups, insurers, and patients, are also involved, sometimes in complex ways. Because of the rapid pace of technological development in medicine and the enormous economic, social, and health stakes involved, ongoing critical analysis of medical products and technologies is important. The complexity and sheer quantity of new developments, however, make it difficult for even well-endowed and powerful nations to monitor them adequately. Developing countries are far less able to evaluate and control the use of new products and technologies, so the regulation of medical products marketed by transnational corporations has become a worldwide problem.

In the United States, the Food and Drug Administration (FDA) regulates pharmaceuticals and has the power to allow or ban their sale and control their labeling; the Federal Trade Commission (FTC) has some additional regulatory authority over the content of advertising claims made for health-related products. In 1938 Congress authorized the FDA controls, but a "grandfather" clause exempted preexisting drugs from scrutiny. Drug regulations required evidence of safety and truth in labeling and, since 1962, proof of efficacy (for a fascinating account of the politics of FDA regulation, see Silverman and Lee, 1974; Silverman et al., 1992). Because of political pressures on behalf of medical industries, the FDA often relaxes its regulatory control (Collins, 1995). For example, the FDA allowed a nonsteroidal anti-inflammatory drug (such as is used for relief in chronic arthritis) to be marketed, despite the evaluation that its testing for long-term effects (especially cancer-causing effects) was seriously inadequate. In response to political pressure, the FDA further allowed the manufacturer to reword the printed warnings (to patients and their doctors) such that these possible effects—especially for chronic users—were downplayed. The drug subsequently proved seriously harmful, but the FDA did not remove it right away, because the regulatory agency gave benefit of doubt to the drug company rather than to consumers. The degree of trust that regulatory authorities invest in pharmaceutical companies and their research processes leads to inadequate protection to patients/consumers (Abraham, 1995).

Initially, only pharmaceuticals and cosmetics were regulated; in 1976 after tragedies such as the deaths from the Dalkon Shield (intrauterine device used for contraception), the FDA was given authority to regulate medical *devices*. Medical *procedures* such as new forms of surgery are not regulated or even systematically evaluated. Many technologies have not been independently evaluated for safety or effectiveness whatsoever, or they were employed widely prior to systematic evaluation and many continue to be used long after studies resulted in negative assessments. Products and technologies that have been poorly, belatedly, or negatively evaluated include electronic fetal monitors, prenatal ultrasound screening, intrauterine devices, silicon gel breast implants, oral contraceptives, an artificial heart valve, and coronary care units (Ewigman et al., 1993; Foster, 1995; Palley, 1995; Ratcliff, 1989).

Often use of a medical technology is related to a complex web of changes that are not carefully evaluated because of the influence of the *technological imperative* (that is, the belief that if we have the technological capability to do something, then we should do it). Electronic fetal monitor (EFM) technology was introduced in the late 1960s and aggressively marketed in the 1970s (prior to the existence of U.S. regulation of new medical technologies). EFM involves placing monitors (usually external) on the woman in labor to provide machine-recorded measures of fetal heart rate and strength of contractions. Many physicians were sold on the prospect of using EFM to detect early signs of "problem" deliveries, and hospitals invested in the technology as an efficient way to monitor several women in labor simultaneously (Kunisch, 1989).

Thus, long before adequate research on the effectiveness, accuracy, and side effects of EFM technology had been done, the devices had already been widely sold to hospitals throughout the United States and accepted in medical training as "good" obstetrical care. High-tech deliveries also enhanced physicians' professional prestige, legitimated obstetricians' control over the childbirth process, and justified hospital childbirth in an era in which both were being challenged (see Davis-Floyd, 1990; Treichler, 1990). Likewise, hospitals considered themselves up to date if their labor and delivery rooms were equipped with the monitoring machines. The cost of the equipment could be passed on to patients and their insurers, and often hospitals could realize profits through increased use of testing and monitoring technologies.

The decision to *buy* the monitors led almost inexorably to the decision to *use* them for all laboring women, not merely the 10 to 15 percent who might be at risk of problem deliveries. By 1994, EFM was used in 80 percent of all live births (USDHHS, 1996b). Probably the foremost reason that EFM technology became a standard for medical intervention in labor and deliveries is that machine readouts were accepted in courts as evidence against malpractice suits (Kunisch, 1989). The decision to use monitors for all births combined with the fear of malpractice suits led to a rapid increase in the rate of delivery by Caesarian section, which involves major abdominal surgery on the mother. In the first decade of EFM use, the rate of surgical deliveries more than tripled. Although the rates leveled off, the 1990 Caesarian section rate was still 23.5 percent of all deliveries, compared to 16.5 percent in 1980 before widespread use of EFM (USDHHS, 1992: 232).

Because 98.9 percent of EFM alarms are false, much of this surgery is medically unnecessary and potentially harmful to the mother (Nelson et al., 1996). Research on the accuracy and effectiveness of EFM technology, as well as the appropriateness of Caesarian sections as medical intervention, came *after* the technologies and standard procedures were already in place. Indeed, the first large-scale trial of EFM came more than 15 years after monitors had first been marketed. Despite research assessments of EFM that concluded the technology provided little benefit in low-risk labors and greatly increased rates of costly and dangerous surgery (Kunisch, 1989; see also Foster, 1995; Leary, 1995b), rates of utilization of EFM continued to increase (USDHHS, 1996b).[5] Nevertheless,

---

[5] Recent studies suggest that EFM-provoked Caesarian sections were not even preventing birth defects, as doctors hoped; babies delivered by EFM-triggered surgery were just as likely as those delivered vaginally to have cerebral palsy (Nelson et al., 1996).

because employment of EFM technology is motivated by complex and unexamined *non*medical factors, physicians and hospitals resist utilizing EFM only for high-risk cases (Banta, 1995).

Medical technologies often have harmful or undesirable side effects. They may even cause illness (iatrogenesis) and death. The evaluation of their safety is difficult, however, partly because it may take years for harmful effects to become evident. For example, in the 1940s and 1950s, unaware of the dangers of radiation, many physicians and dentists used X-rays and other radiological imaging frequently and indiscriminately, thus delivering relatively large doses of radiation to their patients. Because the effects of such radiation are cumulative and may take many years to culminate in disease, which even then may be attributable to multiple causes, the safety of early radioactive technologies was not readily questioned.

Unfortunately, although regulatory agencies have developed requirements of testing for safety before approval for marketing, there is virtually no systematic or mandatory postmarketing surveillance of adverse effects in the United States (unlike Britain, where doctors routinely report patients' experience with a particular drug). After the widespread sale of oral contraceptives, for example, it took years for the FDA to realize these drugs' role in certain cancers and sometimes fatal blood clots, because there was no coordinated monitoring of already approved drugs (Frazier and Colditz, 1995).

Safety is also always relative. The risks of dangerous side effects of a drug or procedure must be weighed against the probabilities and risks of the condition itself as well as of alternative therapies (Banta, 1995). For example, oral contraceptives carry the risk of unpleasant, dangerous, and even fatal side effects, but pregnancy and childbirth create serious health risks too. Regulators have not yet figured how to deal with the fact that safety is also relative to certain characteristics of the patient population. Regulations often restrict drugs that are unsafe for children, for example, but fail to limit those that are unsafe for the elderly (Avorn, 1995; Ray et al., 1990a). Risks must also be weighed against the potential health benefits. Dangerous side effects might be more acceptable in a drug for potentially fatal AIDS than in one for baldness, weight loss, or acne.

The importance of the powerful regulation of these new products and technologies is amply illustrated by the tragedies created by several dangerous products. Between 1958 and 1962, some 10,000 children were born with severe birth defects as a result of thalidomide, a sedative prescribed for their mothers to reduce nausea in pregnancy. The drug was not approved in the United States due to the tenacious efforts of a single medical officer with the FDA. The thalidomide disaster in Europe spurred the passage of the U.S. Drug Act of 1962 (and similar regulatory reform in the United Kingdom, where the drug had been approved) and changed the criteria for testing drug safety (Abraham, 1995; Silverman and Lee, 1974).

A similar tragedy occurred in the United States and elsewhere for children whose mothers took prescribed diethylstilbestrol (DES) during pregnancy. Between 1943 and 1970, DES, a synthetic estrogen, was widely prescribed for women in the United States, despite early and growing evidence that it was cancer causing and ineffective for preventing miscarriages. It was advertised in medical journals in the mid-1950s as "recommended as routine prophylaxis in *all* pregnancies" (quoted in Brody, 1997, emphasis in original ad). Subsequently, researchers found that DES caused iatrogenic disease in the children born to pregnant recipients and several million sons and daughters may have been thus affected (Weiss, 1983). Thus far, DES has been responsible for several hundred cases of cancers of the vagina, cervix, or testicles, but researchers are now discovering more insidious side effects, including immune system defects, urological and genital defects, and reproductive problems (Brody, 1997; Mastroiani et al., 1994).

The case of DES children illustrates the effects of poor scientific analysis and shoddy clinical trials, lack of regulatory control over doctor experimentation with unapproved drugs, and the readiness of a portion of the medical community to prescribe a potent substance that was not fully understood or proven safe and effective (Dutton et al., 1988; see also Bale, 1990; Bell, 1986, 1994; Direcks and Hoen, 1986; Apfel and Fisher, 1984). It also illustrates the difficult problem of how to adequately regulate and control an industry capable of producing dire iatrogenic effects.

The tragedies caused by the Dalkon Shield illustrate the need for greater regulation of medical devices, as well as pharmaceuticals. In 1968 the shield was entrepreneurially promoted for birth control by a respected gynecologist, who later sold the patent to Robins, a large pharmaceutical company. The government then had no effective regulation for medical devices. No agency checked the doctor's claims of safety and effectiveness, and the manufacturer had no legal accountability for using those inaccurate claims in its advertising. Several million women in the United States and overseas had the device inserted. Despite numerous reports of health- and life-threatening side effects due to the IUDs, massive infections, and dangerous abnormal pregnancies, the company did not issue physicians any warnings about its dangers until after the first documented death (Perry and Dawson, 1985; see also Dowie and Johnston, 1987; LaCheen, 1986; Yanoshik and Norsigian, 1989).

Robins continued international sales of the device for two years after lawsuits and deaths forced them to cease U.S. sales. The company offered the U.S.-sponsored development agency, AID, a 48 percent discount on bulk packages of unsterilized shields. Dalkon shields were still being inserted in new patients in developing nations through 1980 (Hartmann, 1987). In the face of extensive U.S. lawsuits (by about 200,000 eligible claimants), Robins filed for bankruptcy, limited its liability by paying $2.3 billion to a trust, and simultaneously provided its shareholders the highest rate of appreciation of any security on the New York Stock Exchange. The terms of the trust provided that some injured women would receive some payment with the amount depending, not on degree of injury, but on the number of eventual claims sharing the trust and whether the trust funds were depleted. However, there was virtually no provision for foreign women injured by the product (Sobol, 1991).

Although some evidence pertaining to safety (and effectiveness) can be deduced from the chemical properties of substances and devices, and further data can be gained from experiments on animals, medical industries and the FDA need to test innovations on human subjects. Early procedures for drug approval allowed clinical trials done under uncontrolled circumstances to be used as evidence of safety and effectiveness. Any licensed physician was permitted to experiment on patients with drugs before FDA approval, and pharmaceutical companies provided large quantities of free samples for so-called clinical trials. There are numerous professional incentives for doctors to experiment to find new applications for approved drugs; such results were publishable sources of professional prestige. Only in the 1970s, however, were experimenters required to obtain the informed consent of patients; previously many subjects did not even know that they were taking experimental drugs. Because of the great medical and commercial interest in the many aspects of women's reproductive lives, women–especially poor and Third World women–have been disproportionately used as guinea pigs in medical research (Ford, 1986; Marcelis and Shiva, 1986; Ward, 1986).

Profits and Products

The free enterprise model of technological development and marketing in the United States means the profit motive is a particularly important influence in the creation and marketing of new drugs and technologies. One critic argued that the proliferation of technological innovation is inevitable because "expansion is an absolute necessity for capitalist enterprises" (Waitzkin, 1979: 1263).

On the one hand, the quest for profits has motivated some impressive research; many technological advances of bioscientific medicine might not have occurred were it not for the investment of much research time and money. Private enterprise is not the only way a society could organize its research incentive, however. We gain much–perhaps most–of our medical advances from *government*-supported research in universities and government research centers.

On the other hand, the profit orientation has greatly *limited* the scope of research and development; the medical industries are understandably interested only in new developments that will produce marketable commodities. In recent years, the profit incentive has influenced even university and medical school research centers, which are licensing patents, becoming partners with corporate interests that manufacture and market new devices and procedures, and seeking to develop "technology parks" on their campuses. Thus, academic research centers jeopardize their ability to evaluate new technologies objectively (Wright, 1987).

Even when scientists and clinicians are not directly employed by medical industries, these corporations indirectly control their work or compromise their scientific neutrality. For example, the researcher who published an article on Retin-A (an acne medication), claiming it could reverse skin wrinkles, had received over $1 million in research and honoraria monies from Ortho Pharmaceuticals' parent company (Bell, 1992; Crossen, 1994). The British pharmaceutical manufacturer of Synthroid (taken daily by some 8 million Americans for hypothyroidism) paid University of California at San Francisco researchers to do a study that could demonstrate its superiority to similar, less expensive drugs. But when the study found that the rival drugs were just as effective, the corporation suppressed for several years, the publication of the researchers' findings which had been accepted by the *Journal of the American Medical Association* (Altman, 1997a, 1997b; King, 1996).

Another problem is that drugs to meet people's *actual* health needs are often of limited commercial interest. The industry is not likely to fund research on a cheap, readily available remedy, even when it may be the best treatment for a condition. For a drug to be profitable, it must be patentable; natural substances and shelf chemicals are not, so they are not researched, even if they may be highly effective. The search for patentable commodities also means that much research is directed to substitute drugs and/or technologies. Many "new" drugs are in fact existing drugs that are only marginally changed to justify a new patent, obtain and hold a market share, or create a new market (for instance, home use and not just hospital use).

Marketability increasingly depends on whether the cost of the drug or technology will be reimbursed by third-party payment. If HMOs and Medicare are not likely to pay for a new treatment, then companies are not likely to invest in its development (Pear, 1988). Drugs for developing nations are likewise of little commercial interest; although large numbers of people need some of these medications, researching and producing them would not be profitable. There is a worldwide surge in tuberculosis that is resistant to previously effective cures, but pharmaceutical corporations are unwilling to invest in developing new drugs, because only a tiny portion of the 8 million persons who get tuberculosis each year live in developed nations and could afford pay for expensive drugs (Altman, 1995).

This general profit orientation does not mean that individual companies always gauge all policies to maximize profits. For example, when a drug developed by Merck for parasitic worms in livestock turned out to be a safe and effective treatment for a human parasitic infection causing river blindness among more than 18 million people in Africa, Merck made the drug available without charge through the World Health Organization (Leary, 1991).

Pharmaceutical companies avoid investing in new drugs for small markets; government research institutes do most of what research is done. The federal government also heavily subsidizes and gives private industry special incentives for the production of needed pharmaceuticals for small markets, called "orphan drugs" (Asbury, 1981). Unfortunately, these government incentives led to high drug prices and windfall profits by eliminating competition without controlling prices. The 1983 Orphan Drug Act granted seven-year market monopolies to companies developing treatment for relatively rare diseases. For example, Genentech was granted orphan-drug status for its version of the human growth hormone. Its research and development costs were $45 million, but sales in the first six years of its monopoly were an estimated $580 million. Some orphan drugs, like Ceredase (the only treatment for a rare hereditary disease), are actually discovered and initially tested by nonprofit researchers rather than drug companies. Nevertheless, a monopoly for their production is protected by the Orphan Drug Act, so the producer is allowed to set whatever price it chooses. Ceredase could cost $550,000 for the first year of treatment at the recommended dosage (Arno et al., 1995).

Many drugs for AIDS-related symptoms were granted "orphan" designation, even after it became obvious that the potential market was large. Ironically, few of these drugs were actual innovations; rather, they had been tested or approved for other uses and manufacturers had only to test their effectiveness for AIDS. For example, the maker of pentamidine increased its price by 400 percent after obtaining orphan-drug protection to formulate the drug for AIDS-related pneumonia (Arno et al., 1995). As a result of such market monopolies, AIDS drugs have become far too expensive ($10,000 to 18,000 a year) for patients and their insurers; patients are forced to exhaust their resources or go without treatment (Altman, 1996; Kolata, 1996; Pear, 1997).

The U.S. government uses tax monies (more than $10 billion annually) to subsidize the research and development of drugs. For example, 34 of the 37 cancer drugs approved between 1955 and 1994 were developed with government research support. In 1995, however, the government relinquished the rights to require "reasonable pricing" on drugs thus researched, so taxpayers are not benefiting from government subsidization (Leary, 1995a; *New York Times*, 1994b).

In the United States, much medical research and new medical technological developments have been directed toward maximizing profits. Sometimes the interests of these corporations coincide with the needs of the sick, but there is no structural reason for this to occur. A market-oriented, profit-maximizing industry does not give first priority to the actual needs of the citizenry.

SOCIAL POLICY AND HUMAN RIGHTS

> Everyone has the right to a standard of living adequate for the health and well-being of himself and of his family, including food, clothing, housing and medical care and necessary social services, and the right to security in the event of unemployment, sickness, disability, widowhood, old age or other lack of livelihood in circumstances beyond his control. Motherhood and childhood are entitled to special care and assistance. . . . [Article 25 of the Universal Declaration of Human Rights, adopted and proclaimed by the General Assembly of the United Nations on 10 December, 1948]

Our society needs to consider the means to health as a basic human right that a government should provide for its citizens, just as it protects citizens' human rights to freedom of religion and freedom from political repression. To how much and what kind of health care or medical care do people have a right? Does a country not have obligations to provide universal health care, comparable to universal education? What priority should health care expenditures have, relative to other national spending on the military, education, highways, and the environment? How do we balance citizens' rights to affordable health—both the maintenance of health and the treatment of illness—against the interests of the many corporations and individuals who profit from the health care system?

Our society's health policy reflects the larger values of the nation: What kind of a people do we want to be? Perhaps the current crisis in the American health system will encourage public discourse on these broader moral and political issues.

Throughout this book, we have outlined numerous ideas about how society affects the body, health, and illness. These ideas, however, are not mere abstractions, removed from people's actual lives. Real people get sick, experience afflictions, and try to find help; real people also enjoy health, and successfully use their bodies to enrich their lives and to fulfill their goals. Even seemingly abstract social factors, such as social control, economic organization and cultural practices, are—for individuals—very real in their consequences.

The issues we raise in this text suggest the diverse points at which social arrangements might be changed to help reach the goal of a healthier society. We hope we have stimulated readers to consider many ways to promote health in this society and globally. It is necessary to have a genuinely holistic understanding of the connections between the mind, body, and society to envision the far-ranging possibilities for enhancing health. We need to go way beyond narrow medical conceptions of health and to appreciate the entire web of socioenvironmental contexts that promote health. From such a holistic perspective, we might not only imagine changes in obvious problem areas, such as nutrition, water pollution, occupational health, and health care financing, but also consider possible health-promoting alterations in areas such as urban landscapes, automobile design, dependent care programs, media messages, and uses of leisure. A broad, holistic perspective to health transforms our ways of thinking about what is relevant to health and to illness prevention.

Similarly, we have suggested points of influence for improvements in the prevention and treatment of illness. Because power is such a pivotal factor in both illness causation and treatment, when we envision healthier alternative social arrangements, we should give special attention to considering changes in the exercise of power and to social arrangements that encourage the *empowerment* of individuals. Likewise, we have noted the importance of access to resources to stay healthy or to get well. Alternative scenarios for a healthier society need to pay close attention to *social inequalities* and the way we choose to distribute the resources necessary to be well or to be alive.

Although the social arrangements that influence our health may seem remote and objectlike, they are human products and as such can be humanly changed. It is necessary, however, for us to move beyond the boundaries of our individual lives to effect many measures that potentially have a wide-ranging ability to prevent illness and death. Our purpose in examining the institutional sources of illness and problems in health care is not to blame but rather to suggest some of the points at which social structure and social policy can be changed. Understanding the complex interrelationships of these arrangements prevents naïve notions that an isolated new program, policy change, or medical innovation will alone produce dramatic changes in people's health. Although most envisioned changes are matters of policy and social organization, some needed changes are embedded in cultural values and stubbornly change-resistant social structures; while still human products, they often change more slowly. Nevertheless, becoming aware of the human sources of the social arrangements that shape our lives is a first step in making effective efforts to change those forces.

SUMMARY

As American medicine has become increasingly specialized and reliant on advanced technology, large-scale organizations such as hospitals, insurance companies, health maintenance organizations, and medical industries have consolidated their power and economic interests. The corporatization of hospitals has changed the economic situation for patients and affected the autonomy of physicians and other health care professionals. Insurance companies and managed care corporations have become powerful agents in the health care system, creating regulations and controlling access to health services. In an array of poorly articulated programs, government agencies are also significant third-party payers and direct providers of health services. Medical industries, especially those researching and developing new pharmaceuticals and technologies, have substantial economic interests in health-related markets. Always a loosely regulated, relatively unplanned, laissez-faire arrangement, the American health system is now powerfully dominated by large for-profit industries.

This system has resulted in major problems of access and cost. The quality of care available under the system is mixed; much is outstanding, but much is terrible. Although the poor receive generally lower-quality medical care, spending lots of money on medical services does not guarantee good quality. Structural incentives, which are related to profitability, are responsible for both the achievements and failures of the American medical system. The problems of the American system clearly illustrate a key theme emphasized throughout this volume: Health and illness are socially produced, especially by structural features of power and stratification.

RECOMMENDED READINGS

Articles

H. DAVID BANTA, "Technology assessment in health care," pp. 401–421 in A. R. Kovner, ed., *Jonas's Health Care Delivery in the United States*. New York: Springer, 1995.
THOMAS BODENHEIMER AND KEVIN GRUMBACH, "Paying for health care," pp. 273–281 in P. Conrad, ed., *The Sociology of Health and Illness*. New York: St. Martin's Press, 1997.
KAREN DAVIS, "Inequality and access to health care." *The Milbank Quarterly* 69(2), 1991: 253–273.
JAMES R. KNICKMAN AND KENNETH E. THORPE, "Financing for health care," pp. 267–293 in A. R. Kovner, ed., *Jonas's Health Care Delivery in the United States*. New York: Springer, 1995.
J. WARREN SALMON, "A perspective on the corporate transformation of health care." *International Journal of Health Services* 25(1), 1995: 11–42.

Books

BRADFORD GRAY, *The Profit Motive and Patient Care: The Changing Accountability of Doctors and Hospitals*. Cambridge, MA: Harvard University Press, 1991. A useful analysis of various ways the pursuit of profit affects the contemporary health care system.
CHARLES E. ROSENBERG, *The Care of Strangers: The Rise of America's Hospital System*. New York: Basic, 1987. A fascinating social history of hospitals and the place of various medical professions within them; it offers an excellent background for understanding contemporary policy issues.

LITERATURE
IN THE SOCIOLOGY
OF HEALTH AND ILLNESS

I. Social science journals in health and illness

Anthropology and Medicine (Carfax Publishing), quarterly

Culture, Medicine, and Psychiatry (D. Reidel), quarterly

Health: An Interdisciplinary Journal for the Social Study of Health, Illness, and Medicine (Sage Publications), quarterly

International Journal of Health Services (Baywood), quarterly

Journal of Health and Social Behavior (American Sociological Association), quarterly

Medical Anthropology Quarterly (American Anthropological Association and Society for Medical Anthropology), quarterly

Qualitative Health Research (Sage Publications), quarterly

Social Science & Medicine (Pergamon Press [United Kingdom]), 24 issues per year

Sociology of Health and Illness: A Journal of Medical Sociology (Basil Blackwell [United Kingdom]), quarterly

Women and Health (Haworth Press), quarterly

II. Sources on current issues, social policy, and health ethics

Critical Public Health (Carfax Publishers), quarterly

Disability Studies Quarterly (Sawyer School of Management), quarterly

Hastings Center Reports (The Hastings Center), bimonthly

Health/PAC Bulletin (Health Policy Advisory Committee), bimonthly

Health Affairs (Project HOPE), bimonthly

Journal of Health Politics, Policy, and Law (Duke University, Department of Health Administration), quarterly

Milbank Quarterly (Milbank Memorial Fund), quarterly

III. Medical and public health journals

American Journal of Public Health (American Public Health Association), monthly

Journal of Public Health Policy (National Association for Public Health Policy), quarterly

The Lancet (Lancet [United Kingdom]), weekly

Medical Care (American Public Health Association, Medical Care Section), monthly

New England Journal of Medicine (Massachusetts Medical Society), weekly

IV. Periodicals with good coverage of health and health policy issues

The Economist (United Kingdom), monthly
The New York Times, daily
The Wall Street Journal, daily

V. Newsletters and magazines

Berkeley Wellness Letter, University of California, School of Public Health, monthly
Ragged Edge (Advocado Press), bimonthly
Health Facts (Center for Medical Consumers), monthly
Health Letter (Public Citizen's Health Research Group), monthly
The Network News (National Women's Health Network), bimonthly
Rehab Brief (U.S. Department of Education, National Institute on Disability and Rehabilitation Research), monthly
The Swedish Information Service, occasional fact sheets

VI. Sources of current statistical data

United Nations Educational, Scientific and Cultural Organization:
    Statistical Yearbook, annual
U.S. Department of Commerce, Bureau of the Census:
    Statistical Abstract of the United States, annual
    U.S. Census of Population, every ten years
    Current Population Reports, occasional reports between decennial censuses
U.S. Department of Health and Human Services, Public Health Service, Centers for Disease Control, National Center for Health Statistics:
    Advance Data, regular reports of data from Vital and Health Statistics, with analysis
    Health, United States, annual compendium of data on health and health care
    Monthly Vital Statistics Report
    Morbidity and Mortality Weekly Report (publication of the Center for Disease Control in Atlanta, Georgia)
    Vital Statistics of the United States, annual report
    Vital and Health Statistics, occasional reports

B

VISUAL RESOURCES

We have found visual resources, such as films and videos, to be invaluable in teaching the sociology of health and illness. Many of these resources are available in multiple formats (film, VHS, 3/4-inch video). Listed here are the formats we have used, but distributors or film libraries may offer others.

Asbestos: The Way to Dusty Death. ABC News Production, 1978, 16 mm, 52 minutes, color. Depicts effects of asbestos, environmental and occupational health issues, and the politics of regulation.

Borderline Medicine. Baxley Media, 1991, VHS, 58 minutes, color. Examines Canadian National Health Insurance as a model for the United States.

Brain, The. WNET, 1984, VHS, each episode 60 minutes, color. The fourth episode, "Stress and Emotion," describes the physiology of stress and how one's sense of control affects capacity to deal with stresses.

Can't Afford to Grow Old. Filmakers Library, 1990, VHS, 55 minutes, color. Examines the social policy issues surrounding long-term care, Medicare and Medicaid, and a medicalized old age and death.

Captives of Care. Australian Film Commission, 1973, 16 mm, 50 minutes, color. Docudrama that dramatizes the struggles for autonomy and independence of residents of an institution for persons with disabilities, many of whom were involved in making the film.

Clockwork. California Newsreel, 1982, VHS, 25 minutes, color. Demonstrates the impact of factory production management techniques, from early Taylorism to contemporary computer-assisted regulation.

Crisis at General Hospital. PBS Video, 1984, VHS, color. Examines the impact of inadequate funding for health care, especially for hospitals serving the urban, underinsured poor populations.

Deadly Deception: The Tuskegee Study of Untreated Syphilis in the Negro Male, The. WGBH/Films for the Humanities and Sciences, 1993, VHS, 56 minutes, color. Documentary on a large-scale ethically questionable biomedical research project and its social aftermath.

D.E.S.: An Uncertain Legacy. National Film Board of Canada and University of California, 16 ram, 3/4-inch video, and VHS, 58 minutes, color. Examines the development, use, and subsequent iatrogenic problems of the artificial hormone diethylstilbestrol.

Doctors and Dollars. PBS, 1993, VHS, 57 minutes, color. Depicts the issues involved in doctors' self-referral and conflicts of interest.

Does Doctor Know Best? Annenberg/CPB, 1989. VHS, 60 minutes, color. Using a case study, panel discusses critical ethical and medical issues in doctor-patient relationships.

Ending Hunger in the Garden State: Recommendations and Reform. New Jersey Commission on Hunger, 1987, VHS, 35 minutes, color. Probes the extent of the problem of hunger and various responses in one of the wealthiest states.

Famine Within. Direct Cinema, Ltd., 1990, VHS, 50 minutes, color. Documentary about women, food, body image, and eating disorders.

Healing and the Mind. PBS/Ambrose Video, 1993, VHS, color. Five-part series. Bill Moyers explores Chinese healing approaches, research on mind-body connections, nonmedical therapies, and U.S. experiences with the importance of the social-emotional factors in health and healing.

Health Care Rationing. PBS, 1991, VHS, 58 minutes, color. Compares the case of Oregon's efforts to devise a fair system for rationing health care for the poor with the situation of Chicago inner-city poor people whose access to health care is denied by the de facto system of rationing according to who can pay.

Hospice: An Alternative Way to Care for the Dying. Billy Budd Films, 1979, 16 mm, 25 minutes, color. Documents the hospice movement, which emphasizes holistic caring for the dying patient and family, typically in the home.

Inventing Reality. PBS/Millennium series, no. 8, 1992, VHS, 60 minutes, color. Depicts the healing approaches of a Mexican Huichol shaman, in comparison with an innovative Canadian cancer treatment center, underlining differences of underlying assumptions of nonbiomedical healing systems.

Medicine at the Crossroads. WNET and BBE Productions, 1993, VHS eight-part series, each episode 60 minutes, color. The episodes "The Code of Silence" on doctor-patient communication and "Life Support" on the ethics of death and aging in various countries are very relevant.

Mind, The. WNET, 1988, VHS, each episode 60 minutes, color. The episodes "Aging" and "Pain and Healing" are particularly useful.

Pharmaceuticals: For Export Only. Richter Productions, VHS (English and Spanish versions), 57 minutes, color. Discusses pharmaceuticals that have been banned or highly restricted in the United States, but are still produced here for export to Third World countries, which have little effective means to control or ban these substances that harm public health.

Plagued: A Series on Disease and Society. Film Australia (distributed by Filmakers Library), 1994, four 52-minute videos, color. A historical and cross-cultural analysis of plagues and new diseases. Part 1 is disappointing and of questionable accuracy; parts 2 and 3 are good for the social history of epidemics; part 4 discusses AIDS and syphilis in a comparative perspective.

Politics of Food, The. Yorkshire Television, 1988, VHS, 2 hours, color. Covers political sources of hunger and famine, problems with food aid, politics and agricultural policies, and alternative political approaches.

Prescriptions for Profit. PBS, 1989, VHS, 60 minutes, color. Questions marketing practices of the pharmaceutical industry.

Setting Limits. Medical University of South Carolina, 1988, VHS, 47 minutes. Lecture by ethicist Daniel Callahan about the proper ends of medicine and appropriate medical care for the aged and dying.

Skin Horse, The. Central Independent Television PIC, 1983, VHS, 60 minutes, color. Evocative documentary that deals with sexuality and disability.

Social Status and Health. Films for the Humanities and Sciences, 1997, VHS, 25 minutes, color. Illustrates some of the research (described in Chapters 2 and 3) on how important socioeconomic status is as a factor in health and illness.

Song of the Canary. New Day Films, 1978, 16 mm, 57 minutes, color. Provocatively examines occupational health problems, using case studies of chemical and textile workers.

Taking Our Bodies Back: The Women's Health Movement. Cambridge Documentary Films, 1974, 16 mm, 33 minutes, color. Examines the development and issues of the women's health movement; contains graphic material about self-help techniques and abortion.

Titticut Follies. Zipporah Films, 1967, 16 mm, 89 minutes, black and white. Frederick Wiseman's controversial cinéma verité documentary (no narration) about a hospital for the criminally insane that illustrates a total institution, with different worlds of staff and inmates.

To Taste a Hundred Herbs. New Day Films, 1986, 16 mm, 58 minutes, color. Portrays the linkage of traditional Chinese medicine, religion, Chinese village life, and the role of the doctor.

When Billy Broke His Head and Other Tales of Wonder. Fanlight Productions, 1994, VHS, 57 minutes, color. Narrated and directed by Billy Golfus who was brain injured, this video looks at the "invisibility" of people with disabilities and barriers to access and social inclusion they encounter.

Who Lives, Who Dies. Public Policy Productions, 1987, VHS, 60 minutes, color. Explores the crisis in the U.S. health care system, and raises issues of health care spending, equity, rationing, and priorities in national spending.

APPENDIX

BIBLIOGRAPHY

ABEL, EMILY K.
1991 *Who Cares for the Elderly? Public Policy and the Experiences of Adult Daughters.* Philadelphia: Temple University Press.

ABEL-SMITH, BRIAN
1992 "Cost containment and new priorities in the European Community," *The Milbank Quarterly* 70(3): 393–415.

ABLON, JOAN
1986 "Reactions of Samoan burn patients and families to severe burns," pp. 163–180 in C. Currer and M. Stacey, eds., *Concepts of Health, Illness and Disease.* Leamington Spa: Berg.

ABRAHAM, JOHN
1995 *Science, Politics and the Pharmaceutical Industry: Controversy and Bias in Drug Regulation.* London: UCL Press.

ADAMS, MIRIAM E.
1995 "Kidney transplantation," pp. 79–91 in H. S. Frazier and F. Mosteller, eds., *Medicine Worth Paying For: Assessing Medical Innovations.* Cambridge, MA: Harvard University Press.

ADAMS, ORVILL
1993 "Understanding the health care system that works," pp. 113–141 in A. Bennett and O. Adams, eds., *Looking North for Health: What We Can Learn from Canada's Health Care System.* San Francisco: Jossey-Bass.

ADER, ROBERT, DAVID L. FELTEN, AND NICHOLAS COHEN
1991 *Psychoneuroimmunology* (2nd ed.). New York: Academic Press.

AIKEN, LINDA H., JULIE SOCHALSKI, AND GERARD F. ANDERSON
1996 "Downsizing the hospital nursing workforce," *Health Affairs* 15(4): 88–92.

ÅKERSTEDT, TORBJÖRN
1990 "Psychological and psychophysiological effects of shift work," *Scandinavian Journal of Work, Environment and Health* 16 (supplement): 67–73.

AKULA, JOHN L.
1997 "Insolvency risk in health carriers: Innovation, competition, and public protection," *Health Affairs* 16(1): 9–33.

ALBRECHT, GARY L., AND JUDITH A. LEVY
1982 "The professionalization of osteopathy: Adaptation in the medical marketplace," *Research in the Sociology of Health Care* 2: 161–202.

ALBRECHT, GARY L., DAVID SLOBODKIN, AND ROBERT J. RYDMAN
1996 "The role of emergency departments in American health care," *Research in the Sociology of Health Care* 13B: 289–316.

326

ALEXANDER, JACQUI
1988   "The ideological construction of risk: An analysis of corporate health programs in the 1980s," *Social Science and Medicine* 26(5): 559–567.

ALEXANDER, LINDA
1982   "Illness maintenance and the new American sick role," pp. 351–367 in N. J. Chrisman and T. W. Maretzki, eds., *Clinically Applied Anthropology*. Dordrecht, Netherlands: D. Reidel.

ALTMAN, LAWRENCE K.
1988   "U.S. moves to improve death certificate," *New York Times*, October 18.
1995   "As TB surges, drug producers face criticism," *New York Times*, September 18.
1996   "New AIDS therapies arise, but who can afford the bill?" *New York Times*, February 6.
1997a   "Drug firm, relenting, allows unflattering study to appear," *New York Times*, April 16.
1997b   "Experts see bias in drug data," *New York Times*, April 29.

ALTMAN, LAWRENCE, AND ELISABETH ROSENTHAL
1990   "Changes in medicine bring pain to healing profession," *New York Times*, February 18.

ALTMAN, STUART H., AND MARC A. RODWIN
1988   "Halfway competitive markets and ineffective regulation: The American health care system," *Journal of Health Politics, Policy and Law* 13(2): 323–339.

AMERICAN AUTOMOBILE MANUFACTURERS ASSOCIATION
1996   *Motor Vehicle Facts and Figures*. Detroit: American Automobile Manufacturers Association.

AMERICAN PSYCHIATRIC ASSOCIATION
1987   *Diagnostic and Statistical Manual of Mental Disorders* (3rd ed., rev.). Washington, DC: American Psychiatric Association.

ANDERSON, RONALD, MEEI-SHIA CHEN, LU ANNE ADAY, AND LLEWELLYN CORNELIUS
1987   "Health status and medical care utilization," *Health Affairs* 6(1): 136–156.

ANDREWS, AHMED, AND NICK JEWSON
1993   "Ethnicity and infant deaths: The implications of recent statistical evidence for materialist explanations," *Sociology of Health and Illness* 15(2): 137–156.

ANGEL, RONALD
1989   "The health of the Mexican origin population," pp. 82–94 in P. Brown, ed., *Perspectives in Medical Sociology*. Belmont, CA: Wadsworth.

ANGEL, RONALD, AND PEGGY THOITS
1987   "The impact of culture on the cognitive structure of illness," *Culture, Medicine, and Psychiatry* 11(4): 465–494.

ANGIER, NATALIE
1991   "Cancer increases among children," *International Herald Tribune*, June 27: 5.
1997   "In a culture of hysterectomies, many question their necessity," *New York Times*, February 17.

ANSPACH, RENEE
1988   "Notes on the sociology of medical discourse: The language of case presentation," *Journal of Health and Social Behavior* 29: 357–375.
1993   *Deciding Who Lives: Fateful Choices in the Intensive-Care Nursery*. Berkeley: University of California Press.

ANTONOVSKY, AARON
1979 *Health, Stress and Coping.* San Francisco: Jossey-Bass.
1984 "The sense of coherence as a determinant of health," *Advances* 1(3): 37–50.
1987 *Unraveling the Mystery of Health: How People Manage Stress and Stay Well.* San Francisco: Jossey-Bass.
1990 "Personality and health: Testing the sense of coherence model," pp. 155–177 in H. S. Friedman, ed., *Personality and Disease.* New York: Wiley.

APFEL, ROBERTA, AND SUSAN M. FISHER
1984 *To Do No Harm: DES and the Dilemmas of Modern Medicine.* New Haven: Yale University Press.

ARIÈS, PHILIPPE
1974 *Western Attitudes Toward Death: From the Middle Ages to the Present.* Baltimore: Johns Hopkins University Press.

ARIES, NANCY, AND LOUANNE KENNEDY
1986 "The health labor force: The effects of change," pp. 196–207 in P. Conrad and R. Kern, eds., *The Sociology of Health and Illness.* New York: St. Martin's Press.

ARMSTRONG, DAVID
1983 *Political Anatomy of the Body: Medical Knowledge in Britain in the Twentieth Century.* Cambridge: Cambridge University Press.

ARNO, PETER S., KAREN BONUCK, AND MICHAEL DAVIS
1995 "Rare diseases, drug development, and AIDS: The impact of the Orphan Drug Act," *The Milbank Quarterly* 73(2): 231–251.

ARONOWITZ, ROBERT A.
1991 "Lyme disease: The social construction of a new disease and its social consequences," *The Milbank Quarterly* 69(1): 79–112.

ASBURY, CAROLYN H.
1981 "Medical drugs of limited commercial interest: Profit alone is a bitter pill," *International Journal of Health Services* 11(3): 451–462.

ASHTON, HEATHER
1991 "Psychotropic drug prescribing for women," *British Journal of Psychiatry* 158 (S10): 30–35.

ATKINSON, PAUL
1978 "From honey to vinegar: Lévi-Strauss in Vermont," pp. 168–188 in P. Morley and R. Wallis, eds., *Culture and Curing.* Pittsburgh: University of Pittsburgh Press.

ATKINSON, THOMAS, RAMSAY LIEM, AND JOAN LIEM
1986 "The social costs of unemployment: Implications for social support," *Journal of Health and Social Behavior* 27: 317–331.

ATTIE, ILANA, AND J. BROOKS-GUNN
1987 "Weight concerns as chronic stressors in women," pp. 218–254 in R. Barnett, L. Biener, and G. K. Baruch, eds., *Gender and Stress.* New York: Free Press.

AVORN, JERRY
1995 "Medication use and the elderly," *Health Affairs* 14(1): 276–287.

BACK, AARON
1981 *Occupational Stress: The Inside Story.* Oakland, CA: Institute for Labor and Mental Health.

BADGLEY, ROBIN F.
1991   "Social and economic disparities under Canadian health care," *International Journal of Health Services* 21(4): 659–671.
BAER, HANS A.
1984   "A comparative view of a heterodox health system: Chiropractic in America and Britain," *Medical Anthropology* 8: 151–168.
1992   "The potential rejuvenation of American naturopathy as a consequence of the holistic health movement," *Medical Anthropology* 13: 369–383.
BAIRD, VANESSA
1992   "Difference and defiance," *New Internationalist* 233 (July): 4–7.
BAKAL, DONALD A.
1979   *Psychology and Medicine.* New York: Springer.
BAKER, COLIN, AND JOSEPH NEWHOUSE
1995   "Cost," pp. 155–172 in D. Calkins, R. J. Fernandopulle, and B. S. Marino, eds., *Health Care Policy.* Cambridge, MA: Blackwell Science.
BAKER, DEAN
1981   "The use and health consequences of shift work," pp. 107–122 in V. Navarro and D. M. Berman, eds., *Health and Work Under Capitalism: An International Perspective.* Farmingdale, NY: Baywood.
BAKER, LAURENCE C.
1996   "Differences in earnings between male and female physicians," *The New England Journal of Medicine* 334 (15): 960–964.
BAKER, SUSAN B., STEPHEN TERET, AND ERICH M. DAUB
1987   "Injuries," pp. 177–206 in S. R. Levine and A. Lilienfeld, eds., *Epidemiology and Health Policy.* New York: Tavistock.
BALE, ANTHONY
1990   "Women's toxic experience," pp. 411–439 in R. D. Apple, ed., *Women, Health, and Medicine in America: A Historical Handbook.* New York: Garland.
BANKS, CAROLINE GILES
1992   " 'Culture' in culture-bound syndromes: The case of anorexia nervosa," *Social Science and Medicine* 34(8): 867–884.
BANTA, H. DAVID
1986   "Medical technology and developing countries: The case of Brazil," *International Journal of Health Services* 16(3): 363–373.
1995   "Technology assessment in health care," pp. 401–421 in A. R. Kovner, ed., *Jonas's Health Care Delivery in the United States.* New York: Springer.
BANTA, H. DAVID, AND BRYAN LUCE
1993   *Health Care Technology and Its Assessment: An International Perspective.* Oxford: Oxford University Press.
BARCHAS, PATRICIA, AND SALLY P. MENDOZA, EDS.
1984a   *Social Cohesion: Essays Toward a Sociophysiological Perspective.* Westport, CT: Greenwood.
1984b   *Social Hierarchies: Essays Toward a Sociophysiological Perspective.* Westport, CT: Greenwood.
BARER, MORRIS L.
1995   "So near, and yet so far: A Canadian perspective on U.S. health care reform," *Journal of Health Politics, Policy and Law* 20(2): 463–476.
BARKER-BENFIELD, BEN
1975   "Sexual surgery in late nineteenth-century America," *International Journal of Health Services* 5(2): 279–298.

BARNET, RICHARD J., AND RONALD E. MUELLER
1974   *Global Reach.* New York: Simon & Schuster.

BARNOUW, ERIK
1978   *The Sponsor: Notes on a Modern Potentate.* New York: Oxford University Press.

BARRACLOUGH, SOLON L.
1991   *An End to Hunger? The Social Origins of Food Strategies.* London: Zed Books.

BARRINGER, FELICITY
1992   "Among elderly, men's prospects are the brighter," *New York Times,* November 10.
1993   "Pride in a soundless world: Deaf oppose a hearing aid," *New York Times,* May 16.

BARRON, JAMES
1989   "Unnecessary Surgery," *New York Times Magazine,* April 16, pp. 25–26, 43–46.

BARTON, L., ED.
1996   *Disability and Society.* London: Longman.

BARTROP, R. W., L. LAZARUS, L. LUCKHURST, L. KILOH, AND R. PENNY
1977   "Depressed lymphocyte function after bereavement," *Lancet* 1(8,016): 834–836.

BATES, MARYANN S.
1987   "Ethnicity and pain: A biocultural model," *Social Science and Medicine* 24(1): 47–50.

BECERRA, JOSÉ, CAROL J. R. HOGUE, HANI K. ATRASH, AND NILSA PEREZ
1991   "Infant mortality among Hispanics: A portrait of heterogeneity," *Journal of the American Medical Association* 265(2): 217–221.

BECKER, E. LOVELL
1986   *International Dictionary of Medicine and Biology.* New York: Wiley.

BECKER, GAY, AND ROBERT D. NACHTIGALL
1992   "Eager for medicalisation: The social production of infertility as a disease," *Sociology of Health and Illness* 14(4): 456–471.

BECKER, HOWARD
1963   *Outsiders: Studies in the Sociology of Deviance.* New York: Free Press.
1967   "History, culture, and subjective experience: An exploration of the social bases of drug-induced experiences," *Journal of Health and Social Behavior* 8(3): 163–176.

BECKER, HOWARD, BLANCHE GEER, EVERETT HUGHES, AND ANSELM STRAUSS
1961   *Boys in White.* Chicago: University of Chicago Press.

BECKMAN, HOWARD, AND R. M. FRANKL
1984   "The effects of physician's behavior on the collection of data," *Annals of Internal Medicine* 101(5): 692–696.

BEECHER, HENRY K.
1956   "Relationship of the significance of wound to the pain experience," *Journal of the American Medical Association* 161: 1604–1613.
1959   *Measurement of Subjective Responses: Quantitative Effects of Drugs.* New York: Oxford University Press.

BELL, ROBERT
1992   *Impure Science: Fraud, Compromise and Political Influence in Scientific Research.* New York: Wiley.

BELL, SUSAN E.
1986   "A new model of medical technology development: A case study of DES," *Research in the Sociology of Health Care* 4: 1–32.

1990   "Changing ideas: The medicalization of menopause," pp. 43–63 in R. Formanek, ed., *The Meanings of Menopause: Historical, Medical and Clinical Perspectives.* Hillsdale, NJ: The Analytic Press.

1994   "From local to global: Resolving uncertainty about the safety of DES in menopause," *Research in Sociology of Health Care* 11: 41–56.

BENCOMO, CHRISTOPHER, CARLOS TREJO, AND DAVID CALKINS

1995   "Physicians," pp. 12–39 in D. Calkins, R.J. Fernandopulle, and B.S. Marino, eds., *Health Care Policy.* Cambridge, MA: Blackwell Science.

BENDELOW, GILLIAN A.

1993   "Pain perceptions, emotions and gender," *Sociology of Health and Illness* 15(3): 273–294.

BENDELOW, GILLIAN A., AND SIMON J. WILLIAMS

1995   "Transcending the dualisms: Towards a sociology of pain," *Sociology of Health and Illness* 17(2): 139–165.

BENNETT, JON, AND SUSAN GEORGE

1987   *The Hunger Machine: The Politics of Food.* Cambridge: Polity Press.

BENOIST, JEAN, AND PASCAL CATHEBRAS

1993   "The body: From an immateriality to another," *Social Science and Medicine* 36(7): 857–865.

BERESFORD, ERIC B.

1991   "Uncertainty and the shaping of medical decisions," *Hastings Center Report* (July–August): 6–11.

BERG, MARC

1996   "Practices of reading and writing: The constitutive role of the patient record in medical work," *Sociology of Health & Illness* 18(4): 499–524.

BERGER, PETER

1967   *The Sacred Canopy: Elements of a Sociological Theory of Religion.* Garden City, NY: Doubleday.

BERGER, PETER, AND THOMAS LUCKMANN

1967   *The Social Construction of Reality.* Garden City, NY: Doubleday.

BERGSMA, JURRIT

1982   *Health Care: Its Psychosocial Dimensions.* Pittsburgh: Duquesne University Press.

BERKI, SYLVESTER E.

1986   "A look at catastrophic medical expenses and the poor," *Health Affairs* 5(4): 138–145.

BERKMAN, LISA F., AND S. LEONARD SYME

1979   "Social networks, host resistance, and mortality: A nine-year follow-up study of Alameda County residents," *American Journal of Epidemiology* 109: 186–204.

BERLANT, JEFFREY L.

1975   *Profession and Monopoly: A Study of Medicine in Great Britain and the United States.* Berkeley: University of California Press.

BERLINER, HOWARD S.

1975   "A larger perspective on the Flexner Report," *International Journal of Health Services* 5(4): 573–592.

1976   "Starr wars," *International Journal of Health Services* 13(4): 671–675.

BERMAN, DANIEL M.

1978   *Death on the Job: Occupational Health and Safety Struggles in the United States.* New York: Monthly Review Press.

BIELIAUSKAS, LINAS
    1982   *Stress and Its Relationship to Health and Illness.* Boulder, CO: Westview.
BIRD, CHLOE I.
    1996   "An analysis of gender differences in income among dentists, physicians, and veterinarians in 1987," *Research in the Sociology of Health Care* 13A: 31–61.
BIRD, CHLOE I., AND ALLEN M. FREMONT
    1991   "Gender, time use, and health," *Journal of Health and Social Behavior* 32(2): 114–129.
BIRKE, LYNDA
    1986   *Women, Feminism and Biology: The Feminist Challenge.* New York: Methuen.
BLACK, DOUGLAS
    1980   *Inequalities in Health: Report of a Research Working Group.* London: Department of Health and Social Services.
BLAIR, ALAN
    1993   "Social class and the contextualization of illness experience," pp. 27–48 in A. Radley, ed., *Worlds of Illness.* New York: Routledge.
BLAXTER, MILDRED
    1983   "The causes of disease: Women talking," *Social Science and Medicine* 17: 59–69.
    1990   *Health and Lifestyles.* New York: Tavistock/Routledge.
    1993   "Why do the victims blame themselves?" pp. 124–142 in A. Radley, ed., *Worlds of Illness.* New York: Routledge.
BLAXTER, MILDRED, AND ELIZABETH PATERSON
    1982   *Mothers and Daughters: A Three-Generational Study of Health Attitudes and Behavior.* London: Heinemann.
BLENDON, ROBERT J., KAREN DONELAN, ROBERT LEITMAN, ARNOLD EPSTEIN, JOEL CANTOR, ALAN COHEN, IAN MORRISON, THOMAS MOLONEY, CHRISTIAN KOECK, AND SAMUEL LEVITT
    1993   "Physician perspectives on caring for patients in the United States, Canada, and West Germany," *New England Journal of Medicine* 328 (14): 1011–1016.
BLENDON, ROBERT J., JOHNSON BENSON, KAREN DONELAN, ROBERT LEITMAN, HUMPHREY TAYLOR, CHRISTIAN KOECK, AND DANIEL GITTERMAN
    1995   "Who has the best health care system? A second look," *Health Affairs* 14(4): 220–230.
BLENDON, ROBERT J., ROBERT LEITMAN, IAN MORRISON, AND KAREN DONELAN
    1990   "Satisfaction with health systems in ten nations," *Health Affairs* 9(2): 185–192.
BLOOR, MICHAEL
    1976   "Bishop Berkeley and the adenotonsillectomy enigma: An exploration of variation in the social construction of medical disposals," *Sociology: The Journal of the British Sociological Association* 10(1): 43–61.
    1991   "A minor office: The variable and socially constructed character of death certification in a Scottish city," *Journal of Health and Social Behavior* 32(3): 273–287.
    1995   *The Sociology of HIV Transmission.* Thousand Oaks, CA: Sage.
BLOOR, MICHAEL, M. SAMPHIER, AND L. PRIOR
    1987   "Artefact explanations of inequalities in health: An assessment of the evidence," *Sociology of Health and Illness* 9(3): 231–263.
BLYTON, PAUL
    1985   *Changes in Working Time: An International Review.* New York: St. Martin's Press.

BODENHEIMER, THOMAS S.
1990   "Should we abolish the private health insurance industry?" *International Journal of Health Services* 20(2): 199–220.

BODENHEIMER, THOMAS, AND KEVIN GRUMBACH
1997   "Paying for health care," pp. 273–281 in P. Conrad, ed., *The Sociology of Health and Illness.* New York: St. Martin's Press.

BOGIN, MEG
1982   *The Path to Pain Control.* Boston: Houghton Mifflin.

BOHUS, B., J. M. KOOLHAAS, AND S. M. KORTE
1991   "Psychosocial stress, anxiety and depression: Physiological and neuroen-docrine correlates in animal models," pp. 120–138 in A. R. Genazzani, G. Nappi, F. Petraglia, and E. Martignoni, eds., *Stress and Related Disorders: From Adaptation to Dysfunction.* Park Ridge, NJ: Parthenon.

BOLOGH, ROSLYN
1981   "Grounding the alienation of self and body: A critical, phenomenological analysis of the patient in western medicine," *Sociology of Health and Illness* 3(2): 188–206.

BOLTON, RALPH
1989   "Introduction: The AIDS pandemic, a global emergency," *Medical Anthropology* 10: 93–104.

BOND, PATRICK, AND ROBERT WEISSMAN
1997   "The costs of mergers and acquisitions in the U.S. health care sector," *International Journal of Health Services* 27(1): 77–87.

BOOKCHIN, MURRAY
1962   *Our Synthetic Environment.* New York: Harper & Row.

BORDO, SUSAN
1990   "Reading the slender body," pp. 83–112 in M. Jacobus, E. F. Keller, and S. Shuttleworth, eds., *Body/Politics: Women and the Discourses of Science.* New York: Routledge.
1993   *Unbearable Weight: Feminism, Western Culture, and the Body.* Berkeley: University of California Press.

BOSTON WOMEN'S HEALTH COLLECTIVE
1992   *Our Bodies, Our Selves* (rev. ed.). New York: Simon & Schuster.

BOTKIN, DANIEL B., AND EDWARD A. KELLER
1982   *Environmental Studies.* Columbus, OH: Charles E. Merrill.

BOWLES, CHERYL L.
1990   "The menopausal experience: Sociocultural influences and theoretical models," pp. 157–175 in R. Formanek, *The Meanings of Menopause: Historical, Medical and Clinical Perspectives.* Hillsdale, NJ: Analytic Press.

BRADSHER, KEITH
1995   "Rise in uninsured becomes an issue in Medicaid fight," *New York Times,* August 27.

BRAITHWAITE, VALERIE
1991   *Bound to Care.* Sydney: Allen & Unwin.

BRANDON, ROBERT M., MICHAEL PODHORZER, AND THOMAS H. POLLAK
1991   "Premiums without benefits: Waste and inefficiency in the commercial health insurance industry," *International Journal of Health Services* 21(2): 265–283.

BRANNON, ROBERT L.
1994   *Intensifying Care: The Hospital Industry, Professionalization, and the Reorganization of the Nursing Labor Process.* Amityville, NY: Baywood.

1996   "Restructuring hospital nursing: Reversing the trend toward a professional work force," *International Journal of Health Services* 26(4): 643–654.

BRAUDEL, FERNAND
1973   *Capitalism and Material Life: 1400–1800.* New York: Harper & Row.

BRAVERMAN, HARRY
1974   *Labor and Monopoly Capital.* New York: Monthly Review Press.

BRAVERMAN, PAULA, GERALDINE OLIVA, MARIE GRISHAM MILLER, RANDY REITER, AND SUSAN EGARTON
1989   "Adverse outcomes and lack of health insurance among newborns in an eight-county area of California, 1982 to 1986," *New England Journal of Medicine* 321 (8): 508–513.

BRENNAN, TROYEN A., LUCIAN L. LEAPE, NAN M. LAIRD, LIESI HEBERT, A. RUSSELL LOCALIO, ANN G. LAWTHERS, JOS. P. NEWHOUSE, PAUL C. WILDER, AND HOWARD LIBIT
1991   "Incidence of adverse events and negligence in hospitalized patients–results of the Harvard Medical Practice Study I," *New England Journal of Medicine* 324(6): 370–376.

BRIGHTBILL, TIM
1991   "Political Action Committees: How much influence will $7.7 million buy?" *International Journal of Health Services* 21(2): 285–290.

BRINDLE, DAVID
1996   "Shaky step forward," *The Guardian*, November 27:6–7

BRODEUR, PAUL
1974   *Expendable Americans.* New York: Viking.

BRODY, ELAINE M.
1994   "Women as unpaid caregivers: The price they pay," pp. 67–86 in E. Friedman, *An Unfinished Revolution: Women and Health Care in America.* New York: United Hospital Fund.

BRODY, HOWARD
1992   *The Healer's Power.* New Haven: Yale University Press.

BRODY, JANE E.
1975   "Physicians' views unchanged on use of estrogen therapy," *New York Times*, December 5.
1983   "Research lifts blame from many of the obese," *New York Times*, March 24.
1995   "Despite reductions in exposure, lead remains a danger to children," *New York Times*, March 21.
1997   "Prenatal exposure to DES can also hurt men, and they should be vigilant," *New York Times*, July 30.

BROOKE, JAMES
1993   "A hard look at Brazil's surfeits: Food, hunger and inequality," *New York Times*, June 6.

BROOM, DOROTHY H., AND ROSLYN V. WOODWARD
1996   "Medicalisation reconsidered: Toward a collaborative approach to care," *Sociology of Health and Illness* 18(3): 357–378.

BROWN, CAROL A.
1978   "The division of laborers: Allied health professions," pp. 73–82 in S. Wolfe, ed., *Organization of Health Workers and Labor Conflict.* Farmingdale, NY: Baywood.
1983   "Women workers in the health service industry," pp. 105–116 in E. Fee, ed., *Women and Health: The Politics of Sex in Medicine.* Farmingdale, NY: Baywood.

BROWN, E. RICHARD
1979   *Rockefeller Medicine Men: Medicine and Capitalism in America.* Berkeley: University of California Press.

BROWN, KAREN MCCARTHY
1991   *Mama Lola: A Vodou Priestess in Brooklyn.* Berkeley: University of California Press.

BROWN, LEIGH PATRICIA
1988   "Designs take heed of human frailty," *New York Times,* April 14.

BROWN, LESTER, WILLIAM U. CHANDLER, CHRISTOPHER FLAVIN, JODI JACOBSON, CYNTHIA POLLOCK, SANDRA POSTEL, LINDA STARKE, AND EDWARD C. WOLF
1987   *State of the World, 1987.* New York: W.W. Norton.

BROWN, PETER J., AND MARCIA C. INHORN
1990   "Disease, ecology and human behavior," pp. 187–214 in T. M. Johnson and C. F. Sargent, eds., *Medical Anthropology: A Handbook of Theory and Method.* New York: Greenwood.

BROWN, PHIL
1995a   "Naming and framing: The social construction of diagnosis and illness," *Journal of Health and Social Behavior* 33: 267–281.
1995b   "Popular epidemiology, toxic waste and social movements," pp. 91–112 in J. Gabe, ed., *Medicine, Health and Risk.* Oxford: Blackwell.

BROWN, PHIL, AND STEVEN C. FUNK
1986   "Tardive dyskinesia: Barriers to the professional recognition of an iatrogenic disease," *Journal of Health and Social Behavior* 27: 116–132.

BROWN, PHIL, AND EDWIN J. MIKKELSEN
1990   *No Safe Place: Toxic Waste, Leukemia and Community Action.* Berkeley: University of California Press.

BRUMBERG, JOAN
1988   *Fasting Girls: The Emergence of Anorexia Nervosa as a Modern Disease.* Cambridge, MA: Harvard University Press.

BRUNNER, ERIC
1996   "The social and biological basis of cardiovascular disease in office workers," pp. 272–299 in G. Blane, E. Brunner and E. Wilkinson, eds., *Health and Social Organization.* London: Routledge.

BRZUZY, STEPHANIE
1997   "Deconstructing disability: The impact of definition," *Journal of Poverty* 1(1): 81–91.

BUDD, SUSAN, AND URSULA SHARMA, EDS.
1994   *The Healing Bond: The Patient-Practitioner Relationship and Therapeutic Responsibility.* New York: Routledge.

BULLINGER, MONIKA
1990   "Environmental stress: Effect of air pollution on mood, neuropsychological function and physical style," pp. 244–250 in S. P. Allegra and A. Oliverio, eds., *Psychobiology of Stress.* Boston: Kluwer Academic.

BUNTON, ROBIN, SARAH NETTLETON, AND ROGER BURROWS
1995   *The Sociology of Health Promotion: Critical Analyses of Consumption, Lifestyle and Risk.* London: Routledge.

BURKHOLDER, JOHN R.
1974   "The law knows no heresy: Marginal religious movements and the courts," pp. 27–52 in I. Zaretsky and M. Leone, eds., *Religious Movements in Contemporary America.* Princeton: Princeton University Press.

BURKITT, DENIS P.
  1973   "Some disease characteristics of modern Western civilisation," *British Medical Journal* 1: 274–278.
BURRIS, BEVERLY H.
  1993   *Technocracy at Work*. Albany: State University of New York.
BURROS, MARIAN
  1994   "Despite awareness of risks, more in U.S. are getting fat," *New York Times*, July 17.
BURT, MARTHA R.
  1992   *Over the Edge: The Growth of Homelessness in the 1980s*. New York: Russell Sage Foundation.
BURY, MICHAEL
  1982   "Chronic illness as biographical disruption," *Sociology of Health and Illness* 4(2): 167–182.
  1988   "Meanings at risk: The experience of arthritis," pp. 89–116 in R. Anderson and M. Bury, eds., *Living with Chronic Illness: The Experience of Patients and Their Families*. London: Unwin Hyman.
  1991   "The sociology of chronic illness: A review of research and prospects," *Sociology of Health and Illness* 13(4): 451–467.
BUSHNELL, OSWALD A.
  1993   *The Gifts of Civilization: Germs and Genocide in Hawaii*. Honolulu: University of Hawaii Press.
BUTLER, ROBERT N.
  1996   "On behalf of older women: Another reason to protect Medicare and Medicaid," *New England Journal of Medicine* 334(12): 794–796.
BUTLER, SAMUEL
  [1901] 1960 *Erewhon*. New York: New American Library.
BUYTENDIJK, JACOBUS
  1974   *Prolegomena to an Anthropological Physiology*. Pittsburgh: Duquesne University Press.
BYRNE, PATRICK S., AND BARRIE E. LONG
  1976   *Doctors Talking to Patients*. London: Her Majesty's Stationery Office.
CAHILL, JANET, AND PAUL A. LANDSBERGIS
  1996   "Job strain among post office mailhandlers," *International Journal of Health Services* 26(4):731–750.
CALIFANO, JOSEPH A.
  1989   "Billions blown on health," *New York Times*, April 12.
CALLAHAN, DANIEL
  1987   *Setting Limits: Medical Goals in an Aging Society*. New York: Simon & Schuster.
CALLAHAN, TAMARA L., AND RONALD DAVID
  1995   "Access," pp. 173–193 in D. Calkins, R. J. Fernandopulle, and B. S. Marino, eds., *Health Care Policy*. Cambridge, MA: Blackwell Science.
CALNAN, MICHAEL
  1984   "Clinical uncertainty: Is it a problem in the doctor-patient relationship?" *Sociology of Health and Illness* 6(1): 74–85.
  1987   *Health and Illness: The Lay Perspective*. New York: Tavistock.
CAMERON, H. M., AND E. MCGOOGAN
  1981   "Prospective study of 1152 hospital autopsies: Inaccuracies in death certification," *Journal of Pathology* 133: 273–283.

CANNON, WALTER B.
  1929   *Bodily Changes in Pain, Hunger, Fear, and Rage.* New York: Harper & Row.
  1942   " 'Voodoo' death," *American Anthropologist* 44: 169–181.
CANT, SARAH L., AND MICHAEL CALNAN
  1991   "On the margins of the medical marketplace? An exploratory study of alter-
         native practitioners' perceptions," *Sociology of Health and Illness* 13(1): 39–57.
CANTOR, JOEL C., STEPHEN H. LONG, AND M. SUSAN MARQUIS
  1995   "Private employment-based health insurance in ten states," *Health Affairs* 14(2):
         199–209.
CAPLAN, ROBERT D.
  1972   "Organizational stress and individual strain: A sociopsychological study of
         risk factors in coronary heart disease among administrators, engineers, and
         scientists." Unpublished Ph.D. dissertation, University of Michigan.
CARPENTER, EUGENIA S.
  1980   "Children's health care and the changing role of women," *Medical Care* 18(12):
         1208–1218.
CARTLAND, JENIFER D. C., AND BETH K. YUDKOWSKY
  1993   "State estimates of uninsured children," *Health Affairs* 12(1): 144–151.
CARTWRIGHT, ANNE
  1967   *Patients and Their Doctors.* New York: Atherton.
CARTWRIGHT, SAMUEL A.
  1851   "Report on the diseases and physical pecularities of the Negro race," *New
         Orleans Medical and Surgical Journal* 7: 691–715.
CASH, THOMAS F., BARBARA WINSTEAD, AND LOUIS JANDA
  1986   "The great American shape-up," *Psychology Today* 20(4): 30–37.
CASSEDY, JAMES H.
  1977   "Why self-help? Americans alone with their diseases, 1800–1850," pp. 31–48
         in G. Risse, R.L. Numbers, and J.W. Leavitt, eds., *Medicine Without Doctors:
         Home Health Care in American History.* New York: Science History.
CASSELL, ERIC J.
  1976   "Disease as an 'it': Concepts of disease revealed by patients' presentation of
         symptoms," *Social Science and Medicine* 10: 143–146.
  1982   "The nature of suffering and the goals of medicine," *New England Journal of
         Medicine* 306: 639–645.
  1986   "Ideas in conflict: The rise and fall (and rise and fall) of new views of disease,"
         Daedalus: Journal of the American Academy of Arts and Sciences 115(2): 19–41.
CASSELL, JOAN
  1991   *Expected Miracles: Surgeons at Work.* Philadelphia: Temple University Press.
CASSIDY, CLAIRE M., HANS BAER, AND BARBARA BECKER
  1985   "Selected references on professionalized heterodox health systems in English-
         speaking countries," *Medical Anthropology Quarterly* 17(1): 10–18.
CENTER FOR PHILOSOPHY AND PUBLIC POLICY
  1985   "Air pollution: The role and limits of consent," *Report from the Center for
         Philosophy and Public Policy,* volume 5, number 5. Hyattsville, MD: University of
         Maryland.
CENTER FOR PUBLIC INTEGRITY
  1995   "Well-healed: Inside lobbying for health care reform, part II," *International
         Journal of Health Services* 25(4): 593–632.

CENTER FOR STUDY OF RESPONSIVE LAW
1982   *Eating Clean: Food Safety and the Chemical Harvest.* Washington, DC: Center for Study of Responsive Law.

CHAPMAN, SIMON, RON BORLAND, DAVID HILL, NEVILLE OWEN, AND STEPHEN WOODARD
1990   "Why the tobacco industry fears the passive smoking issue," *International Journal of Health Services* 20(3): 417–427.

CHARLES, NICKE, AND MARION KERR
1987   "Food for feminist thought," *Sociological Review* 34(3): 537–572.

CHARMAZ, KATHY
1983   "Loss of self: A fundamental form of suffering of the chronically ill," *Sociology of Health and Illness* 4: 167–182.
1987   "Struggling for a self: Identity levels of the chronically ill," *Research in the Sociology of Health Care* 4: 167–182.
1991   *Good Days, Bad Days: The Self in Chronic Illness and Time.* New Brunswick, NJ: Rutgers University Press.
1995   "Identity dilemmas of chronically ill men," pp. 266–291 in D. Sabo and D.F. Gordon, eds., *Men's Health and Illness.* Thousand Oaks, CA: Sage.

CHASSIN, MARK R., JACQUELINE KOSECOFF, R. E. PARK, CONSTANCE WINSLOW, KATHERINE KAHN, NANCY MERRICK, JOAN KEESEY, ARLENE FINK, DAVID SOLOMON, AND ROBERT BROOK
1987   "Does inappropriate use explain geographic variations in the use of health care services? A study of three procedures," *Journal of the American Medical Association* 258(18): 2533–2537.

CHAVKIN, WENDY, ED.
1984   *Double Exposure: Women's Health Hazards on the Job and at Home.* New York: Monthly Review Press.

CHERFAS, JEREMY, AND ROGER LEWIN, EDS.
1980   *Not Work Alone: A Cross-Cultural View of Activities Superfluous to Survival.* Beverly Hills, CA: Sage.

CHERNIN, KIM
1981   *The Obsession: Reflections on the Tyranny of Slenderness.* New York: Harper & Row.

CHESNEY, MARGARET A.
1991   "Women, work-related stress, and smoking," pp. 139–155 in M. Frankenhaeuser, V. Lundberg, and M. Chesney, eds., *Women, Work and Health.* New York: Plenum Press.

CHRISLER, JOAN C.
1994   "Reframing women's weight: Does thin equal healthy?", pp. 330–338 in A.J. Dan, ed., *Reframing Women's Health.* Westport, CT: Auburn House.

CHRISMAN, NOEL J.
1977   "The health-seeking process: An approach to the natural history of illness," *Culture, Medicine and Psychiatry* 1: 351–377.

CHRISTIANSON, JON B., DOUGLAS R. WHOLEY, AND SUSAN M. SANCHEZ
1991   "State responses to HMO failures," *Health Affairs* 10(4): 78–92.

CICOUREL, AARON V.
1983   "Hearing is not believing: Language and the structure of belief in medical communication," pp. 221–239 in S. Fisher and A. Todd, eds., *The Social Organization of Doctor-Patient Communication.* Norwood, NJ: Ablex.

CLASSEN, CONSTANCE
1994   *Aroma: The Cultural History of Smell.* London: Routledge.

COBB, LEONARD A., GEORGE THOMAS, DAVID H. DILLARD, K. ALVIN MERENDINO, AND ROBERT A. BRUCE
1959   "An evaluation of internal mammary artery ligation by a double-blind technic," *New England Journal of Medicine* 260: 1115–1118.

COBURN, DAVID, AND C. LESLEY BIGGS
1986   "Limits to medical dominance: The case of chiropractic," *Social Science and Medicine* 22: 1035–1046.

COBURN, DAVID, GEORGE M. TORRANCE, AND JOSEPH M. KAUFERT
1983   "Medical dominance in Canada in historical perspective: The rise and fall of medicine?" *International Journal of Health Services* 13(3): 407–432.

COCKBURN, ALEXANDER
1988   "Live souls," *Zeta Magazine* 1(2): 5–15.

COCKERHAM, WILLIAM C.
1978   *Medical Sociology.* Englewood Cliffs, NJ: Prentice-Hall.

COHEN, MARC J., AND RICHARD J. HOEHN
1991   *Hunger.* Washington, DC: Bread for the World Institute on Hunger and Development.

COHEN, STANLEY, AND LAURIE TAYLOR
1976   *Escape Attempts: The Theory and Practise of Resistance to Everyday Life.* London: Allen Lane.

COLLINS, CATHERINE FISHER
1996   "Commentary on the health and social status of African-American women," pp. 1–10 in C. F. Collins, ed. *African-American Women's Health and Social Issues.* Westport, CT: Auburn House.

COLLINS, GLENN
1995   "Making gains on the winds from Washington," *New York Times,* March 26.

COMAROFF, JEAN
1978   "Medicine and culture: Some anthropological perspectives," *Social Science and Medicine* 12B: 247–254.

1982   "Medicine: Symbol and ideology," pp. 49–68 in P. Wright and A. Treacher, eds., *The Problem of Medical Knowledge: Examining the Social Construction of Medicine.* Edinburgh: Edinburgh University Press.

1984   "Medicine, time, and the perception of death," *Listening* 19(2): 155–169.

1985   *Body of Power, Spirit of Resistance: The Culture and History of a South African People.* Chicago: University of Chicago Press.

COMAROFF, JEAN, AND PETER MAGUIRE
1981   "Ambiguity and the search for meaning: Childhood leukaemia in the modern clinical context," *Social Science and Medicine* 15B(2): 115–123.

CONRAD, PETER
1985   "The meaning of medications: Another look at compliance," *Social Science and Medicine* 20: 29–37.

1986   "The social meaning of AIDS," *Social Policy* 17(1): 51–56.

1987   "The experience of illness: Recent and new directions," *Research in the Sociology of Health Care* 6: 1–31.

1988   "Worksite health promotion: The social context," *Social Science and Medicine* 26(5): 485–489.

1996   "Medicalization and social control," pp. 137–162 in P. Brown, ed., *Perspectives in Medical Sociology*. Prospect Heights, IL: Waveland Press.

CONRAD, PETER, AND JOSEPH W. SCHNEIDER
1992   *Deviance and Medicalization: From Badness to Sickness*. Philadelphia: Temple University Press.

CONRAD, PETER, AND DIANA WALSH
1992   "The new corporate health ethic: Lifestyle and the social control of work," *International Journal of Health Services* 22(1): 89–111.

CONSUMER REPORTS
1990   "A look at the Canadian alternative" (September): 614–617.

COOMBS, ROBERT H.
1978   *Mastering Medicine: Professional Socialization in Medical School*. New York: Free Press.

COOMBS, ROBERT H., SANGEETA CHOPRA, DEBRA R. SCHENK, AND ELAINE YUTAN
1993   "Medical slang and its functions," *Social Science and Medicine* 36(8): 987–998.

COOPER, MARC
1997   "The heartland's raw deal," *The Nation* 264(4):11–17.

COREA, GENA
1992   *The Invisible Epidemic*. New York: HarperCollins.

CORIN, E.
1994   "The social and cultural matrix of health and disease," pp. 93–132 in R. G. Evans, M. L. Barer, and T. R. Marmor, eds., *Why Are Some People Healthy and Others Not?: The Determinants of Health of Populations*. New York: Aldine de Gruyter.

COULTER, HARRIS L.
1984   "Homoeopathy," pp. 57–79 in J. W. Salmon, ed., *Alternative Medicines: Popular and Policy Perspectives*. New York: Tavistock.

COULTER, IAN D., RON D. HAYS, AND CLARK D. DANIELSON
1996   "The role of the chiropractor in the changing health care system," *Research in the Sociology of Health Care* 13A: 95–117.

COUNCIL ON SCIENTIFIC AFFAIRS
1991   "Hispanic health in the United States," *Journal of the American Medical Association* 265(2): 248–252.

COUSINS, NORMAN
1989   *Headfirst: The Biology of Hope*. New York: Dutton.

COWIE, BILL
1976   "The cardiac patient's perception of his heart attack," *Social Science and Medicine* 10: 87–96.

CRAWFORD, ROBERT
1977   "You are dangerous to your health: The ideology and politics of victim blaming," *International Journal of Health Services* 7(4): 663–680.
1984   "A cultural account of 'health': Control, release, and the social body," pp. 60–103 in J. B. McKinlay, ed., *Issues in the Political Economy of Health Care*. New York: Tavistock.

CREWE, NANCY M., AND IRVING K. ZOLA, EDS.
1983   *Independent Living in America*. San Francisco: Jossey-Bass.

CRITTENDEN, ANN
1981   "Bangladesh hunger linked to feudal system," *New York Times*, December 11.

CROSSEN, CYNTHIA
1994   *Tainted Truth: The Manipulation of Fact in America*. New York: Simon & Schuster.

CSIKSZENTMIHALYI, MIHALY
1990   *Flow: The Psychology of Optimal Experience.* New York: HarperCollins.
CSORDAS, THOMAS J.
1994   *The Sacred Self: A Cultural Phenomenology of Charismatic Healing.* Berkeley: University of California Press.
CSORDAS, THOMAS J., AND ARTHUR KLEINMAN
1996   "The therapeutic process," pp. 3–20 in C. F. Sargent and T. M. Johnson, eds., *Medical Anthropology: Contemporary Theory and Method.* Westport, CT: Praeger.
CULYER, A. J., AND BENGT JONSSON, EDS.
1986   *Public and Private Health Services: Complementaries and Conflicts.* Oxford: Basil Blackwell.
CUMMINGS, JUDITH
1984   "Restrictions on smoking spreading across U.S.," *New York Times,* February 1.
DAHLGREN, GOERAN, AND FINN DIDERICHSEN
1986   "Strategies for equity in health: Report from Sweden," *International Journal of Health Services* 16(4): 517–537.
DANIELS, ARLENE K.
1969   "The captive professional: Bureaucratic limitations in the practice of military psychiatry," *Journal of Health and Social Behavior* 10(4): 255–265.
1972   "Military psychiatry: The emergence of a subspecialty," pp. 145–162 in E. Freidson and J. Lorber, eds., *Medical Men and Their Work.* Chicago: Aldine Atherton.
DANIELS, CYNTHIA R.
1993   *At Women's Expense: State Power and the Politics of Fetal Rights.* Cambridge, MA: Harvard University Press.
DARTMOUTH MEDICAL SCHOOL CENTER FOR THE EVALUATIVE CLINICAL SCIENCES
1996   *The Dartmouth Atlas of Health Care.* American Hospital Association.
DAVIES, CELIA
1995   *Gender and the Professional Predicament in Nursing.* Buckingham: Open University Press.
DAVIS, JOEL
1984   *Endorphins: New Waves in Brain Chemistry.* Garden City, NY: Doubleday.
DAVIS, KAREN
1991   "Inequality and access to health care," *The Milbank Quarterly* 69(2): 253–273.
DAVIS, MARGARET H., AND SALLY T. BURNER
1995   "Three decades of Medicare: What the numbers tell us," *Health Affairs* 14(4): 231–242.
DAVIS-FLOYD, ROBBIE
1987   "Obstetric training as a rite of passage," *Medical Anthropology Quarterly* 1(3): 288–318.
1990   "The role of obstetrical rituals in the resolution of cultural anomaly," *Social Science and Medicine* 31(2): 175–189.
1992   *Birth as an American Rite of Passage.* Berkeley: University of California Press.
1994   "The technocratic body: American childbirth as cultural expression," *Social Science and Medicine* 38(8): 1125–1140.
DEFRIESE, GORDON H., GLENN WILSON, THOMAS C. RICKETTS, AND LYNN WHITENER
1992   "Consumer choice and the national rural hospital crisis," pp. 206–225 in W. M. Gesler and T. C. Ricketts, eds., *Health in Rural North America.* New Brunswick, NJ: Rutgers University Press.

DEMBE, ALLARD E.
1996   *Occupation and Disease.* New Haven, CT: Yale University Press.

DEPPE, HANS-ULRICH
1992   "German unification and European integration," *Health/PAC Bulletin* (Spring): 22–27.

DERBER, CHARLES
1984   "Physicians and their sponsorship: The new medical relations of production," pp. 217–254 in J. B. McKinlay, ed., *Issues in the Political Economy of Health Care.* New York: Tavistock.

DEY, ACHINTYA N.
1996   "Characteristics of elderly home health care users: Data from the 1994 national home and hospice care survey," *Advance Data* 279.

DIAMOND, MARIAN CLEEVES
1988   *Enriching Heredity: The Impact of the Environment on the Anatomy of the Brain.* New York: Free Press.

DILL, ANN, PHIL BROWN, DESIRÉE CIAMBRONE, AND WILLIAM RAKOWSKI
1995   "The meaning and practice of self-care by older adults," *Research on Aging* 7(1): 8–41.

DIMATTEO, M. ROBIN, AND HOWARD S. FRIEDMAN
1982   *Social Psychology and Medicine.* Cambridge, MA: Oelgeschlager, Gunn, and Hain.

DINGWALL, ROBERT
1976   *Aspects of Illness.* New York: St. Martin's Press.

DIRECKS, ANITA, AND ELLEN'T HOEN
1986   "DES: The crime continues," pp. 41–49 in K. McDonnell, ed., *Adverse Effects: Women and the Pharmaceutical Industry.* Toronto: Women's Educational Press.

DOHERTY, WILLIAM J., AND THOMAS L. CAMPBELL
1988   *Families and Health.* Beverly Hills, CA: Sage.

DOHRENWEND, BARBARA, AND LEONARD PEARLIN
1982   "Report on stress and life events," pp. 55–88 in G. R. Elliott and C. Eisdorfer, eds., *Stress and Human Health.* New York: Springer.

DOLAN, ANDREW K.
1980   "Antitrust law and physician dominance of other practitioners," *Journal of Health, Politics, and Law* 4: 675–689.

DONAHUE, JOHN M.
1986   *The Nicaraguan Revolution in Health.* South Hadley, MA: Bergin and Garvey.
1989   "International organizations, health services, and nation building in Nicaragua," *Medical Anthropology Quarterly* 3(3): 258–269.

DONAHUE, JOHN M., AND MEREDITH B. MCGUIRE
1995   "The political economy of responsibility in health and illness," *Social Science and Medicine* 40(1): 47–53.

DONELAN, KAREN, ROBERT J. BLENDON, JOHN BENSON, ROBERT LEITMAN, AND HUMPHREY TAYLOR
1996   "All payer, single payer, managed care, no payer: Patients' perspectives in three nations," *Health Affairs* 15(2): 263–265.

DONOVAN, JENNY L., AND DAVID R. BLAKE
1992   "Patient compliance: Deviance or reasoned decision-making?" *Social Science and Medicine* 34(5): 507–513.

DONOVAN, REBECCA
1987 "Poorly paid home health care workers subsidize an industry" [letter to the editor], *New York Times*, May 16.

DOUGLAS, MARY
1966 *Purity and Danger: An Analysis of Concepts of Pollution and Taboo.* London: Routledge and Kegan Paul.
1970 *Natural Symbols: Explorations in Cosmology.* London: Barrie and Jenkins.

DOW, JAMES
1986 "Universal aspects of symbolic healing: A theoretical synthesis," *American Anthropologist* 88(1): 56–69.

DOWIE, MARK, AND TRACY JOHNSTON
1987 "A case of corporate malpractice and the Dalkon Shield," pp. 629–637 in H. D. Schwartz, ed., *Dominant Issues in Medical Sociology.* New York: Random House.

DOYAL, LESLEY
1983 "Women, health and the sexual division of labour: A case study of the women's health movement in Britain," *Critical Social Policy* 7: 1–33.
1995 *What Makes Women Sick.* New Brunswick, NJ: Rutgers University Press.

DREW, CHRISTOPHER
1995 "In the productivity push, how much is too much?" *New York Times*, December 17.

DRICKAMER, MARGARET A., AND MARK S. LACHS
1992 "Should patients with Alzheimer's disease be told their diagnosis?" *New England Journal of Medicine* 326(18): 947–951.

DRINKA, GEORGE FREDERICK
1984 *The Birth of Neurosis: Myth, Malady, and the Victorians.* New York: Simon & Schuster.

DROGE, DAVID, PAUL ARNTSON, AND ROBERT NORTON
1986 "The social support function in epilepsy self-help groups," *Small Group Behavior* 17(2): 139–163.

DUBOS, RENÉ
1959 *The Mirage of Health.* Garden City, NY: Doubleday.
1968 *Man, Medicine and Environment.* Baltimore: Penguin.

DUFFIE, MARY K.
1996 "Intrapsychic autonomy and the emotional construction of biocultural illness: A question of balance," pp. 47–71 in J. Subedi and E.B. Gallagher, eds., *Society, Health and Disease.* Upper Saddle River, NJ: Prentice Hall.

DULL, DIANA, AND CANDACE WEST
1991 "Accounting for cosmetic surgery: The accomplishment of gender," *Social Problems* 38(3): 54–70.

DUNNELL, KAREN, AND ANN CARTWRIGHT
1972 *Medicine Takers, Prescribers, and Hoarders.* London: Routledge and Kegan Paul.

DURKHEIM, EMILE
[1893] 1964 *The Division of Labor in Society.* New York: The Free Press.
[1895] 1938 *Rules of the Sociological Method.* New York: The Free Press.
[1897] 1951 *Suicide: A Study in Sociology.* New York: The Free Press.
[1915] 1965 *The Elementary Forms of the Religious Life.* New York: Collier/Macmillan.

DUTTON, DIANA
1986 "Social class, health and illness," pp. 31–62 in L. Aiken and D. Mechanic, eds., *Applications of Social Science to Clinical Medicine and Health Policy.* New Brunswick, NJ: Rutgers University Press.

DUTTON, DIANA, THOMAS A. PRESTON, AND NANCY E. PFUND
1988   *Worse Than the Disease: Pitfalls of Medical Progress.* New York: Cambridge University Press.

DYE, JAMES W.
1981   "Man a machine: A philosophical critique," *Journal of Biological Experience: Studies in the Life of the Body* 3(2): 44–60.

EASTWELL, HARRY D.
1982   "Voodoo death and the mechanism for dispatch of the dying in East Arnheim, Australia," *American Anthropologist* 84(1): 5–18.

ECKHOLM, ERIK
1977   *The Picture of Health: Environmental Sources of Disease.* New York: W. W. Norton.
1989   "River blindness: Conquering an ancient scourge," *New York Times Magazine,* January 8.
1993   "Health plan is toughest on doctors making most," *New York Times,* November 7.

EDGAR, HAROLD
1992   "Outside the community," *Hastings Center Report* 22(6): 32–35.

EHRENREICH, BARBARA, AND JOHN EHRENREICH
1978   "Hospital workers: Class conflicts in the making," pp. 41–49 in S. Wolfe, ed., *Organization of Health Workers and Labor Conflict.* Farmingdale, NY: Baywood.

EHRENREICH, BARBARA, AND DEIRDRE ENGLISH
1973   *Witches, Midwives, and Nurses: A History of Women Healers.* Old Westbury, NY: The Feminist Press.
1978   *For Her Own Good: 150 Years of the Experts' Advice to Women.* Garden City, NY: Doubleday.

EICHENWALD, KURT
1995a   "Death and deficiency in kidney treatment," *New York Times,* December 4.
1995b   "Doctors' highest-paid skill: Steering in kidney patients," *New York Times,* December 5.
1995c   "Making incentives work in kidney patients' favor," *New York Times,* December 6.
1996   "Long neglected, the quality of kidney dialysis now may get U.S. guidelines," *New York Times,* January 14.

EISENBERG, DAVID M., THOMAS L. DELBANCO, CATHERINE S. BERKEY, TED J. KAPTCHUK, BRUCE KUPELNICK, JACKIE KUHL, AND THOMAS C. CHALMERS
1993a   "Cognitive behavioral techniques for hypertension: Are they effective?" *Annals of Internal Medicine* 118: 964–972.

EISENBERG, DAVID M., RONALD C. KESSLER, CINDY FOSTER, FRANCES E. NORLOCK, DAVID R. CALKINS, AND THOMAS L. DELBANCO
1993b   "Unconventional medicine in the United States," *New England Journal of Medicine* 328(4): 246–252.

ELIAS, NORBERT
1985   *The Loneliness of Dying.* Oxford: Basil Blackwell.
1994   [1978] *The Civilizing Process,* Vols. 1 and 2. Oxford: Basil Blackwell.

ELLING, RAY H.
1986   *The Struggle for Workers' Health: A Study of Six Industrialized Countries.* Farmingdale, NY: Baywood.

EMERSON, JOAN P.
1970   "Behavior in private places: Sustaining definitions of reality in gynecological examinations," pp. 74–97 in H. P. Dreitzel, ed., *Recent Sociology #2: Patterns of Communicative Behavior.* New York: Macmillan.

ENGEBRETSON, TILMER O., AND CATHERINE M. STONEY
1995   "Anger expression and lipid concentrations," *International Journal of Behavioral Medicine* 2(4): 281–298.
ENGEL, GEORGE L.
1971   "Sudden and rapid death during psychological stress: Folklore or folk wisdom?" *Annals of Internal Medicine* 74: 771–782.
1977   "The need for a new medical model: A challenge for biomedicine," *Science* 196: 129–136.
ENGELS, FRIEDRICH
[1845] 1973 *The Conditions of the Working Class in England in 1844*. Moscow: Universal.
ENGLEHARDT, H. TRISTAM
1978   "The disease of masturbation: Values and the concept of disease," pp. 15–24 in J. W. Leavitt and R. L. Numbers, eds., *Sickness and Health in America*. Madison: University of Wisconsin Press.
ENGLER, RICK
1986   "Political power aids health and safety," in *These Times*, January 15–21: 16–17.
ENGLISH-LUECK, JUNE ANNE
1990   *Health in the New Age: A Study in California Holistic Practices*. Albuquerque: University of New Mexico.
EPSTEIN, PAUL, AND RANDALL PACKARD
1987   "Ecology and immunity," *Science for the People* 19(1): 10–20.
EPSTEIN, SAMUEL S.
1978   *The Politics of Cancer*. San Francisco: Sierra Club Books.
1990a   "Losing the war against cancer: Who's to blame and what to do about it," *International Journal of Health Services* 20(1): 53–71.
1990b   "Corporate crime: Why we cannot trust industry-derived safety studies," *International Journal of Health Services* 20(3): 443–458.
ETTORRE, ELIZABETH, AND ELIANNE RISKA
1995   *Gendered Moods: Psychotropics and Society*. London: Routledge.
EVANS, ROBERT G.
1974   "Supplier-induced demand: Some empirical evidence and implications," pp. 162–173 in M. Perlman, ed., *The Economics of Health and Medical Care*. London: Macmillan.
EVANS, ROBERT G., MORRIS L. BARER, AND THEODORE R. MARMOR, EDS.
1994   *Why Are Some People Healthy and Others Not?: The Determinants of Health of Populations*. New York: Aldine de Gruyter.
EVANS, ROBERT G., M. HODGE, AND I. B. PLESS
1994   "If not genetics then what? Biological pathways and population health," pp. 161–189 in R.G. Evans, M. L. Barer, and T. R. Marmor, eds., *Why Are Some People Healthy and Others Not?: The Determinants of Health of Populations*. New York: Aldine de Gruyter.
EVERETT, MELISSA
1984   "Coffee: How it gets to your cup," *Whole Life Times*, January-February: 20–23.
EWAN, CHRISTINE, EVA LOWY, AND JANICE REID
1991   " 'Falling out of culture': The effects of repetition strain injury on sufferers' roles and identity," *Sociology of Health and Illness* 13(2): 168–192.
EWIGMAN, BERNARD G., JAMES P. CRANE, FREDRIC D. FIGOLETTO, MICHAEL L. LeFEVRE, RAYMOND P. BAIN, DONALD MCNELLIS, AND RADIUS STUDY GROUP
1993   "Effect of prenatal ultrasound screening on perinatal outcome," *New England Journal of Medicine* 329(12): 821–827.

EYER, JOSEPH
  1984   "Capitalism, health and illness," pp. 23–58 in J. B. McKinlay, ed., *Issues in the Political Economy of Health Care.* New York: Tavistock.
EYER, JOSEPH, AND PETER STERLING
  1977   "Stress-related mortality and social organization," *Review of Radical Political Economics* 9(1): 1–44.
FAGERHAUGH, SHIZUKO, AND ANSELM STRAUSS
  1977   *Politics of Pain Management: Staff-Patient Interaction.* Reading, MA: Addison-Wesley.
FALLON, APRIL E., AND PAUL ROZIN
  1985   "Sex differences in perception of desirable body shape," *Journal of Abnormal Psychology* 94(1): 102–105.
FANON, FRANZ
  1963   *The Wretched of the Earth.* New York: Grove.
FARB, PETER, AND GEORGE ARMELAGOS
  1980   *Consuming Passions: The Anthropology of Eating.* Boston: Houghton Mifflin.
FEATHERSTONE, MIKE
  1991   "The body in consumer culture," pp. 170–196 in M. Featherstone, M. Hepworth, and B. S. Turner, eds., *The Body: Social Process and Cultural Theory.* London: Sage.
FEDER, BARNABY
  1996   "Increase in teen-age smoking sharpest among black males," *New York Times,* May 24.
FEIGENBAUM, SUSAN
  1987   "Risk bearing in health care finance," pp. 105–144 in C. J. Schramm, ed., *Health Care and Its Costs.* New York: Norton.
FEIN, ESTHER B., AND ELISABETH ROSENTHAL
  1996   "Patients haunted by delay of New York H.M.O. in paying claims," *New York Times,* April 1.
FEIN, RASHI
  1986   *Medical Care, Medical Costs: The Search for a Health Insurance Policy.* Cambridge, MA: Harvard University Press.
FELDMAN, PENNY HOLLANDER, WITH ALICE M. SAPIENZA AND NANCY M. KANE
  1990   *Who Cares for Them? Workers in the Home Care Industry.* New York: Greenwood Press.
FENN, RICHARD
  1978   *Toward a Theory of Secularization. SSSR Monograph Series, No. 1.* Storrs, CT: Society for the Scientific Study of Religion.
  1982   *Liturgies and Trials: The Secularization of Religious Language.* Oxford: Basil Blackwell.
FETTNER, ANN GUIDICI
  1987   "Where there's smoke, there's ire," *Village Voice* 32(5): 25.
FIELD, MARK G.
  1973   "The concept of the 'health system' at the macrosociological level," *Social Science and Medicine* 7: 763–785.
FIELD, MARK G., ED.
  1989   *Success and Crisis in National Health Systems: A Comparative Approach.* New York: Routledge.
FIELDING, JONATHAN E., AND KENNETH J. PHENOW
  1988   "Health effects of involuntary smoking," *New England Journal of Medicine* 319(22): 1452–1460.

FIELDING, STEPHEN L.
1995　"Changing medical practice and medical malpractice claims," *Social Problems* 42(1): 38–55.
FIFE, BETSY L.
1994　"The conceptualization of meaning in illness," *Social Science and Medicine* 38(2): 309–316.
FIGERT, ANNE E.
1995　"The three faces of PMS: The professional, gendered, and scientific structuring of a psychiatric disorder," *Social Problems* 42(1): 56–73.
FIGLIO, KARL
1982　"How does illness mediate social relations?: Workmen's compensation and medico-legal practices, 1890–1940," pp. 174–217 in P. Wright and A. Treacher, eds., *The Problem of Medical Knowledge: Examining the Social Construction of Medicine.* Edinburgh: Edinburgh University Press.
FINDLAY, STEVEN
1988　"There's no place like home," *U.S. News and World Report,* January 25: 68–70.
FINE, DORIS R.
1988　"Women caregivers and home health workers: Prejudice and inequity in home health care," *Research in the Sociology of Health Care* 7: 105–117.
FINE, MICHELLE, AND ADRIENNE ASCH
1988　"Disability beyond stigma: Social interaction, discrimination and activism," *Journal of Social Issues* 44(1): 3–21.
FINKLER, KAJA
1989　"The universality of nerves," pp. 171–179 in D. Davis and S. Low, eds., *Gender, Health, and Illness: The Case of Nerves.* New York: Hemisphere.
1994　*Women in Pain: Gender and Morbidity in Mexico.* Philadelphia: University of Pennsylvania Press.
FISCHER, CLAUDE
1983　"The friendship cure-all," *Psychology Today* 17(1): 74–78.
FISHER, SUE
1983　"Doctor talk/Patient talk: How treatment decisions are negotiated in doctor-patient communication," pp. 135–157 in S. Fisher and A. Todd, eds., *The Social Organization of Doctor-Patient Communication.* Norwood, NJ: Ablex.
1986　*In the Patient's Best Interest: Women and the Politics of Medical Decisions.* New Brunswick, NJ: Rutgers University Press.
1994　"Is care a remedy? The case of nurse practitioners," pp. 301–329 in A. J. Dan, ed., *Reframing Women's Health.* Thousand Oaks, CA: Sage.
1995　*Nursing Wounds: Nurse Practitioners, Doctors, Women Patients and the Negotiation of Meaning.* New Brunswick, NJ: Rutgers University Press.
FLEXNER, ABRAHAM
1910　*Medical Education in the United States and Canada. Bulletin, Number 4.* New York: Carnegie Foundation for the Advancement of Teaching.
FONAGY, PETER
1996　"Patterns of attachment, interpersonal relationships and health," pp. 125–151 in D. Blane, E. Brunner, and R. Wilkinson, eds., *Health and Social Organization.* London: Routledge.
FONTENOT, WONDA L.
1994　*Secret Doctors: Ethnomedicine of African Americans.* Westport, CT: Bergin & Garvey.

FORD, ANNE ROCHON
1986   "Hormones: Getting out of hands," pp. 27–40 in K. McDonnell, ed., *Adverse Effects: Women and the Pharmaceutical Industry.* Toronto: Women's Educational Press.

FOSTER, PEGGY
1995   *Women and the Health Care Industry: An Unhealthy Relationship?* Buckingham: Open University Press.

FOUCAULT, MICHEL
1973   *The Birth of the Clinic: An Archaeology of Medical Perception.* New York: Tavistock.
1978   *The History of Sexuality: An Introduction.* New York: Pantheon.
1979   *Discipline and Punish: The Birth of the Prison.* Hammondsworth: Penguin.

FOX, RENÉE C.
1957   "Training for uncertainty," pp. 207–241 in R. K. Merton, G. C. Reader, and P. L. Kendall, eds., *The Student Physician.* Cambridge, MA: Harvard University Press.

FRANK, JEROME D.
1973   *Persuasion and Healing.* New York: Shocken.

FRANKE, RICHARD W., AND BARBARA H. CHASIN
1992   "Kerala state, India: Radical reform as development," *International Journal of Health Services* 22(1): 139–156.

FRANKEL, GLENN
1986   "Even the diseases are segregated," *International Herald Tribune,* July 17.

FRANKENHAEUSER, MARIANNE
1981   "Coping with stress at work," *International Journal of Health Services* 11(4): 491–510.
1991   "The psychophysiology of sex differences as related to occupational status," pp. 39–61 in M. Frankenhaeuser, U. Lundberg, and M. Chesney, eds., *Women, Work and Health.* New York: Plenum Press.

FRANKENHAEUSER, MARIANNE, AND BERTIL GARDELL
1976   "Underload and overload in working life: Outline of a multidisciplinary approach," *Journal of Human Stress* 2(3): 35–46.

FRAZIER, HOWARD S., AND GRAHAM A. COLDITZ
1995   "Oral contraceptives: Post-marketing surveillance and rare, late complications of drugs," pp. 212–219 in H. S. Frazier and F. Mosteller, eds., *Medicine Worth Paying For: Assessing Medical Innovations.* Cambridge, MA: Harvard University Press.

FRAZIER, HOWARD S., AND FREDERICK MOSTELLER, EDS.
1995   *Medicine Worth Paying For: Assessing Medical Innovations.* Cambridge, MA: Harvard University Press.

FREIDSON, ELIOT
1970   *Profession of Medicine: A Study of the Sociology of Applied Knowledge.* New York: Dodd, Mead.

FREUDENHEIM, MILT
1987a   "Debate widens over expanding use and growing cost of medical tests," *New York Times,* May 30.
1987b   "Specialty health care booms," *New York Times,* November 24.
1989   "Maxicare Health seeks bankruptcy protection," *New York Times,* March 17.
1993   "Drug makers propose self-control on prices," *New York Times,* March 16.
1994   "Pharmaceutical giant is buying operator of drug-benefit plan," *New York Times,* July 12.

1995a "Drug makers' managed-care ties questioned," *New York Times*, November 10, 1995.
1995b "Penny-pinching H.M.O.'s showed their generosity in executive paychecks," *New York Times*, April 11.
1995c "Profit levels stagnating at hospitals," *New York Times*, February, 6.
1995d "Some drugs rise in price at fast pace," *New York Times*, March 16.
1996 "Drug makers raise profits 20% or more," *New York Times*, April 17.
1997a "Columbia/HCA makes new, cash offer for Value Health," *New York Times*, April 16.
1997b "Dragging out HMO payments," *New York Times*, April 17.
1997c "H.M.O.'s beginning to ease the rules on specialty care," *New York Times*, February 2.
1997d "For teaching hospitals, multiple complications," *New York Times*, May 20.
FREUND, PETER E. S.
1982 *The Civilized Body: Social Domination, Control and Health.* Philadelphia: Temple University Press.
1990 "The expressive body: A common ground for the sociology of emotions and health and illness," *Sociology of Health and Illness* 12(4): 452–477.
1998 "Social performances and their discontents: Reflections on the biosocial psychology of role playing," pp. 393–430 in G. A. Bendelow and S. J. Williams, eds., *Emotions in Social Life: Social Theories and Contemporary Issues.* London: Routledge.
FREUND, PETER E. S., AND GEORGE MARTIN
1993 *The Ecology of the Automobile.* Montreal: Black Rose.
FRIEDMAN, EMILY
1996 "Capitation, integration, and managed care," *Journal of the American Medical Association* 275(12): 957–962.
FRIEDMAN, GARY D.
1987 *Primer of Epidemiology* (3rd ed.). New York: McGraw-Hill.
FRIEDMAN, SAMUEL R.
1993 "A.I.D.S. as a sociohistorical phenomenon," pp. 19–36 in G. L. Albrecht and R. S. Zimmerman, eds., *Advances in Medical Sociology, Vol. III: The Social and Behavioral Aspects of A.I.D.S.* Greenwich, CT: JAI Press.
FRIEDMANN, GEORGES
1961 *The Anatomy of Work.* Glencoe, IL: The Free Press.
FRIES, JAMES F.
1990 "An introduction to the compression of morbidity," pp. 35–41 in P. R. Lee and C. L. Estes, eds., *The Nation's Health.* Boston: Jones and Bartlett.
FROMM, ERIC
1965 *Escape from Freedom.* New York: Avon Books.
FRYER, GEORGE E., JR.
1991 "The United States medical profession: An abnormal form of the division of labor," *Sociology of Health and Illness* 13(2): 213–230.
FUCHS, VICTOR R., AND JAMES S. HAHN
1990 "How does Canada do it?" *New England Journal of Medicine* 323(13): 884–890.
FULDER, STEPHEN
1993 "The impact of non-orthodox medicine on our concepts of health," pp. 105–117 in R. Lafaille and S. Fulder, eds., *Towards a New Science of Health.* London: Routledge.

FUNKENSTEIN, DANIEL, S. H. KING, AND M. E. DROLETTE
1957   *Mastery of Stress*. Cambridge, MA: Harvard University Press.

GABE, JONATHAN
1997   "Continuity and change in the British National Health Service," pp. 492–504 in P. Conrad, ed., *The Sociology of Health and Illness*. 5th ed. New York: St. Martin's Press.

GABEL, JOHN R., AND MICHAEL A. REDISCH
1979   "Alternative physician payment methods: Incentives, efficiency, and National Health Insurance," *Milbank Memorial Fund Quarterly* 57(1): 38–59.

GAINES, ATWOOD D.
1992   "From DSM-I to III-R: Voices of self, mastery and the other: A cultural constructivist reading of U.S. psychiatric classification," *Social Science and Medicine* 35(1): 3–24.

GAMLIEL, SANDY, ROBERT M. POLITZER, MARC L. RIVO, AND FITZHUGH MULLAN
1995   "Managed care on the march: Will physicians meet the challenge?" *Health Affairs* 14(2): 131–145.

GANZ, PATRICIA A.
1992   "Treatment options for breast cancer—beyond survival," *New England Journal of Medicine* 326(17): 1147–1149.

GARRISON, VIVIAN
1977   "Doctor, espiritista, or psychiatrist: Health-seeking behavior in a Puerto Rican neighborhood of New York City," *Medical Anthropology* 1(2): 67–183.

GARSON, BARBARA
1988   *The Electronic Sweatshop*. New York: Simon & Schuster.

GARTNER, ALAN, AND TOM JOE
1987   "Introduction," pp. 1–6 in A. Gartner and T. Joe, eds., *Images of the Disabled, Disabling Images*. New York: Praeger.

GELLHORN, ERIC
1969   "The consequences of the suppression of overt movements in emotional stress: A neurophysiological interpretation," *Confinia Neurologica* 32: 289–299.

GEORGE, SUSAN
1982   *How the Other Half Dies*. Montclair, NJ: Allanheld, Osmun.

GERRITY, MARTHA S., JO ANNE L. EARP, ROBERT F. DEVELLIS, AND DONALD W. LIGHT
1992   "Uncertainty and professional work: Perceptions of physicians in clinical practice," *American Journal of Sociology* 97(4): 1022–1051.

GERTMAN, PAUL M.
1981   "Physicians as guiders of health services use," pp. 258–279 in J. B. McKinlay, ed., *Health Care Consumers, Professionals, and Organizations*. Milbank Reader, No. 2. Cambridge, MA: MIT Press.

GIBSON, ROBERT
1980   "National Health Expenditures, 1979," *Health Care Financing Review* 2(1): 1–36.
1982   "National Health Expenditures," *Health Care Financing Trends* 2(5): 1–9.

GIBSON, ROBERT, DANIEL WALDO, AND KATHERINE LEVIT
1982   "National health expenditures, 1982," *Health Care Financing Review* 5(1): 13–15.

GILBERT, EVELYN
1997   "Achoo, baby!" *Village Voice* (January 28):42–43.

GILL, DEREK, AND STANLEY R. INGMAN
1986   "Geriatric care and distributive justice: Problems and prospects," *Social Science and Medicine* 23(12): 1205–1215.

GILL, SAM D.
1981   *Sacred Words: A Study of Navajo Religion and Prayer.* Westport, CT: Greenwood.
GINGOLD, JUDITH
1996   "Adventures in liposuction," *The Atlantic Monthly,* March: 89–106.
GINZBERG, ELI
1991   "Access to health care for Hispanics," *Journal of the American Medical Association* 165(2): 238–241.
GLASER, BARNEY, AND ANSELM STRAUSS
1968   *Time for Dying.* Chicago: Aldine.
GLASER, WILLIAM A.
1991   "Paying the hospital: American problems and foreign solutions," *International Journal of Health Services* 21(3): 389–399.
GLASS, DAVID
1977   "Stress behavior patterns and coronary disease," *American Scientist* 65: 177–187.
GLASSMAN, MARJORIE
1980   "Misdiagnosis of senile dementia: Denial of care to the elderly," *Social Work* 25(4): 288–292.
GLASSNER, BARRY
1989   "Fitness and the postmodern self," *Journal of Health and Social Behavior* 30: 180–191.
1995   "In the name of health," pp. 159–175 in R. Bunton, S. Nettleton, and R. Burrows, eds., *The Sociology of Health Promotion.* London: Routledge.
GLAZER, NONA Y.
1990   "The home as workshop: Women as amateur nurses and medical care providers," *Gender and Society* 4(4): 479–499.
1993   *Women's Paid and Unpaid Labor: The Work Transfer in Health Care and Retailing.* Philadelphia, PA: Temple University Press.
GLIEDMAN, JOHN
1979   "The wheelchair rebellion," *Psychology Today* 13(3): 59–64, 99–101.
GLIEDMAN, JOHN, AND WILLIAM ROTH
1980   "The unexpected minority: Why society is so mystified by handicap," *New Republic* 182(5): 26–30.
GOFFMAN, ERVING
1959   *The Presentation of Self in Everyday Life.* Garden City, NY: Doubleday.
1961   *Asylums.* Garden City, NY: Doubleday.
1963   *Stigma: Notes on the Management of Spoiled Identity.* Englewood Cliffs, NJ: Spectrum/Prentice Hall.
GOLDOFTAS, BARBARA
1991   "Hands that hurt," *Technology Review* 94(1): 42–50.
GOLDSMITH, FRANK, AND LORIN E. KERR
1982   *Occupational Safety and Health.* New York: Human Sciences Press.
GOLDSMITH, JEFF
1993   "Hospital/physician relationships: A constraint to health care reform," *Health Affairs* 12(3): 160–169.
GOLDSTEIN, AMY
1995   "Public hospitals vulnerable to cuts," *Washington Post,* October 19.
GOLDSTEIN, MICHAEL S.
1992   *The Health Movement: Promoting Fitness in America.* New York: Twayne.

GOLDSTEIN, MICHAEL S., DENNIS JAFFE, CAROL SUTHERLAND, AND JOSIE WILSON
  1987   "Holistic physicians: Implications for the study of the medical profession," *Journal of Health and Social Behavior* 28(2): 103–119.

GOOD, BYRON T.
  1977   "The heart of what's the matter: The semantics of illness in Iran," *Culture, Medicine, and Psychiatry* 1: 25–58.
  1994   *Medicine, Rationality, and Experience.* Cambridge: Cambridge University Press.

GOOD, BYRON, AND MARY-JO DELVECCHIO GOOD
  1981   "The meaning of symptoms: A cultural hermeneutic model for clinical practice," pp. 165–196 in A. Kleinman and L. Eisenberg, eds., *The Relevance of Social Science for Medicine.* Dordrecht, Netherlands: D. Reidel.
  1993   " 'Learning Medicine': The constructing of medical knowledge at Harvard Medical School," pp. 81–107 in S. Lindenbaum and M. Lock, eds., *Knowledge, Power, and Practice.* Berkeley: University of California Press.

GOOD, CHARLES M.
  1987   *Ethnomedical Systems in Africa: Patterns of Traditional Medicine in Rural and Urban Kenya.* New York: Guilford.

GOOD, MARY-JO DELVECCHIO
  1995   *American Medicine: The Quest for Competence.* Berkeley: University of California Press.

GOOD, MARY-JO DELVECCHIO, AND BYRON GOOD
  1982   "Patient requests in primary care clinics," pp. 275–295 in N. J. Chrisman and T. W. Maretzki, eds., *Clinically Applied Anthropology.* Dordrecht, Netherlands: D. Reidel.

GOOD, MARY-JO DELVECCHIO, BYRON J. GOOD, ARTHUR KLEINMAN, AND PAUL E. BRODWIN
  1992   "Epilogue," pp. 198–207 in M. J. Delvecchio Good, B. J. Good, A. Kleinman, and P. E. Brodwin, eds., *Pain as Human Experience: An Anthropological Perspective.* Berkeley: University of California Press.

GORDON, DEBORAH
  1988   "Tenacious assumptions in Western medicine," pp. 19–56 in M. Lock and D. R. Gordon, eds., *Biomedicine Examined.* Dordrecht, Netherlands: Kluwer.

GORDON, SUZANNE
  1995   "Is there a nurse in the house?" *The Nation,* February 13: 199–202.

GORE, SUSAN
  1978   "The effect of social support in moderating the health consequences of unemployment," *Journal of Health and Social Behavior* 19: 157–165.

GOTTLIEB, MARTIN, AND KURT EICHENWALD
  1997   "A hospital chain's brass knuckles, and the backlash," *New York Times,* May 11.

GOULD-MARTIN, KATHERINE, AND CHORSWANG NGIN
  1981   "Chinese Americans," pp. 130–171 in A. Harwood, ed., *Ethnicity and Medical Care.* Cambridge, MA: Harvard University Press.

GRAHAM, HILARY
  1985   "Providers, negotiators, and mediators: Women as the hidden carers," pp. 25–52 in E. Lewin and V. Oleson, eds., *Women, Health, and Healing: Toward a New Perspective.* New York: Tavistock.

GRAY, ALASTAIR MCINTOSH
  1982   "Inequalities in health, The Black Report: A summary and comment," *International Journal of Health Services* 12(3): 349–380.

GRAY, BRADFORD H.
1991   *The Profit Motive and Patient Care: The Changing Accountability of Doctors and Hospitals.* Cambridge, MA: Harvard University Press.
1997   "Trust and trustworthy care in the managed care era," *Health Affairs* 16(1): 34–48.

GREEN, JEREMY
1983   "Detecting the hypersusceptible worker: Genetics and politics in industrial medicine," *International Journal of Health Services* 13(2): 247–264.

GREEN, LINDA BUCKLEY
1989   "Consensus and coercion: Primary health care and the Guatemalan state," *Medical Anthropology Quarterly* 3(3): 246–257.

GRIFFITH, JAMES L., AND MELISSA E. GRIFFITH
1994   *The Body Speaks.* New York: Basic Books.

GRITZER, GLENN
1981   "Occupational specialization in medicine: Knowledge and market explanations," *Research in the Sociology of Health Care* 2: 251–283.

GRONEMAN, CAROL
1995   "Nymphomania: The historical construction of female sexuality," pp. 219–249 in J. Terry and J. Urla, eds., *Deviant Bodies.* Bloomington: Indiana University Press.

GROOPMAN, LEONARD C.
1987   "Medical internship as moral education: An essay on the system of training physicians," *Culture, Medicine, and Psychiatry* 11: 207–227.

GROSS, EDITH B.
1994   "Health care rationing: Its effects on cardiologists in the United States and Britain," *Sociology of Health and Illness* 16(1):19–37.

GROSSINGER, RICHARD
1990   *Planet Medicine.* Berkeley, CA: North Atlantic Books.

GRUCHOW, WILLIAM
1979   "Catecholamine activity and infectious disease episodes," *Journal of Human Stress* 5(3): 11–17.

GUARASCI, RICHARD
1987   "Death by cotton dust," pp. 76–92 in S. L. Hills, ed., *Corporate Violence.* Totowa, NJ: Rowman and Littlefield.

GUARNACCIA, PETER, AND PABLO FARIAS
1988   "The social meaning of nervios: A case study of a Central American woman," *Social Science and Medicine* 26(12): 1223–1231.

GUARNACCIA, PETER J., VICTOR DELACANCELA, AND EMILIO CARRILLO
1989   "The multiple meanings of *ataques de nervios* in the Latino community," *Medical Anthropology* 11: 47–62.

GUELL, ROBERT C., AND MARVIN FISCHBAUM
1995   "Toward allocative efficiency in the prescription drug industry," *The Milbank Quarterly* 73(2): 213–230.

GUILLEMIN, JEANNE H., AND L. L. HOLMSTROM
1986   *Mixed Blessings: Intensive Care for Newborns.* New York: Oxford University Press.

GURALNIK, JAMES M., AND EDWARD L. SCHNEIDER
1990   "The compression of morbidity: A dream which may come true, someday!" pp. 42–53 in P. R. Lee and C. L. Estes, eds., *The Nation's Health.* Boston: Jones and Bartlett.

GUSFIELD, JOSEPH R.
 1981   *The Culture of Public Problems: Drinking-Driving and the Symbolic Order.* Chicago: University of Chicago Press.

GUSSOW, JOAN DYE, ED.
 1978   *The Feeding Web: Issues in Nutritional Ecology.* Palo Alto, CA: Bull.

HABER, SUZANNE N., AND PATRICIA BARCHAS
 1984   "The regulatory effect of social rank on behavior after amphetamine administration," pp. 119–132 in P. Barchas and S. P. Mendoza, eds., *Social Hierarchies: Essays Toward a Sociophysiological Perspective.* Westport, CT: Greenwood.

HAEHN, KLAUS-DIETER
 1980   "Heilpraktikerbesuche chronisch Kranker: Frequenz und Motivation," *Diagnostik* 13: 145–146.

HAFFERTY, FREDERIC W., AND DONALD W. LIGHT
 1995   "Professional dynamics and the changing nature of medical work," *Journal of Health and Social Behavior* (extra issue): 132–153.

HAHN, HARLAN
 1988   "The politics of physical differences: Disability and discrimination," *Journal of Social Issues* 44(1): 39–47.
 1994   "The minority group model of disability: Implications for medical sociology," *Research in the Sociology of Health Care* 11:3–24.

HAHN, ROBERT A.
 1995   *Sickness and Healing: An Anthropological Perspective.* New Haven, CT: Yale University Press.

HAHN, ROBERT A., AND ARTHUR KLEINMAN
 1983   "Biomedical practice and anthropological theory: Frameworks and directions," *American Review of Anthropology* 12: 305–333.

HAMMOND, PHILLIP E.
 1974   "Religion, pluralism, and Durkheim's integration thesis," pp. 115–142 in A. Eister, ed., *Changing Perspectives in the Scientific Study of Religion.* New York: Wiley.

HARASZTI, MIKLOS
 1978   *A Worker in a Worker's State.* New York: Universe.

HARBURG, ERNEST, JOHN C. ERFURT, LOUISE HAUNSTEIN, CATHERINE CHAPE, WILLIAM SCHULL, AND M. A. SCHORK
 1973   "Socio-ecological stress, suppressed hostility, skin color, and black-white male blood pressure, Detroit," *Psychosomatic Medicine* 35: 276–296.

HARDING, JIM
 1981   "The pharmaceutical industry as a public-health hazard and as an institution of social control," pp. 274–291 in D. Coburn, C. D'Arcy, P. Ness, and G. M. Torrance, *Health and Canadian Society: Sociological Perspective.* Pickering, Ont.: Fitzhenry and Whiteside.
 1986   "Mood-modifiers and elderly women in Canada: The medicalization of poverty," pp. 51–86 in K. McDonnell, ed., *Adverse Effects: Women and the Pharmaceutical Industry.* Toronto: Women's Educational Press.

HARKIN, MICHAEL
 1994   "Contested bodies: Affliction and power in Heiltsuk culture and history," *American Ethnologist* 21 (3): 586–605.

HARRINGTON, CHARLENE
 1984   "The nursing home industry," pp. 144–154 in M. Minkler and C. L. Estes, eds., *Readings in the Political Economy of Aging.* Farmingdale, NY: Baywood.

1996   "The nursing home industry: Public policy in the 1990s," pp. 515–534 in P. Brown, ed., *Perspectives in Medical Sociology*. Prospect Heights, IL: Waveland Press.

HARRIS, MARVIN
1985   *The Sacred Cow and the Abominable Pig: Riddles of Food and Culture*. New York: Simon & Schuster.

HARRISON, JAMES, JAMES CHIN, AND THOMAS FICARROTTO
1992   "Warning, masculinity may be dangerous to your health," pp. 271–285 in M. S. Kimmel and M. A. Mesner, eds., *Men's Lives*. New York: Macmillan.

HART, PETER
1990   *A Nationwide Survey of Attitudes on Health Care and Nurses*. Washington, DC: Peter Hart Organization.

HARTMANN, BETSY
1987   *Reproductive Rights and Wrongs: The Global Politics of Population Control and Contraceptive Choice*. New York: Harper & Row.

HARWOOD, ALAN
1977   *Rx: Spiritist as Needed: A Study of a Puerto Rican Community Mental Health Resource*. New York: Wiley.
1981a   "Mainland Puerto Ricans," pp. 397–481 in A. Harwood, ed., *Ethnicity and Medical Care*. Cambridge, MA: Harvard University Press.

HATFIELD, ELAINE, AND SUSAN SPRECHER
1986   *Mirror, Mirror . . . : The Importance of Looks in Everyday Life*. Albany: State University of New York Press.

HAY, IAIN
1992   *Money, Medicine and Malpractice in American Society*. New York: Praeger.

HAYES, DENNIS
1989   *Behind the Silicon Curtain: The Seductions of Work in a Lonely Era*. Boston: South End Press.

HAYNES, SUZANNE G.
1991   "The effect of job demands, job control and new technologies on the health of employed women," pp. 157–169 in M. Frankenhaeuser, U. Lundberg, and M. Chesney, eds., *Women, Work and Health*. New York: Plenum Press.

Health Letter
1987   "Tranquilizing air traffic controllers," 3(12): 11–12.

HEGGENHOUGEN, KRIS, PATRICK VAUGHAN, EUSTACE MUHONDWA, AND J. RUTABANZIBWA-NGAIZA
1987   *Community Health Workers: The Tanzanian Experience*. Oxford: Oxford Medical Publications, Oxford University Press.

HELLANDER, IDA, DAVID U. HIMMELSTEIN, STEFFIE WOOLHANDLER, AND SIDNEY WOLFE
1994   "Health care paper chase, 1993: The cost to the nation, the states, and the District of Columbia," *International Journal of Health Services* 24(1): 1–9.

HELLANDER, IDA, JAMALUDDIN MOLOO, DAVID U. HIMMELSTEIN, STEFFIE WOOLHANDLER, AND SIDNEY M. WOLFE
1995   "The growing epidemic of uninsurance," *International Journal of Health Services* 25(3): 377–392.

HELMAN, CECIL
1978   " 'Feed a cold, starve a fever'–Folk models of infection in an English suburban community and their relation to medical treatment," *Culture, Medicine, and Psychiatry* 2: 107–137.

1985 "Communication in primary care: The role of patient and practitioner explanatory models," *Social Science and Medicine* 20(9): 923–931.

HENLEY, NANCY M.
1977 *Body Politics.* Englewood Cliffs, NJ: Prentice Hall.

HERZLICH, CLAUDINE
1973 "Health and illness: A social-psychological analysis," *European Monographs in Social Psychology, vol. 5.* London: Academic Press.

HERZLICH, CLAUDINE, AND JANINE PIERRET
1987 *Illness and Self in Society.* Baltimore: Johns Hopkins University Press.

HESS, JOHN L.
1987 "Malthus then and now," *Nation,* 244(15): 496–500.

HEURTIN-ROBERTS, SUZANNE, AND EFRAIN REISIN
1990 "Folk models of hypertension among black women: Problems in illness management," pp. 222–250 in J. Coreil and J. D. Mull, eds., *Anthropology and Primary Health Care.* Boulder, CO: Westview Press.

HEYWARD, WILLIAM L., AND JAMES W. CURRAN
1988 "The epidemiology of A.I.D.S. in the U.S.," *Scientific American* 259(4): 72–81.

HIBBARD, JUDITH H., AND CLYDE R. POPE
1993 "The equality of social roles as predictors of morbidity and mortality," *Social Science and Medicine* 36(3): 217–225.

HILBERT, RICHARD A.
1984 "The acultural dimensions of chronic pain: Flawed reality construction and the problem of meaning," *Social Problems* 31(4): 365–378.

HILFIKER, DAVID
1983 "Allowing the debilitated to die: Facing our ethical choices," *New England Journal of Medicine* 308: 718.
1984 "Making medical mistakes," *Harper's Magazine* 268(1606): 59–65.
1986 "A doctor's view of modern medicine," *New York Times Magazine,* February 23.
1994 *Not All of Us Are Saints: A Doctor's Journey with the Poor.* New York: Hill and Wang.

HILL, JOANNA M.
1989 "Neuropeptides and their receptor as the biochemicals of emotion," pp. 61–74 in D. Palermo, ed., *Coping with Uncertainty: Behavioral and Developmental Perspectives.* Hillsdale, NJ: Erlbaum.

HILL, ROLLA B., AND ROBERT ANDERSON
1988 *The Autopsy: Medical Practice and Public Policy.* Boston: Butterworth.
1991 "The autopsy crisis reexamined: The case for a national autopsy policy," *The Milbank Quarterly* 69(1): 51–78.

HILL, SHIRLEY A.
1995 "Taking charge and making do: Childhood chronic illness in low-income black families," *Research in the Sociology of Health Care* 12: 141–156.

HILLMAN, MAYER, JOHN ADAMS, AND JOHN WHITELEGG
1990 *One False Move—A Study of Children's Independent Mobility.* London: Policy Studies Institute.

HILLS, STUART L., ED.
1987 *Corporate Violence.* Totowa, NJ: Rowman and Littlefield.

HILTS, PHILIP J.
1996 "Most doctors with violations keep their license," *New York Times,* March 29.

HIMMELSTEIN, DAVID, AND STEFFIE WOOLHANDLER
    1986   "Cost without benefit: Administrative waste in U.S. health care," *New England Journal of Medicine* 134(7): 441–445.
    1996   "U.S. health reform: Unkindest cuts," *The Nation* 262(3): 16–20.
HIMMELSTEIN, DAVID, STEFFIE WOOLHANDLER, MARTHA HARNLY, MICHAEL BADER, RALPH SILBER, HOWARD BACKER, AND ALICE JONES
    1984   "Patient transfers: Medical practice as social triage," *American Journal of Public Health* 74: 494–496.
HIMMELSTEIN, DAVID, STEFFIE WOOLHANDLER, AND SIDNEY M. WOLFE
    1992   "The vanishing health care safety net: New data on uninsured Americans," *International Journal of Health Services* 22(3): 381–396.
HINDS, MICHAEL DE COURCY
    1987   "Consumer Groups' Dishonor Roll of '87," *New York Times*, December 5.
HOCHSCHILD, ARLIE
    1983   *The Managed Heart: Commercialization of Human Feeling*. Berkeley: University of California Press.
    1989   *The Second Shift*. New York: Viking Penguin.
HOKANSON, J. E., AND M. BURGESS
    1962   "The effects of three types of aggression on vascular processes," *Journal of Abnormal and Social Psychology* 648: 446–449.
HOLAHAN, JOHN, COLIN WINTERBOTTOM, AND SHRUTI RAJAN
    1995   "A shifting picture of health insurance coverage," *Health Affairs* 14(4): 253–264.
HOLDEN, JOHN M.
    1989   "Maxicare posts $17.2 million loss; regulators contest Chapter 11 status," *American Medical News*, April 21.
HOLTZ KAY, JANE
    1997   *Asphalt Nation*. New York: Crown.
HOMOLA, SAMUEL
    1968   *Backache: Home Treatment and Prevention*. West Nyack, NY: Parker.
HOOYMAN, NANCY R., AND JUDITH GONYEA
    1995   *Feminist Perspectives on Family Care*. Thousand Oaks, CA: Sage.
HOROBIN, GORDON, AND JIM MCINTOSH
    1983   "Time, risk, and routine in general practice," *Sociology of Health and Illness* 5(3): 312–331.
HORTON, ELIZABETH
    1985a   "Unfriendly persuasion," *Science Digest* 93(12): 214.
    1985b   "Why don't we buckle up?" *Science Digest* 93(2): 22.
HORWITZ, JILL, AND TROYEN BRENNAN
    1995   "Medical malpractice," pp. 307–327 in D. Calkins, R. J. Fernandopulle, B. S. Marino, eds., *Health Care Policy*. Cambridge, MA: Blackwell Science.
HORWITZ, RALPH I., CATHERINE M. VISCOLI, LISA BERKMAN, ROBERT M. DONALDSON, SARAH M. HORWITZ, CAROLYN J. MURRARY, DAVID F. RANSOHOFF, AND JODY SINDELAR
    1990   "Treatment adherence and risk of death after a myocardial infarction," *The Lancet* 136 (September 1): 542–545.
HOTZ, ROBERT LEE
    1993   "Experiment to aid growth of short children resumes," *Los Angeles Times*, June 29.

HOUBEN, GERARD J.
1991   "Production control and chronic stress in work organizations," *International Journal of Health Services* 21(2): 309–327.

HOUSE, JAMES S.
1981   *Work Stress and Social Support.* Reading, MA: Addison-Wesley.

HOUSE, JAMES S., RONALD C. KESSLER, A. REGULA HERZOG, RICHARD P. MERO, ANN M. KINNEY, AND MARTHA J. BRESLAW
1990   "Age, socioeconomic status and health," *The Milbank Quarterly* 68(3): 383–411.

HOUSE, JAMES S., KARL R. LANDIS, AND DEBRA UMBERSON
1988   "Social relationships and health," *Science* 214 (July): 540–545.

HOWARD, ROBERT
1985   *Brave New Workplace.* New York: Penguin.

HOY, ELIZABETH W., RICHARD E. CURTIS, AND THOMAS RICE
1991   "Change and growth in managed care," *Health Affairs* 10(4): 18–36.

HUGHES, DAVID
1988   "When nurse knows best: Some aspects of nurse/doctor interaction in a casualty department," *Sociology of Health and Illness* 10(1): 1–22.

HUGHES, JAMES J.
1996   "Managed care, university hospitals, and the doctor-nurse division of labor," *Research in the Sociology of Health Care* 13A: 63–92.

Hunger, U.S.A.: A Report by the Citizens' Board of Inquiry into Hunger and Malnutrition in the United States.
1968   Boston: Beacon.

HUNT, LINDA, M., BRIGITTE JORDAN, AND SUSAN IRWIN
1989   "Views of what's wrong: Diagnosis and patients' concepts of illness," *Social Science and Medicine* 28(9): 945–956.

HUNT, SONJA M.
1989   "The public health implications of private cars," pp. 100–115 in C. J. Martin and D. V. McQueen, eds., *Readings for a New Public Health.* Edinburgh: Edinburgh University Press.

HUROWITZ, JAMES C.
1993   "Toward a social policy for health," *New England Journal of Medicine* 329(2): 130–133.

IGLEHART, JOHN K.
1993   "The American health care system: The End Stage Renal Disease Program," *New England Journal of Medicine* 328(5): 366–371.

ILLICH, IVAN
1975   *Medical Nemesis: The Expropriation of Health.* London: Calder and Boyars.

INGLEBY, DAVID
1982   "The social construction of mental illness," pp. 123–143 in P. Wright and A. Treacher, eds., *The Problem of Medical Knowledge: Examining the Social Construction of Medicine.* Edinburgh: Edinburgh University Press.

INSTITUTE FOR WOMEN'S POLICY RESEARCH
1994   *Women's Access to Health Insurance.* Washington, DC: Institute for Women's Policy Research.

INSTITUTE OF MEDICINE
1986   *For-Profit Enterprise in Health Care.* Washington, DC: National Academy Press.

IRWIN, SUSAN, AND BRIGITTE JORDAN
1987   "Knowledge, practice, and power: Court-ordered Cesarean section," *Medical Anthropology Quarterly* 1(3): 319–334.

IVEREM, ESTHER
  1988 "New York's home health-care system facing a labor crisis," *New York Times*, January 28.
JACKALL, ROBERT
  1977 "The control of public faces in a commercial work situation," *Urban Life* 6(3): 277–302.
JACKSON, JEAN
  1994 "Chronic pain and the tension between the body as subject and object," pp. 201–228 in T. J. Csordas, ed., *Embodiment and Experience*. Cambridge: Cambridge University Press.
JACKSON, MICHAEL
  1983 "Knowledge of the body," *Man* 18: 327–345.
JACOBSON, ALAN M., AND JOAN B. LEIBOVICH
  1984 "Psychological issues in diabetes mellitus," *Psychosomatics* 25(1): 7–15.
JAMES, VERONICA, AND JONATHAN GABE, EDS.
  1996 *Health and the Sociology of Emotions*. Oxford: Blackwell.
JANES, CRAIG
  1986 "Migration and hypertension: An ethnography of disease risk in an urban Samoan community," pp. 175–211 in C. Janes, R. Stall, and S. Gifford, eds., *Anthropology and Epidemiology: Interdisciplinary Approaches to the Study of Health and Disease*. Dordrecht, Holland: D. Reidel.
JEFFERY, ROGER
  1979 "Normal rubbish: Deviant patients in casualty departments," *Sociology of Health and Illness* 1(1): 90–107.
JENSEN, GAIL A., MICHAEL A. MORRISEY, SHANNON GAFFNEY, AND DEREK K. LISTON
  1997 "The new dominance of managed care: Insurance trends in the 1990s," *Health Affairs* 16(1): 125–136.
JOHANNESSEN, HELLE, LAILA LAUNSØ, SØREN GOSVIG OLESEN, AND FRANTS STAUGÅRD
  1994 *Studies in Alternative Therapy 1: Contributions from the Nordic Countries*. Odense (Denmark): INRAT/ Odense University Press.
JOHNSON, ALLEN
  1978 "In search of the affluent society," *Human Nature* 1: 50–59.
JOHNSON, DANIEL M., J. SHERWOOD WILLIAMS, AND DAVID BROMLEY
  1986 "Religion, health and healing: Findings from a southern city," *Sociological Analysis* 47(1): 66–73.
JOHNSON, ERNEST H., AND LARRY M. GANT
  1996 "The association between anger-hostility and hypertension," pp. 95–116 in H. W. Neighbors and J. S. Jackson, eds., *Mental Health in Black America*. Thousand Oaks, CA: Sage.
JOHNSON, THOMAS M.
  1987 "Premenstrual syndrome as a Western culture-specific disorder," *Culture, Medicine, and Psychiatry*, 11: 337–356.
JOHNSON, THOMAS M., AND CAROLYN F. SARGENT
  1990 *Medical Anthropology: A Handbook of Theory and Method*. New York: Greenwood Press.
JONES, JAMES H.
  1981 *Bad Blood: The Tuskegee Syphilis Experiment*. New York: Free Press.
JONES, KATHRYN
  1993 "A hospital giant comes to town, bringing change," *New York Times*, November 21.

JONES, R. KENNETH
   1985   "The development of medical sects," pp. 1–22 in R. K. Jones, ed., *Sickness and Sectarianism: Exploratory Studies in Medical and Religious Sectarianism.* London: Gower.
JONES, RUSSELL A.
   1982   "Expectations and illness," pp. 145–167 in H. S. Friedman and M. R. DiMatteo, eds., *Interpersonal Issues in Health Care.* New York: Academic.
Journal of the American Medical Association
   1996   "Tobacco—The growing epidemic in China," *Journal of the American Medical Association* 275(21): 163.
KANE, ROSALIE A.
   1993   "Delivering and financing long term care in Canada's ten provinces," pp. 89–101 in A. Bennett and O. Adams, eds., *Looking North for Health: What We Can Learn from Canada's Health Care System.* San Francisco: Jossey-Bass.
KAPLAN, HOWARD, ROBERT JOHNSON, CAROL BAILEY, AND WILLIAM SIMON
   1987   "The sociological study of AIDS: A critical review of the literature and suggested research agenda," *Journal of Health and Social Behavior* 28: 140–157.
KAPLAN, JAY, STEPHEN MANUCK, THOMAS CLARKSON, FRANCES LUSSO, DAVID TAUB, AND ERIC MILLER
   1983   "Social stress and atherosclerosis in normocholesterolemic monkeys," *Science* 220(4,598): 733–735.
KARASEK, ROBERT, AND TÖRES THEORELL
   1990   *Healthy Work: Stress, Productivity and the Reconstruction of Working Life.* New York: Basic Books.
KASL, STANISLAV V.
   1975   "Issues in patient adherence to health care regimens," *Journal of Human Stress* 1(1,975): 5–17.
KASL, STANISLAV V., AND SIDNEY COBB
   1966   "Health behavior, illness behavior, and sick role behavior," *Archives of Environmental Health* 12: 246–266.
KASSIRER, JEROME P.
   1989   "Our stubborn quest for diagnostic certainty: A cause of excessive testing," *New England Journal of Medicine* 320: 1489–1491.
   1995   "Our ailing public hospitals," *New England Journal of Medicine* 333(20): 1348–1349.
KASSIRER, JEROME P., AND G. A. GORRY
   1978   "Clinical problem solving: A behavioral analysis," *Annals of Internal Medicine* 89: 245–255.
KASTENBAUM, ROBERT
   1971   "Getting there ahead of time," *Psychology Today* 5: 52–54, 83–84.
KATES, ROBERT W.
   1996   "Population, technology and the human environment: A thread through time," *Daedalus* 125(3), Summer: 43–71.
KATZ, ALFRED
   1979   "Self-help groups: Some clarifications," *Social Science and Medicine* 13A: 491–494.
KATZ, ALFRED, HANNAH L. HEDRICK, D. H. ISENBERG, L. M. THOMPSON, T. GOODRICH, AND A. H. KUTSCHER, EDS.
   1992   *Self-Help: Concepts and Applications.* Philadelphia: The Charles Press.

KATZ, ALFRED, AND LOWELL LEVIN
1980 "Self-care is not a solipsistic trap: A reply to critics," *International Journal of Health Services* 10: 329–336.

KAUFERT, PATRICIA
1988 "Menopause as process or event: The creation of definitions in biomedicine," pp. 331–349 in M. Lock and D. R. Gordon, eds., *Biomedicine Examined*. Dordrecht, Netherlands: Kluwer.

KAUFERT, PATRICIA, AND SONJA M. MCKINLAY
1985 "Estrogen-replacement therapy: The production of medical knowledge and the emergence of policy," pp. 113–138 in E. Lewin and V. Olesen, eds., *Women, Health, and Healing: Toward a New Perspective*. London: Tavistock.

KAUFMAN, CAROLINE
1987 "Rights and the provision of health care: A comparison of Canada, Great Britain, and the United States," pp. 491–510 in H. D. Schwartz, ed., *Dominant Issues in Medical Care*. New York: Random House.

KAUFMAN, MARTIN
1971 *Homeopathy in America: The Rise and Fall of a Medical Heresy*. Baltimore: Johns Hopkins University Press.

KAUFMAN, SHARON R.
1988 "Toward a phenomenology of boundaries in medicine: Chronic illness experience in the case of stroke," *Medical Anthropology Quarterly* 2(4): 338–354.

KAUR, NARINDER
1990 "Impact of consumer culture on health," pp. 131–143 in B. Chaudhuri, ed., *Cultural and Environmental Dimensions on Health*. New Delhi: Inter India.

KEARL, MICHAEL
1993 "Dying American style: From moral to technological rite of passage," *American Journal of Ethics & Medicine* (Fall): 12–18.

KELLY, MICHAEL P., AND DAVID FIELD
1996 "Medical sociology, chronic illness and the body," *Sociology of Health and Illness* 18(2): 241–257.

KEMPER, VICKI, AND VIVECA NOVAK
1993 "What's blocking health care reform?" *International Journal of Health Services* 23(1): 69–79.

KENNEDY, BRUCE P., ICHIRO KAWACHI, AND DEBORAH PROTHROW-STITH
1996 "Income distribution and mortality: Cross-sectional ecological study of the Robin Hood Index in the United States," *British Medical Journal* 312: 1004–1007.

KERR, PETER
1991a "Chain of mental hospitals faces inquiry in 4 states," *New York Times*, October 22.
1991b "Mental hospital chains accused of much cheating on insurance," *New York Times*, November 24.
1992 "Centers for head injury accused of earning millions for neglect," *New York Times*, March 16.

KIECOLT-GLASER, JANET K., AND RONALD GLASER
1991 "Stress and immune function in humans," pp. 849–867 in R. Ader, D. Felten, and N. Cohen, eds., *Psychoneuroimmunology* (2nd ed.). New York: Academic Press.

KIEV, ARI
1968 *Curanderismo: Mexican-American Folk Psychiatry*. New York: Free Press.

KILBORN, PETER
1996   "Factories that never close are scrapping the 5-day week," *New York Times*, June 4: A1.
KING, PATRICIA A.
1992   "The dangers of difference," *Hastings Center Report* 22(6): 35–38.
KING, RALPH T., JR.
1996   "How a drug firm paid for university study, then undermined it," *Wall Street Journal*, April 25.
KINLEY, DAVID, ARNOLD LEVINSON, AND FRANCES MOORE-LAPPÉ
1981   "The myth of humanitarian foreign aid," *Nation* 233(2): 41–43.
KIRCHER, TOBIAS, JUDITH NELSON, AND HAROLD BURDO
1985   "The autopsy as a measure of accuracy of the death certificate," *New England Journal of Medicine* 313: 1263–1269.
KIRMAYER, LAURENCE J.
1988   "Mind and body as metaphors: Hidden values in biomedicine," pp. 57–94 in M. Lock and D. R. Gordon, eds., *Biomedicine Examined*. Dordrecht, Netherlands: Kluwer.
KLEIN, DAVID, JACKOB NAJMAN, ARTHUR KOHRMAN, AND CLARKE MUNRO
1982   "Patient characteristics that elicit negative responses from family physicians," *Journal of Family Practice* 14(5): 881–888.
KLEINMAN, ARTHUR
1978   "The failure of Western medicine," *Human Nature* 1: 63–68.
1980   *Patients and Healers in the Context of Culture: An Exploration of the Borderland Between Anthropology, Medicine, and Psychiatry*. Berkeley: University of California Press.
1984   "Indigenous systems of healing: Questions for professional, popular, and folk care," pp. 138–164 in J. W. Salmon, ed., *Alternative Medicine: Popular and Policy Perspectives*. New York: Tavistock.
1988   *The Illness Narratives: Suffering, Healing, and the Human Condition*. New York: Basic.
1992   "Pain and resistance: The delegitimation and relegitimation of local worlds," pp. 169–197 in M. Delvecchio Good, P. E. Brodwin, B. J. Good, and A. Kleinman, eds., *Pain as Human Experience: An Anthropological Perspective*. Berkeley: University of California Press.
1995   *Writing at the Margin: Discourse between Anthropology and Medicine*. Berkeley: University of California Press.
KLEINMAN, ARTHUR, AND JOAN KLEINMAN
1991   "Suffering and its professional transformation: Toward an ethnography of interpersonal experience," *Culture, Medicine and Psychiatry* 15(3): 275–301.
KLINKENBORG, VERLYN
1997   "Awakening to sleep," *New York Times Magazine* (January 5).
KNICKMAN, JAMES R., AND KENNETH E. THORPE
1995   "Financing for health care," pp. 267–293 in A. R. Kovner, ed., *Jonas's Health Care Delivery in the United States*. New York: Springer.
KNUTSSON, ANDER S., BJORN G. JONSSON, TORBJÖRN ÅKERSTEDT, AND KRISTINA ORTH-GOMER
1986   "Increased risk of ischemic heart disease in shift workers," *The Lancet* 2: 86–92.
KOENIG, BARBARA
1988   "The technological imperative in medical practice: The social creation of a 'routine' treatment," pp. 465–496 in M. Lock and D. R. Gordon, eds., *Biomedicine Examined*. Dordrecht, Netherlands: Kluwer.

KOGAN, MONROE D., GREG R. ALEXANDER, MARTHA A. TEITELBAUM, BRIAN W. JACK, MILTON KOTELCHUCK, AND GREGORY PAPPAS
1995   "The effects of gaps in health insurance on continuity of a regular source of care among preschool-aged children in the United States," *Journal of the American Medical Association* 274(18): 1429–1435.

KOLATA, GINA
1994   "Study says 1 in 5 Americans suffers from chronic pain," *New York Times*, October 21.
1996   "AIDS patients slipping through safety net," *New York Times*, September 15.

KONNER, MELVIN
1987   *Becoming a Doctor: A Journey of Initiation in Medical School*. New York: Viking.

KOPRIVA, PHYLLIS
1995   "Women in medicine," pp. 123–133 in E. Friedman, ed., *An Unfinished Revolution: Women and Health Care in America*. New York: United Hospital Fund.

KOTARBA, JOSEPH A.
1975   "American acupuncturists: The new entrepreneurs of hope," *Urban Life* 4(2): 149–177.
1977   "The chronic pain experience," pp. 257–272 in J. Douglas, ed., *Existential Sociology*. Cambridge: Cambridge University Press.

KOTZSCH, RONALD
1985   "How our food choices affect the world," *East West Journal*, June: 15–19.

KRAUT, ALAN M.
1994   *Silent Travelers: Germs, Genes, and the "Immigrant Menace."* New York: Basic Books.

KRIEGER, NANCY
1994   "Epidemiology and the web of causation: Has anyone seen the spider?" *Social Science and Medicine* 39(7): 887–903.

KRIEGER, NANCY, AND ELIZABETH FEE
1994   "Man-made medicine and women's health: The biopolitics of sex/gender and race/ethnicity," *International Journal of Health Services* 24(2): 265–283.

KRISTOF, NICHOLAS D.
1997   "For Third World, water is still a deadly drink," *New York Times*, January 9.

KROHNE, HEINZ WALTER
1990   "Personality as a mediator between objective events and their subjective representation," *Psychological Inquiry* 1(1): 26–29.

KUHN, THOMAS S.
1970   *The Structure of Scientific Revolutions. International Encyclopedia of Unified Science, Vol. 2, No. 2.* Chicago: University of Chicago Press.

KUNISCH, JUDITH R.
1989   "Electronic fetal monitors: Marketing forces and the resulting controversy," pp. 41–60 in K. S. Ratcliff, ed., *Healing Technology: Feminist Perspectives*. Ann Arbor: University of Michigan Press.

KUNITZ, STEPHEN, AND JERROLD LEVY
1981   "Navajos," pp. 337–396 in A. Harwood, ed., *Ethnicity and Medical Care*. Cambridge, MA: Harvard University Press.

KUNZLE, DAVID
1981   *Fashion and Fetishism: A Social History of the Corset, Tight-Lacing and Other Forms of Body Sculpture in the West*. London: Rowan and Littlefield.

KUTNER, NANCY
    1982   "Cost-benefit issues in U.S. national health legislation: The case of the end-stage renal disease program," *Social Problems* 30(1): 51–63.

LACHEEN, CARY
    1986   "Population control and the pharmaceutical industry," pp. 89–136 in K. McDonnell, ed., *Adverse Effects: Women and the Pharmaceutical Industry*. Toronto: Women's Educational Press.

LACK, DOROTHEA Z.
    1982   "Women and pain: Another feminist issue," *Women and Therapy* 1(1): 55–63.

LADERMAN, CAROL, AND MARINA ROSEMAN, EDS.
    1995   *The Performance of Healing*. New York: Routledge.

LAGNADO, LUCETTE
    1997   "Hospitals profit by 'upcoding' illnesses," *Wall Street Journal*, April 17: B1, 10.

LAING, RONALD, AND AARON ESTERSON
    1965   *Sanity, Madness and the Family*. New York: Basic.

LAKOFF, ROBIN T., AND RAQUEL L. SCHERR
    1984   *Face Value: The Politics of Beauty*. Boston: Routledge and Kegan Paul.

LANDEFELD, C. SETH, MARY-MARGARET CHEN, ANN MYERS, RICHARD GELLER, STANLEY ROBBINS, AND LEE GOLDMAN
    1988   "Diagnostic yield of the autopsy in a university hospital and a community hospital," *New England Journal of Medicine* 318 (19): 1249–1254.

LANDEFELD, C. SETH, AND LEE GOLDMAN
    1989   "The autopsy in clinical medicine," *Mayo Clinic Proceedings* 64(9): 1185–1189.

LAPLANTE, MITCHELL P.
    1996   "Health conditions and impairments causing disability," *Disability Statistics Abstract* 16 (September).

LARDY, NICHOLAS R.
    1983   *Agriculture in China's Modern Economic Development*. Cambridge: Cambridge University Press.

LAROCCO, JAMES M., AND JAMES S. HOUSE
    1980   "Social support, occupational stress and health," *Journal of Health and Social Behavior* 21: 202–218.

LARSON, MAGALI SARFATTI
    1979   "Professionalism: Rise and fall," *International Journal of Health Services* 9(4): 607–627.

LASSEY, MARIE L., WILLIAM R. LASSEY, AND MARTIN J. JINKS
    1997   *Health Care Systems around the World*. Upper Saddle River, NJ: Prentice Hall.

LATHAM, MICHAEL C.
    1987   "Strategies for the control of malnutrition and the influence of the nutritional sciences," pp. 330–345 in J. Price, G. Hinger, J. Leslie, and C. Hoisington, eds., *Food Policy: Integrating Supply, Distribution and Consumption*. Baltimore: Johns Hopkins University Press.

LATOUR, BRUNO, AND STEVE WOOLGAR
    1979   *Laboratory Life: The Social Construction of Scientific Fact*. Beverly Hills, CA: Sage.

LATTIMER, MARK, AND SIMON GARFIELD
    1996   "Going private at your expense," *The Guardian*, October 12: 2.

LA VEIST, THOMAS A.
    1992   "The political empowerment and health status of African Americans: Mapping a new territory," *American Journal of Sociology* 97(4): 1080–1095.

1993   "Segregation, poverty and empowerment: Health consequences for African Americans," *The Milbank Quarterly* 71(1): 41–64.

LAW, SYLVIA
1974   *Blue Cross—What Went Wrong?* New Haven: Yale University Press.

LAWRENCE, LINDA, AND THOMAS MCLEMORE
1983   "1981 National Ambulatory Medical Care Survey," *Advance Data, Report Number 88.*

LAWRENCE, PHILIP
1958   "Chronic illness and socioeconomic status," pp. 37–49 in E. G. Jaco, ed., *Patients, Physicians and Illness.* New York: Free Press.

LAZARUS, ELLEN S.
1988   "Theoretical considerations for the study of the doctor-patient relationship: Implications of a perinatal study," *Medical Anthropology Quarterly* 2(1): 34–58.

LAZARUS, RICHARD, ED.
1966   *Psychological Stress and the Coping Process.* New York: McGraw-Hill.

LEAR, DANA
1996   "Women and A.I.D.S. in Africa: A critical review," pp. 276–301 in J. Subedi and E. B. Gallagher, eds., *Society, Health and Disease.* Upper Saddle River, NJ: Prentice Hall.

LEARY, WARREN E.
1991   "With one disease defeated, another is attacked," *New York Times,* December 6.
1995a   "Government gives up right to control prices of drugs it helps develop," *New York Times,* April 12.
1995b   "Routine electronic monitoring of fetuses is challenged in study," *New York Times,* October 25.

LEATH, BRENDA A.
1995   "Homeless children: A growing and vulnerable population," pp. 208–227 in D. L. Adams, ed., *Health Issues for Women of Color.* Thousand Oaks, CA: Sage.

LEDER, DREW
1984   "Medicine and paradigms of embodiment," *Journal of Medicine and Philosophy* 9: 29–43.

LEICHTER, HOWARD M.
1991   *Free to Be Foolish.* Princeton, NJ: Princeton University Press.

LEIDERMAN, DEBORAH, AND JEAN-ANNE GRISSO
1985   "The GOMER phenomenon," *Journal of Health and Social Behavior* 26: 222–231.

LENNERLOF, LENNART
1988   "Learned helplessness at work," *International Journal of Health Services* 18(2): 207–222.

LENNON, MARY CLARE
1994   "Women, work and well-being," *Journal of Health and Social Behavior* 35:235–247.

LERNER, MICHAEL
1992   *Surplus Powerlessness.* Atlantic Highlands, NJ: Humanities Press, Intl.

LESLIE, CHARLES, ED.
1976   *Asian Medical Systems: A Comparative Study.* Berkeley: University of California Press.

LETSCH, SUZANNE W.
1993   "National health care spending in 1991," *Health Affairs* 12(1): 94–110.

LEVI, LENNART
   1978   "Quality of the working environment: Protection and promotion of occupational mental health," *Working Life in Sweden* 8.
   1981   *Preventing Work Stress.* Reading, MA: Addison-Wesley.
LEVIN, LOWELL S., AND ELLEN L. IDLER
   1981   *The Hidden Health Care System: Mediating Structures and Medicine.* Cambridge, MA: Ballinger.
LEVINE, JON D., N. C. GORDON, AND H. FIELDS
   1978   "Mechanism of placebo analgesia," *Lancet* 2(23): 654–657.
LEVINE, SOL R., AND ABRAHAM LILIENFELD, EDS.
   1987   *Epidemiology and Health Policy.* New York: Tavistock.
LEVINS, RICHARD, AND RICHARD LEWONTIN
   1985   *The Dialectical Biologist.* Cambridge, MA: Harvard University Press.
LEVIT, KATHERINE R., MARK S. FREELAND, AND DANIEL R. WALDO
   1989   "Health spending and ability to pay: Business, individuals, and government," *Health Care Financing Review* 3: 10–12.
LEVIT, KATHERINE R., HELEN C. LAZENBY, AND LEKHA SIVARAJAN
   1996   "Health care spending in 1994: Slowest in decades," *Health Affairs* 15(2): 130–144.
LEWIN, TAMAR
   1987   "Company sues its workers' doctors," *New York Times,* June 9.
LEWIN, TAMAR, AND MARTIN GOTTLIEB
   1997   "In hospital sales, an overlooked side effect," *New York Times,* April 27.
LEWIS, CHARLES E.
   1969   "Variance in the incidence of surgery," *New England Journal of Medicine* 281: 880–884.
   1976   "Health maintenance organizations: Guarantors of access to medical care?" pp. 220–240 in C. Lewis, R. Fein, and D. Mechanic, eds., *A Right to Health: The Problem of Access in Primary Care.* New York: Wiley-Interscience.
LEWIS, IOAN M.
   1971   *Ecstatic Religion: An Anthropological Study of Spirit Possession and Shamanism.* Harmondsworth, England: Penguin.
LIGHT, DONALD W.
   1980   *Becoming Psychiatrists: The Professional Transformation of Self.* New York: Norton.
   1992   "Excluding more, covering less: The health insurance industry in the U.S.," *Health/PAC Bulletin,* Spring: 7–13.
   1993   "Countervailing powers," pp. 69–79 in F. W. Hafferty and J. B. McKinlay, eds., *The Changing Character of the Medical Profession.* New York: Oxford University Press.
   1997   "Comparative models of 'health care' systems," pp. 467–482 in P. Conrad, ed., *The Sociology of Health and Illness.* New York: St. Martin's Press.
LIGHT, DONALD W., AND ALEXANDER SCHULLER, EDS.
   1986   *Political Values and Health Care: The German Experience.* Cambridge, MA: MIT Press.
LILIENFELD, DAVID E.
   1991   "The silence: The asbestos industry and early occupational cancer research—a case study," *American Journal of Public Health* 81(6): 791–800.
LINDHEIM, ROSLYN
   1985   "New design parameters for healthy places," *Places* 2(4): 17–27.

LINDORFF, DAVE
1992   *Marketplace Medicine: The Rise of the For-Profit Hospital Chain.* New York: Bantam Books.
LINK, BRUCE G., AND JO PHELAN
1995   "Social conditions in fundamental causes of disease," *Journal of Health and Social Behavior* (Extra Issue): 80–94.
LINK, BRUCE G., EZRA SUSSER, ANN STUEVE, JO PHELAN, ROBERT E. MOORE, AND ELMER STRUENING
1994   "Lifetime and five-year prevalence of homelessness in the United States," *American Journal of Public Health* 84: 1907–1912.
LITTLE, MARILYN
1982   "Conflict and negotiation in a new role: The family nurse practitioner," *Research in the Sociology of Health Care* 2: 31–59.
LITVA, ANDREA, AND JOHN EYLES
1994   "Health or healthy: Why people are not sick in a southern Ontarian town," *Social Science and Medicine* 39(8): 1083–1091.
LIVNEH, HANOCH
1991   "On the origins of negative attitudes toward people with disabilities," pp. 181–196 in R. P. Marinelli and A. E. Dell, eds., *The Psychological and Social Impact of Disability* (3rd ed.). New York: Springer.
LOCK, MARGARET
1990   "On being ethnic: The politics of identity breaking and making in Canada, or, Nevra on Sunday," *Culture, Medicine and Psychiatry* 14(2): 237–254.
1991   "Contested meanings of the menopause," *The Lancet* 337 (May 25): 1270–1272.
1993   "The politics of mid-life and menopause: Ideologies for the second sex in North America and Japan," pp. 330–363 in S. Lindenbaum and M. Lock, eds., *Knowledge, Power, and Practice.* Berkeley: University of California Press.
LOCK, MARGARET, AND NANCY SCHEPER-HUGHES
1990   "A critical-interpretive approach in medical anthropology: Rituals and routines of discipline and dissent," pp. 47–72 in T. M. Johnson and C. F. Sargent, *Medical Anthropology: A Handbook of Theory and Method.* New York: Greenwood.
LOCKE, STEVEN, ROBERT ADER, HUGO BESEDOVSKY, NICOLAS HALL, GEORGE SOLOMON, AND TERRY STROM, EDS.
1985   *Foundations of Psychoneuroimmunology.* New York: Aldine.
LOCKER, DAVID
1981   *Symptoms and Illness: The Cognitive Organization of Disorder.* New York: Tavistock.
LOHR, KATHLEEN, R. H. BROOK, C. J. KAMBERG, G. GOLDBERG, A. LEIBOWITZ, J. KEESEY, D. REBOUSSIN, AND J. P. NEWHOUSE
1986   *Use of Medical Care in the Rand Health Insurance Experiment: Diagnosis and Service-Specific Analysis in a Randomized Control Trial.* Santa Monica, CA: Rand.
LOHR, STEVE
1996   "White House pushing rules on repetitive motion injury," *New York Times,* December 11.
LONGMORE, PAUL K.
1987   "Screening stereotypes: Images of disabled people in television and motion pictures," pp. 65–78 in A. Gartner and T. Joe, eds., *Images of the Disabled, Disabling Images.* New York: Praeger.
LONSDALE, SUSAN
1990   *Women and Disability: The Experiences of Physical Disability among Women.* New York: Macmillan.

LOW, SETHA M.
1985   *Culture, Politics, and Medicine in Costa Rica.* Bedford Hills, NY: Redgrave.
1994   "Embodied metaphors: Nerves as lived experience," pp. 139–162 in T. J. Csordas, ed., *Embodiment and Experience.* Cambridge: Cambridge University Press.

LOWE, MARIAN, AND RUTH HUBBARD, EDS.
1983   *Woman's Nature.* New York: Pergamon.

LOWENBERG, JUNE S., AND FRED DAVIS
1994   "Beyond medicalisation-demedicalisation: The case of holistic health," *Sociology of Health and Illness* 16(5): 579–599.

LUFT, HAROLD
1983   "Economic incentives and clinical decisions," pp. 103–123 in B. Gray, ed., *The New Health Care for Profit: Doctors and Hospitals in a Competitive Environment.* Washington, DC: National Academy Press.

LUKOFF, DAVID, FRANCIS LU, AND ROBERT TURNER
1992   "Toward a more culturally sensitive DSM-IV: Psychoreligious and psychospiritual problems," *The Journal of Nervous and Mental Disease* 180: 673–682.

LUNDBERG, ULF
1976   "Urban commuting: Crowdedness and catecholamine excretion," *Journal of Human Stress* 2(3): 26–31.

LUNDBERG, ULF, ROLAND KADEFORS, BO MELIN, GUNNAR PALMERUD, PETER HASSMÉN, MARGARETA ENGSTRÖM, AND INGELA ELFSBERG DOHNS
1994   "Psychophysiological stress and EMG activity of the trapezius muscle," *International Journal of Behavioral Medicine* 1(4): 354–370.

LUPTON, DEBORAH
1994   *Medicine as Culture.* Thousand Oaks, CA: Sage.
1995   *The Imperative of Health: Public Health and the Regulated Body.* Thousand Oaks, CA: Sage.
1996   *Food, Body, and the Self.* Thousand Oaks, CA: Sage.

LURIE, ELINORE E.
1981   "Nurse practitioners: Issues in professional socialization," *Journal of Health and Social Behavior* 22: 31–48.

LYALL, SARAH
1997   "For British health system, bleak prognosis," *New York Times,* January 30.

LYNCH, JAMES J.
1979   *The Broken Heart.* New York: Basic.
1985   *The Language of the Heart.* New York: Basic.

LYNCH, JAMES J., AND PAUL J. F. ROSCH
1990   "The heart of dialogue: Human communication and cardiovascular health," pp. 31–52 in H. Balner, ed., *A New Medical Model: A Challenge for Biomedicine?* Amsterdam: Swets and Zeitlinger.

LYNCH, MARTY, AND MEREDITH MINKLER
1997   "Impacts of the proposed restructuring of Medicare and Medicaid on the elderly," *International Journal of Health Services* 27(1):57–75.

LYON, MARGOT L.
1990   "Order and healing: The concept of order and its importance in the conceptualization of healing," *Medical Anthropology* 12(10): 249–268.

LYONS, BARBARA, ALINA SALGANICOFF, AND DIANE ROWLAND
1996   "Poverty, access to health care, and Medicaid's critical role for women," pp. 273–295 in M. M. Falik and K. S. Collins, eds., *Women's Health: The Commonwealth Fund Survey.* Baltimore: Johns Hopkins University Press.

MACALISTER, MALCOLM
1992 "The $225,000 habit," *Observer Magazine* (November 8): 22.
MACINTYRE, SALLY
1993 "Gender differences in the perceptions of common cold symptoms," *Social Science and Medicine* 36(1): 15–20.
MACLENNAN, CAROL A.
1988 "From accident to crash: The auto industry and the politics of injury," *Medical Anthropology Quarterly* 2(3): 233–250.
MACMAHON, BRYAN, AND THOMAS F. PUGH
1970 *Epidemiologic Principles and Methods.* Boston: Little, Brown.
MAIRS, NANCY
1987 "Hers," *New York Times,* July 9.
MAKINSON, LARRY
1992 "Political contributions from the health and insurance industries," *Health Affairs* 11(4): 120–134.
MALTHUS, THOMAS ROBERT
[1798] 1965 *Essay on the Principle of Population as It Affects the Future Improvements of Society,* reprinted as *First Essay on Population,* 1798. New York: Kelley.
MANSOUR, JARED
1987 "Eating culture: Food as junk commodity," *Critique* 25: 14–16.
MARCELIS, CARLA, AND MIRA SHIVA
1986 "EP drugs: Unsafe by any name," pp. 11–26 in K. McDonnell, ed., *Adverse Effects: Women and the Pharmaceutical Industry.* Toronto: Women's Educational Press.
MARETZKI, THOMAS, AND EDUARD SEIDLER
1985 "Biomedicine and naturopathic healing in West Germany: A historical and ethnomedical view of a stormy relationship," *Culture, Medicine, and Psychiatry* 9(4): 383–421.
MARKS, NADINE F.
1996 "Socioeconomic status, gender and health at midlife," *Research in the Sociology of Health Care* 13(A):135–152.
MARMOR, THEODORE R.
1993 "Patterns of fact and fiction in the use of the Canadian experience," *American Review of Canadian Studies* 23(1): 47–64.
1994 *Understanding Health Care Reform.* New Haven: Yale University Press.
MARMOR, THEODORE R., AND JERRY L. MASHAW
1997 "Canada's health insurance and ours: The real lessons, the big choices," pp. 482–492 in P. Conrad, ed., *The Sociology of Health and Illness.* New York: St. Martin's Press.
MARMOR, THEODORE, WAYNE L. HOFFMAN, AND THOMAS C. HEAGY
1983a "National Health Insurance: Some lessons from the Canadian experience," pp. 165–186 in T. Marmor, ed., *Political Analysis and American Medical Care.* Cambridge: Cambridge University Press.
MARMOR, THEODORE, DONALD WITTMAN, AND THOMAS C. HEAGY
1983b "The politics of medical inflation," pp. 61–75 in T. Marmor, ed., *Political Analysis and American Medical Care.* Cambridge: Cambridge University Press.
MARMOT, MICHAEL G.
1996 "The social pattern of health and disease," pp. 42–67 in D. Blane, E. Brunner, and R. Wilkinson, eds., *Health and Social Organization.* London: Routledge.
MARMOT, MICHAEL G., M. KOGEVINAS, AND M. A. ELSTON
1987 "Social/economic status and disease," *Annual Review of Public Health* 8: 111–135.

MARMOT, MICHAEL G., AND J. F. MUSTARD
  1994 "Coronary heart disease from a population perspective," pp. 189–214 in R. G. Evans, M. L. Barer, and T. R. Marmor, eds., *Why Are Some People Healthy and Others Not?: The Determinants of Health of Populations*. New York: Aldine de Gruyter.

MARQUIS, M. SUSAN
  1984 *Cost-Sharing and the Patient's Choice of Provider*. Santa Monica, CA: Rand.

MARTIN, EMILY
  1987 *The Woman in the Body: A Cultural Analysis of Reproduction*. Boston: Beacon.

MASTROIANNI, ANNA C., RUTH FADEN, AND DANIEL FEDERMAN, EDS.
  1994 *Women and Health Research, Vol. 1: Ethical and Legal Issues of Including Women in Clinical Studies*. Washington, DC: National Academy Press/ Institute of Medicine.

MAUSNER, JUDITH S., AND ANITA BAHN
  1985 *Epidemiology: An Introductory Text* (2nd ed.). Philadelphia, PA: Saunders.

MAY, CLIFFORD
  1985 "Reporter's notebook: Images far from Ethiopia's famine," *New York Times*, April 7.

MCAULIFFE, EILISH
  1996 "AIDS: Barriers to behavior change in Malawi," pp. 371–386 in H. Grad, A. Blanco, and J. Georgas, eds., *Key Issues in Cross-Cultural Psychology*. Exton, PA: Swets and Zeitlinger Publishers.

MCCARTY, RICHARD, KARIN HORWATT, AND MARIA KONARSKA
  1988 "Chronic stress and sympathetic-adrenal medullary responsiveness," *Social Science and Medicine* 26(3): 333–341.

MCCREA, FRANCES
  1983 "The politics of menopause: The discovery of a deficiency disease," *Social Problems* 13(1): 111–123.

MCDADE, THOMAS
  1996 "Prostates and profits: The social construction of benign prostatic hyperplasia in American men," *Medical Anthropology* 17: 1–22.

MCDONOUGH, JOHN E.
  1997 "Tracking the demise of state hospital rate systems," *Health Affairs* 16(1): 142–149.

MCELROY, ANN, AND PATRICIA K. TOWNSEND
  1985 *Medical Anthropology in Ecological Perspective*. Boulder, CO: Westview.

MCGUIRE, MEREDITH B.
  1982 *Pentecostal Catholics: Power, Charisma, and Order in a Religious Movement*. Philadelphia, PA: Temple University Press.
  1983 "Words of power: Personal empowerment and healing," *Culture, Medicine, and Psychiatry* 7: 221–240.
  1985 "Religion and Healing," pp. 268–284 in P. Hammond, ed., *The Sacred in a Secular Age*. Berkeley: University of California Press.
  1988 *Ritual Healing in Suburban America*, with the assistance of Debra Kantor. New Brunswick, NJ: Rutgers University Press.
  1996 "Religion and healing the Mind/Body/Self," *Social Compass* 43(1): 101–116.
  1997 *Religion: The Social Context* (4th ed.). Belmont, CA: Wadsworth.

MCGUIRE, MEREDITH B., AND DEBRA J. KANTOR
  1987 "Belief systems and illness experiences: The case of non-medical healing groups," *Research in the Sociology of Health Care* 6: 221–248.

MCINTOSH, ALEX WM.
  1995 "World hunger as a social problem," pp. 35–63 in D. Maurer and J. Sobal, eds., *Eating Agendas: Food and Nutrition as Social Problems*. New York: Aldine de Gruyter.

MCINTOSH, JIM
1974   "Processes of communication, information-seeking, and control associated with cancer," *Social Science and Medicine* 8A: 157–187.
MCKEOWN, THOMAS
1979   *The Role of Medicine: Dream, Mirage, or Nemesis?* Princeton: Princeton University Press.
MCKINLAY, JOHN B.
1975   "Who is really ignorant—Physician or patient?" *Journal of Health and Social Behavior* 16: 3–11.
1996   "Some contributions from the social system to gender inequalities in heart disease," *Journal of Health and Social Behavior* 37(March): 1–26.
1997   [1974] "A case for refocusing upstream: The political economy of illness," pp. 519–533 in P. Conrad, ed., *The Sociology of Health and Illness*. New York: St. Martin's Press.
MCKINLAY, JOHN B., AND SONJA M. MCKINLAY
1977   "The questionable effect of medical measures on the decline of mortality in the United States in the twentieth century," *Milbank Memorial Fund Quarterly* 55: 405–428.
MCKINLAY, JOHN B., SONJA MCKINLAY, AND ROBERT BEAGLE ROLE
1989   "Trends in death and disease and the contribution of medical measures," pp. 14–45 in H. E. Freeman and S. Levine, eds., *Handbook of Medical Sociology* (4th ed.). Englewood Cliffs, NJ: Prentice Hall.
MCKINLAY, JOHN B., AND JOHN D. STOECKLE
1988   "Corporatization and the social transformation of doctoring," *International Journal of Health Services* 18(2): 191–205.
MCKINLAY, SONJA M., D. J. BRAMBILLA, N. E. AVIS, AND JOHN B. MCKINLAY
1991   "Women's experience of the menopause," *Current Obstetrics and Gynaecology* 1: 3–7.
MCNEILLY, MAYA DOMINGUEZ, ELWOOD L. ROBINSON, NORMAN B. ANDERSON, CARL F. PIEPER, AKBAR SHAH, PAUL S. TOTH, PAMELA MARTIN, DREAMA JACKSON, TERRENCE D. SAULTER, CYNTHIA WHITE, MARGARATHA KUCHIBATLA, SHIRLEY M. COLLADO, AND WILLIAM GERIN
1995   "Affects of racist provocation and social support on cardiovascular reactivity in African American women," *International Journal of Behavioral Medicine* 2(4): 321–338.
MECHANIC, DAVID
1976   "Illness, illness behavior, and help-seeking," pp. 161–175 in D. Mechanic, ed., *The Growth of Bureaucratic Medicine*. New York: Wiley.
1978   *Medical Sociology*. New York: Free Press.
1995   "The Americanization of the British National Health Service," *Health Affairs* 14(2): 51–67.
MEDVEDEV, Z., AND R. MEDVEDEV
1971   *A Question of Madness*. New York: Knopf.
MEIER, BARRY
1993   "Doctors' investments in home care grow, raising fears of ethical swamp," *New York Times*, March 19.
MELAMED, ELISSA
1983   *Mirror, Mirror: The Terror of Not Being Young*. New York: Linden.
MELOSH, BARBARA
1982   *The Physician's Hand: Work, Culture, and Conflict in American Nursing*. Philadelphia: Temple University Press.

MELZACK, RONALD, AND PETER WALL
1983   *The Challenge of Pain.* New York: Basic.
MEMBERS OF THE WORKING PARTY
1975   "Occupational accidents," pp. 65–90 in Members of the Working Party, eds., *Research for a Better Work Environment: A Summary of Reports on Four Central Research Areas.* Stockholm: LiberFörlag.
MENGES, LOUWRENS J.
1994   "Beyond the Anglophone world: Regular and Alternative medicine," *Social Science and Medicine* 39(6): 871–873.
MERTON, ROBERT K., GEORGE C. READER, AND PATRICIA L. KENDALL, EDS.
1957   *The Student Physician.* Cambridge: Harvard University Press.
MEYER, MADONNA HARRINGTON, AND ELIZA K. PAVALKO
1996   "Family, work and access to health insurance among mature women," *Journal of Health and Social Behavior* 37: 311–325.
MICHAELS, DAVID
1988   "Waiting for the body count: Corporate decision-making and bladder cancer in the U.S. dye industry," *Medical Anthropology Quarterly* 2(3): 215–232.
MILIO, NANCY
1985   "Health policy and the emerging tobacco reality," *Social Science and Medicine* 21(6): 603–613.
MILLER, FRANCES H.
1983   "Secondary income from recommended treatment: Should fiduciary principles constrain physician behavior?" pp. 153–169 in B. Gray, ed., *The New Health Care for Profit: Doctors and Hospitals in a Competitive Environment.* Washington, DC: National Academy Press.
MILLMAN, MARCIA
1976   *The Unkindest Cut: Life in the Backrooms of Medicine.* New York: Morrow.
1980   *Such a Pretty Face: Being Fat in America.* New York: Norton.
MILLON, THEODORE, CATHERINE GREEN, AND ROBERT MEAGHER, EDS.
1982   *Handbook of Clinical Health Psychology.* New York: Plenum.
MILLS, C. WRIGHT
1956   *White Collar.* New York: Oxford University Press.
1959   *The Sociological Imagination.* New York: Oxford University Press.
MINTZ, SIDNEY
1979   "Time, Sugar, and Sweetness," *Marxist Perspectives* 8: 56–73.
MISHLER, ELLIOTT
1984   *The Discourse of Medicine: Dialectics of Medical Interviews.* Norwood, NJ: Ablex.
MITCHELL, JEAN M., AND ELTON SCOTT
1992   "Physician self-referral: Empirical evidence and policy implications," *Advances in Health Economics and Health Services Research* 13: 27–42.
MITCHELL, JEAN M., AND JONATHAN SUNSHINE
1992   "Consequences of physicians' ownership of health care facilities—Joint ventures in radiation therapy," *New England Journal of Medicine* 327(21): 1497–1501.
MIYAJI, NAOKO T.
1993   "The power of compassion: Truth-telling among American doctors in the care of dying patients," *Social Science and Medicine* 36(3): 249–264.
MIZRAHI, TERRY
1986   *Getting Rid of Patients: Contradictions in the Socialization of Physicians.* New Brunswick, NJ: Rutgers University Press.

MOELLER, DADE W.
1992   *Environmental Health.* Cambridge, MA: Harvard University Press.

MOERMAN, DANIEL
1979   "Anthropology of symbolic healing," *Current Anthropology* 20(1): 59–66.
1983   "Physiology and symbols: The anthropological implications of the placebo effect," pp. 156–167 in L. Romanucci-Ross, D. Moerman, and L. Tancredi, eds., *The Anthropology of Medicine: From Culture to Method.* South Hadley, MA: Bergin and Garvey.

MONTGOMERY, KATHLEEN
1992   "Professional dominance and the threat of corporatization," *Current Research on Occupations and Professions* 7: 221–240.

MONTINI, THERESA, AND SHERYL RUZEK
1989   "Overturning orthodoxy: The emergence of breast cancer treatment policy," *Research in the Sociology of Health Care* 8: 3–32.

MOORE, J. STUART
1993   *Chiropractic in America: The History of a Medical Alternative.* Baltimore: Johns Hopkins University Press.

MOORE-LAPPÉ, FRANCES, AND JOSEPH COLLINS
1986   *World Hunger, Twelve Myths.* New York: Grove.

MOOS, RUDOLF H., AND RALPH SWINDLE, JR.
1990   "Person-environment transactions and the stressor-appraisal-coping process," *Psychological Inquiry* 1(1): 30–32.

MORANTZ-SANCHEZ, REGINA M.
1985   *Sympathy and Science: Women Physicians in American Medicine.* New York: Oxford.

MORGAN, LYNN
1989   " 'Political will' and community participation in Costa Rican primary health care," *Medical Anthropology Quarterly* 3(3): 232–245.

MORGAN, MYFANWY, D. PATRICK, AND J. CHARLTON
1984   "Social network and psychological support among disabled people," *Social Science and Medicine* 19: 489–497.

MORGANTHAU, TOM, AND ANDREW MURR
1993   "Inside the world of an HMO," *Newsweek*, April 5: 34–40.

MORONE, JAMES A.
1990   "American political culture and the search for lessons from abroad," *Journal of Health Politics, Policy and Law* 15(1): 129–143.
1995   "Nativism, hollow corporations, and managed competition: Why the Clinton health care reform failed," *Journal of Health Politics, Policy and Law* 20(2): 391–398.

MORONE, JAMES A., AND JANICE M. GOGGINS, EDS.
1995   *European Health Policies: Welfare State in a Market Era*: special issue of *Journal of Health Politics, Policy and Law* 20(3).

MORONEY, ROBERT M.
1980   *Families, Social Services, and Social Policy: The Issue of Shared Responsibility.* U.S. Department of Health and Human Services (DHHS Publication No. [ADM] 80–846). Washington, DC: Government Printing Office.

MOSS, GORDON ERVIN
1973   *Illness, Immunity, and Social Interaction.* New York: Wiley.

MULLEN, KENNETH
1994   "Control and responsibility: Moral and religious issues in lay health accounts," *The Sociological Review* 42(3): 414–437.

MULLER, JESSICA H., AND BARBARA A. KOENIG
    1988   "On the boundary of life and death: The definition of dying by medical residents," pp. 351–374 in M. Lock and D. R. Gordon, eds., *Biomedicine Examined.* Dordrecht, Netherlands: Kluwer.

MUMFORD, LEWIS
    1963   *Technics and Civilization.* New York: Harcourt, Brace, and World.

MURPHY, ROBERT F.
    1987   *The Body Silent.* New York: Henry Holt.

MURRAY, CHRISTOPHER J. L., AND ALAN D. LOPEZ
    1996   "The global alternative epidemiological perspectives, discount rates, age-weights and disability weights," pp. 227–257 in Christopher J. L. Murray and Alan D. Lopez, eds., *The Global Burden of Disease.* Cambridge, MA: Harvard University Press.

MUTCHLER, JAN E., AND JEFFREY A. BURR
    1991   "Racial differences in health and health care service utilization in later life: The effect of socioeconomic status," *Journal of Health and Social Behavior* 32(6): 342–356.

MUWAKKIL, SALIM
    1991   "Living fast, dying young in America's inner cities," *In These Times* 15(7): 7.
    1996a "Moving mountains," *In These Times* 20(7), February 19.
    1996b "The silent catastrophe," *In These Times* 21(1), November 25.

NAJMAN, JAKE M.
    1993   "Health and poverty: Past, present and future," *Social Science and Medicine* 36(2): 157–166.

NATIONAL INSTITUTE ON ALCOHOL ABUSE AND ALCOHOLISM AND THE NATIONAL INSTITUTE OF MENTAL HEALTH
    1992   *Homeless Families with Children: Research Perspectives.* Rockville, MD: U.S. Department of Health and Human Services.

NATIONAL INSTITUTE ON DISABILITY AND REHABILITATION RESEARCH
    1986   "Rehabilitation of nonwhite disabled people," *Rehab Brief* IX(20).
    1987   "Low back pain," *Rehab Brief* IX(9).
    1993   "Disability statistics," *Rehab Brief* XIV(8).

NATIONAL SAFE WORKPLACE INSTITUTE
    1990   *Beyond Neglect: The Problem of Occupational Disease in the U.S.* Chicago: Author.

NAVARRO, VICENTE
    1981   "Work, ideology, and science: The case of medicine," pp. 11–38 in V. Navarro and D. M. Berman, eds., *Health and Work Under Capitalism: An International Perspective.* Farmingdale, NY: Baywood.
    1988   "Professional dominance or proletarianization?: Neither," *Milbank Quarterly* 66(supplement 2): 57–75.
    1989   "Race or class, or race and class," *International Journal of Health Services* 19(2): 311–314.
    1991   "Race or class or race and class: Growing mortality differentials in the United States," *International Journal of Health Services* 21(2): 229–235.

NAVARRO, VICENTE, AND DANIEL M. BERMAN, EDS.
    1981   *Health and Work Under Capitalism: An International Perspective.* Farmingdale, NY: Baywood.

NEAL, HELEN
    1978   *The Politics of Pain.* New York: McGraw-Hill.

NELKIN, DOROTHY, AND MICHAEL S. BROWN
1984   *Workers at Risk: Voices from the Workplace.* Chicago: University of Chicago Press.
NELSON, KARIN B., JAMES M. DAMBROSIA, TRICIA Y. TING, AND JUDITH K. GRETHEN
1996   "Uncertain value of electronic fetal monitoring in predicting cerebral palsy,"
       New England Journal of Medicine 334(10): 613–618.
NETTLETON, SARAH, AND ROBIN BUNTON
1995   "Sociological critiques of health promotion," pp. 41–58 in R. Bunton, S. Nettleton,
       and R. Burrows, eds., *The Sociology of Health Promotion.* London: Routledge.
NEWACHECK, PAUL W., DANA C. HUGHES, AND MIRIAM CISTERNAS
1995   "Children and health insurance," *Health Affairs* 14(1): 244–254.
NEWTON, THOMAS
1995   *Managing Stress: Emotion and Power at Work.* London: Sage.
New York Times
1986   "Your cigarettes or your job, workers are told," January 25.
1989   "For mothers, elderly present second burden," May 13.
1991   "Global checkup: Views in 10 nations," May 2.
1992   "74% of Democrats and 53% of Republicans favor a national health insurance
       financed by tax money: The voters' views," November 4.
1994a "17 American workers a day died on the job during the 80's," January 15.
1994b "Taxpayers may be paying twice for some drugs," July 12.
1994c "Hmong protest girl's forced chemotherapy," October 19.
1996a "Ritalin maker opens drive to end abuse," March 28.
1996b "U.S. Healthcare to end limits on doctors' advice to patients," February 6.
NICHTER, MARK
1987   "Kyasanur forest disease: An ethnography of a disease of development,"
       Medical Anthropology Quarterly 1(4): 406–423.
NICHTER, MARK, AND ELIZABETH CARTWRIGHT
1991   "Saving the children for the tobacco industry," *Medical Anthropology Quarterly*
       5(3): 236–256.
NIGHTINGALE, FLORENCE
1860   *Notes on Nursing: What It Is, and What It Is Not.* New York: Appleton.
NOBLE, BARBARA PRESLEY
1993   "Pushing nurses to a breaking point," *New York Times,* January 10.
NOBLE, KENNETH B.
1986   "Certain numbers can kill," *New York Times,* December 28.
NORBECK, EDWARD, AND MARGARET LOCK, EDS.
1987   *Health, Illness, and Medical Care in Japan.* Honolulu: University of Hawaii Press.
NORDEN, MARTIN F.
1995   "Politics, movies and physical disabilities," *Kaleidoscope* Number 30 (Winter-
       Spring): 6–14.
NORRIS, RUTH, ED.
1982   *Pills, Pesticides, and Profits: The International Trade in Toxic Substances.* Croton-on-
       Hudson, NY: North River Press.
NOTZON, FRANCIS C.
1990   "International differences in the use of obstetric interventions," *Journal of the
       American Medical Association* 263 (24): 3286–3291.
NOVACK, DENNIS, ROBIN PLUMER, RAYMOND SMITH, HERBERT OCHITILL, GARY R.
MORROW, AND JOHN M. BENNETT
1979   "Changes in physician attitude toward telling the cancer patient," *Journal of the
       American Medical Association* 241(9): 897–900.

NOVAK, VIVECA
1993 "The other drug lords," *International Journal of Health Services* 23(2): 263–273.

NOVEK, JOEL, ANNALEE YASSI, AND JERRY SPIEGEL
1990 "Mechanization, the labor process, and injury risks in the Canadian meat packing industry," *International Journal of Health Services* 29(2): 281–296.

NUCKOLLS, KATHERINE B., JOHN CASSEL, AND BERTON V. KAPLAN
1972 "Psychosocial assets, life crisis, and the prognosis of pregnancy," *American Journal of Epidemiology* 95: 431–441.

NUMBERS, RONALD L.
1977 "Do it yourself the sectarian way," pp. 49–72 in G. Risse, R. L. Numbers, and J. W. Leavitt, eds., *Medicine Without Doctors: Home Health Care in American History.* New York: Science History.

OAKLEY, ANN
1984 *The Captured Womb: A History of the Medical Care of Pregnant Women.* Oxford: Basil Blackwell.

O'BRIEN, MARTIN
1995 "Health and lifestyle, a critical mess?: Notes on the dedifferentiation of health," pp. 191–205 in R. Bunton, S. Nettleton and R. Burrows, eds., *The Sociology of Health Promotion: Critical Analyses of Consumption, Lifestyle and Risk.* London: Routledge.

O'DONNEL, MARY
1978 "Lesbian health care: Issues and literature," *Science for the People,* May-June: 18–19.

OHRBACH, SUSIE
1981 *Fat Is a Feminist Issue.* New York: Berkeley.

OKEN, DONALD
1961 "What to tell cancer patients—a study of medical attitudes," *Journal of the American Medical Association* 175: 1120–1128.

OLESEN, VIRGINIA, L. SCHATZMAN, N. DROES, D. HATTON, AND N. CHICO
1990 "The mundane ailment and the physical self: Analysis of the social psychology of health and illness," *Social Science and Medicine* 30: 449–455.

OLIVER, MICHAEL
1996 *Understanding Disability.* London: Macmillan.

OMRAN, ABDEL R.
1971 "The epidemiologic transition: A theory of the epidemiology of population change," *Milbank Memorial Fund Quarterly* 49: 509–538.

ONG, L. M. L., J. C. J. M. DE HAES, A. M. HOOS, AND F. B. LAMMES
1995 "Doctor-patient communication: A review of the literature," *Social Science and Medicine* 40 (7): 903–918.

ORGANISATION FOR ECONOMIC CO-OPERATION AND DEVELOPMENT
1990 *Health Care Systems in Transition: The Search for Efficiency.* Paris: Author.
1993 *Health Systems: Facts and Trends (1960–1991).* Paris: Author.
1994 *The Reform of Health Care Systems: A Review of Seventeen OECD Countries.* Paris: Author.

OSHERSON, SAMUEL, AND LORNA AMARASINGHAM
1981 "The machine metaphor in medicine," pp. 218–249 in E. Mishler et al., *Social Contexts of Health, Illness, and Patient Care.* Cambridge: Cambridge University Press.

OSTERWEIS, MARIAN, ARTHUR KLEINMAN, AND DAVID MECHANIC, EDS.
1987 *Pain and Disability: Clinical, Behavioral, and Public Policy Perspectives.* Washington, DC: Institute of Medicine, National Academy Press.

OTS, THOMAS

    1990   "The angry liver, the anxious heart, and the melancholy spleen: The phenomenology of perceptions in Chinese culture," *Culture, Medicine and Psychiatry* 14(1): 21–58.

OVERFIELD, THERESA

    1985   *Biologic Variation in Health and Illness.* Menlo Park, CA: Addison-Wesley.

PAGET, MARIANNE A.

    1983   "On the work of talk: Studies in misunderstandings," pp. 55–73 in S. Fisher and A. Todd, eds., *The Social Organization of Doctor-Patient Communication.* Norwood, NJ: Ablex.

    1988   *The Unity of Mistakes: A Phenomenological Interpretation of Medical Work.* Philadelphia: Temple University Press.

PALLEY, HOWARD A.

    1995   "The evolution of FDA policy on silicone breast implants: A case study of politics, bureaucracy, and business in the process of decision-making," *International Journal of Health Services* 25(4): 573–591.

PAPPAS, GREGORY, SUSAN QUEEN, WILBUR HADDEN, AND GAIL FISHER

    1993   "The increasing disparity in mortality between socioeconomic groups in the United States, 1960 and 1986," *New England Journal of Medicine* 329(2): 103–109.

PARKER, RICHARD

    1981   "Lappé: take dictators off the dole," *Mother Jones* 6(1) January: 12–13.

PARSONS, TALCOTT

    1951   *The Social System.* Glencoe, IL: Free Press.

    1966   *Societies: Evolutionary and Comparative Perspectives.* Englewood Cliffs, NJ: Prentice Hall.

    1972   "Definitions of health and illness in light of American values and social structure," pp. 107–127 in E. G. Jaco, ed., *Patients, Physicians, and Illness.* New York: Macmillan.

PATTISON, ROBERT V., AND HALLIE M. KATZ

    1983   "Investor-owned and not-for-profit hospitals: A comparison based on California data," *New England Journal of Medicine* 309: 347–353.

PAYER, LYNN

    1988   *Medicine and Culture: Varieties of Treatment in the United States, England, West Germany, and France.* New York: Henry Holt.

PAYNE-JACKSON, ARVILLA, AND JOHN LEE

    1993   *Folk Wisdom and Mother Wit: John Lee—an African American Herbal Healer.* Westport, CT: Greenwood Press.

PEAR, ROBERT

    1988   "Fate of newest treatments is often determined by Medicare," *New York Times,* January 14.

    1991   "AMA acts to curb profits from referrals," *New York Times,* December 12.

    1994   "Report finds prescription drugs cost more in U.S. than in Britain," *New York Times,* February 3.

    1997   "Expense means many can't get drugs for AIDS," *New York Times,* February 16.

PEAR, ROBERT, WITH ERIK ECKHOLM

    1991   "When healers are entrepreneurs: A debate over costs and ethics," *New York Times,* June 2.

PEARLIN, LEONARD I.

    1983   "Role strains and personal stress," pp. 3–32 in H.B. Kaplan, ed., *Psychosocial Stress: Trends in Theory and Research.* New York: Academic.

PEARLIN, LEONARD I., AND CARMEN SCHOOLER
1978   "The structure of coping," *Journal of Health and Social Behavior* 19: 2–21.

PEELE, STANTON
1989   *The Diseasing of America: Addiction Treatment Out of Control.* Lexington, MA: Lexington Books.

PELLEGRINO, EDMUND D.
1976   "Prescribing and drug ingestion: Symbols and substances," *Drug Intelligence and Clinical Pharmacy* 10: 624–630.

PELLETIER, KENNETH R.
1985   *Healthy People in Unhealthy Places: Stress and Fitness of Work.* New York: Dell.
1992   *Mind as Healer, Mind as Slayer,* 2nd ed. New York: Dell.

PELLETIER, KENNETH, AND DENISE L. HERZING
1988   "Psychoneuroimmunology: Toward a mind-body model," *Advances: Institute for the Advancement of Health* 5(1): 27–56.

PENDLETON, DAVID, AND STEPHEN BOCHNER
1980   "The communication of medical information in general practice consultations as a function of patients' social class," *Social Science and Medicine* 14A(6): 669–673.

PERRY, SUSAN, AND JIM DAWSON
1985   *Nightmare: Women and the Dalkon Shield.* New York: Macmillan.

PETERSON, CHRIS L.
1994   "Work factors and stress: A critical review," *International Journal of Health Services* 24(3): 495–519.

PETERSON, IVER
1986   "Surge in Indians' diabetes linked to their history," *New York Times,* February 18.

PFEFFER, RICHARD M.
1979   *Working for Capitalism.* New York: Columbia University Press.

PHYSICIANS' TASK FORCE ON HUNGER IN AMERICA
1985   *Hunger in America: The Growing Epidemic.* Middletown, CT: Wesleyan University Press.

PIERRET, JANINE
1993   "Constructing discourses about health and their social determinants," pp. 9–26 in A. Radley, ed., *Worlds of Illness.* New York: Routledge.

PILISUK, MARC, AND SUSAN H. PARKS
1986   *The Healing Web: Social Networks and Human Survival.* Hanover, NH: University Press of New England.

PINCUS, HAROLD A., ALLEN FRANCIS, WENDY WAKEFIELD DAVIS, MICHAEL B. FIRST, AND THOMAS A. WIDIGEN
1992   "DSM-IV and new diagnostic categories: Holding the line on proliferation," *American Journal of Psychiatry* 149(1): 112–117.

PINDER, RUTH
1988   "Striking balances: Living with Parkinson's disease," pp. 67–88 in R. Anderson and M. Bury, eds., *Living with Chronic Illness: The Experience of Patients and Their Families.* London: Unwin Hyman.
1995   "Bringing back the body without the blame?: The experience of ill and disabled people at work," *Sociology of Health and Illness* 17(5): 605–631.

PINNER, ROBERT W., STEVEN M. TEUTSCH, LONE SIMONSEN, LAURA A. KLUG, JUDITH M. GRABER, MATTHEW J. CLARKE, AND RUTH L. BERVELMAN
1996   "Trends in infectious diseases mortality in the United States," *Journal of the American Medical Association* 275(3), January 17: 189–193.

PODHORZER, MICHAEL
  1995 "Unhealthy money: Health reform and the 1994 elections," *International Journal of Health Services* 25(3): 393–401.
POLEDNAK, ANTHONY P.
  1989 *Racial and Ethnic Differences in Disease.* New York: Oxford University Press.
POLEFRONE, JOANNA M., AND STEPHEN B. MANUCK
  1987 "Gender differences in cardiovascular and neuroendocrine responses to stressors," pp. 13–38 in R. Barnett, L. Biener, and G. K. Baruch, eds., *Gender and Stress.* New York: Free Press.
POLOMA, MARGARET
  1985 "An empirical study of perception of healing among Assemblies of God members," *Pneuma* 7(1): 61–82.
POOLE, C. J. M., G. R. EVANS, A. SPURGEON, AND K. W. BRIDGES
  1992 "Effects of a change in shift work on health," *Occupational Medicine* 42: 193–199.
POPAY, JENNIE, AND MEL BARTLEY
  1989 "Conditions of labor and women's health," pp. 89–97 in C. J. Martin and D. V. McQueen, eds., *Readings for a New Public Health.* Edinburgh: Edinburgh University Press.
POPE, GREGORY C., AND JOHN E. SCHNEIDER
  1992 "Trends in Physician Income," *Health Affairs* 11(1): 181–193.
POPLIN, CAROLINE
  1996 "Mismanaged care," *Wilson Quarterly* 20(3): 12–24.
POPPENDIECK, JANET
  1995 "Hunger in America: Typification and response," pp. 11–34 in D. Maurer and J. Sobal, eds., *Eating Agendas: Food and Nutrition as Social Problems.* New York: Aldine de Gruyter.
POPULATION REFERENCE BUREAU
  1982 *Population Bulletin* 37(2): 30–31.
PORTER, SAM
  1992 "Women in a woman's job: The gendered experience of nurses," *Sociology of Health and Illness* 14(4): 510–527.
POSNER, TINA
  1977 "Magical elements in orthodox medicine," pp. 141–158 in R. Dingwall, C. Heath, M. Reid, and M. Stacey, eds., *Health Care and Health Knowledge.* London: Croom Helm.
POST, STEPHEN G.
  1992 "DSM-III-R and religion," *Social Science and Medicine* 35(1): 81–90.
PRATT, LOIS
  1976 *Family Structure and Effective Health Behavior.* Boston: Houghton Mifflin.
PRESTON, JENNIFER
  1996 "Hospitals look on charity care as unaffordable option of past," *New York Times,* April 14.
PROPAC (PROSPECTIVE PAYMENT ASSESSMENT COMMISSION)
  1988 *Medicare Prospective Payment and the American Health Care System: Report to Congress.* Washington, DC: U.S. Government Printing Office.
PUBLIC CITIZEN HEALTH RESEARCH GROUP
  1993 "Patient dumping continues in hospital emergency rooms," *Health Letter* 9(6): 1–6.
QUICK, ALLISON
  1991 *Unequal Risks: Accidents and Social Policy.* London: Socialist Health Association.

RADLEY, ALAN
1994   *Making Sense of Illness.* Thousand Oaks, CA: Sage.

RAHKONEN, OSSI, EERO LAHELMA, ANTTI KARISTO, AND KRISTINA MANDERBACKA
1993   "Persisting health inequalities: Social class differentials in illness in the Scandinavian countries," *Journal of Public Health Policy* (Spring): 66–81.

RASELL, EDITH
1993   "A bad bargain: Why U.S. health care costs so much and covers so few," *Dollars and Sense* 186 (May): 6–8, 21.

RASELL, EDITH, JARED BERNSTEIN, AND KAINAN TANG
1994   "The impact of health care financing on family budgets," *International Journal of Health Services* 24(4): 691–714.

RATCLIFF, KATHRYN STROTHER
1989   "Health technologies for women: Whose health? Whose technology?" pp. 173–198 in K. S. Ratcliff, ed., *Healing Technology: Feminist Perspectives.* Ann Arbor: University of Michigan Press.

RATLIFF-CRAIN, JEFFREY, AND ANDREW BAUM
1990   "Individual differences and health: Gender, coping and stress," pp. 226–253 in H. S. Friedman, ed., *Personality and Disease.* New York: Wiley.

RAY, WAYNE A., MARIE R. GRIFFIN, AND RONALD I. SHORR
1990a "Adverse drug reactions and the elderly," *Health Affairs* 9(3): 114–122.
1990b "Racism and health: The case of black infant mortality," pp. 34–44 in P. Conrad and R. Kern, eds., *The Sociology of Health and Illness*, 3rd ed. New York: St. Martin's Press.

REED, WORNIE L.
1993   *Health and Medical Care of African-Americans.* Westport, CT: Auburn House.

REID, JANICE, CHRISTINE EWAN, AND EVA LOWY
1991   "Pilgrimage of pain: The illness experiences of women with repetition strain injury and the search for credibility," *Social Science and Medicine* 32(5): 601–612.

REINHARDT, UWE E.
1987   "Resource allocation in health care: The allocation of life styles to providers," *Milbank Quarterly* 65(2): 153–176.
1996   "Spending more through 'cost control': Our obsessive quest to gut the hospital," *Health Affairs* 15(2): 145–153.

REINHOLD, ROBERT
1987   "As hospitals close, rural America tries to cope with a void," *New York Times,* July 6.
1988   "Crisis in emergency rooms: More symptoms than cures," *New York Times,* December 8.

RENNER, MICHAEL
1988   "Rethinking the role of the automobile," *Worldwatch Paper,* No. 84. Washington, DC: Worldwatch Institute.

REVERBY, SUSAN
1987a "A caring dilemma: Womanhood and nursing in historical perspective," *Nursing Research* 36(1): 5–11.
1987b *Ordered to Care: The Dilemma of American Nursing, 1850–1945.* Cambridge: Cambridge University Press.

RHODES, ROBERT P.
1992   *Health Care Politics, Policy, and Distributive Justice: The Ironic Triumph.* Albany: State University of New York Press.

RICE, DOROTHY P.
1990   "The medical care system: Past trends and future projections," pp. 72–93 in
        P. R. Lee and C. L. Estes, eds., *The Nation's Health*. Boston: Jones and
        Bartlett.
1991   "Ethics and equity in U.S. health care: The data," *International Journal of Health
        Services* 21(4): 637–651.
RICHARDSON, JAMES T.
1993   "Religiosity as deviance: Negative religious bias in and misuse of the DSM-
        III," *Deviant Behavior* 14(1): 1–21.
1995   "Two steps forward, one back: Psychiatry, psychology, and the New
        Religions," *International Journal for the Psychology of Religion* 3(3): 181–185.
RICHARDSON, JOHN T. E.
1995   "The premenstrual syndrome: A brief history," *Social Science and Medicine* 41(6):
        761–767.
RICHARDSON, STEPHEN A., NORMAN GOODMAN, ALBERT HASTDORF, AND STANFORD
DORNBUSH
1963   "Variant reactions to physical disabilities," *American Sociological Review* 28:
        429–435.
RICHEY, FERRIS J., WILLIAM C. YOELS, JEFFREY MICHAEL CLAIR, AND RICHARD M.
ALLMAN
1994   "Competing medical and social ideologies and communication accuracy in
        medical encounters," *Research in the Sociology of Health Care* 12: 189–211.
RIES, PETER
1991   "Characteristics of persons with and without health care coverage: United
        States, 1989," *Advance Data* 201 (June 18): 1–9.
RIMER, SARA
1997   "New, reviled college subject: Computer-linked injury," *New York Times*,
        February 9.
RISKA, ELIANNE
1985   *Power Politics and Health: Forces Shaping American Medicine*. Helsinki: The Finnish
        Society of Letters.
RISSE, GUENTER, RONALD L. NUMBERS, AND JUDITH W. LEAVITT, EDS.
1977   *Medicine Without Doctors: Home Health Care in American History*. New York: Science
        History.
RIVO, MARC L., AND DAVID A. KINDIG
1996   "A report card on the physician work force in the United States," *New England
        Journal of Medicine* 334(14): 892–896.
ROBBINS, THOMAS, AND DICK ANTHONY
1982   "Deprogramming, brainwashing, and the medicalization of deviant religious
        groups," *Social Problems* 29(3): 283–297.
ROBERTS, HELEN, SUSAN J. SMITH, AND CAROL BRYCE
1992   "Professionals' and parents' perceptions of A&E use in a children's hospital,"
        Sociological Review 40(1): 109–131.
1995   *Children at Risk? Safety as a Social Value*. Buckingham: Open University Press.
ROBINSON, A. A.
1988   "The motor vehicle, stress, and circulatory system," *Stress Medicine* 4: 73–76.
ROBINSON, JAMES C., AND MITA K. GIACOMINI
1992   "A reallocation of rights in industries with reproductive health hazards," *The
        Milbank Quarterly* 70(4): 587–603.

RODIN, MARI
  1992   "The social construction of premenstrual syndrome," *Social Science and Medicine* 35(1): 49–56.

RODWIN, MARC A.
  1992   "The organized American medical profession's response to financial conflicts of interest: 1890–1992," *The Milbank Quarterly* 70(4): 703–741.
  1993   *Medicine, Money and Morals: Physician Conflicts of Interest.* New York: Oxford University Press.

RODWIN, VICTOR G.
  1989   "New Ideas for Health Policy in France, Canada, and Britain," pp. 265–285 in M. Field, ed., *Success and Crisis in National Health Systems.* London: Routledge.
  1993   *Medicine, Money, and Morals: Physicians' Conflicts of Interest.* New York: Oxford University Press.
  1995   "Comparative Health Systems: A policy perspective," pp. 456–485 in A. R. Kovner, ed., *Jonas's Health Care Delivery in the United States.* New York: Springer.

ROEBUCK, JULIAN, AND ROBERT BRUCE HUNTER
  1975   "Medical quackery as deviant behavior," pp. 72–82 in F. Scarpitti and P. McFarlane, eds., *Deviance: Action, Reaction, Interaction.* Reading, MA: Addison-Wesley.

ROEDER, BEATRICE A.
  1988   *Chicano Folk Medicine from Los Angeles, California. Folklore and Mythology Studies*, vol. 34. Berkeley: University of California Publications.

ROEMER, MILTON I.
  1991   *National Health Systems of the World: The Countries*, vol. I. New York: Oxford University Press.
  1993   *National Health Systems of the World: The Issues*, vol. II. New York: Oxford University Press.

ROMALIS, SHELLY
  1985   "Struggle between providers and recipients: The case of birth practices," pp. 174–208 in E. Lewin and V. Oleson, eds., *Women, Health, and Healing.* New York: Tavistock.

ROSENBERG, CHARLES E.
  1987   *The Care of Strangers: The Rise of America's Hospital System.* New York: Basic.

ROSENBLATT, ROGER A., SHARON A. DOBIE, L. GARY HART, RONALD SCHNEEWEISS, DEBRA GOULD, TINA R. RAINE, THOMAS J. BENEDETTI, MICHAEL J. PIRANI, AND EDWARD B. PERRIN
  1997   "Interspecialty differences in the obstetric care of low-risk women," *The American Journal of Public Health* 87(3): 344–351.

ROSENBLOOM, SANDRA
  1988   "The mobility needs of the elderly," pp. 21–71 in *Transportation in an Aging Society: Improving Mobility and Safety for Older Persons*, Vol. 2. Washington, DC: Transportation Research Board, National Research Council, Special Report 218.

ROSENHAN, DAVID L.
  1973   "On being sane in insane places," *Science* 179: 250–258.

ROSENTHAL, ELISABETH
  1991   "In Canada, a government system that provides health care to all," *New York Times*, April 30.
  1993   "Drug companies' profits finance more promotion than research," *New York Times*, February 21.

1994   "At ailing public hospital in Brooklyn, healing mission is undone by decay," *New York Times*, February 28.
1996   "Reduced H.M.O. fees cause concern about patient care," *New York Times*, November 25.
1997a   "Older doctors and nurses see jobs at stake," *New York Times*, January 26.
1997b   "When a healer is asked, 'Help me die,'" *New York Times*, March 13.
ROSENTHAL, MARILYN M.
1987   *Health Care in the People's Republic of China: Moving Toward Modernization.* Boulder, CO: Westview Press.
1988   *Dealing with Medical Malpractice: The British and Swedish Experience.* Durham, NC: Duke University Press.
1995   *The Incompetent Doctor: Behind Closed Doors.* Buckingham: Open University Press.
ROSENTHAL, MARILYN M., AND MARCEL FRENKEL, EDS.
1992   *Health Care Systems and Their Patients.* Boulder, CO: Westview Press.
ROSS, H. LAURENCE, AND GRAHAM HUGHES
1986   "Drunk driving: What not to do," *Nation* 243(20): 663–664.
ROSS, JERRY, AND GARY L. ALBRECHT
1995   "Escalation in health care delivery," *Research in the Sociology of Health Care*, 12: 241–260.
ROSSER, SUE V.
1994   "Gender bias in clinical research: The difference it makes," pp. 253–264 in A. J. Dan, ed., *Reframing Women's Health.* Thousand Oaks, CA: Sage.
ROTH, JULIUS
1972   "Some contingencies of the moral evaluation and control of clientele: The case of the hospital emergency service," *American Journal of Sociology* 77: 839–856.
1976   *Health Purifiers and Their Enemies: A Study of the Natural Health Movement in the United States with a Comparison to Its Counterpart in Germany.* London: Croom Helm.
1984   "The application of 'sociological wisdom' to issues of cost escalation and cost containment," *Research in the Sociology of Health Care* 3: 257–280.
ROTHE, J. PETER
1991   *The Trucker's World: Risk, Safety and Mobility.* New Brunswick, NJ: Transaction.
ROWLAND, DIANE
1991   "Health status in East European countries," *Health Affairs* 10(3): 202–215.
ROWLAND, DIANE, B. SALGANICOFF, AND P. LONG
1994   "Profile of the uninsured in America," *Health Affairs* 13(2): 283–287.
ROYAL COMMISSION ON ENVIRONMENTAL POLLUTION
1994   *Transport and the Environment.* London: HMSO.
ROYER, ARIELA
1995   "Living with chronic illness," *Research in the Sociology of Health Care* 12: 25–48.
RUBEL, ARTHUR, CARL O'NELL, AND ROLANDO COLLADO-ARD'ON
1984   *Susto: A Folk Illness.* Berkeley: University of California Press.
RUBIN, BETH
1996   *Shifts in the Social Contract: Understanding Change in American Society.* Thousand Oaks, CA: Pine Forge Press.
RUBIN, HAYA R., BARBARA GANDEK, WILLIAM H. ROGERS, MARK KOSINSKI, COLLEEN A. MCHORNEY, AND JOHN E. WARE
1993   "Patients' ratings of outpatient visits in different practice settings," *Journal of the American Medical Association* 270(7): 835–840.

RUGGIE, MARY
  1992   "The paradox of liberal intervention: Health policy and the American welfare state," *American Journal of Sociology* 97(4): 919–944.
RUTLEDGE, ROBERT, THOMAS C. RICKETTS, AND ELIZABETH BELL
  1992   "Emergency medical services in rural areas," pp. 226–248 in W. M. Gesler and T. C. Ricketts, *Health in Rural North America: The Geography of Health Care Services and Delivery.* New Brunswick, NJ: Rutgers University Press.
RUZEK, SHERYL B.
  1979   *The Women's Health Movement.* New York: Praeger.
RYAN, WILLIAM
  1971   *Blaming the Victim.* New York: Vintage.
SACKS, KAREN
  1988   *Caring by the Hour: Women, Work and Organizing at Duke Medical Center.* Urbana: University of Illinois.
SACKS, OLIVER
  1984   *A Leg to Stand On.* New York: Summit.
SAGAN, LEONARD
  1987   *The Health of Nations.* New York: Basic.
SAKS, MIKE, ED.
  1992   *Alternative Medicine in Britain.* Oxford: Clarendon Press.
SALMON, J. WARREN
  1995   "A perspective on the corporate transformation of health care," *International Journal of Health Services* 25(1): 11–42.
SALTMAN, RICHARD B.
  1991   "Emerging trends in the Swedish health system," *International Journal of Health Services* 21(4): 615–623.
SALTONSTALL, ROBIN
  1993   "Healthy bodies, social bodies: Men's and women's concepts and practices of health in everyday life," *Social Science and Medicine* 36(1): 7–14.
SANDELOWSKI, MARGARETE
  1991   "Compelled to try: The never-enough quality of conceptive technology," *Medical Anthropology Quarterly* 5(1): 29–47.
SANDLER, DALE, RICHARD B. EVERSON, AND ALLEN WILCOX
  1988   "Passive smoking in adulthood and cancer rise," *American Journal of Epidemiology* 121(1): 37–48.
SAPOLSKY, ROBERT M.
  1982   "The endocrine stress-response and social status in the wild baboon," *Hormones and Behavior* 16: 279–292.
  1989   "Hypercortisolism among socially subordinate wild baboons originates at the CNS level," *Archives of General Psychiatry* 46: 1047–1051.
  1990   "Stress in the wild," *Scientific American* 252: 116–123.
SCHACHTER, STANLEY
  1968   "Obesity and Eating," *Science* 16: 751–756.
SCHEDER, JO C.
  1988   "A sickly-sweet harvest: Farmworker diabetes and social equality," *Medical Anthropology Quarterly* 2(3): 251–277.
SCHENSUL, STEPHEN L., AND JEAN J. SCHENSUL
  1982   "Healing resource use in a Puerto Rican community," *Urban Anthropology* 11(1): 59–79.

SCHEPER-HUGHES, NANCY
1992   *Death Without Weeping.* Berkeley: University of California Press.
SCHEPER-HUGHES, NANCY, AND MARGARET M. LOCK
1986   "Speaking 'truth' to illness: Metaphor, reification, and a pedagogy for patients," *Medical Anthropology Quarterly* 17: 137–140.
1991   "The message in the bottle: Illness and the micropolitics of resistance," *Journal of Psychohistory* 18(4): 409–432.
SCHEPERS, RITA
1985   "The legal and institutional development of the Belgian medical profession in the nineteenth century," *Sociology of Health and Illness* 7(3): 314–341.
SCHIEBER, GEORGE I., JEAN-PIERRE POULLIER, AND LESLIE M. GREENWALD
1991   "Health care systems in twenty-four countries," *Health Affairs* 10(3): 22–38.
SCHIFF, ROBERT L., DAIV ANSELL, JAMES SCHLOSSER, AHAMED IDRIS, ANN MORRISON, AND STEVEN WHITMAN
1986   "Transfers to a public hospital," *New England Journal of Medicine* 314(9): 552–559.
SCHLESINGER, MARK, JUDY BENTKOVER, DAVID BLUMENTHAL, ROBERT MUSACCICO, AND JANET WILLER.
1987   "The privatization of health care and physicians' perceptions of access to hospital services," *Milbank Quarterly* 65(1): 25–58.
SCHMALE, ARTHUR H.
1972   "Giving up as a final common pathway to changes in health," pp. 20–40 in Z. Lipowski, ed., *Advances in Psychosomatic Medicine*, Vol. 8. Basel: S. Karger.
SCHMECK, HAROLD M.
1985   "73% of Americans suffer headaches," *New York Times*, October 22.
SCHNALL, PETER L., AND ROCHELLE KERN
1981   "Hypertension in American society: An introduction to historical materialist epidemiology," pp. 73–89 in P. Conrad and R. Kern, eds., *The Sociology of Health and Illness* (2nd ed.). New York: St. Martin's Press.
SCHNEIDER, JOSEPH W., AND PETER CONRAD
1980   "In the closet with illness: Epilepsy, stigma potential, and information control," *Social Problems* 28(1): 32–45.
1983   *Having Epilepsy: The Experience and Control of Illness.* Philadelphia: Temple University Press.
SCHNEIDER, KEITH
1987   "New product on farms in Midwest: Hunger," *New York Times*, September 29.
SCHNEIDER, MICHAEL
1975   *Neurosis and Civilization: A Marxist-Freudian Synthesis.* New York: Seabury.
SCHOR, JULIET B.
1992   *The Overworked American.* New York: Basic Books.
SCHOTT, THOMAS, AND BERNHARD BADURA
1988   "Wives of heart attack patients: The stress of caring," pp. 117–136 in R. Anderson and M. Bury, eds., *Living with Chronic Illness: The Experience of Patients and Their Families.* London: Unwin Hyman.
SCHREIBER, JANET M., AND JOHN HOMIAK
1981   "Mexican Americans," pp. 264–336 in A. Harwood, ed., *Ethnicity and Medical Care.* Cambridge, MA: Harvard University Press.
SCHWARTZ, BARRY
1973   "Waiting, exchange, and power: The distribution of time in social systems," *American Journal of Sociology* 79: 841–870.

SCHWARTZ, HILLEL
 1986   *Never Satisfied: A Cultural History of Diets, Fantasies, and Fat.* New York: Macmillan.
SCHWARTZ, MIRIAM
 1984   "A sociological reinterpretation of the controversy over 'unnecessary surgery',"
        Research in the Sociology of Health Care 3: 159–200.
SCITOVSKY, ANNE A.
 1994   " 'The high cost of dying' revisited," *The Milbank Quarterly* 72(4): 561–591.
SCOTCH, RICHARD K.
 1988   "Disability as the basis for a social movement: Advocacy and the politics of
        definition," *Journal of Social Issues* 44(1): 159–172.
SCULLY, DIANA
 1980   *Men Who Control Women's Health: The Miseducation of Obstetrician-Gynecologists.*
        Boston: Houghton Mifflin.
SECCOMBE, KAREN
 1996   "Health insurance coverage among the working poor," *Research in the Sociology of
        Health Care* 13A: 199–227.
SECCOMBE, KAREN, AND CHERYL AMEY
 1995   "Playing by the rules and losing: Health insurance and the working poor,"
        Journal of Health and Social Behavior 36: 168–181.
SEGAL, DAVID
 1996   "Blurring the line between doctors and hospitals," *Washington Post,* national
        weekly edition, January 15–21: 31.
SEGALL, ALEXANDER, AND LANCE W. ROBERTS
 1980   "A comparative analysis of physician estimates and levels of knowledge among
        patients," *Sociology of Health and Illness* 2(3): 317–334.
SELIGMAN, MARTIN
 1992   *Helplessness: On Depression, Development, and Death.* San Francisco: Freeman.
SELIK, RICHARD M., KENNETH G. CASTRO, MARGUERITE PAPPAIVANOU, AND JAMES W.
BUEHLER
 1989   "Birthplace and the risk of AIDS among Hispanics in the United States,"
        American Journal of Public Health 79(7): 836–839.
SELYE, HANS
 1956   *The Stress of Life.* New York: McGraw-Hill.
 1975   *Stress Without Distress.* New York: New American Library.
SHABECOFF, PHILIP
 1987   "Vast changes in environment seen," *New York Times,* November 4.
SHAKESPEARE, TOM
 1996   "Power and prejudice: Issues of gender, sexuality and disability," pp. 191–214
        in L. Barton, ed., *Disability and Society.* London: Longman.
SHAPIRO, JOSEPH P.
 1993   *No Pity: People with Disabilities Forging a New Civil Rights Movement.* New York:
        Random House.
SHARMA, URSULA
 1992   *Complementary Medicine Today: Practitioners and Patients.* London: Tavistock/
        Routledge.
 1995   "The homeopathic body: 'Reification' and the homeopathic 'gaze'," pp. 33–49
        in H. Johannessen, S. G. Oleson, and J. O. Andersen, eds. *Studies in Alternative
        Therapy,* vol. 2. Odense, DK: Odense University Press.

SHILTS, RANDY
    1987   *And the Band Played On: Politics, People, and the AIDS Epidemic.* New York: St. Martin's Press.

SHORTER, EDWARD
    1982   *A History of Women's Bodies.* New York: Basic.

SHULMAN, LAWRENCE C., AND JOANNE E. MANTELL
    1988   "The AIDS crisis: A United States health care perspective," *Social Science and Medicine* 26(10): 979–988.

SICHERMAN, BARBARA
    1978   "The uses of a diagnosis: Doctors, patients, and neurasthenia," pp. 25–38 in J. Leavitt and R. L. Numbers, eds., *Sickness and Health in America.* Madison: University of Wisconsin Press.

SIDEL, VICTOR W.
    1993   "New lessons from China: Equity and economics in rural health care," *American Journal of Public Health* 83(12): 1665–1666.

SIEGRIST, JOHANNES, AND DANIEL A. KLEIN
    1990   "Occupational stress and cardiovascular reactivity in blue-collar workers," *Work and Stress* 4(4): 295–304.

SIGERIST, HENRY B.
    1960   *On the History of Medicine.* New York: M. D. Publications.

SILVERMAN, MILTON, AND PHILIP R. LEE
    1974   *Pills, Profits, and Politics.* Berkeley: University of California Press.

SILVERMAN, MILTON, MIA LYDECKER, AND PHILIP R. LEE
    1992   *Bad Medicine: The Prescription Drug Industry in the Third World.* Stanford, CA: Stanford University Press.

SILVERSTEIN, BRET
    1984   *Fed Up.* Boston: South End.

SIMMONS, ROBERTA G., AND SUSAN KLEIN MARINE
    1984   "The regulation of high cost technology medicine: The case of dialysis and transplantation in the U.K.," *Journal of Health and Social Behavior* 25: 320–334.

SIMON, CAROL J., AND PATRICIA H. BORN
    1996   "Physician earnings in a changing managed care environment," *Health Affairs* 15(3): 124–134.

SIMON, PHILIP J.
    1983   *Reagan in the Workplace: Unraveling the Health and Safety Net.* Washington, DC: Center for Study of Responsive Law.

SIMONELLI, JEANNE M.
    1987   "Defective modernization and health in Mexico," *Social Science and Medicine* 24(1): 23–36.

SINGER, MERRILL, AND HANS BAER
    1995   *Critical Medical Anthropology.* Amityville, NY: Baywood.

SKOLNICK, ANDREW A.
    1995   "Along U.S. southern border, pollution, poverty, ignorance, and greed threaten nation's health," *Journal of the American Medical Association* 273(19): 1478–1482.

SKULTANS, VIEDA
    1974   *Intimacy and Ritual: A Study of Spiritualism, Mediums, and Groups.* London: Routledge and Kegan Paul.

SLOAN, FRANK A.
1988 "Property rights in the hospital industry," pp. 103–141 in H. E. Frech and R. Zeckhauser, eds., *Health Care in America: The Political Economy of Hospitals and Health Insurance.* San Francisco: Pacific Research Institute for Public Policy.

SMITH, BARBARA ELLEN
1981 "Black lung: The social production of disease," *International Journal of Health Services* 11(3): 343–359.
1987 *Digging Our Own Graves: Coal Miners and the Struggle over Black Lung Disease.* Chicago: University of Chicago Press.

SMITH, DAVID G.
1992 *Paying for Medicare: The Politics of Reform.* New York: Aldine de Gruyter.

SMITH, JAMES MONROE
1996 *AIDS and Society.* Upper Saddle River, NJ: Prentice Hall.

SMITH, ROBERT C., AND GEORGE ZIMMY
1988 "Physicians' emotional reactions to patients," *Psychosomatics* 29(4): 392–397.

SMOTHERS, RONALD
1991 "Employers becoming targets of suits in the fight to halt drunken driving," *New York Times,* May 26.

SNELL, BRADFORD
1982 "American ground transport," pp. 316–338 in J. H. Skolnick and E. Currie, eds., *Crisis in American Institutions.* Boston: Little, Brown.

SNOW, JOHN
[1855] 1936 *On the Mode of Communication of Cholera,* reprinted as *Snow on Cholera.* New York: Hafner.

SNOW, LOUDELL F.
1993 *Walkin' Over Medicine.* Boulder, CO: Westview Press.

SNYDER, PATRICIA
1983 "The use of nonprescribed treatments by hemodialysis patients," *Culture, Medicine, and Psychiatry* 7: 57–76.

SOBAL, JEFFERY
1995 "The medicalization and demedicalization of obesity," pp. 67–90 in D. Maurer and J. Sobal, eds., *Eating Agendas: Food and Nutrition as Social Problems.* New York: Aldine de Gruyter.

SOBOL, RICHARD B.
1991 *Bending the Law: The Story of the Dalkon Shield Bankruptcy.* Chicago: University of Chicago Press.

SOLDO, BETH J.
1985 "In-home services for the dependent elderly," *Research on Aging* 7: 281–304.

SOLOMON, GEORGE F.
1985 "The emerging field of psychoneuroimmunology," *Advances: Journal of the Institute for the Advancement of Health* 2(1): 6–19.

SORKIN, ALAN L.
1986 *Health Care and the Changing Economic Environment.* Lexington, MA: D.C. Heath.

SPARROW, MALCOLM K.
1996 *License to Steal: Why Fraud Plagues America's Health Care System.* Boulder, CO: Westview Press.

SPICKARD, JAMES V., AND MELISSA JAMESON
 1995   "Health care in rural El Salvador: Healing the wounds of war," pp. 213–229
        in E. B. Gallagher and J. Subedi, eds., *Global Perspectives on Health Care.*
        Englewood Cliffs, NJ: Prentice Hall.

SPRUIT, INGEBORG P., AND DAAN KROMHOUT
 1987   "Medical sociology and epidemiology: Convergences, divergences, and legiti-
        mate boundaries," *Social Science and Medicine* 25(6): 579–587.

STAFFORD, RANDALL S.
 1991   "The impact of nonclinical factors on repeat caesarean sections," *Journal of the
        American Medical Association* 265(1): 59–63.

STALK, JEFFREY
 1992   "At issue in the Netherlands: Is sex for the disabled a right?" *International Herald
        Tribune,* August 4.

STANNARD, CHARLES
 1973   "Old folks and dirty work: The social conditions for patient abuse in a nursing
        home," *Social Problems* 20(3): 329–342.

STARR, PAUL
 1982   *Social Transformation of American Medicine.* New York: Basic.

ST. CLAIR, JEFFREY
 1997   "Blowing smoke," *In These Times* 21(6): 24–26.

STEARNS, CAROL ZISOWITZ, AND PETER N. STEARNS
 1986   *Anger: The Struggle for Emotional Control in America's History.* Chicago: University
        of Chicago Press.

STEBBINS, KENYON RAINIER
 1986   "Curative medicine, preventive medicine, and health status: The influence of
        politics on health status in a rural Mexican village," *Social Science and Medicine*
        23(2): 139–148.
 1991   "Tobacco, politics and economics: Implications for global health," *Social Science
        and Medicine* 33(12): 1317–1326.
 1994   "Making a killing south of the Border: Transnational cigarette companies in
        Mexico and Guatemala," *Social Science and Medicine* 38(1): 105–115.

STEIN, HOWARD F.
 1986   " 'Sick people' and 'trolls': A contribution to the understanding of the dynamics
        of physician explanatory models," *Culture, Medicine, and Psychiatry* 10: 221–229.

STEIN, LEONARD I.
 1967   "The doctor-nurse game," *Archives of General Psychiatry* 16: 699–703.

STEIN, LEONARD I., D. T. WATTS, AND T. HOWELL
 1990   "The doctor-nurse game revisited," *New England Journal of Medicine* 322: 546–549.

STEINMETZ, SUZANNE K.
 1988   *Duty Bound: Elder Abuse and Family Care.* Newbury Park, CA: Sage.

STELLMAN, JEANNE
 1977   *Women's Work, Women's Health.* New York: Pantheon.

STELLMAN, JEANNE, AND SUSAN M. DAUM
 1971   *Work Is Dangerous to Your Health.* New York: Pantheon.

STELLMAN, JEANNE, AND MARY SUE HENIFIN
 1983   *Office Work Can Be Dangerous to Your Health.* New York: Random House.

STERLING, THEODOR D., ELIA STERLING, AND HELEN D. WARD
 1983   "Building illness in the white collar workplace," *International Journal of Health
        Services* 13(2): 277–287.

STEVENS, WILLIAM K.
1988   "Diarrhea kills surprising rate of U.S. young," *New York Times*, December 9.
STEWART, DAVID C., AND THOMAS J. SULLIVAN
1982   "Illness behavior and the sick role in chronic disease: The case of MS," *Social Science and Medicine* 16: 1397–1404.
STILLION, JUDITH M.
1995   "Premature death among males," pp. 46–67 in D. Sabo and D. F. Gordon, eds., *Men's Health and Illness*. Thousand Oaks, CA: Sage.
STIMSON, GERRY, AND BARBARA WEBB
1974   "Obeying doctor's orders: A view from the other side," *Social Science and Medicine* 8A: 97–104.
1975   *Going to See the Doctor*. London: Routledge and Kegan Paul.
STONE, DEBORAH A.
1979a   "Diagnosis and the dole: The function of illness in American distributive politics," *Journal of Health Politics, Policy and Law* 4(3): 570–591.
1979b   "Physicians as gatekeepers: Illness certification as a rationing device," *Public Policy* 27(2): 227–254.
STOUT, H. R.
1885   *Our Family Physician*. Peoria, IL: Henderson and Smith.
STRAHAN, GENEVIEVE W.
1997   "An overview of nursing homes and their current residents: Data from the 1995 National Nursing Homes Survey," *Advance Data* (USDHHS) 280.
STRAUB, LAVONNE A.
1990   "Financing rural health and medical services," *Journal of Rural Care* 6(4): 467–484.
STRAUS, MURRAY A., RICHARD J. GELLES, AND SUZANNE K. STEINMETZ
1980   *Behind Closed Doors: Violence in the American Family*. New York: Doubleday.
STRAUSS, ANSELM
1975   *Chronic Illness and the Quality of Life*. St. Louis, MO: C.V. Mosby.
STREET, RICHARD L., JR.
1991   "Information-giving in medical consultations: The influence of patients' communicative styles and personal characteristics," *Social Science and Medicine* 32(5): 541–548.
1992   "Communicative styles and adaptations in physician-parent consultations," *Social Science and Medicine* 34(10): 1155–1163.
STRUCK, MIRIAM
1981   "Disabled doesn't mean unable," *Science for the People*, September-October: 24–28.
STRYKER, JEFF
1996   "Life after Quinlan: Right to die," *New York Times*, March 31.
SUDNOW, DAVID
1967   *Passing On: The Social Organization of Dying*. Englewood Cliffs, NJ: Prentice Hall.
SULLIVAN, CYNTHIA B., AND THOMAS RICE
1991   "The health insurance picture in 1990," *Health Affairs* 10(2): 104–15.
SULLIVAN, DEBORAH A.
1993   "Cosmetic surgery: Market dynamics and medicalization," *Research in the Sociology of Health Care* 10: 97–115.
SULLIVAN, MARK
1986   "In what sense is contemporary medicine dualistic?" *Culture, Medicine and Psychiatry* 10: 331–350.

SUMMER, LAURA
1994 "The escalating number of uninsured in the United States," *International Journal of Health Services* 24(3): 409–413.

SUNDQUIST, JAN
1995 "Ethnicity, social class and health: A population-based study on the influence of social factors on self-reported illness in 223 Latin American refugees, 333 Finnish and 126 South European labour migrants and 841 Swedish controls," *Social Science and Medicine* 40(6): 777–787.

SUSMAN, JOAN
1993 "Disability, stigma and deviance," *Social Science and Medicine* 38(1): 15–22.

SUSSER, MERVYN, WILLIAM WATSON, AND KIM HOPPER
1985 *Sociology in Medicine* (3rd ed.). New York: Oxford University Press.

SUTER, STEVE
1986 *Health Psychophysiology: Mind-Body Interactions in Wellness and Illness.* Hillsdale, NJ: Lawrence Erlbaum.

SUTHERLAND, ALLAN T.
1981 *Disabled We Stand.* Bloomington: Indiana University Press.

SUTHERLAND, PRUDY
1987 "I want sex—just like you," *Village Voice* 32(14): 25.

SVARSTAD, BONNIE L.
1976 "Physician-patient communication and patient conformity with medical advice," pp. 220–238 in D. Mechanic, ed., *The Growth of Bureaucratic Medicine.* New York: Wiley.

SVENSSON, ROLAND
1996 "The interplay between doctors and nurses—negotiated order perspective," *Sociology of Health and Illness* 18(3): 379–398.

SWARTZ, KATHERINE
1994 "Dynamics of people without health insurance," *Journal of the American Medical Association* 271(1): 64–66.

SWEDLOW, ALEX, GREGORY JOHNSON, NEIL SMITHLINE, AND ARNOLD MILSTEIN
1992 "Increased cost and rates of use in the California workers' compensation system as a result of self-referral by physicians," *New England Journal of Medicine* 327(21): 1502–1506.

SYME, S. LEONARD
1996 "To prevent disease: The need for a new approach," pp. 21–31 in D. Blane et al., eds., *Health and Social Organization.* London: Routledge.

SYME, S. LEONARD, AND LISA F. BERKMAN
1976 "Social class, susceptibility, and sickness," *American Journal of Epidemiology* 104: 1–8.

SYME, S. LEONARD, AND JACK M. GURALNIK
1987 "Epidemiology and health policy: Coronary heart disease," pp. 85–116 in S. R. Levine and A. Lilienfeld, eds., *Epidemiology and Health Policy.* New York: Tavistock.

SYTKOWSKI, PAMELA, WILLIAM B. KANNEL, AND RALPH B. D'AGOSTINO
1990 "Changes in risk factors and the decline in mortality from cardiovascular disease," *New England Journal of Medicine* 322(23): 1635–1641.

SZASZ, ANDREW
1983 "The reversal of federal policy toward worker safety and health," *Science and Society* 1(Spring): 25–51.

SZASZ, THOMAS S.
1970   *The Manufacture of Madness.* New York: Dell.
TARAGIN, MARK I., L. R. WILLETT, A. P. WILCZEK, R. TROUT, AND J. L. CARSON
1992   "The influence of standard of care and severity of injury on the resolution of medical malpractice claims," *Annals of Internal Medicine* 117(9): 780–784.
TAUSSIG, MICHAEL T.
1980   "Reification and the consciousness of the patient," *Social Science and Medicine* 14B: 3–13.
TAYLOR, FREDERICK
[1911] 1947   *Principles of Scientific Management.* New York: Norton.
TAYLOR, KATHRYN M.
1988   " 'Telling bad news': Physicians and the disclosure of undesirable information," *Sociology of Health and Illness* 10(2): 109–132.
TAYLOR, ROSEMARY C. P.
1984   "Alternative medicine and the medical encounter in Britain and the United States," pp. 191–228 in J. W. Salmon, ed., *Alternative Medicines: Popular and Policy Perspectives.* New York: Tavistock.
TELLES, JOEL LEON, AND MARK HARRIS POLLACK
1981   "Feeling sick: The experience and legitimation of illness," *Social Science and Medicine* 15A: 243–251.
THEORELL, TÖRES
1991   "On cardiovascular health in women," pp. 187–204 in M. Frankenhaeuser, U. Lundberg, and M. Chesney, eds., *Women, Work and Health.* New York: Plenum Press.
THOITS, PEGGY A.
1983   "Dimensions of life events that influence psychological distress: An evaluation and synthesis of the literature," pp. 33–103 in H. B. Kaplan, ed., *Psychosocial Stress: Trends in Theory and Research.* New York: Academic.
THOMAS, CAROL
1995   "Domestic labour and health: bringing it all back home," *Sociology of Health and Illness* 17(3): 328–352.
THOMAS, K. J., L. WESTLAKE, AND B. T. WILLIAMS
1991   "Use of non-orthodox and conventional health care in Great Britain," *British Medical Journal* 302: 207–210.
THOMAS, V. J., AND F. D. ROSE
1991   "Ethnic differences in the experience of pain," *Social Science and Medicine* 32(9): 1063–1066.
THRUPP, LORI ANN
1991   "Sterilization of workers from pesticide exposure: The causes and consequences of DBCP-induced damage in Costa Rica and beyond," *International Journal of Health Services* 21(4): 731–757.
TIEFER, LEONORE
1992   "In pursuit of the perfect penis: The medicalization of male sexuality," pp. 450–465 in M. S. Kimmel and M. A. Messner, eds., *Men's Lives.* New York: Macmillan.
1994   "Women's sexuality: Not a matter of health," pp. 151–162 in A.J. Dan, ed., *Reframing Women's Health.* Thousand Oaks, CA: Sage.
TIERNEY, JOHN
1988   "Wired for stress," *New York Times Magazine,* May 15.

TIPTON, STEVEN M.
1982   *Getting Saved from the Sixties: The Transformation of Moral Meaning in American Culture by Alternative Religious Movements.* Berkeley: University of California Press.

TODD, ALEXANDRA
1983   "Discourse in the prescription of contraception," pp. 159–187 in S. Fisher and A. Todd, eds., *The Social Organization of Doctor-Patient Communication.* Norwood, NJ: Ablex.

TOLCHIN, MARTIN
1988a   "Curbs on tuition for doctors raising fears for care of poor," *New York Times,* July 25.
1988b   "Shift on Medicare to hurt hospitals in the inner cities," *New York Times,* October 19.
1989   "Hospitals give record pay rise to attract nurses," *New York Times,* March 26.

TONER, ROBIN
1996   "Health cares: Harry and Louise were right, sort of," *New York Times,* November 24.

TOOMBS, KAY S.
1995   "Sufficient unto the day: A life with multiple sclerosis," pp. 3–23 in K. S. Toombs, D. Marnard, and R. A. Carson, eds., *Chronic Illness: From Experience to Policy.* Bloomington: Indiana University Press.

TOTMAN, RICHARD
1979   *Social Causes of Illness.* New York: Pantheon.

TOWNSEND, JOHN M., AND CYNTHIA L. CARBONE
1980   "Menopausal syndrome: Illness or social role–a transcultural analysis," *Culture, Medicine, and Psychiatry* 4: 229–248.

TOWNSEND, PETER
1990   "Individual or social responsibility for premature death: Current controversies in the British debate about health," *International Journal of Health Services* 29(3): 373–392.

TREICHLER, PAULA A.
1990   "Feminism, medicine, and the meaning of childbirth," pp. 113–138 in M. Jacobus, E. F. Keller, and S. Shuttleworth, eds., *Body/Politics: Women and the Discourses of Science.* New York: Routledge.

TREVIÑO, FERNANDO, M. EUGENE MOYER, R. BURCIAGA VALDEZ, AND CHRISTINE A. STROUP-BENHAM
1991   "Health insurance coverage and utilization of health services by Mexican Americans, Mainland Puerto Ricans, and Cuban Americans," *Journal of the American Medical Association* 265(2): 233–237.

TROSTLE, JAMES A.
1988   "Medical compliance as an ideology," *Social Science and Medicine* 27(12): 1299–1308.

TROSTLE, JAMES A., W. ALLEN HAUSER, AND IDA SUSSER
1983   "The logic of noncompliance: Management of epilepsy from the patient's point of view," *Culture, Medicine, and Psychiatry* 7: 35–56.

TROTTER, ROBERT T., AND J. A. CHAVIRA
1981   *Curanderismo: Mexican-American Folk Healing.* Athens: University of Georgia Press.

TSING, ANNA L.
1990   "Monster stories: Women charged with perinatal endangerment," pp. 113–138 in F. Ginsburg and A. L. Tsing, eds., *Uncertain Terms: Negotiating Gender in American Culture.* Boston: Beacon.

TUDIVER, SARI
1986 "The strength of links: International Women's Health Network in the eighties," pp. 187–214 in K. McDonnell, ed., *Adverse Effects: Women and the Pharmaceutical Industry*. Toronto: Women's Educational Press.

TURNER, BRYAN S.
1977 "Confession and social structure," *Annual Review of the Social Sciences of Religion* 1: 29–58.
1982 "The government of the body: Medical regimens and the rationalization of diet," *British Journal of Sociology* 33(2): 254–269.
1984 *The Body and Society: Exploration in Social Theory*. Oxford: Basil Blackwell.
1992 *Regulating Bodies: Essays in Medical Sociology*. London: Routledge.

TURNER, VICTOR W.
1968 *The Drums of Affliction*. Oxford: Clarendon.
1969 *The Ritual Process*. Chicago: Aldine.

TURSHEN, MEREDITH
1989 *The Politics of Public Health*. New Brunswick, NJ: Rutgers University Press.

TWADDLE, ANDREW C.
1981 *Sickness Behavior and the Sick Role*. Cambridge, MA: Schenkman.

TWADDLE, ANDREW C., AND RICHARD M. HESSLER
1986 "Power and change: The Swedish Commission of Inquiry on Health and Sickness Care," *Journal of Health Politics, Policy, and Law* 11(1): 19–40.

TYNES, SHERYL
1996 *Turning Points in Social Security: From Cruel Hoax to Social Entitlement*. Palo Alto, CA: Stanford University Press.

UNITED NATIONS DEVELOPMENT PROGRAMME (UNDP)
1995 *Human Development Report, 1995*. New York: Oxford University Press.

U.S. BUREAU OF THE CENSUS
1975 *Historical Statistics of the United States, Colonial Times to 1970*. Bicentennial edition, part 2. Washington, DC.
1992 *Statistical Abstract of the United States: 1992*. Washington, DC.
1993 *Current Population Survey*. Washington, DC: Bureau of the Census.
1995 *Statistical Abstract of the United States: 1995*. Washington, DC.

U.S. DEPARTMENT OF HEALTH AND HUMAN SERVICES (USDHHS)
1987 *Health, United States, 1986*. Hyattsville, MD: National Center for Health Statistics.
1989 *International Classification of Diseases*. Public Health Service, Health Care Financing Administration. Washington, DC: Government Printing Office.
1992 *Health, United States, 1991*. Hyattsville, MD: National Center for Health Statistics.
1995 *Health United States, 1994*. Hyattsville, MD: National Center for Health Statistics.
1996a *Health United States, 1995*. Hyattsville, MD: National Center for Health Statistics.
1996b *Monthly Vital Statistics Report* 44(11S): 15–16, 68.

U.S. DEPARTMENT OF LABOR
1981 "Workers on Late Shifts," Bureau of Labor Statistics, September Summary: 81–103.

VÅGERÖ, DENNY
1992 "Women, work and health in Sweden," *Current Sweden* 387 (January): 1–8.

VÅGERO, DENNY, AND RAYMOND ILLSLEY
1992　"Inequality, health and policy in East and West Europe," *International Journal of Health Services* 3 (3–4): 225–239.

VALACH, LADISLAV
1995　"Coping and human agency," pp. 249–265 in I. Markova and R. M. Farr, eds., *Representations of Health, Illness and Handicap*. London: Harwood.

VERBRUGGE, LOIS M.
1986　"From sneezes to adieux: Stages of health for American men and women," *Social Science and Medicine* 22: 1195–1212.

1990　"Longer life but worsening health?: Trends in health and mortality of middle-aged and older persons," pp. 14–34 in P. R. Lee and C. L. Estes, eds., *The Nation's Health*. Boston: Jones and Bartlett.

1992　"Pathways of health and death," pp. 41–79 in R. D. Apple, ed., *Women, Health and Medicine in America*. New Brunswick, NJ: Rutgers University Press.

VERBRUGGE, LOIS M., AND FRANK J. ASCIONE
1987　"Exploring the iceberg: Common symptoms and how people care for them," *Medical Care* 25(6): 539–569.

VINES, GAIL
1993　*Raging Hormones*. Berkeley: University of California Press.

VOGEL, VIRGIL
1970　*American Indian Medicine*. Norman: University of Oklahoma Press.

VOLICER, BEVERLY
1977　"Cardiovascular changes associated with stress during hospitalization," *Journal of Psychosomatic Research* 22: 159–168.

1978　"Hospital stress and patients' reports of pain and physical status," *Journal of Human Stress* 4: 28–37.

WADSWORTH, MICHAEL
1996　"Family and education as determinants of health," pp. 152–170 in D. Blane et al., eds., *Health and Social Organization*. London: Routledge.

WAGGONER, PAUL E.
1996　"How much land can ten billion people spare for nature?" *Daedalus* 125(3), Summer: 73–93.

WAGNER, MELINDA BOLLAR
1983　*Metaphysics in Midwestern America*. Columbus: Ohio State University Press.

WAID, WILLIAM M.
1984　*Sociophysiology*. New York: Springer-Verlag.

WAITZKIN, HOWARD B.
1971　"Latent functions of the sick role in various institutional settings," *Social Science and Medicine* 5: 45–75.

1979　"A Marxian interpretation of the growth and development of coronary care technology," *American Journal of Public Health* 69(12): 1260–1268.

1984　"The micropolitics of medicine: A contextual analysis," *International Journal of Health Services* 14: 339–378.

1985　"Information giving in medical care," *Journal of Health and Social Behavior* 26: 81–101.

1989　"A critical theory of medical discourse: Ideology, social control, and the processing of social context in medical encounters," *Journal of Health and Social Behavior* 30(2): 220–239.

1991　*The Politics of Medical Encounters: How Patients and Doctors Deal with Social Problems*. New Haven: Yale University Press.

WAITZKIN, HOWARD B., AND JOHN D. STOECKLE
   1972   "The communication of information about illness," *Advances in Psychosomatic Medicine* 8: 180–215.

WALDRON, INGRID
   1976   "Why do women live longer than men?" *Social Science and Medicine* 10: 349–362.
   1991   "Effects of labor force participation on sex differences in mortality and morbidity," pp. 17–38 in M. Frankenhaeuser, U. Lundberg, and M. Chesney, eds., *Women, Work and Health*. New York: Plenum Press.
   1994   "What do we know about causes of sex differences in mortality?" pp. 42–55 in P. Conrad and R. Kern, eds., *The Sociology of Health and Illness* (4th ed.). New York: St. Martin's Press.

WALLSTON, BARBARA S., S. W. ALAGNA, B. M. DEVELLIS, AND R. B. DEVELLIS
   1983   "Social support and physical health," *Health Psychology* 2: 367–391.

WALSH, DIANA CHAPMAN
   1987   *Corporate Physicians: Between Medicine and Management.* New Haven: Yale University Press.

WALTERS, VIVIENNE
   1982   "Company doctors' perceptions of and responses to conflicting pressures from labor and management," *Social Problems* 30(1): 1–12.

WARD, MARTHA C.
   1986   *Poor Women, Powerful Men: America's Great Experiment in Family Planning.* Boulder, CO: Westview.

WARDWELL, WALTER I.
   1993   *Chiropractic History and Evolution of a New Profession.* St. Louis, MO: Mosby-Year Books.
   1994   "Alternative Medicine in the United States," *Social Science and Medicine* 38 (8): 1061–1068.

WARE, JOHN E., JR., MARTHA S. BAYLISS, WILLIAM H. ROGERS, MARK KOSINSKI, AND ALVIN R. TARLOV
   1996   "Differences in 4-year health outcomes for elderly and poor, chronically ill patients treated in HMO and fee-for-service systems," *Journal of the American Medical Association* 276(13): 1039–1047.

WARE, NORMA C.
   1992   "Suffering and the social construction of illness: The delegitimation of illness experience in chronic fatigue syndrome," *Medical Anthropology Quarterly* 6(4): 347–361.

WARNOCK, JOHN W.
   1987   *The Politics of Hunger: The Global Food System.* Toronto: Methuen.

WAXLER, NANCY E.
   1980   "The social labeling perspective on illness and medical practice," pp. 283–306 in L. Eisenberg and A. Kleinman, eds., *The Relevance of Social Science for Medicine.* Dordrecht, Netherlands: D. Reidel.
   1981   "Learning to be a leper: A case study in the social construction of illness," pp. 169–194 in E. Mishler, L. AmaraSingham, S. Hauser, R. Liem, S. Osherson, and N. Waxler, *Social Contexts of Health, Illness, and Patient Care.* Cambridge: Cambridge University Press.

WAXLER-MORRISON, NANCY, T. GREGORY HISLAP, BRONWEN MEARS, AND LISA KAN
   1991   "Effects of social relationships on survival for women with breast cancer: A prospective study," *Social Science and Medicine* 33(2): 177–183.

WAY, KAREN
1995   "Never too rich . . . or too thin: The role of stigma in the social construction of anorexia nervosa," pp. 91–113 in D. Maurer and J. Sobal, eds., *Eating Agendas: Food and Nutrition as Social Problems*. New York: Aldine de Gruyter.

WEBER, MAX
[1904] 1958   *The Protestant Ethic and the Spirit of Capitalism*. New York: Charles Scribner's Sons.
[1922] 1963   *The Sociology of Religion*, trans. E. Fischoff. Boston: Beacon.

WEEKS, JOHN R.
1986   *Population: An Introduction to Concepts and Issues*. Belmont, CA: Wadsworth.

WEIL, ANDREW
1988   *Health and Healing* (rev. ed.), Boston: Houghton Mifflin.

WEIL, ANDREW, AND WINIFRED ROSEN
1993   *From Chocolate to Morphine* (rev. ed.), Boston: Houghton Mifflin.

WEINER, HERBERT
1992   *Perturbing the Organism: The Biology of Stressful Experience*. Chicago: University of Chicago Press.

WEIR, DAVID, AND MARK SHAPIRO
1981   *Circle of Poison*. San Francisco: Institute for Food Development Policy.

WEISS, JAY M.
1972   "Psychological factors in stress and disease," *Scientific American* 226(6): 104–113.

WEISS, KAY
1983   "Vaginal cancer: An iatrogenic disease?" pp. 59–75 in E. Fee, ed., *Women and Health: The Politics of Sex in Medicine*. Farmingdale, NY: Baywood.

WELCH, W. PETE, DIANA VERRILLI, STEVEN J. KATZ, AND ERIC LATIMER
1996   "A detailed comparison of physician services for the elderly in the United States and Canada," *Journal of the American Medical Association* 275(18): 1410–1416.

WELLMAN, BEVERLY
1995   "Lay referral networks: Using conventional medicine and alternative therapies for low back pain," *Research in the Sociology of Health Care* 12: 213–238.

WERTZ, RICHARD W., AND DOROTHY C. WERTZ
1979   *Lying-In: A History of Childbirth in America*. New York: Schocken.

WEST, CANDACE
1983   " 'Ask me no questions . . .': An analysis of queries and replies in physician-patient dialogues," pp. 75–106 in S. Fisher and A. Todd, eds., *The Social Organization of Doctor-Patient Communication*. Norwood, NJ: Ablex.
1984   *Routine Complications: Troubles with Talk Between Doctors and Patients*. Bloomington: Indiana University Press.
1993   "Reconceptualizing gender in physician-patient relationships," *Social Science and Medicine* 36(1): 57–66.

WEST, PATRICK B.
1979   "Making sense of epilepsy," pp. 162–169 in D. J. Osborne, M. M. Greenberg, and J. R. Eiser, eds., *Research in Psychology and Medicine: Social Aspects, Attitudes, Communication, Care, and Training*, Vol. 2. New York: Academic.

WESTLEY, FRANCES
1983   *The Complex Forms of the Religious Life: A Durkheimian View of New Religious Movements*. Chico, CA: Scholars Press.

WETHINGTON, ELAINE, AND RONALD C. KESSLER
1986   "Perceived support, received support, and adjustment to stressful life events," *Journal of Health and Social Behavior* 27: 78–89.

WHITE, WILLIAM D., J. WARREN SALMON, AND JOE FEINGLASS
1994   "The changing doctor-patient relationship and performance monitoring: An agency perspective," pp. 195–224 in J. W. Salmon, ed., *The Corporate Transformation of Health Care # 2*. Amityville, NY: Baywood.

WHITEIS, DAVID, AND J. WARREN SALMON
1987   "The proprietarization of health care and underdevelopment of the public sector," *International Journal of Health Services* 17(1): 47–64.

WHITNEY, CRAIG R.
1991   "British Health Service, much beloved but inadequate, is facing change," *New York Times,* June 9.

WHYTE, SUSAN, AND BENEDICTE INGSTAD
1995   "Disability and culture: an overview," pp. 3–31 in B. Ingstad and S.R. Whyte, eds., *Disability and Culture*. Berkeley: University of California Press.

WIJKMAN, ANDERS, AND LLOYD TIMBERLAKE
1988   *Natural Disasters: Acts of God or Acts of Man?* Philadelphia: New Society Publishers.

WIKLER, DANIEL, AND NORMA J. WIKLER
1991   "Turkey-baster babies: The demedicalization of artificial insemination," *The Milbank Quarterly* 69(1): 5–40.

WILKES, MICHAEL S., AND MIRIAM SHUCHMAN
1989   "Pitching doctors," *New York Times Magazine*, November 5.

WILKINSON, RICHARD G.
1986a   "Income and mortality," pp. 88–114 in R. Wilkinson, ed., *Class and Health: Research and Longitudinal Data*. New York: Tavistock.
1986b   "Socio-economic differences in mortality: Interpreting the data on their size and trends," pp. 1–21 in R. Wilkinson, ed., *Class and Health: Research and Longitudinal Data*. New York: Tavistock.
1996   *Unhealthy Societies*. London: Routledge.

WILLEN, RICHARD S.
1983   "Religion and law: The secularization of testimonial procedures," *Sociological Analysis* 44(1): 53–64.

WILLIAMS, DAVID R., AND CHIQUITA COLLINS
1995   "U.S. socioeconomic and racial differences in health: Patterns and explanations," *Annual Review of Sociology*, 21, Palo Alto, CA: Annual Reviews: 349–386.

WILLIAMS, GARETH, JENNIE POPAY, AND PAUL BISSELL
1995   "Public health risks in the material world: Barriers to social movements in health," pp. 113–132 in J. Gabe, ed., *Medicine, Health and Risk*. Oxford: Blackwell.

WILLIAMS, RORY
1990   *A Protestant Legacy: Attitudes to Death and Illness among Older Aberdonians*. Oxford: Clarendon Press.

WILLIAMS, SIMON, AND GILLIAN BENDELOW
1996   "Emotions, health and illness: The missing link in medical sociology?" pp. 25–53 in V. James and J. Gabe, eds., *Health and the Sociology of Emotions*. Oxford: Blackwell.

WILLIS, EVAN
1983   *Medical Dominance: The Division of Labour in Australian Health Care*. Sydney: Allen and Unwin.

WILSFORD, DAVID
    1991   *Doctors and the State: Politics of Health Care in France and the United States.* Durham, NC: Duke University Press.

WILSON, SHARON
    1991   "The unrelenting nightmare: Husbands' experiences during their wives' chemotherapy," pp. 237–313 in J. M. Morse and J. L. Johnson, eds., *The Illness Experience: Dimensions of Suffering.* Newbury Park: Sage.

WISE, YACQUI
    1996   "Work? It makes me sick," *The Guardian* (October 8): 11.

WOLFE, KATHI
    1995   "Bashing the disabled," *The Progressive* (November): 24–27.

WOLFE, SAMUEL
    1990   "Importing health care reform?: Issues in transposing Canada's health care system to the United States," *Health/PAC Bulletin,* 20(2): 27–33.

WOLINSKY, FREDERICK, AND SALLY WOLINSKY
    1981   "Background, attitudinal, and behavioral patterns of individuals occupying eight discrete health states," *Sociology of Health and Illness* 3: 31–48.

WOLPE, PAUL ROOT
    1985   "The maintenance of professional authority: Acupuncture and the American physician," *Social Problems* 32 (June): 409–424.
    1990   "The holistic heresy: Strategies of ideological challenge in the medical profession," *Social Science and Medicine* 31(8): 913–923.

WOODROW, K. M., G. D. FRIEDMAN, A. B. SIEGELAUB, AND M. F. COLLEN
    1972   "Pain differences according to age, sex, and race," *Psychosomatic Medicine* 34: 548–556.

WOODS, NANCY FUGATE
    1995   "Women and their health," in C. I. Fogel and F. G. Woods, eds., pp. 1–22, *Women's Health Care: A Comprehensive Handbook.* Thousand Oaks, CA: Sage.

WOOLHANDLER, STEFFIE, AND DAVID U. HIMMELSTEIN
    1997   "Costs of care and administration at for-profit and other hospitals in the United States," *New England Journal of Medicine* 336(11): 769–774.

WOOLHANDLER, STEFFIE, DAVID U. HIMMELSTEIN, AND JAMES P. LEWONTIN
    1993   "Administrative costs in U.S. hospitals," *New England Journal of Medicine* 329(6): 400–403.

WORLD HEALTH ORGANIZATION
    1981   "Self-help and health: Report on a W.H.O. consultation," Report Number ICP HED 014, 6484 B, Copenhagen: World Health Organization.

WRIGHT, BARBARA DRYGULSKI
    1987   "Women, work, and the university-affiliated technology park," pp. 352–370 in B. D. Wright, ed., *Women, Work, and Technology: Transformations.* Ann Arbor: University of Michigan Press.

YAGO, GLENN
    1985   "U.S. lacks transportation policy," *In These Times* 9(15): 7.

YANOSHIK, KIM, AND JUDY NORSIGIAN
    1989   "Contraception, control, and choice: International perspectives," pp. 61–92 in K. S. Ratcliff, ed., *Healing Technology: Feminist Perspectives.* Ann Arbor: University of Michigan Press.

YATES, ALAYNE
    1991   *Compulsive Exercise and the Eating Disorders.* New York: Brunner/Mazel.

YELIN, EDWARD
  1986   "The myth of malingering: Why individuals withdraw from work in the presence of illness," *Milbank Quarterly* 64(4): 622–649.
YOELS, WILLIAM C., AND JEFFREY MICHAEL CLAIR
  1995   "Laughter in the clinic: Humor as social organization," *Symbolic Interaction* 18: 39–58.
YOUNG, ALLAN
  1976   "Some implications of medical beliefs and practices for social anthropology," *American Anthropologist* 78(1): 5–24.
  1978   "Mode of production of medical knowledge," *Medical Anthropology* 2: 97–124.
  1980   "The discourse of stress and the reproduction of conventional knowledge," *Social Science and Medicine* 14B: 133–146.
YOUNG, ERNIE, AND DAVID K. STEVENSON
  1990   "Limiting treatment for extremely premature, low-birth-weight infants (500–750 g.)," *American Journal of Diseases of Children* 144(5): 549–552.
YOUNG, JAMES HARVEY
  1992   *American Health Quackery.* Princeton: Princeton University Press.
ZARLING, EDWIN J., HAROLD SEXTON, AND PERVIS MILNOR, JR.
  1983   "Failure to diagnose acute myocardial infarction: The clinicopathologic experience at a large community hospital," *Journal of the American Medical Association* 250(9): 1177–1181.
ZBOROWSKI, MARK
  1952   "Cultural components in response to pain," *Journal of Social Issues* 8: 16–30.
  1969   *People in Pain.* San Francisco: Jossey-Bass.
ZOLA, IRVING K.
  1982   *Missing Pieces: A Chronicle of Living with a Disability.* Philadelphia: Temple University Press.
  1983   *Socio-Medical Inquiries: Recollections, Reflections, and Reconsiderations.* Philadelphia: Temple University Press.
  1993   "Self, identity and the naming question: Reflections on the language of disability," *Social Science and Medicine* 36(2): 167–173.
ZUSSMAN, ROBERT
  1996   "The patient in the intensive care unit," pp. 535–547 in P. Brown, ed., *Perspective in Medical Sociology* (2nd ed.). Prospect Heights, IL: Waveland Press.

AUTHOR INDEX

SUBJECT INDEX

Folk healing (*see* Indigenous healing)
Folk illness, 89, 123, 131, 186, 236, 239
Food and Drug Administration (FDA), 196, 310, 312, 314–16

G

Gender (*see also* Men; Women):
  differences in chronic illness and pain, 142, 149, 151
  differences in stress and coping, 83, 86, 131–32
  and eating disorders, 52–54
  illness as dissent, 131–32
  and medical social control, 129–32
  morbidity and mortality rates, 28–30
  stratification of medical work, 270–76
  and violence, 113–14
  and work roles, 173–76
Genetic factors in morbidity and mortality, 29–31

H

Haitian Americans, 14–15, 32
Handicap (*see* Disability)
Healing (*see* Alternative [non-medical] healing; Asian healing systems; Indigenous healing; Spiritual healing; Symbolism)
Health care policy (*see* Social policy)
Health care systems:
  British National Health Service, 250, 253, 264
  Canadian National Health Insurance, 250–54, 297, 299–301
  in developing countries, 249–50
  hidden health care system, 170–77 (*see also* Home health care)
  in industrialized countries, 249–55
  Japanese, 254
  rural and urban health care delivery, 306–9
  Swedish, 250
  types of, 250
  United States, 249–55
Health insurance, 256, 260, 279–89 (*see also* Medicaid; Medicare)
Health Maintenance Organizations (HMOs), 265–66, 284–88, 292–94
Help seeking and health, 166–70, 176–78
Hispanic Americans (*see also* Cuban Americans, Haitian Americans, Mexican-Americans, Puerto Ricans):
  access to medical care, 307
  AIDS rates, 25
  environmental health hazards, 64
  folk illnesses, 123
  in health occupations, 271, 276
  lack of insurance, 296

morbidity and mortality rates of, 31
HIV (Human Immunodeficiency Virus)
  infection, 21, 24–26 (*see also* AIDS)
Home health care, 170–76, 275–76
Homeopathy, 178–79, 207, 210
Homosexuality, 24–25, 112, 128
Hospitals:
  choosing, 256–57
  conditions of nurses' work, 273–75
  conditions of physicians' work, 259, 264–65
  corporatization, 258, 302–3
  and development of nursing profession, 270–73
  ethical issues and "perverse incentives" for, 264–67, 305
  financing, 303–9
  for-profit (proprietary), 302–3, 305
  history, 301–3
  and professional dominance, 210–11
Human rights and health, 318
Hydrotherapy, 179, 207

I

Iatrogenesis, 16, 196–97, 254, 269
Ideology and medical ideas, 198–206 (*see also* Social construction of knowledge)
Illness:
  as deviance, 118–19, 124–30
  as dissent, 131–32
  lay conceptions of, 144–47, 186
  and self, 101–3, 107–15, 139–43
  social factors in defining, 139, 144, 193–206
Indigenous healing, 180–84
Industry (*see* Corporate interests)
Infants (*see also* Childbirth; Children):
  commercial formulas for, 47–48
  diarrheal dehydration in, 40
  intensive care for, 245
  mortality of, 17, 30, 32
Institutional differentiation, 135, 211
Irish Americans, 150
Italian Americans, 32, 150

J

Jewish Americans, 29, 150

L

Labeling of deviance, 118–19, 126 (*see also* Deviance; Diagnosis; Stigma)
Labeling of patients, 223–24, 230–33, 235, 239
Laypersons:
  advice, 166
  conceptions of health and illness, 143–47, 166–70, 186
  help seeking and advice, 166–70
  mutual help, 176–77